The Dictionary of
Garden Plants

in colour

with House and Greenhouse Plants

Roy Hay and Patrick M. Synge

with Foreword by
The Lord Aberconway v.m.h.

Published in collaboration with The Royal Horticultural Society

EBURY PRESS AND MICHAEL JOSEPH

First published 1969
Reprinted 1969
Third Printing 1970
© George Rainbird Ltd 1969

This book was designed and produced by
GEORGE RAINBIRD LIMITED
Marble Arch House, 44 Edgware Road, London w2
for Ebury Press and Michael Joseph

House editor: Tom Wellsted
Designer: Ronald Clark

Printed by
Jolly & Barber Limited, Hillmorton Road, Rugby,
Warwickshire
Bound in Great Britain

7181 4020 6

Contents

Foreword

The Dictionary of Garden Plants in Colour will fill a gap that exists in the range of gardening books, and should meet a wide and ready response. The existing 'Dictionary of Gardening' sponsored and prepared by the Royal Horticultural Society has become a standard and indispensable book of reference, but it contains no coloured plates. The Dictionary of Garden Plants in Colour has, as its name implies, many coloured plates, admirable in quality.

Descriptions alone can never compete with descriptions accompanied by coloured illustrations, and this book will make less difficult the choice that frequently faces all of us, as to which plants to grow. To see what they should (and we hope will!) look like is both an encouragement and a challenge.

Although the two thousand coloured plates cover only a small proportion of the plants described in the R.H.S. Dictionary, they represent, in the opinion of the authors, the best. Most of the plants are easily obtainable, and, as demand creates supply, the rest should soon be readily available.

The two authors are distinguished plantsmen and gardeners. Roy Hay is well known for his broadcasts and newspaper articles on gardening: until recently he edited the Gardener's Chronicle, and he is Gardening Correspondent of The Times. Patrick Synge has for more than twenty years been the Royal Horticultural Society's Editor: as such he has not only sponsored and corrected the work of others, but has written many articles himself. But no two men, certainly not men so intelligent as these, can claim to cover the whole field of worthwhile plants; and accordingly the authors have not hesitated to bring in experts in various genera to advise and write from their particular knowledge. In addition the most skilled and best known of our horticultural photographers have contributed to make this book one of outstanding quality.

Indeed the Royal Horticultural Society seeks to limit the books, which they publish or are prepared to sponsor, to those which they are confident will be of outstanding quality. The Dictionary of Garden Plants in Colour fulfils this requirement, and I commend it with confidence to all who wish to identify their plants, and to grow the best.

ABERCONWAY
President
Royal Horticultural Society

Introduction

Descriptions of plants are often difficult to write and may differ, especially with regard to colour, from writer to writer. Black and white photographs may adequately show the form or habit of a plant but not the shade of pink its flowers may have or how its foliage may contrast with other plants. The selection of colour photographs that follow is intended to help in these respects. They have nearly all been taken from plants growing in the garden though some exceptionally fine plants have been specially photographed at exhibitions, particularly at the Royal Horticultural Society's Shows. In some cases photographs have been taken of plants in front of a plain background for comparative purposes, as with many of the daffodils where their differing characteristics would not have shown so well when photographed growing in the open. The plates have been put into sections, each section designated by a symbol at the top of each plate:

- 🌼 for Alpine and Rock Garden plants,
- 🌸 for Annual and Biennial plants,
- 🌿 for Greenhouse and House plants,
- 🌷 for Hardy Bulbous plants,
- 🌺 for Perennial plants,
- and 🌳 for Trees and Shrubs, a section sub-divided with 🍃 Climbers and 🌲 Conifers separately grouped.

The selection of so few plants, two thousand and forty-eight, amongst the thousands now cultivated by gardeners may have left a reader's favourite out: a sacrifice to the economics of space and the reasonable retail price of such a book as this.

Following this introduction are general notes on the cultivation of the various groups of plants into which the pictures have been divided. The notes are general because this book is not intended to be a treatise on cultivation nor on particular specialities such as Chrysanthemums. Specialised books and societies should be consulted for further information on such subjects. These groups are not absolute and cannot be so. For instance a dwarf daphne, more suited to a rock garden than planting in a shrubbery will be found illustrated in the Alpine and Rock Garden group and not in the Tree and Shrub group, though taller growing daphnes will be found in the Tree and Shrub group. Similarly not all bulbs are illustrated in the Bulb group – some will also be found in the Greenhouse and House Plant group. At the end of the book, however, all the plants are described under their respective genera, and all the daphnes will be found together under *Daphne*. The genera are given in strict alphabetic order, as most of the species

and cultivars are also, but in some cases, especially where several types of one genus are of a different nature as with irises, a genus which includes herbaceous and bulbous plants, the species and their varieties have been divided into sections. In genera which have been highly developed, this has been carried on to include the main types of hybrid in separate sections, as with rhododendrons where the notes start with the species and the differing types of hybrid follow – Rhododendron Hybrids, Evergreen Azalea Hybrids and Deciduous Azalea Hybrids. This system has been used generally throughout the notes but in some cases where the genus is divided naturally into sections, such as with the previously mentioned irises, the system may apply in part only. The descriptions of the plants themselves are brief and given as useful notes to the pictures. Also included, where it has been considered useful, are brief descriptions of unillustrated plants for comparison or general interest: in some cases such notes follow the descriptions of the illustrated species even though these 'extra plants' will be out of specific alphabetic order. The nomenclature has presented a particularly difficult problem, especially with regard to the alphabetisation. Some plants are so well known under a particular name that a change has been thought inadvisable for ease of reference, so with the plant now known to some botanists as *Crinitaria linosyris* a cross reference is given under this name to the main note which will be found under the more generally used name *Aster linosyris*. On the other hand where there is considered to be little foundation for using the commonly known name, which has possibly become more or less a 'common' name, the plant will appear under its usual botanic name, as with the plant generally called Gloxinia which is cross referred to the main note under *Sinningia*. The cross referencing has been designed to iron out this type of problem, as would any good index, and all synonyms of reasonably common use as well as the more usual common names from the British Isles and the United States are included. Where it has been possible, the differing *English* cultivar names are also given, as with the rose called 'Super Star' throughout the world except in the United States where it is known as 'Tropicana'. An American from the United States would, on looking up 'Tropicana' in the Hybrid Tea section under *Rosa*, be referred to 'Super Star'.

The intention of this book is therefore simply to show in colour some of the plants one hears and reads about. Not a treatise on any particular subject and if you, the reader, grow a particular plant better than one illustrated: good. But if not, then it may be possible to find something else which will grow better in your locality and climate and look as good, possibly even better.

Cultural Notes

Alpine and Rock Garden plants

The word 'alpine' when applied to plants refers to the dwarf plants from any of the higher mountains of the world. It is not restricted to those coming from the European Alps only. The main characteristics of such plants are the dwarf compact habit with short stems and leaves closely packed together and reduced in size, usually occasioned by the strong winds of their native habitats, by a great freedom of flowering and often by very intense colouring in the flowers. There is probably no other group of flowers with a greater intensity of flower colour than the spring gentians from the European Alps or the autumn ones from the Himalayas.

Such plants have a short season of growth combined with a long resting period under the snow in their native haunts. During this resting period they remain dry and consequently winter wet may be far more damaging to the higher alpines than cold. For this reason some are best suited to alpine house culture where they may be kept dry in winter. On the other hand they must not be dessicated. During their growing season they need plenty of moisture but few of them will stand it as stagnant or standing water. Good drainage is the most essential of the factors for growing many of the choicer alpines.

Alpine plants are usually associated in gardens with rock gardens and often they look best nestling into rocks or cascading over them as in their native habitat. Some also are saxatile, growing in rocks, and like some of the androsaces, silver saxifrages and ramondas, are best grown in vertical crevices where the water does not rest on their rosettes. For growing many alpines though, it is not strictly necessary to have a rock garden. A low raised bed at the foot of, or on top of, a wall or the crevices in a dry wall will suit them well. Good examples of beds supported by flat pieces of stone and raised about two feet in the air can be seen in the Savill Garden in Windsor Great Park and in several other gardens. They are excellent for growing alpines and the smaller choice bulbs and they take up little space in the small garden. Weeding is easy, especially if they are surfaced with peat moss or fine shingle and maintenance is also kept to a minimum.

Many plants, however, such as the helianthemums, alyssums or iberis are included in this section but in their habitat are more sub-alpine than alpine. They are easy to grow in the front of any sunny border and look well spreading in loose groups over the flat stones which may have been used to edge the border.

The range of alpine plants is very great and their beauty of flower and foliage and their dwarf, or in some cases, miniature habit appeals to many gardeners, especially to those with limited space. It is possible to grow a very large range of alpine plants in a comparatively small back garden of a quarter of an acre or even less and such is probably the most interesting use of such a space for a keen grower. The cultivation of many of the higher alpines gives also a challenge which stimulates the care and enthusiasm of the gardener.

Wild collected plants and seeds also play a large part in the alpine plantsman's garden. In the alps many of these plants are in such abundance that it seems a few may well be collected, and so it is; but in the case of plants of greater scarcity there are now proper restrictions on collecting and the gardener should be sparing, taking only a cutting or a little seed. It is only too easy for collectors to denude an area of a particular rarity and then it hardly ever returns. The modern polythene bags enable the collector to bring back his plants in good condition. They must not, however, be put into the bags moist or rotting is likely. Many more alpine plants are lost after collection through being packed too wet than too dry.

Another good method of growing alpine plants from the more acid regions of the mountains is in a peat wall garden. Good examples may be seen in the Royal Horticultural Society's garden at Wisley in Surrey or in the Royal Botanic Garden, Edinburgh. Peat is especially suitable for nearly all ericaceous plants such as dwarf rhododendrons and also for many of the choicer primulas and gentians which resent becoming dry in the summer. Such a garden may be made in tiers, with small terraced beds between, and some of the plants may well be grown in the cracks between the peat blocks. These peat blocks must be soaked thoroughly before the building is completed since once they are really dry it is very difficult to get them saturated again. In time the blocks will tend to break down and disintegrate but by then the plants will largely have grown over them and it will not matter too much.

For the plants which come from the higher screes and moraines and require unusual drainage probably the safest method of growing is still in pans, in the alpine house and frame, and wonderful specimens may be grown in this way for exhibition but they do require constant attention and watering. Soil mixtures for the pans usually include a high proportion of coarse sand with large grains which ensure good drainage and the pots must be well crocked at the base with an inch or so of crocks and some shingle or coarse sand above. Some loam and peat should also be mixed into the compost and the pans are usually surfaced with fine shingle or grit; both to give a clean appearance and to stop water collecting around the neck of the plant just below the rosettes. Cushion plants such as the aretian androsaces and some primulas should not be watered on top of the cushions but the pans should be immersed in a basin or shallow tray of water so that it seeps up from below.

The alpine house is generally built with more ventilation than the usual greenhouse and should have a continuous row of windows along the top and also plenty side ventilators. These should be kept open for most of the year only being closed in very extreme frost or in fog. Plants in pans are more sensitive to freezing than plants growing in the ground but the majority of alpines will stand some frost and certainly do not need any artificial heating.

The growing of such specimen plants can be a great test of the skill and patience of the grower but is very rewarding. A large number of pans of choice alpines may be accommodated in quite a small alpine house and the interest increased if the house is supplemented by several frames in which plants may be kept for most of the year being brought into the alpine house for their flowering. The frames will also need constant ventilation. Pans of alpines should never be placed on bare greenhouse slats but should always be plunged in sand or shingle so that they retain some moisture. The plants of the high mountains develop tremendous root systems relative to their branches and leaves and this enables them to draw in moisture from a large area in their native habitats, so large pans are needed for the older plants.

There is much fascination in the perfection of these miniature flowers, often making up in abundance of flower for the lack of size and among them are to be found some of the most graceful and beautiful of all garden plants. They are nearer to the wild plants of the world also than the majority of plants we grow in our gardens and often remind us of pleasant holidays spent among the mountains.

There are alpines requiring the greatest care any gardener can give while others are among the easiest and least demanding of plants. Cultivation may vary in different parts of the world but the principles and main requirements of alpine plants do not vary wherever one may garden. The wise gardener conditions his choice of plants to those which grow best in his area but still for some of his favourite alpines he will make exceptions and take up their challenge.

Annual and Biennial plants

A great many flowers may be grown from seed but those illustrated on plates 225–400 are plants which are normally grown either as annuals or biennials.

Botanically an annual is a plant which completes its life cycle from seed to seed within one growing season – which of course may only be a matter of four or five months. The gardener however considers any plant that he can sow and have in flower inside twelve months as an annual. Some biennials and even some perennials such as antirrhinums are normally treated as annuals.

Remembering this, one can divide the annuals into three groups – hardy, half hardy and tender. The hardy annuals are those which will withstand a considerable amount of frost; they are usually sown in the open in March or April, but some, such as larkspurs and calendulas, may be sown in the autumn. With autumn-sown annuals it is best to defer thinning the seedlings until the spring as slugs and other enemies may decimate them.

Half-hardy annuals will not withstand frost and are normally sown in a heated greenhouse or a cold frame in April or outdoors in May. Only in favourable districts and in good seasons will they grow and flower well before the autumn frosts arrive if sown in the open.

Tender annuals are those which are sown in a heated greenhouse and either planted out for a short time in the height of summer, or grown on to flower in the greenhouse – celosias, schizanthus, cinerarias and calceolarias, are examples.

A biennial is a plant that is raised from seed sown in the early summer – May or June of one year and which will flower usually in the early spring or summer of the following year. The spring bedding plants – wallflowers, *Cheiranthus allionii*, myosotis, and honesty, are among the most popular.

Where there is plenty of room in a garden, a border entirely composed of annual flowers is attractive for many weeks and as seeds are relatively cheap, it does not cost a great deal of money. But it does entail a good deal of time spent in preparing the soil, sowing the seeds, thinning the seedlings and weeding. Such a border may be composed of a mixture of hardy and half-hardy annuals. The hardy kinds are sown in situ in late March or early April and gaps are left to receive the asters, zinnias, nemesias and others which are raised under glass and planted out when danger of frost has passed.

The soil for annual flowers should be reasonably fertile but not too rich. In very rich soils some annuals such as nasturtiums tend to produce too much foliage and too few flowers. The surface has to be raked down to a fine tilth. The seeds may be sown on the surface in irregular patches and lightly raked in, but a better way is to mark out the patches with a pointed stick. Then again with a pointed stick or wooden label draw shallow drills ½ inch deep across the patches in parallel lines say 4 to 6 inches apart. The seeds are sown very thinly in these drills and lightly covered with fine soil. The advantage of sowing in these short drills is that one can easily distinguish between the seedlings of the annuals and the weed seedlings.

When the annual seedlings are large enough to handle they should be thinned to leave the remaining plants about 2 inches apart. Later they should be thinned to their final distance – 4 to 6 inches apart, or in the case of strong growing annuals such as lavatera or annual sunflowers to 1 foot apart.

Few annual flowers require support if they are grown in an open sunny position. But sometimes in semi-shaded gardens or where the annuals are planted close together or in close proximity with other plants they may sometimes need a few twiggy sticks.

In these days of high labour costs, fewer borders composed entirely of annual flowers are seen, as a good deal of time is needed sowing, thinning and weeding them. But both the hardy and the half hardy kinds are invaluable for filling gaps in borders of perennial plants or to provide temporary colour in borders of flowering shrubs, while the latter are small.

With the proliferation of garden centres the use of half-hardy annuals purchased as young plants is increasing rapidly. They are particularly useful in town gardens and courtyards especially in tubs, window boxes, hanging baskets and other containers.

As cut flowers, sweet peas, calendulas, stocks, asters, antirrhinums, rudbeckias, love-in-a-mist and many more, last well in water. If space permits a small cutting garden of flowers from seed is an excellent investment.

It is not always realized that it is possible to grow such plants as petunias and *Phlox drummondii* in pots indoors and have flowers in the winter or early spring.

Prompt removal of faded flowers to prevent seed formation is essential with these flowers and usually prolongs the flowering season. Especially is this true with sweet peas and if such plants as alyssum, lobelia, and linaria are trimmed over hard after flowering they will produce a second and even, in favourable conditions, a third crop of flowers.

In the main these flowers do not suffer much from pests and diseases. Some, however, are very attractive to slugs in the seedling stage and one should take the precaution of scattering pellets of slug bait containing metaldehyde around the seedlings. The black keeled slug which operates below the ground can cause much damage to young sweet peas just after germination and for this reason it is wise to sow a few seeds in a pot or box as a reserve supply for filling any gaps.

Much work is being done in many countries upon breeding new and better flowers from seed. Many of the new strains are F^1 hybrids – that is they are the result of deliberately crossing two separate pure strains. These hybrids are usually more vigorous, often earlier, or larger flowered than either of their parents and it is always worth while trying a packet of any F^1 variety. But, it is a waste of time trying to save seeds of these F^1 hybrids as the progeny will not resemble the parent.

Greenhouse and House plants

After the second World War it was gloomily accepted by many people that the cultivation of greenhouse plants would never again become an important part of amateur gardening. Scarcity and high cost of labour, and rising costs of fuel, it was thought, would put greenhouse plants out of the reach of all but the wealthiest garden owners. But this did not happen. True, greenhouses, like gardens are smaller now, but there are between two and three million in British gardens and electricity has come to the aid of the gardener.

For houses of up to 30 feet in length and say 10 feet wide electricity is economically justifiable as a means of heating. For larger houses it would still pay to use oil or solid fuel. But for electric heating to be really economical it is essential to combine soil warming with space heating. Most plants the amateur wishes to grow, will grow very well if they have a root temperature of about $55°$ F. $(12\frac{1}{2}°$ C.) and $60°$ F. $(15°$ C.) and an air temperature of about $45°$ F. $(7°$ C.). But to maintain the soil in pots or borders at $55°$ F. by warming the air to that temperature is expensive. To raise the temperature from $45°$ F. to $50°$ F. will double the running costs, and to raise it to $55°$ F. will almost double them again. But by installing soil warming wires on benches, or in borders, the desired root temperature may be achieved at a very low cost and the air temperature is kept thermostatically controlled at $45°$ F.

Naturally there are some plants, certain orchids, and others that need higher temperatures and for them it is possible to section off part of the house, say at the end farthest from the door and keep this part rather warmer.

Ventilation may be taken care of by extractor fans. Small electrically heated propagating cases greatly facilitate the raising of seeds and the rooting of many types of cuttings. But mist propagation, made possible by the use of electricity, has revolutionized the propagation of plants by cuttings. Using the mist technique it is possible to root cuttings more quickly and to root cuttings of plants that could not be rooted, or only with great difficulty, by other methods.

Then plastic pots and seed trays have eased the work. They are much easier to clean than clay pots; also, as water does not evaporate through the plastic pot wall, the frequency of waterings is reduced. It is important however not to mix plastic and clay pots – keep the batches separate.

Supplies of good loam for making seed and potting composts are becoming steadily scarcer. Also the loam needs to be sterilized. So gardeners have welcomed the new seed and potting composts based entirely on peat. Again one has to learn the correct technique of watering these new composts and when potting plants in them the compost should never be firmed.

These developments together with new methods of pest and disease control – automatic aerosols and 'smoke cones' – and various systems of automatic watering have greatly eased the work of greenhouse maintenance.

When deciding upon the type of greenhouse to buy, if there is to be only one house, choose one with glass to the ground. Many plants, those grown for their foliage such as ivies, chlorophytums, pileas and the like are perfectly happy growing under a bench in this type of house and, of course, one can thus pack more plants in. Also it is usually feasible to have a third layer of plants either on shelves near the roof or in hanging baskets suspended from the roof.

If the greenhouse is spacious enough, one can grow such charming plants as hoyas, bougainvilleas, jasmines and the like, trained on wires up the side walls and over part of the roof. In small houses, however, climbers grown this way produce too much shade and it is usually better to grow them in large pots, training them round a framework of bamboo canes.

Most amateur greenhouse owners tend to begin with a mixed collection of plants, also using the house to raise seedlings and cuttings and to grow cut flowers or pot plants to bring into the home or to plant out in the garden for a few months in summer. The extension of the home into the garden by the erection of sun lounges attached to the house and warmed by the domestic heating system has given yet another fillip to greenhouse plants – again usually in a colourful collection.

But there are many types of plant that attract the gardener who likes to specialise – cacti, pelargoniums, perpetual flowering carnations, begonias, fuchsias, and of course, orchids. It is a common fallacy that orchids are difficult to grow, are fearfully expensive to buy and that they need costly high temperatures. As regards cultivation, they are not difficult, merely different in their requirements from those of other greenhouse plants. Probably with no other class of plant is it so important for the beginner to equip himself with a simple elementary book on orchid growing before taking the plunge. Certainly the rarer orchids and the latest new hybrids can be expensive, but many are very reasonable in price, and may be easily increased by the reasonably skilled amateur. Regarding temperatures, here again there are orchids, notably cymbidiums which only need frost protection. But of course some, such as cattleyas need higher temperatures and for them one has a smaller, warmer section of the orchid house.

In the main it is better to grow the different types of orchids in separate houses, but with care, certain orchids, notably cymbidiums and cypripediums can be grown with other plants, but priority in the growing conditions must be given to the orchids.

The uninitiated may find the terminology of orchids a trifle confusing, because of the use of the words 'grex' and 'clonal'. The word 'grex' is used to describe a group of hybrids usually, but not always originating from the crossing of more than two species.

It can however be used to describe the progeny of two varieties of orchid. For example *Cymbidium* Alexanderi crossed with *C.* Kittiwake produces a generation of seedling forms and these are given the 'grex' name Rosanna.

If any of these seedlings is propagated vegetatively, it will, of course, remain constant as to colour and habit. It may then be given a 'clonal' name. Thus we have *Cymbidium* Rosanna 'Pinkie', which is a variety that has been selected from the progeny of the original cross between *C.* Alexanderi and *C.* Kittiwake – the Rosanna grex, and has been propagated vegetatively by dividing the plants when they have produced sufficient pseudo-bulbs.

Orchid growers often use the term 'back bulbs'. By this they mean the pseudo-bulbs produced on the surface of the growing medium which can with care be severed from the parent plant and grown on separately to produce more plants of similar character to the parent.

Hardy Bulbous plants

The majority of the bulbs that we grow are native to countries where the weather enforces on them a dormant resting period underground, in our case the winter; in the case of many bulbs from countries of Asia Minor or those bordering the Mediterranean, the hot dry summer, sometimes both. Therefore they need a quick growing cycle and a means of storing nutriment while they are dormant so that they may have a good start when growth begins again. For this most bulbs are well adapted with large fleshy scales or swollen bases to the stem which absorb nutriment and increase in size during the growing period. A tuber is only another form of the same mechanism. This is relevant to their treatment in the garden. Without their resting period the majority will not succeed.

Bulbs and tubers give us some of our most valuable plants for the garden. For the early months of spring there are the snowdrops and snowflakes, the crocuses, reticulata irises, chionodoxas and scillas and many other small bulbs which are a delight whenever the weather permits and are sufficiently tough to last, largely unharmed, when it is bad. These are followed by the daffodils, hyacinths and tulips and later in summer there are the lilies, surely some of the most beautiful of all flowering plants, the galtonias and crinums while in early autumn we have more crocuses, the crocosmias (including montbretias), the nerines and the amaryllis. There is a great range in all these kinds.

Bulbs may be used in the garden and house in a variety of ways; in most cases the flower is already formed in embryo in the bulb before we buy it, so that providing it is of sufficient size and we treat it reasonably we are likely to get a flower in the first year after planting. There is no other group of plants in which we can be so certain. Consequently for the newly formed garden they are invaluable.

The ways of growing bulbs include formal bedding, less practised today but still invaluable in some larger gardens and in public parks, in the border or rock garden, naturalised in grass or in the wild garden, in the cool or warm greenhouse, in pots or bowls for indoor decoration and for cut flowers. For some of the choicer bulbs from the Mediterranean, the bulb frame where they may be assured of a dry resting period in summer is ideal. Some of the smaller bulbs such as the crocus species are also lovely in the alpine house in spring or in raised sinks where they may easily be seen. They require no extra heat.

While tolerant of a very wide range of conditions, most bulbs will grow and flower better in ground which has been generously prepared although they do not require fresh manure, rather compost or old well rotted manure will suit them better. Some feeding with bonemeal, dried blood and sulphate of potash or with complete artificial fertilisers will benefit them in nearly all cases.

The majority of bulbs such as daffodils, hyacinths, scillas and tulips, should be planted in the autumn. September is not too early to plant daffodils but they may also be planted up till November. Tulips are better planted in October or early November, later than the daffodils; lilies are best when planted early in the autumn, mid-September or early October, but few suppliers deliver so early. Lily bulbs received when the soil is frozen or very wet and cold in winter should not be planted outside then but put into pots or boxes with leafmould or peat and then planted out in early spring. The exact depth of planting is generally not very important within reasonable limits. In general a depth of about twice the height of the bulb is appropriate, i.e. crocuses at two inches, daffodils at three to four inches. In light sandy soils they may be planted deeper than in heavy clay soils. Autumn flowering crocuses and cyclamen are best planted in August while tender bulbs or corms such as those of gladioli should be planted in April or early May so that they do not emerge before the frosts are over. These tender bulbs need to be lifted in autumn and stored in frost-free conditions. Many lift their tulips annually in late June or early July and replant again in October and on damp soils this is certainly advisable.

A few formal beds often seem suitable near the house since they can be arranged so as to give colour at several seasons. If not too large they are not really a great labour or as much trouble as is sometimes suggested. For these hyacinths and tulips are the most common choices. For such beds it is not necessary to buy the largest hyacinth bulbs since their spikes will be so massive as to need individual staking. The medium-sized bulbs are more appropriate. Hyacinths may either be planted in a solid mass on their own or they may be spaced more widely and interplanted with a dwarf spreading plant such as the double white arabis. The best combination with tulips, I think, is still the blue forget-me-not especially with the pink tulips such as 'Mariette' or 'Queen of Bartigons', but dwarf yellow or primrose-coloured wallflowers or again white arabis will look well and will prolong slightly the season of flowering. The Darwin hybrid tulips with their enormous glowing scarlet flowers are excellent for bedding since they have great vigour. Flowering a little earlier than the Darwin tulips, they are over earlier and may be removed to make room for the summer bedding. Some of the dwarf bulbs such as scillas and muscari may also be considered for small beds or for interplanting with dwarf carpeting plants.

Only the larger bulbs are suitable for the border but in a mixed shrub and herbaceous border daffodils and tulips will provide some good spring colour before the other plants are making any show and their foliage will largely have died away before the herbaceous plants flower. Clumps of daffodils planted round the base of climbing or large shrub roses nearly always look well and cover the bare bases of the shrubs. Daffodils also look well naturalised among the grass of an orchard where the grass may be left till the middle of June before cutting to allow the foliage of the bulbs to mature. Tulips are not suitable for planting in grass but crocuses, chionodoxas and snowdrops will make lovely groups of colour before the daffodils are out. The little rosy-purple *Crocus tomasinianus* is usually the first to flower and has the capacity of spreading widely by seeding while for autumn flowering the bluer *Crocus speciosus* will do the same. These are two invaluable bulbs that one would never wish to be without. Naturalised bulbs should always be planted in irregular loose groups rather than in tight symmetrical masses such as are required for formal bedding.

Wherever bulbs are planted, however, and especially in places where they are intended to remain for some time, it is desirable to prepare the ground before planting and to mix in some compost or other feeding material with the soil. In the case of planting in grass, especially in light sandy soils, it is worthwhile to lift the turf, prepare the ground underneath, plant the bulbs and then replace the turf. If bulbs are merely planted in small holes made in the turf they will probably flower well the first year but afterwards will be likely to dwindle in size and effect. Bonemeal and dried blood are good fertilisers for bulbs, the former being slow acting. Sulphate of potash is also desirable for use in building up the bulb if applied about flowering time while the foliage is still green. Complete fertilisers may also be used. A bulb has a limited growing period and so must not be starved.

For the rock garden some of the smaller crocus and iris species are ideal and as long as damage from mice can be prevented, many will increase into lovely natural groups but they need to be planted in places where they will not be damp in summer. Such places as raised ledges or at the base of dwarf conifers or other shrubs are suitable. They combine particularly well with grey or silver-leaved shrubs in most cases and the roots of these will usually keep them dry in summer. Dwarf daffodils may be treated in the same way but do not require to be kept so dry. Dwarf tulips also look very well in such situations but in most areas the bulbs will need lifting each summer.

Another good method of growing these dwarf bulbs, particularly those which require a warm dry period in the summer, is in the raised frame which can be covered and kept dry from mid-June to late September. For such a frame I recommend a compost of one part loam, one part coarse sand and one part peat thoroughly mixed and, if possible, sterilised but this is not absolutely essential. At about 6 inches below the surface and so below the level at which the bulbs are planted, a layer about an inch or two thick of old well rotted manure or compost may be included but fresh manure must not be used. Some prefer to top dress the frame also with a thin layer of shingle which will prevent any moisture accumulating round the stem of the bulb and also give a tidier look to the frame. Fine examples of such frames can be seen by the alpine house in the R.H.S. Garden at Wisley in Surrey and they are most rewarding in the wide range of bulbs which flourish in them, particularly dwarf irises, crocuses and tulips. The glass can be used also to provide some protection from bad weather in winter and the flowers will be the more perfect inside them than in the open ground. The majority of such bulbs are quite tough as far as frost and cold are concerned but are much more sensitive to excessive damp. They should be given good ventilation at all times.

The cool greenhouse can be made lovely in the spring with pots or pans of bulbs which require little heat to bring them into flower a little earlier than those outside and almost any of the bulbs, corms or tubers mentioned will grow well there. If they are grown in a completely unheated house the pots should be plunged in shingle, earth or peat moss as some protection from hard freezing. Lilies are also very magnificent in pots in a cool greenhouse in the summer but they must be planted with good drainage and kept well sprayed against aphis and botrytis. Dwarf bulbs are suitable for growing in pans in the Alpine house and those that require summer resting may be more readily looked after there than in the open ground.

Bulbs such as daffodils, hyacinths and tulips are also grown widely in bulb fibre in undrained bowls for house decoration. They should be planted as early as possible in September or October in damp bulb fibre and the noses of the bulbs can be left above the level of the fibre. This should be only so moist that no water can be squeezed out of it. All such bulbs require a cool period without light after planting during which the roots grow. They should only be brought into the light and warmth of the ordinary living room or greenhouse after the buds or leaves have appeared out of the bulb for about an inch. This is usually early in December or in some cases later. Afterwards they will grow away quickly. Specially prepared bulbs of hyacinths, tulips and daffodils are also usually available in which the ripening period and some of the initial cool period has already been given artificially in the bulb store, so they will grow away more quickly than untreated bulbs. Such bulbs will flower from Christmas onwards and brighten the house during the latter half of the winter and early spring.

Perennial plants

In the strict concept of the herbaceous border, so beloved by former generations, only plants which are cut down to the ground every year after flowering were used. But times and gardening fashions have changed. Gardens are smaller, or in large gardens the features are smaller and usually fewer than in the days when labour was cheap and easily obtainable. So borders of hardy flowers are now planned to allow spaces where patches of bulbs, myosotis and other spring flowering plants may be planted to be followed by annual flowers such as antirrhinums, petunias, and the like, which will continue to provide colour into late summer. These in turn may be replaced by tagetes and dwarf pompon chrysanthemums which have been grown elsewhere in the garden and if well watered before lifting and again after planting may be moved successfully just as they are coming into flower.

Then there is the 'mixed border' consisting of a careful selection of flowering shrubs, or suitable evergreens, dwarf golden conifers, winter flowering heathers and so on, combined with kniphofias, phloxes, Michaelmas daisies, tall or dwarf, or any of a hundred other herbaceous plants, so that there is something of interest in the borders all through the year.

Naturally it is easy enough to plan a border that will be a blaze of glory, say, in June or July, or if desired in September, but it is a more complicated exercise to plant so that there is some colour over many months. These mixed borders will never be a blaze of colour but, especially if one sees them all the time from the house, they will always have something to offer.

Shortage of labour has had another effect on the composition and design of herbaceous or mixed borders. At one time such borders were always planted against a wall, fence or hedge, either to hide the fence, or to make use of the wall or hedge as a background. But plants grown in such a position tend to lean towards the light, away from the wall or hedge and thus become 'drawn' and need some kind of staking. So the idea of the free-standing bed has gained great popularity in recent years. Many plants that would need support in a traditional border against a hedge need no staking in a free-standing bed, or at the most a few pea sticks pushed in around them.

Free-standing beds have other advantages. As one can walk all round them it is usually possible to do any hoeing or weeding from the side without having to penetrate very far into the bed. Also by planting a shrub or two here and there one can create a rather more shady spot for those plants that prefer not to be always in the full glare of the sun.

When planting these types of bed or border it must be remembered that the herbaceous plants will remain without disturbance for several years. Some plants such as paeonies should never be disturbed, but others – phloxes, Michaelmas daisies, erigerons and the like – need to be lifted, divided and replanted every three years or so.

The ground should be thoroughly prepared before planting. All perennial weeds, especially couch grass, ground elder and convolvulus should be eliminated and if these weeds are present it would be wise to dig the site over in spring, wait for a massive crop of foliage on the weeds and then destroy them with applications of the various weedkillers now available. Then in the autumn the ground may be dug, manure or compost incorporated and planting may begin.

For consistently good results it is desirable to make provision for watering. This can be done by using the various types of overhead sprinklers, but these often tend to beat the plants down when they are in full growth and make them look rather bedraggled. Another excellent method and economical of water, is to lay sub-irrigation pipes about 6–8 inches below the surface when preparing the bed or border. One can lay the ordinary 2-inch land drains butted together in lines about 2 feet apart and then with a hose pipe pour water down these lines. It will filter out and keep the soil moist below the surface. Alternatively, one can lay lengths of semi-rigid, punctuated plastic pipes 6–8 inches below the surface. Holes are easily made in this type of plastic pipe about 6 inches apart with a bradawl filed down to about the thickness of a gramophone needle. Applied thus underground the water is not lost by evaporation and the plants' roots are encouraged to go down and search for it.

It is also advisable to mulch these beds or borders with say a 2-inch layer of compost, sawdust, spent hops, peat, mushroom manure, or some similar material. This mulch helps to conserve moisture in the soil, and virtually eliminates hoeing. Any weeds that do appear are usually easily pulled out as the soil is moist beneath. It must be remembered that a mulch tends to keep the soil cold, so it should not be put on too early in the year – the middle to the end of April is soon enough as the soil should have begun to warm up by then. Also, if sawdust is used as a mulch it is desirable to scatter a handful of sulphate of ammonia over each square yard of a two-inch mulch. This is to provide nitrogen, because the soil bacteria will set to work to decompose the sawdust and they need nitrogen. Thus they sometimes rob the soil of nitrogen and symptoms of nitrogen deficiency may appear. This is more likely however, when the sawdust is dug in than when it is merely spread over the surface. If dug in, one should apply 1 cwt of sulphate of ammonia, with each ton of sawdust.

Planting of hardy perennial flowers may be done at any time when the ground is workable from October until the end of April. It is best however to plant the fleshy rooted plants such as lupins, anchusas, and the like in the autumn. When lifting and dividing perennials, discard the worn-out centre of the clump and only replant strong young pieces from the outside of the clump.

Trees and Shrubs

Trees and Shrubs should form the backbone and framework of every garden. Even if it is small there will still be room for one or two and it is important to choose those which will conform to the scale. Since they are intended to be permanent, probably for the life of the owner, great care should be taken in their selection and ample room should be allowed for those which are likely to be long lived or move badly. This will leave a new garden looking rather bare but it is possible to fill in some of the gaps with shrubs that, being ball rooted, will move easily and almost at any size, such as rhododendrons and azaleas, or with those such as cistus which tend to live for some years and then succumb to a bad winter but which are at any rate easily propagated from cuttings. Alternatively the spaces may be filled in with annuals and herbaceous perennials and bulbs which can be moved later. Probably most gardeners will want to do some underplanting with bulbs anyway.

It is important also to consider the balance between evergreen and deciduous trees and shrubs. A garden with no evergreens will look bare and colourless in winter; again trees and shrubs with some yellow in their foliage, such as the golden forms of the Lawson cypress or the variegated *Elaeagnus pungens* such as 'Dicksonii' or even the old golden form of privet, will bring light and colour into the garden in winter. Variegated hollies can give the same effect. Form is also important; the upright growing fastigiate trees such as the Dawyck beech or a flowering cherry such as 'Amanogawa' or a *Libocedrus decurrens* as an evergreen can often find a space where a spreading tree would be too large. One of these will stick up like a spire in the garden and provide contrast to the other more horizontal growing shrubs or herbaceous perennials. One of the finest examples of this contrast planting can be seen in one of the glades at the Westonbirt Arboretum in Gloucestershire. Growing there is a group of the *Libocedrus*, perhaps now 50 feet high but each not more than 6 feet across, flanked by *Parrotia persica* which grows with horizontal branches and flames brilliant oranges and scarlets in the autumn before its leaves drop.

Autumn colour is a very valuable factor to consider when planting, especially in the trees and shrubs which give a dual effect, having a good flowering season and then a good autumn season such as *Prunus sargentii* or *Amelanchier canadensis*. Scarlet leaf colour in autumn shows up much better if it has a good contrasting background of evergreen and again a visit to the Westonbirt Arboretum in the autumn will demonstrate this better than any writing for the planting has been made with great artistry and skill.

The range of trees and shrubs is now enormous although, except for hybrid tea and floribunda roses, new varieties do not pour out in the same incessant stream as do new dahlias or chrysanthemums and many of the finest trees and shrubs are still the species introduced by our great plant collectors. So many of the best trees and shrubs and especially our rhododendrons come from the Himalayas or the mountains of Western China, our finest conifers mostly come from the Pacific coast of North America while the mountains of Chile and South America have given us beauties like *Embothrium* and *Crinodendron* (*Tricuspidaria*), the red lantern bush. From New Zealand came the leptospermums and many of the olearias, while from Australia and Tasmania came the *Eucalyptus* and some of the eucryphias, the remainder of these being South American. It will be found that the South American and New Zealand plants are mostly intolerant of very hot, dry conditions in summer and are rather tender in cold areas, but in milder gardens can be absolutely magnificent. The Mediterranean shrubs such as the *Cistus* and also many of the shrub roses, though flower better where the summers are perhaps a little warmer and drier.

Gardeners who work on soil containing chalk or free lime must avoid a number of the ericaceous plants such as rhododendrons and most heathers; the forms of the winter-flowering *Erica carnea* will, however, tolerate lime. Probably the ideal tree and shrub soil is a deep loam and it will grow the widest range but, apart from the chalk factor, the majority will grow over a great variety of soils. It is difficult to grow the finest rhododendrons on very hot, dry sandy soil without extra watering in summer because they have fine roots which congregate near the surface in balls and do not spread deeply downwards. On such soils the cistus, rock roses and the potentillas will do well.

Since trees and shrubs are likely to be long lasting it is important to take some trouble over the preparation of the site and the planting. For a new tree a hole 3 or 4 feet across and 18 inches deep is not too large. The bottom should be broken up and enriched with compost or well rotted, not fresh, manure, while in hot sandy soils some well dampened peat will help. It is useless to put in dry peat straight from the bag since this may never become sufficiently moist. The roots should be well spread out and the soil or compost worked down among them by a judicious slight shaking of the tree. Some gardeners like to make a small mound towards the centre of the hole and place the centre of the tree on it, spreading the roots downwards and outwards from it. This is also the time to insert a good firm stake to which the tree must be tied, preferably with a rubber tree tie which will not eat into the bark as the trunk expands. This is most important. Then the soil should be filled in and firmed so that it reaches up to the level of the previous planting mark on the trunk. It is dangerous to plant much more deeply than the previous level and this is the cause of many casualties. It is particularly important not to plant rhododendrons too deep. The ball of roots should only be covered with a thin layer of leaf mould or peat.

Early pruning and shaping is also important. As a general rule crossing branches should be taken out. If a straight trunk is required the lower side branches need to be taken out at an early stage but do not remove so much in any one year as to weaken the young tree. Again a double leader, where there is a fork instead of one stem, needs attention and the weaker of the two shoots should be cut out. Observation of the growth of a mature specimen will usually provide a clue as to the form of pruning required. Notes are given in most cases under the particular genera. Where a shrub flowers along the young wood produced in the previous year, such as a philadelphus or a deutzia, it should be pruned immediately after flowering; all the branches which have flowered being cut right out down to the older wood so as to encourage as many young shoots as possible to come from lower down. If one leaves all the old flowering branches, new but normally rather weak shoots will grow from near the top and after a few years the bush will become lanky and straggly and no ornament to the garden. Also it will be likely to flower less well. In the case of these and also in the larger shrub roses it is an advantage to cut out each year a few of the very old and woody branches right down to ground level so as to bring light and air to the younger shoots. A shrub congested like a witch's broom is seldom of any use till it has been pruned drastically. Older trees and large shrubs which flower on the old wood usually only require that any dead wood should be removed by cutting right back to the main trunk or branch. Any unwanted branches should be removed at the same time.

Propagation of trees and shrubs is either from seed, which is usually slow, by cuttings or from layers where a branch may be bent down to soil level or bent down and placed in a raised box of soil. Seed in most cases is sown in pots or boxes in the early spring but in the case of certain large seeds with hard coats, such as those of tree peonies or oaks, it is often an advantage to sow in the autumn and leave outside for the winter frost to soften them up and they may then germinate in the following spring, though in some instances two winters may be needed. Cuttings of shrubs are usually taken towards the end of June with soft shoots of the current year's growth. They should either be cut with a small part of the older tissue as a 'heel' or just below a joint, always with a really sharp knife.

A mist spray installation is a great help where large numbers of cuttings are required to be rooted and often difficult cuttings can be rooted in this way which would not easily be rooted under more normal conditions. Many shrubs, however, such as helianthemums and cistuses are easily rooted on an open greenhouse bench while cuttings of smaller leaved rhododendrons and most camellias are easily rooted in a closed propagating case. This process is hastened though with a small amount of heat below them which is easily supplied by electric wiring. They must never be allowed to dry out while rooting. After rooting, which may take from about three weeks to three months, they should be transferred to individual small pots or planted out in a frame and at this stage they do not require much artificial heat.

Layering is particularly used in the case of rhododendrons and azaleas. The process may take eighteen months or two years before the layers are ready to be separated from the parent plant, but during this time they require little attention. It is important to make a sharp twist, as near right angled as possible, before attaching the younger layer to a stick. Many trees and shrubs also are grafted onto other rootstock. For instance, *Hamamelis mollis* is nearly always grafted onto stock of *H. virginiana* while the majority of roses and flowering cherries sold are grafted onto more vigorous growing stocks. For specimen trees or standards or where only one is required, however, it is usually better for the amateur gardener to buy ready grown specimens from a good nurseryman for these will already have been given their initial shape.

Photographing plants

by Harold D. J. Cole, Hon. FRPS, FIIP

Past President Royal Photographic Society Great Britain

Colour photography is no longer a novelty and something demanding high skill and expensive apparatus. Most people today have accepted the fact that the easiest and most rewarding way of making a permanent colour record of holidays, children, gardens and flowers is to photograph them as colour slides or negatives suitable for colour prints. Good colour photographs may be taken quite easily on inexpensive cameras.

The continuing advances in the manufacture of colour films and processing techniques makes the photographer's job easier. As faster films are made it becomes easier to take pictures in poorer light. A faster film also makes it possible to use a higher shutter speed, which helps to arrest the movement of flowers swaying in the breeze.

Photographing growing plants provides opportunities of showing flowers in many different ways. It is a matter of personal preference whether to show the whole plant, a single bloom, or one or two blooms possibly including some foliage, though the composition of the picture is important. The most common mistake made is the inclusion of too much detail. A good picture must be bold, simple in its construction and be able to impress at once. The arrangement and lighting is a very personal thing which can only be compared with an artist and his interpretations of a particular scene and we should never expect to please everybody all the time. It is important however, when framing the picture in the viewfinder, not to include large areas of unwanted foreground or uninteresting details in the scene.

The condition of the selected flower is always important so take care to photograph the best bloom, in its peak condition. Time spent in 'tidying up' the plant, removing any faded blooms and trimming up the foliage is always worthwhile. When possible I like to include a bud partly opened with some foliage. I feel a flower is not just an object to which the standard routine treatment for photographing the inanimate can be applied. Depending on its character, shape and structure, each flower demands its own individual treatment. For example, if emphasis is to be given to the bloom only and not to show the plant in situ, then it is desirable to isolate the flower. A plain tone background may be provided by standing a piece of board carefully behind the plant and which may be supported by two bamboo canes pressed firmly into the soil. In many cases, especially with close-up studies, sufficient isolation of the flower can be attained without the need for the portable background.

Consideration must also be given to the lighting. This for preference should be the softer light of afternoon rather than the harsh midday lighting or a time when the sun is too low so as not to upset the colour balance of the photograph. Too much red in the light would make the picture too yellow and affect the rendering of other colours – particularly the many shades of blue.

There is not very much difference in the photographic technique for taking flower pictures in monochrome and in colour. Correct exposure sets the seal of quality on any colour photograph and the margin that exists between 'just right' and nearly right' is comparatively narrow. Even in black and white photography where the permissible latitude in exposure variation is considerable, it is always better to aim for a correctly exposed negative. The use of an exposure meter will help to ensure uniformity of exposure over a wide range of different brightness values and the printed slip, which is wrapped round the film in the carton, gives exposure guides for daylight and artificial light pictures and tables a range of readings for different lighting conditions such as bright sun, hazy sun, cloudy and heavy cloud. With very light subjects it is as well to *close* the aperture by $\frac{1}{2}$ stop, and for close-up studies and dark subjects, especially those with heavy dark foliage, *open* the aperture by $\frac{1}{2}$ stop. In practice, colour photographs only give detail within a limited range, or in the part for which the exposure has been calculated.

In close-up photography the distance from subject to lens must be very carefully determined since the depth of field is very small. Where you have to rely upon the viewfinder only the framing seen may not necessarily represent accurately what will be in your picture. The difference, called parallax, is only serious when coming in very close and many cameras have special framelines included, within the normal format, on the viewfinder to help overcome the problem. For close-up work consult your photographic dealer for special attachments or lenses which should be used with your particular camera.

Some mention should be made of flash in flower photography, for when the ordinary available light is poor it may be necessary to add more light to the subject. This is done by using a simple flash gun either fixed to the camera or held slightly away. Colour films are balanced for exposure either to daylight or to artificial light. With the daylight slide film it is necessary to use the blue type flash bulbs but a special filter should be used for the artificial light film if blue bulbs are used in daylight. Details of exposure settings for different films and flash bulbs will be found in the instructions supplied with the flash bulbs and must be carefully studied before exposures are made.

In conclusion I would just like to give a little advice to flower photographers who experience some disappointment in the colour reproduction of some of our blue flowers. Most people react instinctively against a flower well known to them if it is shown in other than its natural colours. Many of us do not suspect until too late that blue flowers often reflect a large amount of red and infra red, in addition to the blue colour normally associated with them. The human eye is relatively very insensitive to the reds, while strongly sensitive to the blues, thus seeing the flower as a pure blue. Most colour films are sensitive to the blue and also to the reds and infra reds and so the flower which appears blue to the eye is rendered a rather unattractive pink or mauve by the film. A very pale blue filter over the camera lens will often help.

These few notes I hope will help to increase the pleasure obtained by many keen garden photographers.

Acknowledgments

Mr Roy Hay has been responsible for the sections on Annuals and Biennials, on Herbaceous perennials and on Greenhouse and House plants including succulents; Mr Patrick Synge for the sections on Alpines, Bulbs, Trees and Shrubs. They would like to acknowledge help received from numerous advisers in particular Mr Richard Gorer (Greenhouse and House plants), Mr Denis Hardwicke (Herbaceous perennials), and Mr Alan Bloom (Herbaceous perennials). Mr H. G. Hillier kindly allowed the use of his excellent catalogue which was of great assistance in compiling the section on Trees and Shrubs. Mr George Kalmbacher, Taxonomist, Brooklyn Botanic Garden, New York, has provided useful advice and information on all sections.

In addition the following authorities nominated by the Royal Horticultural Society, have read the sections as indicated and given advice which is gratefully acknowledged.

Mr E. B. Anderson, VMH – Alpines and Bulbs
Mr C. R. Gould – Annuals and Biennials
Mrs Frances Perry – Herbaceous perennials
Mr John Warren – Greenhouse and House plants
Mr O. E. P. Wyatt, VMH – Trees and Shrubs

Mr T. Wellsted and his staff have undertaken the work of inserting the cross references throughout the text and the authors acknowledge with thanks their help in this heavy task which has added greatly to the value of the book.

This book has only been possible due to the kindness of a great many nurserymen and societies, and the perseverance of the photographers whose pictures appear on the following pages.

In particular the nurserymen, nurseries and others listed below have allowed the photographers access and facilities which at times must have held their own work up considerably and a great debt is owed to them. It is hoped that the pictures of their plants are some recompense.

Allwood Bros, Wivelsfield Nurseries, Haywards Heath, Sussex – Plates 499–510 and 1092–1107.

A. C. Ayton Esq., Pelargonium Nurseries, Southborough, Kent – Plates 586–617.

R. C. Barnard Esq., Cormiston, Milverton, Taunton, Somerset – Plates 1597–1600.

Blackmore & Langdon Ltd, Bath, Somerset – Plates 419–422, 424–430, 1086, 1088–1090.

Walter Blom & Son Ltd, Leavesden, Hertfordshire – Plates 671, 684, 697, 699, 702, 704, 705, 709, 711–714, 730, 731, 732, 737–740, 742, 744, 745, 749–763, 766, 767, 770–772, 777, 778, 780–783, 786–789, 805, 806, 824, 825, 828, 829, 831–833, 840, 861–863, 873, 878, 882, 892, 894, 895, 897, 908, 911–940, 1069, 1076, 1080.

Alan Bloom, Bressingham Gardens, Diss, Norfolk – Plates 954, 956, 959, 963, 1006, 1010, 1055, 1059, 1119, 1124, 1135, 1138, 1140, 1143, 1147, 1148, 1157, 1158, 1161, 1168, 1170, 1172, 1181, 1233, 1241, 1242, 1274, 1302, 1309, 1311, 1315, 1316, 1321, 1329, 1331, 1338, 1340, 1346, 1349, 1350, 1354, 1358, 1362, 1364, 1369, 1372, 1375, 1386, 1388, 1397, 1401, 1402, 1419, 1423.

Broadleigh Gardens, Sampford Arundel, nr Wellington, Somerset – Plates 835, 841, 844, 899.

Charlesworth & Co. Ltd, Haywards Heath, Sussex – Plates 434, 442, 487–491, 493, 494, 497, 498, 522, 557–559, 574–582, 655.

Elm Garden Nurseries, Claygate, Surrey – Plates 431, 451, 453–455, 457, 459, 462–464, 466, 467, 515, 1041, 1044.

J. P. Everett, Esq., Trevcott, Little Clacton – Plates 316, 317, 319–321.

Hillier and Sons, Winchester – Nearly all the Tree and Shrub plates.

Nigel Nicholson, Esq. MBE, Sissinghurst Castle, Kent – Plate 88.

Stuart Ogg, Esq., Swanley, Kent – Plates 1061, 1064, 1067, 1070–1072, 1079, 1083.

Orpington Nurseries Co. Ltd, Orpington, Kent – Plates 658, 677.

The Superintendent, Oxford Botanical Gardens – Plates 567–573.

Thomas Rochford & Sons Ltd, Turnford Hall Nurseries, Hoddesdon, Hertfordshire – Plates 404, 470, 516–518, 543, 552, 622, 626, 628, 629, 642, 643, 647, 649.

The Curator, Royal Botanical Gardens, Kew, Surrey – Plates 984, 995, 1004, 1054, 1058, 1111, 1134, 1146, 1150, 1152, 1229, 1257, 1278, 1288, 1291, 1304, 1319, 1326, 1361, 1377, 1379, 1389, 1390, 1400.

The Director, Royal Horticultural Society Garden, Wisley, Surrey –
Plates 8, 15, 17, 19, 26, 49, 62, 85, 91, 99, 102, 123, 151, 198, 217, 479, 814, 945, 946, 949, 951, 952, 955, 961, 962, 967, 969, 973, 974, 976, 979, 981, 982, 992, 996–998, 1003, 1005, 1008, 1012, 1013, 1018, 1022, 1050–1052, 1056, 1087, 1091, 1108–1110, 1112, 1115, 1117, 1121, 1126, 1127, 1131, 1132, 1137, 1142, 1145, 1149, 1154, 1156, 1159, 1160, 1166, 1167, 1169, 1171, 1173, 1176, 1178, 1179, 1182–1184, 1190, 1225, 1228, 1232, 1235, 1239, 1245, 1249, 1250, 1256, 1258–1261, 1272, 1275, 1276, 1287, 1290, 1297, 1310, 1312, 1317, 1322–1325, 1330, 1332–1336, 1341, 1342, 1344, 1353, 1360, 1361, 1373, 1374, 1376, 1382, 1383, 1385, 1387, 1392, 1399, 1403, 1414, 1415, 1418, 1420, 1422, 1462, 1472, 1475, 1503, 1504, 1652, 1700, 1802.

H. C. Russell Esq., Wells (Merstham) Ltd, Redhill, Surrey – Plates 448–450, 452, 460, 461, 1025–1027, 1029, 1030, 1033, 1034, 1038, 1042, 1043.

Sir Eric Savill, KCVO, and the Crown Estate Commissioners, Savill Garden, Windsor Great Park – Plates 964, 970, 980, 1024, 1128, 1162, 1265, 1270, 1277, 1299, 1307, 1359.

Director of Parks, Slough Borough Council – Plates 415–418.

Messrs Thompson & Morgan (Ipswich) Ltd, Ipswich, Suffolk – Plates 225–231, 233–235, 237, 238, 240, 242, 244, 247–252, 256, 259–261, 263–265, 269–275, 278–282, 284–287, 290, 293–295, 299–304, 306, 308–313, 315, 318, 323, 324, 329–332, 334, 336–340, 346, 350, 354, 355, 357, 360–363, 365–370, 372, 374–376, 378, 379, 383, 386, 391, 392, 397–400, 1305.

Lt-Cdr T. Dorrien-Smith and the Head Gardener, Tresco Abbey Gardens, Isles of Scilly – Plates 1510, 1648.

Messrs Wallace & Barr Ltd, Marden, Kent – Plate 820.

John Waterer Son & Crisp Ltd, The Floral Mile, Twyford, Berkshire – Plates 960, 989, 990, 1120, 1123, 1139, 1153, 1352, 1356, 1417.

The Royal Horticultural Society by allowing the photographers to take pictures at the fortnightly and Chelsea shows, where many nurserymen went out of their way with assistance, has been of inestimable value.

The main bulk of the photography has been done by six photographers over a period of about eighteen months, a commendable feat and great thanks are due to Mr J. E. Downward, FIIP, and Mr Ernest Crowson, FIIP, FRPS, especially for work at the Royal Horticultural Society's shows; Miss Valerie Finnis, whose pictures form most of the Alpine and Rock Garden Section as well as contributing to other sections; Mr John Gapp, whose photographs nearly complete two sections, the Annuals and Biennials and the Greenhouse and House plants; Miss Elsa S. Megson, without whom the border plants in the Perennial Section would be sadly lacking and Mr D. Woodland, who heroically took most of the pictures in the largest section Trees and Shrubs.

Despite the splendid achievements of the above six photographers, gaps were inevitable with so short a time available and the completion of the work would not have been possible without contributions from Mr Bernard Alfieri; Mr Anthony Huxley (Alpine and other plants); Mr H. C. Russell (Chrysanthemums); Mr Harry Smith and Mr Patrick M. Synge. Special contributions were also made by:

Armstrong Nurseries, USA (Roses) – Plates 1865, 1872.

H. Castle-Fletcher (Irises) – Plates 1187, 1189, 1191, 1194, 1196, 1198, 1200, 1201, 1202, 1206, 1208–1210, 1212, 1213, 1215, 1216, 1218–1221.

Mr H. D. J. Cole, Hon. FRPS, FIIP (Irises) – Plates 1205, 1207.

Mr John Goater (Fuchsias) – Plates 534–536.

Mr Jan de Graaff (Lilies) – Plate 815.

Mr George Kalmbacher, Taxonomist, Brooklyn Botanic Garden, New York – Plates 635, 644.

Roses by Fred Edmunds, USA – Plate 1862.

Star Roses, USA – Plate 1884.

Mr G. Wells (Fuchsias) – Plates 537–539.

For the photograph of *Abies forrestii*, Plate 2002, thanks are given to the unknown photographer. Endeavours were made to contact him but without avail and apologies are therefore also tendered for its use.

It would not be just to leave the photographic acknowledgments without mentioning the help given by the photographic firm of Ilford Limited, Ilford, Essex. Their enthusiasm for the project in its early days, their generous contributions of film and processing facilities launched the book. They have also been most generous in allowing the producers of this book to use some of the plates taken from their own series of books – *The Ilford Books of Flower Identification*.

1
Adonis amurensis

2
Aethionema
'Warley Rose'

3
Alyssum saxatile
'Citrinum'

4
Anacyclus depressus

5
Anagallis linifolia
'Grandiflora'

6
Anagallis linifolia
'Monellii'

7
Androsace helvetica

8
Androsace
jacquemontii

9
Androsace
lanuginosa

10
Androsace pyrenaica

11
Androsace villosa
'Arachnoidea'

12
Anthemis cupaniana

13
Arabis albida
'Flore Pleno'

14
Armeria caespitosa
'Bevan's Variety'

15
Armeria maritima
'Vindictive'

16
Asperula suberosa

17
Aster alpinus

18
Astilbe chinensis

19
Aubrieta
'Barker's Double'

20
Aubrieta
'Lavender Queen'

21
Boykinia jamesii

22
Calceolaria darwinii

23
Campanula carpatica

24
Campanula
cochlearifolia
'Alba'

25
Campanula
garganica

26
Campanula
portenschlagiana

27
Campanula zoysii

28
Cassiope
'Edinburgh'

29
Cassiope
lycopodioides

30
Celmisia coriacea

31
Celmisia petiolata

32
Celmisia spectabilis

33
Celsia acaulis

34
Cheiranthus
'Wenlock Beauty'

35
Chrysanthemum
haradjanii

36
Codonopsis ovata

37
Convolvulus
althaeoides

38
Convolvulus
mauritanicus

39
Cornus canadensis

40
Corydalis
cashmeriana

41
Cotyledon
oppositifolia

42
Cyananthus lobatus

43
Cyananthus
microphyllus

44
Cypripedium
calceolus

45
Cytisus ardoinii

46
Cytisus beanii

47
Daphne cneorum

48
Daphne petraea
'Grandiflora'

49
Dianthus alpinus

50
Dianthus deltoides

51
Dianthus
gratianopolitanus

52
Dianthus neglectus

53
Dicentra peregrina
var. pusilla

54
Dimorphotheca
barberiae

55
Dionysia aretioides

56
Dodecatheon alpinum

57
Douglasia vitaliana

58
Draba bryoides var.
imbricata

59
Draba mollissima

60
Dryas octopetala

61
Edraianthus pumilio

62
Edraianthus
serpyllifolius
'Major'

63
Erigeron aureus

64
Erigeron mucronatus

65
Erinacea pungens

66
Eritrichium nanum

67
Erodium corsicum
'Rubrum'

68
Erodium guttatum

69
Euphorbia myrsinites

70
Euryops acraeus

71
Gentiana acaulis

72
Gentiana
'Inverleith'

73
Gentiana
lagodechiana

74
Gentiana saxosa

75
Gentiana sino-ornata

76
Gentiana verna

77
Gentiana verna

78
Geranium cinereum
'Ballerina'

79
Geranium
subcaulescens

80
Glaucidium
palmatum
'Album'

81
Gypsophila repens

82
Haberlea rhodopensis

83
Hacquetia epipactis

84
**Helianthemum
'Ben Hope'**

85
**Helianthemum
'Fire Dragon'**

86
**Helichrysum
frigidum**

87
**Helichrysum
milfordiae**

88
Hepatica × ballardii

89
Hepatica triloba

90
Hypericum
polyphyllum

91
Hypericum
rhodopaeum

92
Iberis saxatilis

93
Iris douglasiana

94
Iris lacustris

95
Iris verna

96
Jankaea heldreichii

97
Jeffersonia dubia

98
**Leontopodium
alpinum**

99
**Leptospermum
scoparium
'Nicholsii Nanum'**

100
**Leucogenes
leontopodium**

101
Lewisia cotyledon

102
Lewisia cotyledon

103
Lewisia howellii

104
Lewisia tweedyi

105
Linum elegans
'Gemmell's Hybrid'

106
Linum elegans

107
Lithospermum
'Grace Ward'

108
Lithospermum
oleifolium

109
Lysimachia
nummularia

110
Mimulus primuloides

111
Moltkia intermedia

112
Morisea monantha

113
Nierembergia
rivularis

114
Omphalodes
cappadocica

115
Omphalodes luciliae

116
Omphalogramma
vinciflorum

117
Orchis elata

118
Orchis maculata

119
Orchis maderensis

120
Origanum amanum

15

121
Orphanidesia
gaultherioides

122
Ourisia elegans

123
Oxalis adenophylla

124
Oxalis depressa

125
Oxalis laciniata

126
Papaver alpinum

127
Penstemon fruticosus
var. crassifolius

128
Penstemon
newberryi

129
Penstemon scouleri
'Alba'

130
Petrocosmea kerrii
'Alba'

131
Phlox adsurgens

132
Phlox amoena

133
Phlox bifida

134
Phlox douglasii
'Beauty of Ronsdorf'

135
Phlox nana var.
ensifolia

136
Phlox subulata
'Temiscaming'

137
Phyteuma comosum

138
Platycodon
grandiflorum
'Mariesii'

139
Pleione formosana

140
Pleione formosana
'Alba'

141
Pleione limprichtii

142
Polygala calcarea

143
Polygala
chamaebuxus
'Rhodoptera'

144
Polygonum affine
'Donald Lowndes'

18

145
Polygonum
vacciniifolium

146
Potentilla nitida
'Rubra'

147
Primula allionii

148
Primula auricula

149
Primula auricula
'Queen Alexandra'

150
Primula denticulata
'Alba'

151
Primula edgeworthii

152
Primula farinosa

153
Primula forrestii

154
**Primula
'Garryarde
Guinevere'**

155
Primula gracilipes

156
Primula nutans

157
**Primula pubescens
'Rufus'**

158
Primula reidii

159
**Primula rosea
'Visser de Greer'**

160
**Primula sieboldii
'Alba'**

161
Primula spectabilis

162
Primula vialii

163
Primula vulgaris

164
Primula whytei

165
Prunus prostrata

166
Pulmonaria
angustifolia

167
Pulsatilla alpina

168
Pulsatilla halleri

169
Pulsatilla sulphurea

170
Pulsatilla vernalis

171
Pulsatilla vulgaris

172
Pulsatilla vulgaris
'Alba'

173
Pulsatilla vulgaris
'Rubra'

174
Punica granatum
'Nana'

175
Ramonda myconii

176
Ranunculus
amplexicaulis

177
Ranunculus ficaria
'Major'

178
Ranunculus glacialis

179
Ranunculus
gramineus

180
Raoulia
lutescens

181
Rhodohypoxis baurei

182
Rhodohypoxis
'Margaret Rose'

183
Roscoea cautleoides

184
Roscoea humeana

185
Salix reticulata

186
Sanguinaria
canadensis
'Plena'

187
Saponaria ocymoides
'Rubra Compacta'

188
Saxifraga aizoon

189
Saxifraga apiculata

190
Saxifraga
burseriana
'Gloria'

191
Saxifraga
burseriana
'Sulphurea'

192
Saxifraga
ferdinandi-coburgii

193
Saxifraga fortunei

194
Saxifraga grisebachii

195
Saxifraga jenkinsae

196
Saxifraga longifolia

197
Saxifraga
oppositifolia
'Splendens'

198
Saxifraga
'Peter Pan'

199
Saxifraga
'Riverslea'

200
Saxifraga umbrosa
'Primuloides'

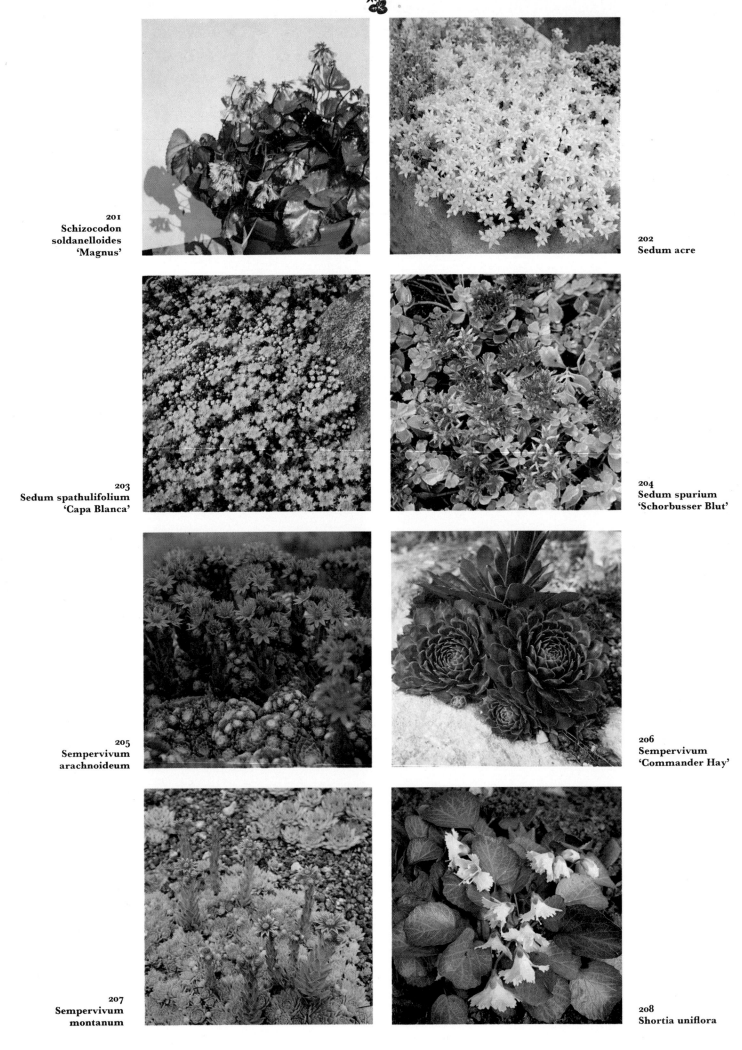

201
Schizocodon
soldanelloides
'Magnus'

202
Sedum acre

203
Sedum spathulifolium
'Capa Blanca'

204
Sedum spurium
'Schorbusser Blut'

205
Sempervivum
arachnoideum

206
Sempervivum
'Commander Hay'

207
Sempervivum
montanum

208
Shortia uniflora

209
Sisyrinchium
bermudiana

210
Soldanella alpina

211
Soldanella montana

212
Soldanella pusilla
'Alba'

213
Thlaspi
rotundifolium

214
Thymus serpyllum
'Coccineus'

215
Trichinium manglesii

216
Tropaeolum
polyphyllum

217
Verbascum
dumulosum

218
Verbascum
spinosum

219
Veronica prostrata

220
Viola gracilis
'Major'

221
Viola tricolor

222
Waldsteinia ternata

223
Weldenia candida

224
Zauschneria
cana

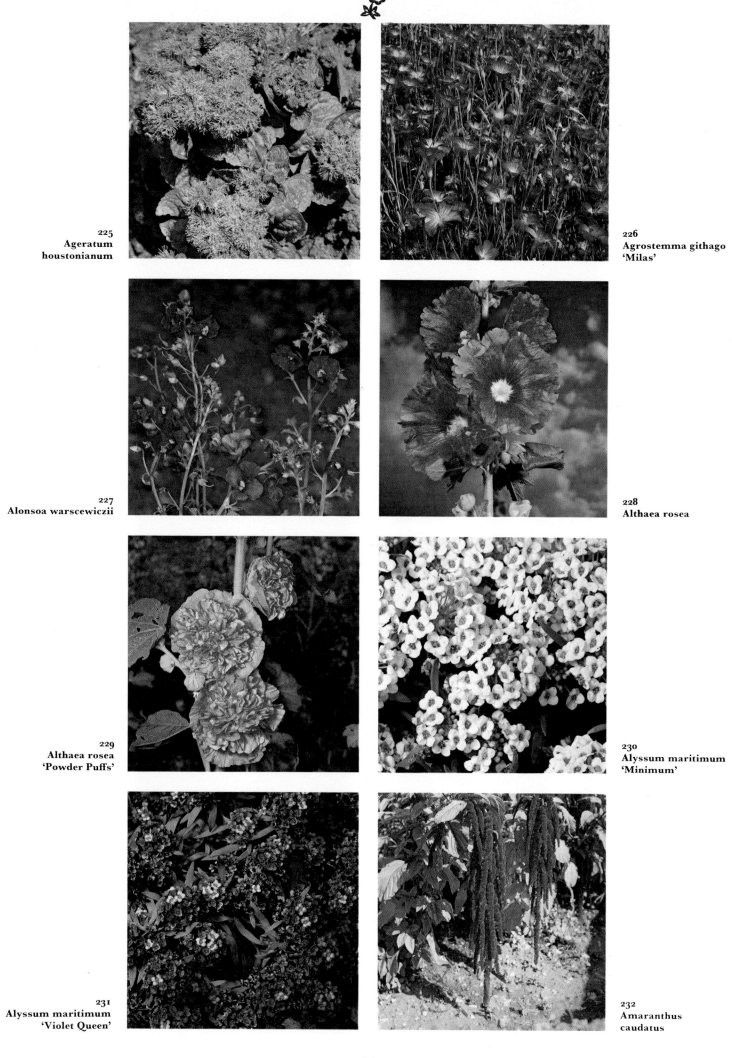

225
Ageratum
houstonianum

226
Agrostemma githago
'Milas'

227
Alonsoa warscewiczii

228
Althaea rosea

229
Althaea rosea
'Powder Puffs'

230
Alyssum maritimum
'Minimum'

231
Alyssum maritimum
'Violet Queen'

232
Amaranthus
caudatus

233
Amaranthus tricolor

234
Ammobium alatum
'Grandiflorum'

235
Anchusa capensis
'Blue Bird'

236
Antirrhinum majus
'Floral Carpet'

237
Antirrhinum majus
'Glamour Shades
Double'

238
Arctotis breviscapa

239
Arctotis hybrida

240
Argemone mexicana

241
Atriplex hortensis

242
Begonia
semperflorens
'Organdy'

243
Bellis perennis
'Pomponette'

244
Brachycome
iberidifolia

245
Briza maxima

246
Calandrinia
umbellata
'Amaranth'

247
Calceolaria ×
multiflora
'Nana'

248
Calendula officinalis
'Geisha Girl'

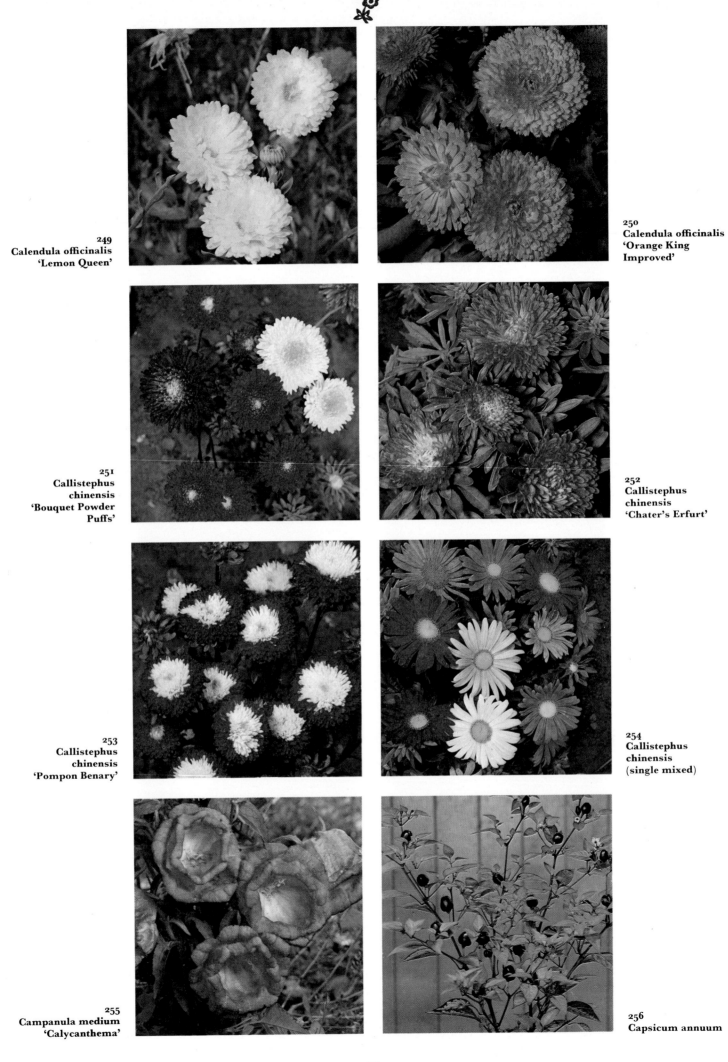

249
Calendula officinalis
'Lemon Queen'

250
Calendula officinalis
'Orange King
Improved'

251
Callistephus
chinensis
'Bouquet Powder
Puffs'

252
Callistephus
chinensis
'Chater's Erfurt'

253
Callistephus
chinensis
'Pompon Benary'

254
Callistephus
chinensis
(single mixed)

255
Campanula medium
'Calycanthema'

256
Capsicum annuum

257
Celosia argentea
'Cristata'

258
Celosia argentea
'Plumosa'

259
Centaurea cyanus
'Julep'

260
Centaurea moschata

261
Cheiranthus allionii
'Lemon Delight'

262
Cheiranthus cheiri

263
Chenopodium
amaranticolor

264
Chrysanthemum
carinatum
'Monarch Court
Jesters'

265
Chrysanthemum
coronarium
'Golden Glory'

266
Chrysanthemum
segetum
'Eastern Star'

267
Cineraria maritima
'Candicans'

268
Cineraria multiflora

269
Clarkia elegans
'Flore Pleno'

270
Cleome spinosa
'Helen Campbell'

271
Collinsia bicolor

272
Convolvulus tricolor
'Royal Ensign'

34

273
Convolvulus tricolor
'Royal Marine'

274
Coreopsis tinctoria
'Dazzler'

275
Cosmos bipinnatus
'Klondyke Early
Gold Crest'

276
Cosmos bipinnatus
'Sensation'

277
Cotula barbata

278
Crepis rubra

279
Cuphea miniata
'Firefly'

280
Dahlia hybrida
'Coltness Scarlet
Gem'

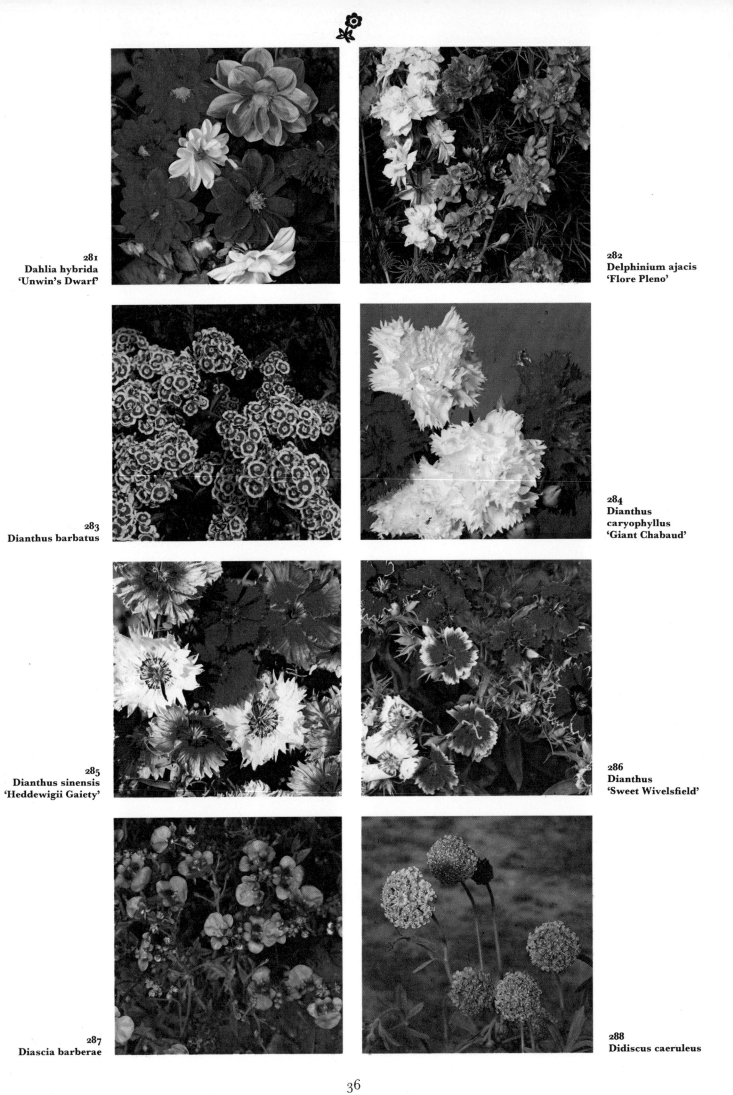

281
Dahlia hybrida
'Unwin's Dwarf'

282
Delphinium ajacis
'Flore Pleno'

283
Dianthus barbatus

284
Dianthus
caryophyllus
'Giant Chabaud'

285
Dianthus sinensis
'Heddewigii Gaiety'

286
Dianthus
'Sweet Wivelsfield'

287
Diascia barberae

288
Didiscus caeruleus

289
Digitalis purpurea
'Excelsior'

290
Digitalis purpurea
'Foxy'

291
Dimorphotheca
aurantiaca hybrids

292
Echium plantagineum
'Blue Bedder'

293
Echium plantagineum
'Dwarf Hybrids'

294
Eschscholzia
californica
'Mission Bells'

295
Eucharidium
concinnum
'Pink Ribbons'

296
Gaillardia pulchella
'Lorenziana'

297
Gazania splendens

298
Gilia hybrida
'French Hybrids'

299
Glaucium flavum
Orange form

300
Godetia grandiflora
'Sybil Sherwood'

301
Godetia grandiflora
'Vivid'

302
Gomphrena globosa
'Nana compacta
Buddy'

303
Gypsophila elegans
'London Market
Strain'

304
Helianthus annuus

305
Helichrysum
bracteatum

306
Heliophila longifolia

307
Helipterum manglesii

308
Hordeum jubatum

309
Humulus scandens
'Variegatus'

310
Iberis umbellata
'Dwarf Fairy'

311
Impatiens balsamina
Camellia flowered

312
Ipomoea tricolor
'Praecox'

313
Kentranthus
macrosiphon

314
Kochia scoparia
'Tricophylla'

315
Lagurus ovatus

316
Lathyrus odoratus
'Anne Vestey'

317
Lathyrus odoratus
'John Ness'

318
Lathyrus odoratus
'Knee-hi'

319
Lathyrus odoratus
'Leamington'

320
Lathyrus odoratus
'Pink Pride'

321
Lathyrus odoratus
'White Ensign'

322
Lavatera trimestris
'Sunset'

323
Layia elegans

324
Leptosyne stillmanii

325
Limnanthes douglasii

326
Limonium sinuatum
'Pacific Giants'

327
Limonium suworowii

328
Linaria maroccana

329
Linum grandiflorum
'Rubrum'

330
Lobelia erinus
'Cambridge Blue'

331
Lobelia erinus
'Mrs Clibran
Improved'

332
Lobelia erinus
'Rosamund'

333
Lunaria annua

334
Lupinus hartwegii

335
Lychnis coeli-rosa
var. oculata

336
Malcolmia maritima

337
Malope trifida

338
Martynia louisiana

339
Matricaria eximia
'Ball's Double White'

340
Matricaria eximia
'Golden Ball'

341
Matthiola incana

342
Mentzelia lindleyi

343
Mesembryanthemum
criniflorum

344
Mimulus variegatus

345
Mirabilis jalapa

346
Moluccella laevis

347
Myosotis alpestris
'Blue Ball'

348
Nemesia strumosa

349
Nemophila menziesii

350
Nicandra physaloides

351
Nicotiana affinis
'Lime Green'

352
Nigella damascena
'Miss Jekyll'

353
Nigella damascena
'Persian Jewels'

354
Nolana acuminata
'Lavender Gown'

355
Papaver rhoeas
Begonia flowered

356
Pennisetum rupellii

357
Perilla frutescens
'Nankinensis'

358
Petunia hybrida
'Blue Bedder'

359
Petunia hybrida
'Pink Satin'

360
Phacelia
campanularia
'Blue Bonnet'

361
Phlox drummondii
'Cuspidata Twinkle'

362
Platystemon
californicus

363
Portulaca grandiflora
'Flore Pleno'

364
Primula
Polyanthus hybrids

365
Reseda odorata
'Goliath'

366
Ricinus communis
'Gibsonii'

367
Ricinus communis
'Zanzibarensis'

368
Rudbeckia hirta
'Gloriosa'

369
Salpiglossis sinuata
'Superbissima'

370
Salvia horminum
'Pink Sundae'

371
Salvia splendens
'Harbinger'

372
Sanvitalia
procumbens

373
Scabiosa
atropurpurea

374
Sedum caeruleum

375
Silene pendula

376
Silybum marianum

377
Specularia speculum

378
Tagetes erecta
'Golden Age'

379
Tagetes erecta
'Spanish Brocade'

380
Tagetes patula
'Dainty Marietta'

381
Tagetes patula
'Harmony'

382
Tagetes tenuifolia
'Golden Gem'

383
Thunbergia alata

384
Thunbergia gregorii

385
Tithonia rotundifolia

386
Torenia fournieri
'Grandiflora'

387
Tropaeolum majus

388
Tropaeolum majus
'Flore Pleno'

389
Ursinia anethoides

390
Ursinia versicolor
'Golden Bedder'

391
Venidium fastuosum

392
Verbena hybrida

49

393
Viola hybrida
'Clear Crystals'

394
Viola hybrida
'Chantreyland'

395
Viola tricolor
Roggli strain

396
Viola tricolor
'Ullswater'

397
Zinnia elegans
(Chrysanthemum
flowered)

398
Zinnia elegans
(Dahlia flowered)

399
Zinnia haageana
'Flore Pleno Persian
Carpet'

400
Zinnia haageana
'Thumbelina'

401
Acalypha hispida

402
Aechmea fulgens

403
Aglaonema
commutatum

404
Aglaonema
'Silver Queen'

405
Aglaonema
treubii

406
Allamanda
cathartica

407
Aloe variegata

408
Anthurium
andreanum

409
Ardisia crispa

410
Aristolochia elegans

411
Arum creticum

412
**Asplenium
nidus-avis**

413
**Begonia hybrida
Pendula hybrid**

414
Begonia masoniana

415
**Begonia socotrana
hybrid 'Ida'**

416
**Begonia socotrana
hybrid 'Mavina'**

417
Begonia socotrana hybrid 'Mrs Leopold de Rothschild'

418
Begonia socotrana hybrid 'Regent'

419
Begonia tuberhybrida 'Buttermilk'

420
Begonia tuberhybrida 'Corona'

421
Begonia tuberhybrida 'Diana Wynyard'

422
Begonia tuberhybrida 'Elaine Tartellin'

423
Begonia tuberhybrida 'Fantasy'

424
Begonia tuberhybrida 'Gold Plate'

425
Begonia tuberhybrida
'Guardsman'

426
Begonia tuberhybrida
'Harlequin'

427
Begonia tuberhybrida
'Mary Heatley'

428
Begonia tuberhybrida
'Red Beacon'

429
Begonia tuberhybrida
'Roy Hartley'

430
Begonia tuberhybrida
'Sugar Candy'

431
Beloperone guttata

432
Billbergia nutans

433
Bomarea kalbreyeri

434
Brassocattleya
cliftonii
'Magnifica'

435
Browallia speciosa
'Major'

436
Brunfelsia calycina
'Macrantha'

437
Caladium candidum

438
Calceolaria ×
multiflora
'Grandiflora'

439
Calceolaria ×
multiflora
'Nana'

440
Campanula isophylla

441
Canna hortensis

442
Cattleya
'Catherine Subod'

443
Cephalocereus senilis

444
Cestrum
aurantiacum

445
Cestrum × newellii

446
Chamaecereus
silvestrii

447
Chlorophytum
comosum
'Variegatum'

448
Chrysanthemum
'Patricia Barnett'

449
Chrysanthemum
'Red Majestic'

450
Chrysanthemum
'William Mascall'

451
Chrysanthemum
'Audrey Shoesmith'

452
Chrysanthemum
'Frances Jefferson'

453
Chrysanthemum
'John Rowe Supreme'

454
Chrysanthemum
'Flash'

455
Chrysanthemum
'Parade'

456
Chrysanthemum
'Fair Lady'

457
Chrysanthemum
'Fred Shoesmith'

458
Chrysanthemum
'Glenshades'

459
Chrysanthemum
'Golden Mayford
Perfection'

460
Chrysanthemum
'Harmony'

461
Chrysanthemum
'Silver Haze'

462
Chrysanthemum
'Marion Stacey'

463
Chrysanthemum
'Yellow Grace Land'

464
Chrysanthemum
'Peggy Stevens'

58

465
Chrysanthemum
'Preference'

466
Chrysanthemum
'Portrait'

467
Chrysanthemum
Rayonnante

468
Cineraria multiflora

469
Cissus antarctica

470
Citrus mitis

471
Clerodendron
speciosissimum

472
Clerodendron
thomsonae

473
Clianthus formosus

474
Clivia miniata

475
Coccoloba uvifera

47⁶
Codiaeum
variegatum
'Pictum'

477
Coelogyne ochracea

47⁸
Coleus blumei

479
Coleus thrysoideus

48o
Columnea gloriosa
'Purpurea'

**481
Cordyline
terminalis**

**482
Coryphantha
arizonica**

**483
Crassula arborescens**

**484
Crassula sarcocaulis**

**485
Cryptanthus
fosterianus
'Foster's Hybrid'**

**486
Cyclamen persicum
'Giganteum'**

**487
Cymbidium Babylon
'Castle Hill'**

**488
Cymbidium
'Ramley'**

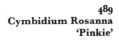

497
Dendrobium
'Stella Hallmark'

498
Dendrobium
'Virginale'

499
Dianthus
'Arthur Sim'

500
Dianthus
'Ballerina'

501
Dianthus
'Brighton Rock'

502
Dianthus
'Brocade'

503
Dianthus
'Edna Samuel'

504
Dianthus
'Flamingo Sim'

505
Dianthus
'Fragrant Ann'

506
Dianthus
'Heather Beauty'

507
Dianthus
'Helios'

508
Dianthus
'Hollywood Sim'

509
Dianthus
'Monty's Pale Rose'

510
Dianthus
'William Sim'

511
Dieffenbachia
amoena

512
Dieffenbachia
arvida
'Exotica'

513
Dieffenbachia picta
'Roehrsii'

514
Dizygotheca
elegantissima

515
Dracaena deremensis
'Bausei'

516
Dracaena fragrans
'Massangeana'

517
Dracaena marginata

518
Dracaena sanderiana

519
Echeveria gibbiflora
'Metallica'

520
Echinocactus
grusonii

521
Echinocactus scheeri

523
Epiphyllum ackermannii

525
Eucharis grandiflora

527
× **Fatshedera lizei 'Variegata'**

522
Epidendrum ibaguense

524
Epiphyllum hybrid

526
Euphorbia fulgens

528
Ficus benjamina

529
Ficus elastica
'Decora'

530
Ficus elastica
'Schryveriana'

531
Ficus pumila

532
Ficus radicans
'Variegata'

533
Fittonia
verschaffeltii

534
Fuchsia
'Coachman'

535
Fuchsia
'Heinrich Heinkel'

536
Fuchsia
'Mission Bells'

537
Fuchsia
'Molesworth'

538
Fuchsia
'Red Spider'

539
Fuchsia
'Television'

540
Gynura aurantiaca

541
Gynura aurantiaca
Purple form

542
Haemanthus
katherinae

543
Hedera canariensis
'Gloire de Marengo'

544
Hedera helix
'Eva'

545
Hedera helix
'Jubilee'

546
Hedera helix
'Little Diamond'

547
× Heliaporus
mallisonii

548
Hibiscus
rosa-sinensis

549
Hippeastrum
aulicum

550
Hippeastrum
× johnsonii

551
Hippeastrum hybrid

552
Impatiens
petersiana

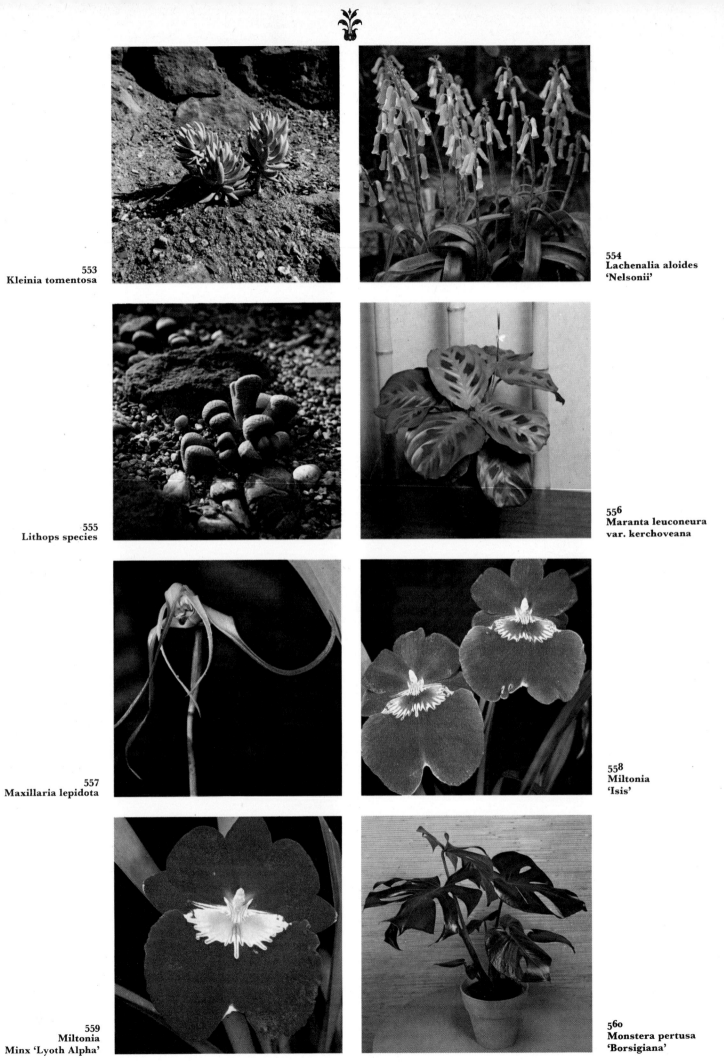

553
Kleinia tomentosa

554
Lachenalia aloides
'Nelsonii'

555
Lithops species

556
Maranta leuconeura
var. kerchoveana

557
Maxillaria lepidota

558
Miltonia
'Isis'

559
Miltonia
Minx 'Lyoth Alpha'

560
Monstera pertusa
'Borsigiana'

561
Neoregelia carolinae
'Tricolor'

562
Neoregelia
marechalii

563
Nerine sarniensis
var. major

564
Nerine sarniensis
'Miss E. Cator'

565
Nidularium
innocentii variety

566
Notocactus
mammulosus

568
Nymphaea capensis
var. zanzibariensis
rosea

567
Nymphaea capensis

569
Nymphaea lotus var.
dentata

570
Nymphaea rubra

571
Nymphaea
'B. G. Berry'

572
Nymphaea
'Daubenyana'

573
Nymphaea
'Dir. Geo. T. Moore'

574
× Odontioda
'Astomar'

575
× Odontioda
'Colwell'

576
× Odontioda
'Marzorka'

577
Odontoglossum
'Alport'

578
Odontoglossum
'Edalva'

579
Odontoglossum
Kopan
'Lyoth Aura'

580
× Odontonia
ampentum
'Regal'

581
× Odontonia Atheror
'Lyoth Majesty'

582
× Odontonia Olga
'Icefall'

583
Opuntia phaeacantha

584
Oscularia deltoides

585
Pamianthe peruviana

586
Pelargonium crispum
'Variegatum'

587
Pelargonium ×
domesticum
'Applause'

588
Palargonium ×
domesticum
'Aztec'

589
Pelargonium ×
domesticum
'Braque'

590
Pelargonium ×
domesticum
'Carisbrooke'

591
Pelargonium ×
domesticum
'Cezanne'

592
Pelargonium ×
domesticum
'Degas'

593
**Pelargonium ×
domesticum
'Doris Frith'**

594
**Pelargonium ×
domesticum
'Grand Slam'**

595
**Pelargonium ×
domesticum
'Renoir'**

596
**Pelargonium ×
domesticum 'Rogue'**

597
**Pelargonium ×
domesticum
'South American
Bronze'**

598
**Pelargonium ×
hortorum
'A Happy Thought'**

599
**Pelargonium ×
hortorum
'Flower of the Day'**

600
**Pelargonium ×
hortorum
'Mrs Henry Cox'**

601
Pelargonium ×
hortorum
'The Czar'

602
Pelargonium ×
hortorum
'Elaine'

603
Pelargonium ×
hortorum
'Elizabeth Angus'

604
Pelargonium ×
hortorum
'Festiva Maxima'

605
Pelargonium ×
hortorum
'Gazelle'

606
Pelargonium ×
hortorum
'Irene Genie'

607
Pelargonium ×
hortorum
'Jane Campbell'

608
Pelargonium ×
hortorum
'Lief'

609
Pelargonium ×
hortorum
'Muriel Parsons'

610
Pelargonium ×
hortorum
'Orangesonne'

611
Pelargonium ×
hortorum
'Xenia Field'

612
Pelargonium ×
hortorum
'Zinc'

613
Pelargonium
peltatum
'Claret Crousse'

614
Pelargonium
peltatum
'Crocodile'

615
Pelargonium
peltatum
'King Edward VII'

616
Pelargonium
peltatum
'L'Elegante'

617
Pelargonium
peltatum
'Trotting Hill'

618
Peperomia argyreia

619
Peperomia caperata

Peperomia
hederaefolia
620

621
Peperomia
obtusifolia
'Variegata'

622
Philodendron
hastatum

623
Philodendron
laciniatum

624
Philodendron
melanochrysum

78

625
Philodendron
scandens

626
Phoenix roebelinii

627
Pilea cadierei
'Nana'

628
Pleomele reflexa
'Song of India'

629
Podocarpus
gracilior

630
Polianthes tuberosa

631
Primula malacoides

632
Primula obconica

633
Rebutia minuscula

634
Rebutia xanthocarpa

635
Rhipsalidopsis rosea

636
Rhoicissus
rhomboidea

637
Saintpaulia ionantha

638
Saintpaulia ionantha

639
Saintpaulia ionantha

640
Saintpaulia ionantha

641
Sansevieria grandis

642
Sansevieria hahnii

643
Sansevieria
trifasciata
'Laurentii'

644
Schlumbergera
gaertneri

645
Scindapsus aureus
'Silver Queen'

646
Sedum sieboldii
'Medio-variegatum'

647
Selaginella caulescens
'Argentea'

648
Sinningia speciosa

**649
Sonerila
margaritacea**

**650
Spathiphyllum
wallisii**

**651
Stephanotis
floribunda**

**652
Streptocarpus
hybridus
'Constant Nymph'**

**653
Streptosolen
jamesonii**

**654
Trichocereus
candicans
'Robustior'**

**655
× Wilsonara
'Lyoth'**

**656
Zygocactus truncatus**

657
Acidanthera bicolor
murielae

658
Allium aflatunense

659
Allium beesianum

660
Allium cernuum

661
Allium christophii

662
Allium flavum

663
Allium karataviense

664
Allium moly

665
Allium
narcissiflorum

666
Allium oreophilum
var. ostrowskianum

667
Allium pulchellum

668
Allium
schoenoprasum

669
Allium siculum

670
Amaryllis belladonna

671
Anemone blanda
'Atrocoerulea'

672
Anemone coronaria
De Caen strain

673
Anemone nemorosa
'Allenii'

674
Anemone pavonina

675
Anemone pavonina
St Bavo strain

676
Arum italicum
marmoratum

677
Brodiaea ida-maia

678
Brodiaea laxa

679
Calochortus uniflorus

680
Camassia cusickii

681
Camassia quamash

682
Cardiocrinum
giganteum

683
Chionodoxa luciliae

684
Chionodoxa luciliae
'Pink Giant'

685
Chionodoxa sardensis

686
Colchicum
autumnale

687
Colchicum cilicicum

688
Colchicum
speciosum

689
Colchicum
speciosum
'Album'

690
Colchicum
speciosum
'The Giant'

691
Corydalis solida

692
× Crinodonna corsii

693
Crinum × powellii

694
Crocosmia
'Jackanapes'

695
Crocosmia
masonorum

696
Crocus aureus

697
Crocus chrysanthus
'Blue Pearl'

698
Crocus chrysanthus
'Cream Beauty'

699
Crocus chrysanthus
'E. A. Bowles'

700
Crocus chrysanthus
'Goldilocks'

701
Crocus chrysanthus
'Lady Killer'

702
Crocus chrysanthus
'Warley'

703
Crocus etruscus

704
Crocus imperati

705
Crocus laevigatus

706
Crocus minimus

707
Crocus sieberi

708
Crocus tomasinianus

709
Crocus tomasinianus
'Whitewell Purple'

710
Crocus vernus
'Vanguard'

711
Crocus
'Kathleen Parlow'

712
Crocus
'Negro Boy'

713
Crocus
'Purpureus
Grandiflorus'

714
Crocus
'Yellow Giant'

715
Crocus nudiflorus

716
Crocus speciosus

717
Crocus speciosus
'Oxonian'

718
Cyclamen cilicium

719
Cyclamen coum

720
Cyclamen
libanoticum

721
Cyclamen
neapolitanum

722
Cyclamen persicum
Wild form

723
Cyclamen
pseudibericum

724
Cyclamen repandum

725
Dierama
pulcherrimum

726
Dracunculus
vulgaris

727
Endymion
non-scripta

728
Eranthis cilicica

729
Eranthis hyemalis

730
Eranthis
tubergeniana

731
Erythronium
dens-canis
'Rose Queen'

732
Erythronium
'White Beauty'

733
Eucomis bicolor

734
Freesia refracta

735
Freesia mixed

736
Fritillaria
acmopetala

737
**Fritillaria imperialis
'Aurora'**

738
**Fritillaria imperialis
'Lutea Maxima'**

739
**Fritillaria meleagris
'Alba'**

740
**Fritillaria meleagris
'Purple King'**

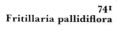

741
Fritillaria pallidiflora

742
Galanthus elwesii

743
Galanthus ikariae

744
Galanthus nivalis

93

745
Galanthus nivalis
'S. Arnott'

746
Galanthus plicatus

747
Galtonia candicans

748
Gladiolus byzantinus

749
Gladiolus nanus
'Charm'

750
Gladiolus nanus
'Robinette'

751
Gladiolus nanus
'Spring Glory'

752
Gladiolus
'Black Jack'

94

753
Gladiolus
'Golden Standard'

754
Gladiolus
'Peter Pears'

755
Gladiolus
'Purple Star'

756
Gladiolus
'Toulouse-Lautrec'

757
Gladiolus
'Chinatown'
(Butterfly)

758
Gladiolus
'Green Woodpecker'
(Butterfly)

759
Gladiolus
'Mokha'
(Butterfly)

760
Gladiolus
'Page Polka'
(Butterfly)

761
Gladiolus primulinus
'Chartres'

762
Gladiolus primulinus
'Sappho'

763
Gladiolus primulinus
'Treasure'

764
Hermodactylus
tuberosus

765
Hyacinthus
amethystinus

766
Hyacinthus
'Cynthella'

767
Hyacinthus
'Cynthella'

768
Hyacinthus mixed

769
Hyacinthus
'Ostara'

770
Hyacinthus
'Perle Brilliant'

771
Hyacinthus
'Princess Margaret'

772
Hyacinthus
'Queen of the Whites'

773
Ipheion uniflorum

774
Iris aucheri

775
Iris bakeriana

776
Iris bucharica

777
Iris danfordiae

778
Iris histrioides
'Major'

779
Iris planifolia

780
Iris reticulata

781
Iris reticulata
'Cantab'

782
Iris reticulata
'Clarette'

783
Iris reticulata
'Harmony'

784
Iris tingitana

785
Iris xiphium

786
Iris xiphium
'Gipsy Girl'

787
Iris xiphium
'King of the Blues'

788
Iris Dutch
'Blue Champion'

789
Iris Dutch
'Lemon Queen'

790
Iris Dutch
'Wedgwood'

791
Iris acutiloba

792
Iris
'Chione'

793
Lapeyrousia cruenta

794
Leucojum aestivum
'Gravetye'

795
Leucojum autumnale

796
Leucojum vernum
var. carpathicum

797
Lilium auratum

798
Lilium Bellingham
hybrids

799
Lilium Bellingham
hybrid
'Shuksan'

800
Lilium
'Black Dragon'

801
Lilium
'Brocade'

802
Lilium canadense

803
Lilium candidum

804
Lilium
'Cinnabar'

805
Lilium
'Destiny'

806
Lilium
'Enchantment'

807
Lilium
Golden Clarion
strain

808
Lilium henryi

809
Lilium ×
hollandicum
'Grandiflorum'

810
Lilium japonicum

811
Lilium
'Limelight'

812
Lilium martagon

813
Lilium pardalinum

814
Lilium ×
parkmannii

815
Lilium
'Pink Glory'

816
Lilium pyrenaicum

817
Lilium regale

818
Lilium
'Royal Gold'

819
Lilium rubellum

820
Lilium speciosum
'Melpomene'

821
Lilium szovitsianum

822
Lilium × testaceum

823
Muscari armeniacum
'Heavenly Blue'

824
Muscari botryoides

825
Muscari botryoides
'Album'

826
Muscari comosum
var. monstrosum

827
Muscari latifolium

828
Muscari
tubergenianum

829
Narcissus asturiensis

830
Narcissus
bulbocodium

831
Narcissus
bulbocodium var.
conspicuus

832
Narcissus
bulbocodium var.
romieuxii

833
Narcissus
cyclamineus

834
Narcissus jonquilla

835
Narcissus juncifolius

836
Narcissus lobularis

837
Narcissus ×
minicycla

838
Narcissus
pseudonarcissus

839
Narcissus
'W. P. Milner'

840
Narcissus triandrus
'Albus'

841
Narcissus triandrus
'April Tears'

842
Narcissus triandrus
'Hawera'

843
Narcissus triandrus
'Silver Chimes'

844
Narcissus watieri

845
Narcissus 1a.
'Kingscourt'

846
Narcissus 1b.
'Preamble'

847
Narcissus 1c.
'Vigil'

848
Narcissus 2a.
'Ceylon'

849
Narcissus 2a.
'Fortune'

850
Narcissus 2b.
'Arbar'

851
Narcissus 2b.
'Tudor Minstrel'

852
Narcissus 3a.
'Chungking'

853
Narcissus 3b.
'Rockall'

854
Narcissus 3c.
'Chinese White'

855
Narcissus 4.
'Double Event'

856
Narcissus 6.
'February Gold'

857
Narcissus 6.
'Charity May'

858
Narcissus 6.
'Dove Wings'

859
Narcissus 6.
'Peeping Tom'

860
Narcissus 7.
'Trevithian'

861
Narcissus 8.
'Cragford'

862
Narcissus 8.
'Grand Soleil d'Or'

863
Narcissus 8.
'Paperwhite
Grandiflora'

864
Narcissus 8.
'Geranium'

865
Nerine bowdenii

866
Nerine bowdenii
'Fenwick's variety'

867
Nomocharis
pardanthina

868
Nomocharis
saluenensis

869
Ornithogalum nutans

870
Ornithogalum
thyrsoides

871
Ornithogalum
umbellatum

872
Pancratium illyricum

873
Puschkinia scilloides

874
Ranunculus asiaticus

875
Romulea
bulbocodium

876
Schizostylis coccinea

877
Schizostylis coccinea
'Mrs Hegarty'

878
Scilla bifolia

879
Scilla peruviana

880
Scilla pratensis

881
Scilla sibirica

882
Scilla tubergeniana

883
Sprekelia
formosissima

884
Sternbergia lutea

885
Tecophilaea
cyanocrocus

886
Tigridia pavonia

887
Trillium
chloropetalum

888
Trillium
grandiflorum

889
Trillium sessile

890
Tropaeolum
tricolorum

891
Tropaeolum
tuberosum

892
Tulipa clusiana

893
Tulipa eichleri

894
Tulipa fosteriana
'Mme Lefeber'

895
Tulipa fosteriana
'Purissima'

896
Tulipa greigii hybrid

897
Tulipa kaufmanniana

898
Tulipa kaufmanniana
'Shakespeare'

899
Tulipa
kolpakowskiana

900
Tulipa linifolia

901
Tulipa praestans

902
Tulipa princeps

903
Tulipa stellata var.
chrysantha

904
Tulipa tarda

905
Tulipa turkestanica

906
Tulipa violacea

907
Tulipa whittallii

908
Tulipa 2.
'Brilliant Star
Maximus'

909
Tulipa 2.
'Keizerskroon'

910
Tulipa 3.
Early double

911
Tulipa 15.
'Eros'

912
'Mt Tacoma'

913
Tulipa 5.
'Mary Housley'

914
Tulipa 5.
'Ringo'

915
Tulipa 9.
'Dyanito'

916
Tulipa 9.
'Mariette'

917
Tulipa 9.
'Queen of Sheba'

918
Tulipa 10.
'Blushing Bride'

919
Tulipa 10.
'Dillenburg'

920
Tulipa 10.
'Marshal Haig'

921
Tulipa 10.
'Mrs John Scheepers'

922
Tulipa 10.
'Artist'

923
Tulipa 10.
'Greenland'

924
Tulipa 6.
'Glacier'

925
Tulipa 6.
'Niphetos'

926
Tulipa 6.
'Sweet Harmony'

927
Tulipa 6.
'Mamasa'

928
Tulipa 6.
'Queen of Bartigons'

929
Tulipa 6.
'Nobel'

930
Tulipa 6.
'Scarlet O'Hara'

931
Tulipa 6.
'La Tulipe Noire'

932
Tulipa 7.
'Apeldoorn'

933
Tulipa 7.
'Gudoshnik'

934
Tulipa 7.
'Jewel of Spring'

935
Tulipa 7.
'Oxford'

936
Tulipa 11.
'Cordell Hull'

937
Tulipa 12.
'Absalon'

938
Tulipa 13.
'May Blossom'

939
Tulipa 14.
'Fantasy'

940
Tulipa 14.
'Orange Parrot'

941
Vallota speciosa

942
Watsonia beatricis

943
Zantedeschia
aethiopica
'Crowborough'

944
Zephyranthes
candida

945
Acanthus spinosus

946
Achillea clypeolata

947
Achillea
filipendulina
'Coronation Gold'

948
Achillea
'Flowers of Sulphur'

949
Achillea millefolium
'Fire King'

950
Achillea
'Moonshine'

951
Achillea ptarmica
'The Pearl'

952
Aconitum napellus
'Newry Blue'

953
Agapanthus
Headbourne hybrids

954
Ajuga pyramidalis

955
Ajuga reptans
'Multicolor'

956
Alchemilla mollis

957
Alstroemeria
aurantiaca

958
Alstroemeria
Ligtu hybrids

959
Amsonia salicifolia

960
Anaphalis nubigena

961
Anaphalis
triplinervis

962
Anaphalis
yedoensis

963
Anchusa azurea
'Loddon Royalist'

964
Anemone hupehensis

965
Anemone × lesseri

966
Anemone
narcissiflora

967
Anthemis
sancti-johannis

968
Anthemis tinctoria
'Grallagh Gold'

969
Anthemis tinctoria
'Perry's variety'

970
Anthemis tinctoria
'Wargrave variety'

971
Anthericum liliago

972
Aponogeton
distachyus

973
Aquilegia hybrida

974
Aquilegia hybrida

975
Arnebia echioides

976
Artemisia
absinthium
'Lambrook Silver'

977
Artemisia lactiflora

978
Artemisia maritima
nutans

979
Aruncus sylvester

980
Aster acris

981
Aster amellus
'King George'

982
Aster amellus
'Rudolf Goethe'

983
Aster frikartii

984
Aster linosyris

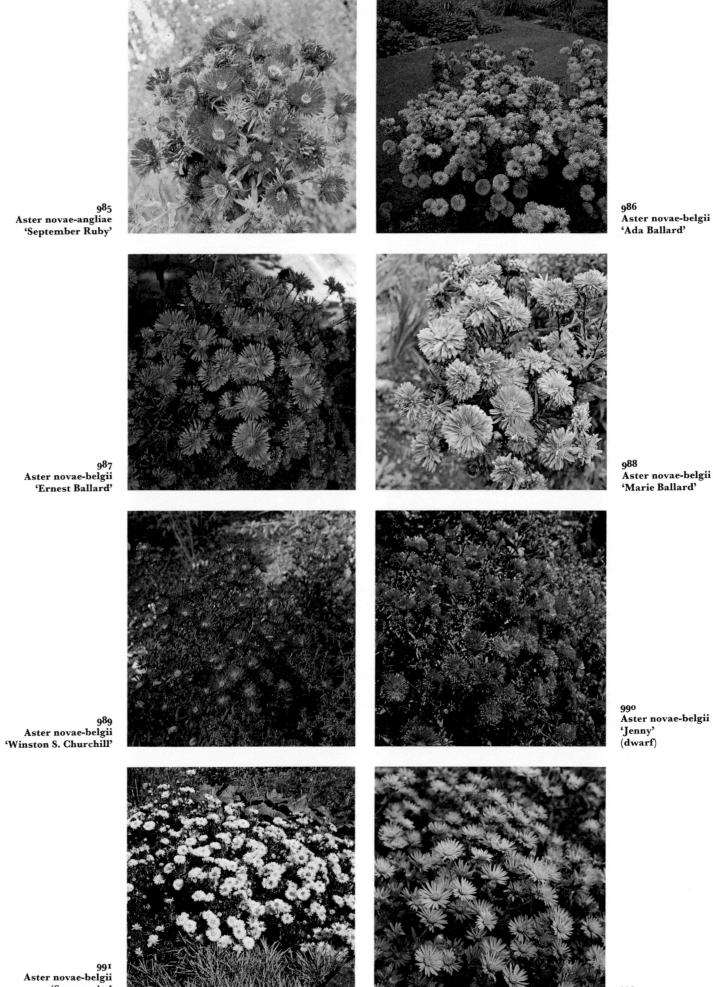

985
Aster novae-angliae
'September Ruby'

986
Aster novae-belgii
'Ada Ballard'

987
Aster novae-belgii
'Ernest Ballard'

988
Aster novae-belgii
'Marie Ballard'

989
Aster novae-belgii
'Winston S. Churchill'

990
Aster novae-belgii
'Jenny'
(dwarf)

991
Aster novae-belgii
'Snowsprite'
(dwarf)

992
Aster spectabilis

993
Aster thomsonii
'Nana'

994
Astilbe × arendsii

995
Astilbe
'Deutschland'

996
Astilbe
'Fanal'

997
Astilbe
'Granat'

998
Astilbe
'Hyacinth'

999
Astrantia maxima

1000
Ballota
pseudo-dictammus

1001
Baptisia australis

1002
Bergenia delavayi

1003
Bergenia
purpurascens

1004
Bletilla striata

1005
Brunnera
macrophylla

1006
Buphthalmum
salicifolia

1007
Butomus umbellatus

1008
Calamintha
nepetoides

1009
Caltha palustris
'Flore Pleno'

1010
Campanula ×
burghaltii

1011
Campanula
glomerata
'Superba'

1012
Campanula
lactiflora
'Loddon Anna'

1013
Campanula
latifolia
'Alba'

1014
Campanula
persicifolia
'Blue Belle'

1015
Campanula
persicifolia
'Telham Beauty'

1016
Catananche coerulea

1017
Cautleya robusta

1018
Centaurea dealbata
'John Coutts'

1019
Centaurea dealbata
'Steenbergii'

1020
Centaurea montana
'Parham'

1021
Cheiranthus cheiri
'Harpur Crewe'

1022
Cheiranthus cheiri
'Moonlight'

1023
Cheiranthus cheiri
'Rufus'

1024
Chelone obliqua

1033
Chrysanthemum
'Incurved Primrose
Evelyn Bush'
(Intermediate
Decorative)

1034
Chrysanthemum
'Joe Edwards'
(Intermediate
Decorative)

1035
Chrysanthemum
'Kathleen Doward'
(Intermediate
Decorative)

1036
Chrysanthemum
'Westfield Bronze'
(Intermediate
Decorative)

1037
Chrysanthemum
'Cameo'
(Pompon)

1038
Chrysanthemum
'Fairie'
(Pompon)

1039
Chrysanthemum
'Grandchild'
(Pompon)

1040
Chrysanthemum
'Jante Wells'
(Pompon)

1041
Chrysanthemum
'Masquerade'
(Pompon)

1042
Chrysanthemum
'Brightness'
(Spray)

1043
Chrysanthemum
'Golden Orfe'
(Spray)

1044
Chrysanthemum
'Gold Treasure'
(Spray)

1045
Chrysanthemum
'Charm Spoon'
(Miscellaneous)

1046
Chrysanthemum
'Garnet Spoon'
(Miscellaneous)

1047
Chrysanthemum
'Hansel'
(Miscellaneous)

1048
Chrysanthemum
'Moonlight Spoon'
(Miscellaneous)

1049
Chrysanthemum
maximum
'Wirral Pride'

1050
Chrysogonum
virginianum

1051
Cimicifuga racemosa

1052
Cirsium rivulare
'Atropurpurea'

1053
Clematis
heracleifolia
'Davidiana'

1054
Clematis recta

1055
Coreopsis grandiflora
'Goldfink'

1056
Coreopsis verticillata
'Grandiflora'

1057
Cortaderia selloana

1058
Crambe cordifolia

1059
Cynoglossum
nervosum

1060
Dahlia II
'Comet'

1061
Dahlia III
'Fashion Monger'

1062
Dahlia III
'Libretto'

1063
Dahlia Va.
'Lavengro'

1064
Dahlia Va.
'Night Editor'

1065
Dahlia Vb.
'Blithe Spirit'

1066
Dahlia Vc.
'Pattern'

1067
Dahlia Vc.
'Terpo'

1068
Dahlia Vd.
'Vigor'

1069
Dahlia Ve.
'David Howard'

1070
Dahlia VIb.
'Rothesay Superb'

1071
Dahlia VII.
'Willo's Violet'

1072
Dahlia VIIIa.
'Poetic'

1073
Dahlia VIIIb.
'Drakenburg'

1075
Dahlia VIIId.
'Doris Day'

1074
Dahlia VIIIc.
'Authority'

1076
Dahlia VIIId.
'Klankstad Kerkrade'

1077
Dahlia IXa.
'Bestevaer'

1078
Dahlia IXb.
'Nantenan'

1079
Dahlia IXb.
'Royal Sceptre'

1080
Dahlia IXc.
'Apache'

1081
Dahlia IXc.
'Fleur de Hollande'

1082
Dahlia IXd.
'Goya's Venus'

1083
Dahlia IXd.
'Marilyn'

1084
Delphinium
brunonianum

1085
Delphinium
'Pink Sensation'
(Belladonna)

1086
Delphinium
'Betty Hay'

1087
Delphinium
'Blackmore's
Glorious'

1088
Delphinium
'Blue Nile'

1089
Delphinium
'Blue Tit'

1090
Delphinium
'Butterball'

1091
Delphinium
'Swan Lake'

1092
Dianthus
'Catherine Glover'
(Border)

1093
Dianthus
'Fiery Cross'
(Border)

1094
Dianthus
'Imperial Clove'
(Border)

1095
Dianthus
'Lustre'
(Border)

1096
Dianthus
'Robin Thain'
(Border)

1097
Dianthus
'Salmon Clove'
(Border)

1098
Dianthus
'Warrior'
(Border)

1099
Dianthus
'Zebra'
(Border)

1100
Dianthus
'Show Beauty'
(Show)

1101
Dianthus
'Show Enchantress'
(Show)

1102
Dianthus
'Show Ideal'
(Show)

1103
Dianthus
'Show Beauty'
(Show)

1104
Dianthus allwoodii
'Doris'

1105
Dianthus allwoodii
'Lilian'

1106
Dianthus allwoodii
'Robin'

1107
Dianthus allwoodii
'Timothy'

1108
Dicentra eximia
'Alba'

1109
Dicentra formosa
'Bountiful'

1110
Dicentra spectabilis

1111
Dictamnus albus
'Purpureus'

1112
Dodecatheon meadia
'Album'

139

1113
Doronicum
caucasicum
'Spring Beauty'

1114
Doronicum cordatum

1115
Echinops ritro
'Veitch's Blue'

1116
Eremurus bungei

1117
Eremurus robustus

1118
Erigeron
'Charity'

1119
Erigeron
'Dignity'

1120
Erigeron
'Felicity'

1121
Erigeron
'Festivity'

1122
Erigeron
'Lilofee'

1123
Erigeron
'Sincerity'

1124
Eryngium alpinum
'Donard'

1125
Eryngium giganteum

1126
Eryngium
tripartitum

1127
Eryngium
variifolium

1128
Eupatorium
purpureum

1129
Euphorbia characias

1130
Euphorbia
epithymoides

1131
Euphorbia griffithii
'Fireglow'

1132
Euphorbia palustris

1133
Euphorbia robbiae

1134
Festuca ovina
'Glauca'

1135
Filipendula
hexapetala
'Flore Pleno'

1136
Filipendula purpurea

1137
Foeniculum vulgare

1138
Gaillardia
'Goblin'

1139
Gaillardia
'Wirral Flame'

1140
Galega officinalis
'Her Majesty'

1141
Galega officinalis
'Lady Wilson'

1142
Gentiana asclepiadea

1143
Geranium ibericum

1144
Geranium ibericum
'Flore Pleno'

1145
Geranium ibericum
'Johnson's Blue'

1146
Geranium
macrorrhizum
'Album'

1147
Geranium pratense
'Flore Pleno'

1148
Geranium
sanguineum

1149
Geranium
sylvaticum
'Mayflower'

1150
Geranium
wallichianum
'Buxton's Blue'

1151
Geum × borisii

1152
Geum chiloense
'Mrs Bradshaw'

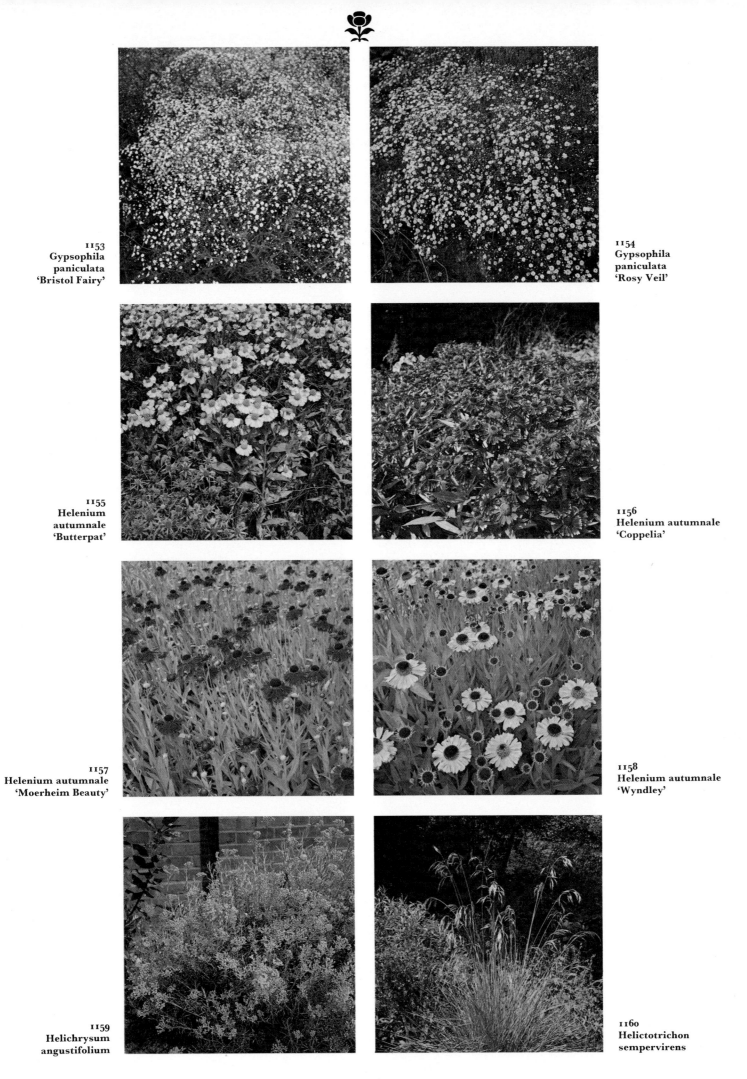

1153
Gypsophila
paniculata
'Bristol Fairy'

1154
Gypsophila
paniculata
'Rosy Veil'

1155
Helenium
autumnale
'Butterpat'

1156
Helenium autumnale
'Coppelia'

1157
Helenium autumnale
'Moerheim Beauty'

1158
Helenium autumnale
'Wyndley'

1159
Helichrysum
angustifolium

1160
Helictotrichon
sempervirens

1161
Heliopsis scabra
'Golden Plume'

1162
Heliopsis scabra
'Light of Loddon'

1163
Helleborus
corsicus

1164
Helleborus niger

1165
Helleborus niger
'Potters Wheel'

1166
Helleborus orientalis

1167
Hemerocallis
'Banbury Canary'

1168
Hemerocallis citrina
'Baronii'

1169
Hemerocallis
'El Magnifico'

1170
Hemerocallis
'Pink Damask'

1171
Hemerocallis
'Pink Prelude'

1172
Heuchera sanguinea
Bressingham hybrid

1173
Heuchera sanguinea
'Scintillation'

1174
Hieraceum villosum

1175
Hosta crispula

1176
Hosta fortunei
'Albopicta'

1177
Hosta plantaginea
'Grandiflora'

1178
Hosta sieboldiana

1179
Hosta undulata

1180
Hylomecon
japonicum

1181
Hyssopus aristatus

1182
Iberis sempervirens
'Snowflake'

1183
Incarvillea delavayi

1184
Incarvillea
grandiflora

1185
Inula ensifolia
'Golden Beauty'

1186
Inula hookeri

1187
Iris delavayi

1188
Iris foetidissima

1189
Iris foliosa

1190
Iris innominata

1191
Iris japonica
'Ledger's variety'

1192
Iris kaempferi
'Geihan'

1193
Iris kaempferi
'Sasameyuki'

1195
Iris laevigata
'Monstrosa'

1197
Iris pallida
'Variegata'

1199
Iris sibirica
'Blue Mere',
'Purple Mere' and
'White Swirl'

1194
Iris laevigata
'Alba'

1196
Iris ochroleuca

1198
Iris pseudacorus

1200
Iris sibirica
'Caesar's Brother'

1201
Iris spuria
'Wadi Zem Zem'

1202
Iris tectorum

1203
Iris unguicularis

1204
Iris unguicularis
'Alba'

1205
Iris versicolor
'Kermesina'

1206
Iris
'Lilli-Bitone'
(Intermediate
Bearded)

1207
Iris
'Scintilla'
(Intermediate
Bearded)

1208
Iris
'Small Wonder'
(Intermediate
Bearded)

1209
Iris
'Arctic Flame'
(Tall Bearded)

1210
Iris
'Dancer's Veil'
(Tall Bearded)

1211
Iris
'Ennerdale'
(Tall Bearded)

1212
Iris
'Esther Fay'
(Tall Bearded)

1213
Iris
'Helen McGregor'
(Tall Bearded)

1214
Iris
'Jane Phillips'
(Tall Bearded)

1215
Iris
'Lady Mohr'
(Tall Bearded)

1216
Iris
'Mary Todd'
(Tall Bearded)

1217
Iris
'Ola Kala'
(Tall Bearded)

1218
Iris
'Olympic Torch'
(Tall Bearded)

1219
Iris
'Rippling Waters'
(Tall Bearded)

1220
Iris
'Starshine'
(Tall Bearded)

1221
Iris
'Velvet Robe'
(Tall Bearded)

1222
Kentranthus ruber

1223
Kirengeshoma
palmata

1224
Kniphofia galpinii

1225
Kniphofia
'Bees' Sunset'

1226
Kniphofia
'H. G. Mills'

1227
Kniphofia
'Maid of Orleans'

1228
Kniphofia
'Royal Standard'

1229
Koeleria gracilis
'Britannica'

1230
Lamium galeobdolon
'Variegatum'

1231
Lamium maculatum
'Roseum'

1232
Lathyrus vernus

1233
Lavatera olbia
'Rosea'

1234
Liatris callilepis

1235
Liatris spicata

1236
Ligularia dentata

1237
Ligularia dentata
'Gregynog Gold'

1238
Ligularia × hessei

1239
Ligularia hodgsonii

1240
Ligularia japonica

1241
Linaria purpurea
'Canon J. Went'

1242
Linum narbonense

1243
Lobelia fulgens

1244
Lotus corniculatus

1245
Lunaria rediviva

1246
Lupinus polyphyllus

1247
Lupinus polyphyllus
'Freedom'

1248
Lupinus polyphyllus
'Harlequin'

1249
Lychnis chalcedonica

1250
Lychnis coronaria

1251
Lychnis flos-jovis

1252
Lychnis × haageana

1253
Lychnis viscaria
'Splendens Plena'

1254
Lysichitum
americanum

1255
Lysichitum
camtschatcense

1256
Lysimachia
ephemerum

1257
Lysimachia punctata

1258
Lythrum salicaria
'The Beacon'

1259
Lythrum virgatum
'Rose Queen'

1260
Macleaya cordata

1261
Macleaya microcarpa

1262
Malva alcea
'Fastigiata'

1263
Meconopsis
betonicifolia

1264
Meconopsis cambrica

1265
Meconopsis grandis
'Branklyn'

1266
Meconopsis
integrifolia

1267
Meconopsis
quintuplinervia

1268
Meconopsis regia

1269
Meconopsis regia

1270
Mertensia virginica

1271
Mimulus × burnetii

1272
Mimulus cupreus
'Whitecroft Scarlet'

1273
Mimulus luteus

1274
Mimulus luteus
'A. T. Johnson'

1275
Miscanthus sinensis

1276
Monarda didyma
'Cambridge Scarlet'

1277
Morina longifolia

1278
Nepeta × faassenii
'Six Hills Giant'

1279
Nymphaea
'Escarboucle'

1280
Nymphaea
'Fire Crest'

1281
Nymphaea
'Gladstoniana'

1282
Nymphaea
'James Brydon'

1283
Nymphaea
'Marliacea
Chromatella'

1284
Nymphaea odorata
'Sulphurea
Grandiflora'

1285
Nymphaea
'Paul Hariot'

1286
Nymphaea
'Sunrise'

1287
Oenothera cinaeus

1288
Oenothera fruticosa

1289
Oenothera
missouriensis

1290
Oenothera tetragona
'Fireworks'

1291
Oenothera tetragona
'Riparia'

1292
Origanum hybridum

1293
Origanum vulgare
'Aureum'

1294
Pachysandra
terminalis
'Variegata'

1295
Paeonia
cambessedesii

1296
Paeonia
'Defender'

1297
Paeonia lactiflora
'Bowl of Beauty'

1298
Paeonia
mlokosewitschii

1299
Paeonia officinalis

1300
Papaver orientale

1301
Papaver orientale
'Mrs Perry'

1302
Papaver orientale
'Sultana'

1303
Peltiphyllum
peltatum

1304
Pennisetum
alopecurioides

1305
Pennisetum villosum

1306
Penstemon barbatus

1307
Penstemon hartwegii
'Firebird'

1308
Penstemon
'Six Hills'

1309
Perovskia
atriplicifolia

1310
Phalaris
arundinacea
'Picta'

1311
Phlox divaricata

1312
Phlox maculata
'Alpha'

1313
Phlox paniculata
'Brigadier'

1314
Phlox paniculata
'Mother of Pearl'

1315
Phlox paniculata
'Norah Leigh'

1316
Phlox paniculata
'Prince of Orange'

1317
Phlox paniculata
'Starfire'

1318
Physalis franchetii

1319
Physostegia
virginiana
'Vivid'

1320
Podophyllum emodii

1329
Potentilla
'Mons. Rouillard'

1330
Potentilla recta
'Warrenii'

1331
Primula beesiana

1332
Primula florindae

1333
Primula helodoxa

1334
Primula japonica

1335
Primula japonica
'Postford White'

1336
Primula pulverulenta

1337
Primula pulverulenta
'Bartley Strain'

1338
Prunella webbiana
'Loveliness'

1339
Puya alpestris

1340
Pyrethrum
parthenium
'White Bonnet'

1341
Pyrethrum roseum
'Brenda'

1342
Pyrethrum roseum
'E. M. Robinson'

1343
Pyrethrum roseum
'Vanessa'

1344
Ranunculus acris
'Flore Pleno'

1345
Ranunculus lingua

1346
Rhazya orientalis

1347
Rheum alexandrae

1348
Rheum palmatum

1349
Rodgersia pinnata
'Superba'

1350
Rodgersia podophylla

1351
Rodgersia tabularis

1352
Rudbeckia fulgida

1353
Rudbeckia laciniata
'Goldquelle'

1354
Rudbeckia purpurea
'Robert Bloom'

1355
Rudbeckia purpurea
'The King'

1356
Rudbeckia sullivantii
'Goldsturm'

1357
Sagittaria sagittifolia
'Flore Pleno'

1358
Salvia haematodes

1359
Salvia sclarea
'Turkestanica'

1360
Salvia × superba

1361
Salvia × superba
'Lubeca'

1362
Salvia × superba
'May Night'

1363
Salvia uliginosa

1364
Sanguisorba
canadensis

1365
Satureia montana
'Coerulea'

1366
Scabiosa caucasica
'Clive Greaves'

1367
Scirpus
tabernaemontanus
'Zebrinus'

1368
Scrophularia nodosa
'Variegata'

1369
Sedum aizoon

1370
Sedum cauticola

1371
Sedum maximum
'Atropurpureum'

1372
Sedum spectabile
'Autumn Joy'

1373
Sedum spectabile
'Meteor'

1374
Sedum spectabile
hybrid 'Ruby Glow'

1375
Senecio doronicum
'Sunburst'

1376
Senecio przewalskii
'The Rocket'

1377
Senecio
'White Diamond'

1378
Serratula shawii

1379
Sisyrinchium
striatum

1380
Smilacina racemosa

1381
Solidago canadensis
'Crown of Rays'

1382
Solidago canadensis
'Goldenmosa'

1383
Solidago canadensis
'Golden Thumb'

1384
Solidago canadensis
'Lemore'

1385
× Solidaster luteus

1386
Stachys lanata

1387
Stachys macrantha

1388
Stachys spicata
'Robusta'

1389
Stipa calamagrostis

1390
Stipa pennata

1391
Stokesia laevis

1392
Stylophorum
diphyllum

1393
Symphytum officinale
'Argenteum'

1394
Teucrium pyrenaicum

1395
Thalictrum
aquilegiifolium

1396
Thalictrum
dipterocarpum
'Hewitt's Double'

1397
Thalictrum lucidum

1398
Tiarella polyphylla

1399
Tiarella wherryi

1400
Tradescantia
virginiana

1401
Tradescantia
virginiana
'Isis'

1402
Tricyrtis stolonifera

1403
Trollius europaeus
'Golden Monarch'

1404
Trollius europaeus
'Orange Princess'

1405
Trollius europaeus
'Superbus'

1406
Trollius ledebourii
'Golden Queen'

1407
Verbascum chaixii

1408
Verbascum hybridum
'Cotswold Queen'

1409
Verbascum hybridum
'Gainsborough'

1410
Verbascum hybridum
'Pink Domino'

1411
Verbena peruviana

1412
Verbena rigida

1413
Verbena tenera
'Mahonettii'

1414
Veronica exaltata

1415
Veronica gentianoides

1416
Veronica incana

1417
Veronica longifolia
'Blue Giant'

1418
Veronica teucrium
'Blue Fountain'

1419
Veronica teucrium
'Crater Lake Blue'

1420
Vinca minor
'Variegata'

1421
Viola cornuta

1422
Viola cornuta
'Ardross Gem'

1423
Viola cornuta
'Northfield Gem'

1424
Viola saxatilis
'Aetolica'

1425
Abelia × grandiflora

1426
Abeliophyllum
distichum

1427
Abutilon
megapotamicum

1428
Abutilon vitifolium

1429
Acacia decurrens
var. dealbata

1430
Acer campestre

1431
Acer griseum

1432
Acer japonicum
'Aureum'

1433
Acer nikoense

1434
Acer palmatum
'Atropurpureum'

1435
Acer palmatum
'Dissectum'

1436
Acer palmatum
'Ozakazuki'

1437
Acer pensylvanicum

1438
Acer plantanoides

1439
Acer pseudoplatanus
'Brilliantissimum'

1440
Acer rubrum
'Schlesingeri'

1441
Aesculus × carnea

1442
Aesculus octandra

1443
Alnus cordata

1444
Amelanchier
canadensis

1445
Amelanchier
canadensis

1446
Aralia elata
'Albo-marginata'

1447
Arbutus ×
andrachnoides

1448
Arbutus ×
andrachnoides

1449
Arbutus menziesii

1450
Arbutus unedo

1451
Arbutus unedo
'Rubra'

1452
Artemisia arborescens

1453
Aucuba japonica

1454
Azara microphylla

1455
Berberis darwinii

1456
Berberis darwinii

1457
Berberis × lologensis

1458
Berberis ×
stenophylla
'Semperflorens'

1459
Berberis thunbergii
'Atropurpurea Nana'

1460
Beschorneria yuccoides

1461
Betula albo-sinensis
var. septentrionalis

1462
Betula pendula

1463
Betula pendula
'Youngii'

1464
Buddleia alternifolia

1465
Buddleia colvilei

1466
Buddleia davidii
'Royal Red'

1467
Buddleia globosa

1468
Buddleia × weyeriana

1469
Bupleurum
fruticosum

1470
Buxus sempervirens

1471
Caesalpinia japonica

1472
Calceolaria
integrifolia
var. angustifolia

1473
Callistemon salignus

1474
Calluna vulgaris

1475
Calluna vulgaris
'Alba Plena'

1476
Calluna vulgaris
'Hammondii Aurea'

1477
Calluna vulgaris
'H. E. Beale'

1478
Calluna vulgaris
'Peter Sparkes'

1479
Camellia japonica
'Adolphe Audusson'

1480
Camellia japonica
'Alba Simplex'

1481
Camellia japonica
'Althaeaflora'

1482
Camellia japonica
'Drama Girl'

1483
Camellia japonica
'Jupiter'

1484
Camellia japonica
'Lady Clare'

1485
Camellia japonica
'Mrs D. W. Davis'

1486
Camellia japonica
'Tricolor'

1487
Camellia reticulata
'Captain Rawes'

1488
Camellia reticulata
'Mary Williams'

1489
Camellia hybrid
'Leonard Messel'

1490
Camellia hybrid
'Cornish Snow'

1491
Camellia × williamsii
'Donation'

1492
Camellia × williamsii
'Inspiration'

1493
Camellia × williamsii
'J. C. Williams'

1494
Camellia × williamsii
'St Ewe'

1495
Carpenteria
californica

1496
Caryopteris ×
clandonensis

1497
Caryopteris ×
clandonensis
'Ferndown'

1498
Catalpa bignonioides

1499
Ceanothus arboreus

1500
Ceanothus
'Delight'

1501
Ceanothus
'Dignity'

1502
Ceanothus 'Gloire de
Versailles'

1503
Ceanothus impressus
'Puget Blue'

1504
Ceanothus thyrsiflorus

1505
Ceratostigma
plumbaginoides

1506
Ceratostigma
willmottianum

1507
Cercis siliquastrum

1508
Chaenomeles speciosa
'Rowallane Seedling'

1509
Chaenomeles superba
'Knap Hill Scarlet'

1510
Chamaerops humilis

1511
Chimonanthus
praecox 'Luteus'

1512
Choisya ternata

1513
Cistus ladaniferus

1514
Cistus laurifolius

1515
Cistus ×
pulverulentus

1516
Cistus ×
purpureus

1517
Clerodendron bungei

1518
Clerodendron
trichotomum

1519
Clerodendron
trichotomum

1520
Clethra barbinervis

1521
Convolvulus cneorum

1522
Cordyline australis

1523
Cordyline indivisa

1524
Cornus alba
'Sibirica'

1525
Cornus alba
'Sibirica'

1526
Cornus florida
var. rubra

1527
Cornus kousa var.
chinensis

1528
Cornus mas

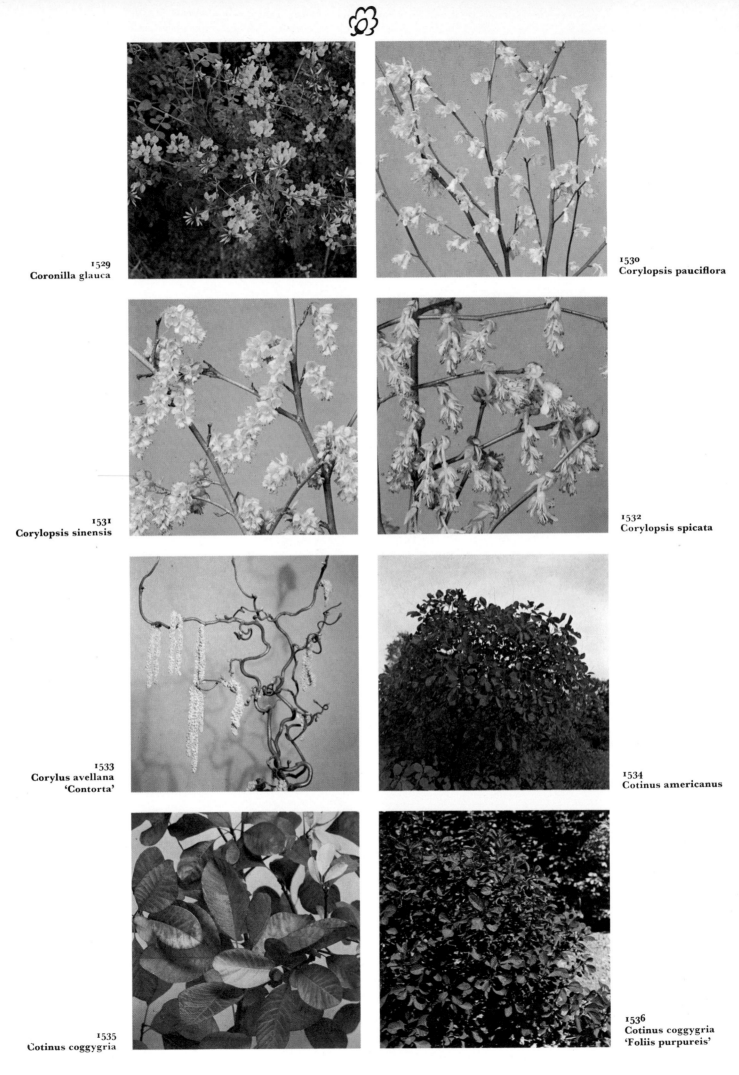

1529
Coronilla glauca

1530
Corylopsis pauciflora

1531
Corylopsis sinensis

1532
Corylopsis spicata

1533
Corylus avellana
'Contorta'

1534
Cotinus americanus

1535
Cotinus coggygria

1536
Cotinus coggygria
'Foliis purpureis'

1537
Cotoneaster
conspicuus
'Decorus'

1538
Cotoneaster
'Cornubia'

1539
Cotoneaster ×
exburyensis

1540
Cotoneaster franchetii
var. sternianus

1541
Cotoneaster
horizontalis

1542
Crataegus × lavallei

1543
Crataegus orientalis

1544
Crataegus oxyacantha
'Coccinea Plena'

1545
Crinodendron
hookerianum

1546
Cytisus battandieri

1547
Cytisus × kewensis

1548
Cytisus scoparius

1549
Daboecia cantabrica

1550
Daphne arbuscula

1551
Daphne blagayana

1552
Daphne collina

1553
Daphne genkwa

1554
Daphne mezereum
'Bowles White'

1555
Daphne odora
'Aureo-marginata'

1556
Daphne retusa

1557
Daphne striata

1558
Davidia involucrata

1559
Decaisnea fargesii

1560
Dendromecon rigidum

1561
Desfontainea spinosa

1562
Deutzia
'Magician'

1563
Deutzia × rosea

1564
Deutzia scabra

1565
Deutzia setchuenensis

1566
Disanthus
cercidifolius

1567
Drimys winteri
var. latifolia

1568
Edgeworthia
papyrifera

1569
Elaeagnus × ebbingei

1570
**Elaeagnus pungens
'Dicksonii'**

1571
**Elaeagnus pungens
'Maculata'**

1572
**Embothrium
coccineum**

1573
**Embothrium
coccineum var.
lanceolatum
'Norquinco'**

1574
**Enkianthus
campanulatus**

1575
Enkianthus cernuus

1576
**Enkianthus cernuus
'Rubens'**

1577
Erica arborea
var. alpina

1578
Erica australis
'Mr Robert'

1579
Erica carnea
'Springwood'

1580
Erica carnea
'Vivellii'

1581
Erica cinerea

1582
Erica cinerea
'Autrorubens'

1583
Erica cinerea
'Rosea'

1584
Erica × darleyensis

1585
Erica lusitanica

1586
Erica tetralix
'Alba'

1587
Erica umbellata

1588
Erica vagans
'Mrs D. F. Maxwell'

1589
Erica vagans
'St Keverne'

1590
Erica × veitchii

1591
Eriobotrya japonica

1592
Erythrina crista-galli

1593
Escallonia
'C. F. Ball'

1594
Escallonia
'Donard Star'

1595
Escallonia
'Peach Blossom'

1596
Escallonia macrantha

1597
Eucalyptus gunnii

1598
Eucalyptus niphophila

1599
Eucalyptus perriniana

1600
Eucalyptus
simmondsii

1601
Eucryphia glutinosa

1602
Eucryphia ×
nymansensis
'Nymansay'

1603
Euonymus alatus

1604
Euonymus europaeus
'Red Cascade'

1605
Euonymus
sachalinensis

1606
Euonymus yedoensis

1607
Exochorda giraldii

1608
Fabiana imbricata

1609
Fagus sylvatica
'Cuprea'

1610
Fatsia japonica

1611
Forsythia ×
intermedia
'Beatrix Farrand'

1612
Forsythia ×
intermedia
'Spectabilis'

1613
Fothergilla gardenii

1614
Fothergilla monticola

1615
Fraxinus excelsior
'Pendula'

1616
Fuchsia
'Mme Cornelissen'

1617
Fuchsia magellanica

1618
Fuchsia
'Mrs Popple'

1619
Garrya elliptica

1620
Gaultheria
procumbens

1621
Genista cinerea

1622
Genista hispanica

1623
Genista lydia

1624
Genista tinctoria
'Royal Gold'

1625
Grevillea sulphurea

1626
Griselinia littoralis

1627
Hakea microcarpa

1628
Halesia monticola

1629
Halimium lasianthum

1630
Hamamelis japonica
var. arborea

1631
Hamamelis japonica
var. zuccariniana

1632
Hamamelis mollis

1633
Hamamelis mollis
'Brevipetala'

1634
Hamamelis mollis
'Pallida'

1635
Hebe
'Autumn Glory'

1636
Hebe brachysiphon

1637
Hebe hulkeana

1638
Hebe 'Pagei'

1639
Hebe speciosa
'La Seduisante'

1640
Hebe speciosa
'Midsummer Beauty'

1641
Hebe speciosa
'Sapphire'

1642
Helichrysum lanatum

1643
Hibiscus syriacus

1644
Hibiscus syriacus
'Blue Bird'

1645
Hibiscus syriacus
'Snow Drift'

1646
Hibiscus syriacus
'Woodbridge'

1647
Hippophae
rhamnoides

1648
Hoheria sexstylosa

1649
Hydrangea
'Blue Wave'

1650
Hydrangea
'Hamburg'

1651
Hydrangea
'Preziosa'

1652
Hydrangea paniculata
'Grandiflora'

1653
Hydrangea serrata
'Acuminata'

1654
Hydrangea villosa

1655
Hypericum
calycinum

1656
Hypericum elatum
'Elstead'

1657
Hypericum patulum
'Hidcote'

1658
Hypericum
'Rowallane Hybrid'

1659
Ilex aquifolium

1660
Ilex aquifolium
'Bacciflava'

1661
Ilex aquifolium
'Golden Queen'

1662
Ilex aquifolium
'Pyramidalis'

1663
Itea ilicifolia

1664
Jasminum nudiflorum

1665
Kalmia latifolia

1666
Kalmia latifolia
'Brilliant'

1667
Kerria japonica
'Flore Pleno'

1668
Kolkwitzia amabilis

1669
Laburnum × vossii

1670
Lagerstroemia indica

1671
Lavandula spica
'Nana Atropurpurea'
(Hidcote)

1672
Lavatera arborea

1673
Leptospermum
cunninghamii

1674
Leptospermum
scoparium
'Keatleyi'

1675
Leycesteria formosa

1676
Lindera triloba

1677
Liquidambar
styraciflua

1678
Liriodendron
tulipifera

1679
Lomatia longifolia

1680
Magnolia campbellii

1681
Magnolia campbellii
'Alba'

1682
Magnolia
'Charles Raffill'

1683
Magnolia denudata

1684
Magnolia grandiflora

1685
Magnolia ×
highdownensis

1686
Magnolia × loebneri
'Merrill'

1687
Magnolia obovata

1688
Magnolia salicifolia

1689
Magnolia sieboldii

1690
Magnolia ×
soulangeana

1691
Magnolia ×
soulangeana
'Alba'

1692
Magnolia ×
soulangeana
'Alexandrina'

1693
Magnolia ×
soulangeana
'Rustica Rubra'

1694
Magnolia stellata
'Water Lily'

1695
Mahonia aquifolium

1696
Mahonia
'Charity'

1697
Mahonia japonica

1698
Mahonia lomariifolia

1699
Malus floribunda

1700
Malus
'Golden Hornet'

1701
Malus
'John Downie'

1702
Malus × lemoinei

1703
Malus × robusta

1704
Malus tschonoskii

1705
Melianthus major

1706
Mimulus glutinosus

1707
Mitraria coccinea

1708
Myrtus luma

1709
Neillia longiracemosa

1710
Nerium oleander

1711
Nothofagus procera

1712
Nyssa sylvatica

1713
Olea europaea

1714
Olearia haastii

1715
Olearia macrodonta
'Major'

1716
Osmanthus delavayi

1717
Oxydendrum
arboreum

1718
Paeonia lutea
var. ludlowii

1719
Paeonia suffruticosa
'Black Pirate'

1720
Paeonia suffruticosa
'Hakuo-Jishi'

1721
Parrotia persica

1722
Paulownia tomentosa

1723
Paulownia tomentosa

1724
Pernettya mucronata

1725
Philadelphus
'Beauclerk'

1726
Philadelphus
'Belle Etoile'

1727
Philadelphus
'Bouquet Blanc'

1728
Philadelphus
coronarius

1729
Philadelphus
'Manteau d'Hermine'

1730
Philesia magellanica

1731
Phlomis fruticosa

1732
Phormium tenax

1733
Photinia beauverdiana

1734
Photinia serrulata

1735
Phygelius aequalis

1736
Phygelius capensis
'Coccineus'

1737
Pieris formosa
var. forrestii

1738
Pieris japonica

1739
Pieris taiwanensis

1740
Pittosporum
crassifolium

1741
Platanus orientalis

1742
Poncirus trifoliata

1743
Poncirus trifoliata

1744
Populus tremula

1745
Potentilla fruticosa
'Elizabeth'

1746
Potentilla fruticosa
'Katherine Dykes'

1747
Potentilla fruticosa
'Mandshurica'

1748
Potentilla fruticosa
'Moonlight'

1749
Potentilla fruticosa
'Tangerine'

1750
Potentilla fruticosa
'Vilmoriniana'

1751
Prostanthera
ovalifolia

1752
Prunus
'Accolade'

1753
Prunus avium
'Plena'

1754
Prunus cerasifera

1755
Prunus conradinae

1756
Prunus incisa hybrid

1757
Prunus mume

1758
Prunus padus

1759
Prunus persica
'Iceberg'

1760
Prunus sargentii

1761
Prunus serrula

1762
Prunus serrulata
'Schimidsu Sakura'

1763
Prunus serrulata
'Tai-Haku'

1764
Prunus serrulata
'Yedo-Zakura'

1765
Prunus subhirtella
'Autumnalis'

1766
Prunus tenella
'Fire Hill'

1767
Prunus triloba
'Flore-Pleno'

1768
Punica granatum

1769
Pyracantha coccinea

1770
Pyracantha
rogersiana 'Flava'

1771
Pyrus salicifolia
'Pendula'

1772
Quercus coccinea
'Splendens'

1773
Rhododendron
albrechtii

1774
Rhododendron
arboreum
var. roseum

1775
Rhododendron
augustinii

1776
Rhododendron
barbatum

1777
Rhododendron
calophytum

1778
Rhododendron
ciliatum

1779
Rhododendron
dalhousiae

1780
Rhododendron
edgeworthii

1781
Rhododendron
ferrugineum

1782
Rhododendron
griersonianum

1783
Rhododendron
kaempferi

1784
Rhododendron
lutescens

1785
Rhododendron
macabeanum

1786
Rhododendron
moupinense

1787
Rhododendron
mucronulatum
var. acuminatum

1788
Rhododendron
obtusum

1789
Rhododendron
pemakoense

1790
Rhododendron
quinquefolium

1791
Rhododendron
racemosum

1792
Rhododendron rex

1793
Rhododendron
sargentianum

1794
Rhododendron
schlippenbachii
'Prince Charming'

1795
Rhododendron
sino-grande

1796
Rhododendron
strigillosum

1797
Rhododendron
sutchuenense

1798
Rhododendron
trichostomum
var. ledoides

1799
Rhododendron
wallichii

1800
Rhododendron
williamsianum

1801
Rhododendron
xanthocodon

1802
Rhododendron
yakusimanum

1803
Rhododendron
'Azor'

1804
Rhododendron
'Britannia'

1805
Rhododendron
'Choremia'

1806
Rhododendron
'Cilpinense'

1807
Rhododendron
'Crest'

1808
Rhododendron
'Elizabeth'

1809
Rhododendron
'Elspeth'

1810
Rhododendron
'Fragrantissimum'

1811
Rhododendron
'Lady Rosebery'

1812
Rhododendron
Loderi
'King George'

1813
Rhododendron
'Mrs G. W. Leak'

1814
Rhododendron
'Penjerrick Cream'

1815
Rhododendron
'Polar Bear'

1816
Rhododendron
'Praecox'

1817
Rhododendron
'Seta'

1818
Rhododendron
'Susan'

1819
Rhododendron
'Tally-Ho'

1820
Rhododendron
'Temple Belle'

1821
Rhododendron
'Addy Wery'

1822
Rhododendron
'Fedora'

1823
Rhododendron
'Hi No Mayo'

1824
Rhododendron
'Daybreak'

1825
Rhododendron
'Hotspur Orange'

1826
Rhododendron
'Hugh Wormald'

1827
Rhododendron
'Ribera'

1828
Rhododendron
'Satan'

1829
Rhododendron
'Scarlet O'Hara'

1830
Rhododendron
'Silver Slipper'

1831
Rhododendron
'Sun Chariot'

1832
Rhus typhina

1833
Ribes sanguineum
'Pulborough Scarlet'

1834
Ribes speciosum

1835
Richea scoparia

1836
Robinia hispida

1837
Romneya coulteri

1838
Rosa ×
cantabrigiensis

1839
Rosa damascena
'Hebes Lip'

1840
Rosa ×
highdownensis

1841
Rosa moyesii

1842
Rosa rubrifolia

1843
Rosa spinossisima
var. altaica

1844
Rosa webbiana

1845
Rosa woodsii
var. fendleri

1846
Rosa
'Blanc Double de
Coubert'

1847
Rosa
'Constance Spry'

1848
Rosa
'Frau Dagmar
Hastrup'

1849
Rosa
'Fritz Nobis'

1850
Rosa
'Frühlingsgold'

1851
Rosa gallica
'Complicata'

1852
Rosa gallica
'Versicolor'

1853
Rosa
'Marguerite Hilling'

1854
Rosa
'Nevada'

1855
Rosa
'Penelope'

1856
Rosa
'Zephirine Drouhin'

1857
Rosa
'Zigeuner Knabe'

1858
Rosa
'Alison Wheatcroft'

1859
Rosa
'Anna Wheatcroft'

1860
Rosa
'Elizabeth of Glamis'

1861
Rosa
'Evelyn Fison'

1862
Rosa
'Golden Slippers'

1863
Rosa
'Iceberg'

1864
Rosa
'Jan Spek'

1865
Rosa
'John S. Armstrong'

1866
Rosa
'Masquerade'

1867
Rosa
'Orangeade'

1868
Rosa
'Pink Parfait'

1869
Rosa
'Queen Elizabeth'

1870
Rosa
'Sarabande'

1871
Rosa
'Blue Moon'

1872
Rosa
'Charlotte
Armstrong'

1873
Rosa
'Christian Dior'

1874
Rosa
'Eden Rose'

1875
Rosa
'Ena Harkness'

1876
Rosa
'Fragrant Cloud'

1877
Rosa
'Gail Borden'

1878
Rosa
'Grandmère Jenny'

1879
Rosa
'Monique'

1880
Rosa
'Peace'

1881
Rosa
'Perfecta'

1882
Rosa
'Prima Ballerina'

1883
Rosa
'Rose Gaujard'

1884
Rosa
'Royal Highness'

1885
Rosa
'Super Star',
'Tropicana' (USA)

1886
Rosa
'Tzigane'

1887
Rosa
'Virgo'

1888
Rosa
'Wendy Cussons'

1889
Rubus
'Tridel'

1890
Ruscus aculeatus

1891
Ruta graveolens
'Jackman's Blue'

1892
Salix alba
'Tristis'

1893
Salix caprea

1894
Salix daphnoides

1895
Salix matsudana
'Tortuosa'

1896
Salvia grahamii

1897
Salvia officinalis
'Tricolor'

1898
Sambucus racemosa
'Plumosa Aurea'

1899
Santolina
chamaecyparissus

1900
Senecio laxifolius

1901
Sinarundinaria
murieliae

1902
Skimmia japonica

1903
Skimmia japonica

1904
Sophora tetraptera

1905
Sorbus aucuparia

1906
Sorbus cashmeriana

1907
Sorbus hupehensis

1908
Sorbus
'Joseph Rock'

1909
Sorbus prattii

1910
Sorbus reducta

1911
Sorbus sargentiana

1912
Sorbus scalaris

1913
Sorbus vilmorinii

1914
Spartium junceum

1915
Spiraea × bumalda
'Anthony Waterer'

1916
Stachyurus chinensis

1917
Stranvaesia davidiana

1918
Styrax hemsleyana

1919
Styrax japonica

1920
Symphoricarpus
albus var.
laevigatus

1921
Syringa × josiflexa

1922
Syringa vulgaris
'Charles X'

1923
Syringa vulgaris
'Firmament'

1924
Syringa vulgaris
'Mme Lemoine'

1925
Syringa vulgaris
'Massena'

1926
Syringa vulgaris
'Primrose'

1927
Tamarix pentandra

1928
Tibouchina
semidecandra

241

1929
Tilia × europaea

1930
Trachycarpus
fortunei

1931
Ulex europaeus
'Plenus'

1932
Ulmus carpinifolia
var. sarniensis
'Aurea'

1933
Vaccinium
corymbosum

1934
Vaccinium
cylindraceum

1935
Vaccinium
glauco-album

1936
Vaccinium
myrsinites

242

1937
Vaccinium
vitis-idaea

1938
Viburnum
betulifolium

1939
Viburnum ×
bodnantense
'Dawn'

1940
Viburnum carlesii

1941
Viburnum davidii

1942
Viburnum fragrans

1943
Viburnum hupehense

1944
Viburnum × juddii

1945
Viburnum opulus

1946
Viburnum opulus
'Sterile'

1947
Viburnum
rhytidophyllum

1948
Viburnum tinus
'St Ewe'

1949
Viburnum
tomentosum
'Mariesii'

1950
Viburnum
tomentosum
'Rowallane'

1951
Vinca major

1952
Weigela
'Eva Rathke'

1953
Weigela
'Newport Red'

1954
Weigela florida

1955
Yucca filamentosa

1956
Yucca gloriosa
'Nobilis'

1957
Actinidia kolomikta

1958
Campsis ×
tagliabuana

1959
Celastrus orbiculatus

1960
Clematis armandii

1961
Clematis ×
jouiniana

1962
Clematis
macropetala

1963
Clematis montana
'Rubens'

1964
Clematis orientalis

1965
Clematis rehderiana

1966
Clematis tangutica

1967
Clematis
'Comtesse de
Bouchaud'

1968
Clematis
'Henryi'

1969
Clematis
'Jackmanii'

1970
Clematis
'Lasurstern'

1971
Clematis
'Nelly Moser'

1972
Clematis
'Ville de Lyon'

1973
Clematis
'Vivyan Pennell'

1974
Clianthus puniceus

1975
Cobaea scandens

1976
Eccremocarpus
scaber

1977
Fremontia californica

1978
Jasminum
polyanthum

1979
Jasminum revolutum

1980
Lonicera ×
americana

1981
Lonicera × brownii
'Fuchsioides'

1982
Lonicera
periclymenum

1983
Lonicera
sempervirens

1984
Mutisia oligodon

1985
Parthenocissus
tricuspidata
'Veitchii'

1986
Passiflora coerulea

1987
Rosa
'Albertine'

1988
Rosa
'Danse du Feu'

1989
Rosa
'Easlea's Golden
Rambler'

1990
Rosa
'Mermaid'

1991
Rosa
'New Dawn'

1992
Rosa
'Wedding Day'

1993
Solanum crispum
autumnale

1994
Tropaeolum
speciosum

1995
Vitis coignetiae

1996
Vitis coignetiae

1997
Vitis vinifera
'Brandt'

1998
Wattakaka sinensis

1999
Wisteria sinensis

2000
Wisteria floribunda
'Macrobotrys'

2001
Abies alba

2002
Abies forrestii

2003
**Cedrus atlantica
'Glauca'**

2004
**Chamaecyparis
lawsoniana
'Allumii'**

2005
**Chamaecyparis
lawsoniana
'Columnaris'**

2006
**Chamaecyparis
lawsoniana
'Fletcheri Nana'**

2007
**Chamaecyparis
lawsoniana
'Lutea'**

2008
**Chamaecyparis
lawsoniana
'Triomphe de
Boskoop'**

2009
Chamaecyparis
obtusa
'Nana Variegata'

2010
Chamaecyparis
obtusa
'Tetragona Aurea'

2011
Cryptomeria
japonica

2012
× Cupressocyparis
leylandii

2013
Cupressus glabra
'Glauca'

2014
Ginkgo biloba

2015
Juniperus communis

2016
Juniperus communis
'Compressa'

2017
**Juniperus communis
'Hibernica'**

2018
**Juniperus
horizontalis**

2019
**Juniperus × media
'Pfitzeriana Aurea'**

2020
**Juniperus recurva
var. coxii
'Castelwellan'**

2021
**Juniperus squamata
meyeri**

2022
Larix decidua

2023
Larix decidua

2024
Libocedrus decurrens

2025
Metasequoia
glyptostroboides

2026
Picea breweriana

2027
Picea glauca var.
albertiana
'Conica'

2028
Picea likiangensis

2029
Picea omorika

2030
Picea pungens
'Glauca'

2031
Pinus ayacahuite

2032
Pinus montezumae

2033
Pinus nigra var.
nigra

2034
Pinus radiata

2035
Pinus sylvestris

2036
Pinus wallichiana

2037
Sciadopitys
verticillata
(lefthand conifer)

2038
Sequoia
sempervirens
'Adpressa'

2039
Sequoiadendron
giganteum

2040
Sequoiadendron
giganteum

2041
Taxodium distichum

2042
Taxus baccata

2043
Taxus baccata
'Fastigiata Aurea'

2044
Thuya orientalis
'Rosedalis Compacta'

2045
Thuya orientalis
'Semperaurea'

2046
Thuya plicata
'Fastigiata'

2047
Thuya plicata
'Zebrina'

2048
Tsuga canadensis

The Dictionary

A

ABELIA (CAPRIFOLIACEAE)

chinensis see under **A. × grandiflora**

floribunda ❋ Summer   *Sh.
Fl. brilliant shocking purplish-magenta, tubular, hanging in pendulous clusters. A very striking plant for a wall position in the warmer areas only, or in a cool greenhouse. Mexico.

× grandiflora ❋ Late Summer–Mid Autumn *Sh.
A hybrid of *A. chinensis* and *A. uniflora. Fl.* white or pale pink with conspicuous calyx of dark purple in clusters. Pendulous. Semi-evergreen. *L.* of rather unusual bright green. Best against a wall except in warmer areas. Valuable as a late flowering shrub. China. **1425**, p. 179.
Other sp. worth growing include:

chinensis ❋ Summer   Sh.
Fl. white, fragrant but less vigorous than *A. × grandiflora.*

schumanii ❋ Summer   Sh.
Fl. rosy-pink. Useful deciduous shrub with pendulous arching branches. For warmer areas or as a wall shrub in central districts. Central China.

triflora ❋ Summer   Sh.
Fl. white and tinged with pink in clusters. Erect, graceful shrub up to 10 ft. Some forms are very fragrant. Apart from *A. × grandiflora* this is the hardiest of the Abelias. N.W. Himalayas.

ABELIOPHYLLUM (OLEACEAE)

distichum ❋ Late Winter–Mid Spring   Sh.

Fl. star-shaped, white with yellow centres, fragrant. Flowering without *l.* Useful as an early flowering shrub. Hardy but *fl.* best against a wall in many places. Prune hard after flowering in order to prevent becoming straggly. Korea. **1426**, p. 179.

ABIES (PINACEAE) Silver Fir

Evergreen trees from North temperate regions of Europe, North Africa, Asia and N. America. Some of our finest forestry and garden sp. come from W. N. America. Conical in outline when young, branches forming flat sprays and bark smooth or with small resin blisters, in older trees deeply furrowed at the base. *L.* dark green or pale green or glaucous beneath, linear and usually short pointed, flattened. The genus is distinguished from allied genera by the base of the old *l.* which leave disc-like scars on the shoots. Male and female cones both borne on the same tree in spring. Male in short catkins from the *l.* axils on underneath of branches. Female cones large and erect usually on upper branches with close overlapping scales which are broad or fan-shaped. Silver Firs grow best in the damper parts of the country but with adequate mulching do reasonably in practically all areas. They are however sensitive to atmospheric pollution in large towns. When young they will withstand some shade. Among main sp. of Silver Firs are:

alba European Silver Fir   Co.
Tall tree up to 150 ft with smooth greyish bark. *L.* arranged in two ranks, lower ones spreading horizontally, upper ones shorter and almost erect on the branchlets, dark shining green. Common Silver Fir of N. Europe particularly in the mountains and used as important forest tree. Now less frequently planted than some of the W. American sp. **2001**, p. 251.

amabilis Red Silver Fir   Co.
Magnificent tree up to 250 ft in native areas but in this country only suited for milder counties and unsuitable for dry situations. Pacific coast of W. N. America.

forrestii   Co.
A very fine Silver Fir and where growing well one

of the most beautiful sp. Stems rusty-red, *l.* dark green above, conspicuously glaucous blue beneath, branches horizontal, cones upright deep blue-mauve. Rarely, however, forms large tree in Britain but most decorative as a young specimen. Often placed as a var. of *A. delavayi* from Western China to which it is close. **2002**, p. 251.

grandis   Co.
One of the finest growing and most popular of the W. American Silver Firs. *L.* horizontally arranged on branches dark shining green up to 2 in. long. Much used as forest tree and can be planted when young in semi-shade. Eventually making one of our largest specimen trees.

nobilis see **A. procera**

procera, syn. **A. nobilis** Noble Fir, Red Fir   Co.
One of the finest Silver Firs reaching 250 ft in Oregon, and specimens well over 100 ft frequently have been grown in Britain. Bark smooth reddish-brown. Leaflets closely set on branches, glaucous green curving upwards. Cones very large up to 10 in. high, cylindrical purplish-brown. One of the finest specimen trees which can be grown in Britain but only suitable for gardens where there is good space, and rarely doing well on chalky soils.

ABUTILON (MALVACEAE)

megapotamicum ❋ Summer   *Sh.
Fl. bell-shaped hanging with red calyx and yellow corolla, prominent purplish-crimson anthers, 2-3 in. Best as a wall shrub in most positions. Prune after flowering. In cold areas give some protection in winter. Up to 10 ft but usually less. Brazil. **1427**, p. 179.

ochsenii ❋ Summer   Sh.
Fl. deeper blue-mauve than in *A. vitifolium* but smaller. Hardy as wall shrub in most areas. Up to 6 ft. Chile.

vitifolium ❋ Summer   *Sh.
Tall shrub up to 10 ft with pale lilac-blue *fl.* in clusters 3–4 in. across. There is also a good white form. *L.* tri-lobed and toothed. Needs warm sunny position. Very fast growing but generally not very long lived. Best form is 'Veronica Tennant'. Propagate by cuttings in early autumn or from seed. Chile. **1428**, p. 179.

ACACIA (LEGUMINOSAE) Mimosa

decurrens var. **dealbata** ❋ Spring   *†T.
Fl. bright yellow in large ball-like clusters and strongly scented. Only suitable for growing as a wall plant in warm areas. *L.* fern-like and much divided. Commonly grown in Mediterranean countries and used as a cut *fl.* To keep *fl.* in water, stems should be scalded for a minute or two. **1429**, p. 179.

ACACIA, FALSE see **Robinia pseudoacacia**

ACACIA ROSE see **Robinia hispida, 1836**, p. 230.

ACALYPHA (EUPHORBIACEAE)

hispida Chenille Plant, Redhot Catstail ❋ Summer   GSh.
Fl. red in drooping tassel-like spikes 12–20 in. long. *L.* evergreen, oval, pointed, 5 in. long, 3 in. wide. Shrub to 10 ft. Rich compost, with very moist warm atmosphere in spring and summer. Winter temp. 60–65°F. A dioecious plant and only the female form appears to be in cultivation. Propagate by cuttings of young wood in 4 at high temps. New Guinea. **401**, p. 51.

wilkesiana 🍂   GSh.
L. ovate-acuminate, mottled and splashed with red on coppery base. Shrub 6–10 ft. Useful foliage plant, sometimes a little coarse. Cultivation as for *A. hispida.* South Sea Islands.

ACANTHUS (ACANTHACEAE) Bears Breeches

mollis ❋ Summer   P.
Fl. white or lilac-pink. *L.* large, narrowly ovate with undulating margin, not spiny. 4–5 ft. Ordinary garden soil in sun or partial shade. Propagate by root cuttings, division in spring or by seed. Italy.

spinosus ❋ Summer   P.
Fl. white and purple with shiny green bracts, on erect stem. *L.* shining dark green, deeply cut, each division spined. 3–4 ft. Sunny position in well-drained soil. Propagate as for *A. mollis.* S. Europe. **945**, p. 119.

ACER (ACERACEAE)

campestre Field Maple   T.
Native British tree up to 15 ft but usually less. Distinguished for its five-lobed *l.* which turn brilliant butter-yellow in autumn. **1430**, p. 179.

griseum Paperbark Maple USA   T.
Deciduous tree up to 40 ft. *L.* trifid with three leaflets and bright crimson colour in autumn but distinguished for its peeling bark leaving shiny mahogany stem. China. **1431**, p. 179.

japonicum 'Aureum' Japanese Maple UK, Fullmoon Maple USA   T.
Deciduous tree up to 30 ft. *L.* up to 5 in. and 7–11 lobed. Distinguished for bright yellow colouring which lasts throughout year. Branching horizontally. **1432**, p. 179.
Other good forms are:
  'Aconitifolium', with *l.* deeply divided and reddish-crimson in autumn;
  'Vitifolium', with *l.* vine-like and brilliant scarlet in autumn.

nikoense Nikko Maple USA   T.
Small tree up to 30 ft. *L.* with three leaflets, distinguished for brilliant orange-scarlet autumn colouring. Rather slow growing. Japan. **1433**, p. 180.

palmatum Japanese Maple   T.
Small tree up to 30 ft but usually less. Distinguished for brilliant autumn colouring. Many hybrids have been raised between this and *A. japonicum.*
Among best forms are:
  'Atropurpureum', *l.* dull purplish-crimson becoming redder in autumn, five to seven-lobed, **1434**, p. 180;
  'Dissectum', *l.* much divided, yellowish-green

Abbreviations and Symbols used in the text.
The following abbreviations may sometimes be used in conjunction as HA. indicating Hardy annual or GBb indicating Greenhouse bulb.

A. = Annual	P. = Perennial
Aq. = Aquatic	R. = Rock or
B. = Biennial	Alpine plant
Bb = Bulb	Sh. = Shrub
C. = Corm	Sp., sp. = Species
Cl. = Climber	Syn. = Synonym
Co. = Conifer	T. = Tree
Fl., fl. = Flower(s)	Tu. = Tuber
G. = Greenhouse or	var. = variety
house plant	× = Hybrid or
H. = Hardy	hybrid parents
HH. = Half-hardy	❋ = Flowering time
L., l. = Leaf, leaves	🍂 = Foliage plant
Mt(s) = Mount,	
mountain(s)	

The following have been used also in the descriptions of Alpines, Bulbs, Trees and Shrubs.

  * = slightly tender
  † = lime hater
  ✿ = highly recommended

The illustration numbers are in **bold type** and the page numbers in light type preceded by p.

throughout summer, becoming deep yellow in
autumn, **1435**, p. 180;
✿ 'Senkaki', with fine coral-red bark on young
twigs, conspicuous in winter, good yellow
autumn colour;
'Dissectum Atropurpureum', *l.* dark maroon-
purple becoming crimson in autumn, usually
a small tree;
✿ *septemlobum* 'Osakazuki', *l.* fiery scarlet in
autumn, probably the most brilliant in colour
and very regular in its colouring, **1436**, p. 180.
All these Maples look well against blue-grey or
dark background, and may be seen superbly placed
in the Westonbirt Arboretum, Gloucestershire.

pensylvanicum Snake-barked Maple UK, Moose-
wood USA T.
Small tree up to 30 ft. Distinguished for its striated
vertical green stem, with white streaks. *L.* up to
7 in. long, 3 lobed and finely toothed. Lower side
shoots should be pruned off when young to give
maximum height of stem. E.N. America. **1437**,
p. 180.

platanoides Norway Maple ✽ Spring T.
Large tree up to 50 ft. Distinguished for bright
yellow *fl.* in clusters flowering before *l.* Fine yellow
autumn colour of *l.* which are large and tri-lobed.
Seeds freely and may become menace. **1438**, p. 180.
'Crimson King', syn. 'Goldsworth Purple', with
dark purplish maroon foliage.

pseudoplatanus Sycamore UK, Sycamore Maple
USA T.
'Brilliantissimum', young *l.* in spring coral-pink
later becoming yellow-green, slow growing
tree up to 20 ft, distinguished for its brilliant
spring colouring of foliage, Britain, **1439**, p. 180;
'Purpureum', deep purple *l.*;
'Spathii', rich, deep purple *l.*

rubrum Scarlet Canadian Maple UK, Red Maple
USA T.
Small tree. *L.* tri-lobed on long pedicels with
brilliant autumn colouring.
'Schlesingeri', is the best form, **1440**, p. 180.

ACHILLEA (COMPOSITAE) Yarrow
A large family varying in height from a few inches
to 4–5 ft for a sunny position in almost any well-
drained soil, with or without lime. The sp. may be
increased by seed, and division in the spring is a
ready method for sp. and hybrids.

clypeolata ✽ Summer P.
Fl. deep gold. *L.* silvery-green, frond like. 9-12 in.
Balkans. **946**, p. 119.

eupatorium see **A. filipendulina**

filipendulina, syn. **A. eupatorium** Fernleaf Yarrow
✽ Summer P.
Fl. mustard-yellow, flat, plate-like heads, 3–4 in.
across. 3 ft. *L.* grey-green, feathery, toothed and
hairy. Caucasus.
Good hybrids include:
'Coronation Gold', 6–9, mustard-yellow, 2½–
3½ ft, **947**, p. 119;
'Gold Plate', 7–9, golden-yellow, 4 ft;
'Parker's Variety', 7–9, bright yellow, 4 ft.

'Flowers of Sulphur' ✽ Summer P.
Fl. soft yellow in large flat heads. *L.* green, strap-
like. 2½ ft. Good cut *fl.* A hybrid of German origin.
948, p. 119.

millefolium ✽ Summer P.
Fl. flat to 3 in. across. *L.* strap-shaped and deeply cut.
2½–3 ft. Plant in ordinary soil and a sunny position.
Increase by division.
A weed on lawns, widely spread in Britain and
Europe but from which some excellent garden
plants have been developed including:
'Cerise Queen', bright cerise, 2½ ft;
'Fire King', deep red, 2½–3 ft, **949**, p. 119.

'Moonshine' ✽ Late Spring–Midsummer P.
Fl. bright yellow in flat heads, 3–4 in. across. *L.*
silver-grey, dense. 2 ft. Garden origin. **950**, p. 119.

ptarmica Sneezewort ✽ Summer P.
Fl. white, borne in quite large corymbs. *L.* narrow,
serrated and smooth. Listed erroneously in some
catalogues under *A. sibirica.* Europe, Britain.
'Perry's White', small, double white, a good
cut *fl.*;
'The Pearl', double white, about ½ in. across,
951, p. 119.

ACIDANTHERA (IRIDACEAE)

bicolor murielae ✽ Autumn *C.
Fl. large, white, with long perianth tube, about 2 in.
across, butterfly- or orchid-like and graceful.
Strongly scented. 2½–3 ft. *L.* like a gladiolus. Should
be planted in a warm sunny place or in boxes in a
cool or cold greenhouse. In most areas should be
lifted in winter like a gladiolus and kept warm.
Often not very free-flowering but so beautiful that
it is well worth growing. Ethiopia. **657**, p. 83.

ACONITE, WINTER see **Eranthis hyemalis**,
729, p. 92.

ACONITUM (RANUNCULACEAE) Monkshood

carmichaelii, syn. **A. fischeri** ✽ Summer P.
Fl. deep purple-blue. *L.* dark, shiny green, deeply
cut. 2½–3 ft. A moist soil and partial shade, but
can be grown in a sunny border so long as the soil
does not dry out. Propagate by division, or by seed
sown in the open in spring. *Aconitum* roots are
poisonous. China.

fischeri see **A. carmichaelii**

lycoctonum Wolf's Bane ✽ Summer P.
Fl. yellow or deep cream. *L.* broadly lobed. 3–4 ft.
Cultivation and propagation as for *A. carmichaelii.*
Europe, N. Asia to China.

napellus ✽ Summer P.
Fl. purple or blue, helmet-like. *L.* deeply cut,
often into fine segments. 3–4 ft. Cultivation and
propagation as for *A. carmichaelii.* Europe, Asia.
Good varieties include:
'Blue Sceptre', blue and white, 2 ft;
'Bressingham Spire', violet-blue, 3 ft;
'Newry Blue', deep blue, 3 ft, **952**, p. 119;
'Spark's Variety', deep violet-blue, 4–5 ft.

wilsonii ✽ Late-Summer–Autumn P.
Fl. amethyst-blue. *L.* three-lobed, short-stalked. 6 ft
or more. Cultivation and propagation as for *A.
carmichaelii.* E. China.
'Barker's Variety', is a deeper blue.

ACTINIDIA (ACTINIDIACEAE)
(Sometimes placed in Ternstroemiaceae)

kolomikta ✽ Early Summer GSh.
Deciduous climber up to 20 ft, best on south or
west wall. *Fl.* greenish-white up to ½ in. across,
fragrant. *L.* ovate-oblong up to 6 in. long by 4 in.
wide, slightly toothed. Distinguished for pink
colouring which sometimes suffuses half *l.* or whole
l., often with distinct line across *l.*, partly white
coloured. Fruit yellow, ovoid, fleshy about 1 in.
long. Grown for pink colouring in *l.* China, Japan.
1957, p. 245.

ADAM'S NEEDLE see **Yucca gloriosa**, **1956**,
p. 245.

ADDER'S TONGUE see **Erythronium**, **731**, **732**,
p. 92.

ADONIS (RANUNCULACEAE)

amurensis ✽ Early Spring RP.
Fl. bright yellow, 2–3 in. across, like a large yellow
globe with central boss of yellow stamens on a very
short stem. *L.* much divided into three segments.
This plant disappears entirely in late summer and

winter and reappears as a fat bud in late *l. Fl.*
open before *l.* are fully developed. Japan, where
numerous forms have been developed including
pink, white, orange and copper coloured ones. A
good double form is also available. Japanese
recommend planting in winter. They also lift
plants in late autumn and force slightly in a cool
frame. Also found in Manchuria, Siberia. **1**, p. 1.

AECHMEA (BROMELIACEAE)
Epiphytes with *l.* in rosette and ephemeral *fl.*
emerging from coloured bracts which persist for
six weeks or more. Compost of peat, leaf-mould,
sand and osmunda fibre in equal parts. The 'vase'
should be kept filled with rain water, which should
be warmed in the winter. Full light needed except
at midsummer, when slight shading may be given.
After flowering the rosettes die off, but occasionally
there are sideshoots at the base, which may be
grown on; otherwise propagation by seed. Winter
temp. 50–55°F. but lower temp. tolerated.

fasciata Urn Plant ✽ Summer GP.
Fl. bluish, fugacious, issuing from rosy-pink bracts,
which also surround the scape. *L.* strap-shaped to
1½ ft long and 4 in. across; grey-green with horizontal grey bands. Rosette to 1 ft high, scape
to 1½ ft or more. Bracts retain their colour for six
months. Probably the most popular *Aechmea* in
cultivation. Plants are sometimes offered under
the name *A. rhodocyanea.* Brazil.

fulgens ✽ Late Summer–Mid-Autumn GP.
Fl. purple, fugacious, emerging from scarlet, berry-
like bracts, which retain their brilliance for two
months. *L.* sword-shaped, to 12 in. long and 2 in.
across; olive green with purple underside in var.
discolor. Rosette to 10 in. high, scape to 20 in.
Guiana, Brazil. **402**, p. 51.

rhodocyanea see **A. fasciata**

AEGLE SEPIARIA see **Poncirus trifoliata**

AESCULUS (SAPINDACEAE) Horse Chestnut

× **carnea** Pink Horse Chestnut ✽ Late Spring T.
Tree up to 50 ft with magnificent panicles of deep
pink *fl.* up to 8 in. long and *l.* in five or seven leaflets.
1441, p. 181.
'Briotii', has slightly deeper coloured *fl.*

Abbreviations and Symbols used in the text.
The following abbreviations may sometimes be
used in conjunction as HA. indicating Hardy
annual or GBb indicating Greenhouse bulb.

A. = Annual	P. = Perennial
Aq. = Aquatic	R. = Rock or
B. = Biennial	Alpine plant
Bb = Bulb	Sh. = Shrub
C. = Corm	Sp., sp. = Species
Cl. = Climber	Syn. = Synonym
Co. = Conifer	T. = Tree
Fl., fl. = Flower(s)	Tu. = Tuber
G. = Greenhouse or	var. = variety
house plant	× = Hybrid or
H. = Hardy	hybrid parents
HH. = Half-hardy	✽ = Flowering time
L., l. = Leaf, leaves	◑ = Foliage plant
Mt(s) = Mount,	
mountain(s)	

The following have been used also in the descriptions of Alpines, Bulbs, Trees and Shrubs.

* = slightly tender
† = lime hater
✿ = highly recommended

The illustration numbers are in **bold type** and
the page numbers in light type preceded by p.

hippocastanum Common Horse Chestnut ❋ Late Spring   T.
One of the most beautiful of large, English, flowering trees. *Fl.* white in tall upright spikes. *L.* divided. Fruits shiny nuts – the conkers loved by little boys.

indica ❋ Early Summer   T.
Also with flushed pink *fl.* in large clusters. A magnificent tree but much more rarely seen than other sp. in England.

octandra ❋ Early Summer   T.
Fl. pale yellow with pinkish calyx. *L.* with good autumn colour. Invaluable small tree. Up to 30 ft but occasionally more. Flowering slightly later then *A. hippocastanum*. S.E. USA. **1442**, p. 181.

parviflora ❋ Summer   T.
Another valuable tree with white *fl.* and red anthers, flowering much later. Usually making small tree or spreading shrub up to 10 ft.

pavia Red Buckeye ❋ Early Summer   Sh.
Shrub, 5–15 ft. *L.* of five radiating leaflets. Valuable for its panicles of red *fl.* at a season when the number of flowering trees and shrubs is rather sparse. The long, slender *fl.*, in large clusters, are remarkable in that calyx, petals and anthers are all of a similar red coloration. Although native to the S.E. USA, it can be grown much farther north.

ETHIONEMA (CRUCIFERAE)

✿ **'Warley Rose'** ❋ Late Spring–Midsummer RP.
Dwarf cress, 4–6 in. high with attractive blue-grey foliage and clusters of deep bluish-pink *fl.* Probably the best in colour among those usually grown of this genus and forming large compact clumps. Best in a sunny and well-drained position. Hardy. Should be propagated from cuttings in 7. Other members of genus grown are *A. grandiflorum* from Lebanon, also hardy, and *A. pulchellum* from Asia Minor which is slightly less hardy. **2**, p. 1.

AFRICAN DAISY see **Arctotis**, **238**, **239**, p. 30.

AFRICAN LILY see **Agapanthus**, **953**, p. 120.

AFRICAN MARIGOLD see **Tagetes erecta**, **78**, **379**, p. 48.

AFRICAN VIOLET see **Saintpaulia**, **637-640**, p. 80.

AGAPANTHUS (LILIACEAE) African Lily

At one time most forms of *Agapanthus* were considered to be varieties of *A. umbellatus*, but these have now been classified as 10 or more separate sp., differing in form of *fl.*, *l.* and vigour. The name *umbellatus* is no longer valid as the sp. had previously been described by botanists as *A. africanus*. The plant sometimes grown in tubs as *A. umbellatus* is now referred to *A. praecox*. It is sometimes now placed in the new family Alliaceae.

africanus ❋ Late Summer   P.
Fl. deep blue-violet to blue in shapely umbels. *L.* evergreen, leathery, about 1½ ft long. Not reliably hardy except in mild districts where it should be planted in deep, well-drained soil in sun or light shade. Once planted should be left undisturbed. Propagate by division in the spring or by seed. Cape Province.

'Headbourne Hybrids' ❋ Summer   P.
Fl. deep violet-blue to pale blue, bell-shaped, borne in umbels on erect stems. *L.* green, strap-like. 2–3 ft. Raised near Winchester by the Hon. Lewis Palmer from crosses of sp. he collected in S. Africa. This hybrid race has proved remarkably hardy and may be seen growing in the open at Wisley and elsewhere in the S. **953**, p. 120.

AGERATUM (COMPOSITAE)

houstonianum, syn. **A. mexicanum** Floss Flower ❋ Summer   HHA.
Fl. in shades of blue, purple, pink and white. *L.* heart-shaped. Grows 6 in.–1½ ft. Sow 2–3 in a warm greenhouse. Plant out late 5. Mexico.
  'Blue Blazer' an F¹ hybrid form, 4 in., uniform, early;
  'Blue Bouquet', 1½ ft, useful for cutting;
  'Blue Chip', an F¹ hybrid form, 6 in., vigorous, free flowering;
  'Blue Mink', 6 in., pale blue;
  'Fairy Pink', 6 in., rose-pink;
  'Florist's Blue', 8 in., lavender-blue, **225**, p. 29;
  'Violet Cloud', 6 in., violet-blue, reddish buds.

mexicanum see **A. houstonianum**

AGLAONEMA (ARACEAE)

Small plants with oblong-lanceolate *l.* which are variegated with grey or silver. They require warm, moist shady conditions and a rich compost. White *fl.* are produced by mature plants in summer and these are followed by red berry-like fruits. Winter temp. 55–60°F. May be used as room plants with minimum of 50°F. if kept dry. Propagate by seed, cuttings or division.

commutatum ➤   GP.
L. 5–9 in. long, 2–3 in. across. Dark green with silvery-grey zones between lateral veins. To 1 ft high. Malaya, Celebes. **403**, p. 51.

robelinii see **A. 'Silver Queen'**

'Silver Queen' ➤   GP.
Either a form of *A. robelinii*, from central Malaya, or a hybrid with that sp. as a parent. *L.* up to 10 in. long and 5 in. across, nearly entirely silver with bright green marks along main veins. **404**, p. 51.

treubii ➤   GP.
L. narrow, to 6 in. long but only 1½ in. across. Dark green with greyish blotches between principal veins. Indonesia. **405**, p. 51.

AGROSTEMMA (CARYOPHYLLACEAE)

githago Corn Cockle ❋ Summer   HA.
Fl. reddish-mauve. *L.* narrow, 2–5 in. long. Height 2–3 ft. Sow in the open 3–5, or 9. The sp. was introduced to the British Isles from S. Europe and became a weed in our cornfields.
  'Milas', rosy-lilac, is a decorative, free-flowering variety, **226**, p. 29.

AJUGA (LABIATAE) Bugle

pyramidalis ❋ Late Spring–Midsummer   P.
Fl. blue or purple forming a compact pyramidal spike. 6 in. *L.* dark green, oval, slightly toothed, almost evergreen. Good ground cover plant for sun or shade where the soil is not too dry. Increase by division, or by seed sown in the open. Europe. **954**, p. 120.

reptans Common Bugle ❋ Late Spring–Midsummer   P.
Fl. deep blue, forming a compact pyramidal spike. *L.* oblong, 1–2 in. shortly stalked. 6–9 in. Increase by division or seed. Europe, including Britain. Good forms include:
  'Atropurpurea', *fl.* blue, *l.* purple;
  'Multicolor', also known as 'Rainbow', *fl.* deep blue, *l.* mottled bronze, **955**, p. 120;
  'Rainbow' see 'Multicolor';
  'Variegata', *fl.* blue, *l.* grey-green and cream.

ALBERTA SPRUCE see **Picea glauca** var. **albertiana** 'Conica', **2027**, p. 254.

ALCHEMILLA (ROSACEAE) Lady's mantle

mollis ❋ Summer   P.
Fl. with yellowish-green calyx, not true petals,

---

about ¼ in. across. *L.* kidney-shaped, 2–6 in., the palmate lobes toothed at the margins. 12–18 in. A native of damp meadows and open woodlands. Easily grown in ordinary moist soil. Comes readily from seed, too readily in some gardens. Asia Minor. **956**, p. 120.

ALDER see **Alnus**, **1443**, p. 181.

ALDER, BLACK see **Ilex verticillata**

ALDER, ITALIAN see **Alnus cordata**, **1443**, p. 181.

ALGERIAN IRIS see **Iris unguicularis**, **1203**, **1204**, p. 151.

ALKANET see **Anchusa**, **235**, p. 30; **963**, p. 121.

ALLAMANDA (APOCYNACEAE)

cathartica ❋ Summer   GCl.
Fl. yellow, funnel-shaped. *L.* in whorls of four, obovate, evergreen. Vigorous climber to 10 ft but variable. Rich potting compost, but more vigorous varieties do better planted out in greenhouse bed. Minimum winter temp. 55°F. Keep dry in winter and prune previous year's growth hard in 1. These prunings can be used as cuttings. Guiana, Brazil. **406**, p. 51.
  'Grandiflora', large yellow *fl.*;
  'Hendersonii', very vigorous.

ALLIUM (LILIACEAE)
(Sometimes now placed in the new family Alliaceae)

aflatunense ❋ Summer   Bb
Fl. star-shaped, large globular heads, rosy-purple. 3–4 ft. *L.* strap-shaped, wide, slightly glaucous. Sunny border or among dwarf shrubs. Central China. **658**, p. 83.
Close are *A. giganteum* and *A. rosenbachianum* both of which have slightly larger *fl.* heads and with *fl.* more densely aggregated. Bulb large, up to 2½ in. across.

albopilosum see **A. christophii**

beesianum ❋ Summer   Bb
Fl. tubular in loose drooping heads, bright blue but

purplish-blue and white forms are also known. 9–12 in. *L.* narrow, grasslike. Rock garden or warm border in sunny but not too dry position, not always very vigorous but an attractive plant. W. China. **659**, p. 83.

bulgaricum see **A. siculum**

cernuum ✳ Summer   Bb
Fl. deep rose to purple, pendulous in loose heads of 30–40 *fl.* Variable in colour. 1–1½ ft. Scent strong. *L.* narrow linear. Full sun in rock garden or front of border. A good grower in most gardens and easy to establish. **660**, p. 83.

✿ **christophii,** syn. **A. albopilosum** ✳ Summer Bb
Fl. in large globular heads like a small football, pale-purplish mauve with a metallic sheen. Up to 80 *fl.* in head. Seedheads also decorative. 1–2 ft. *L.* strap-shaped, grey and hairy. Best in a sunny border, most effective at Sissinghurst Castle below deep purplish-crimson shrub roses. Turkestan, Afghanistan. **661**, p. 83.

flavum ✳ Summer   Bb
Fl. in loose globular heads about 1½–2 in. across with individual *fl.* stalks of uneven length. Bright yellow. 9 in.–1 ft. *L.* narrow, grasslike. Generally spreading freely and useful in the rock garden for later colour. S. Europe, Turkey. **662**, p. 83.

giganteum see **A. aflatunense**

karataviense ✳ Late Spring   Bb
Fl. silvery-white in large round heads about 4 in. across. 6–9 in. Grown chiefly for its very decorative foliage. *L.* are broad, bluish-green, velvety and last for several months. Best in a sunny position. Turkestan. **663**, p. 83.

moly ✳ Summer   Bb
Fl. bright yellow, starlike in heads 2–3 in. across. 9 in.–1 ft. *L.* greyish-green, straplike. Very vigorous and spreading freely to form large clumps so should not be planted among choice and less vigorous plants. S., S.W. Europe. **664**, p. 83.

narcissiflorum ✳ Summer   Bb
Fl. bell-shaped, in small clusters, pendulous or eventually upright, deep rose or rosy-mauve; 8 in.– 1 ft. *L.* strap-shaped, rather narrow. Slightly tender in a cold area, but good for alpine house or sheltered warm place in the rock garden. Described rather euphemistically by Reginald Farrer as 'the glory of its race'. N. Italian Alps. **665**, p. 84.

oreophilum var. **ostrowskianum,** syn. **A. ostrowskianum** ✳ Early Summer   Bb
Dwarf, 6–8 in. with round umbels about 4 in. across of pink starry *fl.* in form 'Zwanenburg' which is recommended, otherwise pinkish-purple. Sunny position in rock garden or border. Needs good summer ripening. Turkestan. **666**, p. 84.

ostrowskianum see **A. oreophilum**

pulchellum ✳ Summer   Bb
Fl. small, reddish-violet, with stamens projecting beyond perianth, in loose heads, with stalks of uneven length. 1–2 ft. *L.* narrow. Sunny position in rock garden and useful for its summer flowering. **667**, p. 84.

rosenbachianum see **A. aflatunense**

schoenoprasum Chives ✳ Summer
Fl. pale lilac in dense globular heads. 6–9 in. *L.* cylindrical in section and very strongly scented, much used as a flavouring in salads, soups and with cheese in place of garlic. Hardy. Sunny position at edge of kitchen garden or border. N. Europe, Alps. **668**, p. 84.

siculum ✳ Early Summer   Bb
Fl. reddish-brown and blue-green in bands, bell-shaped, in loose heads of up to 30 *fl.* per head. 2–2½ ft. *L.* grey-green. A beautiful and distinctive plant but onion smell is very strong if bruised. S. Europe. *A. bulgaricum* is close in form but with yellowish-green *fl.* Easy to grow in sunny position and inclined to spread freely. **669**, p. 84.

triquetrum Wild Garlic ✳ Spring
Fl. white or greenish-white, narrowly tubular and drooping on slender angled stems. 9 in.–1 ft. *L.* grey-green. Scent very strong. Spreading freely by division of bulbs and seeds and may become a menace if planted in rock garden, so only suitable for naturalising in the wild garden. Very vigorous. S. Europe but has become naturalised in parts of England.

ALMOND see **Prunus × amygdalo-persica** 'Pollardii'

ALMOND, DWARF RUSSIAN see **Prunus tenella, 1766**, p. 221.

ALNUS (BETULACEAE) Alder

cordata Italian Alder   T.
Medium-sized tree usually not more than 30 ft but occasionally more. Male *fl.* in catkins 2–3 in. long in 3. Fruit growing erect in large egg-shaped 'cones' up to 1½ in. long and ¾ in. wide. Deep green in colour. *L.* notable for bright green glistening colour. Tree rather upright making pyramidal outline. S. Europe. **1443**, p. 181.

ALOE (LILIACEAE)

variegata Partridge-breasted Aloe ✳ Late Spring– Midsummer   GP.
Up to about 12 in. in *fl. Fl.* red in loose spike, tubular, to 1 in. long. *L.* triangular, closely-packed in three ranks, dark green with bands of white, succulent. Well-drained rather gritty compost. Keep on dry side. Winter temp. 40°F. May be stood outside in full sun in summer with advantage. Propagate by division. S. Africa. **407**, p. 51.

ALONSOA (SCROPHULARIACEAE)

warscewiczii Mask Flower ✳ Summer   HHA.
Fl. bright orange-scarlet. *L.* small, bright green. Height 1½–2 ft. Sow under glass in gentle heat in 3, plant out late 5. Compact scarlet and soft pink forms growing to about 1 ft are also available. Peru. **227**, p. 29.

ALPINE ANEMONE see **Pulsatilla alpina, 167**, p. 21.

ALPINE AURICULA see **Primula auricula, 148, 149**, p. 19.

ALPINE POPPY see **Papaver alpinum, 126**, p. 16.

ALPINE SNOWBELL see **Soldanella alpina, 210**, p. 27.

ALSTROEMERIA (AMARYLLIDACEAE) Peruvian Lily (Sometimes now placed in separate new family Alstroemeriaceae)

aurantiaca ✳ Summer   P.
Fl. orange in loose umbels. *L.* narrow, about 4 in. long, greyish-green beneath. 3 ft. Best in south-facing border with well-drained deep sandy soil but will also grow in E. or W. borders. The fleshy roots may make no top growth the first year. Can be temperamental. Best raised by seed sown as soon as ripe, standing the pans in a cold frame or by division. In exposed areas, young growth must be protected from spring frost. Chile. **957**, p. 120.
Good varieties include:
  'Dover Orange', orange-red, 3 ft;
  'Lutea', bright yellow, 2½ ft.

haemantha see **A. Ligtu Hybrids**

ligtu ✳ Summer   P.
Fl. pale pink, pale lilac or whitish, trumpet-shaped 1½–2 in. long. 2–4 ft. *L.* narrow about 3 in. long. Chile.

Ligtu Hybrids ✳ Summer   P.
Fl. in shades of pink, flame, orange or yellow are a great improvement on the sp. These are the result of crosses of *A. ligtu* and *A. haemantha*. **958**, p. 120.

ALTHAEA (MALVACEAE)

rosea Hollyhock ✳ Summer   HA., P.
Fl. single, **228**, p. 29, and double, **229**, p. 29, in shades of pink, crimson, yellow, also white. *L.* heart-shaped, toothed, rough. Perennial varieties, 5–8 ft, are usually raised from seed sown in the open 6–7. Planted out in the autumn where they are to *fl.*, in a sunny position and well drained soil. The annual varieties, 4–5 ft, are sown under glass and planted out in spring for *fl.* from 7 onwards. Orient. **228**, p. 29.
  'Begonia Flowered', has fringed petals in pastel shades;
  'Chater's double mixed', gives a high percentage of doubles;
  'Powder Puffs', is a new double strain in many beautiful colours, **229**, p. 29.

ALUMINIUM PLANT see **Pilea cadierei, 627** p. 79.

ALYSSUM (CRUCIFERAE)

maritimum, syn. **Lobularia maritima** Sweet Alyssum ✳ Summer–Autumn   HA
Fl. pale blue, white, fragrant. *L.* grey, hairy 3–12 in. Sow in the open 4–5 or 9. S. Europe.
  'Little Dorrit', 4 in., compact, white;
  'Minimum', 3 in., white, **230**, p. 29;
  'Rosie O'Day', 4 in., prostrate, rose-pink;
  'Royal Carpet', 3 in., spreading, deep violet;
  'Snow Cloth', 3 in., spreading, pure white;
  'Violet Queen', 4 in., compact, deep violet, **231** p. 29.

saxatile ✳ Spring   RP
Sub-shrubby crucifer with grey foliage and light yellow cluster of *fl.* 1 ft. Common and easily grown but inclined to become lanky and loose-growing after several years. Should be cut back after flowering. Easily propagated from cuttings. Full sun.
  'Citrinum', pale yellow and preferred by some gardeners, **3**, p. 1;
  'Dudley Neville', pale biscuit coloured;

Abbreviations and Symbols used in the text.
The following abbreviations may sometimes be used in conjunction as HA. indicating Hardy annual or GBb indicating Greenhouse bulb.

A. = Annual	P. = Perennial
Aq. = Aquatic	R. = Rock or
B. = Biennial	Alpine plant
Bb = Bulb	Sh. = Shrub
C. = Corm	Sp., sp. = Species
Cl. = Climber	Syn. = Synonym
Co. = Conifer	T. = Tree
Fl., fl. = Flower(s)	Tu. = Tuber
G. = Greenhouse or	var. = variety
house plant	× = Hybrid or
H. = Hardy	hybrid parents
HH. = Half-hardy	✳ = Flowering time
L., l. = Leaf, leaves	➥ = Foliage plant
Mt(s) = Mount,	
mountain(s)	

The following have been used also in the descriptions of Alpines, Bulbs, Trees and Shrubs.

  * = slightly tender
  † = lime hater
  ✿ = highly recommended

The illustration numbers are in **bold type** and the page numbers in light type preceded by p.

'Flore-pleno', double form which many consider more effective.

ALYSSUM, SWEET see **Alyssum maritimum, 230, 231**, p. 29.

AMARANTH, GLOBE see **Gomphrena globosa, 302**, p. 38.

AMARANTHUS (AMARANTHACEAE)

caudatus Love-lies-bleeding, Tassel Flower ✳ Late Summer–Mid Autumn HA.
Fl. crimson, drooping tassels. *L.* alternate, ovate. Sow in a sunny position in the open 4–5. Self-sown seedlings will often appear the following year. 3 ft. There is a greenish-white form 'Viridis'. Tropics. **232**, p. 29.

tricolor Joseph's Coat ❧ HHA.
Decorative foliage pot plant for cool greenhouse, or window box in summer. There are many good forms with *l.* in shades of crimson, yellow, marbled red and green. The slender *fl.* spikes are insignificant and should be pinched out. 1½ ft. Sow in a warm greenhouse in 3. Tropics. **233**, p. 30.

AMARCRINUM HOWARDII see × **Crinodonna corsii**

AMARYLLIS (AMARYLLIDACEAE)

belladonna Belladonna Lily ✳ Autumn *Bb
Fl. pale pink, trumpet-like, in loose clusters on stem of 2–2½ ft without *l.* at flowering time. Plant in a warm border, preferably with a wall behind, and allow to become as dry as possible in summer after *l.* have died down. Propagate by bulb division or from seed. Best forms are *elata, kewensis, rubra*. Also generally placed under *A. belladonna* are 'Parkeri' and Multiflora strain which are slightly more vigorous with larger heads but may be bigeneric hybrids with *Brunsvigia*. 'Hathor', pure white with yellow throat may also belong to this group. Inclined to be shy-flowering in colder situations. S. Africa. See also × *Crinodonna corsii*. **670**, p. 84.

AMARYLLIS see also **Hippeastrum Hybrids, 551**, p. 69.

AMAZON LILY see **Eucharis grandiflora, 525**, p. 66.

AMELANCHIER (ROSACEAE) Snowy Mespilus

canadensis Shadblow USA ✳ Mid Spring T.
Medium sized tree with large clusters of white *fl.* in spring. Distinguished for brilliant scarlet autumn colouring of foliage thus making a very useful small tree for gardens with double season of beauty. N.E. America. **1444, 1445**, p. 181.

AMERICAN ARBOR-VITAE see **Thuya occidentalis**

AMERICAN ASPEN see **Populus tremuloides**

AMERICAN CYRILLA see **Cyrilla racemiflora**

AMERICAN HOLLY see **Ilex opaca**

AMMOBIUM (COMPOSITAE)

alatum Winged Everlasting US ✳ Summer HHA.
Fl. yellow centre, surrounded by silvery-white bracts. Makes a useful 'everlasting' for winter decorations. *L.* lance-shaped, forming a rosette. Sow under glass, 3. Plant out in sandy, well-drained soil, late 5. 1½ ft. Australia.
'Grandiflorum', is a larger form, **234**, p. 30.

AMPELOPSIS VEITCHII see **Parthenocissus tricuspidata** 'Veitchii'

AMSONIA (APOCYNACEAE)

salicifolia ✳ Summer P.
Fl. light blue in terminal clusters. *L.* slender lance-shaped, hairless. 1½–3 ft. Plant 11–3 in partial shade and ordinary garden soil. Once planted leave undisturbed. Propagate by division in spring, or by cuttings taken in summer. Very similar to *A. tabernaemontana* of which some botanists consider it may be a variety. N. America. **959**, p. 120.

tabernaemontana see **A. salicifolia**

ANACYCLUS (COMPOSITAE)

depressus ✳ Spring–Midsummer †RP,B.
Fl. white with fairly bright red on outside of ray florets, daisy-like. 3–6 in. *L.* finely divided in prostrate rosettes. Free-flowering over quite a long period. Plant in full sun. Good in scree, where it often sows itself. Atlas Mts of Morocco but hardy. **4**, p. 1.

ANAGALLIS (PRIMULACEAE)

✿ **linifolia** ✳ Summer B,A.
Brilliant blue pimpernel, one of the brightest colours available for the rock garden. Height 6 in.–1 ft. Full sun and can be grown as an annual. Slightly tender in cold areas and intolerant of winter wet. Mediterranean regions where it forms large clumps and is perennial.
'Grandiflora', seedsmen's strain with *fl.* of many colours including apricot-orange, mostly with dark eye, usually grown as annuals, **5**, p. 1;
'Monelii', syn. *A. linifolia* var. *phillipsii*, probably the best form with *fl.* in clusters of two to three and up to ½ in. across, **6**, p. 1.

ANAPHALIS (COMPOSITAE) Pearl Everlasting

Grey-foliage plants with heads of small off-white *fl.* which can be cut and dried for winter use. Require a well-drained soil in sun or dry shade. Propagate by division or cuttings taken in the spring.
Good sp. include:

margaritacea ✳ Late Summer P.
Fl. pearly-white, small button-like. *L.* broadly lance-shaped, grey, becoming green. 1½ ft. N. America, N.E. Asia.

nubigena ✳ Late Summer P.
Fl. heads off-white, bunched in small groups. *L.* lance-shaped, woolly, about ½ in. wide. 10 in. Tibet. **960**, p. 120.

triplinervis ✳ Late Summer P.
Fl. similar but larger than *A. nubigena*. *L.* oblong to 8 in. with prominent veins. 1 ft. Tibet. **961**, p. 121.

yedoensis ✳ Late Summer P.
Similar to *A. nubigena* but taller and with *fl.* heads more tightly bunched. 1½ ft. Himalayas. **962**, p. 121.

ANCHUSA (BORAGINACEAE) Alkanet, Bugloss

azurea, syn. **A. italica** ✳ Late Spring–Summer P.
Fl. blue-purple. *L.* lanceolate, 1 ft or more long. 3–5 ft. Plant 11–3 in a sunny position and a deep, well-drained soil. Propagate by root cuttings in the autumn. Caucasus.
'Loddon Royalist', *fl.* early summer, large, gentian blue, **963**, p. 121;
'Morning Glory', *fl.* summer, deep blue, 4–5 ft.

capensis ✳ Summer HA.
Fl. bright blue, forget-me-not-like. *L.* narrow, coarsely haired. Sow in an open, sunny bed 4 or 9. 1½ ft. S. Africa.
'Blue Bird', indigo-blue, **235**, p. 30.

italica see **A. azurea**

myosotidiflora see **Brunnera macrophylla**

ANDROSACE (PRIMULACEAE)

Tussock-forming plants with small, sometimes sessile, *fl.* of white or pink like minute primroses in structure. All need good drainage and the Cushion sp. are best suited for alpine house culture and should not be watered overhead. Keep rather dry in winter. They include some of the most choice plants for the keen connoisseur of alpines, and grow in clefts of rocks high up in the Alps, Pyrenees and Himalayas. They grow well on Tufa rock.

helvetica ✳ Late Spring RP.
Forms a dense cushion up to 4 in. across of small hairy *l.* in rosettes. *Fl.* white about ⅛ in. across but in a good specimen sometimes covering whole cushion, five-petalled. Alpine house or frame. Plant in well drained mixture with plenty of stone chippings. Don't water overhead. Swiss and Austrian Alps. **7**, p. 1.

jacquemontii ✳ Early Summer RP.
3–4 in. *Fl.* pink in clusters on short stems. Rosettes small, hairy about 1 in. across. Suitable for scree in sunny position where should be protected with glass in winter, or alpine house. Sometimes regarded as a variety of *A. villosa*. Himalayas. **8**, p. 1.

lanuginosa ✳ Summer RP.
3–4 in. *Fl.* pale pink or lavender-pink with darker eye in clusters on short stem. Rosettes silvery. Useful for its late flowering and when suited often spreading into large mats over rocks. Himalayas. **9**, p. 2.

pyrenaica ✳ Spring RP.
1–2 in. *Fl.* small, white, almost sessile on dome-shaped tussocks up to 3 in. across. To attain this size may take several years. *L.* are downy and very small and careful watering is necessary. Alpine house. Pyrenees. **10**, p. 2.

sarmentosa ✳ Early Summer RP.
3–4 in. *Fl.* pink or deep pink in clusters on short stems. Rosettes hairy and spreading by stolons and quickly forming large mats. A good plant for rock garden and usually easy to grow successfully in full sun, but invasive with choice plants. Probably the easiest to grow of sp. of this genus. Himalayas.
var. *chumbyi*, very hairy, *fl.* deep pink;
var. *watkinsii*, smaller than type, very hairy;
var. *yunnanensis*, *fl.* slightly larger than type and other vars, vigorous.

Abbreviations and Symbols used in the text.
The following abbreviations may sometimes be used in conjunction as HA. indicating Hardy annual or GBb indicating Greenhouse bulb.

A. = Annual	P. = Perennial
Aq. = Aquatic	R. = Rock or
B. = Biennial	Alpine plant
Bb = Bulb	Sh. = Shrub
C. = Corm	Sp., sp. = Species
Cl. = Climber	Syn. = Synonym
Co. = Conifer	T. = Tree
Fl., fl. = Flower(s)	Tu. = Tuber
G. = Greenhouse or	var. = variety
house plant	× = Hybrid or
H. = Hardy	hybrid parents
HH. = Half-hardy	✳ = Flowering time
L., l. = Leaf, leaves	❧ = Foliage plant
Mt(s) = Mount,	
mountain(s)	

The following have been used also in the descriptions of Alpines, Bulbs, Trees and Shrubs.

    * = slightly tender
    † = lime hater
    ✿ = highly recommended

The illustration numbers are in **bold type** and the page numbers in light type preceded by p.

263

villosa ✳ Early Summer   RP.
2–3 in. *Fl.* white or pale pink with deeper eye. Rosettes small, hairy and forming dense mat. Alpine house or may be grown in rock garden but usually requiring some protection from winter wet.
'Arachnoidea', rounder, hairy *l.*, **11**, p. 2.

ANEMONE (RANUNCULACEAE) Windflower

alpina see **Pulsatilla alpina**

✿ **blanda** Mountain Windflower of Greece ✳ Late Winter–Mid Spring   Tu.
Fl. starry, 1–2 in. across, singly on 4–6 in. stems, pale-deep blue, mauve, pink or white with yellow centres and ruff of divided leaflets below *fl.* Sometimes spreading freely particularly on warm chalky soils. Plant in full sun 2–3 in. deep.
Best forms are:
  ✿ 'Atrocoerulea', syn. 'Ingramii', deep blue, **671**, p. 84;
  'Radar', deep pink;
  scythinica, pale sapphire-blue on outside, inside white, generally flowering later than above and less vigorous, N.E. Turkey:
  'White Beauty', *fl.* very large, nearly twice the size of normal form.

coronaria Poppy Anemone ✳ Spring   Tu.
Fl. 2–3 in. across, white, mauve, scarlet, very variable on stems 6 in.–1 ft. *L.* parsley-like, finely divided. Best in warm situations and requires full sun, cloche protection needed in cold areas. Can be grown either from tubers or seed. Excellent as cut *fl.* Widely sold in florists' shops during winter. Greece and Eastern Mediterranean. Best mixed strains are St Brigid single and de Caen semi-double. **672**, p. 84.
Named cultivars include:
  ✿ 'His Excellency', crimson-scarlet with white centre, single;
  'Mr Fokker', blue, single;
  'Sylphide', mauve, single;
  'The Admiral', deep pink, semi-double;
  'The Bride', white, single;
  'The Governor', scarlet, double.

elegans Pink Japanese Anemone ✳ Late Summer–Autumn   P.
Fl. pink, similar to *A. hupehensis*. May also be found listed as × *hybrida*.
There are numerous named varieties including:
  'Honorine Jobert', syn. *A. japonica* 'Alba', known as the White Japanese anemone, 3 ft;
  'Kriemhilde', rose-pink, semi-double, 3 ft;
  'Margarete', deep pink, semi-double, 2½ ft.

✿ **fulgens** ✳ Spring   Tu.
Fl. scarlet, ray petals starry with dark centre, 2–2½ in. across on 1 ft stem. *L.* less divided than in Poppy Anemone but *fl.* more graceful. Plant in full sun. May be a form of *A. pavonina* (q.v.) or a hybrid from it.

hepatica see **Hepatica triloba**

hupehensis, syn. **A. japonica** Japanese Anemone ✳ Late Summer–Mid Autumn   P.
Fl. mauve or carmine, saucer-shaped, 2 in. or more across. *L.* unequally three-lobed, toothed. 2–3 ft. There is a white form, *A. hupehensis* 'Alba' and named varieties, single and semi-double, in shades of pale pink, rose-pink and purplish-pink. Ordinary garden soil with plenty of leaf-mould or peat, in sun or partial shade. Propagate by root cuttings or division in the autumn. Hupeh. **964**, p. 121.

× **hybrida** see **A. elegans**

japonica see **A. hupehensis**

japonica 'Alba' see **A. elegans** 'Honorine Jobert'

× **lesseri** ✳ Late Spring–Early Summer   P.
Fl. rosy-purple. *L.* roundish, shiny green. 1½–2 ft. Plant 11–3, in partial shade and moist soil. Propagate by root cuttings taken in the late autumn. A hybrid of garden origin. **965**, p. 121.

narcissiflora ✳ Late Spring–Midsummer   P.
Fl. creamy-white, sometimes pinkish, with yellow anthers. *L.* deeply toothed, buttercup-like. 1–2 ft. Plant 11–3, in light shade and a moist soil. Propagate by seed. Europe, Asia, N. America. **966**, p. 121.

nemorosa Wood Anemone ✳ Spring   Tu.
Fl. white or pale mauve, flushed pale pink or mauve outside, 2 in. across on 4–6 in. stems. There is also double white form. Delicate and graceful, they naturalise freely in open woodland, particularly in good loam or clay soils, but are not so good in very dry places. Tuberous rhizomes are slender and should not be allowed to dry out. Transplant soon after flowering. Europe including Britain.
For garden purposes, the selected forms are best, having rather larger *fl.* but need to be sought out in lists or from friends:
  ✿ 'Allenii', pale rosy-lilac outside and soft lavender-blue inside, **673**, p. 85;
  'Robinsoniana', pale lavender-blue;
  'Royal Blue', the deepest blue.

✿ **pavonina** Great Peacock Anemone of Greece ✳ Spring   Tu.
Fl. 2–2½ in. across on stems 1–1½ ft. Scarlet with white eye, scarlet with dark eye, pink, mauve, **674**, p. 85. Generally grown as St Bavo Strain ✿ very variable in colour, **675**, p. 85. Distinguished from Poppy Anemone by leaflets divided into three lobes and more graceful slenderer habit. Plant tubers in full sun or grow from seed. See also *A. fulgens*.

pulsatilla see **Pulsatilla vulgaris**

rivularis ✳ Mid Spring–Early Summer   P.
Similar to *A. narcissiflora*, but with blue anthers, and requiring the same conditions. 1½–2½ ft. India, Ceylon.

vernalis see **Pulsatilla vernalis**

ANEMONE, BUSH see **Carpenteria californica**, **1495**, p. 187.

ANEMONE, DE CAEN see **Anemone coronaria**, **672**, p. 84.

ANEMONE, GREAT PEACOCK see **A. pavonina**, **674**, **675**, p. 85.

ANEMONE, JAPANESE see **A. hupehensis**, **964**, p. 121.

ANEMONE, JAPANESE, PINK see **A. elegans**

ANEMONE, JAPANESE, WHITE see **A. elegans** 'Honorine Jobert'

ANEMONE, PINK JAPANESE see **A. elegans**

ANEMONE, POPPY see **A. coronaria**, **672**, p. 84.

ANEMONE, ST BAVO see **A. pavonina**, **675**, p. 85.

ANEMONE, ST BRIGID see **A. coronaria**, **672**, p. 84.

ANEMONE, WHITE JAPANESE see **A. elegans** 'Honorine Jobert'

ANEMONE, WOOD see **A. nemorosa**, **673**, p. 85.

ANGELICA TREE see **Aralia elata**, **1446**, p. 181.

ANGEL'S TEARS see **Narcissus triandrus** var. **albus**, **840**, p. 105.

ANGEL'S TRUMPET see **Datura suaveolens**, **495**, p. 62.

ANOMATHECA CRUENTA see **Lapeyrousia cruenta**

ANTARCTIC BEECH see **Nothofagus antarctica**

ANTHEMIS (COMPOSITAE)

cupaniana ✳ Summer   RP.
Sub-shrubby, forming large mats of silvery-grey *l.* finely divided and white daisy-like *fl.* 1½–2 in. across, singly on 6 in. stems over a long period. 6–10 in. A stock of cuttings, which strike easily, should be taken each autumn since plants outside may not survive a severe winter. Full sun or semi-shade but can be too invasive of space for a small rock garden. Italy, S. Europe. **12**, p. 2.

sancti-johannis ✳ Summer   P.
Fl. bright orange, solitary, 1½–2 in. across. 1½ ft. *L.* grey-green, hairy. For full sun and a well-drained soil. Propagate by seed sown in 2 in gentle heat, in the open ground in 4, by cuttings taken in summer and inserted in sandy soil in a cold propagating frame or by division in 3. Bulgaria. **967**, p. 121.

tinctoria Ox-eye Chamomile ✳ Summer   P.
Fl. golden-yellow, single, daisy-like, up to 3 in. across. *L.* feathery, downy beneath, deeply cut. 2½ ft. Ordinary well-drained garden soil and full sun. Propagate by division in spring or autumn, or by cuttings in summer inserted in sandy soil in a cold frame. Europe.
Good varieties include:
  'E. C. Buxton', lemon-yellow;
  'Grallagh Gold', deep golden-yellow, **968**, p. 121;
  'Perry's Variety', bright yellow, **969**, p. 122;
  'Wargrave Variety', lemon-yellow, disc-like, **970**, p. 122.

ANTHERICUM (LILIACEAE)

liliago St Bernard's Lily ✳ Early Summer   P.
Fl. white, 1–1½ in. across borne on a slender 1½ ft stem. *L.* narrow, 1–1½ ft long, in tufts. Partial shade and ordinary garden soil which does not dry out in summer. Propagate by division in 9 or by seed sown as soon as ripe. S. Europe. **971**, p. 122.

ANTHURIUM (ARACEAE)

andreanum Flamingo Plant, Painter's Palette ❋ Spring–Autumn GP.
Fl. scarlet, pink or white, spathe about 6 in. long and 3 in. wide; spadix distinct, usually scarlet. *L.* dark green, leathery, oblong heart-shaped up to 8 in. long, 5 in. across. Plant to 2 ft. Needs warm, moist conditions with a very open compost topped with sphagnum moss. Cover new roots with moss as they appear on the surface. Minimum winter temp. 65°F. Shade in summer. Propagate by seed or by division. Colombia. **408**, p. 51.

scherzerianum ❋ Spring–Autumn GP.
Smaller than, but otherwise similar to *A. andreanum*. Will tolerate a winter temp. of 50°F. if kept on the dry side. Guatemala.

ANTIRRHINUM (SCROPHULARIACEAE) Snapdragon

majus ❋ Summer–Autumn HHA.
Fl. crimson, lavender, pink, orange, flame, yellow, white. *L.* narrow, smooth, 1–3 in. long. Sow in a warm greenhouse, 2–3. Plant out in sunny position, late 5. In mild winters some plants are perennial. There are a great many hybrids, tall, intermediate and dwarf, as well as rust-resistant strains, 6 in.–3 ft. Mediterranean.
'Floral Carpet', 8 in., F^1 hybrid, bright colours, **236**, p. 30;
'Glamour Shades Double', 3 ft, pastel shades, **237**, p. 30;
'Magic Carpet mixed', 6 in., very dwarf, creeping habit for rockeries and edging;
'Penstemon Flowered', $1\frac{1}{2}$ ft, a new type with open tubular *fl.*, various colours;
'Tetra mixed', 2 ft, giant ruffled blooms with unusual colours.

APONOGETON (APONOGETONACEAE)

distachyus Cape Pondweed, Water Hawthorn ❋ Late Spring–Mid Autumn Aq.
Fl. white, with black anthers, hawthorn-scented. 3–4 in. *L.* oblong, entire, bright green, floating. Plant in spring in water 6–15 in. deep. Propagate by seed or division of tubers. S. Africa. **972**, p. 122.

APOROCACTUS see × **Heliaporus**

APPLE, GOLDEN see **Poncirus trifoliata**, **1742**, **1743**, p. 218.

APPLE OF PERU see **Nicandra physaloides**, **350**, p. 44.

APRICOT, JAPANESE see **Prunus mume**, **1757**, p. 220.

AQUILEGIA (RANUNCULACEAE) Columbine

hybrida ❋ Early Summer P.
Long-spurred hybrids with *fl.* in many attractive shades of crimson, pink, purple, blue, yellow and white. $1\frac{1}{2}$–2 ft. Best in partial shade and ordinary, moist garden soil. Plant 11–3. Propagate by seed sown in spring, named varieties by division. Of garden origin. **973**, **974**, p. 122.
Good varieties include:
'Crimson Star', crimson and white, with long spurs, 2 ft;
'Rose Queen', soft rose-pink and white, 3 ft;
'Snow Queen', pure white, $1\frac{1}{2}$ ft.
Outstanding strains include:
'Mrs Scott Elliott's', long-spurred hybrids, 2 ft;
'McKana Giant Hybrids', $2\frac{1}{2}$–3 ft.

longissima ❋ Midsummer–Mid Autumn P.
Fl. yellow with exceptionally long spurs. *L.* deeply cut. 2 ft. Texas.

vulgaris Granny's Bonnet, True Columbine ❋ Early Summer P.
Fl. blue, purple, white, single and double, small, with short spurs. 2 ft. *L.* segmented. Europe.

ARABIS (CRUCIFERAE)

A large genus but most of the sp. are too invasive or weed-like for the rock garden. *Fl.* white, pale pink or lilac.

albida Snow-in-summer ❋ Spring RP.
Fl. white in loose clusters on short stems. 6–9 in. Forms a large mat and too invasive for the small rock garden, but can make fine effect of white *fl.* and silvery-grey foliage. Full sun. S.E. Europe, Asia Minor.
'Flore Pleno', probably best form, *fl.* double, slightly less vigorous, **13**, p. 2;
'Rosabelle', *fl.* pale pink.

ARALIA (ARALIACEAE)

elata, syn. **A. chinensis** Angelica Tree ❋ Late Summer T.
Medium-sized tree often suckering with stout rather spiny stems and enormous, rather compound *l.* 3–4 ft long and 2 ft wide. *Fl.* small and white in large panicles. S.E. Asia.
'Albo-marginata', leaflets splashed with white. A most decorative small tree or shrub for conspicuous position, **1446**, p. 181.

elegantissima see **Dizygotheca elegantissima**

japonica see **Fatsia japonica**

sieboldii see **Fatsia japonica**

ARALIA, FALSE see **Dizygotheca elegantissima**, **514**, p. 65.

ARAUCARIA (ARAUCARIACEAE)

Large and wide-spreading evergreen trees confined to the S. Hemisphere usually distinguished by horizontal branches.
Best known and hardiest in Britain is:

araucana, syn. **A. imbricata** Monkey Puzzle, Chilean Pine Co.
Evergreen tree up to 150 ft but rarely so much in Britain. Branches horizontal usually in whorls but curving with a downward pendulous curve towards ends and turning upright nearer tips. *L.* long persistent, spirally arranged, green, particularly stiff and rigid, often remaining on tree after they have turned brown. Male and female cones usually on different trees but occasionally found on the same tree. Male cones solitary or in clusters erect up to 5 in. long and 2 in. wide. Female cones large globular, green with sharp scales, brown when ripe up to 7 in. long by 5 in. in diameter but taking two or three years to mature. One of the most spectacular conifers for its shape but unsuitable for planting in small gardens or close to houses since the branches are wide-spreading. It is however very fine in moister parts. Chile.

ARBOR-VITAE, AMERICAN see **Thuya occidentalis**

ARBOR-VITAE, CHINESE see **Thuya orientalis**, **2044**, **2045**, p. 256.

ARBOR-VITAE, WESTERN see **Thuya plicata**, **2046**, **2047**, p. 256.

ARBUTUS (ERICACEAE) Strawberry Tree

All Arbutus should be planted when young in final sites preferably out of pots since they move badly when older.

× **andrachnoides** ❋ Mid Autumn–Early Winter T.
A hybrid between Greek *A. andrachne* and Killarney Strawberry Tree *A. unedo*. A small tree up to 40 ft distinguished for its cinnamon-red trunk and branchlets. *L.* evergreen and leathery, slightly toothed thus distinguishing it from *A. unedo*. *Fl.* in clusters, small, urn-shaped, whitish-pink, 10–12, growing with fruit which is exactly like small pendulous strawberries. Valuable tree for coloured bark and distinctive twisted system of branching. **1447**, **1448**, p. 181.

✡ **menziesii** Madrona ❋ Spring T.
Large tree up to 50 ft distinguished for its brilliant orange-crimson bark which peels. *Fl.* creamy in large clusters followed by orange-yellow fruits. Hardy but best in sheltered position. W. N. America. **1449**, p. 182.

unedo Killarney Strawberry Tree T.
Small tree up to 30 ft or large bush. Distinguished by creamy-yellow *fl.* and strawberry-like fruits in 9–11, but sometimes lasting throughout winter. *L.* leathery toothed, dark shiny green, thus distinguishing it from *A. andrachne*. Mediterranean and S.W. Ireland. **1450**, p. 182.
'Rubra', *fl.* pale pink, **1451**, p. 182.

ARCTOTIS (COMPOSITAE) African Daisy

breviscapa ❋ Summer HHA.
Fl. in striking shades of orange. *L.* green above, white woolly beneath, lance-shaped. 1 ft. Sow in a warm greenhouse in 2 and 3, plant out in a sunny, well-drained position late 5. S. Africa. **238**, p. 30.

grandis ❋ Autumn HHA.
Fl. pure white with a blue zone, long stemmed. *L.* greyish. 2 ft. Cultivate as for *A. breviscapa*. S. Africa.

hybrida ❋ Summer HHA.
In splendid shades of crimson, red, pink, bronze, yellow, orange, with striking zones of contrasting colours. Also white. The *fl.* are 3–4 in. across and close at dusk. 1–$1\frac{1}{2}$ ft. Of garden origin. **239**, p. 30.

ARDISIA (MYRSINACEAE)

crispa ❋ Summer GSh.
Shrub up to 4 ft, grown principally for its long-persisting berries. *Fl.* reddish-violet, about $\frac{1}{2}$ in. across in terminal clusters, fragrant. *L.* evergreen, elliptic, 2–4 in. long, with waved margins. Berries round, scarlet. Rich compost. Old plants should be

Abbreviations and Symbols used in the text.
The following abbreviations may sometimes be used in conjunction as HA. indicating Hardy annual or GBb indicating Greenhouse bulb.

A.	= Annual	P.	= Perennial
Aq.	= Aquatic	R.	= Rock or Alpine plant
B.	= Biennial	Sh.	= Shrub
Bb	= Bulb	Sp., sp.	= Species
C.	= Corm	Syn.	= Synonym
Cl.	= Climber	T.	= Tree
Co.	= Conifer	Tu.	= Tuber
Fl., *fl.*	= Flower(s)	var.	= variety
G.	= Greenhouse or house plant	×	= Hybrid or hybrid parents
H.	= Hardy	❋	= Flowering time
HH.	= Half-hardy	❧	= Foliage plant
L., *l.*	= Leaf, leaves		
Mt(s)	= Mount, mountain(s)		

The following have been used also in the descriptions of Alpines, Bulbs, Trees and Shrubs.

* = slightly tender
† = lime hater
✡ = highly recommended

The illustration numbers are in **bold type** and the page numbers in light type preceded by p.

hard–pruned in spring and repotted. Winter temp. 45°F. but not under 65°F. in spring and summer. Propagate by seed. E. Indies. **409**, p. 52.

ARGEMONE (PAPAVERACEAE) Prickly Poppy

mexicana ❋ Summer   HA.
Fl. bright lemon-yellow. *L.* light green, with prominent white veins, spiny. 1½–2 ft. Sow in the open 4–5 in light, dryish soil, where they are to *fl.* Tropical America. **240**, p. 30.

ARISAEMA (ARACEAE)

candidissimum ❋ Early Summer   T.
Allied to Lords and Ladies of the British hedgerows. Spathe (outer shield) white, sometimes veined with pink and green, up to 3 in. long. Spadix (central knob) pale greenish-yellow. Slightly scented. *L.* large, three lobed. Best in a dampish position and usually not appearing above ground till early summer. Probably the hardiest and best garden plant in a bizarre genus. W. China.

ARISTOLOCHIA (ARISTOLOCHIACEAE) Birthwort

elegans Calico Plant ❋ Summer   ClGP.
Fl. tube curved, yellowish, 1½ in. long, expanding to cup shape, purple-brown with white marks inside, white with purple veins outside. *L.* kidney-shaped, 2–3 in. long, 2–3 in. wide. Climber. Maintain minimum temp. of 60°F. Water freely in summer, less so in winter. Propagate by seed or cuttings in late winter. Brazil. **410**, p. 52.

ARIZONA CYPRESS, SMOOTH see **Cupressus glabra**, **2013**, p. 252.

ARMERIA (PLUMBAGINACEAE) Thrift

caespitosa ❋ Early Summer   P.
2–3 in. Forms dense cushions of narrow grass-like *l.* slightly domed. *Fl.* pinkish-lilac in clusters on short stems. Sunny position and needs well-drained soil. Spain.
‘Bevan’s Variety’, one of the best forms with deep pink *fl.*, **14**, p. 2.

maritima Sea Pink ❋ Late Spring–Summer   P.
6 in. Larger than preceding. A British native and forming large masses especially along sea coast. *Fl.* pink or pinkish-lilac in varying shades.
‘Vindictive’, with bright crimson *fl.*, **15**, p. 2.

ARNEBIA (BORAGINACEAE)

echioides Prophet Flower ❋ Early Summer   P.
Fl. rich primrose-yellow, tubular, with a black spot at base of each petal, which disappears as the *fl.* matures. *L.* narrow, hairy. 9–12 in. Full sun and a well-drained gritty soil. Propagate by seed or cuttings taken in the autumn with a heel. Armenia. **975**, p. 122.

ARROWHEAD see **Sagittaria**, **1357**, p. 170.

ARTEMISIA (COMPOSITAE)

absinthium Wormwood ❋ Summer & 🌿   P.
Fl. yellow, in short spikes forming leafy panicles. *L.* much divided, clothed in silky white hairs. 3 ft. Does well in poorish soil in sun or partial shade. Propagate by seed or division in the spring. Europe.
‘Lambrook Silver’, an attractive silver-foliage form, 3 ft, **976**, p. 122.

arborescens 🌿   †Sh.
Shrub up to 6 ft but usually less. Distinguished for its finely divided very silvery foliage. Plant in warm sunny position. Propagate any time during summer from cuttings and keep in a cool greenhouse, as in severe winters it may succumb. One of the silver-leaved plants. S. Europe. **1452**, p. 182.

lactiflora White Mugwort ❋ Late Summer–Mid Autumn   P.
Fl. creamy-white in long decorative plumes. 4–5 ft. *L.* deeply cut, 8–9 in. long, deep green. For moist soil and partial shade; admirable for the wild garden. Propagate by division in the spring. China, India. **977**, p. 123.

maritima Sea Wormwood ❋ Late Summer & 🌿 P.
Fl. yellowish to reddish in leafy panicles. 1½–2 ft. *L.* silvery-grey, narrow segments. For poorish light soil and full sun. Propagate by division in the spring. Europe, including Britain.
nutans, similar but with finely cut silvery-white *l.*, 1½–3 ft. Sicily, Canary Islands, **978**, p. 123.

ARUM (ARACEAE)

creticum ❋ Spring   GTu.
Fl. creamy-yellow, to 6 in. long on a 10 in. stem. *L.* arrow-shaped, to 5 in. long, 3 in. wide. Tuberous plant to 1 ft high. The plant is hardy in mild districts. Gritty compost. Winter temp. 40°F. Give good baking from late 6–9. Propagation by seed or by division of tubers. Crete. **411**, p. 52.

dracunculus see **Dracunculus vulgaris**

✧ **italicum marmoratum** ❋ Spring & 🌿   Tu.
Chiefly grown for its decorative highly marbled *l.* which appear in late autumn and are excellent for picking to accompany stylosa irises or other winter bloomers. Spathe pale creamy-green, spadix slightly darker. Seeds contained in fleshy scarlet berries on prominent heads 9–10 thus giving a dual season of interest. Plant in a sunny position. Often spreading freely. Europe, N. Africa. **676**, p. 85.

ARUM, DRAGON see **Dracunculus vulgaris**, **726**, p. 91.

ARUM, IVY see **Scindapsus**, **645**, p. 81.

ARUM, WHITE see **Zantedeschia aethiopica**, **943**, p. 118.

ARUNCUS (ROSACEAE)

sylvester, syn. **Spiraea aruncus** Goat’s Beard ❋ Summer   P.
Fl. creamy-white borne in spiraea-like plumes. *L.* feathery, leaflets 1–3 in. long. 4 ft. For a moist deep soil in partial shade. An attractive plant near water. Propagate by seed or division. For many years this plant was known under its synonym *Spiraea aruncus* and it may still be found under this name in nursery catalogues. N. Hemisphere. **979**, p. 123.

ASH, COMMON see **Fraxinus excelsior**

ASH, MANNA see **Fraxinus ornus**

ASH, MINIATURE MOUNTAIN see **Sorbus reducta**, **1910**, p. 239.

ASH, MOUNTAIN see **Sorbus aucuparia**, **1905**, p. 239.

ASH, WEEPING see **Fraxinus excelsior** ‘Pendula’, **1615**, p. 202.

ASPEN see **Populus tremula**, **1744**, p. 218.

ASPEN, AMERICAN see **Populus tremuloides**

ASPERULA (RUBIACEAE)

suberosa ❋ Summer   *RP.
3–4 in. *Fl.* pale lilac-pink, tubular, opening to small stars. Foliage is silvery and hairy and forms loose mat. Sunny position in rock garden in well-drained

soil but needs some cover to keep off winter wet or alpine house where it makes a good pan plant. Greece. **16**, p. 2.

ASPLENIUM (POLYPODIACEAE)

bulbiferum Spleenwort 🌿   GP.
Fronds 1–2 ft, oblong-deltoid with horizontal pinnae 6 in. long on each side. Plantlets produced on fronds. Tolerates lower temps than *A. nidus-avis*.

nidus-avis Bird’s Nest Fern 🌿   GP.
Fronds entire up to 4 ft long and 8 in. broad, lance-shaped. Best grown in a mixture of equal parts peat and chopped sphagnum. Winter temp. 55–60°F. A very moist atmosphere is essential and shade, although this can be overdone. Propagation by spores. Found more or less throughout the tropics. **412**, p. 52.

ASTER (COMPOSITAE)

A vast and varied genus best known for the great number of Michaelmas Daisy hybrids which have entirely superseded the sp. *A. novae-belgii*. Asters like a sunny, open position and do quite well in ordinary garden soil so long as it does not dry out during the growing season. Planting may be done in autumn or spring, but *A. amellus* varieties should only be moved in the spring and may be increased by division at that time, or by cuttings. Other varieties may be divided in spring or autumn, and by cuttings taken in the spring.

acris ❋ Late Summer   P.
Fl. bright mauve with golden centre, star-like, in clustered heads. *L.* small, bright green. 2–3 ft. Makes a bushy plant for the mid-border. S. Europe. **980**, p. 123.

alpinus ❋ Summer   RP.
Ray florets mauve or rosy-purple, occasionally white, surrounding central disc. *Fl.* head 2–3 in. across. 4–8 in. The common aster of the Alps. **17**, p. 3.
‘Beechwood’, with lavender-blue *fl.* is one of the best forms.

amellus ❋ Autumn   P.
Fl. purple, large, solitary. *L.* oblong lance-shaped, rough. 2–2½ ft. Italy.
Good varieties include:
‘King George’, deep violet-blue, free-flowering, **981**, p. 123;

'Rudolf Goethe', deep lavender, **982**, p. 123;
'Sonia', rosy-pink.

× **frikartii** ✳ Summer   P.
Fl. large, light blue with yellow eye, very freely produced. *L.* oblong, rough, dark green. 2½ ft. Of garden origin, a hybrid from *A. thomsonii* × *A. amellus*. **983**, p. 123.

linosyris, syn. **Crinitaria linosyris** Goldilocks ✳ Autumn   P.
Fl. bright yellow in compact terminal clusters, borne on 2 ft slender stems. *L.* narrow, entire, greyish-green. Given here under its old established name this plant is now known as *Crinitaria linosyris* and may be found in some catalogues under this name. Europe. **984**, p. 123.

novae-angliae New England Aster USA ✳ Late Summer–Mid Autumn   P.
Fl. violet-purple or pink. *L.* lance-shaped, stem-clasping, up to 5 in. long. Taller than *A. novae-belgii*, up to 6 ft. N. America.
The type has given rise to some good hybrids:
    'Barr's Pink', bright rose-pink, 4–5 ft;
    'Harrington's Pink', clear rose-pink, 4 ft;
    'September Ruby', deep rosy-red, 3½–4 ft, **985**, p. 124.

novae-belgii Michaelmas Daisy UK, New York Aster USA ✳ Autumn   P.
Fl. blue. *L.* slender-pointed, 2–5 in. long. Up to 4 ft. E. USA. Numerous hybrids have been developed in a great range of colours and of varying heights.
Tall hybrids include:
    'Ada Ballard', 3 ft, mauve-blue, **986**, p. 124;
    'Ernest Ballard', 3 ft, rosy-crimson, **987**, p. 124;
    'Marie Ballard', 3 ft, light blue, **988**, p. 124;
    'Winston S. Churchill', 2½ ft, glowing ruby-red, **989**, p. 124.
Dwarf hybrids:
    'Audrey', 12 in., pale blue, semi-double;
    'Jenny', 12 in., cerise-red, **990**, p. 124;
    'Snowsprite', 12 in., white, **991**, p. 124.

spectabilis ✳ Late Summer–Mid Autumn   P.
Fl. bright violet, about 1½ in. across. *L.* oval, up to 5 in. long, somewhat toothed. 1½–2 ft. USA. **992**, p. 124.

thomsonii ✳ Late Summer–Mid Autumn   P.
Fl. lavender-blue, freely borne. *L.* almost heart-shaped, toothed, stem-clasping. 1–2 ft. Propagate by seed or cuttings. W. Himalaya.
    'Nana', a dwarf form, to 15 in., **993**, p. 125.

yunnanensis ✳ Early Summer   P.
Fl. solitary, large, bright blue-mauve. 9–12 in. Plant 3–4. Propagate by division in spring. W. China.
    'Napsbury', is a good deep blue and taller form, 15 in.

ASTER, CHINA see **Callistephus**, **251-254**, p. 32.

ASTER, NEW ENGLAND see **Aster novae-angliae**, **985**, p. 124.

ASTER, NEW YORK see **Aster novae-belgii**, **986-991**, p. 124.

ASTER, STOKES' see **Stokesia laevis**, **1391**, p. 174.

ASTILBE (SAXIFRAGACEAE) False Goat's Beard

× **arendsii** ✳ Summer   P.
Fl. in shades of crimson, pink, rosy-lilac and white. 2–3 ft. Plant 10–3, in partial shade or in full sun so long as there is ample moisture at the roots. Propagate by division in the spring. Of garden origin. **994**, p. 125.
    'Deutschland', pure white, **995**, p. 125;
    'Fanal', dark garnet-red in dense panicles, **996**, p. 125;

'Granat', deep crimson-pink in pyramidal trusses, **997**, p. 125;
'Hyacinth', pink, **998**, p. 125.

chinensis ✳ Summer   RP.
Fl. deep pinkish-purple in small plumes on stem up to 1 ft. *L.* divided, fern-like. 8 in.–1 ft. Valuable as a late summer-flowering plant for a moist position. Will grow in semi-shade. A useful miniature of the larger astilbes. China. **18**, p. 3.

davidii ✳ Midsummer   P.
Fl. crimson-magenta in up to 2 ft spikes, height 6 ft. *L.* feathery, coarsely toothed on long stems, bronzy-green when young. Partial shade and ample moisture. China.

ASTRANTIA (UMBELLIFERAE) Masterwort

maxima ✳ Early Summer   P.
Fl. pinkish, with bristly bracts. 1–2 ft. *L.* tripartite, toothed, ovate or broadly lanceolate. In ordinary garden soil in sun or partial shade where there is adequate summer moisture. Propagate by division of the roots in autumn or spring, or by seed sown as soon as harvested. E. Caucasus. **999**, p. 125.

ATRIPLEX (CHENOPODIACEAE)

hortensis Orach ✳ Summer   HA.
Fl. purplish, small, borne on erect spikes. *L.* opposite or alternate, 4–5 in. long. 4–5 ft. Edible, may be used like spinach. Sow in the open in 3–4. Found widely in the Old World. **241**, p. 31.
    'Rubra', has outstanding crimson leaves and colourful violet stems.

ATLAS CEDAR see **Cedrus atlantica**, **2003**, p. 251.

AUBRIETA (CRUCIFERAE)

deltoidea ✳ Spring   RP.
The common aubrietas or aubretias of gardens are most valuable and free-flowering plants forming large mats covered with deep blue, mauve, pinkish or purple star-like *fl.* 3–6 in. tall. They are derived from the Greek *A. deltoidea*. Planted in an open stone wall or on top of it to hang over and in full sun they soon cover large areas. After flowering, cut off with shears all the old *fl.* heads and any straggly shoots. They are easily propagated from cuttings or strains of mixed colours may be grown from seed. Among the best are:
    'Barker's Double', deep rosy-purple, double, long lasting *fl.*, **19**, p. 3;
    'Bressingham Pink', deep pink, semi-double;
    'Dr Mules', deep violet-blue;
    'Lavender Queen', lavender-purple, **20**, p. 3;
    'Magician', bright purple.

AUCUBA (CORNACEAE)

japonica   Sh.
Small shrub up to 5 ft. *L.* leathery, evergreen. Distinguished for its bright scarlet berries in clusters. There is also a form with cream berries. Fruit 8–10. *Fl.* are unisexual, that is male and female *fl.* on separate bushes and so one male plant with *fl.* is inconspicuous among group of females. **1453**, p. 182.

AURICULA, ALPINE see **Primula auricula**, **148**, **149**, p. 19.

AUSTRALIAN SNOW GUM see **Eucalyptus niphophila**, **1598**, p. 200.

AUSTRIAN PINE see **Pinus nigra**, **2033**, p. 255.

AUTUMN CROCUS see **Colchicum autumnale**, **686**, p. 86.

AUTUMN SNOWFLAKE see **Leucojum autumnale**, **795**, p. 100.

AVENA CANDIDA see **Helictotrichon sempervirens**

AVENS see **Geum**, **1151**, **1152**, p. 144.

AZALEA see **Rhododendron** sp. and after **Rhododendron** Hybrids

AZARA (FLACOURTIACEAE)

All species are tender and are best grown against a wall except in very mild areas.

dentata ✳ Midsummer   *Sh.
Shrub with large *l.* and slightly larger *fl.* than the more usually grown *A. microphylla*.

lanceolata ✳ Mid Spring   *Sh.
Undivided narrow *l.* and small mustard-yellow strongly scented *fl.*

microphylla ✳ Mid Spring   *†Sh.
Small tree or wall shrub with divided *l.* and bright yellow *fl.* in clusters like small yellow bells. Strongly scented. Chile. **1454**, p. 182.

B

BABY BLUE-EYES see **Nemophila menziesii**, **349**, p. 44.

BABY'S BREATH see **Gypsophila**, **81**, p. 11; **303**, p. 38; **1153**, **1154**, p. 145.

BACHELOR'S BUTTONS see **Ranunculus acris**, **1344**, p. 168.

BACON AND EGGS see **Lotus corniculatus**, **1244**, p. 156.

BALD CYPRESS see **Taxodium distichum**, **2041**, p. 256.

BALLOTA (LABIATAE)

pseudodictamnus ✳ Late Spring–Midsummer P.
Fl. white with purple spots. *L.* heart-shaped, white woolly. 2 ft. Plant 3–4 in ordinary well-drained

---

Abbreviations and Symbols used in the text.
The following abbreviations may sometimes be used in conjunction as HA. indicating Hardy annual or GBb indicating Greenhouse bulb.

A. = Annual	P. = Perennial
Aq. = Aquatic	R. = Rock or
B. = Biennial	Alpine plant
Bb = Bulb	Sh. = Shrub
C. = Corm	Sp., sp. = Species
Cl. = Climber	Syn. = Synonym
Co. = Conifer	T. = Tree
Fl., fl. = Flower(s)	Tu. = Tuber
G. = Greenhouse or	var. = variety
house plant	× = Hybrid or
H. = Hardy	hybrid parents
HH. = Half-hardy	✳ = Flowering time
L., l. = Leaf, leaves	❧ = Foliage plant
Mt(s) = Mount,	
mountain(s)	

The following have been used also in the descriptions of Alpines, Bulbs, Trees and Shrubs.

    * = slightly tender
    † = lime hater
    ✿ = highly recommended

The illustration numbers are in **bold type** and the page numbers in light type preceded by p.

267

garden soil and a sunny position. Protect from excessive winter wet. Propagate by cuttings or division. Crete. **1000**, p. 125.

BALM OF GILEAD see **Populus candicans**

BALSAM see **Impatiens balsamina**, **311**, p. 39.

BALSAM POPLAR, WESTERN see **Populus trichocarpa**

BAMBOO see **Sinarundinaria**, **1901**, p. 238.

BANE, WOLF'S see **Aconitum lycoctonum**

BAPTISIA (LEGUMINOSAE)

australis ✿ Early Summer   P.
Fl. rich blue, pea-like. L. wedge-shaped, hairless. 4–5 ft. Ordinary garden soil and a sunny position. Propagate by division in autumn or spring, or by seed sown in pans in a cold frame in spring. E. USA. **1001**, p. 126.

BARBERRY see **Berberis**, **1455-1459**, pp. 182, 183.

BARTONIA AUREA see **Mentzelia lindleyi**

BASKET FLOWER see **Hymenocallis narcissi-flora**

BAY, SWEET see **Magnolia virginiana**

BEAN, CHINESE KIDNEY see **Wisteria**, **1999**, **2000**, p. 250.

BEAN TREE, INDIAN see **Catalpa bignonioides**, **1498**, p. 188.

BEARS BREECHES see **Acanthus**, **945**, p. 119 and **Primula auricula**, **148**, **149**, p. 19.

BEAUTY BUSH see **Kolkwitzia amabilis**, **1668**, p. 209.

BEECH see **Fagus**, **1609**, p. 202.

BEECH, ANTARCTIC see **Nothofagus antarctica**

BEECH, COMMON see **Fagus sylvatica**

BEECH, COPPER see **Fagus sylvatica** 'Cuprea', **1609**, p. 202.

BEECH, DAWYCK see **Fagus sylvatica** 'Fastigiata'

BEECH, FERN-LEAF see **Fagus sylvatica** 'Laciniata'

BEECH, ROBEL see **Nothofagus obliqua**

BEECH, SOUTHERN see **Nothofagus**, **1711**, p. 214.

BEECH, WEEPING see **Fagus sylvatica** 'Pendula'

BEGONIA (BEGONIACEAE)

hybrida pendula ✿ Summer   GTu.
Plants with pendulous branches to 1½ ft. long. Fl. scarlet, orange, red, yellow. L. roughly triangular, hairy. Originally based on the cross B.

boliviensis × *B. davisii*, other hybrids have been made with other tuberous sp. but always showing the pendulous stems and long fuchsia-like fl. of B. boliviensis. Treatment the same as other hybrids, see B. tuberhybrida, but must be placed in elevated position or hanging baskets to display their pendulous habit. Propagate by stem cuttings, by cutting tubers or seed. **413**, p. 52.

masoniana Iron Cross ●   GP.
Fl. greenish-white, in clusters. L. roughly triangular, with heart-shaped base, 8 in. long, 6 in. across; grey-green with purple cross-shaped zone in centre. Surface of l. puckered to give mossy effect. Plant to 9 in. Light soil, composed of leaf mould and sand with small amount of loam. Moist shady conditions. Minimum temp. ideally 55°F., but plant will survive, although with l. damage, as low as 45°F. Propagate by seed or by l. cuttings. Introduced by L. Maurice Mason from Singapore Botanic Gardens. Not known in the wild but possibly from Indo-China. **414**, p. 52.

semperflorens ✿ Summer   HHP.
Fl. white, tinged pink. L. pale, shining green, roundish. 6–18 in. Fibrous rooted, Sow the dust-like seed thinly in pans containing finely sifted soil early 2–3 in a warm greenhouse. Plant out early 6. Brazil.
There are a large number of hybrids, including:
'Carmen', 9 in., bright rose fl. bronze foliage;
'Flamingo', 6 in., white fl. with rose picotee edges;
'Galaxy mixed', F¹, 6 in., various colours, uniform dwarf habit with dark bronze foliage;
'Indian Maid', 9 in., bright scarlet fl. and bronze foliage;
'Linda', F¹, 6 in., bright rose, very free flowering;
'Organdy', new F¹, 6 in., a particularly attractive mixture, **242**, p. 31.

socotrana hybrids ✿ Mid Autumn–Early Winter
                                   GP.
Fl. red, pink or white. L. round, dark or light green. To 18 in. A series of hybrids between the winter-flowering, bulbil-bearing B. socotrana × B. dregei. Light compost of equal parts leaf mould and sand most suitable. Winter temperature 50°F. Cuttings of young shoots should be taken in spring, as early as possible and grown on in warm, airy, shady conditions. Give more light after 8. Compost should be kept barely moist, but plants appreciate frequent syringing in hot weather. Larger-flowered hybrids very susceptible to mildew. After flowering, cuttings are taken and the old plant is usually discarded.
Among the most popular winter-flowering varieties are:
'Emita', red;
'Gloire de Lorraine', rosy pink;
'Ida', bright rosy red, **415**, p. 52;
'Mavina', deep rosy red, **416**, p. 52;
'Mrs Petersen', reddish pink with crimson foliage;
'Mrs Leopold de Rothschild', rich pink, **417**, p. 53;
'Regent', rose pink, **418**, p. 53.

tuberhybrida ✿ Summer   GTu.
The hybrid tuberous begonias are of comparatively recent breeding. The first hybrid B. × sedeni was distributed in 1870. It was bred by crossing the tall B. boliviensis with an Andean sp. which had been sent to James Veitch & Sons, but which was not named and may now be lost to cultivation. In all, seven sp. contribute to the strain. Two have already been mentioned, B. boliviensis and the unknown Andean sp. The others were the yellow-flowered B. pearcei, from which all the modern yellow varieties are descended; the handsome scarlet B. veitchii, the similar B. clarkei, the deep pink B. roseflora, and the dwarf compact B. davisii, which was a later introduction, flowering for the first time in Veitch's nursery in 1876 and being introduced to commerce three years later.
The first hybrids concentrated on floriferousness and colour variation, and double flowers when they occurred were not particularly esteemed in Great Britain. In fact the earliest double varieties were

raised in France and Belgium by Lemoine, Felix Crousse (who specialised in these flowers), and Louis van Houtte. In 1875 a noted British hybridiser, John Laing, whose nursery at Forest Hill was renowned, collected the best British and Continental hybrids and started breeding on his own. His results soon equalled, and eventually surpassed, the Continental nurserymen.
The time that the tubers are started depends on the amount of heat available. But it is generally around mid-3, and a temp. of 65°F. is necessary. The tubers are usually laid in boxes (some growers start them upside down) of moist peat and potted up in a light mixture as soon as signs of growth are observed. As growth continues they are potted on. The plants must be shaded from too much direct sunshine. Once in their final pots they can be fed, when the roots have filled the pots. Begonias fl. generally in groups of three, of which the two lateral fl. are female, while the central, much larger one is male. In order to get large fl., the plant should not be allowed to fl. until it is large, and the first buds should be discarded. Great heat is not necessary, unless early flowering is required. Although plenty of water is required when the plants are well-rooted, they must be watered with care in the early stages, and once flowering is over, water is completely withheld and plants are moved into a dry atmosphere. The stems should not be cut, but left until they can be easily pulled off cleanly. The tubers are stored in a mixture of peat and sand, in a temp. around 45–50°F.
There are many varieties of tuberous begonias, and these fall into two classes. First the 'Multiflora' varieties of Continental origin, such as 'Mayor Max', orange-scarlet, double; 'Flamboyant', scarlet; and 'Helen Harms', yellow. They are dwarf, compact, very floriferous, and excellent for bedding. Second there are the large-flowered tuberous begonias which may be bedded out in summer, or grown as specimen plants in the greenhouse or conservatory.
These include:
'Buttermilk', light yellow flushed pink at edge, **419**, p. 53;
'Corona', rich yellow with slightly serrated red edge, **420**, p. 53;
'Diana Wynyard', white, yellow flushed centre, **421**, p. 53;
'Elaine Tartellin', deep rose pink, slightly serrated, **422**, p. 53;

Abbreviations and Symbols used in the text.
The following abbreviations may sometimes be used in conjunction as HA. indicating Hardy annual or GBb indicating Greenhouse bulb.

A. = Annual	P. = Perennial
Aq. = Aquatic	R. = Rock or
B. = Biennial	Alpine plant
Bb = Bulb	Sh. = Shrub
C. = Corm	Sp., sp. = Species
Cl. = Climber	Syn. = Synonym
Co. = Conifer	T. = Tree
Fl., fl. = Flower(s)	Tu. = Tuber
G. = Greenhouse or	var. = variety
house plant	× = Hybrid or
H. = Hardy	hybrid parents
HH. = Half-hardy	✿ = Flowering time
L., l. = Leaf, leaves	● = Foliage plant
Mt(s) = Mount,	
mountain(s)	

The following have been used also in the descriptions of Alpines, Bulbs, Trees and Shrubs.

* = slightly tender
† = lime hater
✿ = highly recommended

The illustration numbers are in **bold type** and the page numbers in light type preceded by p.

'Fantasy', yellow with a slightly pink edge, **423**, p. 53;

'Gold Plate', rich yellow, **424**, p. 53;

'Guardsman', orange-scarlet, **425**, p. 54;

'Harlequin', white with a well defined pink edge, **426**, p. 54;

'Mary Heatley', golden-orange, **427**, p. 54;

'Red Beacon', rich crimson, **428**, p. 54;

'Roy Hartley', soft pink tinged with salmon, **429**, p. 54;

'Sugar Candy', light pink, **430**, p. 54.

BELLADONNA LILY see **Amaryllis belladonna**, **670**, p. 84.

BELLFLOWER see **Campanula**, **23-27**, pp. 3, 4; **255**, p. 32; **440**, p. 55; **1010-1015**, p. 127.

BELLFLOWER, CHILEAN see **Nolana**, **354**, p. 45.

BELLFLOWER, GREAT see **Campanula latifolia**, **1013**, p. 127.

BELLFLOWER, MILKY see **Campanula lactiflora**, **1012**, p. 127.

BELLFLOWER, PEACH-LEAVED see **Campanula persicifolia**, **1014**, **1015**, p. 127.

BELLIS (COMPOSITAE) Daisy

perennis Meadow Daisy, English Daisy USA ✷ Spring   B/P.

Fl. pink, white, red; single and double. L. rounded, 1–3 in. long. A perennial, usually treated as a biennial for bedding purposes. Sow in a cold frame or in the open in 5–6 and plant out in flowering position in autumn. Europe, Britain.

'Monstrosa', giant fl., double, various shades;

'Pomponette'. tightly quilled double, miniature fl. in shades of red, rose and white, **243**, p. 31.

BELLS, CORAL see **Heuchera**, **1172**, **1173**, p. 147.

BELLS OF IRELAND see **Moluccella laevis**, **346**, p. 44.

BELOPERONE (ACANTHACEAE)

guttata Shrimp Plant ✷ Spring-Autumn   GP.

Fl. whitish, concealed in browny-pink bracts. There is also a cultivar in existence in which the bracts are creamy-green with no brown. L. small, ovate. A shrub up to 3 ft. high in the wild, but rarely exceeding 18 in. in cultivation. Easy in a cool greenhouse and often used as a house plant, where it should be given a well-lit position. Minimum winter temp. 45°F. and little water should be given then, nor are large quantities needed when the plant is in growth. Normal potting compost. Propagate by cuttings in heat during summer. Introduced from Mexico as recently as 1936. **431**, p. 54.

BERBERIS (BERBERIDACEAE) Barberry

✿ **darwinii** ✷ Mid Spring   Sh.

Fl. orange-yellow in large clusters. Large shrub up to 10 ft with small leathery shiny l. and rather prickly. One of the most valuable early spring flowering shrubs. Fruit in clusters of bluish-mauve berries in summer. Chile. **1455**, **1456**, p. 182.

× **lologensis** ✷ Spring   *Sh.

A natural hybrid between B. darwinii and B. linearifolia. Fl. deep orange-yellow in large clusters, slightly larger than those of B. darwinii. Less vigorous usually than B. darwinii but with slightly better fl. Chile. **1457**, p. 183.

× **stenophylla** ✷ Mid Spring   *Sh.

Medium sized evergreen shrub with pendulous branchlets and thick small l. Fl. yellowish-orange but paler than those of B. darwinii. May be trimmed as a useful flowering hedge. Parentage B. darwinii and B. empetrifolia.

'Semperflorens', slightly smaller with an extended flowering period, **1458**, p. 183.

thunbergii ☙   Sh.

Medium sized shrub distinguished for brilliant scarlet autumn colouring of foliage. Fruit scarlet berries. Usually a compact grower.

Its varieties include:

'Atropurpurea', with foliage reddish-purple throughout year;

'Atropurpurea Nana', dwarf form of previous sp. **1459**, p. 183.

BERGAMOT see **Monarda didyma**, **1276**, p. 160.

BERGENIA, syn. **MEGASEA** (SAXIFRAGACEAE) Pig Squeak

delavayi ✷ Spring   P.

Fl. rosy-purple in drooping racemes. L. widely oval, green in spring, crimson in winter. 9 in. Plant 9–11. Ordinary garden soil in sun or partial shade. Propagate by division or seed. Very close to B. purpurascens and sometimes regarded as synonymous. China. **1002**, p. 126.

purpurascens ✷ Spring   P.

Fl. purple. L. roundish, erect. 6–9 in. Plant 8–9. Here belongs 'Ballawley' with very large leaves, one of the finest clones. Himalayas, China. **1003**, p. 126.

BESCHORNERIA (AMARYLLIDACEAE)

yuccoides ✷ Early Summer   *Sh.

Shrub up to 4 ft. L. leathery, glaucous. Fl. spikes up to 6 ft long with bright pink succulent stem and bracts, green. In most areas should be grown with a wall against its back. Very conspicuous and unusual plant, worth a little protection in winter. Mexico. **1460**, p. 183.

BETONICA GRANDIFLORA see **Stachys macrantha**

BETONY see **Stachys macrantha**, **1387**, p. 174.

BETULA (BETULACEAE) Birch

albo-sinensis var. **septentrionalis**   T.

Small tree up to 30 ft distinguished for its shiny orange-pinkish bark which also has a slight grey bloom and peels in early summer. L. ovate, rounded at base 2–3 in. long by 1½ in. wide. A tree which should be grown much more widely. China where it grows up to 90 ft. **1461**, p. 183.

pendula Silver Birch   T.

Tree up to 50 ft. Distinguished for its silvery-white bark and graceful habit. Forms should be chosen for their white bark which is absent in some seedlings. **1462**, p. 183.

Among best forms are:

✿ var. dalecarlica, Swedish Birch, tall tree with drooping branches;

'Youngii', which makes a dome-shaped small weeping tree, **1463**, p. 183.

BHUTAN PINE see **Pinus wallichiana**, **2036**, p. 255.

BIG TREE see **Sequoiadendron giganteum**, **2039**, **2040**, p. 255.

BIGNONIA see **Campsis**

BILLBERGIA (BROMELIACEAE)

nutans Queen's Tears USA ✷ Summer   GP.

Fl. bell-shaped, greenish in spike, emerging from pink bracts. L. sword-shaped, evergreen, up to 9 in. long. Up to 1 ft high. Any good potting compost satisfactory. Minimum temp. 45°F or even lower. Propagate by division. Brazil. **432**, p. 54.

× **windii** ✷ Summer   GP.

A more handsome plant than B. nutans, with larger fl. but slightly less hardy. It was produced by crossing B. nutans and B. decora.

BILLBERRY see **Vaccinium myrtillus**

BIRCH see **Betula**, **1461-1463**, p. 183.

BIRD CHERRY see **Prunus padus**, **1758**, p. 220.

BIRD'S EYE PRIMULA see **Primula farinosa**, **152**, p. 19.

BIRD'S-FOOT TREFOIL see **Lotus corniculatus**, **1244**, p. 156.

BIRD'S NEST FERN see **Asplenium nidus-avis**, **412**, p. 52.

BIRTHWORT see **Aristolochia**, **410**, p. 52.

BITTER ORANGE, JAPANESE see **Poncirus trifoliata**, **1742**, **1743**, p. 218.

BLACK ALDER see **Ilex verticillata**

BLACK PINE see **Pinus nigra**, **2033**, p. 255.

BLACK POPLAR see **Populus nigra**

BLACK-EYED SUSAN see **Rudbeckia hirta**, **368**, p. 46 and **Thunbergia alata**, **383**, p. 48.

BLACK ITALIAN POPLAR see **Populus** × **serotina**

Abbreviations and Symbols used in the text.
The following abbreviations may sometimes be used in conjunction as HA. indicating Hardy annual or GBb indicating Greenhouse bulb.

A. = Annual	P. = Perennial
Aq. = Aquatic	R. = Rock or
B. = Biennial	Alpine plant
Bb = Bulb	Sh. = Shrub
C. = Corm	Sp., sp. = Species
Cl. = Climber	Syn. = Synonym
Co. = Conifer	T. = Tree
Fl., fl. = Flower(s)	Tu. = Tuber
G. = Greenhouse or	var. = variety
house plant	× = Hybrid or
H. = Hardy	hybrid parents
HH. = Half-hardy	✷ = Flowering time
L., l. = Leaf, leaves	☙ = Foliage plant
Mt(s) = Mount,	
mountain(s)	

The following have been used also in the descriptions of Alpines, Bulbs, Trees and Shrubs.

* = slightly tender
† = lime hater
✿ = highly recommended

The illustration numbers are in **bold type** and the page numbers in light type preceded by p.

BLACK SNAKE-ROOT see **Cimicifuga racemosa, 1051**, p. 132.

BLANKET FLOWER see **Gaillardia, 1138, 1139**, p. 143.

BLAZING STAR see **Liatris spicata, 1235**, p. 155 and **Mentzelia lindleyi, 342**, p. 43.

BLEEDING HEART see **Dicentra spectabilis, 1110**, p. 139.

BLETIA HYACINTHINA see **Bletilla striata**

BLETILLA (ORCHIDACEAE)

striata, syn. **Bletia hyacinthina** ✳ Summer   P.
Fl. purple, about 1½ in. across. 1 ft. *L.* almost evergreen. For partial shade in well-drained loam and peat. Requires winter protection except in mild districts. Propagate by division of the pseudobulbs after flowering and before they start into growth. There is also a white form. China, Japan. **1004**, p. 126.

BLOOD LILY see **Haemanthus, 542**, p. 68.

BLOODY CRANESBILL see **Geranium sanguineum, 1148**, p. 144.

BLUE LACE FLOWER see **Didiscus caeruleus, 288**, p. 36.

BLUE POPPY, HIMALAYAN see **Meconopsis betonicifolia, 1263**, p. 158.

BLUE SPRUCE see **Picea pungens, 2030**, p. 254.

BLUEBELL see **Endymion non-scripta, 727,** p. 91.

BLUEBELL, SPANISH see **Endymion hispanica**

BLUEBERRY see **Vaccinium corymbosum, 1933**, p. 242 and **V. myrsinites, 1936**, p. 242.

BOCCONIA see **Macleaya**

BOMAREA (AMARYLLIDACEAE)

kalbrayeri ✳ Summer   CIGTu.
Fl. red and orange in terminal umbels. *L.* oblong-acuminate up to 2½ in. long. Deciduous. A tuberous plant with twining stems, that may reach 10 ft. Cool airy conditions are needed and the plant has been grown outside in a few very favoured districts. The plant is related to *Alstroemeria*. Best planted in the greenhouse border, although growing in large pots is possible. A fairly rich mixture is appreciated. Propagation is easiest by seed, although division is sometimes possible. Minimum winter temp. 40°F., when little or no water is needed. The plant should not dry out completely. Colombia. **433**, p. 55.

BORDER CARNATIONS AND PINKS see **Dianthus** after the sp.

BOX see **Buxus, 1470**, p. 184.

BOYKINIA (SAXIFRAGACEAE)

jamesii ✳ Late Spring   †RP.
Fl. deep pink or purplish-pink with five petals surrounding dark disc in raceme on stem 6 in. or slightly more. *L.* kidney-shaped and toothed. Stems pinkish, slightly succulent. 6–9 in. A rather rare alpine but worth an effort to keep it on rock garden. Also suitable for pans in alpine house.

Not suitable for hot dry position or limy soils but requires good drainage. Tends not to *fl.* freely in open. Pike's Peak, Colorado. **21**, p. 3.

BRACHYCOME (COMPOSITAE)

iberidifolia Swan River Daisy ✳ Summer   HHA.
Fl. variable in shades of blue, purple, pink, as well as white. *L.* divided, smooth. 9–12 in. Sow under glass 3–4, or in an open sunny position 5. Makes a decorative pot plant for a cool greenhouse. Australia. **244**, p. 31.

BRAMBLE see **Rubus, 1889**, p. 237.

BRASSAVOLA see × **Brassocattleya**

× **BRASSOCATTLEYA** (ORCHIDACEAE)

hybrids ✳ Summer usually   GP.
Brassavola (now *Rhyncolaelia*) *digbyana*, an orchid with a deeply fringed lip, has been crossed with various *Cattleya* sp. to give the bigeneric hybrids of *Brassocattleya*. Although the *fl.* have the colour and form of the best cattleyas, the lips are fringed and fimbriated to a greater or lesser extent to give an airy appearance to the *fl.* Warm greenhouse.
  cliftonii 'Magnifica', shows rather less of a fringe than do some others of these hybrids, **434**, p. 55.

BREWER'S WEEPING SPRUCE see **Picea breweriana, 2026**, p. 254.

BRIZA (GRAMINEAE) Quaking Grass

maxima ✳ Late Spring–Midsummer   HA.
L. rough above, about ¼ in. wide. 1–1½ ft. Elegant seed heads on slender stems can be cut and dried for winter decoration. Sow in poorish soil in an open position 3–4, or 9. Mediterranean regions. **245**, p. 31.

minor ✳ Summer   HA.
Similar to *B. maxima* but daintier, 9–12 in., and requires the same treatment. W. Europe, naturalised in N. America.

BRODIAEA (LILIACEAE)

coccinea see **B. ida-maia**

ida-maia syn. **B. coccinea, Dichelostemma ida-maia** Californian Fire-Cracker ✳ Early Summer *Bb
Fl. long-tubed, bright crimson-red tipped with yellow and green. A very striking *fl.*, the end of the crimson tube opening to a star of yellowish-green and a white throat. Loose umbels of several drooping *fl.* about 1½ in. long. 1½–2 ft. Slightly tender and needs a very warm position or to be grown as a cold greenhouse plant. **677**, p. 85

laxa syn. **Triteleia laxa** Grass Nut ✳ Summer   Bb
Fl. deep violet-blue, tubular, opening to a star, in a loose umbel up to 20 *fl.* and 1 ft across. 2–3 ft. Probably the finest species for gardens, like a small agapanthus. Sunny position in borders. Quite hardy. California. **678**, p. 85.

BROOM see **Cytisus, 45, 46**, p. 6; **1546-1548**, p. 194.

BROOM, BUTCHER'S see **Ruscus, 1890**, p. 237.

BROOM, MADEIRAN see **Genista virgata**

BROOM, MOONLIGHT see **Cytisus scoparius** 'Sulphureus'

BROOM, MT ETNA see **Genista aetnensis**

BROOM, SPANISH see **Spartium junceum, 1914**, p. 240.

BROOM, YELLOW see **Cytisus scoparius, 1548**, p. 194.

BRONZE LEAF, FEATHERED see **Rodgersia pinnata, 1349**, p. 169.

BROWALLIA (SOLANACEAE)

speciosa 'Major' ✳ Midsummer   GA.
Fl. 2 in. wide, violet with white throat. *L.* lance-shaped, 1½ in. long. Plant 2 ft. Sow in 3 and again in 6 in temp. 55–60°F., barely covering seed. Transplant to 5 in. pots, three or four to a pot. Keep in light position, watering moderately and feeding during 5–6. Colombia. **435**, p. 55.

BRUGMANSIA see **DATURA**

BRUNFELSIA (SOLANACEAE)

calycina   GSh.
Intermittently all year. *Fl.* violet, salver-shaped, 2 in. across in heads. *L.* lanceolate, evergreen, to 3 in. long. Shrub to 3 ft. Any good potting compost will suffice. The plant is slow growing. Ideal minimum temp. 50°F. but plant survives at 45°F. if kept dry in winter. Propagate by cuttings of half-ripened wood in summer. Brazil.
  'Macrantha', is larger than the type in all its parts, from Peru, **436**, p. 55.

BRUNNERA (BORAGINACEAE)

macrophylla, syn. **Anchusa myosotidiflora** ✳ Early Summer   P.
Fl. blue with yellow throat, small, forget-me-not-like. *L.* heart-shaped, up to 6 in. across, rough. 12–18 in. For moist, ordinary soil and partial shade. Propagate by division in early autumn or spring, or by root cuttings in autumn in a cold frame. W. Caucasus. **1005**, p. 126.

BRUNSVIGIA see **Amaryllis belladonna**

BUCKEYE, RED see **Aesculus pavia**

BUCKTHORN, SEA see **Hippophae rhamnoides, 1647**, p. 206.

Abbreviations and Symbols used in the text.
The following abbreviations may sometimes be used in conjunction as HA. indicating Hardy annual or GBb indicating Greenhouse bulb.

A. = Annual	P. = Perennial
Aq. = Aquatic	R. = Rock or
B. = Biennial	Alpine plant
Bb = Bulb	Sh. = Shrub
C. = Corm	Sp., sp. = Species
Cl. = Climber	Syn. = Synonym
Co. = Conifer	T. = Tree
Fl., fl. = Flower(s)	Tu. = Tuber
G. = Greenhouse or	var. = variety
house plant	× = Hybrid or
H. = Hardy	hybrid parents
HH. = Half-hardy	✳ = Flowering time
L., l. = Leaf, leaves	☙ = Foliage plant
Mt(s) = Mount,	
mountain(s)	

The following have been used also in the descriptions of Alpines, Bulbs, Trees and Shrubs.

  * = slightly tender
  † = lime hater
  ✿ = highly recommended

The illustration numbers are in **bold type** and the page numbers in light type preceded by p.

BUDDLEIA (LOGANIACEAE)

alternifolia ❋ Summer　　　　　　　　T.
Small tree up to 20 ft with pendulous branchlets. *Fl.* strongly scented, mauve on branches of previous year. Best grown as a small standard tree with the branches heavily thinned out to show form. Prune after flowering. China. **1464**, p. 183.

colvilei ❋ Early Summer　　　　　　*Sh.,T.
Fl. deep red in large hanging clusters lighter at base. *L.* large slightly felted. Small tree or wall shrub up to 30 ft and rather tender as a young plant. Averse to pruning also. Himalayas. **1465**, p. 184.
　'Kewensis', form with deeper red *fl.*

davidii Butterfly Bush ❋ Summer–Mid Autumn Sh.
Tall shrub up to 10 ft with long racemes up to 2 ft of dark purple, white or bluish-purple *fl.* Should be pruned hard in spring taking out all old wood that has flowered. China.
Amongst best forms are:
　'Magnifica', *fl.* bluish-purple;
　✿ 'Royal Red', *fl.* deep reddish-purple, very strong colour, **1466**, p. 184;
　'Veitchiana', *fl.* deep lavender-purple;
　✿ 'White Bouquet', *fl.* white in enormous panicles each with yellow centre;
　'White Cloud', *fl.* white.

fallowiana ❋ Summer　　　　　　　Sh.
Small shrub 5 ft. Distinguished by silvery-grey foliage. *Fl.* pale lavender-blue in large panicles. China.
　'Alba', form with white *fl.*;
　✿ 'Lochinch', with deep lavender-blue *fl.* but several forms are grown under this name.

globosa Orange Ball Tree ❋ Late Spring　　Sh.
Tall deciduous shrub up to 8 ft. *Fl.* with clusters of small orange balls up to ¾ in. across. Prune in late summer after flowering. **1467**, p. 184.

× **weyeriana** ❋ Summer　　　　　　Sh.
A hybrid between *B. globosa* and *B. davidii. Fl.* in ball-shaped clusters, orange with tints of mauvish-pink. Usually less vigorous than either of its parents. **1468**, p. 184.

BUGLE see **Ajuga**, **954**, **955**, p. 120.

BUGLE, COMMON see **Ajuga reptans**, **955**, p. 120.

BUGLOSS see **Anchusa**, **235**, p. 30; **963**, p. 121.

BUGLOSS, VIPER'S see **Echium**, **292**, **293**, p. 37.

BUPHTHALMUM (COMPOSITAE)

salicifolium Ox-eye ❋ Summer　　　　P.
Fl. yellow, solitary. 1½ in. across. *L.* lance-shaped, smooth or slightly hairy. 1½–2 ft. Ordinary garden soil and full sun. Propagate by division in the spring. Austria. **1006**, p. 126.

BUPLEURUM (UMBELLIFERAE)

fruticosum ❋ Summer　　　　　　　Sh.
Shrub up to 5 ft usually less with dark shiny blue-green *l.* and pale lemon-yellow *fl.* in large umbels. Useful plant for windswept position. S. Europe. **1469**, p. 184.

BURNET see **Sanguisorba canadensis**, **1364**, p. 171.

BURNING BUSH see **Dictamnus albus**, **1111**, p. 139; and **Kochia scoparia** 'Trichophylla', **314**, p. 40.

BUSH ANEMONE see **Carpenteria californica**, **1495**, p. 187.

BUSY LIZZIE see **Impatiens**, **311**, p. 39; **552**, p. 69.

BUTCHER'S BROOM see **Ruscus**, **1890**, p. 237.

BUTOMUS (BUTOMACEAE) Flowering Rush

umbellatus ❋ Summer　　　　　　HAq.
Fl. rose-pink, 1 in. across. *L.* sword-like, bronze-purple when young, becoming green. 2–4 ft. Plant in spring in water 2–4 in. deep in a sunny position. Propagate by division in spring. N. Asia, Europe, Britain. **1007**, p. 126.

BUTTERFLY BUSH see **Buddleia davidii**, **1466**, p. 184.

BUXUS (BUXACEAE) Box

sempervirens　　　　　　　　　Sh,T.
Medium-sized shrub or small tree up to 15 ft. Usually used for hedges or for topiary work. Wind resistant, making a useful evergreen screen. Numerous varieties have been distinguished with yellow markings on the *l.* Europe, N. Africa, W. Asia, probably native in England. **1470**, p. 184.

C

CABBAGE TREE, NEW ZEALAND see **Cordyline australis**, **1522**, p. 191.

CACTI see **Cephalocereus**, **443**, p. 56; **Chamaecereus**, **446**, p. 56; **Coryphantha**, **482**, p. 61; **Echinocactus**, **520**, **521**, pp. 65, 66; **Epiphyllum**, **523**, **524**, p. 66; × **Heliaporus**, **547**, p. 69; **Notocactus**, **566**, p. 71; **Opuntia**, **583**, p. 73; **Rebutia**, **633**, **634**, p. 80; **Rhipsalidopsis**, **635**, p. 80; **Schlumbergera**, **644**, p. 81; **Trichocereus**, **654**, p. 82; **Zygocactus**, **656**, p. 82.

CACTUS, CHRISTMAS see **Zygocactus truncatus**, **656**, p. 82.

CACTUS, EASTER see **Rhipsalidopsis rosea**, **635**, p. 80 and **Schlumbergera gaertneri**, **644**, p. 81.

CACTUS, OLD MAN see **Cephalocereus senilis**, **443**, p. 56.

CACTUS, PEANUT see **Chamaecereus silvestrii**, **466**, p. 56.

CACTUS, WHITSUN see **Schlumbergera gaertneri**, **644**, p. 81.

CAESALPINIA (LEGUMINOSAE)

japonica ❋ Early Summer　　　　* Sh. or T.
Tall loose growing shrub or small tree best grown on a wall in most areas. Notable for prominent spines and bright yellowish-green foliage. Doubly pinnate with twice divided leaflets. *Fl.* 20–30 in a raceme, bright yellow marked with scarlet in centre. China, Japan. **1471**, p. 184.

CALADIUM (ARACEAE)

candidum ❧　　　　　　　　　　GP.
Tuberous plants up to 2 ft high. *Fl.* rarely seen. *L.* heart-shaped, nearly white in *candidum*, but red and orange in other sp. and hybrids. A rich soil is needed with warm, damp conditions, when plants are growing. When *l.* are fully expanded cooler conditions are tolerated and the plants can be used as room ornaments. Winter temp. when tubers are resting 55°F. Tubers should not then be either too wet or too dry, otherwise they rot. When growth begins, temp. of 65°F. or 70°F. required. Propagate

by division of tubers. Sp. from S. America. **437**, p. 55.

CALAMINTHA (LABIATAE)

nepetoides ❋ Summer　　　　　　　P.
Fl. lavender and white. *L.* nepeta-like, slightly aromatic. 12–19 in. Plant 1½–3 in ordinary garden soil and partial shade. Propagate by cuttings or division in the spring. S. Europe. **1008**, p. 126.

CALAMONDIN ORANGE see **Citrus mitis**, **470**, p. 59.

CALANDRINIA (PORTULACACEAE)

umbellata Rock Purslane ❋ Summer　　HHA.
Fl. bright magenta-crimson. *L.* long, narrow, hairy. 6 in. Perennial, but best treated as an annual and sown in the open, 4–5, in light soil and a sunny position. Peru.
　'Amaranth', a good variety, vivid crimson-purple, **246**, p. 31.

CALCEOLARIA (SCROPHULARIACEAE)

darwinii ❋ Summer　　　　　　　†RP.
2–3 in. One of the most exciting and certainly one of the oddest among all the rock plants. *Fl.* solitary or occasionally two-flowered, deep orange-yellow shaped like an open pouch with a broad stripe of white across *fl.* near the base and with some spotting of deep chestnut-red, 1–1¼ in. across. *L.* mostly prostrate, oblong. Alpine house or raised bed in leafmould, peat and sand. Should not be allowed to dry out in summer. Hardy but best with some protection against winter wet. S. America, Patagonia. **22**, p. 3.

integrifolia ❋ Midsummer–Mid Autumn　Sh.
Valuable half-hardy shrub or hardy in warm areas. *Fl.* yellow in clusters, small, pouch shaped, valuable for late summer effect. Easily propagated and retained in cool greenhouse by cuttings taken in late summer. Chile.
　var. *angustifolia, l.* lance-shaped, **1472**, p. 184.

× **multiflora** ❋ Midsummer–Mid Autumn HHA. or GP.
The large multi-coloured calceolarias are hybrids derived principally from *C. crenatiflora* and *C. purpurea*, neither of which are in general cultivation

nowadays. The *multiflora* strain has *C. integrifolia* added to the large flowered hybrids. Seeds are sown in 6 in a cool shady place and the seedlings are kept cool and shaded until 11. They are progressively potted on as they increase in size and are generally flowered in 6 or 7 in. pots. They are brought into the greenhouse before there is a risk of frost and kept at a temp. around 45–50°F. When the sun starts to be powerful towards the end of 2, light shading is necessary to prevent scorching.

'Grandiflora', **438**, p. 55;
'Nana', **247**, p. 31; **439**, p. 55.

CALENDULA (COMPOSITAE)

officinalis Pot Marigold ❋ Summer   HA.
Fl. orange-yellow. *L.* lance-shaped, thick texture. 1–2 ft. Sow in a sunny bed from 3–5, or 9, where they are to *fl.* S. Europe.
There are a large number of striking hybrids including:
'Art Shades', 1½–2 ft, many shades of cream to orange with brown centres;
'Geisha Girl', 2 ft, deep glowing orange, incurved, double, **248**, p. 31;
'Lemon Queen', 1½–2 ft, clear lemon-yellow, **249**, p. 32;
'Orange King Improved', 1½–2 ft, deep orange, double, **250**, p. 32;
'Radio', 1½–2 ft, orange, quilled double.

CALICO BUSH see **Kalmia latifolia**, **1665**, **1666**, p. 209.

CALICO PLANT see **Aristolochia elegans**, **410**, p. 52.

CALIFORNIAN FIRE-CRACKER see **Brodiaea ida-maia**, **677**, p. 85.

CALIFORNIAN LILAC see **Ceanothus**, **1499–1504**, p. 188.

CALIFORNIAN POPPY see **Eschscholzia californica**, **294**, p. 37.

CALIFORNIAN POPPY BUSH see **Dendromecon rigidum**, **1560**, p. 195.

CALLIOPSIS see **Coreopsis**

CALLISTEMON (MYRTACEAE)

salignus ❋ Summer   *Sh.,T.
Evergreen shrub or small tree growing up to 40 ft. but often less in cultivation. The most conspicuous parts of the *fl.* are the bright yellow stamens which in other sp. may be shades of pink, red, crimson, lilac or yellow. In cold areas should be grown in a cold greenhouse. Australia. **1473**, p. 184.

CALLISTEPHUS (COMPOSITAE) China Aster

chinensis ❋ Summer   HHA.
Fl. dark purple in the sp. but the hybrids have been developed to include a wider range from mauve, blue through shades of red and pink to white. *L.* about 3½ in. long, coarsely toothed, wedge-shaped at base. 9 in.–2 ft. Sow in a cool greenhouse 3–4 and plant out in mid-5, or in sheltered gardens sow in the open in late 4 or early 5. A loamy soil in sun or light shade is best. Decorative as pot plants. China, Japan.
There are numerous varieties in a diversity of form, tall, dwarf, single, double and pompon, including:
'Bouquet Powder Puffs', 2 ft, in a wide range of mixed colours, double, **251**, p. 32;
'Chater's Erfurt', 9 in., deep rose, chrysanthemum-flowered, **252**, p. 32;
'Pompon', 1½ ft, mixed or named colours and bicolours as 'Pompon Benary', crimson and white, **253**, p. 32;
'Princess', 2½ ft, various colours, double blooms with quilled centres;
Single, 2 ft, various colours, **254**, p. 32.

CALLUNA (ERICACEAE)

vulgaris, syn. **Erica vulgaris** Heather, Ling
❋ Midsummer–Mid Autumn   †Sh.
Common heather of English moorlands, **1474**, p. 185.
Among some of the best varieties are:
'Alba Plena' Double white, rather dwarf up to 1 ft only, **1475**, p. 185;
'Hammondii Aurea' Taller white with yellow foliage in young growth. **1476**, p. 185;
✿ 'H. E. Beale' One of the most effective of all garden plants. Long spikes of double pale lilac-purple *fl.* 9–10. Spreading freely and very vigorous. **1477**, p. 185;
✿ 'Peter Sparkes' Newer variety *fl.* double pale purplish-pink, vigorous and probably the equal of 'H. E. Beale' in fact some think slightly superior and with slightly deeper colour. **1478**, p. 185.

CALOCHORTUS (LILIACEAE) Mariposa Lily, Globe Tulip

uniflorus ❋ Late Spring–Early Summer   *Bb
Fl. pale lilac-pink, generally darker outside, cup-shaped with a purple spot at base of each petal. 1–1½ ft. Best in alpine house or bulb frame and needing good summer ripening. One of the easier sp. in a genus of very beautiful bulbs, which are regarded as difficult to grow satisfactorily away from their native habitat but this one has been grown satisfactorily in the open in warm situations. California. **679**, p. 85.

CALTHA (RANUNCULACEAE)

palustris Marsh Marigold ❋ Spring   P.
Fl. golden-yellow, borne in profusion on branching stems. *L.* heart-shaped to almost round, 2–3 in. across. 1 ft. An attractive bog plant for the waterside in a sunny position. Propagate by division in spring or immediately after flowering. Europe, N. America, Arctic.
'Alba', a single, white form;
'Flore Pleno', double golden-yellow, **1009**, p. 127.

CALYCANTHUS PRAECOX see **Chimonanthus praecox**

CAMASS, COMMON see **Camassia quamash**, **681**, p. 86.

CAMASSIA (LILIACEAE)

cusickii ❋ Summer   Bb
Fl. pale lilac-blue, star-shaped up to 1½ in. across in long spike. 1½–2 ft. *L.* strap-shaped, broad; bulb large. Best in full sun. W.N. America. **680**, p. 85

esculenta see **C. quamash**

quamash Common Camass ❋ Summer   Bb
Fl. bright violet-blue or mauve, but very variable in colour, star-shaped, 1–2 in. across in spikes of 6–12 *fl.* on 2–3 ft stems. White and double forms are also known. Sunny position near front of border, often a vigorous grower which increases freely. Often listed as *C. esculenta*, a name which must be disregarded as a source of confusion. W. N. America. **681**, p. 86.

CAMELLIA (THEACEAE)

hybrids see under **C. reticulata**

japonica ❋ Late Winter–Mid Spring   †Sh.
Evergreen shrub or small tree up to 30 ft when old, one of the most valuable of all garden shrubs. Quite hardy but flowering early 2–4 so open *fl.* tend to be destroyed by frost. Also good for growing in a cool greenhouse especially the varieties with very large *fl.* or double *fl.* Semi-shade or full sun. Not necessary to plant against a north wall as used to be thought but hot dry situation is unsuitable.
Amongst finest varieties are:

✿ 'Adolphe Audusson', semi-double deep red with prominent yellow stamens in centre. Large up to 5 in. across. Vigorous and flowering for a long season. **1479**, p. 185;
'Alba Simplex', single white with large boss yellow stamens in centre, delightful plant and very resistant to weather. **1480**, p. 185;
'Althaeaflora', also known as 'Childsii', 'Rosette' or 'Blackburniana'. Semi-double rather like small paeony. Bright scarlet-red free flowering an old but still one of the best varieties. **1481**, p. 186.
'Blackburniana' see 'Althaeaflora'.
'Chandleri Elegans' see 'Elegans';
'Childsii' see 'Althaeaflora';
'Compton's Brow White' see 'Gauntlettii';
'Donckelarii', large semi-double crimson-red frequently marbled with white. Vigorous grower;
'Drama Girl', semi-double deep pink very large up to 8 in. across. One of the newer American varieties, excellent for cool greenhouse but not yet thoroughly tested outside. **1482**, p. 186;
✿ 'Elegans', often known as 'Chandleri Elegans'. Large paeony centred, pink *fl.* of perfect form up to 5 in. across. Hardy but excellent as cool greenhouse plant where *fl.* are protected;
'Gauntlettii', also known as 'Sode-gakushi'. Large white, semi-double with conspicuous golden stamens. A very beautiful variety but rather easily damaged by weather and so best in cool greenhouse. Also known as 'Lotus', 'Compton's Brow White' and 'Mrs Sander' but distinct from 'Alba Grandiflora';
'Gloire de Nantes', large semi-double, rose-pink, flowering early. One of the most reliable varieties;
'Jupiter', large single deep pink or geranium lake prominent boss of yellow stamens in centre. Vigorous. **1483**, p. 186;
'Lady Clare', large semi-double pink *fl.* showing few golden stamens in centre. Loose growing shrub with slightly pendulous branches rarely becoming large tree-like. **1484**, p. 186;
'Lotus' see 'Gauntlettii';
'Magnoliaeflora', semi-double shell pink waxy pointed petals. Medium size;
'Mathotiana', large formal double, crimson, again best as cool greenhouse plant;
'Mrs D. W. Davis', very large white or very pale blush pink *fl.* with centre of petaloids and

yellow stamens. Up to 9 in. across. Petals heavy waxy. Probably best in a cool greenhouse. **1485**, p. 186;

'Mrs Sander' see 'Gauntlettii';

'Rosette' see 'Althaeaflora';

'Sieboldii' see 'Tricolor';

'Sode-gakushi' see 'Gauntlettii';

'Tricolor', often known as 'Sieboldii'. Semi-double blush pink, flaked or streaked with deeper red. **1486**, p. 186.

reticulata *Sh.

Probably the finest of all camellias belong to this sp. Usually grown as cool greenhouse shrub but hardy enough in warm areas especially against a wall.

☆ 'Captain Rawes', *fl.* semi-double up to 8 in. across. This semi-double garden form was the first sent from China before wild single type was known. One of the most magnificent of all flowering shrubs. When old makes tree up to 20 ft, spreading. China. **1487**, p. 186;

'Mary Williams', *fl.* semi-double, deep pink with prominent central boss of golden stamens. Nearer single than 'Captain Rawes' and close to wild type of which it is a selected form. **1488**, p. 186.

hybrids

'Cornish Snow', *C. cuspidata × C. saluenensis. Fl.* white small up to 2 in. across single with prominent boss of golden stamens in centre, makes a rather loose growing shrub up to 5 ft. **1490**, p. 187;

'Leonard Messel', *C. reticulata × C. japonica.* Pale pink heavily veined semi-double large *fl.* up to 5 in. across. Hardy in sheltered position and one of the most valuable early flowering plants recently introduced, very free flowering. Also excellent for cool greenhouse, **1489**, p. 187.

williamsii ❋ Winter–Spring Sh.

One of the most valuable groups of garden plants. Very free flowering over long period. Hybrids raised originally at Caerhayes Castle in Cornwall by late Mr J. C. Williams between *saluenensis* and *japonica.* All *williamsii* varieties have advantage of dropping dead *fl.* which are retained by *C. japonica* varieties. Among finest are:

☆ 'Donation', semi-double large pink *fl.* heavily veined with deeper colouring up to 4 in. across. Very free flowering. **1491**, p. 187;

'Inspiration', *fl.* semi-double pink heavily veined. Better as cool greenhouse plant than outside. Most wonderful specimen in temperate house at Savill Gardens, Windsor Great Park, up to 15 ft. **1492**, p. 187;

☆ 'J. C. Williams', *fl.* single very pale blush pink large boss golden stamens and slightly wavy outline. The original plant in this group. With *fl.* like those of a larger but pale Dog Rose. **1493**, p. 187;

'St Ewe', *fl.* slightly cup-shaped deeper pink than 'J. C. Williams' up to 3½ in. across. **1494**, p. 187.

CAMPANULA (CAMPANULACEAE) Bellflower

A large genus ranging from dwarf alpines growing in clefts of alpine rocks to large herbaceous plants. It contains many valuable plants for the rock garden and alpine house.

× **burghaltii** ❋ Summer P.

Fl. satiny grey-blue, large pendant. *L.* dainty, pointed. 2 ft. Any good garden soil in sun or partial shade. Propagate by division or by soft wood cutting, both in 3, or by seed sown in pans of well-drained soil in 6–7 and stood in a cold frame. Of garden origin. **1010**, p. 127.

carpatica ❋ Summer RP.

Fl. variable in colour, white, blue, mauve or lavender-blue; large open bowl-shaped, solitary or several to a stem of 6 in.–1 ft. A valuable and free flowering plant for open or semi-shade position in rock garden. Often forming large clumps. Some selected varieties have been named. E. Europe, Carpathian Mts. **23**, p. 3.

cochlearifolia, syn. **C. pusilla** Fairies Thimbles

❋ Summer RP.

The commonest campanula in the Alps. *F.* bell-shaped, usually single on short wiry stems, very dainty, blue, mauve or white. 2–4 in. In the alps usually a plant of the scree or rock cleft but will grow on the rock garden without scree as long as drainage is good.

'Alba', the white form, **24**, p. 3.

garganica ❋ Summer RP.

Fl. open bell-shaped, deep mauve but paler at base, very numerous. 5–6 in. Stems trailing and quickly forming large mats of small ivy-shaped *l.* In fact, can be too invasive for the small rock garden. It is lovely growing down an open stone wall. Variable including a white variety. S. Italy. **25**, p. 4.

glomerata ❋ Summer P.

Fl. rich violet, funnel-shaped, borne in clusters of erect stems 1–2 ft high. *L.* narrow, 1½–3 in. long, hairy. Any ordinary garden soil that does not dry out excessively. Propagate by division in early spring. Europe including Britain.

Good forms are:

'Alba', white;

'Dahurica', rich violet;

'Superba', deep violet-blue, **1011**, p. 127.

isophylla ❋ Summer GP.

Plant with trailing or pendant stems. *Fl.* cup-shaped, violet-blue, 1½ in. across. *L.* broadly ovate, about 1 in. long. Very nearly hardy, requiring only to be kept frost-free and rather dry in winter. Any good potting compost satisfactory, but drainage must be very good. Propagate by seeds or by cuttings taken in spring. Italy. **440**, p. 55.

'Alba', white;

'Mayi', china-blue.

lactiflora Milky Bellflower ❋ Summer P.

Fl. white to milky blue, single, 1½ in. across. *L.* narrow, sharply toothed. Prefers full sun but will *fl.* in partial shade. 5–6 ft. Requires a deep, moist, fertile soil. Propagate by division of the thick, fleshy roots in spring or by cuttings inserted in sandy soil in the spring. Caucasus.

Good varieties include:

'Alba', pure white, 4 ft;

'Loddon Anna', pale mushroom pink, 4–5 ft, **1012**, p. 127.

latifolia Great Bellflower ❋ Summer P.

Fl. bluish-purple, hairy within, pendant. *L.* heart-shaped up to 6 in. long, upper lanceolate, slender-pointed. 4–5 ft. Cultivation and propagation as for *C. lactiflora.* Europe to Kashmir, including Britain.

Good varieties include:

'Alba', white, 4 ft, **1013**, p. 127;

'Brantwood', violet-purple, 4 ft.

medium Canterbury Bell ❋ Summer HB.

Fl. white and shades of pink, blue, mauve, single, double cup and saucer and hose in hose as in *C.m.* 'Calycanthema'. 1½–3 ft. Sow in the open in 5–6 and transplant to flowering position in early autumn. S. Europe.

'Calycanthema', 2½ ft, white, rose and various shades of blue; a hose in hose form, **255**, p. 32;

'Dwarf Bedding Mixed', 1½ ft, single, various shades, pyramidal habit.

persicifolia Peach-leaved Bellflower ❋ Summer P.

Fl. blue, single 1 in. across. *L.* narrow, peach-like, dark green. 1–3 ft. A good border plant for sun or partial shade. Increase by division in spring or basal cuttings inserted in sandy soil in spring or early autumn. Europe including Britain.

Good varieties include:

'Blue Belle', rich blue, single, **1014**, p. 127;

'Snowdrift', white, single;

'Telham Beauty', light blue, with large single *fl.*, an old favourite, **1015**, p. 127;

'Wirral Belle', rich blue, double.

portenschlagiana ❋ Summer RP.

Fl. upright, open bell-shaped or rather starry, light bluish-mauve, ½–¾ in. across but very abundantly produced. 2–4 in. Quickly forms large clumps or

mats and may be too invasive for small rock gardens, but valuable as a late summer flowering coverer of large areas. Good also hanging down over open stone wall in full sun or semi-shade. S. Europe. **26**, p. 4.

pusilla see **C. cochlearifolia**

zoysii ❋ Summer *RP.

A very choice plant with blue-mauve flask-shaped *fl.* constricted below the mouth and slightly puckered, about 1 in. long and carried usually horizontally on 1 in. stems. *L.* small, obovate or linear. Rhizomes very slender, almost hair-like. Alpine house or fine scree, where it must not be allowed to dry out in growing season. Needs protection against slugs. In winter it appears to die away below ground level. Grows in clefts of rock in N. Italian and Karawan-ken alps. **27**, p. 4.

CAMPION see **Lychnis, 335**, p. 42; **1249-1253**, p. 157.

CAMPION, ROSE see **Lychnis coronaria, 1250**, p. 157.

CAMPSIS (BIGNONIACEAE) Trumpet Creeper

Genus is sometimes placed in Tecoma or Bignonia. All Campsis may be pruned hard in early spring down to ground and will make long shoots.

chinensis see **C. grandiflora**

grandiflora, syn. **chinensis** ❋ Late Summer Cl. Sh.

Deciduous climber up to 30 ft with funnel-shaped orange-red *fl.* slightly smaller and less red than those of *C. × tagliabuana* 'Madame Galen' below.

radicans, syn. **Tecoma radicans**

❋ Late Summer Cl. Sh.

Vigorous climber, self-clinging with small rootlets. *Fl.* in terminal clusters tubular with smaller spreading lobes. S.E. USA.

× **tagliabuana** ❋ Late Summer Cl. Sh.

Vigorous deciduous climber up to 25 ft. *Fl.* funnel-shaped with spreading lobes up to 4 in. long, orange-scarlet in clusters. *L.* pinnate with ovate leaflets, toothed. Valuable for its late flowering but only *fl.* well after warm summer and has had good ripening. Magnificent in S. France and other hot climates. A hybrid between *C. grandiflora × C. radicans.* **1958**, p. 245.

'Madame Galen', is the best form.

Abbreviations and Symbols used in the text.

The following abbreviations may sometimes be used in conjunction as HA. indicating Hardy annual or GBb indicating Greenhouse bulb.

A. = Annual	P. = Perennial
Aq. = Aquatic	R. = Rock or
B. = Biennial	Alpine plant
Bb = Bulb	Sh. = Shrub
C. = Corm	Sp., sp. = Species
Cl. = Climber	Syn. = Synonym
Co. = Conifer	T. = Tree
Fl., fl. = Flower(s)	Tu. = Tuber
G. = Greenhouse or	var. = variety
house plant	× = Hybrid or
H. = Hardy	hybrid parents
HH. = Half-hardy	❋ = Flowering time
L., l. = Leaf, leaves	◑ = Foliage plant
Mt(s) = Mount,	
mountain(s)	

The following have been used also in the descriptions of Alpines, Bulbs, Trees and Shrubs.

* = slightly tender

† = lime hater

☆ = highly recommended

The illustration numbers are in **bold type** and the page numbers in light type preceded by p.

CANADIAN HEMLOCK see **Tsuga canadensis, 2048**, p. 256.

CANADIAN MAPLE, SCARLET see **Acer rubrum, 1440**, p. 180.

CANDYTUFT see **Iberis, 92**, p. 12; **310**, p. 39; **1182**, p. 148.

CANNA (CANNACEAE)

hortensis ❀ Summer　　　　　　　　GP.
Complex hybrids between several sp. from the southern USA and S. and Central America. The large *fl.* show the influence of *C. flaccida*, the purple leaves can come from several sp., but probably from *C. warscewczii*. The plants are used for summer bedding. The rhizomes are over-wintered under cover in soil that is just kept moist. They may be started in heat with the temp. around 60°F., before being planted out. They grow easily from seed. They appreciate rich soil and ample moisture when growing. **441**, p. 56.

CANTERBURY BELL see **Campanula medium, 255**, p. 32.

CAPE COWSLIP see **Lachenalia, 554**, p. 70.

CAPE FIGWORT see **Phygelius capensis, 1736**, p. 217.

CAPE GOOSEBERRY see **Physalis franchetii, 1318**, p. 165.

CAPE PONDWEED see **Aponogeton distachyus, 972**, p. 122.

CAPE PRIMROSE see **Streptocarpus, 652**, p. 82.

CAPSICUM (SOLANACEAE) Red Pepper

annuum, syn. **C. frutescens**　　　　　HHA.
Fl. greenish-white, insignificant. Fruit of varying shape, slender, pointed, bright green ripening to scarlet; round, green, becoming shining black, others large, with basal depressions and wrinkled surface. 2 ft. A useful pot plant for winter decoration, or may be bedded out in a warm border in 6. Shrubs but usually grown as annuals from seed. Sow in a warm greenhouse in 2 or 3. Origin uncertain. **256**, p. 32.

frutescens see **C. annuum**

CARDINAL FLOWER see **Lobelia fulgens, 1243**, p. 156.

CARDIOCRINUM (LILIACEAE)

✿ **giganteum**, syn. **Lilium giganteum** Giant Himalayan Lily ❀ Summer　　　　　Bb
Stem up to 8 ft with numerous drooping large lily-like, white glistening, trumpet *fl.* red at the base, 6 in. long; *l.* heart-shaped, both basal and up stem. A most magnificent plant for a damp position in open woodland. The bulbs usually require more than one year to settle down and increase in size before flowering and it takes five to seven years from seed to flowering size. Benefits from generous feeding. After flowering main bulb dies but usually leaves behind offsets which can be lifted and grown on to flowering size. Differs from true lilies in the heart-shaped instead of linear *l.*, in having bulbs with only a few instead of many scales and in having prominently toothed seed capsules. These are nearly as decorative as the *fl.* Himalayas from Nepal–N.E. Burma.
　　Var. *yunnanense*, slightly smaller and with slight tinge of green in *fl.* W. China, N.W. Burma. **682**, p. 86.

CARNATION see **Dianthus, 49-52**, p. 7; **283-286**, p. 36; **499-510**, p. 63, 64; **1092-1107**, p. 137-139.

CARPENTERIA (SAXIFRAGACEAE)

californica Bush Anemone ❀ Summer　　*Sh.
Fl. white like a small rose with golden anthers at a boss in centre. Usually grown as a wall shrub but makes small tree in warmest areas. Tends to look rather miserable after bad weather but usually recovers quickly. Should be planted in sunny position as possible. California, USA. **1495**, p. 187.

CARYOPTERIS (VERBENACEAE)

× **clandonensis** ❀ Late Summer　　　　Sh.
A hybrid between *C. incana* × *C. mongholica* but appreciably better as a garden plant than either parent. *Fl.* mauve, in clusters. Valuable as late flowering shrub up to 3 ft. Should be pruned hard back each spring, to base of young growth. **1496**, p. 187.
Among named varieties are:
　‘Ferndown’, *Fl.* deep mauve slightly larger in *fl.* than type. **1497**, p. 188;
　‘Heavenly Blue’, *fl.* slightly deeper than type and more upright growing;
　‘Kewensis’, rather similar with deep mauve *fl.*

CASSIOPE (ERICACEAE)　　　　　　　　†
Mat forming sub-shrubby plants with reduced narrow scale-like *l.* and white bell-like *fl.* All need a peaty acid soil and must not be allowed to dry out in summer. They look well on peat wall garden and flower better in an open than in a semi-shady position. Propagate by cuttings in summer.

fastigiata ❀ Spring　　　　　　　　RSh.
6 in.–1 ft. Branches upright with solitary white hanging bell-like *fl.* at top, stem up to 1 ft usually less, *fl.* about ⅓ in. long. Himalayas.
　‘Edinburgh’, is probably a cross between this and *C. wardii* and has several *fl.* in cluster at top of stem, **28**, p. 4.

lycopodioides ❀ Spring　　　　　　RSh.
2–3 in. Large prostrate mats of small branches with scale-like *l.* and small white bell-shaped *fl.* with chestnut brown sepals at base. A well grown specimen may be covered with these. N. America and N.E. Asia including Japan. **29**, p. 4.

mertensiana ❀ Spring　　　　　　　RSh.
6–10 in. *Fl.* slightly larger than preceding sp. A mountain plant generally on N. facing rock in semi-shade. N.W. American States.

selaginoides ❀ Spring　　　　　　RSh.
2–3 in. Prostrate mats with some semi-erect branches. Himalayas, W. China.

wardii ❀ Spring　　　　　　　　　*RSh.
6 in.–1 ft. Upright branches and white bell-like *fl.* comparatively large for the genus, ¼–⅓ in. long. Best as alpine house plant or in a N. facing frame. Probably the finest but the most difficult sp. of the genus. S.E. Tibet.

CASTOR OIL PLANT see **Ricinus communis, 366, 367**, p. 46.

CATALPA (BIGNONIACEAE)

bignonioides Indian Bean Tree ❀ Summer　T.
Small or medium sized tree with large *l.* up to 8 or 9 in. heart-shaped. *Fl.* white with yellow centre, rather like small Foxgloves although more densely collected together. Valuable for its late-flowering also rather late leafing. E. USA. **1498**, p. 188.
　‘Aurea’, valuable and conspicuous throughout season for its greenish-yellow *l.*

CATANANCHE (COMPOSITAE)

coerulea ❀ Summer　　　　　　　　P.
Fl. deep mauve or white, semi-double, with paper-

like bracts, *L.* narrow, hairy. 2–3 ft. Plant in spring in a sunny position and in light, well-drained soil. Propagate by root cuttings in the autumn, or by seed sown in 4 in a cool house or frame. S. Europe. **1016**, p. 127.

CATCHFLY see **Lychnis viscaria, 1253**, p. 157.

CATMINT see **Nepeta, 1278**, p. 160.

CATTLEYA (ORCHIDACEAE)
❀ Spring–Autumn　　　　　　　　　GP.
A spectacular genus of Orchids, most sp. used in hybridising coming from Brazil.
The labiate Cattleyas, which include the most brilliant flowered types, require a winter temp. of 55°–60°F., which can rise to 80°F. with sun heat during the spring and summer. During the growing period a moist, buoyant atmosphere should be maintained and light shading is necessary during the summer. Many of the sp. hybridise in the wild. Propagation is by removing back-bulbs and encouraging them to develop their dormant buds with heat and moisture.
　‘Catherine Subod’ is a typical labiate hybrid, **442**, p. 56.

CAUCASIAN WHORTLEBERRY see **Vaccinium arctostaphylos**

CAUTLEYA (ZINGIBERACEAE)

robusta ❀ Summer　　　　　　　　P.
Fl. yellow, on erect stem. *L.* large, canna-like. 3–4 ft. Plant in moist soil and partial shade. Propagate by division in spring or by seed. Himalayas. **1017**, p. 128.

CEANOTHUS (RHAMNACEAE)
Sometimes known as Californian Lilacs. *Fl.* blue or deep mauve. Some tender and may be short lived; in most parts of Britain grown as wall shrub. Should be pruned after flowering by cutting off dead *fl.* spikes. Mostly evergreen except where mentioned otherwise.

arboreus ❀ Spring　　　　　　　Sh,T.
One of the most tender, small trees or large shrubs.

Abbreviations and Symbols used in the text.
The following abbreviations may sometimes be used in conjunction as HA. indicating Hardy annual or GBb indicating Greenhouse bulb.

A. = Annual	P. = Perennial
Aq. = Aquatic	R. = Rock or
B. = Biennial	Alpine plant
Bb = Bulb	Sh. = Shrub
C. = Corm	Sp., sp. = Species
Cl. = Climber	Syn. = Synonym
Co. = Conifer	T. = Tree
Fl., fl. = Flower(s)	Tu. = Tuber
G. = Greenhouse or	var. = variety
house plant	× = Hybrid or
H. = Hardy	hybrid parents
HH. = Half-hardy	❀ = Flowering time
L., l. = Leaf, leaves	❦ = Foliage plant
Mt(s) = Mount,	
mountain(s)	

The following have been used also in the descriptions of Alpines, Bulbs, Trees and Shrubs.

　　* = slightly tender
　　† = lime hater
　　✿ = highly recommended

The illustration numbers are in **bold type** and the page numbers in light type preceded by p.

Fl. pale china blue or deep blue in large panicles. **1499**, p. 188.

'Trewithen Blue' is the best form for colour and hardier than type.

'Delight' ✳ Spring   Sh.
One of the most valuable hybrids. *Fl.* rich blue-mauve very free flowering excellent as a wall shrub in most areas. **1500**, p. 188.

delilianus see 'Gloire de Versailles'

'Dignity' ✳ Spring   Sh.
Rather close to 'Delight' but *fl.* paler and sometimes flowering also in autumn. **1501**, p. 188.

'Gloire de Versailles' ✳ Summer   Sh.
Fl. china-blue, mauve in late summer. Deciduous. Sometimes known as *delilianus*. Forms part of most valuable group of hybrids between *americanus* and *caeruleus*, another good form is 'Topaz' *fl.* deep blue-mauve. Should be pruned hard in spring before young growth appears. **1502**, p. 188.

✿ **impressus** ✳ Spring   Sh.
Fl. deep blue. One of the most valuable of all wall shrubs, very free flowering. *L.* small. Up to 15 ft on a wall. Also one of the more hardy sp. Sometimes considered a variety of *C. dentatus*.

'Puget Blue' is probably finest form, *fl.* slightly more blue than in type, **1503**, p. 188.

thyrsiflorus ✳ Early Summer   Sh.
One of the more hardy sp. *Fl.* bright blue-mauve. *L.* larger than in *impressus*. *Fl.* in globular clusters. **1504**, p. 188.

'Topaz' see 'Gloire de Versailles'.

CEDAR, ATLAS see **Cedrus atlantica**, **2003**, p. 251.

CEDAR, INCENSE see **Libocedrus decurrens**, **2024**, p. 253.

CEDAR, JAPANESE see **Cryptomeria**, **2011**, p. 252.

CEDAR OF LEBANON see **Cedrus libani**

CEDAR, RED see **Libocedrus decurrens**, **2024**, p. 253.

CEDAR, WESTERN RED see **Thuya plicata**, **2046**, **2047**, p. 256.

CEDAR, WHITE see **Thuya occidentalis**

CEDRUS (PINACEAE) Cedar
Evergreen, large trees usually distinguished by horizontal branching in old specimens. *L.* in clusters usually erect. Cones large, erect and rather barrel-shaped, scales falling apart when mature. Cedars, especially when mature, make some of the most majestic and decorative conifers, especially for growing at edge of a large lawn. All cedars are best transplanted into final position when young and under 4 ft but larger specimens, which have been transplanted regularly in the nursery, may be safely transplanted if care is taken to water them when dry during the next season and if necessary, to protect them from wind shake. There are three sp. usually grown of which *C. atlantica* and *C. libani* are closely related, possibly only geographical races of a single wide-spread and rather variable sp. They are tolerant of a wide range of soils and all are quite hardy but should only be planted where they are given ample space for development.

atlantica Atlas Cedar   Co.
Large tree up to 100 ft or more and as wide-spreading when mature. When young, pyramidal in growth. Distinguished from *C. libani* by the smaller cone, usually not more than 3 in. high by 2 in. wide and by the glaucous *l.* of forms most often grown.

var. *glauca*, with glaucous blue needles, the finest form and perhaps the finest cedar for gardens, Algeria, Morocco, Atlas Mts, **2003**, p. 251.

brevifolia see under **C. libani**

deodara Deodar   Co.
Large evergreen tree which may reach 150 ft in favourable places and grow into the tallest cedar. Distinguished by pendulous habit of leading shoot of young trees and branches. Needles up to 2 in. long, dark green, sharply pointed. Cones barrel-shaped and up to 5 in. long by 3½ in. across. Male and female young cones may be on separate trees but not always so. W. Himalayas, where it is widely distributed.

libani Cedar of Lebanon   Co.
Large and often majestic tree with a tendency to form several trunks from near ground level. Main branches in older trees horizontal. Needles up to 1¼ in. long, dark green or slightly glaucous, in erect clusters. Cones up to 4 in. long but usually less and smaller than those of *C. atlantica*. In young trees, leading shoot may droop near tip. Lebanon and Turkey in Cilician Taurus.

var. *brevifolia*, sometimes regarded as separate sp., is distinguished by shorter needles, smaller cones and less vigorous habit, slow-growing. Of less value horticulturally. Cyprus and W. Turkey in mts.

CELANDINE POPPY see **Stylophorum diphyllum**, **1392**, p. 174.

CELASTRUS (CELASTRACEAE)

orbiculatus, syn. **C. articulatus** ✳ Summer   Cl.
Very vigorous deciduous climber up to 40 ft. *Fl.* small, greenish-yellow. *L.* up to 5 in. long, obovate, slightly toothed with good yellowish autumn colour. Grown chiefly for its brilliant scarlet round seed capsules which contrast with yellow colouring of inside of seed capsule, very freely borne and making distinct effect. It is important to grow form with both sexes of *fl.* on same plant. Fruit very showy and persist through much of winter. May be pruned back hard. Twiner suitable for growing over old trees. S.E. Asia. **1959**, p. 245.

CELMISIA (COMPOSITAE)   †
New Zealand mountain daisy-like plants with large white *fl.* heads and in most cases, silvery foliage. Intolerant of hot dry positions. They grow best on peaty acid soil but will tolerate some lime, and need some protection from winter wet, but when grown well, they are very handsome. Propagate by division or cuttings in summer.

coriacea ✳ Summer   RP.
Fl. heads single, up to 3 in. across with white ray florets and conspicuous yellow disc in centre. *L.* large, silvery, rather stiff, in large rosettes. 10–18 in. Very handsome both in *fl.* and foliage. New Zealand, S. Island. **30**, p. 4.

petiolata ✳ Summer   RP.
Close to *C. spectabilis* and less common in cultivation. Rosettes neat with dark green *l.* of which undersurface is covered with white hairs. *Fl.* heads large on long stems. 1 ft. New Zealand, S. Alps. **31**, p. 4.

spectabilis ✳ Summer   RP.
Rosettes up to 1 ft across and *fl.* among largest of the genus. *L.* very silvery, covered with short hairs, broad but with pointed tip. *Fl.* large white with yellow central disc as in *C. coriacea*. Up to 1½ ft. New Zealand. **32**, p. 4.

CELOSIA (AMARANTHACEAE)

argentea Cockscomb ✳ Summer   HHA.
Fl. heads in shades of glowing crimson, red, scarlet, orange and yellow. *L.* narrow to 2 in. long, almost stalkless. 1–3½ ft. Sow in 3 in warm greenhouse and grow on steadily, moving into larger pots as necessary. Decorative as pot plants or may be bedded out in mid-6. Tropical regions of Asia and Africa.

'Cristata', *C. cristata*, various coloured, crested *fl.* heads, 9 in.–3½ ft, **257**, p. 33;

'Plumosa', *C. plumosa*, mixed colours of *fl.* spikes, 1–2½ ft, **258**, p. 33.

cristata see **C. argentea** 'Cristata'

plumosa see **C. argentea** 'Plumosa'

CELSIA (SCROPHULARIACEAE)

acaulis ✳ Late Spring–Midsummer   RP., B.
A rosette plant with thick puckered *l.* and bright yellow mullein-like *fl.* about 1 in. across on short stem. Centre of *fl.* has boss of orange-red stamens. 4–5 in. Sunny position in scree or well drained soil. Good also as alpine house plant. Often difficult and short lived. Numerous hybrids have been raised between this and *Verbascum phoeniceum*. Greece. **33**, p. 5.

CENIA see **Cotula**

CENTAUREA (COMPOSITAE) Knapweed

cyanus Cornflower ✳ Summer   HA.
Fl. in shades of blue, mauve, crimson, rose-pink, also white. *L.* long, narrow, cottony. 1–3 ft. Sow in a sunny bed in 3–4, or in 9. Europe.
Named dwarf and tall varieties are in cultivation including:

'Blue Diadem', 2½ ft, new, large, double, deep blue;

'Jubilee Gem', 1 ft, compact, double, blue;

'Julep', 1½ ft, a good strain of mixed colours, **259**, p. 33;

'Polka Dot', 1–1½ ft, mixed colours.

dealbata ✳ Midsummer–Mid Autumn   P.
Fl. rosy-purple, buds thistle-like. *L.* pointed, coarsely toothed. 2 ft. Ordinary garden soil on the dry side and sunny bed. Propagate by division in spring or autumn. Caucasus.
Good varieties include:

Abbreviations and Symbols used in the text.

The following abbreviations may sometimes be used in conjunction as HA. indicating Hardy annual or GBb indicating Greenhouse bulb.

A. = Annual	P. = Perennial
Aq. = Aquatic	R. = Rock or
B. = Biennial	Alpine plant
Bb = Bulb	Sh. = Shrub
C. = Corm	Sp., sp. = Species
Cl. = Climber	Syn. = Synonym
Co. = Conifer	T. = Tree
Fl., fl. = Flower(s)	Tu. = Tuber
G. = Greenhouse or	var. = variety
house plant	× = Hybrid or
H. = Hardy	hybrid parents
HH. = Half-hardy	✳ = Flowering time
L., l. = Leaf, leaves	❦ = Foliage plant
Mt(s) = Mount,	
mountain(s)	

The following have been used also in the descriptions of Alpines, Bulbs, Trees and Shrubs.

* = slightly tender
† = lime hater
✿ = highly recommended

The illustration numbers are in **bold type** and the page numbers in light type preceded by p.

'John Coutts', bright pink with a yellow eye, **1018**, p. 128;

'Steenbergii', rosy-crimson, **1019**, p. 128.

montana Mountain Knapweed ❊ Early Summer P.
Fl. purple, cornflower-like. *L.* rough, oblong. 1½ ft.
Ordinary garden soil, in sun or partial shade. Of
spreading habit, particularly in rich soil which
should be avoided. Propagate by division in spring
or autumn. Europe.
Good varieties include:

'Alba', white;

'Parham', lavender-purple, 2 ft, **1020**, p. 128;

'Rubra', rosy-red.

moschata Sweet Sultan ❊ Summer   HA.
Fl. pinkish-purple, rose, yellow and white, fragrant.
L. bright green, lobed and toothed. 1½–2 ft. Sow
3–4 in a sunny bed. E. Mediterranean. **260**, p. 33.

CENTRANTHUS see **Kentranthus**

CEPHALOCEREUS (CACTACEAE)

senilis The Old Man Cactus   GP.
Fl. pink, nocturnal. Very rarely produced in
cultivation. Stem columnar, covered with grey hair-
like bristles, branched. Up to 40 ft. Gritty, open,
well-drained compost. Winter temp. 40°F. Keep
dry in late summer and winter, water freely in late
spring and early summer. Propagate by seed or
cuttings. **443**, p. 56.

CERATOSTIGMA (PLUMBAGINACEAE)

Often known as 'Plumbago' to which they are
closely allied.

plumbaginoides ❊ Late Summer   Sh.
Dwarf shrub up to 1 ft. *Fl.* very bright blue in
clusters on short stems. Spreading laterally freely.
Valuable for its bright colour, also for autumn
colour of foliage. Suitable for large rock garden or
front of shrub border. China. **1505**, p. 189.

willmottianum ❊ Summer   Sh.
Up to 3 ft, usually grown as a wall shrub except in
warmer areas. *Fl.* very bright blue, freely borne.
Foliage tinted red in autumn. One of the most
valuable late flowering shrubs. W. China. **1506**,
p. 189.

CERCIS (LEGUMINOSAE)

canadensis
North America Red Bud, and *C. occidentalis*,
Western Red Bud, from California are rather
similar to *C. siliquastrum* but appear to *fl.* better in
America than in England probably due to lack of
summer ripening of wood.

racemosa ❊ Mid Spring   T.
Fl. pink in drooping racemes. Not such free flowering tree as *siliquastrum* in most gardens. China.

siliquastrum Judas Tree ❊ Spring   T.
Small tree up to 20 ft. *Fl.* deep pink, pea-like, in
clusters on bare branches but in mild season
flowering with young *l.* and less conspicuous. *L.*
rounded with heart-shaped base and attractive
fresh green when young, later blue-green. Usually
making a rather spreading tree with horizontal
branching in old trees. Mediterranean areas. **1507**,
p. 189.

CERIMAN see **Monstera pertusa**

CESTRUM (SOLANACEAE)

Rambling shrubs, needing to be trained to a pillar,
but can be grown outdoors in favoured districts.
Minimum winter temp. 34°F. They require a good
loamy mixture, preferably slightly acid. Propagate
by cuttings of half-ripened shoots. Ample water
required during spring and summer, little in autumn
and winter.

aurantiacum ❊ Summer and Autumn   GSh.
Fl. small, bright orange in terminal and axillary
panicles up to 4 in. across. *L.* ovate about 3 in. long
and 1½ in. wide. The plant is sub-evergreen; old *l.*
persist until new ones have merged. Up to 8 ft high.
Guatemala. **444**, p. 56.

fasciculatum see **C. × newellii**

× newellii ❊ Summer   GSh.
Fl. crimson, 1 in. long in terminal clusters. *L.*
evergreen, oblong-lanceolate up to 5 in. long. The
plant is usually about 6–8 ft high and needs support.
A hybrid of unknown parentage raised by Mr Newell
in the 1920's. One of the parents is probably either
C. fasciculatum or *C. purpureum*. **445**, p. 56.

purpureum see **C. × newellii**

CHAENOMELES (ROSACEAE) Ornamental
Quince

Deciduous shrub or wall plants. Still better known
as Cydonia or as Japonica, all *Chaenomeles* should be
pruned hard in winter or early spring since they
fl. on old wood.

speciosa 'Rowallane Seedling' ❊ Spring   Sh.
Large scarlet-crimson, cup-shaped *fl.* freely produced. **1508**, p. 189.

× superba 'Knap Hill Scarlet' ❊ Spring   Sh.
Fl. bright orange-scarlet, very free flowering. **1509**,
p. 189.

CHAMAECEREUS (CACTACEAE)

silvestrii Peanut Cactus ❊ Early Summer   GP.
Fl. orange-scarlet. Stems cylindrical, prostrate,
spines soft. A monotypic genus. Compost gritty and
open. Winter temp. 40–50°F. Water moderately
3–5, fairly freely 5–7, less 7–9 and keep dry for
remainder of year. Propagate by detaching
branches, which root rapidly. Argentina. **446**, p. 56.

CHAMAECYPARIS (CUPRESSACEAE) False Cypress

Evergreen trees usually pyramidal or conical in
outline. *L.* small opposite scale-like. Male and
female cones borne on same tree, male small
yellow or red, female cones globose with hard
scales like small balls up to 1 in. across.

lawsoniana Lawson Cypress   Co.
The most widely grown sp., native of Oregon,
W. America where it reaches up to 200 ft but no
trees have been recorded in Britain nearly up to
that height. Among forms are some of the most
valuable evergreens for garden purposes and the
majority will stand some cutting:

'Allumii', narrow pyramidal with glaucous blue
foliage, one of the most valuable forms as
specimen or in groups and rarely growing very
wide at the base, **2004**, p. 251;

'Columnaris', also pyramidal, narrow, green and
comparatively slow growing, foliage bluish
glaucous on under surfaces, one of the best
for a narrow space, **2005**, p. 251;

'Erecta', bright green very upright fastigiate
form;

'Erecta Aurea', foliage bright yellow slow growing but erect;

'Fletcheri', slow growing, foliage glaucous
feathery ultimately up to 15 ft and so unsuitable for planting on rock gardens as
sometimes suggested;

'Fletcheri Nana', form of less rapid growth
probably originating from side growth cuttings
and slightly less erect, **2006**, p. 251;

'Green Hedger', see below 'Triomphe de
Boskoop';

'Lutea', foliage golden-yellow, **2007**, p. 251;

'Minima Aurea', syn. 'Minima Aurea Rogersii',
valuable dwarf pyramid with golden-yellow
foliage;

'Triomphe de Boskoop', tall glaucous blue form

fairly fast growing and standing trimming well,
2008, p. 251.
Some forms of *C. lawsoniana* have been used as
hedge plants, probably best is 'Green Hedger' with
dense erect branches and strong green foliage.

obtusa Hinoki   Co.
Large Japanese tree up to 100 ft in wild but slow
growing, bark reddish-brown shed in narrow strips.
L. small closely pressed to stem and in two sizes of
which lateral pair is larger. Sp. distinguished by the
white egg-shaped marking on the underneath of the
l. Many cultivars of this sp. used as dwarfs for rock
garden purposes and among the best of these are:

'Nana', very slow growing dark green mossy
foliage and horizontal tiered branching;

'Nana Variegata', similar but with golden
colouring in some of the *l.* thus producing
mixed effect, a very attractive dwarf growing
conifer, **2009**, p. 252;

'Tetragona Aurea', golden form of slow growing
tree up to 15 ft with feathery branches and
numerous side branches often radially dis-
posed, this is one of the most attractive of
the dwarf conifers and is slow growing, the
green form is now rare in cultivation, **2010**,
p. 252.

CHAMAEROPS (PALMACEAE)

excelsa see **Trachycarpus fortunei**

humilis   T.
Dwarf palm, tender in most areas but can be
grown successfully in southern districts. Usually not
more than 3 ft but occasionally up to 5 ft. *L.* fan-
shaped up to 18 in. across and very decorative.
Plant in as warm and sunny position as possible.
W. Mediterranean districts and N. African coast.
1510, p. 189.

CHAMOMILE, OX-EYE see **Anthemis tinctoria**, **968–970**, pp. 121–122.

CHECKERBERRY see **Gaultheria procumbens**,
1620, p. 203.

CHEIRANTHUS (CRUCIFERAE) Wallflower

allionii, syn. **Erysimum perofskianum** Siberian
Wallflower ❊ Spring   HB.
Fl. bright orange. *L.* up to 3 in. long, toothed.

1–3 ft. Sow 7–8 in the open ground where it is to *fl.* Botanically an *Erysimum* and believed to be a hybrid of garden origin.

There are now several varieties in cultivation, including:

'Apricot Delight', soft apricot, 15 in.;
'Golden Bedder', deep yellow, 15 in.;
'Lemon Delight', clear lemon-yellow, **261**, p. 33.

cheiri ✳ Mid Spring–Summer   HB., P or R.
Fl. vary considerably in colour, very fragrant. *L.* lance-shaped, entire. 9 in. For a sunny bed and a well-drained soil, preferably containing some lime. Many varieties of wallflower are treated as biennial and raised from seed sown in the open in 5–6 and pricked out to 1 ft apart when large enough to handle. Plant out in 10. Particularly good forms are propagated by half-ripe cuttings taken in 6 or 7 and inserted in sandy soil in a cold, shaded frame. Europe, naturalized in Britain. **262**, p. 33.
Good varieties include:
'Harpur Crewe', Mid Spring–Early Summer, golden-yellow, double, makes a small bush, **1021**, p. 128;
'Moonlight' (now *Erysimum alpinus* 'Moonlight'), Late Spring–Summer, pale yellow with brown buds, 1 ft, **1022**, p. 128;
'Rufus', Late Spring–Summer, coppery-red, 9 in., **1023**, p. 128;
'Wenlock Beauty', Spring, coppery-red, 1 ft, **34**, p. 5.

maritimus see **Malcolmia maritima**

CHELONE (SCROPHULARIACEAE) Turtlehead

barbatus see **Penstemon barbatus**

obliqua ✳ Summer   P.
Fl. rosy-purple in terminal clusters, 2 ft. *L.* deep green, broadly oblong, up to 8 in. long. Thrives in well-drained, light loam and in sun or partial shade. Propagate by division in the autumn or early spring, by cuttings taken in the spring and inserted in sandy soil in a cold frame or by seed sown in 3 in light sandy soil under glass. USA. **1024**, p. 128.

CHENILLE PLANT see **Acalypha hispida**, **401**, p. 51.

CHENOPODIUM (CHENOPODIACEAE) Goosefoot

amaranticolor ✳ Summer   HHA.
Fl. long red panicles. Usually grown for its decorative *l.*, triangular and marked purplish-red when young. 6–7 ft. Sow in a warm greenhouse 3 and plant out late 5 or 6. May be used as a substitute for spinach. S. France. **263**, p. 33.

CHERRY, BIRD see **Prunus padus**, **1758**, p. 220.

CHERRY, CORNELIAN see **Cornus mas**, **1528**, p. 191.

CHERRY, CUT-LEAVED see **Prunus incisa**, **1756**, p. 220.

CHERRY, FLOWERING see **Prunus**, **165**, p. 21; **752-1767**, pp. 219–221.

CHERRY, FUJI see **Prunus incisa**, **1756**, p. 220.

CHERRY, JAPANESE FLOWERING see **Prunus serrulata**, **1762-1764**, p. 221.

CHERRY, MANCHU see **Prunus tomentosa**

CHERRY, NANKING see **Prunus tomentosa**

CHERRY PIE see **Heliotropium**

CHERRY PLUM see **Prunus cerasifera**, **1754**, p. 220.

CHERRY, SPRING see **Prunus subhirtella**

CHESTNUT, COMMON HORSE see **Aesculus hippocastanum**

CHESTNUT, HORSE see **Aesculus**, **1441**, **1442**, p. 181.

CHESTNUT, INDIAN HORSE see **Aesculus indica**

CHESTNUT, PINK HORSE see **Aesculus × carnea**, **1441**, p. 181.

CHIASTOPHYLLUM OPPOSITIFOLIUM see **Cotyledon oppositifolia**

CHILEAN BELLFLOWER see **Nolana**, **354**, p. 45.

CHILEAN CROCUS see **Tecophilaea cyanocrocus**, **885**, p. 111.

CHILEAN FIRE BUSH see **Embothrium coccineum**, **1572**, **1573**, p. 197.

CHILEAN LANTERN TREE see **Crinodendron hookerianum**, **1545**, p. 194.

CHILEAN PINE see **Araucaria araucana**

CHILEAN POTATO TREE see **Solanum crispum**, **1993**, p. 250.

CHIMONANTHUS (CALYCANTHACEAE) Wintersweet

praecox, syn. **C. fragrans, Calycanthus praecox** ✳ Winter   Sh.
Fl. pale waxy-yellow with crimson-purple centre appearing on leafless branches. Shrub up to 5 ft usually spreading. Strongly scented, especially when pinched.
'Luteus', deeper yellow form less strongly scented, probably best against a wall but will grow in full exposure, **1511**, p. 189.

CHINA ASTER see **Callistephus**, **251-254**, p. 32.

CHINESE ARBOR-VITAE see **Thuja orientalis**, **2044**, **2045**, p. 256.

CHINESE HOLLY see **Ilex cornuta**

CHINESE KIDNEY BEAN see **Wisteria**, **1999**, **2000**, p. 250.

CHINESE LANTERN see **Physalis franchetii**, **1318**, p. 165.

CHINESE TRUMPET FLOWER see **Incarvillea**, **1183**, **1184**, p. 148.

CHIONODOXA (LILIACEAE)

✿ **luciliae** Glory of the Snow ✳ Spring   Bb
One of the best early spring-flowering bulbs. *Fl.* light-medium blue with white centre, up to ten on 6 in. stem, star-like, ¾ in. across. Often spreads freely from seed. Semi-shade or full sun. Turkey. **683**, p. 86.
'Pink Giant' is a taller form with pinkish *fl.* **684**, p. 86.

✿ **sardensis** ✳ Spring   Bb
Dwarfer and brighter in blue than *C. luciliae* spreading equally freely. Almost Royal blue right to the centre, making a very strong mass of colour once established. 6–8 in. Turkey. **685**, p. 86.

CHIVES see **Allium schoenoprasum**, **668**, p. 84.

CHLOROPHYTUM (LILIACEAE)

capense see **C. comosum**

comosum var. **variegatum** Spider Plant   GP.
Plant to 12 in. high. *L.* long, grassy, about ½ in. across, up to 12 in. long; green with ivory stripes. *Fl.* not always produced, small and white and followed by a tuft of young plantlets. These tufts can be pinned down into small pots, where they will root. Some of these plantlets will be unvariegated but the most typical form has green margins and an ivory centre while others may have the ivory and green portions reversed. Often confused with *C. capense* which has slightly larger *fl.* and is not viviparous. This habit of producing plantlets on the end of the *fl.* scapes fascinated Goethe and its use as a house plant originated with him. Any good compost. Winter temp. 45°F. Well-lit situation, but in greenhouse slight shading needed in summer. S. Africa. **447**, p. 56.

CHOISYA (RUTACEAE)

ternata ✳ Early Summer   Sh.
Sometimes known as Mexican Orange Blossom. Evergreen shrub up to 5 ft, widely spreading. *Fl.* white, in clusters, sweetly scented. *L.* shiny and conspicuous throughout year. Should not be planted in draughty position otherwise hardy enough for most gardens. Propagate from cuttings in late summer of half ripened wood. Mexico. **1512**, p. 189.

CHRISTMAS CACTUS see **Zygocactus truncatus**, **656**, p. 82.

CHRISTMAS ROSE see **Helleborus niger**, **1164**, **1165**, p. 146.

CHRYSANTHEMUM (COMPOSITAE)
This large genus has been divided here into three

Abbreviations and Symbols used in the text.
The following abbreviations may sometimes be used in conjunction as HA. indicating Hardy annual or GBb indicating Greenhouse bulb.

A. = Annual	P. = Perennial
Aq. = Aquatic	R. = Rock or
B. = Biennial	Alpine plant
Bb = Bulb	Sh. = Shrub
C. = Corm	Sp., sp. = Species
Cl. = Climber	Syn. = Synonym
Co. = Conifer	T. = Tree
Fl., fl. = Flower(s)	Tu. = Tuber
G. = Greenhouse or	var. = variety
house plant	× = Hybrid or
H. = Hardy	hybrid parents
HH. = Half-hardy	✳ = Flowering time
L., l. = Leaf, leaves	♣ = Foliage plant
Mt(s) = Mount,	
mountain(s)	

The following have been used also in the descriptions of Alpines, Bulbs, Trees and Shrubs.

* = slightly tender
† = lime hater
✿ = highly recommended

The illustration numbers are in **bold type** and the page numbers in light type preceded by p.

groups. First the sp., second the highly hybridised Indoor Chrysanthemums grown mainly for cutting and show purposes, thirdly the also highly hybridised Outdoor Chrysanthemums.

1 Species

carinatum, syn. **C. tricolor** ❀ Summer HA.
Fl. richly coloured, daisy-like, with striking rings of yellow, purple and red. *L.* divided, fleshy, smooth. 1½–2 ft. Sow in the open in 4 where they are to *fl.* Ordinary garden soil and a sunny position. Morocco.
There are numerous named varieties and mixed strains, including:
'Double mixed', 2 ft, richly coloured fringed petals;
'Monarch Court Jesters', dwarf, 1½ ft, many bright colours, **264**, p. 33.

coccineum see **Pyrethrum roseum**

coronarium ❀ Summer HA.
Fl. pale yellow, single. *L.* finely divided, smooth. 1–3 ft. Cultivated as for *C. carinatum.* Excellent for cutting. Mediterranean region.
'Golden Crown', 3 ft, bright yellow, double;
'Golden Gem', 1–1½ ft, deep yellow, double, dwarf;
'Golden Glory', 2 ft, large, canary-yellow, single, **265**, p. 34.

haradjanii RP.
6–8 in. One of the finest of mat-forming silver-leaved plants. Branches sub-shrubby. *L.* finely divided, fern-like. *Fl.* orange on short stems, but unimportant and often taken off so as not to spoil silvery effect of foliage. Plant in a warm sunny position. Easily propagated by cuttings or division. Sometimes placed in genus *Tanacetum* as *T. densumamani.* Asia Minor. **35**, p. 5.

maximum Shasta Daisy ❀ Summer P.
Fl. large, white, daisy-like, with golden centre. *L.* large, smooth, toothed. 2–3 ft. Plant 10–3 in any ordinary garden soil. Propagate by division in autumn or spring, or cuttings taken in 7–8. Pyrenees.
Good varieties include:–
'Esther Read', large, double white, 2 ft;
'Mayfield Giant', large creamy-white, 3½ ft;
'Wirral Pride', large, double white with anemone centre, 3 ft, **1049**, p. 132.

parthenium
A plant of many synonyms and various forms. The two most important forms have been developed to provide edging plants grown as annuals for their foliage, see *Matricaria eximia*, as well as the hardy perennial Feverfew, see *Pyrethrum parthenium*.

segetum Corn Marigold ❀ Summer HA.
Fl. yellow, single. *L.* oblong, coarsely cut. Cultivate as for *C. carinatum*. Europe, N. Africa.
'Eastern Star', bright yellow with chocolate centre, **266**, p. 34;
'Eldorado', canary-yellow with black centre.

tricolor see **carinatum**

2 Indoor

There are two methods of growing chrysanthemums for flowering under glass in autumn and winter – from cuttings taken early in the year – 2–3 – and grown on as large plants in pots, or from late rooted cuttings purchased in 8–9 and planted direct into a greenhouse border, or grown in pots. The latter method obviously saves a great deal of labour, but is rather more expensive, as one has to buy the rooted cuttings in. Plants from cuttings rooted in the early part of the year are potted in 3 in pots then repotted until they are in their flowering sized pot usually 7–8 in. in size. They are stopped and placed outdoors in 5 on a firm ash based standing ground and staked. The top of the stakes should be tied to wires stretched between pots to prevent the plants being blown over. They are then fed, watered, protected against pests and diseases and brought into the greenhouse in the early autumn. Of the vast range of varieties in the various classifications the following is a representative selection:

Large Exhibition, reflexing and incurving:
'Patricia Barnett', yellow, **448**, p. 56;
'Red Majestic', **449**, p. 57;
'William Mascall', orange, **450**, p. 57.

Exhibition, incurved:
'Audrey Shoesmith', pink, **451**, p. 57;
'Frances Jefferson', light bronze, **452**, p. 57;
'John Rowe Supreme', yellow, **453**, p. 57.

Reflexed decorative:
'Flash', crimson, **454**, p. 57;
'Parade', red, **455**, p. 57.

Intermediate decorative:
'Fair Lady', pink, **456**, p. 57;
'Fred Shoesmith', white, **457**, p. 58;
'Glenshades', bronze, **458**, p. 58;
'Golden Mayford Perfection', **459**, p. 58;
'Harmony', light bronze, **460**, p. 58;
'Silver Haze', rosy lavender, **461**, p. 58.

Anemone flowered:
'Marion Stacey', purple, **462**, p. 58;
'Yellow Grace Land', **463**, p. 58.

Single:
'Peggy Stevens', yellow, **464**, p. 58;
'Preference', pink, pale centre, **465**, p. 59.

Spray:
'Portrait', pink, reflexing, **466**, p. 59.

Spidery-flowered:
Rayonnante, rosy-purple, **467**, p. 59.

3 Outdoor

The early flowering outdoor chrysanthemums have been derived over many years from wild Japanese and Chinese sp. but the original ancestry is not known. It is thought that *C. indicum*, *C. erubescens* and *C. makinoi* had some part in the original parentage. The modern early flowering varieties, of which there are many hundreds, are propagated by cuttings. Old plants of "stools" are lifted in 10–11 and cut down to about 12 in. The soil is washed off the roots and they are then planted in boxes filled with light, moist soil in a greenhouse or a cold frame. Strong young shoots about 3–4 in. long are removed in 3 and placed in small pots or boxes containing a light compost such as John Innes seed compost and placed in a warm greenhouse or frame.
As soon as the cuttings have rooted they may be placed in a cold frame, and hardened off ready for planting out in 5. The old stools are discarded after they have produced sufficient cuttings.
Most modern varieties may be grown to give sprays of *fl.*, or they may be stopped by pinching out the point when the plants are about 12–15 in. high and resulting side shoots are then disbudded to produce one large bloom on each – up to say six blooms to a plant. Grown thus for cut *fl.*, they should be supported by placing 4 in. string mesh over the plants, stretched between canes or posts and raising the mesh as the plants grow. Or they may be supported by tying the growths to bamboo canes. Besides the taller growing varieties grown mainly for cut *fl.* there are many dwarf plants with either single or double *fl.* which are ideal for bedding. These include the Korean, rubellum, spray and pompon varieties.
For the purposes of exhibition at *fl.* shows modern chrysanthemums have been divided into classes with sub-divisions and are listed in the 'British National Register of Chrysanthemums' published by the National Chrysanthemum Society.
Leading varieties in the main classes of interest for garden decoration and cutting include:–

Incurved decoratives, fl. up to 4–6 in. diameter incurving florets:
'Topper', gold yellow, **1025**, p. 129.

Reflexed decoratives, fl. up to 4–6 in. diameter with the reflexing florets:
'Cherry Glow', bright bronzy red, **1026**, p. 129;
'Headliner', deep pink, **1027**, p. 129;
'Regalia', light crimson, **1028**, p. 129;
'Standard', light bronze, **1029**, p. 129;
'Tracey Waller', pink, **1030**, p. 129.

Intermediate decoratives, fl. up to 6 in. diameter:
'Evelyn Bush', white, **1031**, p. 129;
'Harry James', crimson, **1032**, p. 129;
'Incurved Primrose Evelyn Bush', **1033**, p. 130;
'Joe Edwards', pale primrose, **1034**, p. 130;
'Kathleen Doward', pink, **1035**, p. 130;
'Westfield Bronze', **1036**, p. 130.

Pompons and semi-pompons, fl. up to 2 in. diameter, forming a perfect ball of compact hard florets or a flat firm head of florets:
'Cameo', white, **1037**, p. 130;
'Fairie', deep rose, **1038**, p. 130;
'Grandchild', pink, **1039**, p. 130;
'Jante Wells', yellow, **1040**, p. 130;
'Masquerade', deep rose, **1041**, p. 131.

Sprays, fl. up to 2–3 in. diameter; may be pompon, single or reflexing:
'Brightness', russety-red, **1042**, p. 131;
'Golden Orfe', rich yellow, **1043**, p. 131;
'Gold Treasure', light orange, **1044**, p. 131.

Miscellaneous, fl. up to 3 in. diameter, usually double or semi-double:
'Charm Spoon', crimson, **1045**, p. 131;
'Garnet Spoon', wine red, **1046**, p. 131;
'Hansel', deep rose, **1047**, p. 131;
'Moonlight Spoon', yellow, **1048**, p. 131.

CHRYSOGONUM (COMPOSITAE)

virginianum ❀ Late Spring–Summer P.
Fl. yellowish-gold, star-like. *L.* broadly ovate, bluntly toothed. 6–9 in. Moist loam and leaf mould of a somewhat spongy nature, and partial shade. Propagate by division of the roots in early spring. E. N. America. A light coloured form. **1050**, p. 132.

CHUSAN PALM see Trachycarpus fortunei, 1930, p. 242.

CIDER GUM see Eucalyptus gunnii, 1597, p. 200.

CIMICIFUGA (RANUNCULACEAE)

racemosa Black snake-root ❀ Summer P.
Fl. creamy-white, slightly fragrant, borne in feathery plumes. *L.* shiny, green, leaflets deeply cut and toothed. 5–7 ft. Does best in a moist, deep loamy soil, in sun or partial shade. Propagate by division of the roots in spring or by seed as soon as gathered and placed in a cold frame. N. America **1051**, p. 132.

Abbreviations and Symbols used in the text.
The following abbreviations may sometimes be used in conjunction as HA. indicating Hardy annual or GBb indicating Greenhouse bulb.

A.	= Annual	P.	= Perennial
Aq.	= Aquatic	R.	= Rock or Alpine plant
B.	= Biennial	Sh.	= Shrub
Bb	= Bulb	Sp., sp.	= Species
C.	= Corm	Syn.	= Synonym
Cl.	= Climber	T.	= Tree
Co.	= Conifer	Tu.	= Tuber
Fl., fl.	= Flower(s)	var.	= variety
G.	= Greenhouse or house plant	×	= Hybrid or hybrid parents
H.	= Hardy	❀	= Flowering time
HH.	= Half-hardy	❧	= Foliage plant
L., l.	= Leaf, leaves		
Mt(s)	= Mount, mountain(s)		

The following have been used also in the descriptions of Alpines, Bulbs, Trees and Shrubs.

* = slightly tender
† = lime hater
✡ = highly recommended

The illustration numbers are in **bold type** and the page numbers in light type preceded by p.

CINERARIA (COMPOSITAE)

maritima, syn. **Senecio cineraria** Sea Ragwort, Dusty Miller (USA) ✳ Midsummer–Autumn HHP. *Fl.* heads yellow. *L.* 2–6 in. long, deeply cut. 1–1½ ft. Usually treated as a half hardy annual and sown under glass in 2–3. Plant out late 5. Mediterranean regions.

'Candicans', has attractive silvery foliage, **267**, p. 34.

multiflora ✳ Winter–Early Summer HHA. or GA. Cinerarias are derived from the Canary Island *Senecio cruentus*. Although they are technically perennials, they are always treated as annuals. Seed is sown in gentle heat in 3–5 and the plants are potted on and put in frames for the summer. They are brought into the greenhouse before there is a risk of frost and overwintered in gentle heat. If more heat is available, flowering will start earlier. **268**, p. 34; **468**, p. 59.

CINQUEFOIL see **Potentilla**, **146**, p. 19; **1328-1330**, pp. 166-167; **1745-1750**, p. 219.

CIRSIUM (COMPOSITAE)

rivulare ✳ Summer P.
Fl. deep crimson-purple, thistle-like. *L.* deeply cleft, in large tufts. 4 ft. Plant 11–3 in a sunny position, and a moist but well-drained ordinary garden soil. Propagate by seed. Europe, W. Asia. 'Atropurpureum' is rich purple, **1052**, p. 132.

CISSUS (VITACEAE)

antarctica Kangaroo Vine ❧ GCl.
Tendril climber, to 10 ft. *L.* heart-shaped at base, oval, pointed, coarsely toothed, to 4 in. long, 2 in. wide, dark shining green, stalks reddish. Young *l.* pale green. Will withstand low room temp. down to 40°F. Support should be provided. Does not mind partial shade. Water when needed. Australia. **469**, p. 59.

rhombifolia see **Rhoicissus rhomboidea**

CISTUS (CISTACEAE) Rock Roses

All require warm sunny position and grow well in light well-drained sandy soil.

ladaniferus ✳ Summer Sh.
Shrub up to 5 ft with sticky lanceolate *l.* *Fl.* white, large, up to 4 in. across with conspicuous deep crimson blotch at base of petals and large boss of yellow stamens. Requires warm position and unsuitable for cold gardens. **1513**, p. 190.

laurifolius ✳ Summer Sh.
Shrub up to 6 ft, hardier than preceding. *Fl.* white without red blotch. **1514**, p. 190.

× **pulverulentus** ✳ Summer Sh.
Shrub up to 4 ft but often less. *Fl.* deep magenta-pink with rather narrow petals but valuable for striking colour. **1515**, p. 190.

× **purpureus** ✳ Summer Sh.
Tall shrub up to 6 ft. *Fl.* large, deep pink with crimson blotch at base, over long season. One of the best of this genus for general garden purposes. **1516**, p. 190.

salviifolius ✳ Summer Sh.
Small shrub. *Fl.* white without basal blotch. One of the commonest sp. in the wild. Mediterranean regions.

CITRANGE see under **Poncirus**

CITRUS (RUTACEAE)

mitis Calamondin Orange ✳ Mid Autumn–Mid Spring GSh.
Fl. white, starry, about 1 in. across, very fragrant. *L.* evergreen, oval, shining green. Fruits orange about 2 in. in diameter. Grows up to about 2 ft in height.

Winter temp. about 50°F. Should be kept in a moist atmosphere and given ample air when in *fl.* After fruits have fallen, prune back and plunge outside at end of 6 in full sun to ripen new wood. Re-house in late 9. Any good potting compost suitable. Propagate by cuttings. Plants from pips are very slow to come into bearing and are sometimes spiny. Philippines. **470**, p. 59.

trifoliata see **Poncirus trifoliata**

CLARKIA (ONAGRACEAE)

concinna see **Eucharidium concinnum**

elegans 'Flore Pleno' ✳ Summer HA.
Fl. double, salmon-pink, rose-pink, purple, white, in graceful spikes. *L.* lance-shaped, toothed. 1–2 ft. Sow in the open in well cultivated soil and in a sunny position 3–4. Makes a useful cut *fl.* or pot plant for a cool greenhouse. There are numerous named varieties in attractive shades. California. **269**, p. 34.

CLARY see **Salvia sclarea**, **1359**, p. 170.

CLEMATIS (RANUNCULACEAE)

Border perennials and vigorous deciduous or evergreen climbers up to 20 or 30 ft. Clematis seem to flourish best when roots are planted in shade or semi-shade and shoots allowed to reach through to full sun. Climbers excellent for covering old trees or walls; pruned by cutting out old, weak or dead shoots. Late flowering sp. and hybrids should also be pruned by cutting back hard to bud near base in spring.

armandii ✳ Spring *Cl.
Evergreen climber up to 20 ft. *Fl.* in large clusters, white star-shaped each up to 2½ in. across. Leaflets 3, narrowly ovate, lanceolate up to 5 in. long dark glossy green. Hardy in milder areas to cover trees but in other areas usually grown as a wall plant in a sheltered position. China. **1960**, p. 245.

'Apple Blossom', *fl.* tinted pink and *l.* bronzy-green. China.

heracleifolia ✳ Summer P.
Fl. blue, tubular with reflexed tips. *L.* ovate, toothed, slightly hairy. 4 ft. Ordinary garden soil and partial shade. Propagate by division or by seed. China. Good varieties include:–

'Davidiana', deep blue, fragrant, 3–4 ft, **1053**, p. 132;

'Wyevale', flax-blue, fragrant, 4 ft.

integrifolia ✳ Summer P.
Fl. indigo-blue, bell-shaped, pendulous, on long stalks. *L.* up to 4 in. long, stalkless. 3–4 ft. Plant 11–3 in ordinary garden soil. Needs support with short hazel branches. Propagate by division or seed. S. Europe, Siberia.

'Alba', a white form;
'Hendersonii', lavender-blue.

× **jouiniana** ✳ Late Summer Cl.
Vigorous climber up to 20 ft. *Fl.* small white with lilac tint. Leaflets 3–5, ovate. Probably a hybrid of *C. heracleifolia* × *C. vitalba* Traveller's Joy. **1961**, p. 246.

✿ **macropetala** ✳ Spring Cl.
Deciduous vigorous climber of Atragene group, close to *C. alpina*. *Fl.* semi-double up to 4 in. wide blue or violet-blue. *L.* divided into nine leaflets, ovate to lanceolate coarsely toothed. One of the most valuable spring flowering climbers particularly conspicuous covering dark evergreens. China. **1962**, p. 246.

'Maidwell Hall' is one of the best forms;
'Markhamii' is pinkish-purple form.

montana ✳ Spring Cl.
Very vigorous deciduous climber up to 30 ft making thick matted covering or old trees or sheds. *Fl.* white star-like up to 2½ in. across. Leaflets three to a stalk up to 4 in. long, lanceolate, toothed, in a

layer. May be cut back at intervals when over vigorous. Himalayas.

'Rubens', *fl.* rosy-pink and *l.* purplish when young, one of the best forms. **1963**, p. 246.

orientalis ✳ Late Summer Cl.
Deciduous vigorous climber. *Fl.* yellow up to 2 in. across with thick drooping petals. Valuable for its late flowering habit. Seed heads in clusters with long fluffy white tails, as decorative as *fl.* and remaining through much of winter. Prune in spring. Variable when grown from seed. Himalayas, N. China. **1964**, p. 246.

'Orange Peel', is best form with deep orange-yellow *fl.* and petals thick like pieces of orange peel.

recta ✳ Summer P.
Fl. white, about 1 in. across, fragrant, borne freely in branching sprays; there is a double-flowered form and a form with purple foliage in the young stage. 3–6 ft. *L.* deep green, pinnately divided up to 6 in. long. Thrives in a chalky, well-drained loam, and is seen to the best advantage in the border when allowed to scramble up peasticks in a sunny position. Decorative seed heads. Propagate by seed sown in 3 in pans of sandy compost and placed in a cold frame, or by division in early spring. S. and E. Europe. **1054**, p. 132.

rehderiana ✳ Autumn Cl.
Vigorous deciduous climber. *Fl.* small bell-shaped pale yellowish-green but in large nodding clusters, fragrant. Leaflets seven to nine to a stalk, ovate, cordate up to 3 in. long, downy. Foliage looks rather like a Hop. China. **1965**, p. 246.

tangutica ✳ Midsummer Cl.
Deciduous climber. *Fl.* bell-shaped with recurved lobes, pale or deep yellow. Leaflets glaucous up to 3 in. long usually 3-lobed. Seed heads with styles long and feathery and persistent through autumn. China. **1966**, p. 246.

Large-flowered hybrid Clematis Cl.
Among the best are:–

'Comtesse de Bouchaud', soft rose-pink or bluish-pink, ✳ Summer, should be pruned hard in early spring, **1967**, p. 246;

'Henryi', white large-flowered, ✳ Summer, vigorous grower but best pruned by occasional thinning out, **1968**, p. 246;

✿ 'Jackmanii', violet-blue, ✳ Midsummer–Early

Autumn, very deep colour and one of the most vigorous growers which may be pruned hard in early spring, **1969**, p. 247;

'Jackmanii Superba', slightly larger in *fl.* than 'Jackmanii', with violet-purple *fl.*;

'Lasurstern', pale purplish-blue, ✴ Late Spring– Early Autumn, very large, prune by thinning out as needed, **1970**, p. 247;

'Nelly Moser', pale mauvish-pink with deep pink bar down centre of petal, ✴ Late Spring– Early Autumn, one of the most popular and vigorous varieties pruned by thinning out as required, **1971**, p. 247;

'Ville de Lyon', bright carmine-red, ✴ Summer. One of the best red varieties. Prune by thinning out as required. Belongs to *viticella* group, **1972**, p. 247;

'Vivyan Pennell', double, lilac-mauve. Prune by thinning out as required, **1973**, p. 247.

CLEOME (CAPPARIDACEAE)

spinosa Spider Flower ✴ Summer   HHA.
Fl. pale purple, rose and white, with prominent stamens. *L.* oblong, lance-shaped, with spines. 3–4 ft. Sow 2–3 in a warm greenhouse, plant out in late 5 or early 6 in a warm border and a light soil. W. Indies.

'Helen Campbell', 3 ft, white, **270**, p. 34;
'Pink Queen', 3½ ft, apple blossom pink.

CLERODENDRON (VERBENACEAE)

The greenhouse sp. need warm, moist conditions with a minmum of 55°F. in the winter and a rather rich soil mixture of loam, peat and sand. JIP 3 is very suitable. They are pruned after flowering and the prunings may be used as cuttings, though a temp. of at least 70°F. is needed for rooting. Little water is needed in the winter, but once growth is restarted, in 2, it is given increasingly.

bungei ✴ Late Summer   *Sh.
Small shrub. *Fl.* deep pink in clusters at end of horizontal shoots, 3–4 ft. Frequently cut down to ground level in bad winter and some gardeners prune it down to ground level in spring if not otherwise cut. Valuable for its late flowering. China. **1517**, p. 190.

fallax see **C. speciosissimum**

speciosissimum, syn. **C. fallax** ✴ Summer   P.
Fl. scarlet in large panicles. *L.* heart-shaped, up to 12 in. long. Deciduous. Easily raised from seed. Up to 3 ft high. Java. **471**, p. 59.

thomsonae   GCl.
Intermittent summer and autumn or almost continuous at 65°F. or over. *Fl.* in clusters, calyx white fading to pink, corolla crimson. *L.* evergreen, ovate, up to 6 in. long. If a winter temp. of 65°F. or over can be maintained the plant will *fl.* continuously, otherwise flowering is confined to the summer and autumn. A vigorous climber needing ample room. W. Africa. **472**, p. 59.

trichotomum ✴ Late Summer   T.
Small tree up to 10 ft. *Fl.* white star-like in clusters with red calyx. Fruit a conspicuous turquoise blue berry in centre of striking deep crimson-maroon enlarged calyx. Valuable as dual purpose shrub for *fl.* and fruit. Plant in full sun. China, Japan. **1518**, **1519**, p. 190.

CLETHRA (CLETHRACEAE)   †

alnifolia and **arboreus** see under **C. barbinervis**

barbinervis ✴ Summer   Sh.
Medium sized shrub. Deciduous. *Fl.* white in long racemes fragrant. Valuable for its late flowering and also for autumn colour of foliage. Japan. **1520**, p. 190.
Other sp. include *C. alnifolia* the Sweet Pepper Bush which also has pink form and *C. arborea* with magnificent Lily of the Valley *fl.* but too tender

except for Isles of Scilly and very mild areas. Madeira.

fargesii ✴ Midsummer   *Sh.
Fl. white in long racemes. China.

CLIANTHUS (LEGUMINOSAE)

dampieri see **C. formosus**

formosus, syn. **C. dampieri** Glory Pea ✴ Spring– Summer   GP.
Procumbent shrub. *Fl.* large, pea-shaped, red with large black-purple blotch at base, standard 2½ in. long, keel 2 in. in heads of four to six. *L.* evergreen, pinnate, 11–21 leaflets, covered with silky hairs. Rather gritty compost. Survives best if seedlings are grafted on seedlings of *Colutea arborescens*. Minimum temp. 45°F. May be grown as basket plant. Propagate by seed. Keep always on dry side. Even more spectacular than *C. puniceus* but much more tender and difficult to grow satisfactorily. W. Australia. **473**, p. 60.

puniceus Parrot's Bill, Lobster Claw ✴ Summer *Cl.
Evergreen climbing shrub up to 12 ft. *Fl.* in large clusters, pea-like with long keel pointed downwards up to 2½ in. long, sometimes described as canoe-shaped. *L.* pinnate with numerous leaflets each up to 1 in. long. Only suitable for growing outdoors in very warm situations, excellent in S. of France and such areas, otherwise good as cool greenhouse climber, or if grown as a pot plant can be placed outside in summer. New Zealand. **1974**, p. 247.

CLIMBING GAZANIA see **Mutisia**, **1984**, p. 248.

CLIVIA (AMARYLLIDACEAE) Kaffir Lily

miniata ✴ Spring   GBb.
Plant 2 ft high. *Fl.* orange to yellow, trumpet-shaped 2 in. or more long in an umbel of from 12 to 20. Modern hybrids have improved *fl.* colours. *L.* evergreen, strap-shaped, to 2 ft long, 2 in. broad. Fruit berry-like. Any adequate potting compost suitable. Minimum temp. 40–50°F. Best left in pots without disturbance until pot breaks but plants must be given artificial feeding then. Propagate by seed or by division. S. Africa. **474**, p. 60.

CLOTH OF GOLD see **Crocus susianus**

COBAEA (POLEMONIACEAE)

scandens ✴ Midsummer–Mid Autumn   Cl.
Vigorous tender climber, perennial when grown as greenhouse plant but usually grown as annual for planting out of doors in 4–5. *Fl.* pendulous, violet and green, bell-shaped with prominent green calyx, up to 3 in. long, pedicels long up to 6 in. Leaflets ovate about 4 in. long by 2 in. wide. Popular as a very fast growing climber and for its unusual colouring of *fl.* Central and S. America. **1975**, p. 247.

COCCOLOBA (POLYGONACEAE)

uvifera Seaside Grape ➹   GSh.
Tree to 20 ft in wild, a shrub of about 3 ft in cultivation. *Fl.* white in racemes 6 in. long, fragrant; rarely seen in cultivation. *L.* nearly circular 5 in. long, 7 in. wide, shining mid-green, evergreen. Winter temp. 60°F. Rich compost with extra sand. Propagate by cuttings of young wood in early summer. Tropical America. **475**, p. 60.

COCHLIODA see × **Odontioda** and × **Wilsonara**

COCKSCOMB see **Celosia argentea**, **257**, **258**, p. 33.

CODIAEUM (EUPHORBIACEAE) Croton

variegatum 'Pictum' ➹   GSh.
L. variable in shape and colour, most frequently

lanceolate, but some forms have lobed *l.* and others have the *l.* linear. Colours range from nearly black, through red, orange, pink, cream and any combination. *Fl.* whitish, inconspicuous. They require warm, moist conditions with a minimum winter temp. of 60°F. Ample light required to bring out the leaf coloration. Avoid draughts, which cause leaf-drop. Can be brought into cooler conditions for room decoration, but this should be done gradually; sudden temp. changes also cause the lower *l.* to fall. Propagate by stem cuttings in heat. Often used for hedging in tropics. Malaysia. **476**, p. 60.

CODONOPSIS (CAMPANULACEAE)

clematidea see **C. ovata**

ovata ✴ Summer   RP.
Fl. china-blue, open bell-shaped, pendulous on slender curving stems, about 1 in. deep. *L.* small hairy. Root a small tuber. 6 in.–1 ft. A very graceful delicate plant. When bruised all *Codonopsis* give off foxy scent. They move badly and should be planted out as young seedlings. Rather larger is *C. clematidea* with taller stems and pale blue-mauve bells with conspicuous nectaries at base, a more vigorous plant. Himalayas. **36**, p. 5.

COELOGYNE (ORCHIDACEAE)

This genus has a very wide distribution in E. Asia and it is necessary to know the provenance of the sp. to determine their treatment.

ochracea ✴ Spring   GP.
Comes from N.E. India and will respond well to cool house treatment, although needing a temp of 50°F. in the winter. The pseudo-bulbs somewhat resemble gooseberries in shape, and the white *fl.* are deliciously fragrant. Back bulbs can usually be induced to break to give fresh plants. **477**, p, 60.

COFFIN JUNIPER see **Juniperus recurva** var. **coxii**, **2020**, p. 253.

COLCHICUM (LILIACEAE)

autumnale Naked Boys ✴ Autumn   Tu.
Often erroneously known as Autumn Crocus. *Fl.* about 2 in. long with narrow starry segments, soft rosy lilac, pale at base; generally growing in

clusters from tuber and about 4–6 in. high. White and double forms are known. *L.* large and appearing —after *fl.* and not dying down till 5–6, but these should not be trimmed off before they have fully died down. Earlier in *fl.* than *C. speciosum* in autumn. Sun or semi-shade at edge of shrubbery; will grow in grass. Tubers large, often seen sprouting and even flowering on dry shelf of shop. A native plant but commoner in mainland of Europe in sub-alpine meadows. **686**, p. 86.

byzantinum see **C. cilicium**

cilicium ✳ Autumn   Tu.
Fl. dark rosy purple, goblet shaped. Close to *C. byzantinum* but flowering slightly later. One of the finest autumn-flowering sp. *L.* large, appearing soon after *fl.* Full sun to front of border or among shrubs, but does not *fl.* in dense shade. Turkey. **687**, p. 86.

speciosum ✳ Autumn   Tu.
Probably the finest of the genus as a garden plant. *Fl.* large, globose, tulip-like up to 10 in. on long perianth tubes, variable in colour from pale rosy-lilac with a pale or white throat to deep reddish purple. *L.* large, spring to early summer. Plant tubers which are large and irregular in shape in late summer in sun or semi-shade. They will flower same year. Asia Minor, Caucasus. **688**, p. 86.
Numerous forms have been distinguished and among the best available are:
'Album', large white goblets, very beautiful *fl.* **689**, p. 87;
'Disraeli', deep mauve, slightly chequered;
'Lilac Wonder', pinkish-lilac with white throat;
'The Giant', one of the largest, mauvish-pink with white base, **690**, p. 87;
'Water Lily', double, large lilac mauve, very conspicuous but generally falling over.

COLEUS (LABIATAE)

blumei 🍃   GP.
L. ovate with toothed margin to 3 in. long, 1½ in. across in a large range of colours, crimson, bronze, copper, apricot, pink, yellow, often blotched with other colours. Shrubby plant to 18 in. *Fl.* blue and white in autumn, undesirable. Normal potting compost. Usually treated as annuals from seed sown in heat, 60–65°F., in 1. Best forms may be over-wintered at 60°F. or propagated by stem cuttings in spring and summer. *L.* are evergreen, but lose their colour when daylight hours are short and many *l.* drop in winter. Unless seed is wanted all *fl.* spikes should be pinched out as soon as seen. Java. **478**, p. 60.

thyrsoideus ✳ Winter   GP.
Fl. brilliant blue, in panicle about 3 in. long; each *fl.* about ½ in. long, autumn and winter. Leggy plant to 3 ft high. Rich potting compost. Winter temp. 55–60°F. Propagate by cuttings taken in spring. Seed would presumably be effective but is seldom, if ever, offered. Central Africa. **479**, p. 60.

COLLINSIA (SCROPHULARIACEAE)

bicolor ✳ Summer   HA.
Fl. white, in clusters, marked lilac or rose. *L.* ovate, lance-shaped, slightly toothed. 1–1½ ft. Sow in the open 3–4, or in 9, in ordinary garden soil. Will grow in light shade. California. **271**, p. 34.

COLORADO SPRUCE see **Picea pungens**, **2030**, p. 254.

COLUMBINE see **Aquilegia**, **973**, **974**, p. 122.

COLUMBINE, TRUE see **Aquilegia vulgaris**

COLUMNEA (GESNERIACEAE)

gloriosa ✳ Winter–Mid Spring   GP.
Epiphyte with hanging stems, about 2 ft long. *Fl.*

tubular, large, scarlet with yellow throat. *L.* small ovate, dark green. Compost of equal parts leaf mould and grit with good drainage. Minimum temp. 50°F. Propagate by seeds or cuttings of ripened wood. Costa Rica.
'Purpureus' *l.* purplish ageing to bronze, **480**, p. 60.
Other sp. and hybrids all with rather similar *fl.* are grown and include *C. × banksii*, *C. magnifica*, *C. rotundifolia* and *C. × vedrariensis* among the most popular, and they tend to *fl.* later in the year.

COMFREY see **Symphytum**, **1393**, p. 175.

COMFREY, RUSSIAN see **Symphytum peregrinum**

COMMON ASH see **Fraxinus excelsior**, **1615**, p. 202.

COMMON BEECH see **Fagus sylvatica**, **1609**, p. 202.

COMMON GORSE see **Ulex europaeus**, **1931**, p. 242.

COMMON HORSE CHESTNUT see **Aesculus hippocastanum**

COMMON JASMINE see **Jasminum officinale**

COMMON JUNIPER see **Juniperus communis**, **2015-2017**, pp. 252, 253.

COMMON LARCH see **Larix decidua**, **2022**, **2023**, p. 253.

COMMON LAUREL see **Prunus laurocerasus**

COMMON LILAC see **Syringa vulgaris**, **1922-1926**, p. 241.

COMMON MYRTLE see **Myrtus communis**

COMMON OAK see **Quercus robur**

COMMON PRIVET see **Ligustrum vulgare**

COMMON SPINDLE TREE see **Euonymus europaeus**, **1604**, p. 201.

COMMON SPRUCE see **Picea abies**

COMMON YEW see **Taxus baccata**, **2042**, **2043**, p. 256.

CONE FLOWER see **Rudbeckia**, **368**, p. 46; **1352-1356**, pp. 169-170.

CONNEMARA HEATH see **Daboecia cantabrica**, **1549**, p. 194.

CONVOLVULUS (CONVOLVULACEAE)

althaeioides ✳ Mid Spring–Midsummer   *RP.
Prostrate or trailing sub-shrubby. Pinkish-purple rounded *fl.* up to 2 in. across. *L.* much divided, hairy, slightly silvery young stems twining. Up to 1½ ft. Plant in as warm and sunny a position as possible. E. Mediterranean regions, especially near coast where it is common. Close is *C. elegantissimus* but *fl.* are a little smaller and pinker and *l.* are more silvery and with narrow, almost linear lobes. **37**, p. 5.

cneorum ✳ Late Spring–Summer   *Sh.
Small silver leaved shrub. *Fl.* white like small convolvulus with pink divisions where petals join, yellow centre and some pink on outside of buds. Full sun. Best on light sandy soil. Easily propagated

by cuttings in 6–7 and well worth keeping a supply of these since a really hard winter may kill shrub. **1521**, p. 191.

mauritanicus ✳ Summer   *RP.
Trailing. *Fl.* clear blue-mauve, white in centre, 1 in. across freely produced over a long period of summer and spreading freely. Up to 1 ft. Only hardy in warm situations, should be planted in spring, preferably in sunny raised bed. Easily propagated by short cuttings in late summer, which should be wintered in greenhouse. N. Africa. **38**, p. 5.

minor see **C. tricolor**

tricolor, syn. **C. minor** Dwarf Convolvulus or Morning Glory (US) ✳ Summer   HA.
Fl. in shades of blue, rose and pink, funnel-shaped. *L.* egg-shaped, hairy, 6 in.–1½ ft. Sow in the open 3–4, or in 9, in well-drained soil and a sunny position. S.W. Europe.
Varieties include:
'Crimson Monarch', 1 ft, cherry crimson;
'Royal Ensign', 1½ ft, deep blue with golden centre, **272**, p. 34;
'Royal Marine', 6 in., royal blue, **273**, p. 35.

COPPER BEECH see **Fagus sylvatica** 'Cuprea', **1609**, p. 202.

CORAL BELLS see **Heuchera**, **1172**, **1173**, p. 147.

CORDYLINE (LILIACEAE)

australis New Zealand Cabbage Tree   *T.
Small evergreen tree up to 12 ft usually on tall trunk with large mass of very narrow long *l.* up to 2 ft long by 1½ in. broad near top. *Fl.* in long racemes, small, whitish. A distinctive feature of S. Coast gardens in England but hardy in protected situation in other areas. **1522**, p. 191.
Purple-leaved variety sometimes known as *C. australis lentiginosa* and is decorative for sub-tropical gardening in summer.

indivisa   T.
Has broader *l.* glaucous grey with prominent central red or yellow midrib but is much more tender. **1523**, p. 191.

terminalis, syn. **Dracaena terminalis** 🍃 GP.
L. long, oval, to 1 ft long, 4 in. wide. Colours mainly

bright reds and pinks, streaked with green on either side of midrib. 15 in.–3 ft. Grow in rich soil, keep moist during growing period, dryish in winter, minimum temp. 45°F. Propagate by pieces of main stem cut into 1 in. lengths, inserted horizontally to half their depth in sandy compost in 3, temp. 65–70°F. with bottom heat. Tropical Asia. **481**, p. 61.

COREOPSIS (COMPOSITAE) Tickweed

grandiflora ❋ Summer   P.
Fl. bright golden up to 2½ in. across. *L.* lance-shaped, entire. 2–3 ft. Ordinary garden soil and full sun. Rich soil is to be avoided. Propagate by careful division in spring, or by basal side shoots, taken in 7–8 and placed in sandy soil in a cold frame. Seed may be sown in the open in 4. S. USA.
Good varieties include:–
'Badengold', golden-yellow, 3 ft;
'Goldfink', ('Goldfinch'), with bright yellow *fl.* on erect short stems of 6–8 in.; **1055**, p. 132;
'Perry's Variety, semi-double deep yellow, 2–2½ ft.

stillmanii see **Leptosyne stillmanii**

tinctoria, syn. **Calliopsis tinctoria** ❋ Summer   HHA.
Fl. yellow, zoned crimson brown. *L.* narrowly divided. 2–2½ ft. Sow under glass in 3 or in the open ground in 4. N. America.
'Dazzler', 9 in., is one of several dwarf, colourful hybrids. **274**, p. 35.

verticillata ❋ Summer   P.
Fl. yellow, small but prolific. *L.* much divided into thin segments. 1½–2 ft. Plant 11–3 in ordinary garden soil and full sun. Propagate by soft wood cuttings in 7–8, or by division in spring. E. USA.
'Grandiflora', somewhat larger *fl.* and taller, **1056**, p. 132.

CORK OAK see **Quercus suber**

CORKSCREW HAZEL see **Corylus avellana** 'Contorta', **1533**, p. 192.

CORN COCKLE see **Agrostemma githago**, **226**, p. 29.

CORN MARIGOLD see **Chrysanthemum segetum**, **266**, p. 34.

CORN POPPY see **Papaver rhoeas**, **355**, p. 45.

CORNEL see **Cornus**, **39**, p. 5; **1524-1528**, p. 191.

CORNELIAN CHERRY see **Cornus mas**, **1528**, p. 191.

CORNFLAG see **Gladiolus segetum**

CORNFLOWER see **Centaurea cyanus**, **259**, p. 33.

CORNISH HEATH see **Erica vagans**, **1588**, **1589**, p. 199.

CORNUS (CORNACEAE) Dogwood, Cornel

alba Red-barked Dogwood   Sh.
Deciduous shrub usually not more than 5 ft but grown for the crimson or scarlet effect of young stems so best pruned to base each spring.
'Sibirica', best scarlet form sometimes known as 'Westonbirt variety', China, Japan. **1524**, **1525**, p. 191.

canadensis ❋ Summer   †RP.
Up to 6 in. Prostrate creeping rootstick with erect

annual stem up to 6 in. *Fl.* small, greenish-white or purplish in centre of four large creamy-white bracts followed by scarlet berries. Only suited for slightly moist or peaty positions in semi-shade. A lime hater. N. America. **39**, p. 5.

florida North American Flowering Dogwood ❋ Spring   T.
Small tree with conspicuous white petal-like bracts, four to a *fl.* Flowering before *l.* appear.
var. *rubra*, variety with rose-pink bracts is one usually grown in this country and one of our most beautiful flowering trees. N. E. America. **1526**, p. 191.
In W. states replaced by *C. nuttallii* which has slightly larger cream coloured bracts which become flush pink as *fl.* ages. Foliage turns yellow and scarlet. This is probably finest of all the *Cornus* but should only be planted out of pots when young since it establishes badly.

kousa   Sh.
Small shrub up to 10 ft with conspicuous white bracts to *fl.*
var. *chinensis*, has slightly wider bracts. Distinguished also for brilliant scarlet autumn colour. Japan. **1527**, p. 191.

mas Cornelian Cherry ❋ Spring   T.
Small tree up to 30 ft with clusters of acrid yellow small *fl.* on bare twigs. Berries ¾ in. long bright red but rarely seen in Britain. Sun or semi-shade. S. Europe. **1528**, p. 191.

nuttallii see under **C. florida** var. *rubra.*

stolonifera   Sh.
Vigorous suckering shrub with dark red or yellow-barked ('Flaviramea') young twigs giving brilliant colour in winter. N. America.

CORONILLA (LEGUMINOSAE)

emerus ❋ Spring–Autumn   Sh.
Slightly larger than *C. glauca* and slightly more tender. *Fl.* yellow. Central S. Europe.

glauca ❋ Mid Spring   Sh.
Small shrub suitable for warm position with slightly glaucous *l.* and pea-like, yellow *fl.* in clusters. Mostly 4 but flowering intermittently throughout year. Plant in warm sunny position or near S. wall. S. Europe. **1529**, p. 192.

valentina ❋ Spring–Midsummer   Sh.
Up to 1½ ft. Sweetly scented. S. Europe.

CORSICAN HELLEBORE see **Helleborus corsicus**, **1163**, p. 146.

CORTADERIA (GRAMINEAE) Pampas Grass

selloana, syn. **Gynerium argenteum** ❋ Late Summer–Autumn   P.
Fl. silky cream plumes 1½–3 ft long. *L.* narrow, glaucous, arching to 9 ft long. Plant 3–4 in sunny open position and deep well-drained soil. Propagate by division in 4. Argentine. **1057**, p. 133.

CORYDALIS (PAPAVERACEAE)

bulbosa see **C. solida**

cashmeriana ❋ Summer   RP or Tu.
Fl. brilliant greenish-blue held horizontally on short red stems, tubular with long spur and expanded lobes up to ½ in. long. *L.* fern-like, fresh green. Up to 4 in. Prostrate with slender underground rhizome or small tuber and dying away in winter. One of the most beautiful and, in colour, sensational of all alpine plants and occasionally forming large patches, but generally regarded as difficult. Unsuitable for dry hot areas and usually does best in cool position in a peaty or leafy soil and in some shade. It seems to grow more vigorously and easily in Scotland than in S. England. Himalayas, Kashmir. **40**, p. 5.

solida, syn. **C. bulbosa** ❋ Spring   Tu.
Fl. purple with short spur, up to ½ in. long on stem 4 in. *L.* much divided. Tuber solid, round, small and usually growing rather deep. Open or semi-shady position. Europe including Britain but rare. **691**, p. 87.

CORYLOPSIS (HAMAMELIDACEAE)

Closely related to Witch Hazels, *Hamamelis*. All species of *Corylopsis* will grow either in sun or semi-shade but usually not seen on very limy soils.

pauciflora ❋ Spring   Sh.
Small densely branched shrub, usually not more than 4 ft. *Fl.* pale creamy-yellow, scented. Valuable for its early flowering. Japan. **1530**, p. 192.

sinensis ❋ Mid Spring   Sh.
Taller shrub or small tree up to 12 ft. *Fl.* acrid lemon-yellow in long tassel-like pendulous racemes. *L.* hazel-like. One of the best sp. **1531**, p. 192.

spicata ❋ Spring   Sh.
Medium sized shrub up to 6 ft. *Fl.* bright lemon-yellow in tassels of 6 in., fragrant. *L.* roundish leathery and slightly glaucous. **1532**, p. 192.

CORYLUS (CORYLACEAE) Hazel

avellana 'Contorta' Corkscrew Hazel ❋   Sh.
Distinguished for its curious twisted branches. Slow growing shrub up to 10 ft and usually as much across. Catkins up to 4 in. long, lemon-yellow and conspicuous. Attractive and unusual feature in gardens. **1533**, p. 192.

CORYPHANTHA (CACTACEAE)

arizonica ❋ Spring–Early Summer   GP.
Fl. pink large. Stems, globular, covered with tubercles, clump forming, Spines long. Gritty well-drained compost needed. Water freely from 3–6, little from 7–3. Minimum winter temp. 40 °F. Propagate by division. Arizona. **482**, p. 61.

COSMEA see **Cosmos**, **275**, **276**, p. 35.

COSMOS (COMPOSITAE) Cosmea

bipinnatus ❋ Midsummer–Mid Autumn   HHA.
Fl. usually crimson, pink and white, single. Yellow,

orange and double forms have been developed. *L.* narrow, finely cut. 2–4 ft. Sow in 3 under glass and plant out in 5 in a sunny border. Mexico.

   'Klondyke Early Goldcrest', early, double golden-yellow, 2 ft, **275**, p. 35;

   'Klondyke Orange Flare', large, orange, 2 ft;

   'Sensation' types have large *fl.* of clear colour, 3 ft, **276**, p. 35;

   'Sulphureus Sunset', semi-double, rich vermilion, 2½ ft.

COTINUS (ANACARDIACEAE) Smoke Tree

americanus, syn. **Rhus cotinoides** ❋ Summer T. Small deciduous tree up to 15 ft with dense cluster of branches. Distinguished for brilliant autumn colouring of foliage. *Fl.* small in large clusters. **1534**, p. 192.

coggygria, syn. **Rhus cotinus** Venetian Sumach or Smoke Tree ❋ Summer Sh. Shrub up to 10 ft usually less and freely branching. Distinguished both for masses of feathery *fl.* of purplish colour in plume-like inflorescences, for long season turning pink as they fade. Distinguished also for autumn colouring of foliage. **1535**, p. 192.

   'Foliis purpureis', form with dark purple *l.* which change to light red in autumn. Distinctive for its colour throughout the season, and valuable as contrast to silver-leaved shrubs. **1536**, p. 192.

COTONEASTER (ROSACEAE)

Valuable evergreen or deciduous shrubs particularly for autumn fruiting scarlet berries.

conspicuus ❋ Early Summer Sh. Medium sized but wide spreading evergreen shrub up to 5 ft. Berries 8–10. *L.* small. S.E. Tibet.

   ✿ 'Decorus', has more semi-prostrate habit and fruits very freely. Sometimes berries remain on shrub until new year. Especially valuable for covering banks or low walls. **1537**, p. 193.

✿ **'Cornubia'** ❋ Early Summer Sh. Large evergreen shrub up to 15 or 20 ft and wide spreading. A hybrid of *C. frigidus* together with an unknown species. *Fl.* small white in large clusters. Berries shiny scarlet borne in large bunches on short branches. One of the most conspicuous of this genus and valuable where space is available. *L.* broadly lanceolate. **1538**, p. 193.

× **exburyensis** Sh. A hybrid raised at Exbury of *C. salicifolius* × *C. frigidus* 'Fructo-luteo'. Tall evergreen with narrow foliage and large clusters of yellow berries. Frequently retained until new year. **1539**, p. 193. Very close to this is *C.* × *rothschildianus* also with yellow berries but is slightly taller in habit.

franchetii var. *sternianus* ❋ Early Summer Sh. Tall shrub semi-evergreen up to 10 ft. *Fl.* white in small clusters. Berries orange-scarlet frequently remaining on shrub until new year. *L.* rather broad for the genus ovate, sage green, grey underneath. This is often listed as *C. wardii* but the true *C. wardii* is a different plant. Tibet and W. China. **1540**, p. 193

horizontalis Sh. Deciduous shrub of spreading habit up to 5 ft. Branches growing in characteristic herringbone pattern. *L.* small. Berries scarlet freely produced in autumn. Foliage also has brilliant scarlet autumn colour in 10–11 and then in most areas drops. Valuable for covering banks or walls and a conspicuous useful plant. China. **1541**, p. 193.

× **rothschildianus** see under **C.** × **exburyensis**

wardii see **C. franchetii** var. *sternianus*

COTULA (COMPOSITAE)

barbata, syn. **Cenia barbata** Pincushion Plant ❋ Summer HHA. *Fl.* lemon-yellow rounded heads, forming a neat,

---

compact plant. *L.* tufted, narrow, silkily hairy. 4–6 in. Sow under glass in 3 and plant out in 5. S. Africa. **277**, p. 35.

COTYLEDON (CRASSULACEAE)

oppositifolia, syn. **C. simplicifolia**, syn, **Chiastophyllum oppositifolium** Lamb's Tail ❋ Summer RP. Creeping succulent up to 6 in. *Fl.* small, yellow in clusters on crimson arching stem, mostly pendulous. *L.* rather succulent rounded with toothed margin, forming loose rosette and becoming crimsonscarlet as they age. Plant in a sunny position. Hardy. USSR, Caucasus, **41**, p. 6.

simplicifolia see **C. oppositifolia**

COWBERRY see **Vaccinium vitis-idaea**, **1937**, p. 243.

COWSLIP, CAPE see **Lachenalia**, **554**, p. 70.

COWSLIP, HIMALAYAN see **Primula florindae**, **1332**, p. 167.

COWSLIP, VIRGINIAN see **Mertensia virginica**, **1270**, p. 159.

CRAB, FLOWERING see **Malus**, **1699-1704**, p. 213.

CRAB, JAPANESE see **Malus floribunda**, **1699**, p. 213.

CRAB, SIBERIAN see **Malus** × **robusta**, **1703**, p. 213.

CRAMBE (CRUCIFERAE) Seakale

cordifolia ❋ Summer P. *Fl.* white, in loose racemes, gypsophila-like. *L.* greyish-green, heart-shaped. 4–6 ft. Plant 11–3 in ordinary garden soil. Propagate by root cuttings or seed. Caucasus. **1058**, p. 133.

CRANBERRY, MOUNTAIN see **Vaccinium vitis-idaea**, **1937**, p. 243.

CRANESBILL see **Geranium**, **78**, **79**, p. 10; **1143-1150**, pp. 143, 144.

CRANESBILL, BLOODY see **Geranium sanguineum**, **1148**, p. 144.

CRANESBILL, IBERIAN see **Geranium ibericum**, **1143-1145**, pp. 143, 144.

CRANESBILL, MEADOW see **Geranium pratense**, **1147**, p. 144.

CRANESBILL, WOOD see **Geranium sylvaticum**, **1149**, p. 144.

CRAPE MYRTLE see **Lagerstroemia indica**, **1670** p. 209.

CRASSULA (CRASSULACEAE)

A genus of succulent herbs and shrubs. They need gritty soil, full exposure to light and to be kept on the dry side at most times, particularly during winter. Minimum winter temp. 45°F. Propagation by seed, stem or leaf cuttings, taken in summer.

arborescens ❧ GSh. Shrub to 3 ft high. *Fl.* white in panicles, rarely produced in cultivation. *L.* small, round, grey-

---

green with red margins and red dots. S. Africa. **483**, p. 61.

sarcocaulis ❋ Summer GSh. Branched shrub to 1 ft. *Fl.* pink, small in fewflowered cymes. *L.* small, pointed, green. Can be grown outside in favoured districts, but better with protection in regions with high rainfall. S. Africa. **484**, p. 61.

CRATAEGUS (ROSACEAE) Hawthorn, May

Valuable both for *fl.* and for autumn fruiting and in some species for autumn colouring of foliage.

carrierei see **C.** × **lavallei**

crus-gallii and **durobrivensis** see under **C. prunifolia**

× **lavallei**, syn. **C. carrierei** T. A hybrid thought to have been raised from *C. crus-gallii* × *C. pubescens*. Small tree up to 15 or 20 ft. Deciduous. *L.* often remain late on the tree and colour bronzy before dropping. Fruit brilliant scarlet large. Also known under its synonym *C. carrierei* which is sometimes separately listed but probably the two are indistinguishable. One of the best for fruiting. **1542**, p. 193.

mollis and **monogyna** see under **C. prunifolia**

orientalis ❋ Early Summer T. *L.* much divided into deeply cut lobes. Small deciduous tree up to 15 ft often with spreading top. Fruit orange-red to scarlet remaining on tree often till quite late. S.E. Europe, W. Asia. **1543**, p. 193.

oxyacantha Common Hawthorn ❋ Early Summer T. Tree up to 20 ft. *Fl.* white, very freely borne in long panicles.

   'Coccinea Plena', has double scarlet *fl.* often used as a street planting tree. **1544**, p. 193.

prunifolia ❋ Early Summer T. Makes a rounded tree up to 20 ft and is one of the most useful thorns for its free blossoming and its large fruits combined with autumn colour foliage. Other valuable species are *C. crus-gallii* the Cockspur Thorn of E.N. America, *C. durobrivensis* which has very large fruits and prominent spines, *C. mollis* from N. America with scarlet downy fruits. *C. monogyna* is the more common hedgerow Hawthorn and has a number of varieties.

CREAM CUPS see **Platystemon californicus**, **362**, p. 46.

CREEPER, TRUMPET see **Campsis**, **1958**, p. 245.

CREEPER, VIRGINIA see **Parthenocissus**, **1985**, p. 249.

CREEPING JUNIPER see **Juniperus horizontalis**, **2018**, p. 253.

CREEPING WINTERGREEN see **Gaultheria procumbens**, **1620**, p. 203.

CREEPING ZINNIA see **Sanvitalia**, **372**, p. 47.

CREPIS (COMPOSITAE) Hawk's Beard

rubra ✳ Summer   HA.
Fl. light pink with deeper centre, freely produced. L. lance-shaped, toothed. 1 ft. Sow in the open in 3–4 where it is to fl. S. Europe. **278**, p. 35.

CRINITARIA LINOSYRIS see **Aster linosyris**

CRINODENDRON (ELAEOCARPACEAE)

hookerianum, syn. **Tricuspidaria lanceolata**
Chilean Lantern Tree ✳ Early Summer   †T.
Medium sized evergreen tree up to 30 ft but tender and only grows this size in milder South Western or Western areas, but can be grown in a sheltered position near a wall in other regions but not worth growing in cold areas. Distinguished for its deep crimson lantern-like urn-shaped fl. which hang on long pedicles 1 in. deep. L. narrow lanceolate and rather deep green. One of the most valuable shrubs forming large hedges in mild areas. More frequently known in gardens under its synonym *Tricuspidaria lanceolata*. **1545**, p. 194.

✕ **CRINODONNA** (AMARYLLIDACEAE)

corsii, syn. **Amarcrinum howardii** ✳ Autumn *Bb
A bigeneric hybrid group between *Amaryllis belladonna* and *Crinum moorei*. Fl. like the *Amaryllis*, pale pink with white throat but in large clusters on stout stems up to 2½ ft. Fl. about 4 in. across, trumpet-like. Bulb large, ovoid, should be planted about 6 in. deep. L. strap-like, persistent for much of summer. A good summer ripening is important for flowering. **692**, p. 87.

CRINUM (AMARYLLIDACEAE)

✕ **powellii** ✳ Late Summer   Bb
A hybrid between two slightly tender S. African sp. and hardier than either. Fl. lily-like, pink or white, trumpet-like, about 3–4 in. long, slightly drooping, in clusters of six to eight, opening in succession, on stout stems 2–3 ft. L. large, strap-like, light green. Best planted in a sunny border or against a S. wall but the wall is not necessary in warmer areas. In dry seasons, should be watered freely in early 8 before flowering. One of the finest late summer flowering bulbs. These are very large and should be planted with base 6 in. or more deep. In cold areas, cover with ashes or bracken in winter. May be left undivided for many years. **693** p. 87.
Best, rarely listed separately, forms are:–
'Album', pure white;
'Harlemense', pale shell-pink;
'Krelagei', deep pink, large.

CROCOSMIA (IRIDACEAE)

✕ **crocosmiiflora** Garden Montbretia ✳ Late Summer   C.
A large group of variable and valuable late-flowering corms. Fl. lemon-yellow to deep orange,

---

the commonest form being deep orange with rather small fl. on 1½–2 ft stem. This has become naturalised in large masses in parts of the West of England. Sun or semi-shade. Increasing very rapidly and requires division every three years. Some special forms with larger fl. have been selected but unfortunately are less hardy. In cold districts these corms may be lifted and stored like tubers of dahlias.
Among the best of these are:–
'Citronella', lemon-yellow;
'His Majesty', large, orange-scarlet with dark crimson flush on outside of petal;
'Jackanapes', bicoloured, the three outer petals reddish-orange, inner buff yellow, **694**, p. 87;
'Star of the East', pale orange-yellow.

✿ **masonorum** ✳ Summer   C.
Fl. bright reddish-orange, very intense in colour, star-like on stem of 2–2½ ft and arching over at the end so that all fl. face upwards. L. like a montbretia, pleated. Plant in sunny position. Apparently quite hardy and one of best of late summer flowering plants of recent introduction. S. Africa. **695**, p. 87.

CROCUS (IRIDACEAE)

Sun lovers. Plant 2–3 in. deep. They have been grouped according to their flowering seasons below, 1 Winter and early Spring, 2 Autumn.

aureus see 1.	*minimus* see 1.
Autumn see 2 and	*nudiflorus* see 2.
Colchicum autumnale.	*pulchellus* see 2.
chrysanthus see 1.	Saffron see
Cloth of Gold see	*C. sativus* 2.
C. susianus 1.	*sativus* see 2.
corsicus see 1.	*sieberi* see 1.
etruscus see 1.	*speciosus* see 2.
imperati see 1.	*susianus* see 1.
kotschyanus see 2.	*tomasinianus* see 1.
laevigatus see 1.	*vernus* see 1.
Large flowered see	*zonatus* see
C. vernus 1.	*C. kotschyanus* 2.

1 Winter and early Spring   C.

✿ **aureus** ✳ Early Spring sometimes from 1
Wild sp. from which the Dutch 'Yellow Giant' has been derived, but a good garden plant on its own and spreading by self-seeding. Fl. deep golden-yellow, stronger in colour than Dutch Yellow and a little earlier. Greece, W. Asia Minor. **696**, p. 87.

✿ **chrysanthus** ✳ Early Spring
Very variable and a number of forms have been raised and selected. Native form is yellow. Greece. Asia Minor. Nearly all are free-flowering. Colours range from white through pale to deep yellow and golden, pale blue and mauve, many being beautifully feathered with purple on the outside. All are beautiful and grow well in a well-drained sunny place and are also excellent for pans in an alpine house, but no crocuses last indefinitely in pots or pans.
Particularly attractive are:
'Blue Pearl', pale blue with deep orange centre and stigma, **697**, p. 88;
'Cream Beauty', pale creamy yellow with deep orange centre and stigma, large globular, **698**, p. 88;
'E. A. Bowles', deep butter-yellow, heavily feathered outside with bronze towards base, large globular, named after a very famous old gardener and authority on crocus, **699**, p. 88;
'Goldilocks', deep golden-yellow, slightly smaller than 'E. A. Bowles', **700**, p. 88;
'Lady Killer', inner petals white, outer deep mauve, heavily flecked, bordered white, one of most striking forms, **701**, p. 88;
'Warley', large, the three outer petals pale cream heavily marked with deep purplish-blue, inner petals creamy-white with greyish-purple blotches at base, opening white inside with yellow throat, very handsome, **702**, p. 88.

corsicus ✳ Late Winter–Mid Spring
Fl. smaller in size but most beautifully marked. Outer petals pale lilac and heavily feathered with

---

deeper purple, inner petals lilac-mauve. Not quite such an easy sp. to keep as two preceding and requires good drainage and summer ripening. Corsica.

etruscus ✳ Early Spring
Fl. pale lilac-mauve or greyish-lavender, inner petals deeper in colour than outer, throat pale, stigma reddish-orange. Fl. of medium size. Generally free-flowering. Plant in full sun. W. Italy, W. America. **703**, p. 88.

✿ **imperati** ✳ Winter
Sometimes 12 in a warm spell. Fl. large, globular, up to 3 in. across when open. On inside petals are bright mauve but this is only seen when they open in the sun, outside buff-yellow, feathered and veined with deep mauve or purple, throat yellow. Plant in a sunny place, dry in summer. S. Italy, Corsica. **704**, p. 88.

laevigatus ✳ Late Autumn–Mid Winter
A real winter flowerer. Fl. globular, medium in size, pale lilac but beautifully marked with deeper lilac-mauve or purple. Plant where it can be dry in summer. Excellent for bulb frame. Corm unusual in that outer tunic is hard and smooth like a small hazel nut. Greece. Var. *fontenayi* often offered has slightly larger fl. than type which is at any rate variable. **705**, p. 89.

minimus ✳ Spring
Fl. small but most beautifully marked, like a slightly smaller C. corsicus but a little darker mauve. Outer petals lilac and heavily feathered with deep purple, inner petals lilac-purple. A real gem best suited to alpine house or bulb frame. Corsica, Sardinia. **706**, p. 89.

✿ **sieberi** ✳ Early Spring
Fl. medium-large. The form usually sold has pale lilac rather globular fl. but deeper mauve forms also occur and 'Violet Queen' is recommended as one of the deepest in colour although fl. are smaller than in type. This sp. can always be distinguished by the deep yellow colour at its base. Greece, a mountain plant. Particularly lovely wild varieties are *tricolor* from Mt Chelmos which has a wide band between mauve of upper part and yellow of base; var. *versicolor*, also known as var. *heterochromus* from mts of Crete has the outer petals beautifully feathered with deep purple against a light ground and in markings it is infinitely variable. Unfortunately both of these varieties are rare in cultivation

---

and may be slow to increase. They need good summer ripening to maintain them from year to year. **707**, p. 89.

✡ **susianus** Cloth of Gold ✳ Early Spring
Fl. small-medium in size, deep orange with dark mahogany streaks on outside of three outer petals. Very brilliant and strong in colour and very early-flowering, rather dwarf. Quite hardy and vigorous but also good as an alpine house plant where its *fl.* are protected. No crocuses do well with any appreciable artificial warmth. S.W. Russia.

✡ **tomasinianus** ✳ Mid Winter–Early Spring
Fl. medium in size and slender in bud, pale suede-like mauvish-blue on outside but bright lilac-mauve inside. Very hardy and *fl.* open freely both in borders and in grass. One of the plants one would never wish to be without since it *fl.* so early. Rather variable. Several selected forms with stronger colours have been named and are much recommended. The bulbs are always among cheapest of crocuses to buy, an investment which increases prodigiously from year to year, they seem to be impervious to their beds being dry or worked over. S. Italy. **708**, p. 89.
  'Barr's Purple', rich purplish-lilac inside, outside of three outer petals pale mauvish-grey, large;
  'Taplow Ruby', reddish-purple, the colour being darkest towards tip;
  'Whitewell Purple', purplish-mauve, paler inside, a very beautiful and free-flowering form available in nearly all lists and recommended as the best one to obtain, **709**, p. 89.

✡ **vernus** ✳ Late Winter–Mid Spring
This is the wild crocus of the Alpine meadow and infinitely variable in colour. Unfortunately wild collected corms are seldom successful in cultivation. It is thought, however, that the common large-flowered garden crocuses have been derived from it and they are much more vigorous in growth and the *fl.* are much larger. They *fl.* later than most of the sp. described. Good in beds or in short grass where corms may be left to increase for many years. Numerous forms have been named and all are good. The following are a small selection of good ones which can be found in most bulb merchants' lists:
Pale lilac-mauve without stripes:
  'Haarlem Gem', early, pale lilac-mauve, smaller than other forms;
  'Queen of the Blues', larger, later, bluish-lavender;
  'Vanguard', also early and valuable for this, pale silvery-lilac, specially recommended, **710**, p. 89.
White:
  'Kathleen Parlow', pure white with large orange stigma, **711**, p. 89;
  'Snowstorm', large, white.
Pale-mauve with darker stripes:
  'Pickwick', pale lilac, heavily striped from base with deep purple;
  'Striped Beauty', almost white with strong purple markings.
Deep purple:
  'Negro Boy', one of the deepest and finest purples, earlier than the next, **712**, p. 89;
  'Purpureus Grandiflorus', deep rich purple, large, with an attractive satin-like sheen to petals, **713**, p. 90;
  'The Bishop', deep reddish-purple like wine, free-flowering, very vigorous.
Golden-yellow:
  'Yellow Giant' or 'Dutch Yellow', one of the earliest, preceding the mauve, purple and white forms but slightly later than *C. aureus*, bright golden-yellow, very free-flowering and much recommended but some protection from the pecking of birds is often advisable such as black cotton stretched low over or among *fl.* and supported on short twigs, **714**, p. 90.

2 Autumn-flowering crocuses C.

✡ **kotschyanus**, syn. **C. zonatus** ✳ Early Autumn
This is the sp. better known as *C. zonatus*, which was a very apt name for the pale lilac *fl.* which have two

orange-yellow blobs at the base of each petal making a different coloured zone and merging into each other. The throat at the base of the *fl.* is also yellow. Generally the earliest of the autumn-flowering crocuses. A good garden plant which often spreads freely but not so large or conspicuous as *C. speciosus*.

nudiflorus ✳ Autumn
Fl. deep mauve or purple, appearing without *l.* Petals long and *fl.* rather slender. Stigmas bright orange, finely divided and conspicuous. White forms are also found. Almost unique among crocuses in its habit of spreading by stolons which produce new corms at their ends. Generally does well in dampish position where it should be left undisturbed. Corms smaller than in most sp. **715**, p. 90.

pulchellus ✳ Autumn
Fl. large, pale lavender with some slight deeper veining. Usually a little later than *C. speciosus* and rather paler in colour, base deep yellow. Corm also rather small. Asia Minor, Turkey.

sativus Saffron Crocus ✳ Autumn
Fl. large, globular, variable in colour and markings, generally rosy-lilac-purple or even deep purplish-mauve, generally deeper towards base. Distinguished by its large feathery stigmas which are very bright in colour. In England plant in as warm and sunny a position as possible where it can get good ripening. The Saffron dye of the Middle Ages was obtained from this plant by crushing the large orange-red stigmas. Curiously it is now a shy-flowering plant in England and it is rather mysterious how enough was obtained to make the dye. It was also used as a drug but the price was always high. S. Europe, Asia Minor.

✡ **speciosus** ✳ Autumn
The autumn counterpart of the spring-flowering *C. tomasinianus*. *Fl.* large, pale blue-mauve, veined with deeper colour but variable. Very free-flowering when *l.* are only slightly developed. Much recommended and one of the most valuable garden plants since it spreads freely both by seed and from the small cormlets and is tolerant of forking over in its bed. **716**, p. 90.
  'Oxonian', is the deepest coloured form but it is not so vigorous as the type, **717**, p. 90.

zonatus see **C. kotschyanus**

CROSS-LEAFED HEATH see **Erica tetralix**, **1586**, p. 199.

CROTON see **Codiaeum**, **476**, p. 60.

CROWN IMPERIAL see **Fritillaria imperialis**, **737**, **738**, p. 93.

CRYPTANTHUS (BROMELIACEAE)

fosterianus 'Foster's Hybrid' 🌿 GP.
Stemless plant. *L.* stiff, 6 in. long, 1–1½ in. wide, wavy-edged, greyish-green, purplish-brown or reddish towards the base, banded with brown. *L.* form a rosette. *Fl.* small, white, inconspicuous. May be grown in moss on sections of tree trunk. Keep moist in summer, dryish in winter. Propagate by offsets, in spring. **485**, p. 61.

CRYPTOMERIA (TAXODIACEAE) Japanese Cedar

japonica Co.
Tall evergreen tree usually rather narrow in growth up to 100 ft but usually less. Branchlets drooping. *L.* small scale-like dark green. Cones small globular up to ¾ in. across. Best in slightly damp soil and superficially resembling the *Sequoiadendron*. Bark reddish, fibrous and coming away in long shreds. One of the best of the dwarf conifers but unsuitable for dry positions. **2011**, p. 252.
  'Elegans', is form in which foliage has retained juvenile feathery form turning reddish-bronzy

in autumn making beautiful tree, but in old trees trunk tends to fall to horizontal position with erect branches.

CUPHEA (LYTHRACEAE)

miniata ✳ Summer HA.
Fl. bright red. *L.* slender-pointed. 1 ft. Sow in 3 in a warm greenhouse and do not plant out until early 6, choosing a sheltered sunny bed. Perennial and evergreen in its native Mexico.
  'Firefly', bright cerise-red, **279**, p. 35.

CUPID'S DART see **Catananche coerulea**, **1016**, p. 127.

× **CUPRESSOCYPARIS** (CUPRESSACEAE)

leylandii Co.
A valuable intergeneric hybrid between *Cupressus macrocarpa* and *Chamaecyparis nootkatensis*. One of the fastest growing conifers available forming dense evergreen columnar tree and rapidly attaining 40 ft or more. Much used for screening, also used for tall hedge and will stand some clipping. Tolerant of chalky soils and windy conditions. More closely resembles *Chamaecyparis nootkatensis* of its parents. Foliage deep glaucous green. **2012**, p. 252.

CUPRESSUS (CUPRESSACEAE) Cypress
Evergreen and usually rather fastigiate trees with upright branching. Distinguished from *Chamaecyparis* by rounded instead of flattened branchlets and larger cones, and sp. grown mostly less hardy.

arizonica see **C. glabra**

glabra Smooth Arizona Cypress Co.
Most trees grown under name *C. arizonica* in gardens should now be referred to this sp. Fastigiate or pyramidal evergreen trees up to 50 ft but usually much less. Foliage glaucous. Unsuitable for very exposed positions. Arizona, USA.
  'Glauca', form with slightly more glaucous foliage. Syn. *C. arizonica* 'Glauca', **2013**, p. 252.

macrocarpa Monterey Cypress Co.
Fast growing bright green evergreen tree. Foliage resinous. Makes a valuable shelter especially in coastal districts, sometimes grown as a hedging plant but not so suitable as *Chamaecyparis lawsoniana* or

---

Abbreviations and Symbols used in the text.
The following abbreviations may sometimes be used in conjunction as HA. indicating Hardy annual or GBb indicating Greenhouse bulb.

A. = Annual		P. = Perennial
Aq. = Aquatic		R. = Rock or
B. = Biennial		Alpine plant
Bb = Bulb		Sh. = Shrub
C. = Corm		Sp., sp. = **Species**
Cl. = Climber		Syn. = Synonym
Co. = Conifer		T. = Tree
Fl., fl. = Flower(s)		Tu. = Tuber
G. = Greenhouse or		var. = variety
house plant		× = Hybrid or
H. = Hardy		hybrid parents
HH. = Half-hardy		✳ = Flowering time
L., l. = Leaf, leaves		🌿 = Foliage plant
Mt(s) = Mount,		
mountain(s)		

The following have been used also in the descriptions of Alpines, Bulbs, Trees and Shrubs.

  * = slightly tender
  † = lime hater
  ✡ = highly recommended

The illustration numbers are in **bold type** and the page numbers in light type preceded by p.

Thuya plicata since it is often intolerant of clipping. Old trees are very distinctive with horizontal branching.

'Donard Gold', has deep golden foliage and is a more compact plant.

sempervirens Italian Cypress   Co.
Slender columnar tree with dark green foliage, slightly tender especially in cold areas. Grown throughout Mediterranean where it forms one of the most conspicuous trees of the landscape up to 40 ft.

var. *horizontalis*, form restricted to Crete Mts with horizontal branching.

CURRANT, FLOWERING see Ribes, 1833, 1834, p. 230.

CUSHION SPURGE see Euphorbia epithymoides, 1130, p. 142.

CUT-LEAVED CHERRY see Prunus incisa, 1756, p. 220.

CYANANTHUS (CAMPANULACEAE)

integer see **C. microphyllus**

lobatus ❊ Summer   RP.
Spreading prostrate herbaceous plant up to 4 in. forming large mats. *Fl.* deep violet-blue or white with spreading lobes, freely borne. *L.* small rounded. Forms a conspicuous late flowering plant if planted in cool leaf-mould. Probably unsuitable for very chalky soils and certainly for hot positions. Will tolerate some lime if there is humus in soil. Does better in Scotland than in S. England. Propagate by cuttings in late summer or seed. Himalayas. **42**, p. 6.

microphyllus, syn. **C. integer** ❊ Summer   RP.
Spreading matlike plant. *Fl.* deep violet with 5 prominent lobes. *L.* small, almost heath-like. Slightly smaller and usually less vigorous than preceding sp. but a beautiful plant where it grows satisfactorily. Requires cool moist position. Himalayas. **43**, p. 6.

CYCLAMEN (PRIMULACEAE)

Sun or semi-shade. Plant 2–4 in. deep.

atkinsii see **C. coum**

✿ **cilicium** ❊ Autumn   Tu.
Fl. pale pink with a prominent red spot at the base of each petal, 3–5 in. Scented. Each tuber bears a number of *fl. L.* roundish with irregular silvery markings, slightly toothed and about size of a halfpenny, appearing after the first *fl.* have opened. Suitable for a sunny position in rock garden or alpine house. Apparently quite hardy and a beautiful sp. spreading freely by seed. Smaller, daintier than *C. neapolitanum* and should be more widely grown. S. Turkey, **718**, p. 90.

✿ **coum** ❊ Mid Winter–Mid Spring   Tu.
This name is now accepted to cover all those spring-flowering sp., with marbled rounded *l.* and with plain *l.*, which have been grown under a multitude of names including *C. orbiculatum, C. hiemale, C. ibericum, C. vernum,* and *C. atkinsii.* The plants are very variable, with white or pink *fl.* on stems 2–5 in. *Fl.* always dumpy and squarish and without scent. Quite hardy and valuable as one of the first *fl.* of spring. Some forms are a strong magenta-pink with a deeper blotch at base of each petal and when growing freely can be very striking in the garden. Grows in full sun or semi-shade. Excellent also for pans in the alpine house and these may be completely dried off in summer. N. Turkey, Asia Minor. **719**, p. 90.

✿ **europaeum** ❊ Summer   Tu.
Fl. deep pink or carmine, 3–4 in. tall, scented, distinguished from *C. neapolitanum* by the absence of auricles at the base of the *fl.*, by the round *l.* and by the earlier season of flowering. Hardy in all except very cold gardens where the tuber may be protected by placing under a rock. Tuber rooting all over. White form beautiful but very rare. The wild cyclamen of sub-alpine and Central European woods.

hiemale see **C. coum**

ibericum see **C. coum**

libanoticum ❊ Spring   *Tu.
Fl. pale pink with a deeper crimson blotch at base of each petal, larger than in *C. coum* and not so squat. Tender except in warm areas but does well in alpine house or bulb frame. A very beautiful sp. Lebanon. **720**, p. 90.

✿ **neapolitanum** ❊ Autumn   Tu.
Fl. white or pink with bead-like auricles around the tip about ½ in. in height on 4–6 in. stem, resembling a ballet dancer pirouetting on one leg. *L.* ivy-shaped but infinitely variable, in fact no two tubers seem to produce *l.* identical in shape or markings. The earliest *fl.* appears before the *l.* Tubers round and flattish like a thickened saucer and producing roots from *upper* surface only together with short nobbly flowering branches. It is very important to plant this side uppermost. Usually there is a slight depression in upper surface. Mulch when dormant in early 7–8. The most reliable autumn-flowering sp. and a plant that should find a place in every garden. One of the few plants which will flourish in shade of beech trees since main *l.* are made during winter when *l.* are off the trees. S. Italy, Greece. **721**, p. 91.

orbiculatum see **C. coum**

persicum ❊ Spring   *Tu.
Fl. white or pink, generally with a darker rim at base, petals up to 1 in. long, slightly twisted or waved on stem 6–8 in. well above *l.* Very fragrant. *L.* ivy-shaped or rounded, marbled in varying degrees. Not quite hardy but a fine plant for alpine house or cool greenhouse. Dry off or plunge outside in summer. The wild parent of the florists' strains of greenhouse cyclamen, see 'Giganteum' below, much smaller but larger in *fl.* than preceding sp. and with a grace and charm that has been lost in larger strains. E. Mediterranean, Asia Minor including Lebanon, Palestine, N. Africa. **722**, p. 91.

'Giganteum' ❊ Winter–Spring   GTu.
Fl. large, crimson, red, salmon, purple or white. *L.* kidney-shaped, dark green, often marbled. Plant to 1 ft high. Any good potting compost. Plants rarely kept after flowering. Seeds sown in 8–9 to *fl.* 16 months later. Keep cool airy conditions. Minimum winter temp. 45–50°F. and summer temp. not above 70°F. Giant form of E. Mediterranean plant appeared in several nurseries in 1870. **486**, p. 61.

✿ **pseudibericum** ❊ Late Winter–Mid Spring *Tu.
Fl. large, deep crimson-carmine or purplish-red, always with deep crimson spot at base, petals ¾–1 in. long, like a larger *C. coum. L.* heart-shaped, broadly toothed around edge and slightly marbled, deep crimson below. Hardy in warm situations where the tuber is left dry in summer. Excellent for alpine house. Many forms are to be seen each spring in Wisley alpine house. S. Turkey. **723**, p. 91.

✿ **repandum** ❊ Spring   *Tu.
Fl. slightly later than above. Petals longer and narrower, giving a less dumpy *fl.* White, pink or crimson, scented. *L.* ivy-shaped. Tuber round and rooting from *lower* surface in middle only. Hardy in mild areas and excellent as an alpine house plant where tuber will live for many years and produce a vast number of *fl.* Italy, central and S. **724**, p. 91.

vernum see **C. coum**

CYDONIA see Chaenomeles, 1508, 1509, p. 189.

CYMBIDIUM (ORCHIDACEAE)

hybrids ❊ Spring   GP.
A genus of semi-terrestial orchids. The sp. from which the popular hybrids have been bred come mainly from Burma and Annam. They require a fairly rich mixture, probably including leaf mould or some similar vegetable compost, and can tolerate low temp. in the winter; 45°F. is quite sufficient, although slightly higher readings are preferable. During the summer, high temps. are needed, and many growers feel that the production of *fl.* spikes is encouraged by heat and the absence of shading. The young growths are somewhat susceptible to sun scorch, but once the *l.* have matured they can tolerate strong sunshine. Flowering season is early spring. The pink shaded hybrids are derived from *C. insigne.* The white shades are principally derived from *C. erythrostylum* and *C. eburneum,* while the green, and yellow shades come from *C. lowianum* and *C. tracyanum.* The hybridity is now so involved that it is not easy to recognise the components by looking at the hybrid. Propagation is by detaching back bulbs and inducing them to develop their dormant buds.

Among the very many hybrids the following are recommended:
Alexanderi 'Westonbirt', a good white;
Babylon 'Castle Hill', a very fine rosy pink, with distinctive large lip marked with red spotting, **487**, p. 61;
Baltic, a good green;
'Ramley', mainly green with reddish markings on the lip, **488**, p. 61;
Rosanna 'Pinkie', a fine pink which shows the scarlet column characteristic of *C. erthyrostylum,* **489**, p. 62;
Swallow 'Exbury', yellow with a little red spotting on the lip, **490**, p. 62;
Vieux Rose, very variable, amber, pink and khaki shades, **491**, p. 62.

CYNOGLOSSUM (BORAGINACEAE)

nervosum ❊ Summer   P.
Fl. blue, small but of remarkable intensity, borne on branching stems 1½–2 ft high. *L.* narrow, about 8 in. long, rough and hairy. Moderately rich well-drained loam and a sunny position. Propagate by division in spring or by seed sown in the open then. Himalaya. **1059**, p. 133.

Abbreviations and Symbols used in the text.
The following abbreviations may sometimes be used in conjunction as HA. indicating Hardy annual or GBb indicating Greenhouse bulb.

A. = Annual	P. = Perennial
Aq. = Aquatic	R. = Rock or
B. = Biennial	Alpine plant
Bb = Bulb	Sh. = Shrub
C. = Corm	Sp., sp. = Species
Cl. = Climber	Syn. = Synonym
Co. = Conifer	T. = Tree
Fl., fl. = Flower(s)	Tu. = Tuber
G. = Greenhouse or	var. = variety
house plant	× = Hybrid or
H. = Hardy	hybrid parents
HH. = Half-hardy	❊ = Flowering time
L., l. = Leaf, leaves	✿ = Foliage plant
Mt(s) = Mount,	
mountain(s)	

The following have been used also in the descriptions of Alpines, Bulbs, Trees and Shrubs.

   * = slightly tender
   † = lime hater
   ✿ = highly recommended

The illustration numbers are in **bold type** and the page numbers in light type preceded by p.

CYPERUS (CYPERACEAE) Galingale

alternifolius Umbrella Plant ◆ GP.
Probably now the most widely grown sp. Stems up to $2\frac{1}{2}$ ft high, crowned by numerous narrow *l.* Useful plant in a 5 in. pot. Madagascar.

papyrus Papyrus ◆ GP.
Fl. sedge-like, inconspicuous. *L.* grass-like in an umbel at the top of stem, which may reach 10 ft. Requires warm conditions, with a minimum winter temp. of 55°F. and should be planted in shallow water in rather rich soil. Propagation by division. The papyrus of the ancient Egyptians was made from the pith of the stems. Egypt. **492**, p. 62.

CYPRESS see **Cupressus, 2013**, p. 252.

CYPRESS, BALD see **Taxodium distichum, 2041**, p. 256.

CYPRESS, DECIDUOUS see **Taxodium distichum, 2041**, p. 256.

CYPRESS, FALSE see **Chamaecyparis, 2004-2010**, pp. 251, 252.

CYPRESS, ITALIAN see **Cupressus sempervirens**

CYPRESS, LAWSON see **Chamaecyparis lawsoniana, 2004-2008**, p. 251.

CYPRESS, MONTEREY see **Cupressus macrocarpa**

CYPRESS, SMOOTH ARIZONA see **Cupressus glabra, 2013**, p. 252.

CYPRESS, SUMMER see **Kochia**

CYPRESS, SWAMP see **Taxodium distichum, 2041**, p. 256.

CYPRIPEDIUM (ORCHIDACEAE)

calceolus Lady's Slipper Orchid ❋ Summer RP.
A very rare British native, but found more often in sub-alpine woodlands. Always a protected plant. *Fl.* single to a stem, with large yellow labellum pouch and chocolate brown sepals, up to 3 in. across. *L.* broad, ribbed. 12–15 in. A handsome orchid forming clumps where it has conditions to suit it and then long-lived. Plant in a well-drained leafy soil that does not dry out in semi-shade. Hardy. **44**, p. 6.

reginae ❋ Summer †RP.
Up to $1\frac{1}{2}$ ft. *Fl.* those of a slipper orchid, pouch pale purplish-pink, much inflated, sepals and upper petals white, broad, sometimes flushed with pink, large up to 3 in. across, 1–2 per stem. *L.* broad, pleated. Requires damp peaty conditions and must not be allowed to dry out during summer. N. USA.
Greenhouse varieties:
Known correctly botanically as *Paphiopedilum*, these slipper orchids are hybrids from sp. found in S.E. Asia from India to the Philippines. These with unmarked *l.* need comparatively cool conditions, while the more delicate forms with mottled *l.* need warmth and constant moisture. The colours are predominantly green, yellow and white with crimson blotches. The flowering season is late autumn.
Good varieties include:
Alma Gaevert, green with green and white striped dorsal sepal, **493**, p. 62;
Paeony 'Regency', a fully rounded *fl.* with broad petals the upper portions reddish-brown and lower portions greenish-yellow with mahogany streakings, the dorsal sepal is purple with a wide white margin and the pouch mahogany, **494**, p. 62;
W. N. Evans 'Brilliance', reddish-purple with a white margin to the dorsal sepal and yellow edging to the pouch and petals.

CYRILLA (CYRILLACEAE)

racemiflora Leatherwood UK, American Cyrilla USA ❋ Midsummer Sh.
Shrub, exceptional at flowering time with drooping clustered tassels of small white *fl.* Deciduous in the N., where bright green *l.* turn orange and scarlet in late autumn. This rich colouring against some of the lively green of the *l.* makes a striking contrast as the colouring begins to take effect. When planting, use plenty of peat moss. S.E. USA, West Indies to S. America.

CYTISUS (LEGUMINOSAE) Broom

ardoinii ❋ Spring RSh.
Small deciduous semi-prostrate shrublet, 6 in., forming thick mats. *Fl.* deep yellow, pea-like in clusters. *L.* small, with three leaflets grey-green, hairy. Compact grower and suitable for hot sunny position on rock garden. Maritime Alps. **45**, p. 6.

✡ **battandieri** ❋ Summer Sh.
A medium sized shrub up to 8 ft or taller when grown against a wall. Distinguished for its shining silvery foliage. *L.* divided into three leaflets. *Fl.* deep yellow in thick clustered racemes up to 4 in. long. Very strongly scented of pineapple. Unsuitable for very cold areas except against a wall, but in home counties grows well in open. Not easily moved when mature so should be planted young out of a pot. Morocco. **1546**, p. 194.

× **beanii** ❋ Late Spring Sh.
Probably *C. ardoinii* × *C. purgans*. Dense, much branched semi-procumbent, deciduous bush up to $1\frac{1}{2}$ ft. *Fl.* deep yellow, covering bush. *L.* undivided hairy, narrow. Sunny position on large rock garden or near front of border. A valuable hybrid which is quite hardy and *fl.* abundantly and regularly. Rather larger in growth than *C. ardoinii*. **46**, p. 6.
Other dwarf later-flowering brooms for the rock garden are:

decumbens, syn. **C. prostratus** ❋ Early Summer
4 in. with yellow *fl.* S. Europe.

demissus ❋ Early Summer
3 in. with yellow *fl.* stained brown. S.E. Europe.

× **kewensis** ❋ Spring Sh.
Dwarf or medium sized shrub up to 3 ft but spreading more widely. *Fl.* white, borne in great profusion. One of the most valuable of the early flowering brooms and suitable for large rock gardens. Should be pruned hard after flowering. **1547**, p. 194.

prostratus see **C. decumbens**

scoparius Yellow Broom ❋ Early Summer Sh.
Small shrub up to 6 ft or more. Native in its yellow form but this is also valuable for gardens. **1548**, p. 194.
Numerous deeply coloured forms have been grown or mixed forms can be grown from seed. Of named forms to be recommended are 'Andreanus' brown, crimson and orange; 'C. E. Pearson' apricot-yellow, red and rose; 'Cornish Cream' like Common Yellow Broom but paler in growth; 'Dorothy Walpole' rich velvety crimson; 'Firefly' yellow and scarlet; 'Golden Sunset' deep yellow; 'Lady Moore' rich red wings and keel with light buff standard rose on the reverse; 'Lord Lambourne' wings crimson-scarlet and standard pale cream; 'Sulphureus' the Moonlight Broom also known as *pallidus*, deep cream very free flowering. All these brooms should be pruned hard after flowering otherwise they tend to become straggly and are not usually very long lived beyond eight to ten years.

D

DABOECIA (ERICACEAE)

cantabrica Irish Heath ❋ Summer–Autumn †Sh.
Spreading evergreen shrub growing 18 in.–3 ft. *Fl.* rosy-purple or white, larger than *Erica*. Requires same conditions as *Erica*. S.W. Europe, W. Ireland and Azores. **1549**, p. 194.

DAFFODIL see **Narcissus, 829-864**, pp. 104-108.

DAFFODIL, CHALICE-CROWNED SEA see **Hymenocallis narcissiflora**

DAHLIA (COMPOSITAE) Tu.
Tuberous-rooted half-hardy perennial plants. The sp., of Mexican origin, are not grown as garden plants but have given rise to a vast number of hybrids of diverse colour, form and height. Propagation is easy from seed which is evident from the great number of varieties. Seed should be sown thinly in boxes containing light soil and germinated in a greenhouse or frame in 2–3 in a temp. of about 65°F. (18°C.). Germination takes about 10 days. Prick off the seedlings when large enough to handle into deep boxes or singly into 3 in. pots. This is a ready means of raising dwarf bedding dahlias, but named varieties are increased by cuttings or by careful division of the tubers in the spring.
To obtain cuttings place the tubers in boxes of light, moist soil in a warm greenhouse in 3–4. Sturdy young shoots should be taken when about 3 in. long and inserted in small pots containing a sandy compost and rooted in a warm propagating frame. Where large numbers of plants are required the cuttings may be inserted in a bed of sharp silver sand, with gentle bottom heat. As there is no nourishment in the sand such cuttings must be potted singly as soon as sufficient roots have formed. When no more cuttings are required the tubers may be carefully divided so that each piece has several young shoots or 'eyes'. These divisions may be grown on in boxes until planted out in the open towards the end of 5. In mild, frost-free districts, tubers may be left in the ground during the winter so long as the soil is well drained.
In the 'Classified List of Dahlias' published by the National Dahlia Society modern hybrid dahlias are divided into ten classes, with some of the larger classes sub-divided into various sections.

Abbreviations and Symbols used in the text.
The following abbreviations may sometimes be used in conjunction as HA. indicating Hardy annual or GBb indicating Greenhouse bulb.

A. = Annual	P. = Perennial
Aq. = Aquatic	R. = Rock or Alpine plant
B. = Biennial	Sh. = Shrub
Bb = Bulb	Sp., sp. = Species
C. = Corm	Syn. = Synonym
Cl. = Climber	T. = Tree
Co. = Conifer	Tu. = Tuber
Fl., *fl.* = Flower(s)	var. = variety
G. = Greenhouse or house plant	× = Hybrid or hybrid parents
H. = Hardy	❋ = Flowering time
HH. = Half-hardy	◆ = Foliage plant
L., *l.* = Leaf, leaves	
Mt(s) = Mount, mountain(s)	

The following have been used also in the descriptions of Alpines, Bulbs, Trees and Shrubs.

* = slightly tender
† = lime hater
✡ = highly recommended

The illustration numbers are in **bold type** and the page numbers in light type preceded by p.

Leading varieties in the main classes include:

Class I. Single:

'Kokette', red and white bicolor;

'Domingo', reddish-orange.

Class II. Anemone-flowered, *fl.* with one or more outer rings of ray-florets surrounding a dense group of tubular florets and showing no disc:

'Comet', ('Oosten'), dark red, **1060**, p. 133.

Class III. Collerette, *fl.* with a single outer ring of generally flat ray-florets, with a ring of small florets, the centre forming a disc:

'Fashion Monger', claret on pale yellow centre disc, **1061**, p. 133;

'Libretto', dark red and white, **1062**, p. 133.

Class IV. Paeony-flowered:

'Bishop of Llandaff', crimson, dark coppery foliage;

'Grenadier', bright red.

Class VA. Giant-flowered Decorative, *fl.* over 10 in. (254 mm.) across:

'Lavengro', lilac-purple, **1063**, p. 133;

'Night Editor', purple, **1064**, p. 133.

Class VB. Large-flowered Decorative, *fl.* over 8 in. (203 mm.) across, but not usually exceeding 10 in.:

'Blithe Spirit', red and white bicolor, **1065**, p. 134.

Class VC. Medium-flowered Decorative, *fl.* over 6 in. (152 mm.) across, not usually over 8 in.:

'Pattern', lavender and white bicolor, **1066**, p. 134;

'Terpo', red, **1067**, p. 134.

Class VD. Small-flowered Decorative, *fl.* over 4 in. (102 mm.) across but not usually exceeding 6 in.:

'Vigor', yellow, **1068**, p. 134.

Class VE. Miniature-flowered Decorative, *fl.* usually not exceeding 4 in. (102 mm.) across:

'David Howard', orange-bronze blend, **1069**, p. 134.

Class VIB. Miniature Ball, *fl.* up to 4 in. (102 mm.) across:

'Rothesay Superb', red, **1070**, p. 134.

Class VII. Pompon, *fl.* globular, not exceeding 2 in. (51 mm.) across:

'Andrew Lockwood', white;

'Willo's Violet', deep violet, **1071**, p. 134.

Class VIIIA. Giant-flowered Cactus, *fl.* over 10 in. (254 mm.) across:

'Poetic', dark pink and cream blend, fimbriated, **1072**, p. 134.

Class VIIIB. Large-flowered Cactus, *fl.* over 8 in. (203 mm.) across, but not usually exceeding 10 in.:

'Drakenburg', purple bronze blend, **1073**, p. 135.

Class VIIIC. Medium-flowered Cactus, *fl.* over 6 in. (152 mm.) across, but not usually exceeding 8 in.:

'Authority', bronze orange blend, **1074**, p. 135.

Class VIIID. Small-flowered Cactus, *fl.* not exceeding 4 in. (102 mm.) across:

'Doris Day', cardinal red, **1075**, p. 135;

'Klankstad Kerkrade', sulphur yellow, **1076**, p. 135.

Class IXA. Giant-flowered Semi-Cactus, *fl.* over 10 in. (254 mm.) across:

'Bestevaer', red, **1077**, p. 135.

Class IXB. Large-flowered Semi-Cactus, *fl.* over 8 in. (203 mm.) across, not usually over 10 in.:

'Nantenan', yellow, **1078**, p. 135;

'Royal Sceptre', orange-yellow blend, **1079**, p. 135.

Class IXC. Medium-flowered Semi-Cactus, *fl.* over 6 in. (152 mm.) across, not usually over 8 in.:

'Apache', red, fimbriated, **1080**, p. 135;

'Fleur de Hollande', red, **1081**, p. 136.

Class IXD. Small-flowered Semi-Cactus, *fl.* over 4 in. (102 mm.) across, not usually over 6 in.:

'Goya's Venus', bronze violet blend, **1082**, p. 136;

'Marilyn', dark and light pink, **1083**, p. 136.

Miscellaneous:

'Giraffe', orchid-flowered with elegant narrow florets, orange underside spotted crimson;

'Pink Giraffe', pink with red spots.

Coltness varieties ✳ Midsummer–Autumn   HHP.
Fl. crimson, scarlet, pink, yellow or white, single. *L.* opposite, pinnate. 1–1½ ft. Sow in 2–3 in a warm greenhouse and plant out in a sunny position in ordinary garden soil, late 5 or early 6. The tuberous roots should be lifted in the autumn, cleaned, dried and stored in a frost-free place. Of garden origin.

'Coltness Scarlet Gem', scarlet, 1½ ft, **280**, p. 35;

'Unwin's dwarf hybrids', produce double and semi-double *fl.* in many attractive shades, 1 ft, **281**, p. 36.

DAISY, AFRICAN see **Arctotis**, **238**, **239**, p. 30.

DAISY, ENGLISH or **MEADOW** see **Bellis perennis**, **243**, p. 31.

DAISY, KINGFISHER see **Felicia bergeriana**

DAISY, LIVINGSTONE see **Mesembryanthemum criniflorum**, **343**, p. 43.

DAISY, MICHAELMAS see **Aster novae-belgii**, **986-991**, p. 124.

DAISY, NAMAQUALAND see **Venidium**, **391**, p. 49.

DAISY, SHASTA see **Chrysanthemum maximum**, **1049**, p. 132.

DAISY, SWAN RIVER see **Brachycome iberidifolia**, **244**, p. 31.

DAISY BUSH see **Olearia**, **1714**, **1715**, p. 215.

DAPHNE (THYMELAEACEAE)

arbuscula ✳ Early Summer   Sh.
Small evergreen shrub up to 1½ ft but spreading more widely. Branchlets crowded. *Fl.* deep pink. Close to *D. cneorum* but with *l.* arranged in more crowded clusters at the ends of branches and *fl.* slightly larger. Suitable for rock garden in sunny position. S. Europe, Hungary. **1550**, p. 194

blagayana ✳ Summer   Sh.
Evergreen procumbent shrub up to 1 ft. *Fl.* creamy-white in large clusters, very fragrant. Prostrate branchlets should be covered with stones or soil to keep rooting. Valuable plant for rock garden. S. Europe, Yugoslavia. **1551**, p. 194.

× **burkwoodii** ✳ Early Summer   Sh.
A hybrid of *D. cneorum* × *D. caucasica*. Semi-evergreen and rather fast growing shrub up to 3 ft and as much across. *Fl.* white or pale blush-pink with deeper pink buds in clusters. One of the best of the Daphnes for the shrub border and usually longer lived than many other Daphnes. Sweetly scented. Best form is 'Somerset'.

cneorum Garland Flower ✳ Early Summer   RSh.
Dwarf semi-prostrate, evergreen shrub spreading to a large mat up to 8 in. *Fl.* pink, deeper in bud in clusters up to 1½ in. across, strongly scented. One of the finest dwarf shrubs for the rock garden. Easily propagated from cuttings in late summer. Central and S. Europe. **47**, p. 6.

✿ 'Eximia', best form with deeper pink *fl.* and buds;

'Pygmaea', is more prostrate.

collina ✳ Early Summer   Sh.
Small evergreen shrub up to 1½ ft but often less. *Fl.* deep bluish-pink or pale purple, very fragrant. Excellent shrub for the rock garden but rather slow growing. S. Europe, Italy, Sicily, Crete, Asia Minor. **1552**, p. 194.

Close to this is hybrid *neapolitana*.

genkwa ✳ Spring   *Sh.
Small deciduous shrub up to 3 ft. *Fl.* lilac, on bare wood. *L.* lanceolate 1–2 in. long. Unusual in genus for its colour but regarded often as short lived in England. In spite of cold winters, however, it seems to do better in E. States of N. America where it gets stronger summer ripening. **1553**, p. 195.

mezereum Mezereon ✳ Early Spring   Sh.
Deciduous bush up to 5 ft but usually less. *Fl.* deep rosy-purple or white. Berries fleshy 9–10 scarlet or purple forms and yellow in white forms. Europe, Asia Minor.

One of the finest forms is:—

✿ 'Bowles' White', usually not a long lived shrub and should be planted when small but comes freely from seed, sweetly scented and valuable for its winter flowering habit, **1554**, p. 195.

neapolitana see under **D. collina**

odora ✳ Mid Winter–Early Spring   Sh.
Dwarf shrub up to 3 ft and spreading. *L.* narrow. *Fl.* very fragrant in crowded heads white with reddish-purple tube and bud. China, Japan.

✿ 'Aureo-marginata', best and hardiest form, with yellow margin to *l.*, valuable for its very fine scent in winter, should be planted in sunny sheltered position, **1555**, p. 195.

petraea, syn. *D. rupestris* ✳ Early Summer *RSh.
Dwarf evergreen shrub, rarely over 6 in. high, very slow growing with thick gnarled branches. *Fl.* deep pink, waxy, with wide lobes up to ⅓ in. across in a good specimen covering bush with solid *fl.*, very fragrant. *L.* small, spathulate or oblong, leathery. One of the most prized alpines, usually grown as an alpine house plant. It should never be allowed to dry out and is often planted in a cleft or hole in a piece of tufa rock. Usually supplied as a grafted plant. N. Italy in mts around Lake Garda.

'Grandiflora', is form with slightly larger *fl.* and a little more vigorous, **48**, p. 6.

retusa ✳ Early Summer   Sh.
Evergreen bushy shrub up to 3 ft with thick branchlets. *Fl.* white or blush pink with deeper rosy purple buds and tube in clusters, petals rather fleshy. Makes a valuable small shrub for large rock garden or front of border but slow growing. W. China. **1556**, p. 195.

rupestris see **D. petraea**

striata ✳ Early Summer   Sh.
Small shrub up to 1½ ft. Sometimes prostrate. *Fl.* deep pink or purplish-pink in large clusters, sweetly scented. Closely related to *D. cneorum* but differing in its looser habit and smooth un-hairy *Fl.* and unfortunately more difficult to grow satisfactorily. European Alps from W. France to Carpathians. **1557**, p. 195.

Abbreviations and Symbols used in the text.
The following abbreviations may sometimes be used in conjunction as HA. indicating Hardy annual or GBb indicating Greenhouse bulb.

A. = Annual	P. = Perennial
Aq. = Aquatic	R. = Rock or
B. = Biennial	Alpine plant
Bb = Bulb	Sh. = Shrub
C. = Corm	Sp., sp. = Species
Cl. = Climber	Syn. = Synonym
Co. = Conifer	T. = Tree
Fl., *fl.* = Flower(s)	Tu. = Tuber
G. = Greenhouse or	var. = variety
house plant	× = Hybrid or
H. = Hardy	hybrid parents
HH. = Half-hardy	✳ = Flowering time
L., *l.* = Leaf, leaves	❧ = Foliage plant
Mt(s) = Mount,	
mountain(s)	

The following have been used also in the descriptions of Alpines, Bulbs, Trees and Shrubs.

* = slightly tender

† = lime hater

✿ = highly recommended

The illustration numbers are in **bold type** and the page numbers in light type preceded by p.

tangutica ❋ Early Summer   Sh.
Closely allied to *D. retusa* but with slightly longer *l.* and rather similar *fl.* clusters.

DATURA, syn. BRUGMANSIA (SOLANACEAE)

suaveolens, syn. **Brugmansia suaveolens** Angel's Trumpet ❋ Summer   GT.
Fl. white, pendant, fragrant. *L.* oblong-ovate 6–10 in. long. Can reach a height of 10–12 ft. Evergreen in the wild, but frequently deciduous in cultivation. Keep cool and dry during winter at temp. around 45°F., but in summer as much sun heat as is available is appreciated and the plant needs ample water. After flowering is complete prune hard back. Young plants need less severe pruning, until a good framework is formed. Large pots are required for mature plants or they can be planted out in the greenhouse beds. Propagate by cuttings of side-shoots with a heel at a temp. of 60°F. or over. Mexico. **495**, p. 62.
Two other sp. are very similar and require the same treatment. These are the Mexican *D. cornigera* (*D. knightii*) and *D. arborea* from Peru.

DAVIDIA (CORNACEAE)

involucrata Pocket-Handkerchief Tree, Dove Tree, Ghost Tree ❋ Late Spring   T.
Deciduous tree up to 50 ft. Distinguished for its large white bracts two to each *fl.* cluster in 5 but often long lasting. Larger bract up to 5 in. long is below *fl.* cluster and smaller one above. Pure white and conspicuous when waving in wind. *L.* broadly ovate up to 6 in. long. Fruit pear-shaped 1½ in. long green with purplish bloom in autumn. Unsuitable for very dry positions but very hardy. W. China. **1558**, p. 195.
Sometimes distinguished are varieties:
laeta, with *l.* slightly yellowish-green beneath;
vilmoriniana, with *l.* smooth and glaucous beneath; but for garden value there is probably little difference.

DAWN REDWOOD see **Metasequoia, 2025**, p. 254.

DAWYCK BEECH see **Fagus sylvatica** 'Fastigiata'.

DAY LILY see **Hemerocallis, 1167-1171**, pp. 146, 147.

DEAD NETTLE see **Lamium, 1230, 1231**, p. 154.

DEAD NETTLE, SPOTTED see **Lamium maculatum, 1231**, p. 154.

DECAISNEA (LARDIZABALACEAE)

fargesii ❋ Early Summer   Sh.
Deciduous shrub with clusters of tall direct shoots up to 10 ft. *Fl.* yellow-green in pendulous racemes. Fruit is the main feature of plant in hanging metallic-blue pods like those of a broad bean, 9–11. *L.* large pinnate up to 2½ ft. Should be planted in sunny position or semi-shade and left unmoved. China. **1559**, p. 195.

DECIDUOUS CYPRESS see **Taxodium distichum, 2041**, p. 256.

DELPHINIUM (RANUNCULACEAE)

ajacis Larkspur ❋ Summer   HA.
Fl. blue, pink, rose and white. *L.* deeply cut. 1½–3 ft. Sow in the open in a sunny position in 3–4, or in 9, where they are to *fl.* The hyacinth-flowered varieties, both tall and dwarf, and the double flowered 'Flore Pleno' mixed are delightful when

sown in liberal groups. The 'Giant Imperial' strain, 3 ft, with tall spikes of double *fl.* is available in mixed or separate colours and is good for cutting. S. Europe. **282**, p. 36.

brunonianum ❋ Summer   P.
Fl. violet, shading to purple. *L*, kidney-shaped, sharply cut, hairy. 10–15 in. Plant in a sunny position and well-drained soil. Propagate by seed or division in the spring. Afghanistan, Tibet. **1084**, p. 136.

Belladonna hybrids ❋ Summer   P.
Fl. in shades of blue, rose-pink, also white, on slender spikes. *L.* larkspur-like. 2½–4 ft. Propagate as for large-flowered hybrids. Of garden origin.
'Blue Bees', light blue;
'Moerheimi', white;
'Pink Sensation', light pink, **1085**, p. 136;
'Wendy', gentian blue.

Large-flowered hybrids ❋ Summer   P.
4½–6 ft. Plant 11–3 in a deep rich soil and sunny position or in spring in heavy soil. Propagate by cuttings taken in the spring or by division in 3.
There are many named varieties:
'Betty Hay', pale sky blue with a white eye, **1086**, p. 136;
'Blackmore's Glorious', a blend of mauve and pale blue with a white eye, **1087**, p. 136;
'Blue Nile', deep blue with white eye, **1088**, p. 136;
'Blue Tit', deepest blue with black eye, dwarf 3 ft, **1089**, p. 137;
'Butterball', white with cream centre, **1090**, p. 137;
'Swan Lake', white with a black eye, **1091**, p. 137.

DENDROBIUM (ORCHIDACEAE) ❋ Usually Early Summer

There are not a great number of epiphytic orchids that are deciduous and the genus *Dendrobium* is the largest and most attractive. The sp. are found over a wide range from India to China and Japan in the east and to the Philippines, New Guinea, and Australia in the south.
Although not all the sp. are deciduous, the majority are, and this fact makes them easier to cultivate in some ways, although their treatment in winter is different from that of the majority of epiphytic orchids. Growth starts in the spring and is rapid, so that the plant requires high temperatures and plenty of moisture during this period. Once the pseudobulbs have matured, they require ripening, so that less water is now required and as the *l.* yellow and drop it can be reduced to a minimum. The plants are overwintered in full light in a cool atmosphere; ideally around 50°F. The *fl.* buds appear among the upper nodes of the old pseudobulbs.

nobile   GP.
Found over a large area from India to China, has many different forms, all attractive, and is the parent of many hybrids.
Montrose 'Lyoth Gold', shades of yellow with a mahogany blotch, **496**, p. 62;
'Stella Hallmark', white, edged lilac-pink, blotch crimson, **497**, p. 63;
'Virginale', white with cream throat, **498**, p. 63.

victoriae-reginae   GP.
A curious climbing sp. with purplish *fl.* passing to white at base. It requires warmer conditions than *D. nobile* as do other sp. from the Philippines.

DENDROMECON (PAPAVERACEAE)

rigidum Californian Poppy Bush ❋ Summer   *Sh.
Shrub up to 10 ft but usually grown in Britain as a wall shrub. *Fl.* deep yellow four-petalled about 3–4 in. across. *L.* glaucous. Although tender this beautiful plant has from time to time survived some years against a sunny wall. Useful for the depth of yellow colour in the *fl.* It is very resentful of moving and young plants should be planted out of their pots with the minimum of disturbance. *Fl.* produced on

quite small plants. Said to do best in soil with mortar rubble and some sand. Propagation from cuttings in late summer planted singly in small pots in moderate heat. **1560**, p. 195.

DEODAR see **Cedrus deodara**

DESFONTAINEA (LOGANIACEAE)

spinosa ❋ Summer   *Sh.
Evergreen shrub up to 6 ft occasionally more especially against a wall. *Fl.* long tubular, scarlet with yellow tips and open lobes. *L.* holly-like. Out of *fl.* bush is easily mistaken for Holly. Valuable for its late flowering but only suitable for mild areas. Chile. **1561**, p. 196.

DEUTZIA (SAXIFRAGACEAE)

All Deutzias should be pruned after flowering or in early spring by having the flowering shoots cut right out or back to good bud.

crenata see **D. scabra**

'Magician' ❋ Summer   Sh.
Deciduous shrub up to 6 ft. *Fl.* in clusters star-shaped blush pink with deeper purplish-pink buds and outside of *fl.* *L.* lanceolate. Useful for its mid-summer flowering. Probably a hybrid from *D. longifolia* from China. **1562**, p. 196.

× **rosea**   Sh.
A hybrid of *D. gracilis* × *D. purpurascens.* Deciduous shrub up to 6 ft. *Fl.* with broader petals than above in small clusters, white or blush pink. **1563**, p. 196.
Various forms are known including:
'Campanulata', white, *fl.* with purple calyx;
'Carminea', deeper rose-carmine *fl.*;
'Venusta', large white *fl.*

scabra, syn. **D. crenata** ❋ Summer   Sh.
Deciduous shrub up to 6 ft. *Fl.* white in medium sized clusters. **1564**, p. 196.
Often grown in double forms:
'Candidissima', pure white;
'Plena', often known as 'Pride of Rochester', white suffused rose-purple outside;
'Pride of Rochester' see 'Plena'.

setchuenensis ❋ Summer   Sh.
Shrub up to 5 ft. *Fl.* white starry in small clusters. Very free flowering and loose growing rather

---

slender shrub valuable for its late flowering habit. China. **1565**, p. 196.

DIANTHUS (CARYOPHYLLACEAE)

This genus is divided below into four main sections:–
1 Alpine and Rock garden Pinks;
2 Annual and Biennial Plants;
3 Border Pinks and Carnations;
4 Perpetual Carnations for the greenhouse.

1 Alpine and Rock Garden Pinks

Compact tussocky plants with narrow evergreen foliage, often glaucous. *Fl.* white, pink or crimson, in midsummer, in some cases over a long period. All do well on chalk and also by the seaside in full sun. They are less good on hot sandy soils. The sp. are easily grown from seed, all may be propagated from cuttings or slips in late summer.

alpinus ❋ Summer RP.
Fl. large up to 1¼ in. across, pink or deep rose with a central ring of spots flecking of deep purplish-crimson, on a light or whitish ground, petals fringed at ends, solitary and practically unscented. *L.* grass-green not glaucous and forming a small mat. Up to 4 in. tall. One of the finest sp. but needs very good drainage. Excellent for alpine house or scree frame. E. Alps. **49**, p. 7.

caesius see **D. gratianopolitanus**

deltoides Maiden Pink ❋ Summer RP.
Fl. several to a stem, 6–9 in. tall in succession, white, pink or crimson up to ½ in. across, unscented. *L.* grass-like and green forming a loose mat. One of the easiest sp. for the rock garden. N. Europe including Britain. **50**, p. 7.
  'Brilliant', deep pink;
  'Hansen's Red', *fl.* bright crimson, one of the finest forms but not a very common plant, sometimes listed as 'Steriker'.

gratianopolitanus, syn. **D. caesius** The Cheddar Pink ❋ Summer RP.
Fl. pale–deep pink, very numerous covering tussock. Strongly scented, up to 1 in. across, petals fringed, stem up to 8 in., single-flowered. *L.* narrow, grass-like, stiff, slightly glaucous. One of the best sp. and usually easy to grow in well-drained sunny position. Central Europe including Britain. **51**, p. 7.

neglectus ❋ Summer RP.
Fl. bright pink, large up to 1¼ in., petals slightly fringed and uniform pink with buff colouring on reverse, on short stems up to 4 in., frequently covering compact tussock of grass-like *l.* One of the finest sp. and a favourite of alpine gardeners, needs good drainage and unsuitable for chalk. European Alps including Tyrol. **52**, p. 7.

2 Annual and Biennial Plants

barbatus Sweet William ❋ Late Spring–Summer HB.
Fl. crimson, scarlet, pink and white, single and double. *L.* broadly lance-shaped. 4 in.–2 ft. Sow in a seed bed in the open from 4–7, prick out 6 in. apart in rows, and transplant to sunny flowering positions from late 9 onwards, in well-drained soil. S. and E. Europe. **283**, p. 36.
Good forms include:
  'Auricula Eyed', 1½–2 ft, brightly marked *fl.* with contrasting zones of colour;
  'Dwarf Red Monarch', 9 in., large scarlet heads of *fl.*, may be grown as an annual;
  'Indian Carpet', 1 ft, compact, various colours;
  'Wee Willie', 4 in., very dwarf annual mixed.

caryophyllus Carnation ❋ Late Summer HB.
Fl. red, pink, crimson, yellow, white. 1–2 ft. Sow in a warm greenhouse in 2–3, plant out in 5. Of garden origin. Some good strains are:
  'Dwarf Pygmy mixed', 1 ft, new compact double strain for pots and bedding, fragrant;
  'Enfant de Nice', 1½–2 ft, large double *fl.* in self and striped colours;
  'Giant Chabaud', 1½ ft, various colours, double fringed *fl.*, **284**, p. 36.

chinensis see **D. sinensis**

sinensis 'Heddewigii', syn. **D. chinensis** 'Heddewigii' Japanese Pink ❋ Summer HHA.
Fl. crimson, salmon, pink, white, both double and single. 6 in.–1 ft. Sow under glass in 3 and plant out in 5. The sp. is from Japan.
  'Baby Doll', 6 in., dwarf habit, very large single *fl.* with various coloured markings;
  'Bravo', 1 ft, single dazzling scarlet;
  'Gaiety', 1 ft, has large fringed *fl.* in many colours, **285**, p. 36.

× **Sweet Wivelsfield** ❋ Summer HHA.
Fl. crimson, red, pink, white. 1½ ft. Sow in a warm greenhouse in 3 and plant out in 5, or in the open in 4 in well-drained soil and a sunny position. Of garden origin D. allwoodii × D. barbatus. **286**, p. 36.

3 Border Pinks and Carnations

Many sp. and hybrids which enjoy full sun, a well-drained soil and most appreciate some lime. A wide range of pinks have been evolved from *D. plumarius* (S.E. Europe) and border carnations from *D. caryophyllus* (S. France, N. Italy). The hybrid race *D.* × *allwoodii* is the result of crosses made between old fashioned garden pinks and perpetual-flowering carnations.
Propagation. Seed may be sown in spring in pans containing light sandy soil in gentle heat or in a cold frame. Cuttings or pipings of pinks should be inserted in sandy soil in a cold frame in summer, Border carnations by layering in 7–8.

Border Carnations: P.
  'Catherine Glover', yellow edged and barred scarlet, a show variety, rather than a border plant, **1092**, p. 137;
  'Fiery Cross', brilliant scarlet, a reliable border and exhibition variety, **1093**, p. 137;
  'Imperial Clove', violet-carmine, clove scented, **1094**, p. 137;
  'Lustre', golden-apricot, **1095**, p. 137;
  'Robin Thain', white striped rosy-crimson, clove scented, **1096**, p. 137;
  'Salmon Clove', soft salmon-pink, clove scented, **1097**, p. 138;
  'Warrior', white ground, flecked bright crimson, **1098**, p. 138;
  'Zebra', maize-yellow, striped crimson, an old favourite, **1099**, p. 138.

Show Pinks: P.
  'Show Beauty', deep pink, maroon centre, **1100**, p. 138;
  'Show Enchantress', salmon self, free flowering, **1101**, p. 138;
  'Show Ideal', creamy-pink with a salmon-red central ring, **1102**, p. 138;
  'Show Pearl', pearly white, **1103**, p. 138.

× **allwoodii** P.
  'Doris', delicate pink with a deep pink eye, **1104**, p. 138;
  'Lilian', pearly white, fragrant, free-flowering, **1105**, p. 139;
  'Robin', bright scarlet tinged orange, **1106**, p. 139;
  'Timothy', silvery pink, flecked cerise, **1107**, p. 139.

4 Perpetual Carnations for the Greenhouse GP.

It would seem that the first perpetual-flowering carnation was raised in France in 1750, but little notice was taken of this. It was in 1830 that a M. Dalmais raised the first plants that were to be further developed. No one is sure of the ancestry of these plants, but the late Montague Allwood who spent a lifetime in raising new Dianthus was of the opinion that they derived from the Border Carnation (*Dianthus caryophyllus*), being pollinated by the China pink (*D. sinensis*). The modern carnation needs cool greenhouse treatment in this country and is chiefly grown by commercial growers for the cut flower trade. For this purpose it is necessary to breed plants that will flower well in winter, when prices are most advantageous, and with strong stems, so that they will not be weighed down by the *fl.* and can be arranged satisfactorily. If the *fl.* are too double, they are liable to burst their calices and

this is also not required. Commercial growers have greenhouses entirely planted with carnations and and it is not too easy to grow them satisfactorily in the mixed greenhouse that most amateurs have. Many enthusiastic growers have shown however that it is not impossible. Cuttings of ripe side growths can be taken at any time of the year, and the plant will break naturally without having to be stopped. Some support is needed when the *fl.* stems start to elongate and they will probably need disbudding. At one time the range of possible colours was larger than it is today, although it is interesting to see that the striped Picotees are now coming back into favour. The soil for carnations should not be too rich, and a little lime is appreciated. If possible the temp. should be kept as constant as possible around 50–60°F. Too great a heat will cause the stems to be weak. In the old days, the Picotees and Fancies always had weak stems and these had to be supported with wire when the *fl.* were cut. If the temp. falls too low, it will not damage the plants, provided they are not frosted, but it will delay flowering. A good yellow carnation has yet to be bred but 'Helios' is quite satisfactory, although the colour is not as deep a yellow as some other cultivars. The best whites are usually not very large flowered and there is room for improvement here. Pinks and reds are the most common colours, and all the Sim's varieties are noted for their neat *fl.* and stiff stems. *Fl.* with a few white blotches are less popular and apart from the graceful Picotees, it is the self-colours that are most popular.
The following are among the best varieties and the heights given indicate the approximate height after two years:
  'Arthur Sim', white, lightly marked with scarlet, 6 ft, **499**, p. 63;
  'Ballerina', glowing cerise, short and compact, 4 ft, **500**, p. 63;
  'Brighton Rock', soft salmon ground, heavily marked with scarlet, 5 ft, **501**, p. 63;
  'Brocade', white with a heavy overlay of crimson, 5 ft, **502**, p. 63;
  'Edna Samuel', deep salmon-pink, free flowering, 5 ft, **503**, p. 63;
  'Flamingo Sim', bright pink, strong grower, 6 ft, **504**, p. 63;
  'Fragrant Ann', large white, strongly scented, 4 ft, **505**, p. 64;
  'Heather Beauty', large, mauve-pink, fragrant, 4 ft, **506**, p. 64;

Abbreviations and Symbols used in the text.
The following abbreviations may sometimes be used in conjunction as HA. indicating Hardy annual or GBb indicating Greenhouse bulb.

A. = Annual	P. = Perennial
Aq. = Aquatic	R. = Rock or
B. = Biennial	Alpine plant
Bb = Bulb	Sh. = Shrub
C. = Corm	Sp., sp. = Species
Cl. = Climber	Syn. = Synonym
Co. = Conifer	T. = Tree
Fl., *fl.* = Flower(s)	Tu. = Tuber
G. = Greenhouse or	var. = variety
house plant	× = Hybrid or
H. = Hardy	hybrid parents
HH. = Half-hardy	❋ = Flowering time
L., *l.* = Leaf, leaves	☙ = Foliage plant
Mt(s) = Mount,	
mountain(s)	

The following have been used also in the descriptions of Alpines, Bulbs, Trees and Shrubs.

  * = slightly tender
  † = lime hater
  ☼ = highly recommended

The illustration numbers are in **bold type** and the page numbers in light type preceded by p.

'Helios', primrose-yellow, robust grower, 6 ft, **507**, p. 64;

'Hollywood Sim', large, scarlet, flushed pink, 6 ft, **508**, p. 64;

'Monty's Pale Rose', pale rose-pink, fragrant, 5 ft, **509**, p. 64;

'William Sim', bright scarlet, neat habit, 6 ft, **510**, p. 64.

DIASCIA (SCROPHULARIACEAE)

barberae Twinspur ❋ Summer   HHA.
Fl. rose-pink. *L.* egg-shaped, bluntly toothed. 9–12 in. Sow in 3–4 under glass and plant out in late 5 in a sunny position. Makes a decorative pot plant. S. Africa. **287**, p. 36.

DICENTRA (PAPAVERACEAE)

(Sometimes now placed in separate family Fumariaceae)

eximia Fringed Bleeding Heart ❋ Late Spring–Summer   P.
Fl. rosy-purple on graceful drooping stems. *L.* fern-like, greyish-green, freely produced. *L.* 1½ ft. For sun or partial shade where the soil is of good depth, moist, but well-drained. Propagate by division in early spring or by root cuttings taken in 3 and placed in boxes in a cold frame. E. USA. 'Alba' is a good white form, **1108**, p. 139.

formosa ❋ Late Spring–Early Summer   P.
Fl. pink to light red. *L.* somewhat coarser than *D. eximia* and tufted. 1–1½ ft. Cultivation and propagation similar to *D. eximia*. W. and N. USA. 'Bountiful', has large deep pink *fl.* in spring and often again in autumn, **1109**, p. 139.

peregrina var. **pusilla** ❋ Late Spring–Early Summer   *†RP.
Fl. deep pink with reflexed white-edged petals and long anther cone, singly on 3 in. stems. Like small 'bleeding hearts'. *L.* glaucous, finely divided, fern-like. One of the choicest alpines, but with a reputation for difficulty and a short life. A lime-hater but needing very good drainage. Japanese growers recommend very dilute feeding while in growth. Best in alpine house. Japan, Siberia. **53**, p. 7.

spectabilis Bleeding Heart, Dutchman's Breeches ❋ Late Spring–Early Summer   P.
Fl. rosy-pink with white tips, dangling gracefully from arching stems. *L.* glaucous, deeply cut. 1½–2 ft. Cultivation and propagation as for *D. eximia*. Siberia, Japan. **1110**, p. 139.
'Alba', is a rare white form.

DICHELOSTEMMA IDA-MAIA see **Brodiaea ida-maia**

DICKSON'S GOLDEN ELM see **Ulmus carpinifolia** var. **sarniensis** 'Aurea', **1932**, p. 242.

DICTAMNUS (RUTACEAE) Burning Bush, Dittany

albus, syn. **D. fraxinella** ❋ Summer   P.
Fl. white, borne on erect spikes. *L.* light green, smooth, aromatic. 2–3 ft. Plant 11–3 in ordinary garden soil and a sunny position. Once planted leave undisturbed. Propagate by seed sown in the open ground or by division. E. Europe, Asia.
'Purpureus', a purplish-pink form with large individual *fl.*, **1111**, p. 139.

fraxinella see **D. albus**

DIDISCUS (UMBELLIFERAE)

caeruleus, syn. **Trachymene caerulea** Blue Lace Flower ❋ Midsummer–Mid Autumn   HHA.
Fl. lavender-blue on erect stems. *L.* usually tripartite, toothed. 1½–2 ft. Sow under glass in 3–4 and plant out in light, sandy soil and a warm position in 5. W. Australia. **288**, p. 36.

DIEFFENBACHIA (ARACEAE) Dumb Cane

L. large, oblong, pointed at tips, generally variegated in some way. If allowed to persist the plants can eventually reach a height of 8 ft, with a curiously corkscrew-shaped trunk. They are usually seen as plants about 18 in. high and when they get too tall are cut up for propagation. Each ring of the trunk is bisected and placed in a temp. of 80°F. They need warm, moist conditions and should be kept growing continuously as, although evergreen, the individual *l.* are not long-lived. A compost of equal parts of loam, peat and leaf-mould suits them well, but ample drainage must be arranged. The plants are extremely poisonous. *Fl.* not seen in cultivation.

amoena   GP.
L. up to a foot long, dark green, with blotches of cream and pale yellow along the principal veins. Tolerates lower temps. than most other sp. Minimum winter temp. 55°F. S. American tropics. **511**, p. 64.

arvida, syn. **D. hoffmannii**   GP.
L. up to 6 in. long and 3 in. across. When young marbled along principal veins, but when mature, marbling covers most of the upper surface. Costa Rica.
'Exotica', is a selected clone found at Rio Ysidho in Costa Rica, a good room plant, but like all sp. intolerant of draughts or oil fumes, minimum winter temp. 60°F., **512**, p. 64.

hoffmannii see **D. arvida**

picta   GP.
L. very variable in colour, mostly green with a quantity of cream or silver blotches, up to 9 in. long and 3 in. across. Minimum winter temp. 65°F. Brazil, Colombia.
'Roehrsii', has wider *l.* than most other vars. and the surface is mainly yellowish-green, **513**, p. 65.

DIERAMA (IRIDACEAE)

pulcherrimum Wand Flower ❋ Summer   C.
Fl. like hanging bells in purple, mauve, wine-red or white, suspended from slender arching stem up to 5 ft in height. Dwarf forms up to only 2 ft can also be grown. *L.* narrow, iris-like. Not completely hardy in cold areas and also unsuitable for dry hot areas. Dieramas are touchy over moving when mature and may take years to recover so corms should either be planted out of pots or planted out as seedlings into their final position. S. Africa. **725**, p. 91.

DIERVILLA AMABILIS and D. FLORIDA see **Weigela florida**

DIGITALIS (SCROPHULARIACEAE) Foxglove

purpurea ❋ Summer   HB.
Sow in the open in 5 and 6 for flowering in the following year. Ordinary garden soil in sun or partial shade. Europe, Asia.
'Excelsior hybrids', shades of pink, primrose, cream and white, with the individual *fl.* held horizontally all around the stem, 5–6 ft, **289**, p. 37;
'Foxy', *fl.* carmine, pink, cream and white, heavily spotted maroon, may be flowered as an annual from sowings under glass in 2–3 and planted out in 5 and 6, 2½ ft, **290**, p. 37.

DIMORPHOTHECA (COMPOSITAE) Star of the Veldt, African Daisy

aurantiaca ❋ Summer   HHP.
Fl. bright orange. *L.* alternate, variously cut. Perennial but usually treated as an annual. 1 ft. Hybrid strains of *D. sinuata, D. calendulacea* and *D. aurantiaca* are available in shades of orange, yellow, pale salmon, buff-apricot, also white. Sow in a cool greenhouse in 3–4 and plant out in mid-5, or sow in the open in 4 where they are to *fl.* in a

sunny position and in well-drained soil. S. Africa. **291**, p. 37.

barberiae ❋ Summer   RP.
Fl. heads daisy-like, bright purplish-pink, up to 2½ in. across, on stems up to 1 ft, numerous and flowering over long season from 6–9. *L.* narrow up to 4 in. Plant in a warm sunny position. Easily propagated from cuttings in late summer and overwintered in frame or cool greenhouse. S. Africa. **54**, p. 7.
var. *compacta*, more dwarf with *fl.* heads on stems up to 9 in. and hardier.

ecklonis ❋ Summer   HHP.
Fl. white, with blue disc, in heads 3 in. across. *L.* lance-shaped, slightly cut. 2 ft. Cultivate as for *D. aurantiaca*. S. Africa.

DIONYSIA (PRIMULACEAE)

aretioides, syn. **D. demavendica** ❋ Spring   *RP.
Cushion plant with loose green tussocks, *l.* small, slightly grey underneath. *Fl.* with long tube and spreading lobes, deep yellow up to 1½ in. across. Probably best as alpine house plant, planted in gritty scree mixture. Only recently reintroduced but it promises to be the easiest to grow of this genus of rather difficult connoisseurs' plants. Should not be watered overhead. Iran, Afghanistan. **55**, p. 7.

demavendica see **D. aretioides**

DIPLACUS GLUTINOSUS see **Mimulus glutinosus**

DISANTHUS (HAMAMELIDACEAE)

cercidifolius ☙   †Sh.
Deciduous rather slender shrub up to 10 ft. *Fl.* small purplish and inconspicuous. Chiefly grown for beautiful autumn foliage. *L.* roundish heart-shaped at base, deep crimson or carrot-red with some scarlet *l.* in autumn. One of the finest of autumn colouring shrubs. Does best in peaty soil and unsuitable for very dry positions. Japan. **1566**, p. 196.

DITTANY see **Dictamnus**, **1111**, p. 139.

Abbreviations and Symbols used in the text.
The following abbreviations may sometimes be used in conjunction as HA. indicating Hardy annual or GBb indicating Greenhouse bulb.

A. = Annual	P. = Perennial
Aq. = Aquatic	R. = Rock or
B. = Biennial	Alpine plant
Bb = Bulb	Sh. = Shrub
C. = Corm	Sp., sp. = Species
Cl. = Climber	Syn. = Synonym
Co. = Conifer	T. = Tree
Fl., fl. = Flower(s)	Tu. = Tuber
G. = Greenhouse or house plant	var. = variety
	× = Hybrid or hybrid parents
H. = Hardy	❋ = Flowering time
HH. = Half-hardy	☙ = Foliage plant
L., l. = Leaf, leaves	
Mt(s) = Mount, mountain(s)	

The following have been used also in the descriptions of Alpines, Bulbs, Trees and Shrubs.

* = slightly tender
† = lime hater
✿ = highly recommended

The illustration numbers are in **bold type** and the page numbers in light type preceded by p.

DIZYGOTHECA (ARALIACEAE)

elegantissima, syn. **Aralia elegantissima** False Aralia ✿ GP.
Shrub to 10 ft or more, very slow-growing. *L.* hand-shaped on long stems. Leaflets 7–10; thread-like in juvenile plants (as in illustration) up to 2 in. broad in mature specimens; up to 1 in. long: reddish-brown, darkening to nearly black. Needs warm, moist conditions; very susceptible to Red Spider if atmosphere too dry. Minimum winter temp. 60°F. Avoid draughts and sudden changes of temp. Propagate by seed, also by cuttings in bottom heat. New Hebrides. **514**, p. 65.

DODECATHEON (PRIMULACEAE)

alpinum Shooting Star ✳ Early Summer RP.
Fl. pendulous, bright purplish-crimson with yellow ring at base, reflexed petals like those of a cyclamen and protruding anther cone up to 7 in. a small umbel on 8–10 in. stems. *L.* oblong, slightly fleshy and glabrous. All shooting-stars are plants of damp places and must not be allowed to dry out in cultivation. Probably best in semi-shade. Plant dies away soon after flowering and does not re-appear till spring. USA, California. **56**, p. 7.

meadia ✳ Early Summer P.
Fl. rosy, in clusters, with bright yellow anthers and reflexed petals. *L.* in rosettes near the ground, about 6 in. long, slightly toothed. 1–1½ ft. Requires partial shade and a moist soil. Propagate by division in the autumn, or by seed sown in pans of light sandy soil and placed in a cold frame in 9 or 3. N. America.
‘Album’, is a most graceful white form, **1112**, p. 139.

DOG-TOOTH VIOLET see **Erythronium denscanis**, **731**, p. 92.

DOGWOOD see **Cornus**, **39**, p. 5; **1524-1528**, p. 191.

DONDIA EPIPACTIS see **Hacquetia epipactis**

DORONICUM (COMPOSITAE) Leopard's Bane

caucasicum ✳ Spring P.
Fl. deep yellow, about 2 in. across, solitary. *L.* kidney-shaped, deeply toothed. 1–1½ ft. In sun or partial shade where the soil is of good depth and moist. Propagate by division of the roots in early autumn. Europe, Asia.
Good varieties include:
‘Magnificum’, a larger form with *fl.* up to 3½ in. across;
‘Spring Beauty’, raised in Germany as ‘Frühlingspracht’, deep yellow, fully double, **1113**, p. 140.

cordatum ✳ Mid Spring–Early Summer P.
Fl. golden-yellow, solitary. *L.* heart-shaped. 6 in. Cultivation and propagation as for *D. caucasicum*. S.E. Europe, W. Asia. **1114**, p. 140.

plantagineum ✳ Mid Spring–Early Summer P.
Fl. yellow, daisy-like, good for cutting. *L.* heart-shaped, toothed. 2½–3 ft. Cultivation and propagation as for *D. caucasicum*. W. Europe.
Good varieties include:
‘Excelsum’, syn. ‘Harpur Crewe’, golden-yellow, 3 ft;
‘Miss Mason’, yellow, free flowering, 2 ft.

DOROTHEANTHUS BELLIDIFLORUS see **Mesembryanthemum criniflorum**

DOUGLASIA (PRIMULACEAE)

vitaliana ✳ Late Spring–Summer *RP.
Mat forming dwarf plant with small greyish-green narrow linear *l. Fl.* bright yellow, about ½ in. across with long tube, almost sessile. Probably best as an alpine house or scree frame plant. Requires very good drainage and outside should be planted in full sun. Alps and Pyrenees at fairly high altitudes. **57**, p. 8.

DOVE TREE see **Davidia**, **1558**, p. 195.

DRABA (CRUCIFERAE)

bryoides var. **imbricata**, syn. **D. imbricata** ✳ Spring *RP.
Small green dome-shaped cushion plants. *Fl.* bright yellow small in clusters of 3–4 on 2–3 in. stems. *L.* small, oblong in dense rosettes. Usually grown as an alpine house or scree frame plant but a good crevice plant in open. Do not water overhead in winter. USSR, Caucasus. **58**, p. 8.

imbricata see **D. bryoides** var. **imbricata**

mollissima ✳ Spring *RP.
Domed cushion plant, when old up to 8 in. across, *fl.* small yellow, star-like in small clusters on 1–2 in. stem. Rosettes covered with short grey hairs. Usually grown as an alpine house plant, should be watered from below by plunging pan or round side of pan. USSR, Caucasus. **59**, p. 8.

DRACAENA (LILIACEAE)

A genus of shrubs or small trees with sword-like *l.*, giving a palm-like appearance. Much used for indoor decoration as house plants. A good potting compost, such as JIP suits them well. Propagation by stem cuttings, which need a temp. of 80°F. to root.

deremensis ✿ GSh.
To 15 ft in wild. *L.* sword-like to 1½ ft long, 2 in. across, edged dark green then two silver stripes and grey-green centre. Minimum winter temp. 55°F. Keep on dry side in winter. Africa.
‘Bausei’, the centre of the *l.* is silver, **515**, p. 65.

fragrans ‘Massangeana’ ✿ GSh.
Up to 20 ft in wild, sometimes branched. Rarely more than 3 ft in cultivation. *L.* strap-shaped, to 18 in. long and 4 in. across. Margins emerald green, centre of *l.* golden. Treatment as for *D. deremensis*. Guinea. **516**, p. 65.

marginata ✿ GSh.
10–15 ft in wild, about 2–3 ft in cultivation. *L.* sword-like, up to 15 in. long but only 1 in. across; dark green with very narrow red margins. Winter temp. 45–50°F. Keep dry in winter, moderately moist at other times. Madagascar. **517**, p. 65.

sanderiana ✿ GSh.
Slender plant to 3 ft, branched at base. *L.* sword-shaped, undulant, 1 in. across; 7–10 in. long, striped grey and silver. Keep on dry side in winter. Minimum temp. 50°F., survives with little damage at 45°F. Congo. **518**, p. 65.

terminalis see **Cordyline terminalis**

DRACUNCULUS (ARACEAE)

vulgaris, syn. **Arum dracunculus** Dragon Arum ✳ Early Summer Tu.
A very striking arum lily, an enormous Lords and Ladies, with a large reddish-maroon spathe like a back shield, 1 ft long and up to 8 in. across. Spadix almost black and often longer than spathe when mature, looking like the clapper of a bell or a Jack in the Pulpit. As they go over, *fl.* tend to smell rather offensively. Stems up to 2 ft, strikingly spotted. *L.* large and deeply divided. Roundish tuber should be planted in as warm a place as possible. Doubtfully hardy in cold areas. S. Europe, Mediterranean regions. **726**, p. 91.

DRAGON ARUM see **Dracunculus vulgaris**, **726**, p. 91.

DREGEA SINENSIS see **Wattakaka sinensis**

DRIMYS (MAGNOLIACEAE)

winteri ✳ Late Spring *Sh.,T.
Evergreen shrub or small tree to 25 ft. with aromatic bark. *Fl.* white and fragrant. *L.* large, magnolia-like. S. America.
var. *latifolia*, similar to type but slightly hardier and with larger *fl.* **1567**, p. 196.

DROOPING JUNIPER see **Juniperus recurva**, **2020**, p. 253.

DROPWORT see **Filipendula**, **1135**, **1136**, p. 142.

DRYAS (ROSACEAE)

octopetala ✳ Spring RP.
Mat forming evergreen sub-shrubby plant. *Fl.* white with egg-yellow centre, up to 1½ in. across like a small anemone. *L.* small, deeply lobed and dark green above, greyish below. Useful for covering rocks in sunny position and usually a vigorous grower but rarely in cultivation *fl.* as freely as it does in the Alps where it is abundant. A rare native of Scotland and W. of Ireland also. **60**, p. 8.
var. *minor*, less spreading.

DUMB CANE see **Dieffenbachia**, **511-513**, pp. 64, 65.

DUNKELD LARCH see **Larix × eurolepis**

DURMAST OAK see **Quercus petraea**

DUSTY MILLER see **Cineraria maritima**, **267**, p. 34.

DUTCH HONEYSUCKLE, see **Lonicera periclymenum** ‘Belgica’ and ‘Serotina’

DUTCHMAN'S BREECHES see **Dicentra spectabilis**, **1110**, p. 139.

DWARF SNOWBELL see **Soldanella pusilla**, **212**, p. 27.

DWARF RUSSIAN ALMOND see **Prunus tenella**, **1766**, p. 221.

DYER'S GREENWEED see **Genista tinctoria**, **1624**, p. 203.

Abbreviations and Symbols used in the text.
The following abbreviations may sometimes be used in conjunction as HA. indicating Hardy annual or GBb indicating Greenhouse bulb.

A. = Annual	P. = Perennial
Aq. = Aquatic	R. = Rock or
B. = Biennial	Alpine plant
Bb = Bulb	Sh. = Shrub
C. = Corm	Sp., sp. = Species
Cl. = Climber	Syn. = Synonym
Co. = Conifer	T. = Tree
Fl., *fl.* = Flower(s)	Tu. = Tuber
G. = Greenhouse or	var. = variety
house plant	× = Hybrid or
H. = Hardy	hybrid parents
HH. = Half-hardy	✳ = Flowering time
L., *l.* = Leaf, leaves	✿ = Foliage plant
Mt(s) = Mount,	
mountain(s)	

The following have been used also in the descriptions of Alpines, Bulbs, Trees and Shrubs.

* = slightly tender
† = lime hater
☆ = highly recommended

The illustration numbers are in **bold type** and the page numbers in light type preceded by p.

E

EARLY DUTCH HONEYSUCKLE see **Lonicera periclymenum** 'Belgica'

EASTER CACTUS see **Rhipsalidopsis rosea**, **635**, p. 80, and **Schlumbergera gaertneri**, **644**, p. 81.

EASTERN HEMLOCK see **Tsuga canadensis**, **2048**, p. 256.

ECCREMOCARPUS (BIGNONIACEAE)

scaber ❋ Summer   *Cl.
Semi-woody but fast growing climber climbing by tendrils. *Fl.* in clusters, narrowly tubular and contracted at mouth 1 in. long, bright orange-red, some forms have yellow *fl.* and others deeper red. Leaflets doubly pinnate with tendrils at end of main stalks. Useful as a wall climber but except in very warm areas usually cut to ground each winter. May be grown as an annual by planting seed in 2 in warm greenhouse and planting out in 5. As a greenhouse plant forms a woody base and grows vigorously. Chile. **1976**, p. 247.

ECHEVERIA (CRASSULACEAE)

gibbiflora 'Metallica' ❋ Summer   G sub-Sh.
Fl. scarlet. *L.* ovate, fleshy, grey-green with metallic flush in rosettes at ends of branches. Minimum winter temp. 45°F. Keep dry in winter and water fairly sparingly in spring and summer. Propagate by cuttings taken in spring. Mexico. **519**, p. 65.

ECHINACEA PURPUREA see Rudbeckia purpurea

ECHINOCACTUS (CACTACEAE)

grusonii   GP.
Fl. yellow, rarely produced in cultivation. Stem globose, deeply ribbed, up to 3 ft high. Slow-growing. Spines golden-yellow, up to 2 in. long. Compost mainly of coarse grit. Winter temp. 40°F. Water moderately in early spring, more copiously in summer but start to water less in 8 and keep dry during autumn and winter. Propagation by seed. Mexico. **520**, p. 65.

ECHINOCEREUS (CACTACEAE)

scheeri ❋ Late Spring–Midsummer   GP.
Fl. purple. Stems cylindrical, ribbed, spiny. Gritty well-drained soil and practically no water between 10 and 3; only moderate amounts 3–5 and 8–10. Winter temp. 45°F. Propagate by rooting branches, which are produced freely. Mexico, southern USA. **521**, p. 66.

ECHINOPS (COMPOSITAE) Globe Thistle

ritro ❋ Summer   P.
Fl. steely-blue. *L.* much divided, downy on the underside. 3 ft. Plant 10–3 in ordinary garden soil, sun or shade. Propagate by division or by root cuttings. E. Europe.
  'Veitch's Blue', a bright, deep blue, **1115**, p. 140.

ECHIUM (BORAGINACEAE) Viper's Bugloss

lycopsis see **E. plantagineum**

plantagineum ❋ Summer   HA.
Fl. deep purplish-violet. *L.* oblong, hairy. 1–3 ft. Sow in the open in 3–4, where it is to *fl.*, does quite well in poor, dry soil. Well known as *E. plantagineum*, this plant is now correctly *E. lycopsis*. Mediterranean region.
  'Blue Bedder', sometimes listed under *E. vulgare*, 1 ft, compact, bright blue, **292**, p. 37;

'Dwarf Hybrids', 1 ft, in shades of blue, lavender, pink, **293**, p. 37.

EDGWORTHIA (THYMELAEACEAE)

papyrifera, syn. **E. chrysantha** ❋ Late Winter–Mid Spring   *Sh.
Deciduous shrub up to 5 ft. Young shoots clothed with silky hairs. *Fl.* in dense clusters, tubular buff-yellow deeper inside, sometimes rather pendulous and at ends of short branches. Fragrant. Valuable for its early flowering but only suitable for milder areas. Closely related to *Daphne*. Grown widely in Japan where it is used for making paper. China. **1568**, p. 196.

EDRAIANTHUS (CAMPANULACEAE)

pumilio, syn. **Wahlenbergia pumilio** ❋ Early Summer   *RP.
Dwarf loose cushion plant. *Fl.* upright, bell-shaped, strong violet-blue, almost sessile, up to ¾ in. across. *L.* very narrow, forming tufts of cushion. Suitable for limestone scree in full sun or alpine house where it often *fl.* very freely covering cushions. Balkans, Dalmatia. **61**, p. 8.

serpyllifolius, syn. **Wahlenbergia serpyllifolius** ❋ Early Summer   RP.
Dwarf loose mat-forming plant. *Fl.* upright, bell-shaped, violet-blue even more intense than previous sp., solitary, up to 1 in. across with petals reflexed at mouth on short stems up to 4 in. *L.* narrow, up to 1 in. forming tufts. Plant in full sun in limestone scree or in alpine house. Requires warm position and very good drainage.
  'Major', *fl.* slightly larger and more vigorous, **62**, p. 8.

EDWARDSIA MICROPHYLLA see Sophora tetraptera var. microphylla

EGYPTIAN LOTUS see Nymphaea lotus, 569, p. 72.

ELAEAGNUS (ELAEAGNACEAE)

× **ebbingei**   Sh.
A hybrid between *E. glabra* × *E. pungens*. Evergreen shrub up to 8 ft. Very fast growing. *Fl.* small inconspicuous. *L.* large up to 5 in., shiny with rustiness underneath. Valuable as wind break and for providing shelter in windy areas especially in S. and W. **1569**, p. 197.

pungens   Sh.
Shrub up to 10 ft usually less. Grown for its conspicuously variegated *l.* which are in a number of forms.
  'Dicksonii', deep yellow and green variegations, rather slow growing. **1570**, p. 197;
  'Maculata', *l.* liberally splashed with deep golden-yellow, green at edges. Valuable for winter effect, **1571**, p. 197.

ELDER, ROSE and WATER see Viburnum opulus, 1945, 1946, p. 244.

EMBOTHRIUM (PROTEACEAE)

coccineum Chilean Fire Bush ❋ Summer   †*Sh.
Evergreen or in some areas nearly deciduous. Shrub or small tree up to 30 ft. *Fl.* in clusters of short racemes along end of branches. Most brilliant scarlet. **1572**, p. 197.
The following have been sometimes distinguished as separate sp. but are probably only var. of the one polymorphic sp. S. America, Chile but extending over long range.

  ✿ var. **lanceolatum** 'Norquinco' ❋ Early Summer
Fl. orange-scarlet very freely produced clothing all ends of branches, long tubular. One of the most conspicuous plants which can be grown in milder areas. **1573**, p. 197.

var. **longifolium**, with narrower *l.*

ENDYMION (LILIACEAE)

hispanicus, syn. **Scilla campanulata, S. hispanica** Spanish Bluebell ❋ Spring   Bb
Like a large bluebell. *Fl.* tubular, pendulous, white, pale blue, deep blue, pale rosy-purple or pink. Forms large clumps and may be naturalised in semi-wild positions or in the border or open woodland, a better garden plant than the bluebell. It is often placed under *Scilla* in catalogues.
Among good selected forms are:
  'Excelsior', deep blue, large;
  'King of the Blues', deep sky-blue;
  'Mount Everest', white;
  'Myosotis', sky-blue;
  'Queen of the Pinks', deep rose-pink;
  'White Triumphator', white, large in *fl.*

non-scripta, syn. **Scilla nutans, S. non-scripta** Bluebell ❋ Spring   Bb
Lovely for naturalising in open woodland among shrubs such as deciduous azaleas, but rather too invasive for the garden, making large clumps and spreading by seeding. An English native. **727**, p. 91.

ENGLISH DAISY see Bellis perennis, 243, p. 31.

ENGLISH ELM see Ulmus procera

ENGLISH HOLLY see Ilex aquifolium, 1659-1662, p. 208.

ENGLISH IVY see Hedera helix, 544-546, pp. 68, 69.

ENGLISH LAVENDER see Lavandula spica, 1671, p. 209.

ENKIANTHUS (ERICACEAE)

campanulatus ❋ Early Summer   †Sh.
Shrub up to 8 ft but usually less. *Fl.* open bell-shaped in small pendulous clusters, creamy-white at base, purplish-pink nearer tips. Also valuable for autumn colouring. **1574**, p. 197.

Abbreviations and Symbols used in the text.
The following abbreviations may sometimes be used in conjunction as HA. indicating Hardy annual or GBb indicating Greenhouse bulb.

A. = Annual	P. = Perennial
Aq. = Aquatic	R. = Rock or
B. = Biennial	Alpine plant
Bb = Bulb	Sh. = Shrub
C. = Corm	Sp., sp. = Species
Cl. = Climber	Syn. = Synonym
Co. = Conifer	T. = Tree
Fl., fl. = Flower(s)	Tu. = Tuber
G. = Greenhouse or	var. = variety
house plant	× = Hybrid or
H. = Hardy	hybrid parents
HH. = Half-hardy	❋ = Flowering time
L., l. = Leaf, leaves	❧ = Foliage plant
Mt(s) = Mount,	
mountain(s)	

The following have been used also in the descriptions of Alpines, Bulbs, Trees and Shrubs.

  * = slightly tender
  † = lime hater
  ✿ = highly recommended

The illustration numbers are in **bold type** and the page numbers in light type preceded by p.

---

cernuus Sh.

Shrub up to 5 ft often less. Valuable for brilliant autumn colouring of its small *l*. In 9–10 these are claret coloured then later becoming fiery red. Japan. **1575**, p. 197.

'Rubens' is best form with red *fl*., **1576**, p. 197.

EPIDENDRUM (ORCHIDACEAE)

ibaguense, syn. **E. radicans** ❋ Throughout the year GP.

Scandent plant up to 10 ft. *Fl*. orange-scarlet, to 1½ in. across on long-lasting racemes, lip bright red. *L*. strap-shaped. Usual orchid compost of osmunda and sphagnum, or other media. Winter temp. 45–50°F. Propagation by cutting plant up, any section of the stem will make growth. Guatemala. **522**, p. 66.

radicans see **E. ibaguense**

EPIPHYLLUM (CACTACEAE)

A genus of showy-flowered Cacti, epiphytic in nature. Stems flattened and spines very small or absent. This, with the related genera of *Schlumbergera* and *Zygocactus*, with which Epiphyllum are often hybridised, needs rather richer soil than the desert cacti and appreciates warmer and moister conditions and shading in the summer. A minimum winter temp. of 50°F. is desirable. The plants should be kept on the dry side in the winter, but syringed from time to time. If a temp. of 50°F. cannot be maintained, they must be kept dry and although they will shrivel, they will plump out again when it is safe to water again. Propagation by cuttings of joints. Seed is unlikely to come true.

ackermannii ❋ Late Summer GP.

Fl. crimson, large. Stems flat and thin with a few spines. Plant usually about 2 ft tall. Thought now not to be a true sp., but a hybrid. Mexico. **523**, p. 66.

hybrids ❋ Late Summer GP.

A large number of hybrids have been raised among the sp. themselves and with related genera. A wide range of colours has been developed. They require similar treatment to the sp. **524**, p. 66.

Among the best named hybrids are:

'Cooperi', white, large flowered, strongly scented, not very free-flowering;

'Duchess', pale mauve, reasonably free-flowering;

'Eden', white, free-flowering, but not scented;

'Janus', orange, not scented, medium to large flowered;

'London Beauty', flame red, azalea-pink in autumn, free-flowering, medium sized;

'London Glory', orange-red with an overlay of magenta which gives the appearance of a blue sheen; medium sized *fl*., not scented;

'London Magic', pale pink, medium sized *fl*., the colour deepens with age;

'London Sunshine', yellow *fl*. paling to cream in centre;

'London Surprise', orange *fl*. medium to large strongly scented;

'Professor Ebert', deep mauve, free-flowering;

'Reward', even yellow, medium sized *fl*., not so free-flowering as 'London Sunshine'.

ERANTHIS (RANUNCULACEAE)

cilicica ❋ Early Spring Tu.

Similar to *E. hyemalis* but with a ruff below the *fl*. of more finely divided leafy bracts. Cilicia. **728**, p. 91.

hyemalis Winter Aconite ❋ Early Spring Tu.

One of the earliest and brightest of our spring *fl*. *Fl*. bright golden-yellow, cup-shaped like a buttercup on short stems 2–3 in. Below *fl*. is a ring of bright divided leafy bracts which frame the *fl*. like a Toby dog's ruff. Tuber nobbly, should be planted 9 or 10 only 2–3 in. deep. They do best in a fairly moist situation, where they will often spread freely and naturalise themselves. **729**, p. 92.

× **tubergenii** ❋ Early Spring Tu.

A hybrid between our common Winter Aconite and the Cilician sp. Stems slightly taller than in *E. hyemalis* and *fl*. larger and more globe-shaped and slightly deeper in colour. **730**, p. 92.

One of the best forms is 'Guinea Gold'.

EREMURUS (LILIACEAE) Foxtail Lily

bungei, syn. **E. stenophyllus** ❋ Early Summer P.

Fl. bright yellow in closely packed spike. 2–3 ft. *L*. sword-shaped. Plant 10 in a well-drained soil and a sunny position. Propagate by division or by seed. Persia. **1116**, p. 140.

Highdown Hybrids ❋ Early Summer P.

Fl. in shades of pink, amber, orange, yellow and copper. 5–6 ft. Cultivation and propagation see *E. bungei*. Raised by the late Sir Frederick Stern in his garden at Highdown, Sussex.

robustus ❋ Early Summer P.

Fl. soft pink or white, 7–9 ft. *L*. bright green, up to 4 ft long, Cultivation and propagation see *E. bungei*. Turkestan. **1117**, p. 140.

ERICA (ERICACEAE) Heath

All Heaths are best pruned by cutting over with shears or secateurs immediately after flowering otherwise they tend to become rather straggly. Easily propagated from short cuttings in summer. Sometimes also called Heather.

arborea Tree Heath ❋ Spring *†Sh.

Bushy shrub up to 20 ft in favourable locality but usually rather less. *Fl*. whitish very fragrant.

var. *alpina* hardiest form which makes a large shrub in home counties and rarely suffers from any frost. *Fl*. white. Foliage distinguished by the fresh mossy-green. Native from Spain in the mts and distinct from *arborea*, **1577**, p. 198.

australis Spanish Heath ❋ Mid Spring–Early Summer *†Sh.

Shrub up to 4 ft occasionally more. *Fl*. slightly larger than those of *E. arborea*, pink or rosy-purple or white in form known as 'Mr Robert'. Spain, Portugal.

'Mr Robert' is a slightly hardier variety than typical *E. australis*, **1578**, p. 198.

carnea Winter Heath ❋ Mid Winter–Early Spring Sh.

Only Heath which will grow satisfactorily on lime. Low spreading shrub up to 1 ft often less. One of the most valuable groups of plants for winter flowering. Usually very long season of flower.

There are many named forms, among the best are:

'Atrorubra', deep pink *fl*. later in *fl*. than others;

'Eileen Porter', rich carmine-red often starting in 10;

'King George', deep pink rather dwarf and early flowering;

'Queen Mary', deep rose-red;

✿ 'Springwood', finest white variety with long spikes of urn-shaped white *fl*. Spreading freely forming large masses. One of the most valuable winter flowering plants, **1579**, p. 198;

'Springwood Pink', with rose-pink *fl*.;

'Vivellii', deep carmine dwarfer than type, **1580**, p. 198;

'Winter Beauty', rose-pink flowering winter–early spring.

cinerea Scotch or Grey Heath ❋ Summer *Sh.

Low shrub up to 1½ ft spreading widely. One of commonest British native Heaths. Not suitable for limy soils. Typical form is deep purplish-pink. **1581**, p. 198.

Other named forms are:

'Alba', white;

'Atrorubens', deeper purplish-red than type very bright colour, **1582**, p. 198;

'Rosea', deep rose-pink, **1583**, p. 198.

× **darleyensis** ❋ Winter–Spring *Sh.

A hybrid between *E. carnea* × *E. mediterranea*. Small spreading shrub up to 1½ ft covered with spikes of rosy-purple *fl*. Very valuable as ground cover plant in sunny or semi-shady positions forming large mats of colour in winter and will tolerate some lime. Slightly taller in growth than *E. carnea*. **1584**, p. 198.

lusitanica Portuguese Heath ❋ Late Winter–Mid Spring *Sh.

Erect shrub up to 10 ft. *Fl*. white rather like those of *E. arborea* but slightly larger. S.W. Europe. Rather less hardy than *E. australis* or *E. arborea alpina* but valuable in S.W. counties. **1585**, p. 199.

tetralix Cross-leaved Heath ❋ Summer–Mid Winter †Sh.

Low shrub spreading up to 18 in. *Fl*. rose-coloured. Distinguished by *l*. arranged in whorls of four forming a cross, narrow. Dark green. One of the most abundant of the Heaths. Unsuitable for very dry areas. A British native and ranging across N. and W. Europe.

'Alba', *fl*. white, **1586**, p. 199;

'Mollis', with light grey *l*. and white *fl*.;

'Pink Glow', grey foliage and pink *fl*.;

'Rosea', deeper rose-pink.

umbellata ❋ Late Spring–Early Summer *†Sh.

Dwarf shrub up to 3 ft but usually less. *L*. usually in threes. *Fl*. 3–6 at ends of shoots, deep pink or reddish-purple. Only suitable for S. and W. districts in England. Spain, Portugal, N.W. Africa. **1587**, p. 199.

vagans Cornish Heath ❋ Summer–Mid Autumn †Sh.

Dwarf spreading shrub up to 2 ft usually less. *Fl*. rosy-pink or white near ends of short direct branches but usually with tip of green above *fl*. Valuable for its late summer flowering.

'Alba', white;

'Kevernensis' see 'St Keverne';

'Lyonesse', pure white, larger than 'Alba';

'Mrs D. F. Maxwell', deep cerise-pink, an old favourite, **1588**, p. 199;

'St Keverne', sometimes known as 'Kevernensis', clear light rose-pink spreading freely into large mass, **1589**, p. 199.

× **veitchii** Tree Heath ❋ Spring *†Sh.

A hybrid between *E. arborea* × *E. lusitanica*. Shrub up to 6 ft but usually less. *Fl*. white in long racemes very freely produced. Valuable for its early flowering in milder districts of S. and W. but too tender for very cold areas. **1590**, p. 199.

vulgaris see **Calluna vulgaris**

ERIGERON (COMPOSITAE) Fleabane

aureus ❋ Early Summer RP.
Fl. bright golden yellow, daisy-like but with double row of ray-florets, up to 1 in. across on stem of up to 3 in. *L.* small, spathulate. Plant in full sun in well-drained position or in sunny scree. W. N. America. **63**, p. 8.

mucronatus ❋ Summer RP.
Fl. heads white or pink, like small daisies on rather long stems up to 6 in., a very dainty *fl. L.* lanceolate, small. Tends to spread and *fl.* abundantly nearly all summer and grows well in crevices of a wall or at edge of path. Unsuitable for very small rock gardens. In very hard winters it may be killed back to ground level but is seldom lost once established. Mexico. **64**, p. 8.

Garden hybrids ❋ Summer–Mid Autumn P.
A wide range of hybrid erigerons have been raised in England and in Germany with *fl.* in many shades of pink, lilac, purple and mauve.
The following are among the best and range from 1½–2 ft high:
    'Charity', light pink, **1118**, 140;
    'Dignity', violet-mauve, **1119**, p. 140;
    'Felicity', deep pink, **1120**, p. 140;
    'Festivity', lilac-pink, **1121**, p. 141;
    'Lilofee', violet-mauve, **1122**, p. 141;
    'Sincerity', large, mauve-blue, **1123**, p. 141.

ERINACEA (LEGUMINOSAE)

pungens, syn. **Anthyllis erinacea** Hedgehog Broom
❋ Early Summer *RSh.
    Tender, very spinous small tussocky shrublet up to 2 ft in height but in old plants sometimes more across. *Fl.* pale lilac-blue, pea-like, up to 1 in. across, in small clusters, often covering bush. *L.* small and inconspicuous, their place being taken by the dense green or silvery-grey branchlets. Requires very warm sunny position or alpine house culture.

ERIOBOTRYA (ROSACEAE)

japonica Loquat ❋ Mid Autumn–Mid Spring *T.
Evergreen tree or large wall shrub up to 20 ft but usually less. *Fl.* white, usually in winter. *L.* large up to 1 ft long by 5 in. wide, under surface brownish, upper glossy green. Fruit rarely produced in England, yellow pear-shaped up to 1½ in. long. One of the most decorative evergreens for its large foliage. In S. Europe ripens freely and is used for dessert. China, Japan. **1591**, p. 199.

ERITRICHIUM (BORAGINACEAE)

nanum The King of the Alps ❋ Early Summer †RP.
Small, hairy, grey tussock. *Fl.* deep sky-blue, like a small but deeper blue forget-me-not, almost sessile. *L.* small, hairy in close rosettes. A high level alpine which has a peculiar fascination and challenge for alpine gardeners and climbers, but it is so difficult to establish satisfactorily from collected plants that it is better left in its native habitat. May be sometimes grown from seed, but must be watered very carefully, usually attempted in two pots, one inside the other, of granitic chips, coarse sand and loam and watered between rim of the two pots, and even then generally short lived. European Alps in clefts of granitic rocks only and so probably a lime-hater. **66**, p. 9.

rupestre var. **pectinatum,** syn. **E. strictum**
Much easier to grow in scree than *E. nanum* but it has upright stems of 8 in. or more and paler blue *fl.* and does not have the same fascination for alpine gardeners.

strictum see **E. rupestre** var. **pectinatum**

ERODIUM (GERANIACEAE)

corsicum ❋ Summer RP.
Mat-forming perennial but too tender for cold

areas, not difficult in alpine house. *Fl.* pale magenta-pink, cup-shaped, upright on 3 in. stems. *L.* silvery grey-green, deeply lobed. Needs a warm sunny position and good drainage. Corsica at near sea level.
    'Rubrum', deeper pink with white centre, **67**, p. 9.

guttatum ❋ Summer RP.
Fl. white or very pale rosy-lilac, two upper petals blotched with deep lilac-purple, all petals veined with deeper colour, up to 1 in. across on 4–6 in. branching stems. *L.* silvery grey-green, many lobed. Often forming a large clump from a sub-shrubby base. Plant in full sun. S.W. Europe. **68**, p. 9.

ERYNGIUM (UMBELLIFERAE) Sea Holly

alpinum ❋ Summer P.
Fl. metallic blue, teasel-like. *L.* deeply cut and toothed, long-stalked. 1½–2 ft. Full sun and a dryish soil. Propagate by root cuttings in autumn or winter in boxes of sandy soil placed in a cold frame, by division in autumn or spring, or the sp. by seed sown in 4–5 in a cold frame. Europe.
    'Donard', has metallic blue and silver *fl.* heads, **1124**, p. 141.

giganteum ❋ Summer P,B.
Fl. silvery blue with large bracts. *L.* and stems silvery. 3–4 ft. Propagate by seed sown in late spring. Biennial, once established, usually reproduced from self-sown seedlings. Caucasus. **1125**, p. 141.

tripartitum ❋ Summer P.
Fl. blue-grey, teasel-like, small but freely produced. *L.* wedge-shaped, coarsely toothed, less spiny than other varieties. Cultivation and propagation as for *E. alpinum.* Origin uncertain, probably a hybrid. **1126**, p. 141.

variifolium ❋ Summer P.
Fl. bluish. *L.* heart-shaped, upper deeply cut, marbled and veined silver. 2 ft. Cultivation and propagation as for *E. alpinum.* Europe. **1127**, p. 141.

ERYSIMUM ALPINUM 'MOONLIGHT' see Cheiranthus cheiri 'Moonlight'

ERYSIMUM PEROFSKIANUM see Cheiranthus allionii

ERYTHRINA (LEGUMINOSAE)

crista-gallii Coral Tree ❋ Late Spring–Midsummer *Sh.
    Usually grown as a wall shrub, rarely seen over 6 ft and often cut back to ground level in winter. *Fl.* deep crimson-scarlet with conspicuous standard, growing in large terminal racemes. Valuable where it can be grown, it should be treated as a very tender plant. Leaflets slightly glaucous, leathery. Brazil. **1592**, p. 199.

ERYTHRONIUM (LILIACEAE) Adders Tongue, Trout Lily USA

✿ **dens-canis** Dog-Tooth Violet ❋ Spring Tu.
Fl. pink, crimson-purple or white. Petals recurved like a Turks-cap lily with a ring of orange-red markings around base. A most beautiful and graceful *fl.* well set off by its lovely bluish marbled *l.* Suitable for woodland or more open places and often increases fast, the clumps of tubers requiring division every third or fourth year. Hardy. European and sub-alpine woodlands.
Some good named forms are available and are recommended such as:
    'Franz Hals', light reddish-violet;
    'Congo', deep rosy-purple;
    'Rose Queen', clear pink, **731**, p. 92;
    'Snowflake', a good white.

✿ **'Kondo'** ❋ Mid Spring Tu.
A fairly new hybrid taller and larger than the ordinary Dog-tooth violets. Petals primrose-yellow,

opening flat and then recurving with darker markings near base on stems 1 ft tall. *L.* unmottled. Tubers large. Similar is 'Pagoda' but with deeper yellow *fl.* several to a stem. Excellent for the rock garden.

oregonum see **E. 'White Beauty'**

'Pagoda' see **E. 'Kondo'**

revolution see **E. 'White Beauty'**

tuolumnense ❋ Spring Tu.
Fl. deep yellow two to three on stem of 8–10 in. but rather small for height of stem. *L.* green, unmottled. Vigorous and often forming large clumps.

✿ **'White Beauty'** ❋ Mid Spring Tu.
Fl. white with dark red markings at base. One or two on a 5–6 in. stem. Probably a form or hybrid of *E. oregonum,* one of the finest trout lilies of W. N. America but often listed under *E. revolutum* which has pink *fl.* Frequently establishes well in a dampish position and well worth cherishing. A real beauty. **732**, p. 92.

ESCALLONIA (SAXIFRAGACEAE)

hybrids ❋ Summer Sh.
Valuable evergreen shrubs or small trees. *Fl.* from ¼–½ in. wide in terminal panicles. Slightly tender in cold positions and all are excellent in seaside areas. Useful for late flowering. South America, mainly from Chile.
Most of those grown are garden raised hybrids and among the best are:–
    'Apple Blossom', *fl.* pink and white, more erect stiff shrub than most other hybrids;
    'C. F. Ball', crimson-rose, tall growing, **1593**, p. 200;
    'Donard Radiance', *fl.* deep pink;
    'Donard Star', *fl.* shell pink, large waxy, **1594**, p. 200;
    'Peach Blossom', *fl.* white towards base, deep pink to tips and on buds, close to 'Apple Blossom', **1595**, p. 200.

macrantha ❋ Summer Sh.
Tall evergreen up to 10 ft much used as a hedge plant by the sea and very resistant to salt spray. *L.* large, glossy, deep green. *Fl.* deep pink or red. Unsuitable growing away from sea or in cold areas. **1596**, p. 200.

Abbreviations and Symbols used in the text.
The following abbreviations may sometimes be used in conjunction as HA. indicating Hardy annual or GBb indicating Greenhouse bulb.

A. = Annual	P. = Perennial
Aq. = Aquatic	R. = Rock or
B. = Biennial	Alpine plant
Bb = Bulb	Sh. = Shrub
C. = Corm	Sp., sp. = Species
Cl. = Climber	Syn. = Synonym
Co. = Conifer	T. = Tree
Fl.,fl. = Flower(s)	Tu. = Tuber
G. = Greenhouse or	var. = variety
house plant	× = Hybrid or
H. = Hardy	hybrid parents
HH. = Half-hardy	❋ = Flowering time
L., l. = Leaf, leaves	❧ = Foliage plant
Mt(s) = Mount,	
mountain(s)	

The following have been used also in the descriptions of Alpines, Bulbs, Trees and Shrubs.

    * = slightly tender
    † = lime hater
    ✿ = highly recommended

The illustration numbers are in **bold type** and the page numbers in light type preceded by p.

ESCHSCHOLZIA (PAPAVERACEAE)

californica Californian Poppy ❀ Summer   HA.
Fl. bright orange, yellow, carmine, creamy-white. *L.* grey-green, finely divided. 9 in.–1½ ft. Sow in 3–4, or in 9, in ordinary garden soil and in a sunny position. N.W. America.
There are numerous named hybrids in brilliant colours, tall and dwarf, double and single, and including:
> 'Mission Bells', 9 in., compact, large *fl.* in a good range of colour, **294**, p. 37.

EUCALYPTUS (MYRTACEAE) Gum Tree, Iron-bark Tree

Tall trees up to 70 ft but usually less in this country, or large evergreen shrubs. Distinguished by peeling bark and by very fast growth. Eucalyptus also distinguished by difference between juvenile and adult foliage. Juvenile *l.* being mostly heart-shaped, stalkless, more glaucous and standing out horizontally while the adult *l.* tend to hand down vertically and are much narrower and longer and less grey. Valuable as foliage plants in the milder parts of the country but some species from the higher regions of Australia and Tasmania proving hardy in many areas. Excellent in S. Europe and other areas where there is a hot summer. Australia, Tasmania.
The following sp. can be recommended:

coccifera ❀ Early Summer N. Hemisphere, Winter, sometimes Summer, Australia   *T.
Small tree up to 30 ft. *L.* very blue, glaucous up to 1½ in. long, roundish, grey-green and narrower in adult foliage. *Fl.* in groups of about seven, urn-shaped white with boss of yellow stamens.

gunnii Cider Gum ❀ Autumn N. Hemisphere, Winter Australia   T.
Evergreen tree up to 70 ft but rarely so. Juvenile foliage, glaucous rounded up to 2½ in., notched and rounded where it joins to stem. *Fl.* late, white with boss of yellow stamens. **1597**, p. 200.

✿ **niphophila** Australian Snow Gum ❀ Summer N. Hemisphere, Winter Australia   T.
One of the hardiest species. *L.* more elongated than rounded up to 4 in. long, glaucous. Distinguished also by its grey peeling bark. One of the hardiest and most beautiful sp. *Fl.* white produced on quite young plants. **1598**, p. 200.

perriniana ❀ Summer N. Hemisphere, Mid Winter–Early Spring Australia   T.
Distinguished for its orbicular *l.* which clasp the stem in pairs, very glaucous. A very useful small tree for making good foliage effect, can be kept pollarded in order to make constant young growth. *Fl.* white. **1599**, p. 200.

simmondsii ❀ Early Winter Australia   *T.
L. longer, green or sub-glaucous lanceolate ovate only in young plants. Rough fibrous bark. *Fl.* white freely produced. Young stems reddish. Tasmania. **1600**, p. 200.

EUCHARIDIUM (OENOTHERACEAE)

concinnum, syn. **Clarkia concinna** ❀ Summer   HA.
Fl. rose-pink ribbon-like petals. *L.* small, oblong. 1–2 ft. Sow in the open in 3–4, or in 9 in a sunny border. California.
> 'Pink Ribbons', a deep rose-pink form, 1 ft, **295**. p. 37.

EUCHARIS (AMARYLLIDACEAE)

amazonica see **E. grandiflora**

grandiflora, syn. **E. amazonica** Amazon Lily ❀ Mid Spring–Early Summer   *GBb.
Fl. snow-white, four to six on a stem, large up to 5 in. across, drooping from a 2 ft stem. A central cup in the *fl.* is surrounded by broad spreading lobes, sometimes slightly tinged with green, very strongly scented. One of the finest bulbs for a warm greenhouse and frequently used for forcing. Several bulbs may be placed in a large pot and they need frequent watering while growing in a temperature of 65°–70°F. S. America, Andes. **525**, p. 66.

EUCOMIS (LILIACEAE)

bicolor ❀ Summer   *Bb.
Fl. light greenish-yellow, starlike, in a dense spike 1–1½ ft tall which has a small rosette of green *l.* at top. Stem fleshy. An unusual plant valuable for its late flowering and always attracting attention and curiosity. Needs a warm situation, preferably under a south wall, but easy in a cool greenhouse. **733**, p. 92.
Close to this is *E. comosa* with slightly larger spikes on spotted purplish fleshy stems. S. Africa.

comosa see **E. bicolor**

EUCRYPHIA (EUCRYPHIACEAE)

cordifolia ❀ Late Summer   *T.
Evergreen tree up to 40 ft but usually much less. *L.* leathery cordate oblong up to 3 in. *Fl.* white solitary in leaf axils but clustered near ends of shoots 2½ in. across with central boss of stamens. Hardy only in warmer areas but valuable as an evergreen throughout year. Chile.

glutinosa, syn. **E. pinnatifolia** ❀ Late Summer   T.
Deciduous or partly evergreen large shrub or small tree up to 15 ft. *L.* divided, pinnate with three to five leaflets which are regularly toothed and dark shining green. *Fl.* singly or in pairs at ends of shoots, 2½ in. across rounded with fine boss of yellow stamens in centre. Unsuitable for chalky soils or very dry situations. One of the most valuable shrubs for late summer flowering and the hardiest sp. of this genus. Chile. **1601**, p. 201.

× **nymansensis** ❀ Early Autumn   T.
Evergreen tree rather erect up to 30 ft. Valuable hybrid between *E. cordifolia* and *E. glutinosa* which arose by chance at Nymans a famous garden in Sussex. *Fl.* 2½ in. across rounded with overlapping petals and boss of yellow anthers. Hardier than *E. cordifolia* and tolerant of some chalk in the soil. Best forms are:
> 'Mount Usher', raised at a famous garden in Ireland;
> 'Nymansay', the original, **1602**, p. 201.

pinnatifolia see **E. glutinosa**

EUGENIA APICULATA   see   **Myrtus luma**

EULALIA JAPONICA see **Miscanthus sinensis**

EUONYMUS (CELASTRACEAE) Spindle Tree

Trees or shrubs, evergreen or deciduous. Inconspicuous in *fl.* which are small and greenish-white but valuable garden plants for brilliant autumn colour of foliage and strongly coloured scarlet fruits in late autumn.

alatus Winged Spindle Tree   Sh.
Deciduous shrub wide-spreading up to 8 ft but usually less, known as Winged Spindle Tree from corky wings up to ½ in. wide on branches. *L.* narrow up to 3 in. long brilliantly coloured rosy-purple becoming pinkish-scarlet in autumn. One of the most valuable autumn colouring shrubs. China, Japan. **1603**, p. 201.

europaeus Common Spindle Tree   T.
Deciduous shrub or small tree up to 20 ft usually less. Valuable for its brilliant fruit which is scarlet-crimson in autumn in capsule which opens to show orange-scarlet seeds. Seed capsules are pendulous in clusters of 2–3. Europe including Britain.
> 'Red Cascade' is among finest forms and also has good autumn colouring and brilliant scarlet fruits, **1604**, p. 201.

kiautschovicus, syn. **E. patens.** Spreading Euonymus.   Sh.
Evergreen shrub, in the N. part of its horticultural range half-evergreen. To 9 ft. Fruits showy, pinkish to red in 10–11. In America carried by many nurseries. China.

latifolius   T.
Larger fruit than *E. europaeus* but otherwise similar. Europe.

patens see **E. kiautschovicus**

planipes see **E. sachalinensis**

sachalinensis, syn. **E. planipes**   T.
Distinguished for large seed capsules, seeds hanging singly on long stalks up to 1½ in. across rosy-scarlet five angled. Seeds are darker crimson-red. *L.* obovate up to 5 in. long and larger than in most other sp. of the genus. Japan. **1605**, p. 201.

yedoensis
Deciduous small tree up to 10 ft. *L.* obovate or oval and tapered at both ends up to 5 in. long and about 2 in. wide. Brilliant autumn colouring. Also valuable for its orange-scarlet seed coats and pink seeds in autumn. Good autumn colouring shrub. Japan. **1606**, p. 201.

EUONYMUS, SPREADING see E. kiautschovicus

EUPATORIUM (COMPOSITAE) Joe Pye Weed

purpureum ❀ Late Summer   P.
Fl. purplish-pink borne erect on stiff stems. *L.* slender-pointed, in whorls. 3–6 ft. Plant 11–3 in moist soil and partial shade in the wild garden. Propagate by seed sown where it is to *fl.* or by division. N. America. **1128**, p. 141.

EUPHORBIA (EUPHORBIACEAE) Spurge

characias ❀ Early Summer   P.
Fl. sulphur-yellow with paper-like bracts borne as large terminal heads. *L.* blue-grey, evergreen in mild winters. 3–4 ft. Does quite well in poor soil in sun or partial shade. Increase by seed sown in the open as soon as gathered, by cuttings taken immediately after flowering or by division. Should be planted out when young as older plants resent disturbance. Europe. **1129**, p. 142.

Abbreviations and Symbols used in the text.
The following abbreviations may sometimes be used in conjunction as HA. indicating Hardy annual or GBb indicating Greenhouse bulb.

A. = Annual	P. = Perennial
Aq. = Aquatic	R. = Rock or
B. = Biennial	Alpine plant
Bb = Bulb	Sh. = Shrub
C. = Corm	Sp., sp. = Species
Cl. = Climber	Syn. = Synonym
Co. = Conifer	T. = Tree
Fl., fl. = Flower(s)	Tu. = Tuber
G. = Greenhouse or	var. = variety
house plant	× = Hybrid or
H. = Hardy	hybrid parents
HH. = Half-hardy	❀ = Flowering time
L., l. = Leaf, leaves	🍃 = Foliage plant
Mt(s) = Mount,	
mountain(s)	

The following have been used also in the descriptions of Alpines, Bulbs, Trees and Shrubs.

> * = slightly tender
> † = lime hater
> ✿ = highly recommended

The illustration numbers are in **bold type** and the page numbers in light type preceded by p.

epithymoides, syn. **E. polychroma** Cushion spurge ❈ Spring　　　　P.
Fl. bright gold bracts in rounded heads, fading to green. L. fresh green. 1 ft. Cultivation and propagation as for E. characias. Europe. **1130**, p. 142.

fulgens Scarlet Plume ❈ Winter　　　　GP.
Shrubs to 3 ft. Fl. in small clusters, surrounded by scarlet petal-like bracts. L. elliptic, about 1¼ in. long, dark green, evergreen. Rich compost needed; minimum winter temp. 55°F. Prune hard after flowering is over. Propagate by cuttings of young shoots in early spring. Keep shaded and free from draughts. Mexico. **526**, p. 66.

griffithii ❈ Early Summer　　　　P.
Fl. bright yellow. L. bright green. 1½ ft. Cultivation and propagation as for E. characias. Himalaya. 'Fireglow', has brilliant orange-red bracts, **1131**, p. 142.

myrsinites ❈ Spring　　　　RP.
Trailing plant with slightly succulent blue-grey l. Fl. with conspicuous yellowish-green bracts in large umbels up to 3 in. across on stems up to 1 ft but with prostrate stems. Useful for growing over rocks in hot sunny position. Tender in cold areas. Easily grown from seed. S. Europe. **69**, p. 9.

palustris Fen or Bog spurge ❈ Early Summer　P.
Fl. sulphur-yellow borne in a large, flattish heads. L. lush green. 3–4 ft. Makes a plant where there is plenty of moisture, otherwise requires the same conditions for cultivation and propagation as for E. characias. Europe. **1132**, p. 142.

polychroma see **E. epithymoides**

pulcherrima Poinsettia　　　　GSh.
Deciduous shrub up to 10 ft. L. elliptical to lanceolate. Fl. yellow, insignificant, bracts bright vermilion. Popular Christmas decoration. Mikkelsen strain is an improvement on other forms. Propagation by stem cuttings.

robbiae ❈ Summer　　　　P.
Fl. pale yellow, bracts pale green. L. evergreen, leathery, dark green, up to 4 in. long. 2–2½ ft. Cultivate and propagate as for E. characias. N.W. Asia Minor. **1133**, p. 142.

wulfenii, syn. **E. venata** ❈ Spring–Midsummer P.
Fl. greenish-yellow in large, terminal beads. L. bluish-green, oblong, hairy. 4 ft. Increase by seed sown in the open or in a cold frame as soon as ripe. E. venata is considered by most botanists now as the correct name but most references in literature and catalogues still give this plant as E. wulfenii. Europe.

EUROPEAN SILVER FIR see **Abies alba**, **2001**, p. 251.

EUROPS (COMPOSITAE)

acraeus, syn. **E. evansii** ❈ Summer　　　　RP.
It was introduced under its synonym E. evansii and by which name it is grown. Dense silvery shrublet up to 1 ft high and as much across. Fl. heads like yellow daisies on 3 in. stems. L. linear, very brightly silvered with dense short hairs. Suitable for a sunny position and appears to be quite hardy but dislikes excessive dampness. Also good as alpine house plant. May be propagated from short cuttings or suckers in late summer. S. Africa. **70**, p. 9.

EVENING PRIMROSE see **Oenothera**, **1287-1291**, pp. 161–162.

EVERGREEN BLUEBERRY see **Vaccinium myrsinites**, **1936**, p. 242.

EVERGREEN OAK see **Quercus ilex**

EVERLASTING see **Helichrysum**, **86**, **87**, p. 11; **305**, p. 39; **1159**, p. 145; **1642**, p. 206; and **Helipterum**, **307**, p. 39.

EVERLASTING, PEARL see **Anaphalis**, **960-962**, pp. 120–121.

EVERLASTING, WINGED see **Ammobium alatum**, **234**, p. 30.

EXOCHORDA (ROSACEAE)

giraldii ❈ Late Spring　　　　Sh.
Deciduous shrub up to 10 ft. Fl. white with five petals, obovate and narrow at base. Branches tend to curve downwards and near ends are covered in racemes of white fl. up to 2 in. across. L. ovate to oblong, pointed. N.W. China. **1607**, p. 201.

F

FABIANA (SOLANACEAE)

imbricata ❈ Early Summer　　　　*Sh.
A small evergreen shrub rather slender growing up to 6 ft usually less. Fl. white tubular, funnel-shaped near mouth arranged along young branches, numerous. About ¼ in. across and ½ in. long. L. small scale-like rather like those of a Heather. Chile. **1608**, p. 201.
　violacea, wider spreading evergreen shrub. Fl. pale lilac-mauve, occasionally recorded as blue-mauve. Chile.

FAGUS (FAGACEAE) Beech

sylvatica Common Beech　　　　T.
One of the finest British deciduous trees, up to 60 ft or 70 ft and widespreading.
Numerous varieties have been described including:
　'Cuprea', Copper Beech, with foliage dark purplish-red or pinkish-crimson with light shining through, magnificent tree, **1609**, p. 202;
　'Fastigiata', Dawyck Beech, columnar and narrow in growth, erect;
　'Heterophylla' see 'Laciniata';
　'Laciniata', 'Heterophylla', Fernleaf Beech, l. divided, one of our finest ornamental trees;
　'Pendula', Weeping Beech, branches pendulous and curving.

FALSE ACACIA see **Robinia pseudoacacia**

FALSE ARALIA see **Dizygotheca elegantissima**, **514**, p. 65.

FALSE CYPRESS see **Chamaecyparis**, **2004-2010**, pp. 251, 252.

FALSE GOAT'S BEARD see **Astilbe**, **18**, p. 3; **994-998**, p. 125.

FALSE SPIKENARD see **Smilacina racemosa**, **1380**, p. 173.

× FATSHEDERA (ARALIACEAE)

lizei ❈ Late Autumn　　　　GSh.
Evergreen scandent shrub with dark green l. Fl. greenish-white in large spikes in late autumn. A bigeneric hybrid between Fatsia japonica var. moseri and Hedera hibernica first raised in 1912 by Lizé Freres at Nantes. Used for room decoration, but will tolerate some frost. Likes some shade.
　'Variegata', has l. boldly margined cream when young but the margin narrows as the l. age, **527**, p. 66.

FATSIA (ARALIACEAE)

japonica, syn. **Aralia japonica, Aralia sieboldii** ❈ Autumn　　　　Sh.
Evergreen shrub up to 12 ft but usually less. Fl. creamy-white in globular clusters. L. large deeply lobed, shiny up to 15 in. across. One of the most

valuable evergreens for foliage effect and growing well in open districts. Japan. **1610**, p. 202.

FEATHER GRASS see **Stipa pennata**, **1390**, p. 174.

FEATHERED BRONZE LEAF see **Rodgersia pinnata**, **1349**, p. 169.

FELICIA (COMPOSITAE)

bergeriana Kingfisher Daisy ❈ Summer　HHA.
Fl. intense sky-blue with yellow centres. L. narrow, hairy, 6 in. Sow in 2–3 in heat and plant out in sunny position in 5–6. Useful for rockery and edging. S. Africa.

FENNEL see **Foeniculum vulgare**, **1137**, p. 143.

FERN, BIRD'S NEST see **Asplenium nidus-avis**, **412**, p. 52.

FERNLEAF BEECH see **Fagus sylvatica** 'Laciniata'

FERNLEAF YARROW see **Achillea filipendulina**, **947**, p. 119.

FESCUE, SHEEP'S see **Festuca ovina**, **1134**, p. 142.

FESTUCA (GRAMINEAE)

ovina Sheep's Fescue ❈ Late Spring–Midsummer P.
Fl. in panicles, purplish. L. grey-blue, slender, forming dense tufts. 9 in. Useful edging plant for a sunny position. Propagate by division or seed. Europe.
　'Glauca', the l. are more blue than the type, **1134**, p. 142.

FEVERFEW see **Matricaria eximia**, **339**, **340**, p. 43; and **Pyrethrum parthenium**, **1340**, p. 168.

FICUS (MORACEAE) Fig

A remarkably diverse genus, ranging from large

Abbreviations and Symbols used in the text.
The following abbreviations may sometimes be used in conjunction as HA. indicating Hardy annual or GBb indicating Greenhouse bulb.

A. = Annual	P. = Perennial
Aq. = Aquatic	R. = Rock or
B. = Biennial	Alpine plant
Bb = Bulb	Sh. = Shrub
C. = Corm	Sp., sp. = Species
Cl. = Climber	Syn. = Synonym
Co. = Conifer	T. = Tree
Fl., fl. = Flower(s)	Tu. = Tuber
G. = Greenhouse or	var. = variety
house plant	× = Hybrid or
H. = Hardy	hybrid parents
HH. = Half-hardy	❈ = Flowering time
L., l. = Leaf, leaves	❧ = Foliage plant
Mt(s) = Mount,	
mountain(s)	

The following have been used also in the descriptions of Alpines, Bulbs, Trees and Shrubs.

* = slightly tender
† = lime hater
✿ = highly recommended

The illustration numbers are in **bold type** and the page numbers in light type preceded by p.

trees to small prostrate creepers. The tender sp. cultivated are grown for their attractive foliage.

benjamina 🌿 GT.
Large tree in tropics, seldom over 10 ft in cultivation, much branched. *L.* evergreen, oblong-oval, to 4 in. long and 1½ in. across, pale green willow-like, not persisting long. Keep moist at all times, but water sparingly in winter. Winter temp. 50°F. or more if possible. Propagate by stem cuttings, rooted in heat or by seed. India. **528**, p. 66.

elastica Indian Rubber Tree 🌿 GT.
Tree to 50 ft in wild, seldom more than 10 ft in cultivation. *L.* oblong, evergreen, lance-shaped, green, leathery, to 12 in. long, 7 in. wide. The type has been superseded by the var. *decora*. Fairly rich compost needed. Winter temp. ideally about 55°F., but lower readings possible if plant kept dry. Water sparingly at all times, but give moist atmosphere. Propagate by stem or *l.* cuttings, with great heat, at least 80°F. Tropical Asia.
   'Decora', has larger *l.* and a red sheath covering the growing tip, **529**, p. 67;
   'Schryveriana', is one of the best variegated forms which have occurred; it is somewhat more delicate, **530**, p. 67.

lyrata 🌿 GT.
Often cultivated, has large *l.* shaped like a violin. Africa.

pumila, syn. **F. repens** 🌿 GCl.
Trailer or climber, supporting itself by aerial roots. *L.* heart-shaped, small, evergreen; 1 in. long, ½ in. across. Hardy in sheltered spots in British Isles. Never allow to dry out and keep well shaded. Fruiting branches have larger *l.* and no aerial roots but are rarely produced indoors. Winter temp. 40°–45°F. Propagate by cuttings in heat. China. **531**, p. 67.

radicans 'Variegata' 🌿 GCl.
Trailer or climber with aerial roots. *L.* evergreen oblong, pointed, up to 2½ in. long and 1 in. across. Winter temp. 55°–60°F. Keep moist and provide moist atmosphere but beware of overwatering. Avoid direct sunlight. Propagate by stem cuttings under heat. E. Indies. **532**, p. 67.

repens see **F. pumila**

FIELD MAPLE see **Acer campestre**, **1430**, p. 179.

FIG see **Ficus**, **528-532**, pp. 66, 67.

FIGWORT, CAPE see **Phygelius capensis**, **1736**, p. 217.

FIGWORT, KNOTTED see **Scrophularia nodosa**, **1368**, p. 171.

FILIPENDULA (ROSACEAE)
hexapetala, syn. **F. vulgaris, Spiraea filipendula** Dropwort 🌼 Summer P.
Fl. creamy-white on erect stems, 2–3 ft. *L.* fern-like in neat tufts. Ordinary soil, even dryish, and a sunny position. Propagate by division or by seed sown under glass in the autumn. Europe.
   'Flore Pleno', double flowered and a better plant than the type, to 1½ ft, **1135**, p. 142.

palmata see **F. purpurea**

purpurea, syn. **F. palmata rubra, Spiraea palmata** (of gardens) 🌼 Summer P.
Fl. pinkish-purple in flat heads, 2–2½ ft. *L.* large, five or seven-lobed. Plant 10–3 in moist soil and partial shade. Propagate by division or by seed sown in the autumn under glass. Considered by some authorities to be a hybrid of *F. multijuga* × *F. auriculata*. Japan. **1136**, p. 142.

rubra, syn. **Spiraea lobata** Queen of the Prairie 🌼 Summer P.
Fl. deep pink, in bold feathery plumes. *L.* large,

lobed, deep green. 4–8 ft. A deep moist soil in sun or partial shade. Propagate by division in the spring. Eastern USA. Good forms are:
   'Magnifica', large heads of carmine-pink, 6 ft;
   'Venusta', deep pink, 4 ft.

vulgaris see **F. hexapetala**

FIR, EUROPEAN SILVER see **Abies alba**, **2001**, p. 251.

FIR, NOBLE see **Abies procera**

FIR, RED see **Abies procera**

FIR, RED SILVER see **Abies amabilis**

FIR, SILVER see **Abies**, **2001, 2002**, p. 251.

FIR, WATER see **Metasequoia**, **2025**, p. 254.

FIRE BUSH, CHILEAN see **Embothrium coccineum**, **1572**, p. 197.

FIRETHORN see **Pyracantha**, **1769, 1770**, p. 222.

FITTONIA (ACANTHACEAE)
argyroneura 🌿 GP.
Considered by some authorities as a variety of and similar in appearance to *F. verschaffeltii*, but with silvery veins, needs similar conditions but the minimum temp. in winter should be 60°F. Peru.

verschaffeltii 🌿 GP.
Prostrate creeping plant. *L.* oblong-oval, up to 4 in. long and 3 in. across, dark green with all veins crimson, producing netted effect. Warm, moist shady conditions required with a minimum of 55°F. Sometimes offered as room-plant, but only suitable in closed containers. Avoid draughts and sudden temp. changes. Propagate by cuttings, usually taken in spring. S. America. **533**, p. 67.

FLAME FLOWER, SCOTTISH see **Tropaeolum speciosum**, **1994**, p. 250.

FLAMINGO PLANT see **Anthurium andreanum**, **408**, p. 51.

FLAX see **Linum**, **105, 106**, p. 14; **329**, p. 42; **1242**, p. 156.

FLAX, NEW ZEALAND see **Phormium tenax**, **1732**, p. 217.

FLORENCE COURT YEW see **Taxus baccata** 'Fastigiata'

FLOSS FLOWER see **Ageratum houstonianum**, **225**, p. 29.

FLOWER OF JOVE see **Lychnis flos-jovis**, **1251**, p. 157.

FLOWERING CHERRY see **Prunus**, **1752-1767**, pp. 219-221.

FLOWERING CHERRY, JAPANESE see **Prunus serrulata**, **1762-1764**, p. 221.

FLOWERING CRAB see **Malus**, **1699-1704**, p. 213.

FLOWERING CURRANT see **Ribes**, **1833, 1834**, p. 230.

FLOWERING RUSH see **Butomus umbellatus**, **1007**, p. 126.

FLOWERS OF THE WESTERN WIND see **Zephyranthes candida**, **944**, p. 118.

FOAM FLOWER see **Tiarella**, **1398, 1399**, p. 175.

FOENICULUM (UMBELLIFERAE)
vulgare Fennel 🌼 Late Summer–Mid Autumn P.
Fl. yellow borne in umbels. *L.* finely cut, used fresh or dried for flavouring for fish dishes; there is a bronze foliage form. 4–6 ft. Seed aromatic. It is unwise to let the plant seed as it may become widespread. Propagate by seed sown in the open, 4–5. Thrives on chalky soil. S. Europe, Britain. **1137**, p. 143.

FORGET-ME-NOT see **Myosotis**, **347**, p. 44.

FORSYTHIA (OLEACEAE)
All Forsythias should have old wood pruned out after flowering. In some areas they also need some protection from birds which are inclined to take the buds.

× **intermedia** Common Forsythia 🌼 Spring Sh.
A hybrid of *F. suspensa* × *F. viridissima*. A quick growing shrub up to 9 ft. *Fl.* deep yellow, clustering along branches very abundant. Tubular at base with star-shaped lobes.
Among best forms are:
   ✿ 'Beatrix Farrand', *fl.* deep canary-yellow exceptionally large often an inch across, very freely and densely borne, **1611**, p. 202;
   'Lynwood', *fl.* with broad petals, rich yellow. One of the finest forms;
   'Spectabilis', *fl.* large, deep yellow profusely borne, **1612**, p. 202.

suspensa 🌼 Spring Sh.
A rambling shrub with slender hanging branches. Best form is:
   atrocaulis, young stems dark purple appearing black contrasting with pale lemon-yellow *fl.*;
   fortunei, is most vigorous form of this sp. with stout arching branches.

FOTHERGILLA (HAMAMELIDACEAE)

alnifolia see **F. gardenii**

alnifolia 'Major' see **F. major**

carolina see **F. gardenii**

gardenii, syn. **F. alnifolia, F. carolina** ❋ Spring Sh.
Small deciduous shrub up to 3 ft with numerous crossing, rather slender, branches. *Fl.* white without petals and consisting of white stamens and yellow anthers in globular clusters at ends of branches 1–1½ in. across. *L.* oval or obovate up to 2½ in. long, rounded at base. Colouring to beautiful carrot-crimson in autumn. S.E. USA. **1613**, p. 202.

major, syn. **F. alnifolia** 'Major' ❋ Late Spring Sh.
A deciduous shrub up to 10 ft. *Fl.* in erect spikes of stamens, white and yellow. *L.* larger than in preceding sp. up to 4 in. long broadly ovate, colouring brilliant scarlet in autumn. S.E. USA.

monticola ❋ Late Spring Sh.
A deciduous shrub up to 6 ft usually more open and spreading than preceding sp. *Fl.* white and yellow in clusters up to 2 in. across also without petals. *L.* up to 4 in. long, roundish or obovate heart-shaped at base, colouring brilliant scarlet or crimson in autumn. One of our finest autumn colouring plants. S.E. USA. **1614**, p. 202.

FOUNTAIN GRASS see **Pennisetum ruppellii, 356**, p. 45.

FOXGLOVE see **Digitalis, 289, 290**, p. 37.

FRAXINUS (OLEACEAE)

excelsior Common Ash T.
Deciduous tree, very valuable for timber, up to 100 ft, not too large for planting in majority of gardens. *Fl.* greenish-white in clusters on bare branches. *L.* pinnate up to 1 ft long with leaflets up to 4½ in. long. Fruit in pendant clusters 1½ in. long. Best form for gardens is:
'Pendula', Weeping Ash, which makes fine specimen tree on lawn. Branches very pendulous, wide-spreading but must be top grafted in order to make satisfactory tree, **1615**, p. 202.

ornus The Manna Ash ❋ Late Spring T.
Medium sized tree. *Fl.* with clusters of greenish-yellow heads.

FREESIA (IRIDACEAE)

❋ Winter–Mid Spring Indoors, ❋ Summer–Mid Autumn Outdoors *C or GC.
The modern race of Freesias, used so freely for cut *fl.* are derived from S. African sp. *F. refracta* which has much smaller creamy-white *fl.* Many colours have now been developed covering a range from snowy-white through creamy-yellow to orange and crimson, while blue and mauve forms are also grown. Freesias are grown either from corms in the case of named cultivars and some mixtures from seeds where the crop will show some variation. Corms are planted 8–9 for winter-flowering in a heated greenhouse. Seeds should be sown in early spring, the seedlings being grown on directly to *fl.* During the summer they may be stood out of doors but must not be allowed to dry out. **734, 735**, p. 92. Among the many selected and named cultivars the following may be recommended by colours:
White:
'Snow Queen', 'White Swan';
Cream and pale yellow:
'Buttercup', 'Fantasy', double and especially long-lasting;
Deep yellow and pale orange:
'Orange Favourite', 'Orange Sun';
Pink:
'Pink Giant', medium dark cerise-pink;
'Red Bird', deep salmon-pink with a yellow throat;

Blue:
'Sapphire', delicate shade of pale lavender-blue with a white throat.

FREMONTIA (STERCULIACEAE)

californica ❋ Late Spring–Midsummer *Sh., T.
Deciduous or semi-evergreen wall shrub. In native country grown as a small tree and may be so grown as greenhouse shrub. *Fl.* deep yellow with wide overlapping petals up to 3 in. across. *L.* up to 3 in. wide, lobed, dull green. Easily grown from seed and fast growing but not usually long lived in this country although specimens on warm walls up to 20 ft high and as much across have been grown. One of the finest summer flowering wall plants where it is possible to grow it. USA. **1977**, p. 248.
'California Glory', is probably a hybrid of *F. californica* and *F. mexicana* and the most valuable form for size and freedom of *fl.*

FRENCH LAVENDER see Lavandula stoechas

FRENCH MARIGOLD see Tagetes patula, 380, 381, p. 48.

FRINGED BLEEDING HEART see Dicentra eximia, 1108, p. 139.

FRITILLARIA (LILIACEAE)

✿ **acmopetala** ❋ Mid Spring Bb
Fl. 1–3 nodding bells, slightly recurved towards lower end of bell, three inner segments maroon-brown, three outer segments jade-green 1–1¼ in. deep and about the same across, on slender stems up to 1½ ft. *L.* glaucous. One of the most delightful and graceful sp. and one of the easiest to grow. Suitable for rock garden or alpine house. The bulbs should if possible be ripened off in summer. Asia Minor. **736**, p. 92.

✿ **imperialis** Crown Imperial ❋ Spring Bb
A favourite of the old Dutch *fl.* painters. *Fl.* lemon-yellow or orange-red on stout stems up to 4 ft. The bells hang in a circle below the top rosette of *l.* and are 2–2½ in. deep and nearly as much across. At the base of each is a ring of dark shiny spots, the nectaries and many legends have been associated with this, notably that it was the one *fl.* which would not bow its head as Jesus passed to Calvary and ever after bowed its head with unshed tears which are represented by the nectaries. The bulbs are large and fleshy and if damaged give out a strong and unpleasant foxy smell. Plant in full sun and leave undisturbed as far as possible. They become dormant in midsummer so their position should be marked. The typical form is orange-red but the lemon-yellow is more spectacular in the garden.
Selected cultivars include:
'Aurora', deep reddish-orange, vigorous, **737**, p. 93;
'Lutea Maxima', deep lemon-yellow, **738**, p. 93;
'Rubra Major', rusty-red, slightly deeper in colour than 'Aurora'.

libanotica see **F. persica**

meleagris Snake's Head Fritillary, Guinea Flower ❋ Mid Spring Bb
One of the most beautiful of British native *fl.* *Fl.* nodding, a broad bell on a slender stem, purple, reddish-purple, patterned with a chequering of white. Grows best in damp places where it can be naturalised as in Christ Church meadow, Oxford. **739**, p. 93.
Selected forms which can be recommended include:
'Aphrodite', white, a strong grower;
'Charon', dark purple;
'Purple King', dusky vinous purple, **740**, p. 93;
'Saturnus', light reddish-purple, large.

pallidiflora ❋ Mid Spring Bb
Fl. pale creamy-yellow or greenish-yellow, inside

flecked with reddish dots, bell-shaped, large, up to 12 to a head in axils of upper whorls of *l.* Stem stout, fleshy, up to 2 ft. *L.* broad, slightly glaucous. Bulb large for the genus. One of the easiest sp. for front of a sunny border. USSR, S. Siberia. **741**, p. 93.

persica ❋ Spring Bb
Tall stems up to 2½ ft with many rather small dark maroon-purple bells covered with a whitish bloom in a loose spike. In Lebanon the forms generally have pale jade-green *fl.* and used to be separated as *F. libanotica*. Bulb large, egg-shaped, *l.* glaucous arranged up the stem. Suitable for a sunny and well drained position or alpine house. N.W. Persia through Iraq, Syria to Lebanon, Jordan, Israel.

pyrenaica ❋ Spring Bb
Stems up to 1½ ft with one or two dark maroon-purple bells, sometimes almost appearing black but inside they are yellow and chequered with crimson-purple. Very variable. Rock gardens or open woodland. One of the easiest garden plants in the genus. Pyrenees, N. Spain.

FRITILLARY see Fritillaria, 736-741, pp. 92–93.

FUCHSIA (ONAGRACEAE)

hybrida ❋ Summer GSh.
Shrubs usually of 2–3 ft, but can be larger. *Fl.* composed of tube with four spreading sepals subtending a corolla in various colour combinations of red, white and purple. *L.* ovate, varying in size. Plants are usually raised annually from stem cuttings of soft wood that can be taken at any time. However plants can be dried off, overwintered at a temp. of 40°F. and pruned, repotted and restarted in early spring at a temp. of 55°F. The main parents are the hardy *F. magellanica* with crimson sepals and a purple corolla and *F. fulgens* with scarlet-green tipped sepals and a scarlet corolla. The white-sepalled varieties are derived from 'Venus Victrix', raised in the 1840's from an unknown sp. with a white corolla which was subsequently lost and has not been rediscovered. In the early years of this century, the tender but exceedingly floriferous *F. triphylla* was used to produce a low-growing bedding plant; 'Gartenmeister Bonstedt' is one of these *triphylla* hybrids. The hybrids with rather weak, pendulous stems may have *F. corymbiflora* in their ancestry. All the hybrids will thrive out of doors in the summer and, if kept in the greenhouse, need

---

Abbreviations and Symbols used in the text.
The following abbreviations may sometimes be used in conjunction as HA. indicating Hardy annual or GBb indicating Greenhouse bulb.

A. = Annual	P. = Perennial
Aq. = Aquatic	R. = Rock or
B. = Biennial	Alpine plant
Bb = Bulb	Sh. = Shrub
C. = Corm	Sp., sp. = Species
Cl. = Climber	Syn. = Synonym
Co. = Conifer	T. = Tree
Fl., fl. = Flower(s)	Tu. = Tuber
G. = Greenhouse or	var. = variety
house plant	× = Hybrid or
H. = Hardy	hybrid parents
HH. = Half-hardy	❋ = Flowering time
L., l. = Leaf, leaves	◗ = Foliage plant
Mt(s) = Mount,	
mountain(s)	

The following have been used also in the descriptions of Alpines, Bulbs, Trees and Shrubs.

* = slightly tender
† = lime hater
✿ = highly recommended

The illustration numbers are in **bold type** and the page numbers in light type preceded by p.

slight shade and full ventilation. *F. magellanica* is native to Chile and the Falkland Islands, *F. fulgens* to Mexico. New varieties may be raised from seed, otherwise propagation is by stem cuttings. Among the best modern varieties are:

'Coachman', orange-red corolla, pink sepals, **534**, p. 67;

'Heinrich Heinkel', purple corolla, long red tube and sepals, **535**, p. 67;

'Mission Bells', purple corolla, red sepals, **536**, p. 67;

'Molesworth', white corolla, red sepals, **537**, p. 68;

'Red Spider', red corolla, long tube and sepals paler, **538**, p. 68;

'Television', dark purple corolla, white sepals, **539**, p. 68.

magellanica ❋ Summer–Mid Autumn   Sh.
Deciduous shrub or small tree up to 12 ft. Tender except in S. and W. areas but even if cut to base in winter will spring up and *fl.* next season. *Fl.* crimson-red with spreading calyx and central petaloid cup with purple centre and long protruding stigma and stamens, pendulous. Has a long season. This is the wild fuchsia of hedges. **1617**, p. 203.
Developed from it have been numerous forms and hybrids of which the best are:

'Madame Cornelissen', with red sepals and white petaloid cup, **1616**, p. 202;

'Mrs Popple', similar to type but with larger *fl.* Very reliable garden plant, **1618**, p. 203;

'Riccartonii', with more spreading calyx and deeper purple centre cup. Frequently used as a hedging plant in mild districts.

FUJI CHERRY see **Prunus incisa**, **1756**, p. 220.

FULLMOON MAPLE see **Acer japonicum**, **1432**, p. 179.

FUNKIA see **Hosta**

FURZE see **Ulex europaeus**, **1931**, p. 242.

G

GAILLARDIA (COMPOSITAE) Blanket Flower

aristata ❋ Summer–Mid Autumn   P.
Fl. yellow and red. *L.* oblong, toothed. 2 ft. A sunny position and light well-drained soil; unsuitable for heavy wet soils. Propagate by division in the spring or by root cuttings. The parent of many colourful hybrids. W. N. America.
Good varieties include:

'Burgundy', deep red, 2 ft;

'Goblin', crimson and cream, dwarf, 6 in., **1138**, p. 143;

'Tommy', bright tangerine self, 2½ ft;

'Wirral Flame', deep orange-red, 2½–3 ft, **1139**, p. 143.

pulchella ❋ Summer   HHA.
Fl. yellow with crimson base, single. *L.* lance-shaped, coarsely toothed. 1–2 ft. Sow under glass in 3 and plant out in a sunny position and in a well-drained soil in 5. N. America.

'Indian Chief', deep orange-scarlet, single, 2 ft;

'Lorenziana' hybrids, including crimson, orange, yellow and white, double, 2 ft, **296**, p. 37.

GALANTHUS (AMARYLLIDACEAE) Snowdrops

In all sp. the *fl.* are white, globular or bell-shaped and drooping, the three inner segments of the *fl.* being smaller than the outer and joined into a small cup. All are suitable for sun or semi-shade and grow as well on chalk as in acid soils. Lovely when naturalised which they do best in cool slightly moist and not too sandy places. Among the best sp. and forms are:

elwesii Giant Snowdrop ❋ Winter   Bb
One of the largest *fl.* in genus, distinguished by broad green markings at base of inner segments. Rather late. *L.* broad and glaucous. W. Turkey. **742**, p. 93.

ikariae ❋ Early Spring   Bb
Fl. large with broad green markings on inner segment. Distinguished by broad green *l.* Close to *G. ikariae* subsp. *latifolius* but larger in *fl.* Semi-shade. Only so far found on Isle of Nikaria in E. Mediterranean. **743**, p. 93.

nivalis Common Snowdrop ❋ Winter   Bb
Good for quick increase. Britain. **744**, p. 93.
Large-flowered selected forms or hybrids of *nivalis* type, which are also more vigorous, are:

'Atkinsii', named after a famous snowdrop grower and usually earlier than 'S. Arnott' below;

'S. Arnott', also named after a famous grower, occurred in his garden in Scotland, **745**, p. 94.

plicatus 'Warham' ❋ Spring   Bb
The finest form of *G. plicatus*. *Fl.* large. Distinguished by the glaucous *l.* being folded back at the margins. This form was collected during the Crimean War and is the only snowdrop so far to have received a First Class Certificate from The Royal Horticultural Society, their highest award for a plant. S. Russia. **746**, p. 94.

GALEGA (LEGUMINOSAE) Goat's Rue

officinalis ❋ Summer   P.
Fl. white or mauve, pea-shaped. *L.* short-stalked, pinnate. 3–5 ft. Ordinary garden soil in sun or light shade. Propagate by seed sown in the open in 4 or by division in the spring. S. Europe, Asia.
Good varieties include:

'Alba', white;

'Her Majesty', soft lilac-blue, **1140**, p. 143;

'Lady Wilson', lilac-blue, **1141**, p. 143.

GALEOBDOLON LUTEUM see **Lamium galeobdolon**

GALINGALE see **Cyperus**, **492**, p. 62.

GALTONIA (LILIACEAE)

✿ **candicans**, syn. **Hyacinthus candicans** Giant Summer Hyacinth ❋ Summer   Bb
Fl. white, bell-shaped and pendulous, slightly tinged with green, numerous on stout stems up to 4 ft. A very valuable summer-flowering bulb. *L.* strap-shaped and glaucous. Often grown in herbaceous border. Full sun. S. Africa. **747**, p. 94.

GARDENER'S GARTERS see **Phalaris arundinacea** 'Picta', **1310**, p. 164.

GARLIC, WILD see **Allium triquetrum**

GARRYA (GARRYACEAE)

elliptica ❋ Winter–Early Spring   Sh.
Evergreen shrub or even small tree up to 15 ft. Young wood downy pubescent. *Fl.* densely borne in pendulous catkins. Dioecious, that is male and female catkins on separate bushes. The male ones are superior, up to 6 in. long, suede grey. *L.* oval to roundish up to 3 in. long, leathery, dark green above and grey beneath. A very valuable evergreen expecially for its winter-flowering habit. Hardy in most areas but in cold areas best grown as a wall shrub. Plant preferably out of pot when small since it moves badly. Propagate from cuttings in late summer. USA. **1619**, p. 203.

GAULTHERIA (ERICACEAE)

procumbens Checkerberry, Creeping Wintergreen ❋ Autumn   Sh.
Dwarf procumbent creeping shrub, usually not more than 6 in. high. Evergreen. *Fl.* small, flask-shaped, white and pink followed by pink to crimson berries in clusters. *L.* leathery, thick, up to 1½ in. long by 1 in. across. Makes an excellent ground cover, preferably in non-limy soils. Oregon, California. **1620**, p. 203.
Other good sp. are:

forrestii ❋ Late Spring   Sh.
Fl. in racemes, white, waxy, fragrant. Blue berries. China, Yunnan.

hookeri ❋ Spring   Sh.
With blue-black fruits. E. Himalayas.

nummularioides ❋ Summer   Sh.
Procumbent small shrub up to 1 ft with shiny *l.* arranged in two ranks. Fruits blue-black in layers. Himalayas.

semi-infera   Sh.
With large indigo-blue grape-like fruits. Himalayas, Yunnan.

shallon ❋ Early Summer   Sh.
Larger sp. very vigorous forming thickets up to 5–6 ft high. Fruits dark purple. *Fl.* pink. Spreads so freely that may be a menace in small areas. W. N. America.

wardii ❋ Early Summer   Sh.
Fruits milky-blue. S.E. Tibet.

GAYFEATHER see **Liatris spicata**, **1235**, p. 155.

GAYFEATHER, KANSAS see **Liatris callilepis**, **1234**, p. 155.

GAZANIA (COMPOSITAE)

× **splendens** ❋ Summer–Autumn   HHP.
Fl. golden-orange, spotted with brown or mauve around the centre. Hybrids include pink, bronze and ruby shades. *L.* long, narrow, silky-white beneath. 6–9 in. Half-hardy perennial which can be increased by cuttings, but often grown as an annual. Sow in a warm greenhouse in 3. Plant out in late 5 or early 6 in a sunny open position and a light sandy soil. Of garden origin. **297**, p. 38.

GAZANIA, CLIMBING see **Mutisia**, **1984**, p. 248.

Abbreviations and Symbols used in the text.
The following abbreviations may sometimes be used in conjunction as HA. indicating Hardy annual or GBb indicating Greenhouse bulb.

A. = Annual	P. = Perennial
Aq. = Aquatic	R. = Rock or
B. = Biennial	Alpine plant
Bb = Bulb	Sh. = Shrub
C. = Corm	Sp., sp. = Species
Cl. = Climber	Syn. = Synonym
Co. = Conifer	T. = Tree
Fl., *fl.* = Flower(s)	Tu. = Tuber
G. = Greenhouse or	var. = variety
house plant	× = Hybrid or
H. = Hardy	hybrid parents
HH. = Half-hardy	❋ = Flowering time
L., *l.* = Leaf, leaves	♣ = Foliage plant
Mt(s) = Mount,	
mountain(s)	

The following have been used also in the descriptions of Alpines, Bulbs, Trees and Shrubs.

* = slightly tender
† = lime hater
✿ = highly recommended

The illustration numbers are in **bold type** and the page numbers in light type preceded by p.

GEAN see **Prunus avium, 1753**, p. 220.

GENISTA (LEGUMINOSAE)

aetnensis see **G. cinerea**

✿ **cinerea** ✼ Summer   Sh.
Tall deciduous shrub up to 10 ft. *Fl.* deep yellow very freely produced, frequently covering whole of upper part of shrub making yellow billows of colour. Plant in any sunny position and prune flowering shoots after flowering otherwise all brooms should not be pruned too hard. W. N. Africa and W. Mediterranean regions from Spain to Italy. **1621**, p. 203.
> Close to this are *G. virgata* the Madeiran Broom and *G. aetnensis*, Mt Etna Broom, the latest broom to *fl.* in 7–8, which has loose pendulous growth.

hispanica Spanish Gorse ✼ Summer   Sh.
Dwarf spiny shrub up to 3 ft usually less, spreading freely, excellent for ground cover in large rock garden. Deep golden-yellow in clusters. Sunny position. Spain, S.W. Europe. **1622**, p. 203.

✿ **lydia** ✼ Early Summer   Sh.
Dwarf shrub up to 3 ft with pendulous branches, covered with deep yellow *fl.* so that shrub looks like a billowing mound of yellow, very rich colour. Good in front for training down over a low wall or in large rock garden. Hardly ever fails to flower freely. Sunny position. E. and S.E. Europe. **1623**, p. 203.

tinctoria Dyer's Greenwood, Waxen Woad ✼ Summer   Sh.
Dwarf, erect shrub up to 3 ft, usually less, with slender young shoots. *Fl.* deep yellow in racemes. Sunny position towards front of border or in large rock garden. S. Europe and Britain.
> Various named forms are available of which 'Royal Gold' is one of the best, **1624**, p. 203.

virgata see **G. cinerea**

GENTIAN see **Gentiana, 71–77**, pp. 9, 10; **1142**, p. 143.

GENTIANA (GENTIANACEAE) Gentian

acaulis Trumpet Gentian ✼ Mid Spring–Early Summer   RP.
Fl. bright blue, trumpets up to 2 in. long and 1 in. across, throat usually speckled at base. *L.* dark green, strap-shaped and forming small mats where happy. 2–3 in. *G. acaulis* is the name usually given to the garden forms grown. Its origin is uncertain but is variable and probably derived from the two wild alpine sp. *G. clusii* which grows on limestone rocks and soils and *G. kochiana* which grows on igneous rocks and soils which are acid or neutral. Both are widespread in Alps and Pyrenees. *G. acaulis* has the repuation of fickleness in flowering, in some gardens doing this regularly and freely while in others also quite close it will not *fl.* at all and no reason has yet been discovered. Wild collected plants of the alpine sp. rarely *fl.* well in cultivation. **71**, p. 9.
> var. *dinarica*, probably the finest form from the E. Alps.

asclepiadea Willow Gentian ✼ Late Summer   P.
Fl. deep blue or rarely white, tubular, on arching stems. *L.* lance-shaped, prominently veined, opposite. 1½–2 ft. Partial shade and moist soil with plenty of leaf mould. Once planted leave undisturbed. Propagate by seed sown in pans as soon as ripe. Europe. **1142**, p. 143.

bavarica see **G. verna**

farreri ✼ Late Summer–Mid Autumn   RP.
Fl. greenish bright sky-blue with greenish-blue markings inside and on outside of tube and white base, funnel shaped, upright up to 1½ in. long and 1 in. across. *L.* linear, grass-like, forming small

mats where plant is suited but less vigorous than *G. sino-ornata*. 3–5 in. Best planted in peaty soil with a little grit and good drainage, but will tolerate a little liminess in soil which most other members of this group of gentians will not do. One of the most sensational autumn-flowering rock plants because of its unique colour. May be propagated by division of thong-like roots in spring or grown from seed, but seedlings may vary in colour. Parent of several very good hybrids. S.E. Tibet, W. China.

'Inverleith' see **G. sino-ornata**

lagodechiana ✼ Summer   RP.
Fl. deep blue, not so bright as in *G. acaulis*, trumpet-funnel-shaped with spreading lobes, green speckled in throat, 1½ in. long. singly on the ends of short upright branches, up to 8 in. *L.* ovate up to 1 in. long. One of the easiest gentians to grow successfully and usually free-flowering in open sunny position on rock garden. USSR, Caucasus. **73**, p. 10.

'Macaulayi' see **G. sino-ornata**

saxosa ✼ Summer   RP.
2–4 in. *Fl.* white, upright, cup-shaped, often dark veined on short dark stems, up to ¾ in. across. *L.* spathulate, dark green forming a small mat. Often not a very long-lasting plant in English gardens. New Zealand where all gentians are white. **74**, p. 10.

septemfida ✼ Summer   RP.
Close to *G. lagodechiana* but with trumpet *fl.* in clusters on longer trailing stems which turn upright before flowering. It is equally successful as a garden plant. N.E. Turkey, Asia Minor.

✿ **sino-ornata** ✼ Late Summer–Mid Autumn †RP.
Fl. deep gentian-blue, upright, large trumpets up to 2 in. long and 1½ in. across, streaked with green outside. *L.* narrow grass-like and where suited forming large mats. Only suitable for moist acid peaty or leaf mould soils and will grow in semi-shade. One of the most valuable and spectacular autumn-flowering alpine plants but in growth it must never be allowed to dry out. Easily propagated by division of thong-like roots in spring. S.E. Tibet, W. China. **75**, p. 10.
> *G. veitchiorum* is close but with wider opening trumpets. Several valuable hybrids have been raised which resemble *G. sino-ornata* but are rather more vigorous growers and with slightly larger *fl.* These include ✿ 'Inverleith' (*G. farreri* × *G. veitchiorum*), **72**, p. 9, and ✿ 'Macaulayi' (*G. farreri* × *G. sino-ornata*).

verna Spring Gentian ✼ Mid Spring–Early Summer   RP.
Fl. short trumpets with five star-like lobes, 1 in. long, variable in colour from strongest and brightest blue of all gentians to pale sky blue or occasionally white. *L.* lanceolate forming small tufts. Plant in well-drained soil or on scree. Excellent in pots in alpine house. Fresh stocks should be raised at intervals from seed which usually germinates freely after winter freezing. Alps and Pyrenees where it is abundant and Mts of Asia Minor. **76, 77**, p. 10. High level, closely allied sp. is *G. bavarica* with most brilliant deep blue *fl.* on very short stems often in large clumps but difficult in cultivation, and *G. verna* var. *angulosa* which has winged calyx and is easier in cultivation. They require scree or alpine house conditions.

GERANIUM (GERANIACEAE) Cranesbill

A large family of hardy border plants with some suitable for the rock garden, not to be confused with bedding geraniums (*Pelargonium*), mostly thriving in a sunny position and in well-drained ordinary garden soil. Easily propagated by seed, sown in the spring in pans of sandy soil placed in a cold frame, or sown in the open in a sunny bed in 4, and in most cases by division in autumn or spring.

armenum see **G. psilostemon**

cinereum ✼ Summer   RP.
3–6 in. *Fl.* variable from deep pink, purplish-pink to white, open saucer-shaped, generally veined

with deeper purplish-crimson and maroon at base, up to 1 in. across, on short stems. *L.* deeply lobed, slightly glaucous. A valuable and easily grown plant for an open sunny position, on rock garden. Pyrenees.
> 'Ballerina', is a specially selected form with pale rosy-purple *fl.* deeply veined and with deep crimson base, **78**, p. 10.

cinereum var. **subcaulescens** see **G. subcaulescens**

ibericum Iberian Cranesbill ✼ Summer   P.
Fl. violet-blue about 1 in. across in open panicles. *L.* roundish, deeply cleft, woolly. 1½–2 ft. Caucasus. **1143**, p. 143.
> Good varieties include:
> 'Alba', 2 ft, white;
> 'Flore Pleno', 2 ft, double, violet-blue, **1144**, p. 143;
> 'Johnson's Blue', 2 ft, bright blue, **1145**, p. 144.

macrorrhizum ✼ Late Spring–Midsummer   P.
Fl. bright red, veined. *L.* smooth, five-lobed, aromatic. 1–1½ ft. S. Europe.
> Good varieties are:
> 'Album', pure white, 15 in., **1146**, p. 144;
> 'Ingwersen', large, rosy-pink, 15 in.

pratense Meadow Cranesbill ✼ Summer   P.
Fl. blue, variable shades, 1 in. or more across. *L.* roundish, coarsely toothed. 1½–3 ft. N. Europe, Britain.
> Good varieties include:
> 'Album', pure white, 2 ft;
> 'Album Plenum', double white, 2 ft;
> 'Flore Pleno', double blue, 2 ft, **1147**, p. 144;
> 'Mrs Kendall Clarke', single, pale opal blue, 2 ft.

psilostemon, syn. **G. armenum** ✼ Summer   P.
Fl. magenta-red with very dark centre. *L.* heart-shaped, five-lobed. 2–3 ft. Plant 10–3. A very spectacular plant, forming large clumps in full sun. Armenia.

sanguineum Bloody Cranesbill ✼ Summer   P.
Fl. intense magenta. *L.* opposite, neatly lobed. 18 in. Europe. **1148**, p. 144.
> Good varieties include:
> 'Album', white, 9 in.;
> var. *lancastriense*, clear rose pink, 6 in.

subcaulescens, syn. **G. cinereum** var. **subcaulescens** ✼ Summer   RP.
6 in. *Fl.* very bright magenta-crimson, a very strong

colour, up to 1 in. across, open bowl-shaped with dark centre. *L.* deeply divided, green but slightly glaucous below. An easy and striking plant for open sunny position. Mts of E. Europe, Balkans, N.E. Turkey. **79**, p. 10.

sylvaticum Wood Cranesbill ❋ Summer   P.
Fl. variable, bluish-purple to pink. *L.* roundish, deeply lobed. 2 ft. Plant 11–3. Does well in partial shade. Europe, including Britain.
Good varieties include:
'Album', white, pinkish in the bud stage, 2 ft;
'Mayflower', light blue, 2 ft, **1149**, p. 144.

wallichianum ❋ Late Summer   P.
Fl. violet-blue. *L.* and stem covered with silky hairs, 1 ft, of spreading habit. Partial shade and a moist ordinary soil. Himalaya.
'Buxton's Blue', also known as 'Buxton's Variety', is a deeper shade, **1150**, p. 144.

GERANIUM see also **Pelargonium**, **586-617**, pp. 74-78.

GEUM (ROSACEAE) Avens

× **borisii** ❋ Late Spring–Summer   P.
Fl. orange-scarlet. *L.* wedge-shaped, deeply toothed. 1 ft. In sun or dappled shade and ordinary garden soil. Propagate by division or seed. Of garden origin, *G. bulgaricum × reptans*. **1151**. p. 144.

chiloense ❋ Summer   P.
Fl. scarlet in erect panicles. *L.* three-parted, deeply cut. 1–2 ft. Cultivation and propagation as for *G. × borisii*.
Good varieties include:
'Lady Stratheden', 2 ft, yellow, semi-double;
'Mrs Bradshaw', 2 ft, crimson, semi-double, **1152**, p. 144;
'Prince of Orange', 1–1½ ft, orange-yellow, double.

rivale Water Avens ❋ Summer   P.
Fl. reddish, nodding, on hairy stems. *L.* feathery at base. 1 ft. For moist position beside a stream or pool. Propagate by division or seed. Europe, including Britain.
'Leonard', is a good form with salmon, orange tinted *fl.*, 1½ ft.

GHOST TREE see **Davidia involucrata**, **1558**, p. 195.

GIANT HIMALAYAN LILY see **Cardiocrinum giganteum**, **682**, p. 86.

GIANT RAGWORT see **Ligularia japonica**, **1240**, p. 155.

GIANT SUMMER HYACINTH see **Galtonia candicans**, **747**, p. 94.

GILIA (POLEMONIACEAE)

hybrida, syn. **Leptosiphon hybridus** ❋ Summer   HA.
Fl. golden-yellow, bright rose, cream, orange, red, star-like. *L.* narrowly parted, marginally hairy. 6–9 in. Sow in the open in 3–4, where they are to flower, and in a sunny position and ordinary garden soil. Various mixed strains, including 'French Hybrids', 6 in., **298**, p. 38, are most colourful. California.

GINKGO (GINKGOACEAE)

biloba Maidenhair Tree   Co.
Unique deciduous tree up to 100 ft but usually less. *L.* fan-shaped yellowish-green. Cones, the two sexes are borne on different trees. The tree is single survivor of family of trees which in prehistoric times were fertilised by mobile sperm cells. Often known as Maidenhair Tree from resemblance of *l.*

to Maidenhair Fern. Valuable for its yellow autumn colouring of foliage. One of the finest trees is at Kew while there is famous avenue in Washington. Has long been regarded as a sacred tree in the Far East. China, but doubtful whether it still exists as a wild tree. **2014**, p. 252.

GLADIOLUS (IRIDACEAE)

byzantinus ❋ Summer   C.
Distinct for its bright magenta pink *fl.* and that it is hardy in sunny warm situations and often spreads freely by seeding. *Fl.* spike up to 2½ ft but *fl.* are smaller than in the large-flowered hybrids. A white form is known but is difficult to *fl.* and requires hot position. E. Mediterranean. **748**, p. 94.

colvillei see **G. nanus**

nanus (including those often known as **G. colvillei**) ❋ Mid Spring–Early Summer   C.
Early flowering hybrid group*
Smaller in *fl.* than the later flowering hybrids. 1½–2 ft. Tender, best cultivated in cool greenhouse but if planted in late autumn rather deep and covered with a pile of ashes for winter they will often last satisfactorily outside. Much used by florists and a delightful cut *fl.* generally white or pale pink with a deeper blotch.
Among best forms are:
'Ackerman', bright orange-scarlet with darker flecking around throat, one of the oldest but still worth growing;
'Blushing Bride', white with bright carmine fleckings;
'Charm', cerise-pink with creamy-white blotch and markings on lower petals, **749**, p. 94;
'Nymph', white with crimson flecks;
'Peach Blossom', shell-pink;
'Robinette', deep cerise-pink with small cream blotch on lower petals edged with deeper crimson, **750**, p. 94;
'Spitfire', deep salmon-orange with small violet flecks, a striking *fl.*;
'Spring Glory', salmon pink with white blotch on three lower petals, each blotch surrounded by darker zone of crimson-red, **751**, p. 94;
'The Bride', white.
Large-flowered standard varieties ❋ Summer   C.
3–4 ft. Plant in spring in sunny position 3–4 in. deep:
'Black Jack', deep ruby-crimson velvet, lighter towards centre, **752**, p. 94;
'Golden Standard', deep golden yellow, **753**, p. 95;
'Peter Pears', pale orange-pink with creamy ill-defined blotch on lower petal which is slightly streaked with orange-scarlet, **754**, p. 95;
'Purple Star', deep crimson-purple with velvet texture, **755**, p. 95;
'Toulouse-Lautrec', apricot-orange with yellow throat, slightly flecked with crimson, **756**, p. 95.
Butterfly Gladioli ❋ Summer   C.
2½–3½ ft. Slightly smaller in *fl.* than standard varieties, often with fluted petals. Plant as for standard varieties:
'Chinatown', orange-red with deeper red blotch at base, **757**, p. 95;
'Green Woodpecker', yellowish-green with crimson at base, a fascinating colour especially for arrangements, **758**, p. 95;
'Mokha', crimson-maroon with paler centre and velvet texture, **759**, p. 95;
'Page Polka', pale primrose-yellow, slightly deeper on lower petals, **760**, p. 95.
Primulinus Gladioli: C.
2½–3½ ft. *Fl.* smaller than in standard varieties and more loosely spaced:
'Chartres', bright crimson-red with an ivory-white narrow edge to each petal, **761**, p. 96;
'Sappho', ivory-white with pale primrose centre, **762**, p. 96;
'Treasure', blood-red with velvet texture, **763**, p. 96.

segetum Cornflag ❋ Early Summer   *C.
Fl. rosy-purple. Stems more slender and with fewer, more widely spaced *fl.* than in *G. byzantinus* but more graceful. Only hardy in very warm situations. S. Europe where it is frequent in cornfields.

GLAUCIDIUM (PODOPHYLLACEAE)

palmatum ❋ Spring   RP.
8–10 in. Forming clumps. *Fl.* pale lilac or white, cup-shaped or saucer-shaped with wide overlapping petals and boss of deep yellow stamens in centre up to 2 in. across, borne on upright stems up to 10 in. *L.* deeply lobed like vine *l.* usually in pairs from upper part of stem, large up to 6 in. across. A woodland plant for semi-shady part of rock garden in leaf soil or peat. A large clump is much prized by alpine gardeners. Japan. **80**, p. 10.

GLAUCIUM (PAPAVERACEAE)

flavum Horned Poppy ❋ Summer   HA.
Fl. golden-yellow or orange. Seeds in pods up to 1 ft long. *L.* glaucous-green, deeply lobed, thick and fleshy, thinly hairy. Sometimes perennial. 1–3 ft. Sow in the open in 4–5 where it is to *fl.*, in sandy soil and a sunny position. Europe, including Britain, N. Africa; naturalised in E. N. America. **299**, p. 38.

GLEDITSCHIA (LEGUMINOSAE)

triacanthos Honey Locust   T.
Tree, 35 to 70 ft. Thornless forms of this tree have a wide range of uses. Excels as a lawn tree since its delicate fine foliage and loose pattern makes but little shade on the grass below it, and old fallen leaflets 'melt' into the grass. Valuable to those who want a quick-growing tree. Since it is not particular as to soil acidity or alkalinity, heat or cold, it makes a good street tree and is adaptable in difficult areas, such as dry and windy regions. S. to mid-E. USA.
'Moraine', the Moraine Locust; fast-growing, very popular;
'Shademaster', grows even faster;
'Ruby Lace', pronounced new red growth;
'Sunburst', new foliage growth is golden-yellow.

GLOBE AMARANTH see **Gomphrena globosa**, **302**, p. 38.

GLOBE TULIP see **Calochortus**, **679**, p. 85.

Abbreviations and Symbols used in the text.
The following abbreviations may sometimes be used in conjunction as HA. indicating Hardy annual or GBb indicating Greenhouse bulb.

A. = Annual	P. = Perennial
Aq. = Aquatic	R. = Rock or
B. = Biennial	Alpine plant
Bb = Bulb	Sh. = Shrub
C. = Corm	Sp., sp. = Species
Cl. = Climber	Syn. = Synonym
Co. = Conifer	T. = Tree
Fl., fl. = Flower(s)	Tu. = Tuber
G. = Greenhouse or	var. = variety
house plant	× = Hybrid or
H. = Hardy	hybrid parents
HH. = Half-hardy	❋ = Flowering time
L., l. = Leaf, leaves	☙ = Foliage plant
Mt(s) = Mount,	
mountain(s)	

The following have been used also in the descriptions of Alpines, Bulbs, Trees and Shrubs.

* = slightly tender
† = lime hater
✿ = highly recommended

The illustration numbers are in **bold type** and the page numbers in light type preceded by p.

GLORIOSA (LILIACEAE) Glory Lily

rothschildiana see **G. superba**

superba ❋ Summer   *Tu.
A beautiful scrambling plant from E. Africa. *Fl.* deep orange and red or deep clear yellow, variable in colour, very exotic and conspicuous, the petals being recurved like a Turks-cap lily and crimped or wavy along the edge. Stem up to 6 ft but requires support. Tubers need to be started into growth in a warm greenhouse after the winter but may be then plunged outside for the summer, but they are more usually grown as greenhouse plants, where they require plenty of moisture and feeding. Also grown is *G. rothschildiana* which is rather similar but with bright crimson-red *fl.* which are yellow at the base.

GLORY LILY see **Gloriosa**

GLORY PEA see **Clianthus formosus, 473,** p. 60.

GLOXINIA see **Sinningia speciosa, 648,** p. 81.

GOAT WILLOW see **Salix caprea, 1893,** p. 237.

GOAT'S BEARD see **Aruncus sylvester, 979,** p. 123.

GOAT'S BEARD, FALSE see **Astilbe 18,** p. 3; **994-998,** p. 125.

GOAT'S RUE see **Galega, 1140, 1141,** p. 143.

GODETIA (ONAGRACEAE)

grandiflora ❋ Summer   HA.
Fl. dark pink, salmon-orange. lavender, white, single and double. *L.* lance-shaped. 9 in.–2 ft. Sow in the open in 3–4, or 9, where they are to flower. Ordinary garden soil and a sunny position. The species is from Western N. America. There are cultivated varieties and hybrids. Among the best:
   Whitneyi hybrids, dwarf 9 in.–1½ ft. Of garden
      origin, many colours, including:
   'Celestial', compact, lavender paler at centre,
      black anthers, 9 in.;
   'Crimson Glow', crimson, 1 ft;
   'Orange Glory', scarlet orange, 1 ft;
   'Sybil Sherwood', bright pink, edged white, 1½
      ft, **300,** p. 38.
   'Vivid', brilliant cherry-rose, 9 in, **301,** p. 38.

GOLDEN APPLE see **Poncirus trifoliata, 1742, 1743,** p. 218.

GOLDEN ELM, DICKSON'S see **Ulmus carpinifolia** var. **sarniensis** 'Aurea', **1932,** p. 242.

GOLDEN PRIVET see **Ligustrum ovalifolium** under **L. vulgare.**

GOLDEN ROD see **Solidago, 1381-1384,** p. 173.

GOLDEN WILLOW see **Salix alba** 'Vitellina'.

GOLDILOCKS see **Aster linosyris, 984,** p. 123.

GOMPHRENA (AMARANTHACEAE)

globosa Globe Amaranth ❋ Summer   HHA.
Fl. various, purple, pink, yellow, white. *L.* oblong, hairy. 6 in.–1½ ft. Useful 'ever-lasting' flower heads, or bracts. Sow under glass in 3–4 and plant out in ordinary garden soil in 5. India.
   'Nana Compacta 'Buddy'', dwarf, excellent as a
      pot plant, vivid purple, 6 in., **302,** p. 38.

GOOSEBERRY, CAPE see **Physalis franchetii, 1318,** p. 165.

GOOSEFOOT see **Chenopodium, 263,** p. 33.

GORSE, COMMON see **Ulex europaeus, 1931,** p. 242.

GORSE, SPANISH see **Genista hispanica, 1622,** p. 203.

GRANNY'S BONNET see **Aquilegia vulgaris.**

GRAPE HYACINTH see **Muscari, 823-828,** pp. 103, 104.

GRAPE, OREGON see **Mahonia aquifolium, 1695,** p. 212.

GRAPE, SEASIDE see **Coccoloba uvifera, 475,** p. 60.

GRAPE VINE see **Vitis vinifera, 1997,** p. 250.

GRASS, FEATHER see **Stipa pennata, 1390,** p. 174.

GRASS, FOUNTAIN see **Pennisetum ruppellii, 356,** p. 45.

GRASS, HARE'S-TAIL see **Lagurus ovatus, 315,** p. 40.

GRASS, PAMPAS see **Cortaderia, 1057,** p. 133.

GRASS, QUAKING see **Briza, 245,** p. 31.

GRASS, RIBBON see **Phalaris arundinacea** 'Picta', **1310,** p. 164.

GRASS, SHEEP'S FESCUE see **Festuca ovina, 1134** p. 142.

GRASS, SQUIRREL-TAIL see **Hordeum jubatum, 308,** p. 39.

GRASS NUT see **Brodiaea laxa, 678,** p. 85.

GREAT BELLFLOWER see **Campanula latifolia, 1013,** p. 127.

GREAT SPEARWORT see **Ranunculus lingua, 1345,** p. 169.

GREENWEED, DYER'S see **Genista tinctoria, 1624,** p. 203.

GREVILLEA (PROTEACEAE)

alpina see under **G. sulphurea**

rosmarinifolia see under **G. sulphurea**

sulphurea ❋ Summer   *†Sh.
Evergreen shrub up to 6 ft usually considerably less. *Fl.* creamy-yellow, tubular in clusters resembling small pin cushions with the tubes as the pins. *L.* narrow slightly prickly. All Grevilleas need mild conditions being excellent in S.W. districts of England in S. of France and in States such as California. **1625,** p. 204.
Other interesting sp. are:

alpina ❋ Summer   Sh.
Dwarf shrub for areas with red and cream *fl.* over

long period of summer. Excellent in Alpine house or cool greenhouse.

rosmarinifolia ❋ Summer   Sh.
Fl. deep crimson in long terminal racemes during much of summer. New South Wales, Australia.

GREY HEATH see **Erica cinerea, 1581-1583,** p. 198.

GREY POPLAR see **Populus canescens**

GRISELINIA (CORNACEAE)

littoralis ❋ Late Spring   *Sh.
Evergreen shrub or small tree with large oval *l.* up to 3 in. long and nearly as much across, leathery bright shining green. *Fl.* small greenish inconspicuous. Much planted as evergreen screen in milder areas of fairly high rainfall and for this purpose one of the best evergreens available. Fast growing. New Zealand. **1626,** p. 204.

GUELDER ROSE see **Viburnum opulus, 1945, 1946,** p. 244.

GUERNSEY ELM see **Ulmus carpinifolia** var. **sarniensis** 'Aurea', **1932,** p. 242.

GUERNSEY LILY see **Nerine sarniensis, 563, 564,** p. 71.

GUINEA FLOWER see **Fritillaria meleagris, 739, 740,** p. 93.

GUM, AUSTRALIAN SNOW see **Eucalyptus niphophila, 1598,** p. 200.

GUM, CIDER see **Eucalyptus gunnii, 1597,** p. 200.

GUM, SWEET see **Liquidambar styraciflua, 1677,** p. 210.

GUM TREE see **Eucalyptus, 1597-1600,** p. 200.

Abbreviations and Symbols used in the text.
The following abbreviations may sometimes be used in conjunction as HA. indicating Hardy annual or GBb indicating Greenhouse bulb.

A. = Annual	P. = Perennial
Aq. = Aquatic	R. = Rock or
B. = Biennial	Alpine plant
Bb = Bulb	Sh. = Shrub
C. = Corm	Sp., sp. = Species
Cl. = Climber	Syn. = Synonym
Co. = Conifer	T. = Tree
Fl., fl. = Flower(s)	Tu. = Tuber
G. = Greenhouse or	var. = variety
house plant	× = Hybrid or
H. = Hardy	hybrid parents
HH. = Half-hardy	❋ = Flowering time
L., l. = Leaf, leaves	➥ = Foliage plant
Mt(s) = Mount,	
mountain(s)	

The following have been used also in the descriptions of Alpines, Bulbs, Trees and Shrubs.

   * = slightly tender
   † = lime hater
   ✿ = highly recommended

The illustration numbers are in **bold type** and the page numbers in light type preceded by p.

GYNANDRIRIS (IRIDACEAE)

sisyrinchium, syn. **Iris sisyrinchium** ✳ Spring C.
Fl. bright blue or mauve, variable like a little blue butterfly on stems 4–8 in. Very common round the Mediterranean especially in dry and sandy places where each *fl.* only opens for a day. More difficult to *fl.* satisfactorily in this country where the round corms require good summer ripening, but well worth an effort.

GYNERIUM ARGENTEUM see **Cortaderia selloana**

GYNURA (COMPOSITAE)

aurantiaca ➴ GP.
Fl. orange. *L.* shallowly lobed, lance-shaped, up to 6 in. long and 2½ in. across, in some forms covered with violet hairs, as are also the stems. The plant will reach a height of 3 ft and needs pruning back each year after flowering. Winter temp. about 50°F. Light conditions, shaded from direct sun are required. Propagate by cuttings in summer at a temp. of 70°F. Ample water during summer but very little in winter. E. Indies. **540, 541**, p. 68.

sarmentosa, syn. **G. scandens** ➴ GP.
Twining plant reaching 18 in. with small numerous orange *fl.* and *l.*, elliptic, toothed, purplish below, slate-blue flushed purple above. Needs similar treatment to *G. aurantiaca.* India.

scandens see **G. sarmentosa**

GYPSOPHILA (CARYOPHYLLACEAE) Baby's Breath

elegans ✳ Late Spring–Early Autumn HA.
Fl. small white, in dainty sprays, in the *sp.* but many other colours from crimson through pink to various whites have been developed. *L.* grey-green, narrow. 1–1½ ft. Sow in the open in 3–4, or in 9, where it is to *fl.* and in a sunny position in ordinary garden soil, preferably chalky. Asia Minor.
Good varieties include:
  'London Market Strain' amongst the best white, 1½ ft, **303**, p. 38.

paniculata ✳ Late Spring–Summer P.
Fl. white in large branching panicles. 2–3 ft. Plant 3–4 in a sunny position, preferably in chalky soil, but will grow in lime-free soil. Propagate by cuttings taken in 7 and inserted in sandy soil in a cold frame. E. Europe, Siberia. Good varieties include:
  'Bristol Fairy', double white, **1153**, p. 145;
  'Pink Star', more compact than 'Rosy Veil' and slightly deeper in colour;
  'Rosy Veil', ('Rosenschleier'), 9 in., double white becoming light pink, **1154**, p. 145.

repens ✳ Summer RP.
3–6 in. Mat-forming with sub-shrubby base, often reaching several feet across. *Fl.* pale blush-pink or lilac-pink or white, small but often very numerous on short wiry stems. *L.* small, narrow, grass-like. An easy plant for an open sunny position and excellent for covering large rocks. Alps. **81**, p. 11.

H

HABERLEA (GESNERIACEAE)

ferdinandi-coburgi ✳ Mid Spring RP.
Larger, pale lilac *fl.* and plant than *H. rhodopensis.* Requires similar treatment. Balkans.

rhodopensis ✳ Mid Spring RP.
6–8 in. *Fl.* pale lilac, tubular with a wide spreading lip, 1 in. across, several on a short stem. *L.* obovate, hairy and toothed in a loose basal rosette. Often grown as a crevice plant in semi-shade, but suitable for growing in leaf-mould in a pocket in rock garden, in similar position to a *Ramonda.* Both will grow well facing N. N. Greece. **82**, p. 11.
  var. *virginalis*, white, less vigorous than lilac form.

HACQUETIA (UMBELLIFERAE)

epipactis, syn. **Dondia epipactis** ✳ Spring RP.
3–4 in. *Fl.* small, yellow, clustered in centre of an umbel of green leafy bracts. *L.* trifoliate, radical. Forming small clumps but resenting disturbance. Suitable for semi-shady position in rock garden, making useful ground cover. **83**, p. 11.

HAEMANTHUS (AMARYLLIDACEAE) Blood Lily

coccineus ✳ Late Summer *GBb
Fl. bright scarlet in an umbel on short but stout stem of 6–8 in. with upright stamens looking like a large red shaving brush backed by two scarlet bracts. *Fl.* without *l.* which appear later and lie flat on ground, broad and strap-shaped up to 2 ft in length. When these die away in summer bulb should be rested dry. Cool greenhouse. S. Africa.

katherinae ✳ Summer GBb
Fl. scarlet on 1–2 ft stems. *L.* large oblong, on separate stem. Bulb very large and globular and thrives better planted out in greenhouse bed than grown in pots. Minimum winter temp. around 50°F. About three months after flowering the bulbs should be given a rest for a further three months and all water withheld. When growth restarts water sparingly at first, more copiously later. S. Africa. **542**, p. 68.

HAKEA (PROTEACEAE)

microcarpa ✳ Late Spring *Sh.
Evergreen shrub up to 6 ft. *Fl.* in clusters, tubular, yellowish-white. *L.* rounded and spineless. Sunny position but only hardy in very warm parts of S.W. and in Isles of Scilly. Does well in French Riviera gardens and also suitable for California and S. USA. Australia, Tasmania. **1627**, p. 204.

HALESIA (STYRACACEAE) Snowdrop Tree

carolina, syn. **H. tetraptera** ✳ Late Spring Sh.
More shrubby and spreading than *H. monticola* with *fl.* not quite so large, but will grow on lime. Both excellent large garden shrubs or small trees.

monticola ✳ Late Spring †T.
Small tree or large shrub up to 30 ft. *Fl.* white, pendulous bell-shaped borne in clusters of 2–5 about 1 in. long. *L.* broad ovate appearing with *fl.* A beautiful small tree for spring effect. S.E. USA. **1628**, p. 204.
  'Rosea', *fl.* very pale pink.

tetraptera see **H. carolina**

vestita T.
L. slightly downy beneath otherwise close to *H. monticola.*

HALIMIUM (CISTACEAE)

Halimiums are half-way in size between *Helianthemum*, of rock gardens, and *Cistus.*

lasianthum ✳ Summer *Sh.
Dwarf evergreen shrub with silvery foliage up to 3½ ft but usually less but wide-spreading. *Fl.* bright yellow 1½ in. across, petals with maroon-crimson blotch at base. Foliage grey. Valuable plant for large rock garden or for sunny position at front of border. Hardy in most areas. Propagate by cuttings in late summer like a cistus. Portugal. **1629**, p. 204.
  var. *concolor*, *fl.* without basal blotch.

ocymoides, syn. **Helianthemum algarvense** ✳ Early Summer Sh.
Compact shrub up to 3 ft with small grey *l.* and slightly smaller but bright yellow *fl.* with dark maroon blotch at base. Portugal.

HAMAMELIS (HAMAMELIDACEAE) Witch Hazel

All Witch Hazels are hardy and can be grown in full exposure or in semi-shade but generally *fl.* better and make more compact shrubs in the open. They are usually grafted on stock of the N. American sp. *H. virginiana* which has small *fl.* with the *l.* in autumn. All prefer lime free soils but will tolerate some lime where the soil is not too light.

japonica ✳ Winter T.
Small tree or large bush up to 15–20 ft. *Fl.* yellow with narrow waving petals about ¾ in. long and red calyx base, borne on bare twigs. *L.* broad, ovate up to 3 in. long and 2½ in. wide. Japan.
  arborea, the largest of this sp. and the one usually grown, **1630**, p. 204;
  zuccariniana, petals lemon-yellow and calyx green inside. A conspicuous plant in winter but later in *fl.* than other forms, **1631**, p. 204.

☆ **mollis** ✳ Mid Winter–Early Spring T.
A small shrub or tree up to 15 ft. Petals yellow or golden slightly wider than in *H. japonica* and so making more effect. Valuable for its winter *fl.*, in fact one of the finest winter flowering plants we have. Also useful for good yellow autumn colour of *l.* which are broadly ovate up to 3 in. long. China. **1632**, p. 204.
Various forms of *H. mollis* have been developed in recent years and among the best are:
  'Brevipetala', petals shorter and more thick set and deeper orange-gold thus making *fl.* appear in dense clusters 1–3, **1633**, p. 205;
  ☆'Pallida', petals lemon-yellow. One of the most conspicuous plants to *fl.* in winter and probably the best of all the *Hamamelis* for present planting. Named forms such as these can only be grown by grafting or by layering, **1634**, p. 205.

HANDKERCHIEF TREE see **Davidia involucrata**, **1558**, p. 195.

HAREBELL POPPY see **Meconopsis quintuplinervia**, **1267**, p. 159.

HARE'S TAIL GRASS see **Lagurus ovatus**, **315**, p. 40.

HAWK'S BEARD see **Crepis**, **278**, p. 35.

HAWKWEED, SHAGGY see **Hieraceum villosum**, **1174**, p. 147.

HAWTHORN see **Crataegus, 1542-1544**, p. 193.

HAWTHORN, WATER see **Aponogeton distachyus, 972**, p. 122.

HAZEL see **Corylus, 1533**, p. 192.

HAZEL, CORKSCREW see **Corylus avellana** 'Contorta', **1533**, p. 192.

HAZEL, WITCH see **Hamamelis, 1630-1634**, pp. 204, 205.

HEATH see **Daboecia, 1549**, p. 194, and **Erica, 1577-1590**, pp. 198, 199.

HEATH, CONNEMARA see **Daboecia cantabrica, 1549**, p. 194.

HEATH, CORNISH see **Erica vagans, 1588, 1589**, p. 199.

HEATH, CROSS-LEAFED see **Erica tetralix, 1586**, p. 199.

HEATH, GREY see **Erica cinerea, 1581-1583**, p.198.

HEATH, IRISH see **Daboecia cantabrica, 1549**, p. 194

HEATH, PORTUGUESE see **Erica lusitanica, 1585**, p. 199.

HEATH, SCOTCH see **Erica cinerea, 1581-1583**, p. 198.

HEATH, SPANISH see **Erica australis, 1578**, p. 198.

HEATH, TREE see **Erica arborea, 1577**, p. 198 and **E. × veitchii, 1590**, p. 199.

HEATH, WINTER see **Erica carnea, 1579-1580**, p. 198.

HEATHER see **Calluna, 1474-1478**, p. 185; and **Erica, 1577-1590**, pp. 198, 199.

HEBE (SCROPHULARIACEAE)

Evergreen shrubs frequently placed in older lists under *Veronica* from which they are separated botanically by small details of the thickness of the seed capsule. Tender but excellent shrubs for milder and seaside areas. All those discussed come from New Zealand.

'Autumn Glory' ✳ Midsummer–Mid Autumn Sh.
A hybrid of unknown parentage. *Fl.* deep violet over a long season. *L.* small rounded rather leathery. Usually not growing more than 4 ft or less. Less tender than most other plants of this genus. Plant in full sun where possible. **1635**, p. 205.

brachysiphon ✳ Summer Sh.
Often wrongly known as *H. traversii* which name properly belongs to a different plant. A shrub up to 5 ft or sometimes more. *Fl.* lilac-mauve in long racemes. White form is also known as 'White Gem' which makes a compact more dwarf shrub barely over 3 ft. **1636**, p. 205.

hulkeana ✳ Early Summer Sh.
Rather tender only suitable for warm areas or sheltered positions at base of a wall. *Fl.* very pale blue-lilac in long panicles. Shrub occasionally up to 5 ft but usually about half that height, often cut back severely in bad winter. One of the most beautiful sp. where it can be grown. **1637**, p. 205.

'Pagei', syn. **Veronica pagei, V. pageana** ✳ Late Spring Sh.
Dwarf shrub usually not more than 1½ ft, branches semi-procumbent. *Fl.* white in small clusters towards ends of branches. *L.* glaucous, rounded. Valuable shrub for larger rock garden and fairly hardy. Of uncertain wild origin but long cultivated, possibly of hybrid origin, perhaps best regarded as a form of *H. pinguifolia* a variable dwarf shrubby sp. from New Zealand. **1638**, p. 205.

pinguifolia see **H. 'Pagei'**

speciosa ✳ Summer Sh.
Common shrubby Veronica of seaside areas. Up to 5 ft. *Fl.* large in compact bottle-brush racemes in axils of *l.* and at ends of short branches, variable in colour. *L.* deep fresh green.
Among named varieties, all of which below grow well by the seaside, are:
'Alicia Amhurst', frequently known as 'Veitchii' or 'Royal Purple', one of the finest hybrids of this group with deep purple-blue *fl.*;
'La Seduisante', *fl.* deep purplish-red, **1639**, p. 205;
'Midsummer Beauty', purplish-lavender *fl.* very free-flowering over long period 7–9 hardier than preceding forms, **1640**, p. 205;
'Royal Purple', see 'Alicia Amhurst';
'Sapphire', *fl.* rosy-lilac in rather dense clusters, free-flowering, **1641**, p. 206;
'Simon Delaux', rich crimson large racemes, summer, one of the best of the speciosa hybrids, but tender in cold areas;
'Veitchii', see 'Alicia Amhurst'.

traversii see **H. brachysiphon**

HEDERA (ARALIACEAE) Ivy

Used extensively for room decoration and sometimes in the cool greenhouse. Under these circumstances they are frost-tender, but if hardened off will tolerate severe frost without injury. Any good potting compost is effective. Cultivars with green *l.* will grow in heavy shade if necessary, but those with variegated *l.* need ample light. Propagation by cuttings taken in spring or summer.

canariensis ❧ Cl. or Trailer
L. roughly triangular, evergreen, lobed up to 6 in. long, 3 in. across. Usually, only the variegated form is cultivated, sometimes known as 'Gloire de Marengo', with a dark green centre and cream edge. Best effect given by inserting three plants per pot. Some support necessary. Will tolerate up to 55°F. in winter, but lower readings preferred. Take out growing point and any undersized *l.* in spring. Overwatering causes *l.* to yellow and fall. Pot on every three years, but feed for second and third. Canary Is., Madeira, Azores. **543**, p. 68.

'Gloire de Marengo' see **H. canariensis**.

helix English Ivy ❧ Cl. or Trailer
The forms of the common Ivy grown as house plants are generally of the type known as self-branching. *L.* small, variable in shape, but roughly triangular; sometimes deeply-lobed, often variegated.
'Eva', also known as 'Little Eva', is not self-branching and up to three plants are put in each pot, the *l.* are varied in shape, even on a single plant, but generally three-lobed, with the central lobe larger than the rest, the *l.* become greener as they age, **544**, p. 68;
'Jubilee', needs a well-lit position and makes considerable growth before the *l.* expand properly and the golden blotch becomes prominent. This is also not self-branching and pinching out the growing point in spring is recommended, **545**, p. 69;
'Little Diamond', the *l.* are about 1 in. long and practically unlobed, the plant grows slowly, **546**, p. 69.

HELENIUM (COMPOSITAE) Sneezeweed USA

autumnale ✳ Summer P.
Fl. yellow, 1–1½ in. across. *L.* lance-shaped, usually toothed, smooth. 4–6 ft. Free-flowering in ordinary soil and a sunny position. Propagate by division in spring or autumn, or by seed. Canada, E. USA. The parent of many good hybrids:
'Butterpat', clear yellow, 3 ft, **1155**, p. 145;
'Coppelia', late-flowering, deep coppery-orange 3 ft, **1156**, p. 145;
'Moerheim Beauty', bronze-red, 3 ft, **1157**, p. 145;
'Wyndley', coppery-orange, 2 ft, **1158**, p. 145.

HELIACEREUS see × **Heliaporus**

HELIANTHEMUM (CISTACEAE) Rock Rose

algarvense see **Halimium ocymoides**

chamaecistus see **H. nummularium**

nummularium, syn. **H. chamaecistus** ✳ Summer RSh.
6 in.–1 ft. Dwarf sub-shrubby plants spreading widely to form large mats, covered with *fl.* in summer. Wild type has yellow *fl.* ½ in. across but numerous brightly coloured forms have been developed with larger *fl.* 1 in. across, single or double, white, pink, scarlet, crimson, yellow. The rock roses should be planted in full sun in rock garden or front of border. After flowering they should be trimmed of all dead *fl.* heads and lanky growth to keep them compact. Propagate from cuttings in late summer. N. Europe including Britain.
Among best named forms are:
'Ben Afflick', orange-yellow with deeper centre;
'Ben Hope', deep pinkish-crimson, **84**, p. 11;
'Ben Nevis', yellow with orange centre, dwarf;
'Fire Dragon', bright orange-red, grey foliage, **85**, p. 11;
'Mrs Earle', double, red;
'The Bride', white, grey foliage;
'Wisley Pink', clear pink.

HELIANTHUS (COMPOSITAE) Sunflower

annuus Common Sunflower ✳ Summer–Autumn HA.
Fl. yellow, single, 1 ft or more across, with brown central disc. *L.* heart-shaped, coarsely toothed, up to 1 ft long. 3–12 ft. Sow in 4 where they are to *fl.*, in a sunny position in ordinary garden soil. W. USA. **304**, p. 38.

Abbreviations and Symbols used in the text.
The following abbreviations may sometimes be used in conjunction as HA. indicating Hardy annual or GBb indicating Greenhouse bulb.

A. = Annual	P. = Perennial
Aq. = Aquatic	R. = Rock or
B. = Biennial	Alpine plant
Bb = Bulb	Sh. = Shrub
C. = Corm	Sp., sp. = Species
Cl. = Climber	Syn. = Synonym
Co. = Conifer	T. = Tree
Fl., fl. = Flower(s)	Tu. = Tuber
G. = Greenhouse or	var. = variety
house plant	× = Hybrid or
H. = Hardy	hybrid parents
HH. = Half-hardy	✳ = Flowering time
L., l. = Leaf, leaves	❧ = Foliage plant
Mt(s) = Mount,	
mountain(s)	

The following have been used also in the descriptions of Alpines, Bulbs, Trees and Shrubs.

* = slightly tender
† = lime hater
✿ = highly recommended

The illustration numbers are in **bold type** and the page numbers in light type preceded by p.

Named hybrids have been developed, including doubles, from 3–8 ft and in shades of chestnut-brown, sulphur-yellow, golden-yellow and shades of white.

× HELIAPORUS (CACTACEAE)

mallisonii, syn. **H. smithii** ✻ Summer   GP.
Fl. cerise, 2–3 in. wide. Stems pendant, cylindrical, to 1 ft. A bigeneric hybrid between the Rat's Tail Cactus, *Aporocactus flagelliformis* and a sp. of *Heliocereus*. It resembles the *Aporocactus*, but is more vigorous and floriferous. Gritty compost. Winter temp. 45–50°F. Propagate by rooting separate stems. **547**, p. 69.

smithii see **H. mallisonii**

HELICHRYSUM (COMPOSITAE) Everlasting

angustifolium ✻ Summer   P.
Fl. small yellow clusters. *L.* slender, white-downy, strongly aromatic. 9–15 in. Full sun and poorish, well-drained soil. Does not like winter wet. Propagate by cuttings. Useful when dried for winter decorations. S. Europe. **1159**, p. 145.

bellidioides ✻ Summer   RP.
Fl. white on creeping stems. *L.* silvery, up to ½ in. long. 3 in. Requires protection from winter wet. New Zealand.

bracteatum Strawflower ✻ Summer   HHA.
Fl. single, pink or yellow bracts. *L.* lance-shaped, stalkless. 2–3 ft. Sow under glass in 3 or in the open in 4 in mild districts in well-drained soil and a sunny position. Double varieties in shades of red, terracotta and gold make admirable winter decorations when cut and dried. Australia. **305**, p. 39.
    'Dwarf Spangle mixed', 1 ft, is a new strain suitable for bedding.

frigidum ✻ Early Summer   *RSh.
2–3 in. Dwarf silvery prostrate evergreen shrublet. *Fl.* head white ½ in. across, like dwarf everlastings, long lived. *L.* small, silky grey below, downy. Best grown as an alpine house plant in a scree mixture but will sometimes survive outside in a sunny rock crevice. A very choice little plant. Corsica. **86**, p. 11.

lanatum ☙   *Sh.
A small sub-shrub up to 1½–2 ft distinguished for silvery-grey, slightly flannelly, young stems and *l.* which are narrow oblanceolate up to 3 in. long by ½ in. wide. *Fl.* heads bright lemon-yellow in terminal clusters up to 3 in. across; individual *fl.* heads being ½–¾ in. across. Easily propagated by cuttings which should be overwintered in cool greenhouse. Plant in as sunny position as possible. Should be cut hard back after flowering to keep compact habit. One of the most valuable silver-leaved plants. S. Africa. **1642**, p. 206.

marginatum see **H. milfordiae**

milfordiae ☙   RSh.
Dwarf silvery mat-forming sub-shrubby plant. Unopened buds like crimson globules. *Fl.* heads silvery-white with yellow centre and stiff white bracts in double row, 1 in. across, on short stem up to 4 in. *L.* silvery, forming small rosettes. Alpine house or well-drained position in rock garden in full sun. Some gardeners, to encourage flowering, protect it in winter with a pane of glass to keep off wet. Apparently quite hardy. This plant has been confused with *H. marginatum* under which name it has been mistakenly distributed. Basutoland. **87**, p. 11.

HELICTOTRICHON (GRAMINEAE)

sempervirens, syn. **Avena candida** ✻ Summer P.
Seed heads silvery. *L.* blue-grey, evergreen, in dense tufts. 3–4 ft. Plant 3–4 in a sunny position and well-drained soil. Propagate by division in the spring, or by seed. S. Russia, Turkestan. **1160**, p. 145.

HELIOPHILA (CRUCIFERAE)

longifolia ✻ Summer   HHA.
Fl. blue with white or yellow base. *L.* narrow, up to 10 in. long at base. 1–1½ ft. Sow under glass in 3 or in open in 5 in well-drained soil and sunny position where they are to *fl.* Makes an attractive pot plant for a cold greenhouse. S. Africa. **306**, p. 39.

HELIOPSIS (COMPOSITAE)

scabra ✻ Summer   P.
Fl. yellow, sunflower-like, about 3 in. across, terminal, 3–4 ft. *L.* coarsely toothed, rough all over. Any ordinary garden soil and a sunny position. Propagate by division of the roots in spring. N. America. Good hybrids are:
    'Golden Plume', double golden-yellow, well-formed *fl.*, **1161**, p. 146;
    'Light of Loddon', bright yellow, single, free-flowering, **1162**, p. 146;
    'Orange King', bright orange;
    'Summer Sun', orange-yellow.

HELIOTROPE see Heliotropium

HELIOTROPIUM (BORAGINACEAE) Heliotrope, Cherry Pie

peruvianum ✻ Summer   HHP. or GP.
Fl. pale to deep blue and white in large umbels, sweetly scented. *L.* oblong, slightly hairy, green to purplish-green. 1¼–3 ft. Sow under glass in heat in 2–3 and plant out in open sunny position early 6. Makes a useful pot plant for the cool greenhouse. Peru.
    'Royal Marine', 1¼ ft, deep violet-blue, dark foliage.

HELIPTERUM (COMPOSITAE) Everlasting

manglesii, syn. **Rhodanthe manglesii** ✻ Summer   HA.
Fl. bright rose, pink or white, nodding heads. *L.* glaucous, up to 4 in. long. 1–1½ ft. Sow under glass in 3 or in the open in 4 where it is to *fl.* in light, dryish soil. May be cut and dried for winter decoration. W. Australia. **307**, p. 39.
    'Rosea', double, pink, 1 ft.

HELLEBORE see Helleborus, 1163–1166, p. 146.

HELLEBORUS (RANUNCULACEAE) Hellebore

argutifolius see under **H. corsicus**

corsicus, syn. **H. argutifolius**, **H. lividus** sub-sp. **corsicus** Corsican Hellebore ✻ Winter–Spring   P.
Fl. creamy-green, cup-shaped, borne in large trusses. *L.* evergreen, glaucous and spiny. 2 ft. For a shady position with well-drained soil of good depth and add old manure and leaf-mould before planting. Once planted leave undisturbed, except for an occasional top-dressing of compost or old manure. Propagate by division in 3 or by seed sown as soon as ripe in a cold frame or in the open ground. Corsica. **1163**, p. 146.

niger Christmas Rose ✻ Winter   P.
Fl. white, saucer-shaped. *L.* evergreen deep green, leathery, toothed at apex. 1–2 ft. Plant 9–10. Cultivate and propagate as for *H. corsicus*. Central and S. Europe. **1164**, p. 146.
    Good varieties include:
    'Altifolius', large white *fl.* tinted rose-purple on the reverse, 11–12, 1½ ft;
    'Potter's Wheel', pure white with broad petals, 1–2, 1–1½ ft, **1165**, p. 146.

orientalis Lenten Rose ✻ Spring   P.
Fl. variable, white, cream, pink, purple. *L.* evergreen, leathery, up to 15 in. or more across. 2 ft. Cultivate and propagate as for *H. corsicus*. Greece, Asia Minor. **1166**, p. 146.

HEMEROCALLIS (LILIACEAE) Day Lily

citrina ✻ Summer   P.
Fl. pale lemon, tinged brown, slightly fragrant, remains open at night. *L.* dark green up to 2½ ft long. 3½ ft. Any ordinary moist garden soil, or beside water in sun or partial shade. Should be left undisturbed for years. Propagate by division of the clumps in the spring, or by seed. China, Japan.
    'Baronii', a hybrid is very similar but larger and free-flowering, (*H. citrina* × *H. thunbergii*), **1168**, p. 146.

hybrids ✻ Summer   P.
Various sp. have been used by plant breeders with the result that there is now a wide range of colour with large, shapely *fl.*
    Good varieties include:
    'Banbury Canary', large cream and gold trumpets, **1167**, p. 146;
    'Doubloon', bright orange;
    'El Magnifico', large coppery-pink, **1169**, p. 147;
    'Glowing Gold', bright orange;
    'Marion Vaughn', pale lemon;
    'Pink Damask', large glowing pink, **1170**, p. 147;
    'Pink Prelude', a pale pink self, **1171**, p. 147;
    'Stafford', deep crimson.

HEMLOCK and HEMLOCK SPRUCE see Tsuga, 2048, p. 256.

HEPATICA (RANUNCULACEAE)

× ballardii ✻ Spring   RP.
Often found in lists under *Anemone*. Probably a hybrid between *H. triloba* × *H. transsilvanica*. *Fl.* pale china-blue, large up to 1½ in. across, star-like, on long stems up to 4 in. *L.* kidney-shaped, trifoliate. Probably the finest member of the genus. Hepaticas are woodland plants and may be grown in semi-shade or in position in rock garden where root is shaded or protected by rock from drying out in summer. **88**, p. 11.

triloba, syn. **Anemone hepatica** ✻ Spring   RP.
The wild hepatica of sub-alpine woodlands. *Fl.* white, deep blue, pale blue or occasionally pink, usually single but some double forms are in cultivation, star-like, 1 in. across. *L.* trifoliate, kidney-shaped. Open woodland in leaf-mould. Usually takes a year or two to settle after moving. **89**, p. 12.

Abbreviations and Symbols used in the text.
The following abbreviations may sometimes be used in conjunction as HA. indicating Hardy annual or GBb indicating Greenhouse bulb.

A. = Annual		P. = Perennial	
Aq. = Aquatic		R. = Rock or	
B. = Biennial		Alpine plant	
Bb = Bulb		Sh. = Shrub	
C. = Corm		Sp., sp. = Species	
Cl. = Climber		Syn. = Synonym	
Co. = Conifer		T. = Tree	
Fl., *fl.* = Flower(s)		Tu. = Tuber	
G. = Greenhouse or		var. = variety	
house plant		× = Hybrid or	
H. = Hardy		hybrid parents	
HH. = Half-hardy		✻ = Flowering time	
L., *l.* = Leaf, leaves		☙ = Foliage plant	
Mt(s) = Mount,			
mountain(s)			

The following have been used also in the descriptions of Alpines, Bulbs, Trees and Shrubs.

* = slightly tender
† = lime hater
✿ = highly recommended

The illustration numbers are in **bold type** and the page numbers in light type preceded by p.

HERB OF GRACE see **Ruta graveolens, 1891,** p. 237.

HERMODACTYLUS (IRIDACEAE)

tuberosus, syn. **Iris tuberosa** Snake's head Iris ✳ Spring   Tu.
    Fl. with dark purplish-black falls and yellowish-green or yellow standards and haft (centre of fl. and base of fall), single, about 2 in. across. Up to 1 ft. Root, tuberous. Hardy in warm situations but may take a year to establish well. E. Mediterranean regions. **764,** p. 96.

HEUCHERA (SAXIFRAGACEAE) Coral Bells

sanguinea ✳ Summer   P.
    Fl. deep or bright red, small bell-shaped. L. heart-shaped, evergreen, five to seven-lobed. 1½–2 ft. Ordinary well-drained soil in sun or partial shade. A mulch of garden compost or peat in early spring will encourage free flowering. Propagate by division of three or four-year old plants in the spring or by seed which is very variable and only the best coloured seedlings should be kept. Mexico, Arizona. There are numerous named varieties in attractive shades of soft pink, rose-pink, scarlet and white:
        Bressingham Hybrids, pale pink to deep crimson, 2 ft, **1172,** p. 147;
        'Scintillation', bright pink, tipped coral, 2 ft, **1173,** p. 147.

HIBISCUS (MALVACEAE)

rosa-sinensis ✳ Summer   GSh.
    Shrub to 5 ft. Fl. red, pink, orange or yellow, to 5 in. across, trumpet-shaped. Usually single though double forms are also known. L. ovate, coarsely toothed, evergreen unless winter temp. too low. Rich potting compost. Best winter temp. 55°F., but will survive at as low as 45°F., when it must be kept dry and when it will lose its l. Propagate by cuttings of half-ripe wood, taken in early summer if possible. China. **548,** p. 69.

sinosyriacus ✳ Midsummer–Mid Autumn   Sh.
    Worth growing but more tender than H. syriacus and fl. are slightly larger, mostly white or mauve with maroon centres. Only useful in most areas as a wall shrub. China.

syriacus ✳ Midsummer–Mid Autumn   Sh.
    Deciduous shrub up to 10 ft, bushy and broad with rather erect growth. Plant in as sunny position as possible. Fl. varying in colour, open trumpet-shaped. L. ovate deeply lobed. Fl. 3–4 in. across. Distinguished also for its very late leafing usually not before 5. Syria. **1643,** p. 206.
    Among best forms are:
        'Blue Bird', deep blue-mauve with crimson blotch at base. Probably the best single form in this colour at present, **1644,** p. 206;
        'Coeleste', single deep blue-mauve;
        'Hamabo', large pale blush or white with deep crimson basal blotch;
        'Snow Drift', large single white without blotch, **1645,** p. 206;
        'Woodbridge', large deep rosy-pink with maroon blotch at base. A very distinctive and valuable plant for all gardens. Propagate by cutting in late summer, **1646,** p. 206.

trionum ✳ Summer   HA.
    Fl. creamy-white with purple-black centre. L. oval to lobed. 1½ ft. Sow in open sunny beds in 4–5. Tropics.

HIERACIUM (COMPOSITAE)

villosum Shaggy Hawkweed ✳ Summer   P.
    Fl. bright yellow, 2 in. across. L. silvery, shaggy, coarsely toothed. 1 ft. Poorish, well-drained soil and sun. Propagate by division or seed. Central Europe. **1174,** p. 147.

HIGH-BUSH BLUEBERRY see **Vaccinium corymbosum, 1933,** p. 242.

HIMALAYAN BLUE POPPY see **Meconopsis betonicifolia, 1263,** p. 158.

HIMALAYAN COWSLIP see **Primula florindae, 1332,** p. 167.

HIMALAYAN HONEYSUCKLE see **Leycesteria formosa, 1675,** p. 210.

HIMALAYAN KNOTWEED see **Polygonum campanulatum, 1326,** p. 166.

HIMALAYAN LILY, GIANT see **Cardiocrinum giganteum, 682,** p. 86.

HIMALAYAN MAYFLOWER see **Podophyllum emodii, 1320,** p. 165.

HIMALAYAN WHORLFLOWER see **Morina, 1277,** p. 160.

HINOKI see **Chamaecyparis obtusa, 2009, 2010,** p. 252.

HIPPEASTRUM (AMARYLLIDACEAE) Late Winter and Early Spring
    Often incorrectly referred to as Amaryllis. Fl. trumpet-shaped, variously coloured, but usually shades of red, pink or white. L. strap-shaped, very short at inflorescence, elongating to over 12 in. and sometimes persisting for more than one year. The large bulbs need a rich soil mixture, but should not be over-potted. With sufficient heat, growth may be started at any time in the winter and the fl. buds will soon emerge. An air temp. around 55°F. is ideal, but often the pots are plunged to give a bottom heat of 70°F. If these conditions are not available, the plants will start into growth later. When growth is complete, water should be gradually withheld and the bulbs given a rest of two or three months. Watering is resumed about 11, as there is considerable root growth, before any movement is seen in the aerial portions. The bulbs are only half buried in the soil, which should be fairly rich. With feeding, plants should only need repotting every three years. Propagation is by seed or by off-shoots; the latter is the only way to reproduce the hybrids.

aulicum Lily of the Palace ✳ Winter   GBb
    Fl. crimson, about 6 in. long on 18 in. scape. L. strap-shaped and broad. Brazil, Paraguay. **549,** p. 69.

× **johnsonii** ✳ Spring   GBb
    Fl. deep red with white stripe. L. strap-shaped. One of the earliest hybrids raised in 1799. The parentage is H. reginae × H. vittatum and the plant was raised by a watchmaker named Johnson. **550,** p. 69.

Hybrids ✳ Late Winter–Spring   *GBb
    These are the large and very conspicuous fl. often, though erroneously described as Amaryllis. Fl. open trumpet-shaped, two to four on 2 ft stem. Often very large, up to 6 in. long and up to 8 in. across. Deep red, scarlet, pink, white or striped. Warm greenhouse flowering 2–5 depending on temp. and date of planting. Specially prepared bulbs are now marketed which may be flowered satisfactorily on a warm window ledge. Bulbs should be dried off when l. begin to die down. They require generous feeding while in growth. **551,** p. 69.

pratense, syn. **Habranthus pratensis** ✳ Late Spring–Early Summer   *GBb
    Fl. bright scarlet with a yellow base, funnel-shaped. A striking fl., up to 3 in. across. Stem 1 ft with

two to three fl. Tender but may be grown outdoors in a very warm situation, more often grown as a cool greenhouse plant and has been found subject to eelworm. S. America.

rutilum ✳ Spring   GBb
    Small flowered and more graceful than hybrids usually grown. Fl. scarlet. Probably one of the parents of large flowered hybrids. Brazil, Venezuela.

HIPPOPHAE (ELAEAGNACEAE)

rhamnoides Sea Buckthorn ✳ Late Spring   Sh.
    Deciduous shrub up to 10 ft but usually less. Distinguished for silvery young branchlets and foliage. L. narrow up to 2 in. long. Fl. small yellowish inconspicuous, followed by deep orange-yellow berries along branches very freely borne. These are very persistent since they are said to be unpalatable to birds and make a brilliant combination with the silvery foliage. Particularly good on light sandy soils and as a seaside shrub. Should be planted in groups for berries since male and female fl. borne on different plants. N. Europe. **1647,** p. 206.

HOHERIA (MALVACEAE)

glabrata
'Glory of Amlwych'   see under
lyallii   **H. sexstylosa**
populnea

sexstylosa ✳ Summer   T.
    Tall evergreen shrub or small tree up to 20 ft. Fl. white about 1 in. across with large central boss of stamens borne in clusters. L. lanceolate toothed at edges about 3 in. long, grey-green. New Zealand. **1648,** p. 206.
    Other valuable sp. are H. populnea with fl. slightly smaller, H. glabrata tender but with largest fl. in the genus 6–7 and hybrid 'Glory of Amlwych', H. glabrata × H. sexstylosa. This retains foliage during mild winters and has large fl. Usually grown as a wall shrub. New Zealand. H. lyallii close to H. glabrata, distinguished by downy l. flowering slightly later.

HOLLY see **Ilex, 1659-1662,** p. 208.

HOLLYHOCK see **Althaea rosea, 228-229,** p. 29.

Abbreviations and Symbols used in the text.
The following abbreviations may sometimes be used in conjunction as HA. indicating Hardy annual or GBb indicating Greenhouse bulb.

A. = Annual	P. = Perennial
Aq. = Aquatic	R. = Rock or
B. = Biennial	Alpine plant
Bb = Bulb	Sh. = Shrub
C. = Corm	Sp., sp. = Species
Cl. = Climber	Syn. = Synonym
Co. = Conifer	T. = Tree
Fl., fl. = Flower(s)	Tu. = Tuber
G. = Greenhouse or	var. = variety
house plant	× = Hybrid or
H. = Hardy	hybrid parents
HH. = Half-hardy	✳ = Flowering time
L., l. = Leaf, leaves	✿ = Foliage plant
Mt(s) = Mount,	
mountain(s)	

The following have been used also in the descriptions of Alpines, Bulbs, Trees and Shrubs.

        * = slightly tender
        † = lime hater
        ✿ = highly recommended

The illustration numbers are in **bold type** and the page numbers in light type preceded by p.

HOLM OAK see **Quercus ilex**

HOLY THISTLE see **Silybum marianum, 376,** p. 47.

HONESTY see **Lunaria, 333,** p. 42; **1245,** p. 156.

HONEY LOCUST see **Gleditschia triacanthos**

HONEYSUCKLE see **Lonicera, 1980-1983,** p. 248.

HONEYSUCKLE, EARLY DUTCH see **Lonicera periclymenum** 'Belgica'

HONEYSUCKLE, HIMALAYAN see **Leycestaria formosa, 1675,** p. 210.

HONEYSUCKLE, LATE DUTCH see **Lonicera periclymenum** 'Serotina'

HONEYSUCKLE, SCARLET TRUMPET see **Lonicera × brownii, 1981,** p. 248.

HOP see **Humulus scandens, 309,** p. 39.

HORDEUM (GRAMINEAE)

jubatum Squirrel-tail Grass ✼ Summer HA.
L. sharply pointed, rough, tufted. Graceful feathery silvery-grey or brown seed heads, with awns about 2½ in. long. 1-1½ ft. Sow in 3 and 4, or in 9 in dryish garden soil. N. and S. America. **308,** p. 39.

HORNED POPPY see **Glaucium flavum, 299,** p. 38.

HORSE CHESTNUT see **Aesculus, 1441, 1442,** p. 181.

HOSTA, syn. **FUNKIA** (LILIACEAE) Plantain Lily
Hostas have bold foliage, often with variegation, and spikes of lilac, violet or white fl. They thrive in moist soil and partial shade and are particularly attractive near a pool where the l. are reflected in the water. Propagate by dividing the clumps in spring, when new growth is just evident.

crispula ✼ Late Spring P.
Fl. violet, funnel-shaped. L. large, up to 8 in. long, green with a broad white margin. 1½-2½ ft. Japan. **1175,** p. 147.

fortunei ✼ Late Spring P.
Fl. lilac. L. broad, glaucous green. 1½-2 ft. Japan. 'Albopicta', fl. lilac, l. yellowish with green margins in the young stage and an attractive network of veins, 1½ ft, **1176,** p. 147.

glauca see **H. sieboldiana**

plantaginea ✼ Late Summer P.
Fl. white, trumpet-shaped, fragrant. L. oval, up to 18 in. long. heart-shaped. 1½-2 ft. China, Japan. 'Grandiflora', longer trumpets than the type, **1177,** p. 148.

sieboldiana, syn. **H. glauca** ✼ Early Summer P.
Fl. pale lilac. L. blue-green, roundish, elegantly ribbed. 1½-2 ft. Japan. **1178,** p. 148.

undulata ✼ Late Summer P.
Fl. pale lilac. L. large, oval, green heavily splashed with white. 2½ ft. Japan. **1179,** p. 148.

HUMULUS (CANNABINACEAE) Hop

japonicus see **H. scandens**

scandens, syn. **H. japonicus** ☙ HA.
Perennial, but often grown as an annual to provide a quick screen of light green foliage. Climbing to

10 ft or so. Sow under glass in 3-4, or in the open in 5 in ordinary garden soil and a sunny position. China, Japan.
'Variegatus', has attractive silver and white marks on foliage, **309,** p. 39.

HYACINTH see **Hyacinthus, 765-772,** pp. 96, 97.

HYACINTH, GIANT SUMMER see **Galtonia candicans, 747,** p. 94.

HYACINTH, TASSEL see **Muscari comosum** var. **monstrosum, 826,** p. 104.

HYACINTHUS (LILIACEAE)

amethystinus ✼ Spring Bb
Fl. tubular drooping, numerous on 8 in. stem. Cambridge blue like porcelain, one of the most beautiful and delicate of early spring bulbs. A white form is also sometimes seen. Hardy. Pyrenees where it fl. 5-6. **765,** p. 96.

azureus ✼ Spring Bb
Fl. in a dense head more like a grape hyacinth, deep azure-blue. Stem 8 in. Quite hardy and does best in a sunny position. Distinguished from a grape hyacinth by the bells being unconstricted at the mouth. A white form is also known. Asia Minor.

candicans see **Galtonia candicans**

orientalis ✼ Spring Bb
The parent from which all the large florists' hyacinths have been derived, but the wild plant is very beautiful also much slenderer with fewer and smaller bells, but more graceful and with a superb scent. Fl. blue-mauve or white but variable. Hardy but fl. best after summer ripening. E. Mediterranean regions.
Florists' hyacinths Specially precooled bulbs are available for forcing of nearly all those given below. All are suitable for growing in bulb fibre in bowls. All are heavily scented. Start in 9 for forcing but do not bring into heat before mid-11.
Cynthella Miniature early-flowering with fl. loosely spaced on stem, sold usually by colour, red, pink, white, **766,** p. 96, shades of blue, **767,** p. 96, salmon or yellow. Excellent for forcing.
Early-flowering:
Most of these are slightly smaller than the later forms:
'Fairy Blue', pale porcelain blue;
Roman, generally white;
'Rosalie', deep rose-pink, very reliable and always one of the earliest with larger spikes than the Roman hyacinth.
Later-flowering:
mixed for bedding, **768,** p. 96.
Deep Blue:
'King of the Blues';
'Ostara', **769,** p. 97.
Pale Blue:
'Myosotis';
'Perle Brilliante', **770,** p. 97;
'Queen of the Blues';
'Winston Churchill';
Pale Pink:
'Lady Derby';
'Princess Irene';
'Princess Margaret', **771,** p. 97;
Deep pink to scarlet:
'Jan Bos';
'Pink Pearl';
'Tubergen's Scarlet';
Yellow:
'City of Haarlem';
White:
'Edelweiss';
'Hoar Frost';
'L'Innocence';
'Queen of the Whites', **772,** p. 97.

HYDRANGEA (HYDRANGEACEAE)
All hydrangeas grow particularly well by the sea.

macrophylla Common Hydrangea ✼ Summer, earlier when forced Sh.
Normally divided into two groups Lace Caps of which 'Blue Wave' is good variety, **1649,** p. 207, and Hortensia entirely with sterile florets. Deciduous shrub up to 6 ft usually rather less. Fl. in dense heads of which outer florets only are coloured pale blue-mauve. Variable in colour according to soil on more alkaline soils becoming pink.
hortensia
These are the forms with the florets all sterile which make large globular heads and are those sold in florists' shops. Among the finest are:
'Altona', rose-coloured, large florets, may be turned blue by treatment with suitable salts of iron and aliminium;
'Europa', deep pink large fl.;
'Général Vicomtesse de Vibraye', the best blue when treated, otherwise rose;
'Hamburg', deep rose, large heads of fl. up to 1 ft across, **1650,** p. 207;
'La France', rose-coloured with fringed florets;
'Marechal Foch', rosy-red;
'Preziosa', deep pink with paler pink heads as they fade, more dwarf shrub than preceding with smaller heads, **1651,** p. 207.

paniculata ✼ Summer Sh.
Hardy shrub up to 6 ft. Fl. heads large up to 8 in. long by 6 in. across in dense clusters, all sterile, white fading to pink. Both the forms below should be pruned hard in early spring almost back to old wood in order to encourage bushy habit and large fl. heads.
'Grandiflora', the best form, **1652,** p. 207;
'Praecox', fl. slightly earlier.

sargentiana ✼ Summer Sh.
Tall shrub up to 8 ft. Fl. heads large with white rayed-florets. L. very large and velvety, stems bristly and slightly tender but in a sheltered situation in most counties does well. Very distinctive.

serrata 'Acuminata' ✼ Summer Sh.
Shrub up to 4 ft. Ray-florets blue or white occasionally pinkish, free flowering. L. longer and less broad than in macrophylla. **1653,** p. 207.
Other forms are:
'Grayswood', blue;
'Rosalba', white turning crimson.

Abbreviations and Symbols used in the text.
The following abbreviations may sometimes be used in conjunction as HA. indicating Hardy annual or GBb indicating Greenhouse bulb.

A. = Annual	P. = Perennial
Aq. = Aquatic	R. = Rock or
B. = Biennial	Alpine plant
Bb = Bulb	Sh. = Shrub
C. = Corm	Sp., sp. = Species
Cl. = Climber	Syn. = Synonym
Co. = Conifer	T. = Tree
Fl., fl. = Flower(s)	Tu. = Tuber
G. = Greenhouse or house plant	var. = variety
	× = Hybrid or hybrid parents
H. = Hardy	
HH. = Half-hardy	✼ = Flowering time
L., l. = Leaf, leaves	☙ = Foliage plant
Mt(s) = Mount, mountain(s)	

The following have been used also in the descriptions of Alpines, Bulbs, Trees and Shrubs.

* = slightly tender
† = lime hater
✿ = highly recommended

The illustration numbers are in **bold type** and the page numbers in light type preceded by p.

villosa ✱ Summer   *Sh.
Tall shrub up to 9 ft and as much across. *Fl.* heads lilac-blue with large ray-florets and lilac-blue centre becoming pink as they age and in alkaline soils. *L.* velvety, ovate oblong tapering at both ends. One of the most valuable late flowering shrubs for general garden use. **1654**, p. 207.

HYLOMECON (PAPAVERACEAE)

japonicum ✱ Spring   P.
Fl. golden-yellow, about 2 in. across. *L.* fern-like, up to 10 in. long, irregularly toothed. 1 ft. Plant 11–3 in deep, moist soil with plenty of leaf mould. Propagate by division of the creeping rootstock. Japan. **1180**, p. 148.

HYMENOCALLIS (AMARYLLIDACEAE) Spider Lily

calathina see **H. narcissiflora**

narcissiflora Chalice-crowned Sea Daffodil ✱ Summer   *Bb
Fl. white with a large central cup funnel-shaped, edge fringed, outer segments up to 3 in. but narrow and reflexed. Height 1½ ft with up to five *fl.* per stem. Very fragrant. Generally grown as a cool greenhouse plant. Commonest form is 'Advance', also often known under its synonym *H. calathina*, the Basket Flower. S. America.

HYPERICUM (GUTTIFERAE) St John's Wort
(Sometimes placed in separate family as Hypericaceae)

calycinum Rose of Sharon ✱ Summer   Sh.
Deciduous or semi-evergreen small shrub up to 18 in. spreading widely and one of the most valuable ground cover plants available, either in sunny or shady places and in dry places under trees or on dry banks. *Fl.* pale yellow with deeper orange-yellow stamens up to 4 in. across freely borne at ends of short shoots. *L.* ovate oblong up to 3 in. slightly scented when bruised. Should be pruned hard in early spring and may be cut over with shears in order to keep compact. China and Japan but almost naturalised in Britain. **1655**, p. 207.

elatum ✱ Summer   Sh.
Dwarf deciduous shrub up to 4 ft but often less after pruning. *Fl.* deep yellow with prominent stamens. Fruits scarlet narrowly egg-shaped and prominent. *L.* broadly ovate. Should be pruned hard in early spring in order to keep bushy habit. Canary Islands.
    'Elstead', is the best form in which the fruits are particularly brightly coloured and borne in clusters, **1656**, p. 207.

patulum ✱ Summer   Sh.
Deciduous or semi-evergreen shrub up to 6 ft but usually less after pruning. *Fl.* deep yellow rather saucer-shaped with broad overlapping petals and deeper coloured boss of stamens in centre up to 3 in. across. *L.* broad. If pruned hard in spring makes a dense twiggy bush which will be covered with *fl.* in late summer and forms one of our most valuable late flowering summer shrubs.
    ✿'Hidcote', best form with larger *fl.* than type, flowering very freely, **1657**, p. 208.

polyphyllum ✱ Summer   Rsub.Sh.
6 in.–1 ft. Small sub-shrubby plant with tufts or erect stems. *Fl.* deep yellow with five large petals and central boss of golden stamens, up to 1½ in. across, free-flowering, buds often tinged scarlet. *L.* narrowly ovate, small in two ranks along stem. Suitable for sunny position in rock garden. S.W. Asia Minor. **90**, p. 12.
    'Citrinum', is a paler lemon-yellow form.

rhodopaeum ✱ Late Spring–Early Summer   RP.
6 in. Sub-shrubby with prostrate stems, *fl.* stem sometimes ascending up to 6 in. *Fl.* pale or golden-yellow, up to 1¾ in. across, free-flowering. Buds in small clusters but usually only one *fl.* of cluster opening at a time. *L.* downy, slightly glaucous,

ovate, sessile on stem. Sunny position in rock garden. S.E. Europe, Asia Minor. **91**, p. 12.

'Rowallane Hybrid' ✱ Late Summer   Sh.
Probably a hybrid between *H. hookerianum rogersii* and *H. leschenaultii*. Up to 6 ft and evergreen in mild areas but in colder areas cut to ground annually and growing up to 3 or 4 ft. *Fl.* in clusters at ends of branches deep buttercup-yellow 3 in. across bowl or cup-shaped. Valuable shrub but slightly more tender than 'Hidcote'. It arose in garden in N. Ireland. *L.* 2¼ in. long ovate lanceolate dark green but glaucous beneath. One of the most beautiful St John's Worts where it can be grown satisfactorily. **1658**, p. 208.

HYSSOPUS (LABIATEAE) Hyssop

aristatus ✱ Late Summer   P.
Fl. rich blue. *L.* semi-evergreen, aromatic, opposite, narrow. 1 ft. More compact than *H. officinale*, 1–2 ft, to which it is otherwise similar. Plant 3–4 in light, dryish soil and sun. Propagate by cuttings in summer or by seed sown in the open in 4–5. Palestine, **1181**, p. 148.

officinale see **H. aristatus**

I

IBERIAN CRANESBILL see **Geranium ibericum**, **1143-1145**, pp. 143, 144.

IBERIS (CRUCIFERAE) Candytuft

saxatilis ✱ Late Spring–Midsummer   RP.
4–6 in. Small evergreen shrublet. *Fl.* white in flat heads up to 1½ in. at end of short branches. *L.* small, linear. An easy plant for sunny position in rock garden. S. Europe, Pyrenees. **92**, p. 12.

sempervirens ✱ Early Summer   P.
Fl. white rounded heads up to 2 in. across. *L.* evergreen, forming a spreading neat bush. 9–12 in. Ordinary soil in a dry, sunny place, admirable for the top of a dry wall. Propagate by seed or named varieties by cuttings taken with a heel after flowering and inserted in sandy compost in a cold frame. S. Europe. Good varieties include:
    'Little Gem', white, 6 in.;
    'Snowflake', large white heads, 9 in., **1182**, p. 148.

umbellata ✱ Late Spring–Summer   HA.
Fl. variable, in flat heads of purple shades. *L.* slender-pointed. 9–15 in. Sow in the open in 3–4 or in 9 in ordinary garden soil and in a sunny position, where they are to *fl.* Named varieties, both dwarf and tall, are available in shades of mauve, purple, bright rose, rose-pink, also white. S. Europe.
    'Dwarf Fairy', mixed, compact, 9 in., **310**, p. 39.

ICE PLANT see **Sedum maximum**, **1371**, p. 172.

ICELAND POPPY see **Papaver nudicaule**

ILEX (AQUIFOLIACEAE) Holly

aquifolium Common Holly UK, English Holly USA.   T.
Evergreen shrub or small bushy tree up to 20 ft sometimes more. All trees of holly are unisexual and it is necessary to plant female bushes with males for cross pollination. Typical form has scarlet red berries in large clusters. Well known for Christmas decorations. One of the most beautiful British trees in winter. **1659**, p. 208.
Other valuable selected forms are:
    'Bacciflava', with yellow berries in large clusters, **1660**, p. 208;
    'Golden Queen', variegated holly, *l.*, margined with deep yellow or sometimes almost entirely deep yellow. This is valuable evergreen for leaf effect but, being somewhat illogically a male plant, bears no berries, **1661**, p. 208.

'Golden King' on the other hand, with slightly larger variegated *l.*, but more rarely seen, is a female plant.
    'Pyramidalis', makes an upright small tree or shrub. Fruit scarlet and larger than in type. *L.* almost spineless thus making it one of the best hollies to plant in the garden, **1662**, p. 208.

cornuta Chinese Holly   Sh,T.
Shrub or small tree. Unique rather rectangular glossy *l.* with three thorny prongs at the tips 1½ to 4 in. long. The bright red berries are exceptionally large. Long lasting. There are female varieties and kinds that need no male, forming berries without pollination. These berries are seedless. China.

opaca American Holly   Sh,T.
Evergreen tree, 40 and more feet high. Sometimes shrubby. Habit is similar to *Ilex aquifolium*, which is called 'English Holly' in the USA. *L.* are dull on the surface as against the shiny *l.* of *aquifolium*. There are areas in the USA where the climate is too cold for attractive growth of *aquifolium*, and here the American holly is a good counterpart. The berries of the American holly are formed on this year's shoots, whereas the berries of the English holly are formed on last year's shoots. USA.
    'Canary', a yellow-berried form.

verticillata Black Alder, Winterberry   Sh.
A deciduous holly shrub, to 9 ft. Spaced clusters of bright red berries along stems make a nice contrast when *l.* are still green in autumn. but are more attractive when seen on the bare twigs in winter. Plants are also either male or female. E. USA.

IMPATIENS (BALSAMINACEAE) Busy Lizzie, Touch-me-not

balsamina Balsam ✱ Summer–Autumn   HA.
Fl. red, but variable in colour and in size of *l.* 9 in.–2½ ft. Sow in a warm greenhouse in 3–4, or in the open in 5, in a sheltered sunny bed with rich, moist soil. India, China, Malaysia.
    Camellia flowered, these double varieties in shades of rose, scarlet and white, flushed pink are the most showy for a border, **311**, p. 39;
    'Tom Thumb mixed', extra dwarf, large double *fl.*, 9 in.

holstii see under **I. petersiana**

petersiana ✱ Late Spring–Summer   GP.
Fl. scarlet, 2 in. across, flat with long slender spur. *L.*

---

purple-bronze, evergreen, elliptic, to $1\frac{1}{2}$ in. long. To $1\frac{1}{2}$ ft. Rich compost required and ample water in growing season. Winter temp. 55°F. if possible. Will survive at lower temps., but may fail. Much used for room culture, where a well-lit position is required. Young plants more floriferous. Propagate by stem cuttings. Tropical W. Africa. **552**, p. 69.

    I. holstii and *I. sultanii* are very similar to *I. petersiana* and have been heavily hybridised of recent years. F^1 and open pollinated cultivars which come true from seed are now available and widely grown.

sultanii see under **I. petersiana**

INCARVILLEA (BIGNONIACEAE) Chinese Trumpet Flower

    These plants require full sun and good, deeply cultivated soil, enriched with compost or old manure. Propagate by division of the roots in spring or by seed sown in 3 in a temp. of 55°F. or in a cold frame in 4.

delavayi ✳ Early Summer   P.
    Fl. bright rosy, five or six large trumpets on a stem. *L.* dark green, 1–$1\frac{1}{2}$ ft long, ash-like. W. China. **1183**, p. 148.
    'Bees' Pink' is good with soft pink trumpets.

grandiflora ✳ Early Summer   P.
    Fl. deep rosy-red, large, trumpet shaped, with throat suffused yellow. *L.* with rounded leaflets. 1 ft. W. China. **1184**, p. 148.

INCENSE CEDAR see **Libocedrus decurrens**, **2024**, p. 253.

INDIA RUBBER TREE see **Ficus elastica**, **529**, **530**, p. 67.

INDIAN BEAN TREE see **Catalpa bignonioides**, **1498**, p. 188.

INDIAN HORSE CHESTNUT see **Aesculus indica**

INULA (COMPOSITAE)

ensifolia ✳ Summer   P.
    Fl. yellow, long lasting, 2 in. across. *L.* slender, pointed. 1 ft. Ordinary soil that does not dry out in summer and a sunny position. Propagate by division in early autumn or spring, or by seed. Caucasus.
    'Golden Beauty', a good golden-yellow, 2 ft, **1185**, p. 149.

hookeri ✳ Summer   P.
    Fl. lemon-yellow, about 3 in. across, with numerous, slender rays. *L.* 3–4 in. long, finely toothed, downy. 2 ft. Cultivate and propagate as for *I. ensifolia*. Himalaya. **1186**, p. 149.

IPHEION (AMARYLLIDACEAE)

uniflorum Spring Star Flower ✳ Spring   Bb
    Fl. single on a 6 in. stem, white or pale lilac-mauve, trumpet-shaped opening into a star, smelling slightly of garlic. *L.* grasslike with some smell of garlic. Increases freely and forms large clumps. *Fl.* very early in alpine house where it is an effective plant. Hardy. S. America. **773**, p. 97.

IPOMOEA (CONVOLVULACEAE) Morning Glory

rubro-caerulea see **I. tricolor**

tricolor, syn. **I. rubro-caerulea**, **Pharbitis tricolor** ✳ Summer   HHA.
    Fl. large, sky-blue with yellow throat. *L.* slender-pointed. Twining, 5–10 ft. Sow in 2–3 in a warm greenhouse and plant out against a warm wall in late 5, or grow in a cold greenhouse for summer decoration. Tropical America.
    'Praecox', an early variety, good in the open, **312**, p. 39.

IRIS (IRIDACEAE)

    The irises here have been divided into seven groups, the first three of which are comprised of bulbous irises, the next three make up the herbaceous group (tuberous and fibrous rooted sp. and bearded flag irises) and the last rock garden perennials. 1 Small Bulbous, 2 Juno, 3 Xiphium, 4 Oncocyclus and Regelio-cyclus, 5 Herbaceous sp. and forms, 6 Bearded hybrids and 7 Rock garden plants other than in section 1. The numbers in the list below refer the reader to the section where the plant is described.

acutiloba see 4
alata see **I. planifolia** 2
Algerian see **I. unguicularis** 5
attica see 6 (Dwarf)
aucheri see 2
bakeriana see 1
brevicaulis see **I. foliosa** 5
bucharica see 2
chamaeiris see 6 (Dwarf)
cristata var. **lacustris** see **I. lacustris** 7
danfordiae see 1
delavayi see 5
douglasiana see 7
foetidissima see 5
foliosa see 5
histrioides 'Major' see 1
innominata see 5
japonica see 5
Juno see 2
kaempferi see 5
lacustris see 7
laevigata see 5
magnifica and **magnifica** 'Alba' see after **I. planifolia** 2
mesopotamica see 6 (Intermediate)
ochroleuca see 5
Oncocyclus see 4
orchioides see after **I. planifolia** 2
pallida see 5 and also 6 (Intermediate)
Persian see **I. persica**
persica see after **I. planifolia** 2
planifolia see 2
pseudacorus see 5
pumila see 6
Regelia see 4
Regelio-cyclus see 4
reticulata see 1
sibirica see 5
sindjarensis see **I. aucheri**
sisyrinchium see **Gynandriris sisyrinchium**
Snake's Head see **Hermodactylus tuberosus**
spuria see 5
stylosa see **I. unguicularis** 5
tectorum see 5
tingitana see Dutch Irises, 3
tingitana 'Fontanesii' see after Spanish Irises, 3
trojana see 6 (Intermediate)
tuberosa see **Hermodactylus tuberosus**
unguicularis see 5
variegata see 6 (Intermediate)
verna see 7
versicolor see 5
winogradowii see 1
xiphioides see English Irises, 3
xiphium see Dutch and Spanish Irises, 3
Xiphium see 3

1 Small bulbous irises
(Sect. *reticulata*) with round bulbs covered with a net-like coat, early.

bakeriana ✳ Early Spring   Bb
    More slender in *fl.* than *I. reticulata* to which it is close. Generally less vigorous in growth. Pale blue with orange ridge to fall and dark purple blotch at base of fall, but forms are known without dark blotch. Best in alpine house. If planted outside give as sunny a position as possible in a very well-drained position. S.E. Iran, Iraq, E. Turkey. **775**, p. 97.

danfordiae ✳ Winter   Bb
    Fl. rather squat since the standards are much reduced, very bright lemon-yellow, 3–4 in., very early. Usually *fl.* strongly from Dutch grown bulbs

the first year and then the bulbs break up into numerous small bulblets which need to be grown on carefully to flowering size. Requires feeding. Hardy and also excellent in alpine house. **777**, p. 98.

✿ **histrioides 'Major'** ✳ Winter   Bb
    Fl. strong blue with gold and white markings on falls which stick out almost horizontally. Very early. The stoutest and probably the best garden plant in this section. Sometimes produces large and persistent colonies. Very resistant to bad weather. See also *I. reticulata*. **778**, p. 98.

✿ **reticulata** ✳ Early Spring   Bb
    Fl. deep bluish-mauve with gold markings on falls, scented. 6–8 in. *L.* narrow and four-ribbed. A graceful and delicate *fl.*, deservedly popular especially as the bulbs are usually the cheapest of this section. Sunny position on rock garden, alpine house or bulb frame. **780**, p. 98.
    Hybrids between it and *I. histrioides* 'Major' have been developed and are some of the most showy and distinctive *fl.* in this section and are generally more vigorous and persistent than *I. reticulata*. These include:
    'Cantab', pale blue with gold blotch edged with white on falls. 4–5 in. Usually smaller than type, **781**, p. 98;
    ✿'Clarette', violet blue and gentian blue falls marked with white, **782**, p. 98;
    ✿'Harmony', deep sky-blue with prominent gold markings, **783**, p. 98;
    'Joyce', is rather similar to 'Harmony';
    'Royal Blue', darker royal blue with broad fall like *histrioides* and conspicuous yellow patch on the blade;
    'Velvet', deep purple with velvet-like texture and sheen;
    'Violet Beauty', more slender and taller, rich violet-purple with orange crests on falls;
    'Wentworth', deep purplish-blue, taller than the two above.

winogradowii ✳ Early Spring   Bb
    Fl. pale lemon-yellow, dwarf, a handsome sp. but rarer and slower of increase than preceding, resembling a yellow *I. histrioides* in form and size. Falls with an orange ridge. S. Russia.

2 Juno   Bb
    Bubous irises flowering mostly later than preceding. Distinguished by the large fleshy roots below the bulb. It is important not to damage these on transplanting. All require good summer baking.

aucheri, syn. **I. sindjarensis** ✻ Spring   Bb

Fl. pale lilac-blue with yellow ridge to centre of fall. 6 in.–1 ft. *Fl.* emerging from axis of broad fleshy green *l.* Mesopotamia. **774**, p. 97.

bucharica ✻ Spring   Bb

Fl. creamy-white with deep lemon-yellow blade to falls. Six or seven *fl.* in axils of *l.* on stem 1 ft. The standards are small and project horizontally instead of upright, their place in the Iris form being taken by conspicuous crests to the style. *L.* fresh shiny green and keeled, clasping stem at base. **776**, p. 97.

planifolia, syn. **I. alata** ✻ Winter–Early Spring Bb

Fl. large bright lilac-blue with orange and white markings on falls, 3½ in. across, up to three on 8 in.– 1 ft stem. Styles with large fringed crests. A beautiful sp. but rather shy *fl.* in Britain and difficult in open as it *fl.* so early. Best in cold frame. Sicily, N. Africa. **779**, p. 98.

Other good sp. in this section are:

  magnifica, pale silvery-blue;

  magnifica 'Alba', creamy-white, vigorous up to 1½ ft;

  orchioides, golden-yellow, variable and most attractive;

  persica Persian Iris, of which there are many forms and varieties from Turkey and Iran. It seemed to grow better in the time of Clusius, in the sixteenth century, than it does now. It is now practically impossible to grow satisfactorily in open being very sensitive to wet on *l.*

3 Xiphium

These are the bulbous irises of florists' shops, the English, the Spanish and the Dutch, often forced to *fl.* from the New Year to the summer, but in the garden *fl.* 6–mid 7. Their parents came from W. Mediterranean regions, N.W. Africa, Spain, Portugal and the Pyrenees, but the original sp. are seldom grown in gardens today. They are adequately hardy in warmer areas but in cold areas need a little protection in winter such as some dry bracken or cloches. All force easily for early-flowering in pots or boxes in a warm or cool greenhouse and the present range of their colours is considerable.

Dutch Irises ✻ Summer   *Bb

Raised from *I. xiphium* var. *praecox* of Spain and Portugal and crossed with *I. tingitana* of N. Africa, **784**.

Plant bulbs in early autumn 3–4 in. deep in an open, sunny place. Height 1–1½ ft. Range of *fl.* colours includes white, yellow and bronze, blue, mauve and purple. All are equally easy to grow and mostly fairly cheap to buy.

Some of the best include:

  'Blue Champion', bright blue with yellow blotch on falls, **788**, p. 99;

  'Lemon Queen', citron yellow with the falls slightly paler than the standards, **789**, p. 99;

  'Orange King', deep orange self colour;

  'Wedgwood', light blue with a yellow blotch, early, probably the most popular variety for the florist trade and excellent for forcing, **790**, p. 99.

English Irises ✻ Summer   Bb

A little later than Dutch Irises. These are forms and hybrids of *I. xiphioides* of the Pyrenees and range from white through light blue, dark blue, mauve to deep purple. *Fl.* slightly larger and more solid. 1½–2 ft. They do best with some moisture in the soil. The *l.* appear later than in the Spanish irises and for this reason they are slightly more persistant in English gardens. They are often grown as a mixture and blend well together but named forms include:

  'Coombelands', deep blue falls and purplish-blue standards;

  'King of the Blues', dark blue with darker flecking;

  'Mont Blanc', white;

  'The Giant', deep blue, large.

Spanish Irises ✻ Early Summer   Bb

Raised from *I. xiphium* and generally the earliest of the three groups to *fl.* In colder areas they should be lifted after flowering and replanted again in late 9–10. They range from white through the blues to deep purple and often have fine yellow blotches on the falls, while some are self-coloured yellow or bronze and yellow, **785**, p. 99, or even bronze and blue. 1½–2 ft.

Among the selected varieties are:

  'Cajanus, large, golden yellow;

  'Gipsy Girl', purple and grey with an amber blotch, **786**, p. 99;

  'Hercules', fall bronzy-brown with golden blotch, standards purplish-blue and bronze.

  'King of the Blues', deep blue with a yellow blotch on falls, scented, **787**, p. 99;

  'Queen Wilhelmina', snow-white, one of the earliest.

tingitana var. **fontanesii** ✻ Mid Winter–Early Summer   *Bb

Fl. bright violet-blue with golden markings. 2 ft. Much grown for market forcing as a cut *fl.*, suitable for cool greenhouse but will grow satisfactorily in a warm sheltered position in S. England. N.W. Africa, Morocco.

4 Oncocyclus ✻ Early Summer   Tu.

acutiloba

Fl. slate-white with deep chocolate veining, falls borne horizontally 2–3 in. across on stem of 9–12 in., dark chocolate blotch at base of fall. **791**, p. 99. All in this section require adequate summer baking to ensure sufficient ripening and need complete absence of moisture during summer. It contains however some of the most beautiful irises with large *fl.*, heavily veined such as *I. gatesii*, *I. susiana* and *I. hoogiana* which with *I. acutiloba* are the easiest of the section. N.W. Iran, Transcaucasia.

Regelio-cyclus ✻ Early Summer   Tu.

Hybrids between Regelia and Oncocyclus group but much easier to grow, need sunny position and good ripening in summer combined with good drainage. *Fl.* large, blue or purple generally with prominent veining and blotch at base of falls.

  'Chione', standards pale lilac with deeper veining, and prominent dark purple blotch on falls, **792**, p. 99.

5 Herbaceous species and forms

delavayi   P.

Belongs to Apogon or unbearded irises. *Fl.* violet-blue with white patch on falls and golden and white markings, 2½–3 in. across, several to a stem. *L.* narrow, grass-like. 3–4 ft. Best in a moist position. China. **1187**, p. 149.

foetidissima   P.

Fl. yellowish-green and lilac, heavily veined. Plant chiefly grown for its brilliant orange-red seeds which last from 11–1 in open, seed head pendulous on short stem. Excellent for winter floral decorations. Foliage is light green and sword-like. 1–2 ft. Grows easily from seed and may be planted in sun or semi-shade. The stink is derived from roots and is not normally apparent. A British and European native. **1188**, p. 149.

foliosa, syn. **I. brevicaulis** ✻ Summer   P.

Fl. bright blue with gold and white markings on falls, which are held horizontally and are narrow and white at base; *fl.* up to 5 in. across. Dwarf up to 6 in. A sp. which should be more often grown. S.E. USA. **1189**, p. 149.

✿**innominata** ✻ Late Spring–Early Summer   P.

Fl. variable but in shades of yellow from pale cream to deep yellow. Falls usually with deeper veining, about 1½–2 in. across, usually only one to a stem. *L.* grass-like. Dwarf up to 8 in. Plant forms large clumps. Plant in sunny place in Britain but in Oregon it grows in open woodland. Much used as a parent of many valuable dwarf hybrids and much crossed with *I. douglasiana*, and other Pacific Coast irises. Oregon, USA. **1190**, p. 149.

japonica ✻ Spring   P.

One of Evansia section. *Fl.* pale blue or white, 2–4 in. across, several on a branched stem, falls and standards fringed, falls are deep yellow or orange at base and around this colour are dotted and streaked with deep blue. A rather exotic orchid-like *fl.* *L.* bright green, sword-like and growing in a fan. 1–2 ft. Not very hardy so should be planted in a warm sunny position in front of a wall where possible. Japan, China.

  'Ledger's' variety is an improvement on the type, **1191**, p. 149.

kaempferi ✻ Summer   P.

Fl. very variable in colour from white, pale mauve, rosy-purple to deep mauvish or royal purple, very large up to 8 in. across, rather floppy but very decorative. Not very long-lasting but several to a stem. 2–3 ft. Needs damp position and often grows as a bog plant at edge of pond, but will not tolerate standing water in winter. Japan.

There are many varieties:

  'Attraction', purple on a grey ground;

  'Geihan', white, **1192**, p. 149;

  'Juno', single, rosy-purple;

  'Purple Splendour', double, rich purple;

  'Sasameyuki', violet on grey ground, **1193**, p. 150;

  'Swan', double, white.

laevigata ✻ Summer   P.

Fl. deep bluish-purple or white, up to 5 in. across, falls usually horizontal but drooping as they go over. 2 ft. Close to *I. kaempferi* and a moisture loving plant which will actually grow in the water as well as at edge of pond. China.

  'Alba', a fine white, **1194**, p. 150;

  'Monstrosa', striking large blue and white, **1195**, p. 150.

ochroleuca ✻ Summer   P.

One of spuria section. *Fl.* creamy-white with prominent yellow patch on falls, 3–4 in. across and several to a stem. *L.* tall, sword-like and decorative. 3–4 ft. Usually in moist places. Unsuitable for dry places. Asia Minor. **1196**, p. 150.

pallida ✻ Late Spring–Early Summer   P.

Fl. pale lavender, fragrant. *L.* sword-like, pale, glaucous. 2–3 ft. Dalmatia.

  'Variegata', outstanding with its striped *l.*, in two forms, 'Argentea', silver stripes, and 'Aurea', gold stripes, **1197**, p. 150.

pseudacorus Yellow Flag ❋ Late Spring–Early Summer P.

Fl. deep golden-yellow, sometimes pale orange with deeper markings at base of falls. 2–3 ft. Probably origin of the French 'Fleur de Lys'. A British native and widespread in dampish places in N. Europe. **1198**, p. 150.

var. *bastardii*, with lemon-yellow *fl.* without deeper markings at base.

sibirica ❋ Summer P.

Fl. white, variable from deep violet-blue with gold markings or pale blue, 2–3 in. across. 3–4 ft. A moisture lover which will form large clump at edge of pond but does not require as much moisture as *I. kaempferi*. Many named varieties have been developed which are distinct improvement on type.

'Blue Mere', violet-blue, standards lighter than falls, **1199**, p. 150;

'Caesar's Brother', large *fl.* deep violet with broad circular fall and golden markings at base, edged with white, **1200**, p. 150;

'Cool Springs', pale violet-blue with lighter standards and rather heavy veining;

'Purple Mere', deep violet-purple, one of the best of the newer forms, **1199**, p. 150;

'White Swirl', large white *fl.* with broad falls, 1½–2 ft, probably best white form at present available, **1199**, p. 150.

spuria ❋ Summer P.

Fl. cream, yellow or blue, very variable. If blue usually with yellow blotch on falls near base. *L.* tall, sword-like. 2–4 ft. Needs moisture when growing and then good summer ripening. This section *fl.* better in a hot summer.

'Wadi Zem Zem', with deep yellow *fl.* is one of best varieties, excellent in S. states of USA, **1201**, p. 151.

tectorum ❋ Early Summer P.

Dwarf iris with large light blue streaked with dark blue or white *fl.* about 2½–3 in. across on 1 ft stems. A decorative plant, and often a fairly vigorous grower which should be grown more widely. Japan. **1202**, p. 151.

✿ **unguicularis**, syn. **I. stylosa** Algerian or Stylosa Iris ❋ Winter–Early Spring P.

Fl. large lilac-mauve with gold and white markings at base 3–4 in. across. *L.* grass-like. 6–8 in. One of the most valuable winter-flowering plants *Fl.* may be pulled for the house. Plant in as warm a place as possible, preferably against a south wall and do not disturb. Variable in colour. S. and E. Mediterranean regions including Algeria. **1203**, p. 151.

'Alba', is a good white form with prominent deep yellow streaks in centre of fall, **1204**, p. 151;

'Mary Barnard', deep violet-purple with gold markings.

versicolor ❋ Early Summer P.

Fl. light purple with gold markings edged with white on falls, 2–3 in. across. Several to a stem which also bears *l.* 1–1½ ft. N. America.

'Kermesina', *fl.* deep reddish-purple, very rich in colour and strongly marked; sunny position near front of herbaceous border, **1205**, p. 151.

6. Bearded Hybrid Irises:

These are now divided into three classes, Dwarf, Intermediate and Tall.

Dwarf bearded with *fl.* up to 8 in. in 4 and early 5.

Fl. creamy-yellow, golden-yellow, blue, white or purple. They are mostly derived from *I. pumila* and *I. chamaeiris*, both of which are very variable in the wild and are native to S. Europe. *I. attica* of Greece is often regarded as a variety or sub-sp. of *I. pumila*. Plant in full sun at front of border.

Intermediate with stems up to 27 in. These are dwarfer than tall bearded, usually rather smaller in *fl.* and also earlier in mid-5, but some of those more recently developed *fl.* with the tall bearded irises in 6. These and the tall bearded irises have been derived from a number of sp. but as this work has gone on for very many years their origins are obscure. In their parentage *I. variegata*, *I. pallida*, *I. mesopotamica* and *I. trojana* have all played a part. Plant in full sun; among the best are:

'Lilli-Bitone', a bicolor, standard very pale almost white, falls deep purplish-red with light edge, a strong grower, 1–1¼ ft, **1206**, p. 151;

'Scintilla', a bicolor, standard white, falls tawny-brown with white edge, 1½ ft, **1207**, p. 151;

'Small Wonder', bright sky-blue with orange beard and veining, like a small version of 'Helen McGregor', one of the most famous of the tall bearded varieties, sometimes described as a Lilliput iris, **1208**, p. 151.

Tall bearded: ❋ Early Summer

These form the largest and most popular class and the varieties are very numerous. They range from above 27 in. to 3½ or even 4 ft, and the *fl.* are up to 6 in. across. Unfortunately many of the newer varieties with very large *fl.* often require staking. Plant in sunny positions and lift clumps and divide every third or fourth year, preferably either in late 6 or early 7 just after flowering or in 9 when new roots are growing. If possible avoid moving in winter. The rhizomes should be planted on or near the surface; all make firm roots. The beard is the crest of hair along the base and centre of the fall. Among the best are:

'Arctic Flame', white with bright orange-red beard, ruffled edge to fall and standard, **1209**, p. 152;

'Benton Cordelia', pale orchid or lilac-pink with ruffled standard and falls, deep orange beard;

'Cliffs of Dover', white, ruffled edge to falls, a large *fl.* and a good vigorous grower;

'Dancer's Veil', a plicata iris, falls white heavily margined with deep violet-purple and streaked near base, standards deep violet-purple, on a white base, much ruffled at edge, one of the finest irises yet raised in this class, **1210**, p. 152;

'Elleray', deep golden-yellow with lighter patch on falls, tall and vigorous grower;

'Ennerdale', pale lemon-yellow with pale cream centre to falls and paler standards, a very attractive blend of colouring, **1211**, p. 152;

'Esther Fay', pale apricot-pink with deep orange-red beard, ruffled edge, **1212**, p. 152;

'Helen McGregor', pale silvery-blue with ruffled edge, a vigorous grower and a very popular *fl.*, **1213**, p. 152;

'Jane Phillips', medium blue, slightly striated at base, one of the older but still very popular varieties, **1214**, p. 152;

'Lady Mohr', a blended *fl.* with some oncocyclus iris in its parentage but a vigorous grower, standard oyster-white, slightly fluted at edge, falls greenish-yellow, **1215**, p. 152;

'Mary Todd', strong mahogany reddish-brown with tangerine-orange beard, there is a slightly mauvish bloom on falls which are flimsy and ruffled, one of the finest *fl.* yet raised in this class but not a very strong grower, **1216**, p. 152;

'Ola Kala', strong orange-yellow, a vigorous grower, **1217**, p. 153;

'Olympic Torch', apricot-bronze with tangerine beard, a large *fl.* with wavy margins to falls and standard, **1218**, p. 153;

'Rippling Waters', pale lilac-purple with orange beard, a large *fl.* with wavy margins to falls and standards, **1219**, p. 153;

'Sierra Skies', medium self-coloured blue with a pale purplish sheen, on fall, very free-flowering;

'Starshine', a soft pearly blend of deep cream, standards and falls of almost white with orange-brown edging, **1220**, p. 153;

'Velvet Robe', deep mahogany-crimson with velvet texture, ruffled edge to fall, **1221**, p. 153.

7. Rock garden perennials

douglasiana ❋ Early Summer RP.

6 in.–1 ft. Mat or clump forming plant, spreading widely. *Fl.* one or two to sheath on erect stems. Purple or bluish-purple up to 2 in. across, very variable in colour and markings, usually marked with white at base of fall. *L.* evergreen, linear. One of parents with *I. innominata* of widely grown race of Californian dwarf irises. Sun or semi-shade. Should be disturbed as rarely as possible. W. USA, Oregon, California. **93**, p. 12.

lacustris, syn. **I. cristata** var. **lacustris** ❋ Late Spring RP.

2–4 in. Charming dwarf iris with slender rhizome. *Fl.* singly on short stems, falls pale lilac-blue with white and gold central markings, standards erect rather narrower than falls. *L.* yellowish-green, broad, linear. A plant for well-drained but not dry position in rock garden or alpine house. Like a smaller form of *I. cristata*. E. USA. **94**, p. 12.

verna ❋ Spring RP.

Small rhizomatous plant. *Fl.* lilac-mauve with golden crest to falls but without a 'beard', up to 2 in. across. *L.* broadly linear, sword-like, slightly glaucous, about 6 in. long at flowering time. A delightful dwarf iris for a rather warm situation, rarely successful in very cold areas. S. USA. **95**, p. 12.

IRISH HEATH see **Daboecia cantabrica**, **1549**, p. 194.

IRISH JUNIPER see **Juniperus communis** 'Hibernica', **2017**, p. 253.

IRISH YEW see **Taxus baccata** 'Fastigiata'

IRON-BARK TREE see **Eucalyptus**, **1597-1600**, p. 200.

IRON CROSS see **Begonia masoniana**, **414**, p. 52.

IRON TREE see **Parrotia persica**, **1721**, p. 216.

ITALIAN ALDER see **Alnus cordata**, **1443**, p. 181.

ITALIAN CYPRESS see **Cupressus sempervirens**

ITALIAN VERBENA see **Verbena tenera**, **1413**, p. 177.

ITEA (SAXIFRAGACEAE)

ilicifolia ❀ Late Summer — Sh.
Evergreen shrub up to 12 ft, usually less, slightly tender and in colder areas best grown against a wall. *Fl.* in long catkins, up to 1 ft long, pale greenish-yellow. *L.* holly-like but less thick, dark green above paler below, less spiny than holly. Valuable evergreen shrub for milder areas especially for late flowering habit. W. China. **1663**, p. 208.

IVY see **Hedera**, **543-546**, pp. 68, 69.

IVY ARUM see **Scindapsus**, **645**, p. 81.

IVY-LEAVED PELARGONIUM see **Pelargonium peltatum**, **613-617**, pp. 77, 78.

IVY, POISON see **Rhus toxicodendron** after **R. typhina**

IXIA (IRIDACEAE)

❀ Summer — *C.
Rather tender corms but with *fl.* of great brilliance and grace. Stem 1½–2 ft, thin and wiry with narrow grasslike *l. Fl.* several to a stem, star-like in colours varying from white through yellow to scarlet, bright blue, generally with a darker centre like an eye. In warmer areas they may be planted in a warm sunny border in late 10 or even 11 and given a covering of ashes or bracken against severe frosts. In cooler areas they do well as cool greenhouse plants in large pots six or 12 to a pot. Generally grown as a rainbow-like mixture although there are also named varieties of particular colours. S. Africa.

IXIOLIRION (AMARYLLIDACEAE)

montanum ❀ Early Summer — *Bb
Fl. bright blue or lavender-like, star-like, about 2 in. across, several on a 1 ft stem. Plant in a sunny well-drained border. *L.* grasslike. Central Asia, Iran, Turkey.
var. *pallasii* has rosy-purple *fl.*

J

JACOBEAN LILY see **Sprekelia**, **883**, p. 111.

JANKAEA (GESNERIACEAE)

heldreichii ❀ Spring — *RP.
2–3 in. One of the most choice of all alpine plants. *Fl.* pale blue-mauve, two or three to a stem, bell-shaped, pendulous. *L.* downy with short silvery hairs giving appearance of silver, slightly rugulose like those of a Ramonda, ovate and forming small flat rosettes. Usually grown in alpine house in hole in block of tufa or in very well-drained gritty pans. Sensitive of winter wet on *l.* but should not be allowed to dry out completely. Greece, Mt Olympus in gorges, growing in crevices of vertical rocks. **96**, p. 12.

JAPANESE ANEMONE see **Anemone hupehensis**, **964**, p. 121.

JAPANESE ANEMONE, PINK see **Anemone elegans**

JAPANESE ANEMONE, WHITE see **Anemone elegans** 'Honorine Jobert'

JAPANESE APRICOT see **Prunus mume**, **1757**, p. 220.

JAPANESE AZALEA see after **Rhododendron** Hybrids, **1821-1823**, p. 228.

JAPANESE BITTER ORANGE see **Poncirus trifoliata**, **1742**, **1743**, p. 218.

JAPANESE CEDAR see **Cryptomeria**, **2011**, p. 252.

JAPANESE CRAB see **Malus floribunda**, **1699**, p. 213.

JAPANESE FLOWERING CHERRY see **Prunus serrulata**, **1762-1764**, p. 221.

JAPANESE LARCH see **Larix kaempferi**

JAPANESE MAPLE see **Acer japonicum**, **1432**, p. 179; and **A. palmatum**, **1434-1436**, p. 180.

JAPANESE PINK see **Dianthus sinensis** 'Heddewigii', **285**, p. 36.

JAPANESE SNOWBALL BUSH see **Viburnum tomentosum** 'Sterile'

JAPANESE UMBRELLA PINE see **Sciadopitys verticillata**, **2037**, p. 255.

JAPONICA see **Chaenomeles**, **1508**, **1509**, p. 189.

JASMINE see **Jasminum**, **1664**, p. 208; **1978**, **1979**, p. 248.

JASMINE, COMMON see **Jasminum officinale**

JASMINE, MADAGASCAR see **Stephanotis floribunda**, **651**, p. 82.

JASMINE, WINTER see **Jasminum nudiflorum**, **1664**, p. 208.

JASMINUM (OLEACEAE) Jasmine

✩**nudiflorum** Winter Jasmine ❀ Mid Autumn–Early Spring — Sh.
Fl. deep yellow star-like. Deciduous shrub up to 10 ft but when well pruned usually less. Usually grown as a wall shrub and will *fl.* well against a north wall. *Fl.* up to 1 in. across. *L.* opposite trifoliate up to 1 in. long glossy green. Branches four angled rather slender. One of the most valuable winter-flowering plants and very hardy. Should be pruned back nearly to old wood after flowering or prune by picking shoots for house. China. **1664**, p. 208.

officinale Common Jasmine ❀ Summer — Cl.
Semi-evergreen vigorous twining climber, deciduous in colder areas. *Fl.* white, pinkish in bud, in small terminal clusters, very sweetly scented and flowering over a long period. *L.* pinnate with up to seven pairs of small leaflets. Usually grown against a wall or allowed to scramble over a tree. Used for perfume of Jasmine. Iran, through N. India to China.

polyanthum ❀ Early Spring–Early Summer — *Cl.
Very vigorous climber with twining shoots. *Fl.* white, deep pink or crimson in bud, very fragrant, in large many-flowered clusters up to 6 in. across. *L.* pinnate with up to seven leaflets. Usually grown in Britain as cool greenhouse plant, valuable for its early flowering and very strongly sweetly scented *fl.* Season of flowering depending on amount of warmth in greenhouse. In warmer parts such as S. France and in a few S. counties of England grows well against a very warm wall. It grows freely outdoors and buds have deeper pinkish-crimson colouring than is developed in greenhouse plants. Can be pruned hard after flowering and this is necessary in most greenhouses otherwise it tends to be too vigorous. China. **1978**, p. 248.

revolutum ❀ Summer — *Sh.
Evergreen loose growing shrub often grown as wall shrub. *Fl.* yellow with long tubes and spreading lobes up to 1 in. across in large clusters, fragrant. *L.* pinnate composed up to seven leaflets. Afghanistan. **1979**, p. 248.

JEFFERSONIA (BERBERIDACEAE)

dubia, syn. **Plagiorhegma dubia** ❀ Early Summer — RP.
Fl. pale lavender-blue, open bowl-shaped, 1½ in. across, singly on slender wiry stems. *L.* peltate, roundish, two-lobed, slightly glaucous, up to 3 in. across. 6 in. Hardy in semi-shade in woodland soil. A beautiful and delicate plant but unsuitable for dry hot places. In mild spring and generally when grown in shade, *fl.* appear before *l.* which are folded flat when they first appear, otherwise *l.* tend to hide *fl.* Manchuria. **97**, p. 13.

JERSEY ELM see **Ulmus carpinifolia** var. **sarniensis**

JERUSALEM SAGE see **Phlomis fruticosa**, **1731**, p. 217.

JEW'S MALLOW see **Kerria japonica**, **1667**, p. 209.

JOE PYE WEED see **Eupatorium**, **1128**, p. 141.

JONQUIL see **Narcissus jonquilla**, **834**, p. 105.

JONQUIL, CAMPERNELLE see **Narcissus odorus** after **N. jonquilla**

JOSEPH'S COAT see **Amaranthus tricolor**, **233**, p. 30.

JUDAS TREE see **Cercis siliquastrum**, **1507**, p. 189.

JUNIPER see **Juniperus**, **2015-2021**, pp. 252, 253.

JUNIPERUS (CUPRESSACEAE) Juniper

Evergreen trees or sometimes small shrubs, upright

or spreading. Leaflets small, narrow and sharply pointed at the ends. Female cones blue, berry-like when mature containing one or more seeds. Bark often reddish, resinous. Junipers all thrive on limy soils and are easily propagated from seeds or cuttings.

communis Common Juniper   Co.
Small spreading tree or large shrub. Bark reddish-brown scaling in sheets. *L.* awl-shaped persisting narrow needle-like. Female cones green initially, when ripe being covered with blue waxy bloom, globose, berry-like up to ½ in. in diameter. **2015**, p. 252.
Among forms grown:
'Compressa', very slow growing usually small, fastigiate bush taking many years to reach 2 ft and so valuable for rock garden, very glaucous blue, **2016**, p. 252;
'Hibernica', upright columnar form with glaucous green foliage forming larger tree than 'Compressa', sometimes known as Irish Juniper, **2017**, p. 253.

horizontalis, syn. **J. prostrata**, **J. sabina** 'Procumbens' Creeping Juniper   Co.
Branches prostrate and rooting from younger growth and often spreading horizontally over large area. *L.* small scale-like, glaucous. Cones bluish up to ¾ in. long but rarely produced on cultivated plants. N. America. **2018**, p. 253.
Best form is:
'Glauca', with very slender branchlets and steely-blue glaucous foliage, valuable plant for ground cover owing to its horizontal growth, seldom reaching more than 2½ ft high.

× **media**   Co.
Probably a hybrid arising from *J. sabina* × *J. sphaerica*. Often placed under *J. chinensis* and sometimes under *J. sabina*.
'Pfitzeriana', Knap Hill Savin or Pfitzer Juniper, widespreading evergreen shrub with branchlets drooping at tips, valuable for its horizontal growth for covering large areas;
'Aurea', foliage soft yellow with some green in winter, **2019**, p. 253.

recurva Drooping Juniper   Co.
Shrub or small tree up to 30 ft with drooping pendulous branches and peeling bark greyish-brown. *L.* greyish-green narrow, densely overlapping.
var. *coxii*, Coffin Juniper, branchlets longer and more pendulous than in type and foliage darker blue-green, probably also more vigorous. Wood is very resinous and used for incense in Buddhist Temples as well as for coffins for which it commands a very high price; 'Castlewellan', is particularly fine form, showing drooping branches, unsuitable for very cold areas. China, Burma, **2020**, p. 253.

squamata   Co.
Prostrate or horizontal growing shrub with reddish-brown erect branchlets and small overlapping green *l.* Himalayas, Western China.
Form usually grown is:
meyeri, which is more erect with stiff spreading branches and glaucous blue foliage, often grown as rock garden conifer, but has reached a height of 20 ft when older, **2021**, p. 253.

K

KAFFIR LILY see **Clivia**, **474**, p. 60; and **Schizostylis coccinea**, **876**, **877**, p. 110.

KALMIA (ERICACEAE)

latifolia Mountain Laurel, Calico Bush ❋ Late Spring–Early Summer   †Sh.
Evergreen shrub or small tree up to 25 ft but in Britain usually not more than 6 ft. *Fl.* in large terminal clusters pale or deep rose-pink, saucer-shaped 1 in. across with prominent darker stamens making dots on *fl. L.* thick leathery shiny green making it a valuable evergreen shrub at all seasons. E. N. America. **1665**, p. 209.
'Brilliant', one of the finest forms with deeper pink *fl.*, crimson in bud, **1666**, p. 209.

KALOCEDRUS DECURRENS see **Libocedrus decurrens**

KANGAROO VINE see **Cissus antarctica**, **469**, p. 59.

KANSAS GAYFEATHER see **Liatris callilepis**, **1234**, p. 155.

KARO see **Pittosporum**, **1740**, p. 218.

KENTRANTHUS (VALERIANACEAE) Valerian (Also often spelt as *Centranthus* which some botanists prefer)

macrosiphon ❋ Summer   HA.
Fl. rosy-carmine, also a white form. *L.* blue-grey. 1–2 ft. Sow in the open in 2–3. Does quite well in poorish soil, dry soil. Spain. **313**, p. 40.

ruber ❋ Summer   P.
Fl. red, freely produced. *L.* ovate, slightly toothed. 2–3 ft. Plant 11–3 in ordinary well-drained soil, likes lime and sun. Propagate by seed sown in open ground in 3. Europe, naturalised in Britain. **1222**, p. 153.
'Albus', is a white form.

KERMES OAK see **Quercus coccifera**

KERRIA (ROSACEAE) Jew's Mallow

japonica ❋ Spring   Sh.
Deciduous shrub up to 6 ft with deep green branches. *Fl.* orange-yellow singly slightly cup-shaped up to 1½ in. across. Sometimes grown as wall shrub but in most areas this is not necessary. Easily propagated by summer cuttings. Prune in winter in order to keep from getting too straggly. China, Japan.
'Flore Pleno', is form often grown with double globular *fl.* heads about 2 in. across and rather stouter growth, **1667**, p. 209.

KIDNEY BEAN, CHINESE see **Wisteria**, **1999**, **2000**, p. 250.

KILLARNEY STRAWBERRY TREE see **Arbutus unedo**, **1450**, **1451**, p. 182.

KINGFISHER DAISY see **Felicia bergeriana**

KIRENGESHOMA (SAXIFRAGACEAE) Waxbells (Sometimes placed in separate family Hydrangeaceae)

palmata ❋ Late Summer   P.
Fl. pale yellow, drooping, of waxy appearance. *L.* large, roundish, lobed and slightly hairy. 2–4 ft. Plant 11–3 in moist woodland soil and partial shade. Propagate by careful division in the spring. Japan. **1223**, p. 153.

KLEINIA (COMPOSITAE)
tomentosa, syn. **Senecio haworthii** ❧ Summer   GP.
Succulent to about 12 in. *Fl.* rayless, orange-yellow, about 1 in. long. *L.* cylindrical, pointed, ¾ in. thick, to 2 in. long. Plant entirely clothed in white wool. Gritty compost. Water very sparingly in winter and not much at other times. Winter temp. 40–50°F. Propagate by stem cuttings. S. Africa. **553**, p. 70.

KNAP HILL SAVIN see **Juniperus** × **media** 'Pfitzeriana'

KNAPWEED see **Centaurea**, **259**, **260**, p. 33; **1018-1020**, p. 128.

KNIPHOFIA (LILIACEAE) Red Hot Poker

galpinii ❋ Late Summer–Mid Autumn   P.
Fl. orange-flame, drooping, borne on slender stems. *L.* grass-like. 2–2½ ft. A sheltered sunny border and a well-drained soil. Not suitable for exposed gardens. Propagate by division in the spring. Transvaal. **1224**, p. 153.

uvaria ❋ Summer   P.
Fl. coral-red becoming orange, 1–1½ ft in the wild but garden forms up to 7 ft. *L.* grey-green, to 3 ft long. Plant 11–3 in rich deep soil and sun. Propagate by division in spring or autumn. S. Africa.
There are numerous hybrids:
'Bees' Lemon', bright lemon-yellow, 3 ft;
'Bees' Sunset', gold tinged red, 2½–3 ft, **1225**, p. 154;
'H. C. Mills', gold and red, 3–3½ ft, **1226**, p. 154;
'Maid of Orleans', creamy-white, 3½ ft, **1227**, p. 154;
'Royal Standard', bright red and yellow, 3½ ft, **1228**, p. 154.

KNOTTED FIGWORT see **Scrophularia nodosa**, **1368**, p. 171.

KNOTWEED see **Polygonum**, **144**, **145**, pp. 18, 19; **1324-1326**, p. 166.

KOCHIA (CHENOPODIACEAE)

scoparia Summer Cypress   HHA.
Fl. small, greenish, inconspicuous. Attractive foliage plant with *l.* finely cut, tender green. A decorative plant of erect, bushy habit. Usually 2–3 ft but up to 5 ft. Sow in 4 under glass and plant out in late 5 in a sunny position. Europe, Asia.
'Trichophylla', the Burning Bush has *l.* turning rich russet-red, late summer–autumn, **314**, p. 40.

KOELERIA (GRAMINEAE)

gracilis ❋ Summer   P.
Fl. creamy-white in dense spikes, 1–2 ft. *L.* narrow, blue-green, up to 1 ft long. Plant 3–4 in a sunny

---

Abbreviations and Symbols used in the text.
The following abbreviations may sometimes be used in conjunction as HA. indicating Hardy annual or GBb indicating Greenhouse bulb.

A. = Annual	P. = Perennial
Aq. = Aquatic	R. = Rock or
B. = Biennial	Alpine plant
Bb = Bulb	Sh. = Shrub
C. = Corm	Sp., sp. = Species
Cl. = Climber	Syn. = Synonym
Co. = Conifer	T. = Tree
Fl.,fl. = Flower(s)	Tu. = Tuber
G. = Greenhouse or	var. = variety
house plant	× = Hybrid or
H. = Hardy	hybrid parents
HH. = Half-hardy	❋ = Flowering time
L., l. = Leaf, leaves	❧ = Foliage plant
Mt(s) = Mount,	
mountain(s)	

The following have been used also in the descriptions of Alpines, Bulbs, Trees and Shrubs.

* = slightly tender
† = lime hater
✿ = highly recommended

The illustration numbers are in **bold type** and the page numbers in light type preceded by p.

---

position and sandy soil. Propagate by division in spring, or by seed. Central Europe, W. Siberia.

'Britannica', deep cream spikes, foliage forms a blue-green cushion, **1229**, p. 154.

KOLKWITZIA (CAPRIFOLIACEAE)

amabilis Beauty Bush ❋ Early Summer　　　Sh.
Deciduous shrub up to 7 ft. *Fl.* white or pale pink tubular with spreading lobes in clusters 3 in. across. One of the most valuable midsummer flowering shrubs. All old flowering wood should be pruned out after flowering or in winter. China. **1668**, p. 209.

KOWHAI TREE see **Sophora tetraptera, 1904**, p. 238.

KUMQUAT see **Poncirus**

L

LABURNUM (LEGUMINOSAE)

anagyroides Common Laburnum ❋ Early Summer　　　T.
Small deciduous tree up to 20 ft spreading. *Fl.* deep yellow pea-like in large pendulous clusters.

×**vossii** ❋ Early Summer　　　T.
A hybrid of *L. alpinum*, the Scotch Laburnum, and *L. anagyroides*. Racemes longer than in Common Laburnum and narrower but probably the most valuable Laburnum to grow for most gardens. **1669**, p. 209.

LACE FLOWER, BLUE see **Didiscus caeruleus, 288**, p. 36.

LACHENALIA (LILIACEAE) Cape Cowslip

aloides, syn. **L. tricolor** ❋ Spring　　　GBb
Fl. tubular, 1 in. long, 10–20 in spike, yellow or red and green. *L.* broad, strap-shaped to 10 in. long, sometimes spotted purple. Normal potting compost. Pot bulbs beginning of 8, in frames and water sparingly until growth is well advanced. Bring under cover before frosts come. Winter temp. 45°F. Higher temps. undesirable. After flowering is complete, let bulbs ripen and foliage die down and keep dry during 6–7. Repot yearly. Propagation by offsets, or seed. S. Africa.

'Nelsonii' has clear yellow *fl.*, slightly tinged with green, **554**, p. 70.

tricolor see **L. aloides**

LADY TULIP see **Tulipa clusiana, 892**, p. 112.

LADY'S MANTLE see **Alchemilla, 956**, p. 120.

LAGERSTROEMIA (LYTHRACEAE)

indica Crape Myrtle ❋ Summer　　　*T.
Deciduous tree or shrub up to 30 ft. In most areas needs to be grown against a wall and given winter protection. *Fl.* deep pink in large clusters with crinkled petals. Grows and *fl.* freely in warmer states of USA after summer ripening, particularly in California, also valuable in other sub-tropical countries. China. **1670**, p. 209.

'Alba', has white *fl.*

LAGURUS (GRAMINEAE)

ovatus Hare's-tail Grass ❋ Summer　　　HA.
L. narrow, woolly. Plume-like heads are decorative in the garden and when cut and dried. 1–1½ ft. Sow in 4 in the open where they are to grow. W. Europe. **315**, p. 40.

LAMB'S TAIL see **Cotyledon oppositifolia, 41**, p. 6.

LAMB'S TONGUE see **Stachys lanata, 1386**, p. 174.

LAMIUM (LABIATAE) Dead Nettle

galeobdolon, syn. **Galeobdolon luteum** Yellow Archangel ❋ Early Summer　　　P.
Fl. yellow. *L.* slender-pointed, 1½ in. long. 6 in., of spreading habit suitable for the wild garden in partial shade. Plant 11–3. Europe.

'Variegatum', has silver and green *l.*, **1230**, p. 154.

maculatum Spotted Dead Nettle ❋ Late Spring–Midsummer　　　P.
Fl. pink-purple, hooded. *L.* heart-shaped with silver mottling. 9–12 in. For poorish soil and partial shade. May become invasive. Propagate by pieces of underground root transplanted in spring. Europe, including Britain.

Good forms include:

'Aureum', with golden *l.* not so vigorous as the type;

'Roseum', with shell-pink *fl.*, **1231**, p. 154.

LANTERN TREE, CHILEAN see **Crinodendron hookerianum, 1545**, p. 194.

LAPEYROUSIA (IRIDACEAE)

cruenta, syn. **Anomatheca cruenta** ❋ Summer *C.
Fl. crimson-scarlet with a darker blotch at base, star-like, several on a 1 ft stem. *L.* grasslike like those of a freesia but more slender. Corm small. Hardy only in warm gardens but has become naturalised spreading widely in gardens in the Isles of Scilly and on the Riviera. Otherwise suitable for pots in a cool greenhouse or the bulb frame but requires water in summer when it is in active growth. **793**, p. 100.

LARCH see **Larix, 2022, 2023**, p. 253.

LARGER PERIWINKLE see **Vinca major, 1951**, p. 244.

LARKSPUR see **Delphinium, 282**, p. 36; **1084-1091**, pp. 136, 137.

LARIX (PINACEAE) Larch

Tall deciduous trees up to 150 ft. Bark in young trees greyish but brown in older trees and fissured towards base. Needles arranged in whorls like those of the Cedar. Female cones erect up to 2 in. across brown when mature.

decidua, syn. **L. europaea** Common Larch　　　C.
Better known under syn. *L. europaea*. Deciduous tree up to 150 ft, dark brown on main trunk. Leaflets very bright yellow-green when first emerging then deeper green and turning good yellow in autumn before falling. Cones bright red when young becoming dark brown surrounded by short green needles, ovoid up to 1½ in. long and 1 in. wide, scales rounded. Excellent tree for forestry purposes and growing in arboreta, decorative when young from the feathery foliage particularly in spring. Often planted as forest tree and tolerant to a wide variety of conditions but unsuitable for planting in shade. **2022, 2023**, p. 253.

×**eurolepis** Dunkeld Larch　　　Co.
A hybrid between *L. kaempferi* × *L. decidua*. Is often grown as forest tree and is perhaps the most vigorous larch for forestry purposes, also being more free from attack by aphis and fungi.

europaea see **L. decidua**

japonica see **L. kaempferi**

kaempferi, syn. **L. leptolepis, L. japonica** Japanese Larch　　　Co.
Better known under syn. *L. leptolepis* or *L. japonica*. Distinguished from Common larch by more glau-

cous shoots in early spring and wider blue-green *l.* and somewhat broader cones, excellent as a forest tree.

leptolepis see **L. kaempferi**

LASIANDRA MACRANTHA see **Tibouchina semidecandra**

LATE DUTCH HONEYSUCKLE see **Lonicera periclymenum** 'Serotina'

LATHYRUS (LEGUMINOSAE)

odoratus Sweet Pea ❋ Summer　　　HA.
Fl. in a great range of colour, fragrant. *L.* in pairs, sharply pointed. 9 in.–8 ft, dwarf and climbing. Sow in 10 in a cold frame and plant out in deeply dug, rich soil in 3, or sow in the open 2–3. Sowing can also be done under glass in early spring, plants then hardened off and planted out in 4 or early 5 for late flowering. The sp. is a native of Sicily.

Leading varieties:

'Anne Vestey', scarlet, **316**, p. 40;

'John Ness', lavender, **317**, p. 40;

'Knee-hi, strain, new various colours; sow in the spring where they are to *fl.*, 2–2½ ft or 3–4 ft if staked, **318**;

'Leamington', dark lavender, **319**, p. 40;

'Little Sweethearts', 9 in., compact, bushy habit, mixed colours, useful for window boxes;

'Pink Pride', pale pink, white ground, **320**, p. 40;

'White Ensign', **321**, p. 41.

vernus, syn. **Orobus vernus** ❋ Late Spring–Early Summer　　　P.
Fl. variable shades of purple and blue, pea-like. *L.* in two or three pairs, lance-shaped, shiny. 1½–2 ft. Moist deep soil in sun. Europe. **1232**, p. 154.

LAUREL, COMMON see **Prunus laurocerasus**

LAUREL MAGNOLIA see **Magnolia grandiflora, 1684**, p. 211.

LAUREL, MOUNTAIN see **Kalmia latifolia, 1665, 1666**, p. 209.

LAUREL, PORTUGAL see **Prunus lusitanica**

LAURUSTINUS see **Viburnum tinus**, **1948**, p. 244.

LAVANDULA (LABIATAE) Lavender

spica English Lavender ❀ Summer   Sh.
Small evergreen shrub up to 4 ft with stems square and whitish-grey. *Fl.* dark mauve tubular in crowded spikes, very fragrant. Frequently grown as low hedge for which it should be pruned hard in early spring almost back to old wood. Mediterranean region.
One of the finest forms is:
    'Nana Atropurpurea', frequently known as 'Hidcote'. Very compact and free-flowering deep violet. Usually not more than 1½ ft high. Stems and foliage grey downy, **1671**, p. 209.

stoechas French Lavender ❀ Late Spring–Midsummer   *Sh.
Foliage light green. *Fl.* very dark purple in dense heads, usually not growing more than 1 ft. More tender than English Lavender and only suitable for mildest areas. S. Europe.

LAVATERA (MALVACEAE) Mallow

arborea Tree Mallow ❀ Summer   Sh.
Sub-shrubby plant often grown as biennial but reaching 10 ft high in favourable areas. *Fl.* pale rosy-purple up to 3 in. across in clusters at ends of small branches. *L.* hairy and large lobed. One of the most valuable plants for late summer flowering and does best in full sun. S. Europe. **1672**, p. 209.

olbia ❀ Summer–Mid Autumn   HP.
Fl. reddish-purple, hollyhock-like flowers. *L.* woolly, three-lobed, vine-like. 5–6 ft. Ordinary garden soil and in full sun. Not a long-lived plant. Propagate by half-ripe cuttings taken in 7 and inserted in sandy soil in a cold propagating frame, or by seed sown in spring and placed in a cool house. S. France.
    'Rosea', rosy-pink, a more pleasing shade than type, **1233**, p. 155.

trimestris ❀ Summer   HA.
Fl. rosy-pink, trumpet-shaped, also a white form. *L.* roundish, pale green. 2–4 ft. Sow in 3–4 where they are to *fl.* in a sunny position and ordinary garden soil. S. Europe.
    'Loveliness', deep rose;
    'Sunset', a deeper rose, **322**, p. 41.

LAVENDER see **Lavandula**, **1671**, p. 209.

LAVENDER COTTON see **Santolina**, **1899**, 238.

LAVENDER, ENGLISH see **Lavandula spica**, **1671**, p. 209.

LAVENDER, FRENCH see **Lavandula stoechas**

LAVENDER, SEA see **Limonium**, **326, 327**, p. 41.

LAWSON CYPRESS see **Chamaecyparis lawsoniana**, **2004-2008**, p. 251.

LAYIA (COMPOSITAE)

elegans Tidy Tips ❀ Summer   HA.
Fl. yellow, tipped white, daisy-like, 2 in. across, fragrant. There is also a white form. *L.* narrow lance-shaped, divided. 1–1½ ft. Sow in the open in 3–4, in a sunny position and a dryish soil. Useful for cutting. W. N. America. **323**, p. 41.

LEATHERWOOD see **Cyrilla racemiflora**

LENT LILY see **Narcissus pseudonarcissus**, **838**, p. 105.

LENTEN ROSE see **Helleborus orientalis**, **1166**, p. 146.

LEONTOPODIUM (COMPOSITAE)

alpinum Edelweiss ❀ Late Spring–Midsummer RP. 4–6 in. *Fl.* heads surrounded by silvery white flannelly bracts giving star-shaped appearance. *L.* narrow, linear, white in small tufts. Not difficult in sunny well-drained position in rock garden or alpine house and may be raised from seed. European Alps, although becoming rare in many areas owing to over-collection. **98**, p. 13.

sibiricum   RP.
Has larger *fl.* heads than *L. alpinum*. Russia.

LEOPARD LILY see **Lilium pardalinum**, **813**, p. 102.

LEPTOSIPHON × **hybridus** see **Gilia** × **hybrida**

LEPTOSPERMUM (MYRTACEAE)

cunninghamii ❀ Summer   *†Sh.
Silvery-leaved shrub up to 6 ft. More hardy than other sp. *Fl.* white in short spikes. Plant in sunny position preferably in shelter of wall in most areas. Australia, Tasmania. **1673**, p. 210.

scoparium Manuka, Tea-tree ❀ Early Summer *Sh.
Evergreen shrub or small tree up to 10 ft generally growing densely with erect branching. Does well in S.W. gardens otherwise treat as wall shrub. New Zealand.
Among finest forms are:
    'Keatleyi', with large *fl.* up to 1½ in. across pale pink with dark centre. Tender and in most areas only suitable as cool greenhouse plant where it has very long flowering season. *L.* small heather-like, **1674**, p. 210.
    'Nanum', 4–6 in. Dwarf semi-prostrate shrublet form of tall growing Manuka. *Fl.* white, five petalled with large disc-like centre, up to 1 in. across. *L.* small, heather-like. Slightly tender in cold situations and best given some protection in winter. Excellent in alpine house. Unsuitable for very dry or calcareous soils. New Zealand. **99**, p. 13.
    'Nicholsii', *fl.* deep rosy-crimson. *L.* purplish-green;
    'Red Damask', double deep red and very long lasting. Probably as hardy as 'Nicholsii'.

LEPTOSYNE (COMPOSITAE)

stillmanii ❀ Summer   HA.
Fl. bright yellow. *L.* long and narrow. 1–1½ ft. Sow in the open in 4–5, in a sunny position and a light sandy soil. Fast-growing and free-flowering. Some authorities refer this plant to *Coreopsis stillmanii*. California. **324**, p. 41.
    'Golden Rosette', a good double form.

LESSER PERIWINKLE see **Vinca minor**, **1420**, p. 178.

LEUCOGENES (COMPOSITAE)

grandiceps see **L. leontopodium**

leontopodium ❀ Summer   RP.
3–6 in. Forms mats of very silvery small rosettes, sub-shrubby. *Fl.* heads in a dense cluster on short stems, silvery white like a small everlasting, clusters up to 1 in. across. *L.* small, ovate, downy with short silvery hairs. One of the finest silver-leaved plants. Best in a scree or sink or alpine house. New Zealand mts. *L. grandiceps* is rather similar but smaller. **100**, p. 13.

LEUCOJUM (AMARYLLIDACEAE) Snowflakes
They are easily distinguished from *Galanthus*, the

Snowdrops, by the segments of the *fl.* which are all equal in size instead of having the three inner ones smaller than the three outer. All have white *fl.*

aestivum Summer Snowflake, Loddon Lily ❀ Spring   Bb
Despite name a spring *fl.* *Fl.* bell-like about ¾ in. deep and across, several at end of stem 1½–2 ft. *L.* numerous, strap-shaped and bright green, Usually there is a preponderance of *l.*, relative to *fl.* Grows most lushly in damp places. A native plant but local in Oxfordshire and Berkshire. Widely spread in Europe and into Asia Minor.
    'Gravetye', is the best form, **794**, p. 100.

autumnale Autumn Snowflake ❀ Autumn   Bb
Fl. white tinged with pink, small bells, 1–2 on delicate thin stems, 4–6 in. high. Appearing before *l.* which are very narrow and rush like. Best planted in a warm and sunny position. S.W. Europe, N. W. Africa. **795**, p. 100.

✿ **vernum** Spring Snowflake ❀ Early Spring   Bb
Fl. snowy white with green or greenish-yellow tip to petals as in var. *carpathicum*. Stems stout up to 8 in. with generally large bell or often two in var. *carpathicum* and var. *vagneri* which are slightly more vigorous than the type. One of the best of our early-flowering spring bulbs and increases freely in any moisture-retentive soil. European but probably naturalised rather than native in England.
    var. *carpathicum*, **796**, p. 100.

LEWISIA (PORTULACACEAE)
3–9 in. All Lewisias are best grown in vertical crevices between rocks or as alpine house plants and require good drainage being sensitive to damp around collar below rosette. W. N. America.

cotyledon ❀ Spring–Early Summer   RP.
Evergreen rosette plant with fleshy, slightly succulent *l.* *Fl.* pale pink, pink or magenta-pink or white with darker veins, rather variable in colour, opening flat up to 1 in. across, in small sprays on branching stems up to 9 in. Selected forms are often available with clearer colours and slightly larger *fl.* *L.* spathulate, slightly wavy at edge, lying flat. California. **101, 102**, p. 13.

howellii ❀ Early Summer   RP.
Fl. rose-pink or magenta-pink, rather star-like, up to ¾ in. across, in sprays on stems up to 8 in. *L.* fleshy,

oblong to ovate with crisped margins forming flat rosette. Oregon. **103**, p. 13.

tweedyi ✽ Spring–Early Summer   RP.
Fl. pale flesh pink and pale apricot in melting tones, large up to 2½ in. across, singly or in pairs on short stems up to 4 in., petals broader than in other sp. Very freely borne in a good clump. *L.* fleshy, obovate. The beauty of the genus and one of the most choice alpine plants. Usually grown in a deep pot as alpine house plant or in sunny crevice or position on rock garden well surfaced with chips. Washington State. **104**, p. 13.
    'Rosea', pink form.

LEYCESTERIA (CAPRIFOLIACEAE)

formosa Himalayan Honeysuckle ✽ Summer   Sh.
Deciduous shrub, sometimes known as Himalayan Honeysuckle although not resembling honeysuckle superficially. Up to 6 ft with smooth slightly glaucous erect shoots. *Fl.* white in drooping clusters, main feature however is large purplish bracts up to 1½ in. long. Fruit purplish berry generally scattered freely and many seedlings tend to appear throughout garden. *L.* ovate cordate at base up to 7 in. long, downy beneath. Old branches should be cut entirely out allowing younger shoots to ripen. In hard winters it may be cut to the ground but will usually shoot again. Valuable for its fresh green shoots and its free flowering and free seeding habits. Himalayas. **1675**, p. 210.

LIATRIS (COMPOSITAE)

callilepis Kansas Gayfeather ✽ Summer   P.
Fl. bright purple-rose in a closely packed spike. *L.* small, lance-shaped. 2–3 ft. A sunny position in poorish, light soil. Propagate by division of the basal buds in spring or by seed sown in the open in light soil 8–9. E. and S. USA. **1234**, p. 155.

spicata Blazing Star, Gayfeather ✽ Late Summer P.
Fl. reddish-purple, long-lasting. The buds open first at the top of the erect stem which is unusual for spiky plants. *L.* dark green, small, lance-shaped. 1½–2 ft. Does well on poorish, light soil and in full sun. Propagate by division of the curious basal buds in spring or by seed sown in the open in light soil in 8–9. E. and S. USA. **1235**, p. 155.
    'Alba', is a white form.

LIBOCEDRUS (CUPRESSACEAE)

decurrens Incense or Red Cedar   Co.
Tall evergreen rather fastigiate tree sometimes placed by modern authors in separate genus as *Kalocedrus decurrens*. Incense Cedar, sometimes also known as Red Cedar, name which also belongs to *Thuya plicata*. Tree up to 150 ft but usually much less in Britain, always narrow in girth and very erect shaped like large green pencil. In cultivated trees branches are short giving erect columnar outline, for this particularly valuable in gardens to contrast with horizontally branched shrubs. This effect particularly fine in autumn with Parrotias and Japanese Maples. *L.* dark green, decurrent about ½ in. long. Cones ovate, pendulous 1 in. long by ½ in. wide, yellowish or reddish-brown when ripe. W. America, Oregon. **2024**, p. 253.
Various forms have been grown such as:
    'Aureo-variegata', with yellow leaflets;
    'Columnaris', very narrow columnar form;
    'Glauca', with slightly glaucous hue.

LIGULARIA (COMPOSITAE)

dentata, syn. **L. clivorum, Senecio clivorum** ✽ Summer   P.
Fl. orange-yellow in large loose heads, 3–5 ft. *L.* kidney-shaped, coarsely toothed, lower *l.* about 18 in. across. Moist soil or by water in sun or light shade. Propagate by division in the spring. China, Japan. **1236**, p. 155.
Good varieties include:

    'Desdemona', orange, 4 ft;
    'Gregynog Gold', gold with bronze centre, 3 ft, **1237**, p. 155.

× hessei ✽ Summer   P.
Fl. rich orange in large heads, 4–6 ft. *L.* large, kidney-shaped, freely produced. Moist soil in sun or partial shade. A hybrid between *L. dentata* and *L. wilsoniae*. **1238**, p. 155.

hodgsonii ✽ Summer   P.
Fl. orange, 2 ft. *L.* dark green, broadly oval. Plant 11–3 in moist well-drained soil and sun. Propagate by division in the spring. **1239**, p. 155.

japonica, syn. **Senecio japonica** Giant Ragwort ✽ Late Summer   P.
Fl. orange-yellow on branching stems. *L.* 1 ft across, deeply lobed. 5 ft. Plant 11–3. Requires ample moisture, admirable beside a stream. Japan. **1240**, p. 155.

przewalskii see **Senecio przewalskii**

LIGUSTRUM (OLEACEAE) Privet

ovalifolium see **L. vulgare**

vulgare Common Privet ✽ Summer   Sh.,T.
Shrub or small tree up to 10 ft; usually deciduous but in mild areas semi-evergreen. *Fl.* dull white in erect panicles up to 2 in. long. *L.* narrowly oval, usually about 1½ in. long. Golden Privet with strong yellow colouring in *l.* is more valuable for bright effect and is variety of *L. ovalifolium* of Japan. Berries small, black.
Tolerant of dry conditions and wide range of soil. Once much used for hedges since quick growing and easily propagated from slips, but now largely replaced by more decorative plants. Privet roots spread widely and tend to rob soil around of moisture and nutrients to the detriment of other plants close by. N.E. Europe, including Britain.

LILAC see **Syringa, 1921-1926**, p. 241.

LILAC, CALIFORNIAN see **Ceanothus, 1499-1504**, p. 188.

LILAC, COMMON see **Syringa vulgaris, 1922-1926**, p. 241.

LILIES OF THE FIELD see **Sternbergia lutea, 884**, p. 111.

LILIUM (LILIACEAE)

A large genus containing some of the most beautiful bulbous plants that it is possible to grow. *Fl.* from 6–9 they present a great variety of both colour and form, from the regular trumpet shape to the turkscap in which the petals are recurved and the stamens and stigma project. Other *fl.* are bowl or star-shaped; some are borne horizontally, some are pendulous while a few are erect. The bulbs are made up of a number of bare scales without any covering or tunic as in the daffodil or tulip, consequently they must not be allowed to dry out at any time. Their requirements for cultivation are also varied but the one invariable requirement is good drainage. They will not survive in a water-logged soil. Where natural drainage is bad it is advisable to grow the lilies in raised beds, mixing the soil well with compost, leaf mould and very coarse sand, even ashes. Lilies can also be grown satisfactorily in pots and tubs. They are propagated by division in late summer or early autumn, by bulbils which in some kinds form up the stem, by the bulbils which grow on scales detached from the parent bulb and from seed. This section deals only with true lilies and numerous plants such as *Agapanthus, Ixia, Amaryllis* and *Zantedeschia* which have been incorrectly called lilies, will be found under their respective generic names.

'Allegra' see **L. × parkmannii**

✿**auratum** Golden-rayed lily of Japan, Goldband Lily ✽ Summer   †Bb
Often described as the Queen of Lilies. *Fl.* are large, trumpet or bowl-shaped with six to eight or even up to 30 to a stem and each *fl.* may be 8 in. across. The stems grow 5–8 ft. *Fl.* are variable white generally with a central golden or crimson ray to each petal and often heavily spotted with deep crimson or yellow, petals thick and waxy, strongly scented. *L.* narrow and scattered up the stem. *L. auratum* will grow in semi-shade or full sun; the large bulbs are stem rooting and should be planted about 6 in. deep. *L. auratum* crossed with *L. speciosum* has given us the great race of *parkmannii* hybrids, q.v., which grow so magnificently both in N. America and in Australia, New Zealand. **797**, p. 100.
Good varieties of *L. auratum* are:
    pictum, heavily spotted with crimson and with a broad deep yellow and crimson band to each petal;
    platyphyllum, with *l.* wider, often more vigorous and well worth growing;
    rubro-vittatum, heavily spotted and with deep crimson band;
    virginale, almost an albino form with pale yellow band and spots.

× aurelianense see **L. henryi**

Bellingham hybrids ✽ Summer   Bb
A large group of variable hybrid lilies of great vigour and among the easiest to grow, forming large clumps. *Fl.* stem up to 8 ft with 10 or more orange and red *fl.* to a stem, petals strongly recurved in Turks cap form. Derived from crosses between *L. humboldtii, L. pardalinum* and *L, parryi*. **798**, p. 100.
    'Shuksan', summer. One of the best of Bellingham hybrids. *Fl.* yellow, heavily spotted with crimson-maroon. Petals strongly recurved. A tall and vigorous grower often up to 6–7 ft. Semishade, **799**, p. 100.

✿**'Black Dragon'** ✽ Late Summer   Bb
One of the finest of the Oregon raised group of trumpet hybrid lilies. *Fl.* large open trumpet-shaped with thick waxy petals, white heavily flushed with deep maroon on outside, white inside with golden throat. Stems 3–6 ft. Resembles *L. brownii* one of the finest species lilies from China, but is generally regarded as much easier to grow satisfactorily. **800**, p. 100.

'Brocade' ❋ Summer Bb

A hybrid of the group called Marhan, derived from *L. hansonii* and *L. martagon* and one of the finest of this group. *Fl.* butter-yellow, petals slightly recurved and anthers bright orange-red. 3–5 ft. **801**, p. 101.

brownii see **L.** × **'Black Dragon'**

bulbiferum see **L.** × **hollandicum**

'Buttercup' see **L. pardalinum**

canadense ❋ Summer †Bb

One of the most beautiful lilies for its poise and grace, the *fl.* are 3–4 in. across, strong yellow and spotted with deep maroon towards centre, pendulous on long curving pedicels which give a candelabra effect. Stem 4–6 ft with one to many *fl.* to a head, *l.* in whorls. E. N. America including Canada and USA, widespread and variable. Forms with crimson *fl.* are also found. Not suitable for dry or limy position. In the wild it grows in very damp places near the edge of streams. **802**, p. 101.

✿**candidum** The Madonna Lily ❋ Summer Bb

Perhaps the best known and certainly one of the most beautiful of all lilies. *Fl.* white with golden stamens, erect or horizontal. The Madonna Lily should be grown in as warm and sunny a position as is available and should be planted shallowly in late 7 or 8 which is their only dormant season. Basal *l.* are produced in autumn. 3–5 ft high with *l.* up the stem. A rare native in N. Greece (Salonika) and probably also in Syria and Israel, but cultivated from ancient times. **803**, p. 101.

✿**'Cinnabar'** ❋ Summer Bb

One of the best of deep scarlet crimson hybrids with upright *fl.* Stem 2–3 ft with numerous *fl.* to a stem. Plant in full sun. This seems fairly persistent in English gardens. Raised in Oregon. **804**, p. 101.

'Destiny' ❋ Summer Bb

A most valuable hybrid since it has pale lemon-yellow erect *fl.*, heavily spotted towards base of petal. The petals are pointed and recurve gracefully. Full sun or very light semi-shade. This has proved quite a good garden plant and makes large groups in English gardens. Also raised in Oregon. **805**, p. 101.

Empress of China, of India and of Japan see **L.** × **parkmannii**

✿**'Enchantment'** ❋ Summer Bb

One of the most valuable and free-flowering hybrids yet raised with erect *fl.* Most brilliant orange-red. Plant in full sun. Easily propagated from bulbils. **806**, p. 101.

'Excelsior' see **L.** × **parkmannii**

giganteum see **Cardiocrinum giganteum**

Golden Clarion ❋ Summer Bb

A strain of trumpet lilies rich golden yellow inside and deep maroon flushed outside but variable in depth of yellow colouring and amount of maroon on outside. Plant in full sun among low bushes or in semi-shade. Raised in Oregon. **807**, p. 101.

'Sunburst' has been selected from this strain and is a very striking and strong growing lily with stems up to 6 ft.

hansonii Japanese Turks-cap Lily ❋ Summer Bb

Fl. of martagon type but with petals less strongly recurved. Star-shaped. Strong golden-yellow with thick waxy petals. Stems up to 5 ft with large heads of *fl.* This lily is a vigorous grower and clumps are often persistent over many years. Semi-shade such as glades in open woodland. Korea. See also *L.* 'Brocade'.

henryi ❋ Late Summer Bb

Fl. of turkscap type with strongly recurved petals. Bright orange. Petals have numerous small papillae (pimples) near base. A vigorous grower with stems up to 8 ft and numerous *fl.* to a stem, often two *fl.* on each pedicel. Does well on lime. This lily is one of the parents of the great race of *aurelianense* hybrids which have contributed so much to our gardens,

the other parent being *L. sargentiae* a trumpet lily resembling *L. regale*. China. **808**, p. 101.

× **hollandicum** ❋ Summer Bb

A large group of hybrid lilies with orange or red upright *fl.* thought to have arisen from *L. bulbiferum* the orange lily of the alps crossed with *L. maculatum*. They are often known in catalogues as *L. umbellatum*. Stem stout up to 2½ ft with chalice-shaped *fl.* in cluster at top. Rather susceptible to virus disease, but long in cultivation. Full sun or front of shrub border.

Some of finest clones are:

'Erectum', orange-red;

'Golden Fleece', deep yellow;

'Grandiflorum', deep mahogany-red, **809**, p. 102.

humboldtii see **L. Bellingham hybrids**

'Imperial Crimson', 'Imperial Silver' see **L.** × **parkmannii**

japonicum Sasa-yuri or Bamboo Lily ❋ Summer *†Bb

Fl. shell-pink, trumpet shaped, about 4 in. long by 3 in. across, one or two on a stem up to 2½ ft. One of the most beautiful pink trumpet lilies, slightly larger than *L. rubellum* in *fl.* but not so deep a pink. Slightly tender in cold situations, semi-shade in peaty slightly moist situations, often not long-lived. Japan. See also *L.* × *parkmannii.* **810**, p. 102.

'Jillian Wallace' see **L.** × **parkmannii**

✿'Limelight' ❋ Summer Bb

Open trumpet-shaped, pale lemon-yellow flushed with lime green on the outside. Raised in Oregon and one of most lovely of the trumpet hybrids. Plant in semi-shade for best effect. **811**, p. 102.

maculatum see **L.** × **hollandicum**

Marhan see **L. 'Brocade'**

martagon Martagon or Turks-cap Lily ❋ Summer Bb

Fl. variable in colour from light rosy-purple to deep mahogany maroon. Petals strongly recurved. Stem up to 6 ft with numerous pendulous *fl.* Buds downy. In some areas still frequent in subalpine woodlands. One of the best garden lilies even naturalising itself in some areas. Tolerant of chalk as are its hybrids. Plant in semi-shade. The turkscap lily of Northern Europe ranging from the Alps across to Siberia in the USSR. **812**, p. 102.

Varieties include:

✿ *album*, white form, one of the most beautiful lilies;

✿ *cattaniae*, with deep mahogany unspotted *fl.* glistening, the synonym *dalmaticum*, is a name often used for the dark mahogany form. Dalmatia and Balkans;

dalmaticum see var. *cattaniae*;

sanguineo-purpureum, mahogany-coloured form with dark golden-spotted *fl.*

The main hybrids are crosses with *L. hansonii* and many are a pleasant butter-yellow such as 'Brocade', q.v., or 'Sceptre'. Strains of mixed hybrids raised in America include 'Paisley' strain and these are reputed to be more vigorous than the older Backhouse hybrids.

'Paprika' ❋ Summer Bb

Fl. bowl-shaped, glowing scarlet, mahogany, a very brilliant colour, erect or horizontal. Rather a dwarf lily with stem rarely over 2 ft. Raised in Oregon.

monadelphum see **L. szovitsianum**

'Nobility' see **L.** × **parkmannii**

'Paisley' see **L. martagon**

pardalinum Leopard Lily ❋ Summer Bb

Fl. turkscap, orange flushed and spotted with red or maroon, pendulous. Stems tall up to 8 ft. One of the parents of the Bellingham hybrids and one of the easier sp. to grow. W. N. America where it grows in damp places and is unsuitable for dry places. **813**, p. 102.

Varieties include:–

giganteum, the Sunset Lily, is slightly larger than the type and with more brightly coloured *fl.*

'Buttercup', is a beautiful yellow, heavily spotted clone with star-shaped *fl.* only partly recurving and derived as to one parent from *L. pardalinum.*

✿ × **parkmannii** ❋ Summer †Bb

A very rich and variable race of hybrids between *L. auratum* forms and *L. speciosum* forms, q.v. *Fl.* large up to 8 in. across, white, bowl-shaped, generally heavily spotted with yellow or crimson on stems 3–7 ft. Some forms are deeply rayed with crimson or appear crimson almost all over. They do best in full sun or semi-shade in an acid or neutral soil and grow particularly well in W. N. American States and in Australia and New Zealand where the summer sun is warmer than in England but good results can be obtained in England also. **814**, p. 102.

Best strains raised in Oregon are:

'Imperial Crimson', deep crimson-red;

'Imperial Silver', white with light spotting;

'Nobility', very deep ruby-red all over.

Good clones are:

'Allegra', white with slightly recurving petals, thus resembling *L. speciosum* more than *L. auratum*, with green buds in centre, raised at Beltsville Research Station, Maryland;

'Empress of China', very large white *fl.* with crimson spotting, raised in Oregon;

'Empress of India', very large *fl.* up to 10 in. across, dark crimson-red, almost black in centre, outside of petals deep pink;

'Empress of Japan', very large *fl.*, white with golden ray in centre of petals and heavily spotted with deep crimson;

'Excelsior', large pink *fl.* with deeper crimson rays, tall and graceful grower, raised in New Zealand;

'Jillian Wallace', one of the earliest hybrids raised in Australia, *fl.* pale crimson with deeper central rays to petals, striking;

L. × *parkmannii* has also been crossed with *L. rubellum* and *L. japonicum* both pink-flowered species and with the latter has produced the very lovely ✿ Pink Glory strain in which the *fl.* are clear deep pink with some pale crimson spotting and rays. Not such a large *fl.* but a beautiful delicate colour. Open trumpet or bowl-shaped. Up to 5 ft with five or six *fl.* to stem, **815**, p. 102.

Abbreviations and Symbols used in the text.
The following abbreviations may sometimes be used in conjunction as HA. indicating Hardy annual or GBb indicating Greenhouse bulb.

A. = Annual	P. = Perennial
Aq. = Aquatic	R. = Rock or
B. = Biennial	Alpine plant
Bb = Bulb	Sh. = Shrub
C. = Corm	Sp., sp. = Species
Cl. = Climber	Syn. = Synonym
Co. = Conifer	T. = Tree
Fl., fl. = Flower(s)	Tu. = Tuber
G. = Greenhouse or house plant	var. = variety
	× = Hybrid or hybrid parents
H. = Hardy	
HH. = Half-hardy	❋ = Flowering time
L., l. = Leaf, leaves	❧ = Foliage plant
Mt(s) = Mount, mountain(s)	

The following have been used also in the descriptions of Alpines, Bulbs, Trees and Shrubs.

* = slightly tender

† = lime hater

✿ = highly recommended

The illustration numbers are in **bold type** and the page numbers in light type preceded by p.

parryi see **L. Bellingham hybrids**

Pink Glory see **L. × parkmannii**

pyrenaicum Yellow Turks-cap Lily ❋ Summer Bb
Fl. lemon-yellow with orange-red stamens, turks-cap lily with tightly recurved petals and numerous *fl.* of medium size on stem of 2–4 ft, with numerous scattered *l.* up stem. One of the easiest lilies to grow, and early-flowering. Sun or semi-shade. Scent is strong, rather acrid and disliked by some growers. Pyrenees but one of very few lilies which have been naturalised in England. **816**. p. 102.
    rubrum, with orange-red *fl.* rarely seen but a more vigorous and desirable plant than the type.

✿ **regale** ❋ Summer   Bb
Fl. white with yellow throat, trumpet-shaped, flushed maroon on outside, thick waxy petals. One of the easiest to grow and most valuable of all lilies. 3–5 ft with up to eight large trumpet *fl.* to a stem. Sun. Easily raised from seed and will usually *fl.* in second year. Lime tolerant. Introduced by Dr E. H. Wilson, from China, fifty years ago and now one of the most popular lilies. **817**, p. 103.

'Royal Gold' The Golden Regal ❋ Summer   Bb
Fl. strong yellow with maroon flush to outside, trumpet-shaped. Close in appearance to Golden Clarion strain. Larger *fl.* than *L. regale* from which it is said to have been derived. 4–5 ft. Plant in sun. Oregon raised. **818**, p. 103.

rubellum ❋ Summer   †Bb
Fl. deep pink, trumpet-shaped. Rather a dwarf lily, normally not more than 2½ ft, but one of the most beautiful and sometimes long-lasting when once established. Grows best in semi-shade in woodland or moist peaty soil. Intolerant of lime and unsuitable for hot dry places. Japan. See also *L. × parkmannii*. **819**, p. 103.

sargentiae see **L. henryi**

'Sunburst' see **L. 'Golden Clarion'**

'Sceptre' see **L. martagon**

'Shuksan' see **L. Bellingham hybrids**

speciosum ❋ Summer   †Bb
Fl. white or pink with crimson spots, petals thick and waxy with small papillae, strongly recurved, varying in amount of pink or crimson. Stem 3–5 ft with numerous *fl.* Close to *L. auratum* and requires similar conditions. Semi-shade. Intolerant of lime and does well in peaty or woodland soil, also in tubs flowering later than most other lilies. Japan, China. Good forms are:–
    'Album Novum', with white *fl.* slightly spotted with pale yellow;
    'Kraetzeri', *fl.* white slightly spotted with pale yellow;
    'Melpomene', **820**, p. 103;
    rubrum, with deep pink and crimson *fl.*;
    'Uchida', *fl.* deep pink and crimson.

szovitsianum ❋ Summer   Bb
Fl. deep yellow with thick waxy petals partly recurved. A very handsome lily with stem up to 5 ft and up to eight well spaced large pendant *fl.*, variable both in depth of colour and amount of spotting. This lily does well often on heavy clay soils and where there is lime. S. Caucasus, N.E. Turkey. Closely allied to *L. monadelphum* in which anthers are fused together in a tube. **821**, p. 103.

× **testaceum** Nankeen Lily ❋ Summer   Bb
The oldest lily hybrid which is still widely grown. *L. candidum*, the Madonna lily × *L. chalcedonicum* a scarlet-flowered lily from Greece. Stem up to 5 ft. *Fl.* apricot-yellow with orange red anthers, petals somewhat recurved and sometimes twisted. Tolerant of lime and should be grown in a sunny warm position, seems to like richer feeding than most other lilies and in a place in kitchen gardens it often does well. **822**, p. 103.

tigrinum The Tiger lily ❋ Summer   Bb
Fl. deep orange and heavily spotted, with petals recurved, a turks-cap lily and one of commonest but

forms without virus are rare and so it is better grown apart from other lilies. Stems up to 5 ft, dark and with bulbils up stem. Full sun, slightly intolerant of lime. China, Japan, Korea.
    splendens, the most vigorous form with darker *fl.* than type.

umbellatum see **L. × hollandicum**

LILY see **Lilium**

LILY, AFRICAN see **Agapanthus**, **953**, p. 120.

LILY, AMAZON see **Eucharis grandiflora**, **525**, p. 66.

LILY, ARUM see **Arum**, **411**, p. 52, **676**, p. 85; **Dracunculus**, **726**, p. 91; and **Zantedeschia**, **943** p. 118.

LILY, BAMBOO see **Lilium japonicum**, **810**, p. 102.

LILY, BLOOD see **Haemanthus**, **542**, p. 68.

LILY, DAY see **Hemerocallis**, **1167-1171**, pp. 147, 147.

LILY, GIANT HIMALAYAN see **Cardiocrinum**, **682**, p. 86.

LILY, GLORY see **Gloriosa**

LILY, GOLDBAND see **Lilium auratum**, **797**, p. 100.

LILY, GOLDEN RAYED OF JAPAN see **Lilium auratum**, **797**, p. 100.

LILY, GOLDEN REGAL see **Lilium** 'Royal Gold', **818**, p. 103.

LILY, GUERNSEY see **Nerine sarniensis**, **563**, **564**, p. 71.

LILY, JACOBEAN see **Sprekelia**, **883**, p. 111.

LILY, JAPANESE TURKS-CAP see **Lilium hansonii**.

LILY, KAFFIR see **Clivia**, **474**, p. 60 and **Schizostylis coccinea**, **876**, **877**, p. 110.

LILY, LENT see **Narcissus pseudonarcissus**, **838**, p. 105.

LILY, LEOPARD see **Lilium pardalinum**, **813**, p. 102.

LILY, LODDON see **Leucojum aestivum**, **794**, p. 100.

LILY, MADONNA see **Lilium candidum**, **803**, p. 101.

LILY, MARIPOSA see **Calochortus**, **679**, p. 85.

LILY, MARTAGON see **Lilium martagon**, **812**, p. 102.

LILY, NANKEEN see **Lilium × testaceum**, **822**, p. 103.

LILY OF THE NILE see **Zantedeschia aethiopica**, **943**, p. 118.

LILY OF THE PALACE see **Hippeastrum aulicum**, **549**, p. 69.

LILY, PERUVIAN see **Alstroemeria**, **957**, **958**, p. 120.

LILY, PLANTAIN see **Hosta**, **1175-1179**, pp. 147, 148.

LILY, ST BERNARD'S see **Anthericum liliago**, **971**, p. 122.

LILY, SASA YURI see **Lilium japonicum**, **810**, p. 102.

LILY, SCARBOROUGH see **Vallota speciosa**, **941**, p. 118.

LILY, SEA see **Pancratium maritimum**

LILY, SPIDER see **Hymenocallis**

LILY, SUNSET see **Lilium pardalinum** var. **giganteum**

LILY, TIGER see **Lilium tigrinum**

LILY, TOAD see **Tricyrtis**, **1402**, p. 176.

LILY TREE see **Magnolia denudata**, **1683**, p. 211.

LILY, TROUT see **Erythronium**, **731-732**, p. 92.

LILY, TURKS-CAP see **Lilium martagon**, **812**, p. 102.

LILY, TURKS-CAP, JAPANESE see **Lilium hansonii**

LILY, TURKS-CAP, YELLOW see **Lilium pyrenaicum**, **816**, p. 102.

LILY, WATER see **Nymphaea**, **1279-1286**, pp. 160, 161.

Abbreviations and Symbols used in the text.
The following abbreviations may sometimes be used in conjunction as HA. indicating Hardy annual or GBb indicating Greenhouse bulb.

A. = Annual	P. = Perennial
Aq. = Aquatic	R. = Rock or
B. = Biennial	Alpine plant
Bb = Bulb	Sh. = Shrub
C. = Corm	Sp., sp. = Species
Cl. = Climber	Syn. = Synonym
Co. = Conifer	T. = Tree
Fl., fl. = Flower(s)	Tu. = Tuber
G. = Greenhouse or	var. = variety
house plant	× = Hybrid or
H. = Hardy	hybrid parents
HH. = Half-hardy	❋ = Flowering time
L., l. = Leaf, leaves	➧ = Foliage plant
Mt(s) = Mount,	
mountain(s)	

The following have been used also in the descriptions of Alpines, Bulbs, Trees and Shrubs.

    * = slightly tender
    † = lime hater
    ✿ = highly recommended

The illustration numbers are in **bold type** and the page numbers in light type preceded by p.

LILY, YELLOW TURKS-CAP see **Lilium pyrenaicum, 816**, p. 102.

LIME see **Tilia, 1929**, p. 242.

LIMNANTHES (LIMNANTHACEAE)

douglasii Meadow Foam USA. ✳ Late Spring–Summer HA.
Fl. white, with a prominent yellow centre. L. yellowish-green, smooth, much divided. 6–12 in., of spreading habit. Sow in 3–4 or in 9, where it is to fl. in a sunny position and in almost any soil. A useful edging plant. California. **325**, p. 41.

LIMONIA TRIFOLIATA see Poncirus trifoliata

LIMONIUM (PLUMBAGINACEAE) Sea Lavender, Statice

sinuatum, syn. **Statice sinuata** ✳ Late Summer–Autumn HHA.
Fl. blue and white. Separate shades of pink, lavender and deep blue are obtainable in the large-flowered hybrids. L. 6–8 in. long with deeply waved margins. Biennial, but usually treated as half-hardy annual. 1–2 ft. Sow under glass in 2–3 and plant out in a sunny border in mid-5 in well-drained soil. Mediterranean region.
'Art Shades', includes many pastel shades, 1½ ft;
'Pacific Giants', is a colourful mixture excellent for cutting and drying, 1½ ft, **326**, p. 41.

suworowii, syn. **Statice suworowii** ✳ Summer–Autumn HHA.
Fl. rose-pink, in dense spikes. L. up to 10 in. long, wavy margin. 1½ ft. Similar treatment as for L. sinuatum. Turkestan. **327**, p. 41.

LINARIA (SCROPHULARIACEAE) Toadflax

maroccana ✳ Summer HA.
Fl. violet-purple with yellow markings, like miniature snapdragons. L. long and narrow, in whorls. 9–15 in. Sow thinly in 3–4, preferably in light soil and a sunny position where they are to fl. Hybrids are available in separate colours and there are good mixed strains in shades of carmine, crimson, orange, purple, also white. Morocco. **328**, p. 41.
'Excelsior Hybrids', bright colours, 12–15 in.;
'Fairy Bouquet', large fl. in mixed colours, 9 in.

purpurea Purple Toadflax ✳ Summer P.
Fl. bluish-purple, on a slender erect spike. 2½–3 ft. L. blue-green, narrow. Ordinary garden soil, preferably light, and in sun. Propagate by seed, basal cuttings in spring in sandy soil in a cold frame or by division in spring. S. Europe.
'Canon Went', pink with a shade of orange, 2½ ft, **1241**, p. 156.

LINDEN see **Tilia, 1929**, p. 242.

LINDERA (LAURACEAE)

triloba ✳ Early Spring Sh.
Deciduous shrub up to 10 ft. Fl. small, yellowish, inconspicuous, unisexual. L. large obovate tri-lobed at the end, bright green in summer turning deep butter-yellow in autumn. One of the best of the yellow autumn colouring shrubs although still rarely seen in gardens. Japan. **1676**, p. 210.

LING see **Calluna, 1474-1478**, p. 185.

LINUM (LINACEAE) Flax

arboreum ✳ Early Summer RP.
Up to 1 ft. Small sub-shrubby plant, freely branching. Fl. creamy-yellow or bright yellow up to 1 in. across, in small clusters on short stems, opening flat with wide petals. L. narrow, slightly recurved,

Sunny position in rock garden or alpine house. Tender in cold areas. E. Mediterranean, Crete.

elegans, syn. **L. iberidifolium** ✳ Late Spring RP.
Up to 8 in. Small shrublet. Fl. deep golden yellow with broad petals 1¼ in. across, numerous often covering plant. L. spathulate, slightly glaucous. A beautiful plant for alpine house or very warm sunny position on rock garden, needs good drainage. **106**, p. 14.
'Gemmell's Hybrid', is probably a hybrid of L. elegans and L. campanulatum, more dwarf with deeper yellow fl., **105**, p. 14.

grandiflorum ✳ Summer HA.
Fl. red, freely produced in loose panicles. L. narrow, lance-shaped. 1–1½ ft. Sow in the open in 3–4 where they are to fl., in a sunny position. N. Africa.
Outstanding forms include:
'Album', white, crimson centre;
'Roseum', deep pink;
'Rubrum', brilliant scarlet, **329**, p. 42.

iberidifolium see **L. elegans**

narbonense ✳ Summer P.
Fl. clear blue, in panicles on slender, erect stems. L. small, narrow and upstanding. 1½ ft. A light well-drained soil and full sun. Propagate by seed sown in the open in spring or in a cold frame, or division of the roots is sometimes possible in spring. S. Europe. **1242**, p. 156.

LIQUIDAMBAR (HAMAMELIDACEAE)

styraciflua Sweet Gum ☙ T.
Large tree up to 50 ft or more in native country, usually with erect rather pyramidal head. Branchlets as they become older forming corky wings. Fl. inconspicuous. L. maple-like usually with five or seven lobes up to 7 in. across, heart-shaped at base, turning brilliant scarlet or deep crimson in autumn. Unsuitable for very hot or dry situations but in damper ground one of the finest autumn colouring trees. There is a particularly brilliant colouring one at Wisley in the seven acres area.
It is distinguished from true Maple by the arrangement of the l. which is alternate while in Maples the l. are opposite. E. USA. **1677**, p. 210.

LIRIODENDRON (MAGNOLIACEAE)

tulipifera Tulip Tree ✳ Summer T.
Tall tree up to 100 ft. Fl. greenish-white with rather conspicuous orange coloured spot at base, bell-like or tulip-like with petals overlapping. L. large up to 8 in. long and as much in width. Distinguished by broad apex which is cut off almost squarely or occasionally with a shallow notch, turning brilliant butter-yellow in autumn and for this purpose one of the finest autumn colouring large trees. Only suitable for good soils where it will respond quickly to heavy feeding. Should be transplanted early. E. N. America. **1678**, p. 210.

LITHOPS (AIZOACEAE)

Living Stones ☙ GP.
Plants only a few inches high. Fl. inconspicuous. L. very fleshy, resembling pebbles. Very well-drained gritty compost required and the surface is usually covered with pebbles or coarse grit. No water at all should be given from 4 until growth is observed re-starting and very little at other periods. A very sunny position is necessary. Winter temp. 40–50°F. Propagation by seed, occasionally division is possible. S. Africa. **555**, p. 70.
Good sp. include L. lesliei, brown; L. marmorata, grey-green with grey markings; L. olivacea, olive green with darker markings; L. optica var. rubra, with opalescent tips to the plant body, and L. salicola, brown.

LITHOSPERMUM (BORAGINACEAE)

diffusum ✳ Late Spring–Midsummer †RSh.
Mat-forming shrublet, 6 in.; when growing well it

will cover large areas of rock or hang down in an open stone wall. Fl. bright gentian blue, star-shaped up to ½ in. across, with basal tube slightly striped with reddish-violet. L. narrow, hispid, hairy. One of the finest rock garden plants for its strong blue colour but unsuitable for limy areas. Best grown with some peat in soil in sunny position. Propagate by cuttings in late summer. S. Europe.
Best forms are:
'Grace Ward', **107**, p. 14.
'Heavenly Blue'.

intermedium see **Moltkia × intermedia**

oleifolium ✳ Late Spring–Midsummer *RSh.
Dwarf prostrate shrublet. Fl. pale china-blue with deeper base, more tubular than sp. above, up to ½ in. across in clusters on short stems up to 4 in., sometimes variable in colour with some violet-pink in blue. L. oblong, grey, silky beneath. Usually grown as a scree plant or in alpine house. Requires sunny position and very good drainage, and does well with lime in soil. Propagate by cuttings in late summer. Pyrenees. **108**, p. 14.

LIVING STONES see **Lithops, 555**, p. 70.

LOBELIA (CAMPANULACEAE)

erinus ✳ Summer HHA.
Fl. light blue with white or yellowish throat. L. narrow lance-shaped, toothed. 6 in., of trailing habit. Sow thinly in pans in a warm greenhouse in 2–3 and plant out in late 5. S. Africa.
Good forms include:
'Cambridge Blue', light blue, compact, 6 in., **330**, p. 42;
'Crystal Palace', dark blue, dark l., 6 in.;
'Mrs Clibran Improved', brilliant blue, striking white eye, compact 6 in., **331**, p. 42;
'Pendula Blue Cascade', light blue, trailing, excellent for hanging baskets or window boxes;
'Pendula Sapphire', dark blue, white eye, trailing;
'Rosamund', carmine-red with white eye, compact 6 in., **332**, p. 42.

fulgens Cardinal Flower ✳ Summer P.
Fl. brilliant scarlet. L. lance-shaped, toothed. Plant 5–6 in a peaty, moist soil and full sun. 1–3 ft. Not reliably hardy, requiring protection in winter from excess wet and frost. Propagate by division or soft

cuttings in the spring, or by seed sown in 2 in a warm greenhouse. Mexico. **1234**, p. 156.
   'Bees' Flame', intense scarlet;
   'The Bishop', velvety scarlet, bronze foliage.

LOBSTER CLAW see **Clianthus puniceus, 1974,** p. 247.

LOBULARIA MARITIMA see **Alyssum maritimum**

LOCUST see **Robinia pseudoacacia**

LOCUST, HONEY see **Gleditschia triacanthos**

LOCUST, MORAINE see **Gleditschia triacanthos 'Moraine'**

LOMATIA (PROTEACEAE)

ferruginea ❀ Midsummer   *†Sh.
   More tender than *L. longifolia* but useful as a shrub for wind-breaks in milder districts of the S.W. and W. with large pinnate *l.* making evergreen shrub up to 15 or 20 ft. Chile, Patagonia.

longifolia ❀ Midsummer   *†Sh.
   Evergreen shrub up to 6 ft. *Fl.* pale creamy-yellow in clusters, long tubular and shaped like those of a *Grevillea. L.* very narrow linear up to 4 in. long. Australia, New South Wales, Victoria. **1679**, p. 210.

LOMBARDY POPLAR see **Populus nigra** var. **italica**

LONICERA (CAPRIFOLIACEAE) Honeysuckle

× **americana** ❀ Summer   Cl.
   Vigorous deciduous climber. *Fl.* creamy-white with pink colour in bud and on outside of tube in large clusters up to 3 in. across, fragrant. *L.* broad, pointed at tip. Very vigorous climber but may be pruned after flowering or in winter, cutting out old flowering shoots. A hybrid from *L. caprifolium* × *L. etrusca.* **1980**, p. 248.

× **brownii** Scarlet Trumpet Honeysuckle ❀ Summer   *Cl.
   Semi-evergreen climber with less vigour than previous. *Fl.* orange-scarlet long tubular in large clusters. A hybrid of *L. sempervirens* × *L. hirsuta.*
   'Fuchsioides', is close to type but with slightly larger *fl. L.* broad perfoliate slightly glaucous. Succeeds as a wall climber in warmer areas of England and in other milder areas, **1981**, p. 248.

fragrantissima see **L.** × **purpusii**

nitida 🍂   Sh.
   Evergreen shrub with neat small *l.* frequently used for hedging since it grows vigorously and stands clipping well, making dense compact hedge. *Fl.* creamy-white, small but usually not noticeable in hedges. Stands wind well. Quite hardy. W. China.

periclymenum Woodbine ❀ Summer   Cl.
   Fl. creamy-white with pink or crimson buds or tube in large clusters, strongly scented. Britain. **1982**, p. 248.
   Best forms are:
   'Belgica', Early Dutch Honeysuckle, *fl.* 5–6 and often again in 8–9;
   'Serotina', Late Dutch Honeysuckle, *fl.* 7–10 deeper red colour in buds and tube.

× **purpusii** ❀ Late Winter   Sh.
   Deciduous shrub up to 8 ft. *L.* oval up to 3 in long, usually less. *Fl.* creamy-white, fragrant. Grown for winter *fl.* but rarely makes much effect in garden nor do its parents *L. fragrantissima* China and *L. standishii* China.

sempervirens ❀ Summer   *Cl.
   Fl. scarlet tubular, pendulous in clusters up to 3 in. long, tubes very narrow with small lobes. *L.* slightly glaucous perfoliate. Usually grown as a wall climber in milder areas only and needs warm position, S.E. USA. **1983**, p. 248.

standishii see **L.** × **purpusii**

syringantha ❀ Early Summer   Sh.
   Deciduous shrub up to 6 ft, habit spreading. *Fl.* small, pale lilac, distinguished for very strong scent. China.

tragophylla ❀ Summer   Cl.
   Very vigorous, deciduous climber. *Fl.* deep yellow up to 4 in. long, tubular in large clusters but scentless. Grows well over evergreen trees in semi-shade. *L.* large up to 4 in. long. Tender in very cold situations but otherwise sufficiently hardy for English gardens. China.

LOOSESTRIFE see **Lysimachia, 109**, p. 14; **1256, 1257**, pp. 157. 158.

LOOSESTRIFE, PURPLE see **Lythrum salicaria, 1258**, p. 158.

LOQUAT see **Eriobotrya japonica, 1591**, p. 199.

LOTUS (LEGUMINOSAE)

corniculatus Bird's-foot Trefoil, Bacon and Eggs ❀ Late Spring–Summer   P.
   Fl. bright yellow, becoming orange. *L.* short-stalked, divided into three ovate leaflets. Procumbent. Plant 11–3 in ordinary soil and sun. Propagate by seed or division. Europe, including Britain. **1244**, p. 156.
   'Pleniflorus' is a good double gold and copper form.

LOTUS, EGYPTIAN see **Nymphaea lotus, 569**, p. 72.

LOVE-IN-A-MIST see **Nigella, 352, 353**, pp. 44, 45.

LOVE-LIES-BLEEDING see **Amaranthus caudatus, 232**, p. 29.

LUNARIA (CRUCIFERAE) Honesty

annua, syn. **L. biennis** Honesty ❀ Late Spring–Midsummer   HB.
   Fl. violet-lilac to purple, also white. *L.* heart-shaped. There is also a form with a variegated *l.* The empty silvery seed heads are useful for winter decorations. 1½–2 ft. Sow in the open in 5 where it is to *fl.* in light shade. Sweden. **333**, p. 42.

biennis see **L. annua**

rediviva ❀ Late Spring–Early Summer   P.
   Fl. deep mauve, fragrant. *L.* deep green, entire. 3 ft. Plant 11–3, in ordinary well-drained soil and partial shade. Silvery transparent pods are useful as 'everlastings'. Propagate by division or by seed. Europe. **1245**, p. 156.

LUPINE see **Lupinus, 334**, p. 42; **1246-1248**, p. 156.

LUPINUS (LEGUMINOSAE) Lupine or Lupin

hartwegii ❀ Summer   HA.
   Fl. blue, marked white. *L.* long-stalked, hairy. 1–3 ft. Sow in 4–5 in ordinary garden soil where they are to *fl.* Mexico. **334**, p. 42.
   There are several forms:
   'Albus', white, 3 ft;
   'Giant King', dark blue, 3 ft;
   'Tom Thumb', mixed, 1–1½ ft.

polyphyllus ❀ Late Spring–Early Summer   P.
   Fl. deep blue, purple, yellow. 2½–4 ft. Plant 11–2

in light sandy soil, sun or light shade. Propagate by seed sown in the open in 4–5, or named varieties by cuttings taken in 4 with a heel, inserted in sunny soil in a cold frame. N. America. **1246**, p. 156.
Russell and other hybrid lupines are available in a wonderful range of colours but need propagation about every third year as they are not long lived. Good varieties include:
   'Freedom', lavender-blue with white standards, 4 ft, **1247**, p. 156;
   'George Russell', coral pink with cream standards edged pink, 4 ft;
   'Harlequin', deep pink with gold standards, 4 ft, **1248**, p. 156;
   'Josephine', slaty-blue and yellow, 4 ft.

LYCHNIS (CARYOPHYLLACEAE) Campion

chalcedonica Maltese Cross ❀ Summer   P.
   Fl. brilliant scarlet usually but there are white and pink forms, in flat clusters. *L.* ovate, coarsely toothed. 2–3 ft. Plant 11–3 in well-drained soil. Propagate by division or seed sown in the open in 3–4 where they are to *fl.* S. Russia. **1249**, p. 157.

coeli-rosa var. **oculata,** syn. **Viscaria oculata** ❀ Summer–Mid Autumn   HA.
   Fl. lavender, pale blue, pink, carmine and white, 1 in. across. *L.* narrowly oblong, opposite. 6–12 in. Sow in 3–4 in the open in ordinary garden soil in a sunny position. Of hybrid origin. Now considered by some authorities to be *Silene oculata.* **335**, p. 42.
   Named varieties include:
   'Blue Pearl', lavender-blue, 1 ft;
   'Fire King', bright scarlet, 1 ft;
   'Rose Beauty', deep pink, 1 ft;
   'Tom Thumb', dwarf mixed, 6 in.

coronaria Rose Campion ❀ Summer   P.
   Fl. vivid cerise. *L.* oblong, softly woolly, whitish, as are the stems 1½–2 ft. Ordinary well-drained garden soil and sun. Propagate by division in the spring. S. Europe. **1250**, p. 157.
   Good varieties include:
   'Alba', white, 2 ft;
   'Abbotswood Rose', vivid pink, 1½ ft.

flos-jovis Flower of Jove ❀ Summer   P.
   Fl. purple or scarlet, about an inch across. *L.* and stem grey woolly. 1–2 ft. Easily grown in ordinary well-drained soil. Propagate by division in spring or by seed sown in the open. Central Alps. **1251**, p. 157.

Abbreviations and Symbols used in the text.
The following abbreviations may sometimes be used in conjunction as HA. indicating Hardy annual or GBb indicating Greenhouse bulb.

A. = Annual	P. = Perennial
Aq. = Aquatic	R. = Rock or
B. = Biennial	Alpine plant
Bb = Bulb	Sh. = Shrub
C. = Corm	Sp., sp. = Species
Cl. = Climber	Syn. = Synonym
Co. = Conifer	T. = Tree
Fl., fl. = Flower(s)	Tu. = Tuber
G. = Greenhouse or	var. = variety
house plant	× = Hybrid or
H. = Hardy	hybrid parents
HH. = Half-hardy	❀ = Flowering time
L., l. = Leaf, leaves	🍂 = Foliage plant
Mt(s) = Mount,	
mountain(s)	

The following have been used also in the descriptions of Alpines, Bulbs, Trees and Shrubs.

   * = slightly tender
   † = lime hater
   ✿ = highly recommended

The illustration numbers are in **bold type** and the page numbers in light type preceded by p.

Good varieties include:
'Alba', white, 1½ ft;
'Hort's Variety', clear pink, 1 ft.

× **haageana** ❋ Summer   P.
A hybrid of *L. fulgens* × *L. coronata*, producing scarlet, orange-red and salmon shades. *L.* ovate, slightly hairy. 1 ft. Plant 3–4 in well-drained sandy soil in sun or light shade. Propagate by seed or division. **1252**, p. 157.

viscaria, syn. **Viscaria vulgaris** Catchfly ❋ Summer   P.
Fl. rosy-red, on branching stems. *L.* grassy, up to 3 in. long. Stem glutinous, hence the common name. 1½ ft. Propagate by seed sown in the open in spring or by division in spring or early autumn. Europe.
'Splendens Plena', double, carmine-pink, 15 in., **1253**, p. 157.

LYSICHITUM (ARACEAE)

americanum ❋ Spring   P.
Fl. yellow with an unpleasant odour, 1–1½ ft. *L.* 2–3 ft long, develop after the *fl.* Plant in 2–3 by the waterside or in the bog garden, in sun or partial shade. Propagate by division in early spring or by seed. W. N. America. **1254**, p. 157.

camtschatcense ❋ Spring   P.
Fl. white, erect, arum-like spathe 4–6 in. long, unpleasant odour, 18 in. *L.* glaucous-green, blunt-tipped, develop after the *fl.*, up to 3 ft long in summer. For the waterside or bog garden in sun or light shade. Propagate by division of the rhizome in early spring. Japan. **1255**, p. 157.

LYSIMACHIA (PRIMULACEAE) Loosestrife

ephemerum ❋ Summer   P.
Fl. erect slender plumes of white tinged purple. *L.* lanceolate, opposite. 3 ft. Plant 11–3 in moist soil, sun or partial shade. Propagate by division in spring. S.W. Europe. **1256**, p. 157.

nummularia Creeping Jenny ❋ Summer   RP.
2 in. Herb with long trailing stems which may grow several ft. *Fl.* deep yellow, cup-shaped, up to ¾ in. across, numerous, erect on creeping stems. *L.* roundish with short stalks, deep green. Valuable for covering large areas as ground cover plant but too invasive for planting with choice alpines on small rock garden. Will grow in either sun or semi-shade. N. Europe including Britain. **109**, p. 14.

punctata ❋ Summer   P.
Fl. bright yellow, in whorls on erect stems. *L.* oval, pointed 1½–2½ ft. Moist soil in partial shade or sun. Propagate by division in the spring or by seed sown in the open or in a cold frame. Asia Minor. **1257**, p. 158.

LYTHRUM (LYTHRACEAE)

salicaria Purple Loosestrife ❋ Summer   P.
Fl. red-purple borne on erect stems. *L.* lance-shaped, opposite or in whorls. 2½–3 ft. Likes a moist, heavyish soil and partial shade. Attractive beside a pool or stream. There are numerous named varieties in shades of pink to bright rose which are preferable to the type plant. Propagate by cuttings or division in spring. N. Hemisphere, including Britain, also Australia.
Good varieties include:
'Brightness', deep rose, 2½ ft;
'Robert', clear pink, 2 ft;
'The Beacon', bright rose-crimson, 2½ ft, **1258**, p. 158.

virgatum ❋ Summer   P.
Fl. purple borne in slender, graceful spikes. *L.* dark lance-shaped, narrow at the base. 1½–2 ft. Similar treatment as for *L. salicaria*. Taurus.
Good varieties include:
'Dropmore Purple', rosy-purple, 2½ ft;
'Rose Queen', bright rose-red, 1½–2 ft, **1259**, p. 158.

M

MACLEAYA, syn. BOCCONIA (PAPAVERACEAE)
Plume Poppy

cordata ❋ Summer   P.
Fl. white, without petals, in feathery panicles, 6–8 ft. *L.* large, green, white beneath, roundish, deeply veined and lobed. Plant 11–3 in a moist, deep soil in sun or partial shade. Propagate by root cuttings or careful division in the spring. China, Japan. **1260**, p. 158.

microcarpa ❋ Summer   P.
Fl. bronze-yellow, pink buds, borne erect in plume-like panicles, 6–8 ft. *L.* large, prominently veined. Cultivate and propagate as for *M. cordata*. China. **1261**, p. 158.

MADAGASCAR JASMINE see **Stephanotis floribunda**, **651**, p. 82.

MADEIRAN BROOM see **Genista virgata**

MADRONA see **Arbutus menziesii**, **1449**, p. 182.

MAGNOLIA (MAGNOLIACEAE)

campbellii ❋ Spring   T.
One of the most magnificent trees that can be grown in British gardens. Deciduous, up to 60 ft and spreading widely. *Fl.* very large up to 10 in. across; deep pink-crimson outside, white or pale blush-pink inside when open, shaped like a large chalice and freely borne on old trees. *Fl.* tender to frost after the outer coverings have been shed. Unsuitable for very dry areas and probably prefers lime free districts and should be given sheltered position if possible.
Unfortunately this magnificent tree does not *fl.* until it has reached the size of at least 15 or 20 ft after 10–20 years growth. Himalayas. **1680**, p. 210.
   'Alba', fine, large white *fl.*, **1681**, p. 211.
Close is sub-species *mollicomata* from S.E. Tibet, Yunnan and E. Himalayas. *Fl.* of this are slightly less clear in their pink or crimson colouring but tend to be produced on younger plants.
   ✿'Charles Raffill', is a valuable hybrid between these two, flowering younger than either parent. *Fl.* deep pink white inside up to 8 in. across. **1682**, p. 211.

conspicua see **M. denudata**

delavayi ❋ Summer   *T.
Large evergreen tree usually grown against a wall except in milder countries. *Fl.* creamy-white 6–7 in. across. *L.* leathery, very large up to 1 ft in length and 8 in. across. One of the finest evergreen trees that can be grown in Britain. *L.* tend to mask *fl.* Also grows well on chalk. China.

✿ **denudata**, syn. **M. conspicua** Yulan or Lily Tree ❋ Mid Spring   T.
Deciduous tree up to 30 ft usually widespreading. *Fl.* white cup-shaped, smaller than those of *M. campbellii* but up to 4 or 5 in. across when open, freely borne on young trees. One of the most beautiful flowering shrubs and trees for British gardens and quite hardy. China. **1683**, p. 211.

grandiflora Laurel Magnolia ❋ Summer   T.
Evergreen tree often grown as a wall shrub where it flowers more freely especially in warm areas but when seen as a free standing tree is much finer. Hardy in most districts but occasionally cut by very severe winter. *Fl.* very large up to 10 in. across, very fragrant opening to show large boss of golden stamens. *L.* rusty underneath. E. USA., where known as Laurel Magnolia. **1684**, p. 211.
Best varieties are:–
   'Exmouth', tends to *fl.* at a younger age;
   'Goliath', very large *fl.* also produced comparatively early age.

halliana see **M. stellata**

× **highdownensis** ❋ Summer   T.
A supposed hybrid between *M. sinensis* and *M. wilsonii* and slightly more vigorous than either parent. Deciduous large shrub or small tree up to 15 ft. *Fl.* white pendulous with broad overlapping petals and central boss of crimson stamens, borne with the *l.* *L.* broad with slightly pointed apex. Should be planted where one can look up at *fl.* *M. sinensis* is distinguished by broader *l.* without conspicuous apex or point, *M. wilsonii* has narrower *l.* with pointed apex and *fl.* earlier than *M. sinensis*. Both from China. **1685**, p. 211.

hypoleuca see **M. obovata**

✿ × **loebneri** ❋ Spring   Sh.,T.
A hybrid between *M. stellata* × *M. kobus* and probably preferable to either parent. *Fl.* white up to 4 in. across with numerous petals slightly waxy produced on bare twigs. Quick growing shrub or small tree up to 20 ft.
   'Merrill', is probably best form, **1686**, p. 211.

mollicomata see under **M. campbellii**

obovata, syn. **M. hypoleuca** ❋ Early Summer   T.
Tall deciduous tree up to 50 ft. *Fl.* creamy-white up to 8 in. across and fragrant, in centre is ring of crimson stamens. *L.* very large obovate up to 1 ft long and 6 in. across. Fruits large, pendulous, bright crimson 10–11. This makes it valuable dual purpose tree. **1687**, p. 211.

parviflora see **M. sieboldii**

✿ **sargentiana** var. **robusta** ❋ Spring   T.
Tall spreading deciduous tree up to 50 ft. *Fl.* rosy-crimson or purplish-crimson outside, paler within, up to 1 ft across, produced so that they are placed horizontally or facing downwards, thus should be planted where one can look up at the *fl.* One of the most magnificent of the Yulan section. *Fl.* slightly younger than *M. campbellii* and is fast growing in suitable soils. Hardy but *fl.* and buds are tender to late frosts after the outer coverings have been shed. W. China.

salicifolia ❋ Spring   Sh.,T.
Deciduous tree up to 30 ft or large shrub flowering early on bare branches. *Fl.* white or creamy-white, up to 4 in. across, with six petals, wide-spreading, sometimes covering tree like a white cloud. Young branchlets slender and when broken giving a lemon

scent. *L.* narrow, willow-like. Usually this magnolia does not *fl.* when young but it is well worth waiting for its maturity. One of the finest spring-flowering trees, close to *M. kobus* and *M.* × *loebneri* but usually making a more graceful and slender tree. Japan. **1688**, p. 211.

sieboldii, syn. **M. parviflora** ✺ Late Spring–Summer   Sh.
Deciduous spreading shrub up to 10 ft. *Fl.* white, waxy, borne horizontally or pendulous with boss of crimson stamens in centre, fragrant, cup-shaped. *Fl.* intermittently over several weeks. Japan. **1689**, p. 212.

sinensis see in **M.** × **highdownensis**

× **soulangeana** ✺ Spring   Sh.,T.
A hybrid between *M. denudata* × *M. liliflora.* Deciduous shrub or widespreading tree. *Fl.* white stained purple at base, erect very freely borne, cup-shaped but narrower in bud. Probably the most common Magnolia in general cultivation and quite hardy. Should be planted in open site. **1690**, p. 212.
Among best named sorts are:
✡'Alba', also known as 'Alba Superba', *fl.* white with very little rosy colouring at base sometimes none, slightly larger than type and more globular in *fl.*, **1691**, p. 212;
'Alexandrina', close to type with crimson-purple flush towards base. A rather compact dense shrub, **1692**, p. 212;
'Lennei', *fl.* large, globular, rosy-purple outside and white inside, slightly later than type and often appearing with young *l.*;
✿ 'Rustica Rubra', *fl.* chalice-shaped, rosy-crimson outside, large, **1693**, p. 212.

stellata, syn. **M. halliana** ✺ Spring   T.
Deciduous shrub or small spreading tree rather slow growing when young. *Fl.* white with numerous petals opening wide and slightly star-shaped, slightly fragrant. Should be planted in open situation but if possible shielded from late spring frosts which may destroy *fl.* otherwise quite hardy. Japan.
'Water Lily', a selected form with slightly larger *fl.*, **1694**, p. 212.

virginiana Sweet Bay ✺ Summer   Sh.,T.
Loose shrub or small tree, deciduous in its northern horticultural range. Grey bark and its 3–5 in. long *l.*, whitish beneath, are bonuses, its lemony richly fragrant waxy-white *fl.* alone are enough to recommend it. The cup-shaped *fl.*, about 3 in. across, scattered about the tree, *fl.* over a long period during the warm weather. E. USA (coastal areas).

wilsonii see in **M.** × **highdownensis**

MAHONIA (BERBERIDACEAE)

Evergreen shrubs closely related to Berberis in which genus *Mahonia* used to be placed. Distinct in their pinnate foliage and in the absence of spines on the branches although *l.* are usually prickly margined. All are handsome and valuable evergreens.

aquifolium Oregon Grape ✺ Early Spring   Sh.
Evergreen shrub up to 4 ft but usually rather less. Spreading freely by underground suckers and thus making good ground cover. *Fl.* yellow in dense erect racemes about 3–4 in. long. *L.* pinnate, glossy, dark green. Valuable as a glossy evergreen and as cut foliage. W. N. America. **1695**, p. 212.

bealei see **M. japonica**

✿ **'Charity'** ✺ Mid Winter–Early Spring   Sh.
A good hybrid between *M. lomariifolia* and *M. japonica.* Shrub up to 10 ft usually less. *L.* slightly larger than either parent and *fl.* heads densely borne semi-erect, this however is a variable hybrid and different seedlings have been raised. **1696**, p. 212.

✿ **japonica** ✺ Early Spring   Sh.
Taller shrub up to 7 ft usually widespreading with long stems from base. *Fl.* lemon-yellow in long spreading racemes up to 1 ft, sometimes slightly pendulous. Very fragrant smelling like Lilies of the Valley. Close to this and often confused with this is *M. bealei* in which the racemes are shorter and erect. *L.* pinnate, large up to 1 ft or more in length. Hardy. One of the most valuable winter-flowering evergreen shrubs. China, Formosa, long cultivated in Japan. **1697**, p. 213.

lomariifolia ✺ Winter   Sh.
Evergreen shrub up to 8 ft. *Fl.* deep yellow in dense erect racemes up to 8 in. long and six or more to a head. Leaflets lobed and rather prickly. Slightly tender and should be planted in protected situation. W. China. **1698**, p. 213.

MAIDENHAIR TREE see Ginkgo biloba, 2014, p. 252.

MALACOCARPUS MAMMULOSUS see Notocactus mammulosus

MALCOLMIA, MALCOMIA (CRUCIFERAE)

maritima, syn. **Cheiranthus maritimus** Virginian Stock ✺ Spring–Mid Autumn with successive sowings   HA.
Fl. lilac, pink, red or white. *L.* blunt, entire. 6–9 in. Sow from 3–9 where it is to *fl.* Easily grown in crevices in paving and will succeed in sun or partial shade. Obtainable in separate colours or mixed. Mediterranean region. **336**, p. 42.

MALCOMIA see Malcolmia

MALLOW see Lavatera, 322, p. 41; 1233, p. 155; 1672, p. 209; and Malva, 1262, p. 158.

MALLOW, JEW'S see Kerria japonica, 1667, p. 209.

MALLOW, TREE see Lavatera arborea, 1672, p. 209.

MALOPE (MALVACEAE)

grandiflora, a variety of **M. trifida**

trifida ✺ Summer   HA.
Fl. rosy-purple. *L.* slender with pointed lobes, toothed, smooth. 2–3 ft. Sow in 4–5 where they are to *fl.* in a sunny position and a well-drained, preferably light soil. There are also crimson, pink and white forms sometimes listed under *M. grandiflora.* Mediterranean region. **337**, p. 43.

MALTESE CROSS see Lychnis chalcedonica, 1249, p. 157.

MALUS (ROSACEAE) Flowering Crab

Valuable deciduous trees both for their white, pink, red or purplish *fl.* in early spring and for their conspicuous fruits in autumn, most of which are edible. Previously placed in genus *Pyrus* but in catalogues usually now kept separate under *Malus.* All should be planted in sunny position. Hybrids are usually grafted on apple stocks.

floribunda Japanese Crab ✺ Spring   T.
Small round headed tree up to 12 ft with wider spreading head, sometimes grown as a shrub. *Fl.* 1–1½ in. wide in large clusters, rosy-red in bud and pink on opening. Japan but sometimes suspected of being of hybrid origin. **1699**, p. 213.
Various forms of this are grown including:
'Atrosanguinea', with slightly deeper coloured *fl.*;
'Hillieri', probably a hybrid with semi-double *fl.* crimson in bud, bright pink when open.

✿ **'Golden Hornet'** ✺ Late Spring   T.
One of the finest trees for yellow fruits which remain on tree usually long after *l.* have been shed, sometimes up to 1 or 2. Small deciduous tree up to 10 ft with spreading top. *Fl.* white. **1700**, p. 213.

'John Downie' ✺ Late Spring   T.
One of the best fruiting crabs and fruits are valuable for jam making or jellies. *Fl.* white with pinkish outside. Fruits 9–10 deep yellow heavily flushed with scarlet about 1½ in. long, pear-shaped. Makes a small rather erect branched tree up to 15 ft. **1701**, p. 213.

× **lemoinei** ✺ Late Spring   T.
One of the best of hybrid group raised from *M. pumila niedzwetzkyana.* *Fl.* vivid purplish-crimson borne in large clusters with *l.* which are bronzy when young. Small tree up to 15 ft. **1702**, p. 213.
Other members of this group are:
'Aldenhamensis', with vinous red *fl.*;
'Profusion', with *fl.* slightly larger than *lemoinei* and a little later, winy-red, deep pink in bud;
'Wisley Crab', with purple *fl.* is also of similar parentage and so is 'Eleyi', but this is slightly less vigorous and now superseded.

'Red Jade'   T.
A weeping flowering crab tree, up to 20 ft or more. Attractive at any time because of its graceful weeping habit, it is a picture in the spring when free in *fl.* But its glory is the fruiting season with its many glowing strands of numerous small red crab apples. Occasional branches growing up at an angle and any ground suckers should be pruned off. Originated at the Brooklyn Botanic Garden.

✿ × **robusta** Siberian Crab ✺ Autumn   T.
Tree up to 20 ft but usually less with spreading branches. Fruits like large cherries, bright scarlet and usually lasting long on the tree. *Fl.* white with pale pink outside. Probably a cross between *M. baccata* × *M. prunifolia.* **1703**, p. 213.

tschonoskii ✺ Late Spring   T.
Tall erect pyramidal tree up to 40 ft. *Fl.* white with rose tinted buds up to 1¼ in. wide in clusters. *L.* broadly ovate and pointed with very brilliant scarlet autumn colouring which combined with its erect habit makes it a valuable tree for narrow restricted places. Japan. **1704**, p. 213.

Abbreviations and Symbols used in the text.
The following abbreviations may sometimes be used in conjunction as HA. indicating Hardy annual or GBb indicating Greenhouse bulb.

A. = Annual	P. = Perennial
Aq. = Aquatic	R. = Rock or
B. = Biennial	Alpine plant
Bb = Bulb	Sh. = Shrub
C. = Corm	Sp., sp. = Species
Cl. = Climber	Syn. = Synonym
Co. = Conifer	T. = Tree
Fl., *fl.* = Flower(s)	Tu. = Tuber
G. = Greenhouse or	var. = variety
house plant	× = Hybrid or
H. = Hardy	hybrid parents
HH. = Half-hardy	✺ = Flowering time
L., *l.* = Leaf, leaves	☙ = Foliage plant
Mt(s) = Mount,	
mountain(s)	

The following have been used also in the descriptions of Alpines, Bulbs, Trees and Shrubs.

* = slightly tender
† = lime hater
✿ = highly recommended

The illustration numbers are in **bold type** and the page numbers in light type preceded by p.

MALVA (MALVACEAE) Mallow

alcea ✳ Midsummer–Mid Autumn   P.
Fl. rosy-pink tinged purple. *L.* light green, heart-shaped, lobed and downy. 3–4 ft. Ordinary soil in a sunny position. Withstands drought. Propagate by seed sown in spring in pans of sandy soil and placed in a cold frame, or by cuttings. Europe.
   'Fastigiata', *fl.* deeper in colour, 3 ft, **1262**, p. 158.

MAMMOTH TREE see **Sequoiadendron giganteum**, **2039, 2040**, p. 255.

MANCHU CHERRY see **Prunus tomentosa**

MANNA ASH see **Fraxinus ornus**

MANUKA see **Leptospermum scoparium**, **1674**, p. 210.

MAPLE see **Acer**, **1430-1440**, pp. 179, 180.

MARANTA (MARANTACEAE) Prayer Plant

leuconeura 🍂   GP.
   To 6 in. tall. *Fl.* white, inconspicuous. *L.* oblong-oval to 5 in. long and 3½ in. across. They need a rich compost and warm moist, shady condition. Bright sunlight causes the *l.* to fold up. Minimum temp. 55°F., but lower readings tolerated if plants are kept dry. Brazil.
   var. *erythrophylla*, with prominent red markings;
   var. *kerchoveana*, bright green with maroon blotches, **556**, p. 70;
   var. *massangeana*, bright green with the principal veins picked out in white.

MARIGOLD, AFRICAN see **Tagetes erecta**, **378-379**, p. 48.

MARIGOLD, CORN see **Chrysanthemum segetum**, **266**, p. 34.

MARIGOLD, FRENCH see **Tagetes patula**, **380, 381**, p. 48.

MARIGOLD, MARSH see **Caltha palustris**, **1009**, p. 127.

MARIGOLD, POT see **Calendula officinalis**, **248-250**, pp. 31, 32.

MARJORAM see **Origanum vulgare**, **1293**, p. 162.

MARSH MARIGOLD see **Caltha palustris**, **1009**, p. 127.

MARTHA WASHINGTON PELARGONIUM see **Pelargonium × domesticum**, **587-597**, pp. 74, 75.

MARTYNIA (MARTYNIACEAE)

louisiana, syn. **Proboscidea jussieui** Unicorn Plant ✳ Summer   HHA.
   Fl. creamy-white with yellow, green or light red markings in the throat. *L.* alternate, up to 1 ft long, roundish. Fruit ripens to become hard, beak-shaped, hence the common name. 2–3 ft. Sow in a warm greenhouse in 3–4 and plant out in a rich soil and a sunny border in early 6. S. USA. **338**, p. 43.

MARVEL OF PERU see **Mirabilis jalapa**, **345**, p. 44.

MASK FLOWER see **Alonsoa warscewiczii**, **227**, p. 29.

MASTERWORT see **Astrantia**, **999**, p. 125.

MATRICARIA (COMPOSITAE)

eximia, syn. **Chrysanthemum parthenium** Feverfew ✳ Summer   HHA.
   Fl. white with yellow disc. *L.* divided, slightly hairy. 9 in.–3 ft. Perennial but often raised from seed sown in 3 under glass and planted out in 5 to *fl.* the same season. S. Europe.
   The double and dwarf forms make good border plants:
   'Ball's Double White', 1½ ft, **339**, p. 43;
   'Golden Ball', 1 ft, dwarf compact, lemon-yellow, **340**, p. 43;
   'Silver Ball', 1 ft, dwarf compact, pure white;
   'White Stars', 9 in., extra dwarf, double with flat ray petals.

MATTHIOLA (CRUCIFERAE) Stock, Gilliflower

incana, syn. **M. annua, M. graeca** ✳ Summer HHB.
   The original wild types are no longer grown in gardens but many varieties have been produced over the years. *Fl.* double or single in columnar or branching spikes in shades of crimson, pink, salmon, lilac, pale yellow and white. *L.* lanceolate. Height 1–2½ ft. Double *fl.* produce no seed and percentage of double *fl.* varies considerably in different varieties and strains. There are, however, 100% double strains in which it is possible to eliminate the single flowered plants in the seedling stage. Sow in a greenhouse 3–4. Prick out into boxes and plant out 4–5. **341**, p. 43.
   Popular strains include Early Cascade and the ten week strains Column, Giant Imperial, Giant Perfection and Mammoth, all available in mixtures and separate colours.

sinuata ✳ Mid Summer   HB.
   A native British sp. which gave rise to the fairly hardy stocks and the Intermediate and East Lothian varieties. *Fl.* white, purple, mauve, pink, rose scarlet or crimson. Hardy in mild districts. Height 1–1½ ft.

Brompton or Winter flowering ✳ Late Spring–Early Summer   HB.
   Height 1½–2 ft. These are also obtainable in the earlier flowering, 100% double strains.

East Lothian ✳ Early Summer   HB.
   Height 1–1½ ft. The two above are available in separate colours. Sow in greenhouse or frames 8–9 and overwinter in small pots in a cold frame. Plant out in 3–4. In mild districts seeds may be sown in late 7 and the seedlings planted out in 9.

MAXILLARIA (ORCHIDACEAE)

lepidota ✳ Usually Late Spring–Early Summer GP.
   About 9 in. high. *Fl.* yellow, with sepals contracted into tails 2½ in. long. *L.* singly on pseudobulb, lanceolate, to 9 in. long. Usual orchid compost and intermediate conditions; temp. of 55°F. in winter. Moist atmosphere, but ventilate whenever conditions allow. Propagate by back-bulbs. Colombia. **557**, p. 70.

MAY see **Crataegus**, **1542-1544**, p. 193.

MAYFLOWER, HIMALAYAN see **Podophyllum emodii**, **1320**, p. 165.

MAZZARD see **Prunus avium**, **1753**, p. 220.

MEADOW CRANESBILL see **Geranium pratense**, **1147**, p. 144.

MEADOW DAISY see **Bellis perennis**, **243**, p. 31.

MEADOW FOAM see **Limnanthes douglasii**, **325**, p. 41.

MEADOW RUE see **Thalictrum**, **1395-1397**, p. 175.

MECONOPSIS (PAVAVERACEAE)

betonicifolia, syn. **M. baileyi** Himalayan Blue Poppy ✳ Summer   P.
   Fl. rich sky-blue, 2 in. across, almost circular, with golden anthers. *L.* oblong hairy. 2–5 ft. Requires a lime-free, moist soil containing plenty of leaf-mould or peat. In partial shade in the S., but in N. gardens it will grow in full sun so long as the roots are cool. If plants are allowed to *fl.* the first year they usually die after flowering. Easily raised from seed sown in autumn or spring in pans of well-drained sandy loam and peat and placed in a warm greenhouse to germinate. Tibet, Yunan. **1263**, p. 158.

cambrica Welsh Poppy ✳ Summer   P.
   Fl. yellow or orange, nearly round, about 1½ in. across. *L.* deeply cut, somewhat hairy, about 8 in. long. 1 ft. Easily grown in any well-drained garden soil and full sun where it will colonize itself by seed. The double forms are increased by careful division in early spring. W. Europe, including Britain. **1264**, p. 158.

grandis ✳ Early Summer   P.
   Fl. deep blue, large saucer-shaped, purple in the bud stage. *L.* oblong, toothed, with reddish bristles. 1½–3 ft. Plant 11–3 in a moist, but well-drained lime-free soil, shaded from the midday sun. Propagate by division or by seed. Nepal, Tibet.
   There are various forms including:
   'Branklyn', outstanding, rich blue, **1265**, p. 159.

integrifolia ✳ Summer   P.
   Fl. yellow, cup-shaped. *L.* forming golden-haired rosettes which dislike winter wet. 1½ ft. Plant 11–3. Monocarpic, see *M. regia*, and must be increased by seed. Tibet. **1266**, p. 159.

quintuplinervia Harebell Poppy ✳ Late Spring–Early Summer   P.
   Fl. lavender-blue, nodding, usually singly. *L.* bronze, rough, forming a basal rosette. 1–1½ ft. For a sheltered place on the rock garden in moist,

---

Abbreviations and Symbols used in the text.
The following abbreviations may sometimes be used in conjunction as HA. indicating Hardy annual or GBb indicating Greenhouse bulb.

A. = Annual	P. = Perennial
Aq. = Aquatic	R. = Rock or
B. = Biennial	Alpine plant
Bb = Bulb	Sh. = Shrub
C. = Corm	Sp., sp. = Species
Cl. = Climber	Syn. = Synonym
Co. = Conifer	T. = Tree
Fl., fl. = Flower(s)	Tu. = Tuber
G. = Greenhouse or	var. = variety
house plant	× = Hybrid or
H. = Hardy	hybrid parents
HH. = Half-hardy	✳ = Flowering time
L., l. = Leaf, leaves	🍂 = Foliage plant
Mt(s) = Mount,	
mountain(s)	

The following have been used also in the descriptions of Alpines, Bulbs, Trees and Shrubs.

   * = slightly tender
   † = lime hater
   ✿ = highly recommended

The illustration numbers are in **bold type** and the page numbers in light type preceded by p.

but well-drained soil. Propagate by division in the spring of the underground stems. Tibet, W. China. **1267**, p. 159.

regia ❋ Summer   P.
Fl. yellow, on a branching stem. *L.* form a handsome silky-haired rosette, even in winter. 4–5 ft. Plant 9–10 or 3. Propagate by seed. Monocarpic, that is it usually *fl.* the second year and then dies. Nepal. **1268**, **1269**, p. 159.

MEGASEA see **Bergenia**

MELIANTHUS (MELIANTHACEAE)

major ❋ Summer   *Sh.
Spreading shrub up to 7 ft with hollow stems and *l.* in terminal clusters. Chiefly grown as foliage shrub. *L.* slightly glaucous up to 1½ ft long, pinnate with numerous leaflets which are also toothed, fern-like. *Fl.* in terminal erect racemes up to 1 ft in length, reddish-brown. Only suitable for outside planting in milder counties of S. and W. and S.W. Ireland where it is magnificent. Valuable for sub-tropical bedding as well as a pot plant in winter in cool greenhouse for its magnificent foliage. May be cut back to ground level when it becomes too lanky. S. Africa, India. **1705**, p. 214.

MENTZELIA (LOASACEAE)

lindleyi, syn. **Bartonia aurea** Blazing Star ❋ Summer   HA.
Fl. golden-yellow, with attractive mass of feathery stamens, slightly fragrant. *L.* much divided, lance-shaped. 1½–2 ft. Sow in 4–5 in a sunny border where they are to *fl.* California. **342**, p. 43.

MERTENSIA (BORAGINACEAE)

ciliata ❋ Early Summer   P.
Fl. light blue, bell-shaped, in clusters. *L.* large, greyish-green. 2 ft. Plant 11–3 in deep moist soil and partial shade. Propagate by seed or by division in the autumn. N. America.

virginica Virginian Cowslip ❋ Late Spring   P.
Fl. purplish-blue in drooping clusters. *L.* bluish-grey, lance-shaped up to 6 in. long. 2 ft. Plant 11–3. Propagate by division in early spring as soon as young growth is visible or by seed. Virginia, USA. **1270**, p. 159.

MESEMBRYANTHEMUM (AIZOACEAE)

criniflorum, syn. **Dorotheanthus bellidiflorus** Livingstone Daisy ❋ Summer   HHA.
Fl. in shades of pink, carmine, yellow, pale mauve, buff. *L.* almost cylindrical, succulent. 3–4 in., prostrate. Sow under glass in 3–4 and plant out in mid-5, in a sunny position and in well-drained soil. Does well near the sea. The well known generic name, *Mesembryanthemum*, means 'midday flower', as it opens only in bright sunlight but the plant is now correctly known under its original name *Dorotheanthus*. **343**, p. 43.

deltoides see **Oscularia deltoides**

MESPILUS, SNOWY see **Amelanchier**, **1444**, **1445**, p. 181.

METASEQUOIA (TAXODIACEAE) Dawn Redwood, Water Fir

glyptostroboides   Co.
Deciduous tree up to 150 ft in native country but largest trees in Britain so far only reach just over 40 ft. Fast growing with rather narrow conical habit. Trunk reddish-brown, fissured towards base. *L.* small linear, arranged in two ranks horizontally on sides of short shoots, becoming pinkish-brown before falling in autumn thus giving tree very attractive effect, about ½ in. long sometimes longer on young trees, bright yellowish-green. Cones small,

round up to 1 in. across, rarely seen so far in cultivation. Best grown in dampish situations and quite hardy. Easily propagated from cuttings either in summer or in winter. This remarkable tree, the genus being previously only known from fossils, was rediscovered in China in 1941 and collected first and introduced to America and Europe in 1946 through Arnold Arboretum. Very fast growing and one of our most valuable ornamental conifers. W. China, Hupeh. **2025**, p. 254.

MEXICAN ORANGE BLOSSOM see **Choisya ternata**, **1512**, p. 189.

MEXICAN PINE, ROUGH-BARKED see **Pinus montezumae**, **2032**, p. 254.

MEXICAN SUNFLOWER see **Tithonia rotundifolia**, **385**, p. 49.

MEXICAN WHITE PINE see **Pinus ayacahuite**, **2031**, p. 254.

MEZEREON see **Daphne mezereum**, **1554**, p. 195.

MICHAELMAS DAISY see **Aster novae-belgii**, **986-991**, p. 124.

MIGNONETTE see **Reseda odorata**, **365**, p. 46.

MILFOIL see **Achillea millefolium**, **949**, p. 119.

MILK THISTLE see **Silybum marianum**, **376**, p. 47.

MILKY BELLFLOWER see **Campanula lactiflora**, **1012**, p. 127.

MILTONIA (ORCHIDACEAE)

hybrids ❋ Late Spring–Autumn   GP.
Most of the pansy-flowered orchids are forms of the very variable *M. vexillaria* or are hybrids between this sp. and *M. roezlii* and *M. phalaenopsis*. The last-named sp. *fl.* in 5, the other two in autumn and the hybrids may *fl.* at any time between 5 and autumn. Propagation by removing back bulbs, preferably in spring or when repotting. Colours range from the nearly pure white of *M. phalaenopsis* and *M. vexillaria alba* to various shades of pink, red and deep crimson. Winter temp. 55°F., summer temp. best not higher than 70°F. Shade in summer and maintain moist buoyant atmosphere. Amongst the many fine hybrids are:
    'Isis', **558**, p. 70;
    Minx 'Lyoth Alpha', **559**, p. 70.

MIMOSA see **Acacia**, **1429**, p. 179.

MIMULUS (SCROPHULARIACEAE) Musk

× **burnetii** see **M. cupreus**

cupreus ❋ Summer   P.
Fl. coppery-orange, trumpet-shaped, freely borne. *L.* ovate or oblong. 6–9 in. For a moist soil in sun or shade. Propagate by cuttings taken off young shoots in the spring or by seed sown in pans of light soil in the spring under glass. Chile.
There are numerous named hybrids:
    × *burnetii* (*M. cupreus* × *guttatus*), yellow ground heavily spotted and overlaid bronze, 9–12 in., **1271**, p. 159;
    'Red Emperor', bright crimson-scarlet, 6 in.;
    'Whitecroft Scarlet', vermilion, 4 in., **1272**, p. 159.

glutinosus, syn. **Diplacus glutinosus** ❋ Summer   *Sh.
Evergreen shrub up to 5 ft with buff, salmon-

yellow or deep crimson *fl.* like those of a snapdragon. Foliage and stems sticky. Tender and only suitable for warmer areas. Good as a cool greenhouse plant or for summer planting in a warm corner against a wall. Quick growing and easily propagated from cuttings in 7–8. These should be overwintered in cool greenhouse. **1706**, p. 214.

luteus Monkey Flower or Monkey Musk ❋ Late Spring–Summer   P.
Fl. bright yellow. *L.* oblong, glistening green. 1–1½ ft. Thrives beside a pool or stream in a sunny position. N. America, naturalized in Britain. **1273**, p. 160.
    'A. T. Johnson', orange spotted brown, 15 in., **1274**, p. 160.
    var. *guttatus*, with *fl.* spotted with brownish-purple.

primuloides ❋ Summer   RP.
Up to 6 in. *Fl.* deep yellow with narrow throat up to 1 in. across, solitary on short stems. *L.* small, obovate. In boggy positions or at edge of streams on mts of Pacific States. A beautiful little plant which should be more widely grown, but not a ramper. W. USA. **110**, p. 14.

variegatus ❋ Summer   HHA.
Fl. large variable, white or yellow throat, with red or crimson-purple zones. *L.* oblong, veined. 9–12 in. Perennial but often sown in 2–4, under glass and planted out in moist, semi-shade in 5. Chile. **344**, p. 43.
Varieties include:
    'Bonfire', orange-scarlet, 9 in.;
    'Queen's Prize strain', brilliant colours, heavily spotted, 9–12 in.

MINIATURE MOUNTAIN ASH see **Sorbus reducta**, **1910**, p. 239.

MINT BUSH see **Prostanthera**, **1751**, p. 219.

MIRABILIS (NYCTAGINACEAE)

jalapa Marvel of Peru ❋ Midsummer–Mid Autumn   HHA.
Fl. vary from rosy-purple, red, yellow to white, fragrant, funnel-shaped, *L.* entire, large, smooth, oval lance-shaped. Quick growing bushy plants. 2–3 ft. Sow under glass in 2–3, plant out in late 5–6. Perennial in its native W. Indies. **345**, p. 44.

Abbreviations and Symbols used in the text.
The following abbreviations may sometimes be used in conjunction as HA. indicating Hardy annual or GBb indicating Greenhouse bulb.

A. = Annual	P. = Perennial
Aq. = Aquatic	R. = Rock or
B. = Biennial	Alpine plant
Bb = Bulb	Sh. = Shrub
C. = Corm	Sp., sp. = Species
Cl. = Climber	Syn. = Synonym
Co. = Conifer	T. = Tree
Fl., fl. = Flower(s)	Tu. = Tuber
G. = Greenhouse or	var. = variety
house plant	× = Hybrid or
H. = Hardy	hybrid parents
HH. = Half-hardy	❋ = Flowering time
L., l. = Leaf, leaves	❧ = Foliage plant
Mt(s) = Mount,	
mountain(s)	

The following have been used also in the descriptions of Alpines, Bulbs, Trees and Shrubs.

    * = slightly tender
    † = lime hater
    ✿ = highly recommended

The illustration numbers are in **bold type** and the page numbers in light type preceded by p.

MISCANTHUS (GRAMINEAE)

sinensis, syn. **Eulalia japonica** ✻ Late Summer P.
Fl. whitish panicles 8 in.–1 ft long, tinged red. 3–5 ft. *L.* silver-green with whitish mid-stripe, up to 3 ft long in dense clump. The form 'Variegatus' has a creamy mid-stripe. Plant 3–4 in a sunny position and ordinary soil. Propagate by division in the spring. China, Japan. **1275**, p. 160.

MITRARIA (GESNERIACEAE)

coccinea ✻ Summer *Sh.
Loose growing shrub or climber usually grown against a wall, only suitable for milder areas. *Fl.* bright scarlet, tubular up to 1½ in. long, constricted at base. *L.* small, ovate, slightly leathery. Chile. **1707**, p. 214.

MOCK ORANGE see **Philadelphus, 1725-1729,** pp. 216, 217.

MOLTKIA (BORAGINACEAE)

× **intermedia,** syn. **Lithospermum intermedium** ✻ Summer RP.
Probably a hybrid between *M. petraea* and *M. suffruticosa*. Sub-shrubby plant, 10 in., forming clump with erect herb stem. *Fl.* bright gentian blue, pendulous, tubular in loose clusters. *L.* narrow, linear. A very useful summer-flowering plant for sunny position in rock garden. Parents are both S. European. **111**, p. 14.

MOLUCCELLA (LABIATAE)

laevis Bells of Ireland, Shell Flower ✻ Summer HA.
Fl. small, white, surrounded by large cup-shaped, pale green calyces. These make attractive winter decorations when cut and dried. *L.* roundish, coarsely notched. 1–1½ ft. Sow in a warm greenhouse in 3 and plant out in a sunny position in 5, or sow in the open in 4, in well-drained soil and in a sheltered place. Syria. **346**, p. 44.

MONARCH OF THE VELDT see **Venidium fastuosum, 391,** p. 49.

MONARDA (LABIATAE)

didyma Bergamot, Oswego Tea ✻ Summer P.
Fl. scarlet, *L.* roughly hairy, aromatic, cordate at base. 2–3 ft. Thrives in moist soil, sun or partial shade. During drought mulch with garden compost or moist peat. Easily increased by division of the rootstock in spring. N. America.
Good varieties include:
  'Cambridge Scarlet', brilliant scarlet, 2–3 ft, **1276**, p. 160;
  'Croftway Pink', clear rose-pink, 2½ ft;
  'Prairie Glow', purple, 2½ ft;
  'Snow Maiden', white, 2½ ft.

MONKEY FLOWER see **Mimulus luteus, 1273, 1274,** p. 160.

MONKEY MUSK see **Mimulus luteus, 1273, 1274,** p. 160.

MONKEY PUZZLE see **Araucaria araucana**

MONKSHOOD see **Aconitum, 952,** p. 119.

MONSTERA (ARACEAE)

pertusa Ceriman ☙ GP.
Climbing plant to 10 ft. *Fl.* dirty-white, short-lived. Juvenile *l.* heart-shaped, to 4 in. long; mature *l.* oblong-ovate, to 15 in. long, much dissected and irregularly perforated. If put in too heavy a shade the *l.* revert to the juvenile form. Aerial roots formed at every node and best trained

down into pot. Rich compost required. Winter temp. 50°F., but lower readings tolerated. Propagate by stem cuttings, taken at intervals to allow growing points to be formed. Tropical S. America. 'Borsigiana', reasonably compact, is the form usually grown, **560**, p. 70.

MONTEREY CYPRESS see **Cupressus macrocarpa**

MONTEREY PINE see **Pinus radiata, 2034,** p. 255.

MOONLIGHT BROOM see **Cytisus scoparius** 'Sulphureus'

MOOSEWOOD see **Acer pensylvanicum, 1437,** p. 180.

MORAINE LOCUST see under **Gleditschia triacanthos**

MORINA (DIPSACEAE) Himalayan Whorlflower
(Sometimes now placed in separate family Morinaceae)

longifolia ✻ Summer P.
Fl. opening white, becoming pink to crimson, on long spikes. *L.* spiny, thistle-like, large. 2–3 ft. For a sunny position and a sandy loam. Propagate by seed sown in early autumn or by division soon after flowering. Nepal. **1277**, p. 160.

MORISIA (CRUCIFERAE)

hypogaea see **M. monantha**

monantha, syn. **M. hypogaea** ✻ Spring RP.
Densely tufted small rock plant, 1–2 in. *Fl.* strong lemon-yellow, almost sessile, cup-shaped, up to ½ in. across. *L.* deeply divided up to 3 in. long. Best grown in alpine house or in warm sunny scree. Corsica, Sardinia. **112**, p. 14.

MORNING GLORY see **Ipomoea, 312,** p. 39.

MORNING GLORY, DWARF see **Convolvulus tricolor, 272, 273,** pp. 34, 35.

MT ETNA BROOM see **Genista aetnensis**

MOUNTAIN ASH see **Sorbus aucuparia, 1905,** p. 239.

MOUNTAIN ASH, MINIATURE see **Sorbus reducta, 1910,** p. 239.

MOUNTAIN CRANBERRY see **Vaccinium vitis-idaea, 1937,** p. 243.

MOUNTAIN LAUREL see **Kalmia latifolia, 1665, 1666,** p. 209.

MOUNTAIN KNAPWEED see **Centaurea montana, 1020,** p. 128.

MOUTAN see **Paeonia suffruticosa, 1719, 1720,** p. 215.

MUGWORT, WHITE see **Artemisia lactiflora, 977,** p. 123.

MULLEIN see **Verbascum, 217, 218,** p. 28; **1407-1410,** pp. 176, 177.

MUSCARI (LILIACEAE) Grape hyacinth

armeniacum 'Heavenly Blue' ✻ Spring Bb
The grape hyacinth usually seen. A very rapid

spreader and increaser which should be kept away from competition with choicer alpines. *Fl.* bright blue, small plants like bells in rather dense heads on stems 4–8 in. high. *L.* grass-like, produced in autumn. Rock garden or front of sunny border. Clumps are best divided every few years. **823**, p. 103.

✡**botryoides** ✻ Spring Bb
Dwarfer than preceding and spreading less freely, bells almost globular, pale china-blue or white in *M. botryoides* 'Album'. Excellent for the rock garden. Italy and the Balkans. **824, 825,** pp. 103, 104.

comosum var. **monstrosum** (var. **plumosum**) Tassel Hyacinth
The *fl.* are all sterile and malformed into dark mauvish-blue tufts of long tassel or plume-like plants which are attractive and showy. Sunny position in rock garden or front of border. Not known in wild and presumably originated from *M. comosum* which is a common native in S. Europe and Middle East. **826**, p. 104.

  var. **plumosum** see **M. comosum** var. **monstrosum**

latifolium ✻ Spring Bb
Fl. very dark, dusky blue on 1 ft stalk. *L.* broad up to 1 in. across. Asia Minor. **827**, p. 104.

macrocarpum ✻ Spring Bb
Fl. pale or medium yellow, larger and stouter than preceding sp. Stems up to 10 in. with 20 or more *fl.*, slightly fleshy. Very sweetly scented. Bulb larger and with fleshy perennial roots and *l.* wider and strap-shaped. Needs a warm sunny position and good summer ripening, but a lovely and distinctive plant. Aegean Islands.

tubergenianum ✻ Spring Bb
The Oxford and Cambridge grape hyacinth, so named since the top of the spike has dark blue *fl.* and the lower part light blue. Height 4–6 in. Suitable for sunny position on rock gardens. N.W. Persia. **828**, p. 104.

MUSK see **Mimulus, 110,** p. 14; **344,** p. 43; **1271-1274,** pp. 159–160; **1706,** p. 214.

MUTISIA (COMPOSITAE) Climbing Gazania

decurrens ✻ Summer Cl.
Even finer than *M. oligodon* but difficult to establish. *Fl.* heads bright orange or vermilion up to 5 in.

Abbreviations and Symbols used in the text.
The following abbreviations may sometimes be used in conjunction as HA. indicating Hardy annual or GBb indicating Greenhouse bulb.

A. = Annual	P. = Perennial
Aq. = Aquatic	R. = Rock or
B. = Biennial	Alpine plant
Bb = Bulb	Sh. = Shrub
C. = Corm	Sp., sp. = Species
Cl. = Climber	Syn. = Synonym
Co. = Conifer	T. = Tree
Fl., fl. = Flower(s)	Tu. = Tuber
G. = Greenhouse or	var. = variety
house plant	× = Hybrid or
H. = Hardy	hybrid parents
HH. = Half-hardy	✻ = Flowering time
L., l. = Leaf, leaves	☙ = Foliage plant
Mt(s) = Mount,	
mountain(s)	

The following have been used also in the descriptions of Alpines, Bulbs, Trees and Shrubs.

  * = slightly tender
  † = lime hater
  ✡ = highly recommended

The illustration numbers are in **bold type** and the page numbers in light type preceded by p.

across with numerous ray-florets ½ in. wide. *L.* evergreen, narrowly oblong, base decurrent with narrow wings to the stem, up to 5 in. long. Hardy only in mild districts and should be planted with greatest of care out of pot when young. All Mutisias should not be allowed to dry out.

oligodon ✳ Summer   *Cl.
Evergreen climber with young twining shoots rather straggling up to 4 ft. *Fl.* heads with up to 12 ray-florets up to 1 in. across and 1¼ in. long, satiny-pink. *L.* oblong clasping stem up to 1½ in. long coarsely toothed. Only hardy in warmer districts of Britain. Chile in mountainous districts. **1984**, p. 248.

MYOSOTIS (BORAGINACEAE) Forget-me-not

alpestris ✳ Mid Spring–Early Summer   HB.
Fl. in shades of blue, pale pink, also white. *L.* lance-shaped. 6–9 in. More or less perennial, usually sown in moist soil in 5–6 and planted out in early autumn where they are to *fl.* European mountains.
  Named forms come true from seed:
    'Blue Ball', clear blue, compact, 6 in., **347**, p. 44;
    'Carmine King', carmine pink, 6 in.;
    'Royal Blue', dark blue, 9–12 in.;
    'Ultramarine', very dwarf, dark blue, 6 in.

MYROBALAN see **Prunus cerasifera**, **1754**, p. 220.

MYRTLE see **Myrtus**, **1708**, p. 214.

MYRTLE, COMMON see **Myrtus communis**

MYRTLE, CRAPE see **Lagerstroemia indica**, **1670**, p. 209.

MYRTUS (MYRTACEAE) Myrtle

communis Common Myrtle ✳ Midsummer   *Sh.
Evergreen shrub up to 12 ft. *Fl.* white up to ¾ in. across, very fragrant, boss of numerous stamens in centre. *L.* ovate to lanceolate 1½ in. long, dark lustrous green and smelling strongly when bruised. Only suitable as a wall shrub except in very mild areas. Plant in full sun. S. Europe but spreading through to W. Asia.
  var. *tarentina*, *l.* smaller and *fl.* also slightly smaller creamy-white.

luma, syn. **Eugenia apiculata**   *T.
Shrub or small tree up to 25 ft. Distinguished for its reddish-brown peeling bark and in this category one of the finest small trees. Stems often blotched and cinnamon coloured. *L.* evergreen small. *Fl.* solitary less conspicuous than those of Common Myrtle. Only hardy in milder areas of S.W. Chile. **1708**, p. 214.

N

NAMAQUALAND DAISY see **Venidium fastuosum**, **391**, p. 49.

NANKING CHERRY see **Prunus tomentosa**

NARCISSUS (AMARYLLIDACEAE) Daffodil

A large genus ranging from small miniatures only a few in. high to big trumpet daffodils of 2 ft with *fl.* 4 in. across. Of all spring bulbs these are perhaps the most popular and the majority of them are tolerant of a wide range of conditions and soils and may be planted either in full sun or semi-shade. They are natives mainly of Spain, Portugal and N. Africa but the bunch-flowered or tazetta narcissi extend right across Europe and Asia to China. They grow best in places where they can get plenty of moisture at the roots in spring while they are

growing but after the *l.* have died down they can stand quite dry conditions to ripen the bulbs. All daffodils should, if possible, be planted early in 9 or even in 8, since they begin to root early in the autumn. The smaller bulbs of the miniatures, both sp. and hybrids, should be planted from 1½–3 in. deep but the larger-flowered daffodils may be planted deeper, from 3–5 in.

While we associate yellow as the daffodil colour, there are also white ones of great beauty and some with apricot-pink, shell-pink and one or two with scarlet trumpets. Here we will deal first with the wild daffodils which are so lovely to naturalise in the garden or to grow in pots and pans, then with the big hybrids which make such an effect when naturalised. They are also grown in vast quantities for cutting for market and some are grown chiefly for Show purposes. The qualities that make a good Show daffodil are a regular form, smoothness and thickness of the petals, a well proportioned cup or trumpet in relation to the perianth (petals) and clearness of colour.

The Species and miniature hybrids:

asturiensis, syn. **N. minimus** ✳ Early Spring   Bb
The smallest trumpet daffodil. A perfect miniature, 3–5 in. with deep gold petals and trumpet, the mouth of which is frilled or deeply indented. Stem inclines to be weak especially after heavy rain. Very suitable for the rock garden in sunny positions and requiring well-drained soil. Mountains of N.W. Spain. **829**, p. 104.

bulbocodium The Hoop petticoat ✳ Mid Winter–Mid Spring   Bb
A group distinct from other daffodils because of the large funnel-shaped corona (cup) and the narrow and reduced perianth segments (petals). *L.* narrow rush-like and bulb small. 2–5 in. It gets its common name from the resemblance to a small old-fashioned hoop petticoat blown up in the wind. Naturalises best in places moist as in the alpine meadow at Wisley where a mixture of forms grows in thousands and make a lovely spectacle each spring. Spain, Portugal, S.W. France. **830**, p. 104.
  The main varieties are:
    citrinus see var. *conspicuus*;
    ✿ *conspicuus* ✳ Spring, *fl.* deep yellow with widely expanded corona, one of the largest and best forms, and with var. *citrinus* (more lemon-yellow) and their hybrids forms the bulk of the alpine meadow at Wisley, **831**, p. 204;
    romieuxii* ✳ Winter, *fl.* lemon-yellow, opening wider, very early-flowering and so especially suitable for pots in alpine house, requires thorough drying off after flowering and a drier position than those above and as much sun as possible, bulb small, N.W. Africa, Atlas Mts, **832**, p. 104.

✿ **cyclamineus** ✳ Early Spring   Bb
Fl. deep yellow with long tubular coronas and petals reflexed upwards, usually appearing before the hoop petticoats. 4–8 in. *L.* broader than those of the hoop petticoats. Unsuitable for dry and hot places as growing best in really moist conditions. Parent of many fine hybrids when crossed with larger daffodils. Spain, Portugal. **833**, p. 105.

jonquilla The wild Jonquil ✳ Spring   Bb
Fl. yellow with small cup-shaped corona, 1–1½ in. across, several on a stem. *L.* deep green, rush-like. 6 in.–1 ft. Bulb small, very dark brown. Requires hot position to *fl.* well. The strongest and sweetest scented of all daffodils. Spain, Portugal, S. Europe, N.W. Africa. **834**, p. 105.
  flore-pleno is the double jonquil often known as Queen Anne's double jonquil;
  The Campernelle jonquils, *N. odorus* and *N. odorus rugulosus*, are rather larger in *fl.* than *N. jonquilla*. Also very sweet scented and more vigorous. S. Europe, Mediterranean regions.

juncifolius ✳ Spring   Bb
A charming miniature jonquil with deep yellow *fl.* and very short coronas, ½ in. across, one to three on stems up to 6 in. but generally less. A good plant

for pans in alpine house but quite hardy. Spain, Portugal, S.W. France. **835**, p. 105.

lobularis ✳ Early Spring   Bb
Perianth segments paler than trumpet. Dwarf trumpet daffodil on stems 6–10 in. A good plant for rock garden or for naturalising in a meadow. Often regarded as a subsp. of *N. pseudonarcissus*. **836**, p. 105.

× **minicycla** ✳ Early Spring   Bb
Fl. deep yellow on stems 4–8 in. A dwarf hybrid between *N. asturiensis* and *N. cyclamineus*. Variable but generally clearly intermediate between the two, the petals spreading widely. Often occurs naturally where these two sp. are planted close together. Generally less vigorous than either parent. **837**, p. 105.

minimus see **N. asturiensis**

odorus see after **N. jonquilla**

pseudonarcissus The Lent Lily ✳ Late Winter–Mid Spring   Bb
The wild dwarf trumpet narcissus that still survives in a few British woodlands. Perianth paler than trumpet. A beautiful plant for naturalising in meadow or open woodland and flowering earlier than the larger daffodils. **838**, p. 105.
  'W. P. Milner', early spring, a dwarf hybrid trumpet with *fl.* more sulphur-lemon in colour than the above. The trumpets tend to hang down, a good plant for naturalising also, 6–10 in., **839**, p. 105.

triandrus 'Albus' Angel's Tears ✳ Spring   Bb
One of the prettiest dwarf daffodils with pendulous *fl.* creamy-white with large cup-shaped corona and reflexed, sometimes twisted petals. 1–3 in. on 4–6 in. stems. Does well in damp places, but requires good drainage after flowering. A delightful plant for pans in the alpine house or for bringing into the home. N.W. Spain, Portugal. **840**, p. 105.
  'April Tears', Spring, taller than preceding with pale yellow cup and slightly deeper petals, probably a hybrid with a jonquil, with *l.* and stems rush-like, excellent for pans in alpine house but quite hardy, **841**, p. 106;
  'Hawera', Spring, raised in New Zealand and close to 'April Tears' but with *fl.* more lemon-yellow, generally several on a 6–10 in. stem, a lovely plant which, when suited, will make clumps in the rock garden, **842**, p. 106;

'Silver Chimes', Spring, a larger hybrid between *N. triandrus* and the bunch-flowered *N. tazetta*, the *fl.* are creamy-white with pale yellow corona, 1½ in. across, scented, several in a bunch on 1–1½ ft stems. A vigorous grower, suitable for front of the shrub border or larger rock garden, good also for picking for house. *L.* broad and deep green, **843**, p. 106.

watieri ✤ Early Spring   *Bb
A miniature ice-white jonquil with sweet scent. *Fl.* 1¼ in. across with a shallow cup on 3 in. stems. One of the gems of the miniatures but not very vigorous or long lasting in many gardens usually only surviving with some protection. Delightful in alpine house or bulb frame. N. Africa, so needs thorough ripening after flowering. **844**, p. 106.

Large-flowered Hybrid Daffodils ✤ Spring   Bb
These are divided into Divisions for Show purposes, admittedly an artificial classification but a useful one which is followed in many catalogues. These daffodils should be planted 3–6 in. deep and if grown for Show purpose they will need some organic or artificial feeding and must not be left dry while they are growing. Every third or fourth year the bulbs should be lifted and the clumps divided although daffodils naturalised in grass will often last much longer without division.
The following alphabetic list of hybrids gives the division number under which the named hybrids are described.

Actaea 9	Grand Soleil d'Or 8
Arbar 2b	Hunter's Moon 1a
Ardclinis 1c	Kilworth 2b
Armada 2a	King Alfred 1a
Bartley 6	Kingscourt 1a
Blarney 3b	Lanarth 7
Camellia 4	Lapford 1b
Cantatrice 1c	Liberty Bells 5
Carbineer 2a	Lunar Sea 1d
Carlton 2a	Magnificence 1a
Ceylon 2a	Mahmoud 3b
Charity May 6	Moonstruck 1a
Chinese White 3c	Mount Hood 1c
Chungking 3a	Moylena 2b
Cragford 8	Newcastle 1b
Craigywarren 2a	Paperwhite Grandiflora 8
Crocus 2a	Peeping Tom 6
Cromarty 1a	Polindra 2b
Debutante 2b	Preamble 1b
Double Event 4	Rembrandt 1a
Dove Wings 6	Rockall 3b
Empress of Ireland 1c	Salmon Trout 2b
February Gold 6	Scilly Isles White 8
Fermoy 2b	Silver Chimes 5
Fortune 2a	Spellbinder 1d
Frigid 3c	Sun Chariot 2a
Geranium 8	Thalia 5
Glacier 1c	Trevithian 7
Goldcourt 1a	Trousseau 1b
Golden Ducat 4	Tudor Minstrel 2b
Golden Harvest 1a	Ulster Prince 1a
Golden Torch 2a	Vigil 1c

Div. 1. Trumpet daffodils
(a) With corona and trumpet all coloured, the typical golden trumpets.
Good yellow trumpets for cutting are:
  'Cromarty';
  'Goldcourt';
  'Kingscourt', very deep pure gold in colour and with *fl.* of fine smooth texture and very regular form, **845**, p. 106;
  'Rembrandt';
  'Ulster Prince'.
Very attractive lemon-primrose varieties are:
  'Hunter's Moon';
  'Moonstruck'.
Older varieties still good for naturalising in masses and also still much used for forcing for market cut *fl.*, the earliest to *fl.* being 'Magnificence'.
  'Golden Harvest';
  'King Alfred';
  'Magnificence'.

(b) With perianth white and corona coloured.
The bicolor trumpets such as:
  'Lapford';
  'Newcastle', one of the finest show *fl.* of this class but the bulbs are likely to remain expensive;
  'Preamble', an unusually large and fine *fl.* with pale trumpet, **846**, p. 106.
  'Trousseau'.
(c) Perianth and corona white, the corona not being paler than the perianth.
The white trumpets. There are some exceptionally lovely *fl.* in this class and they look well both in vases and in the garden.
Among the older ones still to be recommended for garden use or for growing in bowls are:
  'Ardclinis';
  ✿'Cantatrice';
  'Mount Hood', particularly vigorous but without the smoothness and regular form of 'Cantatrice'.
Newer and more expensive ones of great beauty are:
  'Empress of Ireland', with very large *fl.*;
  'Glacier';
  'Vigil', **847**, p. 106.
(d) Trumpet daffodils with any other colour combination.
This covers the newer lemon-yellow trumpets in which the perianth segments are stronger in colour than the corona as in 'Spellbinder', a big *fl.* with pale lemon or lime-yellow corona paler at base than mouth, perianth sulphur-yellow; very striking in the garden and a vigorous grower. Some very good newer ones have been recently raised in Oregon, USA such as 'Lunar Sea'.

Div. 2. The large-cupped narcissi
These are widely grown for cutting.
(a) Perianth and corona coloured, the corona not being paler than the perianth, i.e., the large-cupped varieties with red or yellow cups.
They are very numerous and among the best are:
Varieties with yellow cups:
  'Carlton', one of the most vigorous and widely grown daffodils;
  'Crocus';
  'Golden Torch'.
Varieties with orange or orange-red in the corona. These are some of the strongest in colour in the cup. Among the best are:
  'Armada';
  'Carbineer';
  ✿'Ceylon', a fine show and garden variety, **848**, p. 106;
  'Craigywarren';
  'Fortune', one of the most famous of plants in this section and still widely grown for market but for quality of *fl.* it is outdated, **849**, p. 107;
  'Sun Chariot'.
(b) Those with perianth white and corona coloured.
  'Arbar', white petals with a large orange-red cup, a very fine variety, **850**, p. 107;
  'Fermoy', white perianth and a very brightly coloured orange-red cup;
  'Kilworth', white with a bright orange-red cup;
  ✿'Polindra', white with yellow cup, vigorous grower;
  ✿'Tudor Minstrel', white perianth and deep yellow cup, a large *fl.* of very fine quality and a plant of great vigour, **851**, p. 107.
Pink-cupped varieties are a recent development and several are now a reasonable price.
Among the best are:
  'Debutante', still rather highly priced;
  'Moylena';
  'Salmon Trout'.

Div. 3. The small-cupped narcissi
(a) Perianth and corona coloured.
  'Chungking', petals deep yellow with a shallow vivid orange-red cup, very fine variety, **852**, p. 107.
(b) Perianth white and corona coloured.
  'Blarney', white perianth, small rather flat cup of salmon-orange with a pale primrose rim, good grower;
  'Mahmoud', white with a small but very vivid orange-red cup;

'Rockall', white with bright orange-red cup, **853**, p. 107.
(c) Perianth and cup white.
  'Chinese White', *fl.* of very fine quality, large perianth with broad overlapping segments and a small, saucer-shaped white cup with a fluted rim and a faint green eye in centre, **854**, p. 107;
  'Frigid', a much smaller *fl.* and usually the latest narcissus to *fl.* in May.

Div. 4. Double narcissi
Some very fine *fl.* have been raised in this section in recent years, including:
  'Camellia', pale yellow double, a lovely *fl.* but often rather heavy in the head for its stem;
  'Double Event', *fl.* with white petals and salmon-orange centre, **855**, p. 107.
  'Golden Ducat', deep yellow double sport from 'King Alfred'.

Div. 5. Triandrus narcissi of garden origin
  'Liberty Bells', a good American raised variety with deep lemon-yellow pendulous *fl.*;
  'Silver Chimes', more fully described under *N. triandrus*, may be placed in this section, **843**, p. 106;
  'Thalia', slightly taller than preceding and has both perianth and corona white.

Div. 6. Cyclamineus narcissi of garden origin
These are mostly early-flowering and include some very lovely *fl.*:
  'Bartley', see 'Peeping Tom' below;
  'Charity May', single flowered slightly later, corona lemon-yellow and perianth paler yellow, larger *fl.* than 'February Gold', **857**, p. 108;
  ✿'Dove Wings', perianth creamy-white and corona pale canary-yellow, lovely *fl.* and one of the best garden plants in this section, **858**, p. 108;
  ✿'February Gold', often flowering in 2, 1–1½ ft with one or two yellow hanging *fl.* on a stem, **856**, p. 107;
  'Peeping Tom', corona very long, good self-coloured deep yellow, **859**, p. 108;
  very close to this is 'Bartley', both are good garden plants, excellent for naturalising.

Div. 7. Jonquil narcissi of garden origin
  'Lanarth', tall with buttercup-yellow perianth and deep orange-yellow corona, one to three *fl.* to a stem, sweet scented;
  'Trevithian', self-coloured *fl.* of deep buttercup-

yellow, strongly scented, good garden plant and also in bowls of fibre, **860**, p. 108.

Div. 8. Tazetta narcissi, showing characteristics of Tazetta group

These include the bunch-flowered narcissi so useful for Christmas forcing such as:

'Cragford', a good early forcing variety with white perianth and orange-red corona, **861**, p. 108;

'Geranium', a popular variety with white perianth and orange-red corona, usually flowering a little later than the other mentioned since it belongs to the Poeticus group in which the other parent is a *poeticus* narcissus, **864**, p. 108;

'Grand Soleil d'Or', with deep yellow *fl.*, **862**, p. 108;

'Paperwhite Grandiflora', **863**, p. 108;

'Scilly Isles White'.

Div. 9. Poeticus narcissi

The Old Poet or Pheasant Eye narcissi. Late flowering. Perianth white with a small cup of orange-red colour and a green rim.

'Actaea', one of finest with snow-white perianth and large cup for this section;

'Geranium', see under Division 8.

NASTURTIUM see **Tropaeolum**, **216**, p. 27; **387**, **388**, p. 49; **890**, **891**, p. 112; **1994**, p. 250.

NEILLIA (ROSACEAE)

longiracemosa ✳ Early Summer   Sh.
Deciduous shrub up to 6 ft with rather slender branches. *Fl.* small rosy-pink in rather drooping racemes. *L.* up to 4 in. irregularly three-lobed and toothed. For pruning, old shoots should be cut right out to base to encourage younger ones. China. **1709**, p. 214.

NEMESIA (SCROPHULARIACEAE)

strumosa ✳ Summer   HHA.
Fl. variable, orange, yellow, carmine, purple, white. *L.* oblong, or lance-shaped, toothed. 6 in.–2 ft. Sow in 3–4 under glass in gentle heat; plant out at the front of a sunny border in late 5–6. Separate colours and some good strains in various colours are available. S. Africa. **348**, p. 44.

'Blue Gem', dwarf, with medium size *fl.* of clear blue, 6–9 in.;

'Carnival', a semi-dwarf mixture, very large *fl.* in a bright colour range, 9–12 in.;

'Triumph', a dwarf compact mixture of all colours, 9 in.

NEMOPHILA (HYDROPHYLLACEAE)

insignis see **N. menziesii**

menziesii, syn. **N. insignis** Baby Blue Eyes ✳ Late Spring–Summer   HA.
Fl. light blue or white. *L.* opposite or alternate, divided. 6–8 in. Sow in the open in 3–4, or for early flowering in 9, where they are to *fl.* in cool, moist ordinary garden soil. Does well in light shade. There are various forms in shades of sky-blue, blue with white eye, blue edged white. Pacific N. America. **349**, p. 44.

NEOREGELIA (BROMELIACEAE)

carolinae 'Tricolor' ✳ Summer and Autumn ☙ GP.
Fl. bluish, small. *L.* strap-shaped, up to 15 in. long and 1 in. across, forming a rosette up to 24 in. across. Outer *l.* are green variegated with cream and pink. Before the *fl.* buds are formed, the central *l.* turn a brilliant red. A mixture of peat, sharp sand and osmunda fibre seems best for all the epiphytic Bromeliads and the central 'vase' should be kept full of rain water. Winter temp. around 55°F., but lower readings tolerated. Shade slightly in summer. Brazil. **561**, p. 71.

marechalii ✳ at any time ☙   GP.
Fl. bluish. *L.* as in *N. carolinae*, but not variegated, flushed with wine-red when young, fading to green, rather more upright than in previous, so that rosette is less spreading. *L.* around *fl.*, bright crimson. Treatment as for *N. carolinae*. Propagation by seed; sometimes offshoots produced, which can be separated from the old plant, which dies after flowering. Brazil. Considered by some authorities to be a cultivar of *N. carolinae*. **562**, p. 71.

NEPETA (LABIATAE) Catmint

× **faassenii**, syn. **N. mussinii** ✳ Late Spring–Summer   P.
Fl. soft lavender. 1–1½ ft. *L.* small, serrated, silvery-grey. For a light soil and sun. Does not survive for long in heavy, poorly-drained soil. Propagate by division in the spring, or by cuttings in spring, or after flowering when the plants have been cut back. Insert the cuttings in sandy soil in a cold frame. Of garden origin.

'Six Hills Giant', violet-blue, 2 ft, this hybrid does not produce seed, **1278**, p. 160.

mussinii see × **faassenii**

NERINE (AMARYLLIDACEAE)

✿**bowdenii** ✳ Early Autumn   Bb
The only really hardy sp. *Fl.* pink, up to eight to a cluster on 2 ft stem. Perianth segments strap-shaped up to 3 in. long, slightly wavy and curving back near ends. Colour varies in different forms and includes forms which are almost white. Plant in a warm border in full sun and leave bulbs undivided until a thick cluster is formed. One of the most valuable of autumn flowering bulbs. Excellent also for cut *fl.*. Easily grown also from seed sown fresh but takes up to five years to *fl.* S. Africa. **865**, p. 109.
Two of the best forms are:

'Fenwick's Variety', taller and larger than type, **866**, p. 109;

'Pink Beauty', slightly deeper pink than type.

corusca see under **N. sarniensis**

sarniensis Guernsey Lily ✳ Autumn   GBb
Fl. vermilion, trumpet-shaped to 2 in. long in umbel, appearing before *l.* *L.* strap-shaped, to 9 in. long, slightly glaucous. When *fl.* buds appear, start to water slightly and increase as *l.* elongate. Start to water less in 4 and let bulbs dry out and have a thorough bake from 6–9. Any ordinary potting compost is suitable. Propagation by offsets or by seed. Many hybrids have been produced in recent years. *N. corusca* is now usually regarded as a variant of *N. sarniensis*. S. Africa.

var. *major* is larger and more brilliant than the type, a beautiful plant in itself and the parent of hybrids with pink, salmon and striped *fl.*, minimum winter temp. 40°F., **563**, p. 71;

'Miss E. Cator', *fl.* deep red, vigorous grower and free-flowering, **564**, p. 71.

NERIUM (APOCYNACEAE)

oleander Oleander, Rose Bay ✳ Summer–Mid Autumn   *Sh.
Evergreen shrub up to 10 ft and bushy when properly pruned. *Fl.* in wild form pale pink or occasionally white, single up to 2 in. across in terminal clusters throughout summer. In cultivated forms *fl.* are often semi-double and vary in colour through deep pink, red, creamy-yellow and pale rosy-purple. Should be treated as cool greenhouse shrub in most parts of the country but may be stood outside during summer. *Fl.* most freely when pruned hard in winter or after flowering. A semi-double form. **1710**, p. 214.

NETTLE, DEAD see **Lamium**, **1230**, **1231**, p. 154.

NEW ENGLAND ASTER see **Aster novae-angliae**, **985**, p. 124.

NEW YORK ASTER see **Aster novae-belgii**, **986-991**, p. 124.

NEW ZEALAND CABBAGE TREE see **Cordyline australis**, **1522**, p. 191.

NEW ZEALAND FLAX see **Phormium tenax**, **1732**, p. 217.

NICANDRA (SOLANACEAE)

physaloides Apple of Peru, Shoo Fly Plant ✳ Summer   HA.
Fl. large, blue, bell-shaped, drooping. *L.* deeply toothed, wavy. Curious, small apple-shaped fruits, giving rise to one common name, but the name Shoo Fly Plant derives from the belief that growing the plant under glass rids the greenhouse of the pest whitefly. 2–3 ft. Sow in the open in 4 in ordinary garden soil. Requires ample space, transplant 2–3 ft apart. Peru. **350**, p. 44.

NICOTIANA (SOLANACEAE) Tobacco Plant

alata, syn. **N. affinis** ✳ Summer–Mid Autumn HHA.
Fl. greenish-yellow, white within, strongly fragrant in the evening. *L.* about 6 in. long, egg-shaped, 2–3 ft. Sow in a warm greenhouse in 2–3 and plant out in late 5 in sun or partial shade. They like a rich soil and adequate moisture. Perennial in country of origin, S. Brazil.

'Daylight', white, remaining open all day;

'Dwarf White Bedder', 1½ ft;

'Lime Green', a delicate shade of greenish-yellow, **351**, p. 44;

'Sensation mixed', many shades, remaining open all day, 2 ft.

hybrida (**N. langsdorffii** × **N. alata**) ✳ Summer–Mid Autumn   HHA.
Fragrant white or mixed coloured *fl.* which remain open during the day, 1½–2 ft.

sanderae (**N. alata** × **N. forgetiana**) ✳ Summer–Mid Autumn   HHA.

'Crimson Bedder', 1½ ft;

'Crimson King', 2½ ft, deep velvety crimson;

'Hybrida', a mixed strain in shades of pink, crimson, mauve and white.

NIDULARIUM (BROMELIACEAE)

innocentii 🌿 GP.
Fl. white, inconspicuous in centre of 'vase'. *L.* strap-shaped, in rosette, to 15 in. long, 1½ in. across; dark green, flecked with purple on upper side, claret-coloured on underside. *L.* before *fl.* appear turn bright crimson in centre of vase. Compost of leaf mould, sand and Osmunda fibre. Winter temp. 50°F. Shade in summer and keep in moist atmosphere. 'Vase' should be kept filled with rain water. Propagate by seed; offshoots occasionally formed which can be rooted, but their presence cannot be guaranteed. Monocarpic. Brazil. A lighter variety is illustrated, **565**, p. 71.

NIEREMBERGIA (SOLANACEAE)

caerulea, syn. **N. hippomanica** 🌸 Summer HHP.
Fl. lavender-blue to purple. *L.* narrow, dark green. 6 in. Sow in 2–3 in heat and plant in sunny position in 5–6. Also makes a useful pot plant. Argentine.
    'Purple Robe', *fl.* cup shaped, deep violet purple with yellow centre.

hippomanica see **N. caerulea**

rivularis, syn. **N. repens** 🌸 Summer RP.
2–3 in. Mat-forming and creeping. *Fl.* white, cup-shaped, up to 1 in. across, numerous. *L.* narrow, rather dark green. A valuable plant for its late summer flowering which looks and grows well in crevices between stones, but does not do well in very dry situations. S. America, Chile. **113**, p. 15.

NIGELLA (RANUNCULACEAE) Love-in-a-Mist

damascena 🌸 Summer HA.
Fl. blue in *sp.* but hybrids with many other colours are cultivated. *L.* Bright green, finely cut, fennel-like. 1½–2 ft. Sow in 3–4 in ordinary garden soil and a sunny position, or in 9 to *fl.* earlier the next year. Admirable for cutting and the seed pods are also decorative when cut and dried. Mediterranean region.
    'Miss Jekyll', cornflower blue, semi-double, **352**, p. 44;
    'Persian Jewels', mixed shades, **353**, p. 45;
    'Persian Rose', apple-blossom pink.

NIKKO MAPLE see **Acer nikoense**, **1433**, p. 180.

NOBLE FIR see **Abies procera**

NOLANA (NOLANACEAE)

acuminata, syn. **N. rupicola** Chilean Bellflower 🌸 Summer HHA.
Fl. blue, yellow and white throat, about 2½ in. across, funnel-shaped. *L.* like a lance head. 4–6 in., trailing. Sow thinly in small pots under glass in 3 and 4, or in the open in 5 in sandy soil and a sunny position where they are to flower. Chile.
    'Lavender Gown', the usually cultivated form with lavender blue *fl.*, 6 in., **354**, p. 45.

rupicola see **N. acuminata**

NOMOCHARIS (LILIACEAE) †

Closely related to the true lilies, these are most beautiful *fl.* resembling *Odontoglossum* orchids in their appearance. Unfortunately in most gardens they do not have the same vigour as many lilies but seem to grow more easily in Scotland. They like a moist peaty soil, enriched but not with fresh manure and are very intolerant of moving. The bulbs are smaller than those of most lilies and have larger but fewer scales, thus bringing them close to fritillaries. They are best propagated from seed. They are native to the high meadows of N. Burma, W. China and S.E. Tibet.

mairei 🌸 Summer Bb.
A very beautiful species, *fl.* pendulous 3–4 in. across,
white, heavily spotted and petals fringed on margin. stem 2–4 ft.

pardanthina 🌸 Summer Bb.
Fl. pendulous, pale pink with deeper centre and small spots around centre, 3–4 in. across. Stem 2–4 ft with up to 10 *fl.*, **867**, p. 109.

saluenensis 🌸 Summer Bb.
Fl. pale rose-pink or white, open bowl-shaped, generally erect but outside *fl.* may be horizontal, stem 2–3 ft, with up to six *fl.* about 3½ in. across, *l.* broader than in two preceding sp., **868**, p. 109.

NORTH AMERICAN FLOWERING DOGWOOD see **Cornus florida**, **1526**, p. 191.

NORTH AMERICAN RED BUD see **Cercis canadensis**

NORWAY MAPLE see **Acer platanoides**, **1438**, p. 180.

NORWAY SPRUCE see **Picea abies**

NOTHOFAGUS (FAGACEAE) Southern Beech

Tall trees, deciduous or evergreen many of which are rather tender, lime haters for the most part. Superficially resembling Beeches or Hornbeams. Among the hardiest are:

antarctica Antarctic Beech 🌸 Late Spring T.
Fast growing tree but liable to straggle. *L.* small, rounded and heart-shaped, glossy. Deciduous. *Fl.* small, produced unisexually. Fruit small nuts.

obliqua Robel Beech T.
Large deciduous tree up to 100 ft in wild but so far much less in Britain. *L.* arranged in two opposite rows ovate to oblong up to 3 in. long. Chile.

procera T.
Large deciduous tree up to 80 ft in wild. *L.* oblong or narrowly oval rounded at apex up to 4 in. long by 1½ in. wide. Distinguished by fine autumn colouring of yellow and scarlet. Chile. **1711**, p. 214.

NOTOCACTUS (CACTACEAE)

mammulosus, syn. **Malacocarpus mammulosus** 🌸 Summer GP.
Fl. yellow. Plant round, ribbed, tuberculate. About 6 in. high, making clumps. Gritty compost. Winter temp. 45–50°F. Keep dry from 10 to end of 2, water moderately until 8, then sparingly until 10. Propagate by seed or by division. S. America from Argentina to Brazil. **566**, p. 71.

NYMPHAEA (NYMPHAEACEAE) Water Lily

Hardy Water Lilies 🌸 Summer Aq.
Numerous sp. and hybrids in shades of pink, crimson, yellow and white. Plant 4–6. Depth of water varies, from 6 in. to 2–3 ft, according to the plant's vigour. Garden pools should be in a sunny open position away from overhanging trees. Propagate by removing 'eyes' or side shoots in 4–5 or by division of rhizomes. Hardy sp. are native of Europe and N. America.
Leading hybrids:
    'Escarboucle', wine-crimson, large, planting depth, 1½–2 ft, **1279**, p. 160;
    'Fire Crest', pink, fragrant, depth, 1–1½ ft, **1280**, p. 160;
    'Gladstoniana', pure white, prominent golden stamens, large, depth, 2–3 ft, **1281**, p. 161;
    'James Brydon', carmine-red, depth, 1½–2 ft, **1282**, p. 161;
    'Marliacea Chromatella', pale lemon yellow with bright yellow stamens, depth 1½–2 ft, **1283**, p. 161;
    odorata 'Sulphurea Grandiflora', deep sulphur-yellow, mottled leaves, depth 1–1½ ft, **1284**, p. 161;

    'Paul Hariot', coppery-rose, becoming coppery-red, depth 6–15 in., **1285**, p. 161;
    'Sunrise', yellow and gold, planting depth 1–2 ft, **1286**, p. 161.

Tropical Water Lilies 🌸 Summer GAq.
The tropical water lilies are very gorgeous, but since they need a pond with the water kept over 70°F. they are not available to many amateurs. In many parts of the USA they are kept in greenhouses over the winter and spring and planted out to *fl.* in the summer in public parks and the blue *N. stellata* is treated in the same way at Wisley. Tropical water lilies flower for many months in summer or into autumn depending of course on conditions. In frost-free places in USA their *fl.* will survive autumn outdoors. Both *N. rubra* from Bengal and *N. lotus* var. *dentata* from Sierra Leone are nocturnal bloomers. *N. capensis* is found over much of tropical S. Africa and the var. *zanzibariensis* in both blue and pink forms, comes, as its name implies, from Zanzibar. In addition to their attractive *fl.* these are also very fragrant. Unlike the hardy sp., tropical water lilies hybridise with ease and many have been raised since the first ones were done in Germany in 1859 when Herr Borsig crossed *N. rubra* with *N. lotus* and then crossed the resultant hybrids back on to *N. lotus*. Those raised by Mr George Pring of Missouri are especially notable. The plants are usually started at the end of 3 and then the tubers are placed in large pots or half wine casks in concrete tanks in shallow water. Eventually about a foot of water should cover the plants. After flowering is completed the plants are left for the tubers to ripen and these are overwintered in their containers which are kept damp, or the tubers are lifted and stored in damp sand. These tubers should be protected from rodents. Plants grow easily from seed, but this must be collected with care, as it floats for only 20 minutes, and it is as well to place a container below the ripening pod. Muslin bags are recommended for this purpose. The seed is sown in shallow water at a temp. of 70°F. and the seedlings potted on and put into deeper water as they develop.

capensis GAq.
Fl. large, bright blue, with blue anthers and yellow filaments; fragrant. *L.* 12–16 in. across, roundish-ovate, toothed. S. and E. Africa, Madagascar. **567**, p. 71.
    var. *zanzibariensis rosea*, *fl.* vary from pink to deep carmine, *l.* red beneath, Zanzibar, **568**, p. 71.

Abbreviations and Symbols used in the text.
The following abbreviations may sometimes be used in conjunction as HA. indicating Hardy annual or GBb indicating Greenhouse bulb.

A. = Annual	P. = Perennial
Aq. = Aquatic	R. = Rock or
B. = Biennial	Alpine plant
Bb. = Bulb	Sh. = Shrub
C. = Corm	Sp., sp. = Species
Cl. = Climber	Syn. = Synonym
Co. = Conifer	T. = Tree
Fl., *fl.* = Flower(s)	Tu. = Tuber
G. = Greenhouse or	var. = variety
house plant	× = Hybrid or
H. = Hardy	hybrid parents
HH. = Half-hardy	🌸 = Flowering time
L., *l.* = Leaf, leaves	🌿 = Foliage plant
Mt(s) = Mount,	
mountain(s)	

The following have been used also in the descriptions of Alpines, Bulbs, Trees and Shrubs.

    * = slightly tender
    † = lime hater
    ✿ = highly recommended

The illustration numbers are in **bold type** and the page numbers in light type preceded by p.

lotus var. **dentata** Egyptian lotus GAq.
Fl. pure white. 6–14 in. across, open at night. *L.* up to 2 ft across. Sierra Leone. **569**, p. 72.

rubra GAq.
Fl. deep red, 5–8 in. across; open at night. *L.* purplish-red when young, green as they age. Bengal. **570**, p. 72.
Among the many hybrids are:
'B. G. Berry', *fl.* large rosy-crimson, night flowering, *l.* large, dark green, **571**, p. 72;
'Daubenyana', *fl.* small pale blue, 3–4 in. across, day-flowering, *l.* green, red veined beneath, this is a viviparous var. producing new plants on the *l.* **572**, p. 72;
'Dir. Geo. T. Moore', *fl.* large, violet purple, 8 in. across, day-flowering, *l.* large, red veined beneath, **573**, p. 72.

NYSSA (NYSSACEAE)

sylvatica Tupelo ✳ Mid Spring T.
Small tree up to 25 ft in Britain but considerably more in its native country. *L.* obovate up to 4 in. long. *Fl.* small greenish inconspicuous. Distinguished for brilliant autumn colouring of foliage which is as bright a scarlet as any other autumn colouring tree. Unsuitable for very limy or dry soils. Raised from seed it shows great variations; fine examples may be seen at Sheffield Park in Sussex, well worth a visit in autumn. E. N. America. **1712**, p. 214.

O

OAK see **Quercus**, **1772**, p. 222.

OAK, COMMON see **Quercus robur**

OAK, CORK see **Quercus suber**

OAK, DURMAST see **Quercus petraea**

OAK, EVERGREEN see **Quercus ilex**

OAK, HOLM see **Quercus ilex**

OAK, KERMES see **Quercus coccifera**

OAK, POISON see **Rhus radicans** after **Rhus typhina**

OAK, RED see **Quercus borealis maxima**

OAK, SCARLET see **Quercus coccinea**, **1772**, p. 222.

OAK, TURKEY see **Quercus cerris**

OBEDIENT PLANT see **Physostegia virginiana**, **1319**, p. 165.

× ODONTIODA (ORCHIDACEAE)

hybrids ✳ Late Spring–Midsummer GP.
Bigeneric hybrids between *Cochlioda densiflora, C. noezliana*, an orchid with rather small *fl.* of a brilliant scarlet and various sp. of *Odontoglossum*. The resulting hybrids have the large *fl.* of the latter and the brilliant reds of *C. densiflora* and have been given the name × *Odontioda*. Some *fl.* approach nearer to the brilliant scarlet of *Cochlioda* though in others the accompanying colour may be white or yellow. They will tolerate slightly more heat than *Odontoglossum* (q.v.), but a dry hot atmosphere is to be deprecated. There are a large number of these hybrids, though they do not differ from each other to any large extent, as may be seen in the illustrated plants:
'Astomar', rosy-mauves, magentas and purples in various patterns, **574**, p. 72;

'Colwell', various shades of red, **575**, p. 72;
'Marzorka', various reds, sometimes marked with white, **576**, p. 72.

ODONTOGLOSSUM (ORCHIDACEAE)

hybrids ✳ Late Spring–Midsummer GP.
This is one of the showiest of orchids, but it is also one of the most difficult to grow successfully. For the most part the plants are found high up in the mountains of Mexico, where they are daily bathed in mist and where the temp. is nearly constant. In the greenhouse a constant temp. summer and winter of 60°F. should be aimed at, although lower readings are permissible in the winter, and the atmosphere should be moist and buoyant. Hot dry conditions are resented by the plants and if persisted in for too long may be lethal. The plants should be sprayed frequently, but growers are advised that moisture should not be allowed to linger on the young growths. A compost of equal parts of chopped Osmunda fibre and chopped sphagnum moss is generally recommended; some growers add some decayed oak *l.* to this compost. Although the various sp. are very beautiful, only the white *O. crispum* is in general cultivation and it is usually the hybrids that are seen. A large number have occurred naturally, including the handsome red and white *O. × warnerianum* (supposedly *O. rossii × O. apterum*). The sp. most usually mentioned, are *O. gloriosum* and *O. triumphans* with mainly yellow *fl.*, and *O. nobile* with white *fl.* blotched with crimson. The red flowered hybrids are generally bigeneric crosses with *Cochlioda densiflora* and known as × *Odontioda* (q.v.). Among the many good hybrids are:
Alport, white with various marks and spots in reds, browns and purples, **577**, p. 73;
Edalva, similar to Alport but the marks and spots often concentrated towards the base of each segment, giving the appearance of a coloured centre, **578**, p. 73;
Kopan 'Lyoth Aura', yellow with brown spots and marks, **579**, p. 73.

× ODONTONIA (ORCHIDACEAE)

Hybrids ✳ Usually Late Spring–Midsummer GP.
Bigeneric crosses between sp. of *Odontoglossum* and *Miltonia*. The differences between the two genera structurally are very slight, but *Miltonia* is usually characterised by larger *fl.*, and particularly by the very large lip. The hybrids generally resemble *Odontoglossum* in colour and habit, but the lips have the larger size of *Miltonia*. Although *Miltonia* likes warmer conditions than most *Odontoglossums*, the hybrids will thrive under the same cool conditions as *Odontoglossum* (q.v.). The only way for amateurs to propagate bigeneric hybrids is by back-bulbs, though other techniques are practised by specialist growers.
Excellent modern varieties include:
ampentum 'Regal', mainly cerise with white margins and tips of *fl.* segments, **580**, p. 73;
Atheror 'Lyoth Majesty', white with cherry basal markings on all segments and apex of lip creamy, **581**, p. 73;
Olga 'Icefall', white, **582**, p. 73.

OENOTHERA (ONAGRACEAE) Evening Primrose

cinaeus ✳ Summer P.
Fl. yellow, funnel-shaped. *L.* spear-shaped, in rosettes, outstanding in spring for the varying shades of purple, crimson and buff. 12–15 in. For a sandy, well-drained soil in sun or dappled shade. Propagate by seed sown in spring in a frame or cool house, by cuttings in spring or summer, or by division in spring. N. America. **1287**, p. 161.

fruticosa ✳ Summer P.
Fl. deep yellow up to 2 in. across, opening in the evening. *L.* mainly spear-shaped. Variable in height up to 2 ft. E. N. America. **1288**, p. 161.

macrocarpa see **O. missouriensis**

missouriensis, syn. **O. macrocarpa** ✳ Summer P.
Fl. lemon yellow, large, funnel-shaped. *L.* lance-shaped on trailing stems. 6–9 in. Well-drained soil in sun or light shade. Propagate by seed. S. Central USA. **1289**, p. 162.

tetragona ✳ Summer P.
Fl. bright yellow, of branching habit. *L.* ovate, up to 8 in. long. 1–2 ft. For a light, well-drained soil in sun or partial shade. Propagate by seed sown in 3–4 in sandy soil in a cold frame, or by division. E. N. America.
Good varieties include:
'Fireworks', yellow, red in the bud stage, 1½ ft, **1290**, p. 162;
'Highlight', large yellow, 1½ ft;
'Riparia', large bright yellow, exceptionally long-flowering, 1½ ft, **1291**, p. 162.

OLD MAN CACTUS see **Cephalocereus senilis**, **443**, p. 56.

OLD POET NARCISSUS see **Narcissus** Div. 9.

OLEA (OLEACEAE)

europaea Olive ✳ Summer *T.
Small tree up to 40 ft in Mediterranean areas but usually much less in cultivation. Only possible to grow outdoors in milder regions of Britain, although there is a fine old specimen in Chelsea Physic Garden, London. *Fl.* small greenish-white but very fragrant, in short racemes. *L.* leathery, grey-green above and silvery glaucous below, giving appearance to tree of grey or silvery nature especially when wind blows. Fruit oily up to 1½ in. long, late autumn, source of olive oil when pressed, also for eating as olives. One of the most important crop of plants of Mediterranean region where old twisted trees with conspicuous bark may be seen as part of landscape. One of the oldest cultivated trees. **1713**, p. 215.

OLEANDER see **Nerium oleander**, **1710**, p. 214.

OLEARIA (COMPOSITAE) Daisy Bush

Shrubs mostly evergreen. Valuable for late flowering in 7–8. They are mostly tender only suitable for warmer or seaside areas but among the hardiest are:

Abbreviations and Symbols used in the text.
The following abbreviations may sometimes be used in conjunction as HA. indicating Hardy annual or GBb indicating Greenhouse bulb.

A. = Annual	P. = Perennial
Aq. = Aquatic	R. = Rock or
B. = Biennial	Alpine plant
Bb = Bulb	Sh. = Shrub
C. = Corm	Sp., sp. = Species
Cl. = Climber	Syn. = Synonym
Co. = Conifer	T. = Tree
Fl., fl. = Flower(s)	Tu. = Tuber
G. = Greenhouse or	var. = variety
house plant	× = Hybrid or
H. = Hardy	hybrid parents
HH. = Half-hardy	✳ = Flowering time
L., l. = Leaf, leaves	☙ = Foliage plant
Mt(s) = Mount,	
mountain(s)	

The following have been used also in the descriptions of Alpines, Bulbs, Trees and Shrubs.

* = slightly tender
† = lime hater
✿ = highly recommended

The illustration numbers are in **bold type** and the page numbers in light type preceded by p.

haastii ❀ Summer Sh.
Evergreen shrub, bushy up to 9 ft but usually less. Young branches greyish-white and downy. *Fl.* small with white ray-florets and small yellow disc-florets but in flattish clusters up to 3 in. across, fragrant like Hawthorn. *L.* oval or ovate up to 1 in. long and ½ in. wide, dark shining green, glabrous above but white-felted beneath. Occasionally cut to ground by hard winter frost but usually springing up again. New Zealand. **1714**, p. 215.

macrodonta 'Major' ❀ Summer Sh.
Evergreen shrub up to 15 ft or making small tree in very mild areas or in wild. Bark peeling in long strips. *Fl.* in large terminal clusters up to 6 in. across, ray-florets white and disc-florets golden-yellow in large centre disc. *L.* greyish, leathery, narrowly oval with toothed margins, rather decorative. Valuable as late flowering shrub and particularly fine by seaside. One of the hardiest members of genus. New Zealand. **1715**, p. 215.

OLIVE see **Olea europaea**, **1713**, p. 215.

OMPHALODES (BORAGINACEAE)

cappadocica ❀ Mid Spring–Early Summer RP.
6–8 in. Forms clumps with creeping rhizomes. *Fl.* bright sky-blue, not unlike forget-me-nots, in sprays, about ½ in. across. *L.* ovate. Does best in semi-shade in rather peaty soil. Valuable for long season of *fl.* Asia Minor, S. Turkey. **114**, p. 15.

luciliae ❀ Late Spring–Summer RP.
Fl. pale china blue combining well with very bluish glaucous *l.* on semi-prostrate trailing or ascending stems. 6–8 in. Needs scree conditions when *fl.* spasmodically from late spring until cut by frost, or best grown in alpine house. A beautiful plant but not always easy to establish and resents disturbance. Greece, Asia Minor. **115**, p. 15.

OMPHALOGRAMMA (PRIMULACEAE)

vinciflorum, syn. **Primula vinciflora** ❀ Late Spring–Early Summer †RP.
Fl. strong blue-violet with long tube and six spreading petals up to 2 in. across and very spectacular. *L.* oval, hairy in basal rosette. 6–8 in. Requires moist peaty position in cool climate and usually much easier to grow satisfactorily in Scotland than in S. England. Best protected with pane of glass from winter wet. W. China, Yunnan. **116**, p. 15.

ONCIDIUM see × **Wilsonara**

ONTARIO POPLAR see **Populus candicans**

OPUNTIA (CACTACEAE) Prickly Pear

phaeacantha GP.
Fl. yellow, rarely produced in cultivation. Stems composed of numerous flat, oval joints with reflexed spines. Any well drained soil seems to suit most of this genus, which tend to make shrubby plants up to 5 ft tall and do not *fl.* when young. The spines are barbed and easily detached, so plants must be handled with care. Detached joints will root easily. They like to be dry in winter and moist during the summer, with water given very sparingly in the autumn. Winter temp. for most sp. 40°F. or even lower. S. USA. **583**, p. 73.

ORACH see **Atriplex hortensis**, **241**, p. 31.

ORANGE BALL TREE see **Buddleia globosa**, **1467**, p. 184.

ORANGE BLOSSOM, MEXICAN see **Choisya ternata**, **1512**, p. 189.

ORANGE, CALAMONDIN see **Citrus mitis**, **470**, p. 59.

ORANGE, JAPANESE BITTER see **Poncirus trifoliata**, **1742**, **1743**, p. 218.

ORANGE, MOCK see **Philadelphus**, **1725-1729**, pp. 216, 217.

ORCHIDS see **Bletilla**, **1004**, p. 126; × **Brassocattleya**, **434**, p. 55; **Cattleya**, **442**, p. 56; **Coelogyne**, **477**, p. 60; **Cymbidium**, **487-491**, pp. 61, 62; **Cypripedium**, **44**, p. 6, **493**, **494**, p. 62; **Dendrobium**, **496-498**, pp. 62, 63; **Epidendrum**, **522**, p. 66; **Maxillaria**, **557**, p. 70; **Miltonia**, **558-559**, p. 70; × **Odontioda**, **574-576**, p. 72; **Odontoglossum**, **577-579**, p. 73; × **Odontonia**, **580-582**, p. 73; **Orchis**, **117-119**, p. 15; **Pleione**, **139-141**, p. 18; × **Wilsonara**, **655**, p. 82.

ORCHIS (ORCHIDACEAE)

elata ❀ Summer RP.
Fl. large, deep purple or violet-purple in dense spike of 8 in. *L.* broad, unspotted. 1–1½ ft. One of the finest terrestial orchids, best in peaty situations in semi-shade and should not be allowed to dry out in summer. Unsuitable for cold situations. N. Africa Algeria, Spain. **117**, p. 15.

foliosa see **O. maderensis**

maculata ❀ Summer RP.
Fl. pale lilac-pink or white, heavily spotted, but very variable with three-lobed flat lip, spike dense, often conical. *L.* lanceolate, usually heavily spotted. 1 ft. N. Europe including Britain, but rarely established for long as a rock garden plant. **118**, p. 15.

maderensis, syn. **O. foliosa** ❀ Summer RP.
Fl. bright reddish-purple in long and dense oblong spike up to 8 in. long. Lip broad, three-lobed. 1–1½ ft. Probably the finest hardy sp. but unsuitable for cold areas. Best in a moist peaty situation in semi-shade. Close to *O. elata.* Madeira. **119**, p. 15.

OREGON GRAPE see **Mahonia aquifolium**, **1695**, p. 212.

ORIENTAL PLANE see **Platanus orientalis**, **1741**, p. 218.

ORIENTAL POPPY see **Papaver orientale**, **1300**, **1301**, **1302**, p. 163.

ORIGANUM (LABIATAE)

amanum ❀ Summer RP.
Fl. deep rosy-lilac with long narrow tube of 1½ in. and spreading corolla lobes, numerous and covering plants. *Fl.* bracts purple. *L.* small, cordate, bright green, hairy at edges. Forms small mats or loose tussocks with thin wiry stems. 2–4 in. A fairly recent introduction which promises to make a good plant for scree or alpine house but may be tender in colder areas; probably it should be trimmed back after flowering. Asia Minor. **120**, p. 15.

hybridum ❀ Late Summer P.
Fl. pink, drooping, solitary or in threes. *L.* downy-grey in neat tufts, 9 in. Well-drained limy soil and sunny position. Easily raised from seed, cuttings or division in spring. Levant. **1292**, p. 162.

vulgare Marjoram ❀ Summer P.
Fl. purple in clusters, not showy. *L.* aromatic, deep green. 9–12 in. Cultivation and propagation as for *O. hybridum.* Europe, including Britain.
'Aureum', is the golden form with neat tufts of golden-green *l.* which is often used effectively for edging, 9 in., **1293**, p. 162.

ORNAMENTAL QUINCE see **Chaenomeles**, **1508**, **1509**, p. 189.

ORNITHOGALUM (LILIACEAE)

arabicum ❀ Early Summer *Bb
Fl. white with a prominent dark centre, about 2 in. across in dense spikes on stem 1½ ft. Bulb large, ovoid, about size of a walnut, *l.* broad. One of the finest members of the genus but tender in all except very warm areas and usually best grown as cool greenhouse plant. Needs good ripening after the foliage has died down. Mediterranean region.

nutans ❀ Spring Bb
Fl. white with prominent green bands on outside, drooping so that much of effect is soft jade green. 1 ft. Distinct in the genus, beautiful and much appreciated for unusual *fl.* arrangements. Hardy in all except very cold areas and does well in semi-shade. S. Europe. **869**, p. 109.

thyrsoides Chincherinchee ❀ Summer in England, Early Winter in S. Africa *Bb
Fl. white with yellow stamens, cup-shaped in dense spikes. 1½ ft. Not hardy but may be planted outside in 4 for summer flowering and the bulbs lifted in autumn. The cut spikes are very long lasting and are exported in large numbers from S. Africa for Christmas. **870**, p. 109.

umbellatum Star of Bethlehem ❀ Spring Bb
Fl. white, star-like, opening flat on short stalks of 3–6 in. They open only late in morning and close again in late afternoon, but only give starry white effect when open. An English native and spreading freely when naturalised, so should not be planted among choice dwarf plants, but lovely under trees or shrubs or in a semi-wild garden. **871**, p. 109.

OROBUS VERNUS see **Lathyrus vernus**

ORPHANIDESIA (ERICACEAE)

gaultherioides ❀ Spring †RP.
Small prostrate shrublet 4–6 in. *Fl.* pale shell-pink, saucer-shaped, up to 2 in. across in small clusters. *L.* oval, leathery, hairy, about 3 in. long by 2 in. across. Best grown in peaty or woodland position in semi-shade and must not be allowed to dry out in summer. Slightly tender in very cold conditions. Easily propagated by layers. N.E. Turkey, N. lower slopes of Pontus range. **121**, p. 16.

Abbreviations and Symbols used in the text.
The following abbreviations may sometimes be used in conjunction as HA. indicating Hardy annual or GBb indicating Greenhouse bulb.

A.	= Annual	P.	= Perennial
Aq.	= Aquatic	R.	= Rock or Alpine plant
B.	= Biennial	Sh.	= Shrub
Bb	= Bulb	Sp., sp.	= Species
C.	= Corm	Syn.	= Synonym
Cl.	= Climber	T.	= Tree
Co.	= Conifer	Tu.	= Tuber
Fl., *fl.*	= Flower(s)	var.	= variety
G.	= Greenhouse or house plant	×	= Hybrid or hybrid parents
H.	= Hardy	❀	= Flowering time
HH.	= Half-hardy	☛	= Foliage plant
L., *l.*	= Leaf, leaves		
Mt(s)	= Mount, mountain(s)		

The following have been used also in the descriptions of Alpines, Bulbs, Trees and Shrubs.

* = slightly tender
† = lime hater
✡ = highly recommended

The illustration numbers are in **bold type** and the page numbers in light type preceded by p.

OSCULARIA (AIZOACEAE)

deltoides, syn. **Mesembryanthemum deltoides**
❋ Summer   GP.
Shrubby plant to 9 in. high. *Fl.* mauve-pink with numerous thread-like petals, ½ in. across. *L.* fleshy, glaucous, triangular, ¾ in. long. Gritty compost. Keep on dry side during winter and water only moderately in summer. Winter temp. 40°F. Will thrive outside in summer. Propagate by stem cuttings, which root quickly. Cape of Good Hope. **584**, p. 73.

OSMANTHUS (OLEACEAE)

delavayi, syn. **Siphonosmanthus delavayi** ❋
Spring   Sh.
Evergreen shrub, densely bushy, up to 10 ft but usually less and as much across. *Fl.* small but very numerous, jasmine like with white corolla tube up to ½ in. and four spreading lobes, very fragrant. *L.* small, leathery, ovate, toothed. One of the most valuable spring flowering shrubs for its fragrant abundance of *fl.* W. China. **1716**, p. 215.

OSWEGO TEA see **Monarda didyma**, **1276**, p. 160.

OURISIA (SCROPHULARIACEAE)

coccinea ❋ Summer   RP.
Fl. bright scarlet-crimson, pendulous, tubular, about 1½ in. long with small spreading lobes, in loose clusters on erect stems. *L.* small, oval, toothed forming a spreading clump. 8–10 in. Should be grown in a cool moist position which does not dry out in summer, but it is sensitive to damp in winter and in damp areas should be given a glass over it. A very striking plant but rarely seen. Usually better in the N. of England and Scotland. Chile, Andes.

elegans ❋ Summer   RP.
Close to *O. coccinea* but a slightly larger plant and with *l.* more heart-shaped. 18 in. Chile. **122**, p. 16.

OXALIS (OXALIDACEAE)

adenophylla ❋ Spring   RP.
Fl. funnel-shaped with spreading lobes, lilac-pink, whitening towards base, 1 in. long, numerous. *L.* with many drooping clover-like leaflets, greyish-green. 4 in. Base a small corm-like rounded rhizome covered with coarse fibres. A good plant for well-drained position in rock garden or alpine house. Quite hardy, but disappearing below ground in winter. Chile, Andes. **123**, p. 16.

depressus see **O. inops**

inops, syn. **O. depressus** ❋ Late Spring–Early
Summer   RP.
Fl. shell-pink, yellow at base with a whitish band between, about 1 in. across, numerous, on short stems. *L.* with three broad leaflets like a trefoil. 2–3 in. Sunny position in rock garden where it appears to be quite hardy. S. Africa, Basutoland. **124**, p. 16.

laciniata ❋ Late Spring–Early Summer   RP.
Fl. variable in colour, pink, bluish-mauve or deep lilac or deep violet-mauve, cup-shaped, about 1½ in. across, often with deeper veining, on very short stems, scented. *L.* small, glaucous, compound with up to 12 leaflets. 2–3 in. A recent introduction but a very beautiful miniature for sunny place in rock garden or scree. Hardy but dies back in late summer and winter to a knobbly small rhizome. S. America, Patagonia. **125**, p. 16.

OX-EYE see **Buphthalmum salicifolium**, **1006**, p. 126.

OX-EYE CHAMOMILE see **Anthemis tinctoria**, **968–970**, pp. 121, 122.

OXYDENDRUM (ERICACEAE)
(Sometimes spelt **OXYDENDRON**)

arboreum ❋ Summer   †T.
Small tree up to 20 ft. *Fl.* small, white, but in long pendulous racemes. *L.* narrow, lanceolate up to 6 in. long and 2½ in. wide but usually less. Valuable for its very brilliant scarlet autumn foliage. Unsuitable for very dry or for limy areas. E. USA. **1717**, p. 215.

P

PACHYSANDRA (BUXACEAE)

terminalis ❋ Early Spring   P.
Fl. greenish-white, insignificant. *L.* evergreen, shiny, coarsely toothed. 9–12 in. Useful ground-cover plant for dryish soil beneath trees. Propagate by division in spring. Japan.
  'Variegata', is a silver-leaf form, 9 in., **1294**, p. 162.

PAEONIA (RANUNCULACEAE) Peony
(Sometimes included in new family Paeoniaceae)

Handsome border plants for sun or partial shade. Before planting the ground should be deeply dug and manured, and once planted the woody roots should be left undisturbed. They start into growth early and some varieties are liable to damage by frost, therefore it is wise to plant them where they are not exposed to the early morning sun which may ruin the opening buds. Named varieties are propagated by division in early 10 and the sp. increased by seed.

albiflora see **P. lactiflora**

cambessedesii ❋ Spring   P.
Fl. single, rose pink with prominent yellow anthers. *L.* glossy deep green above, purple beneath. 1½ ft. Does best where protected by taller shrubs. Propagate by seed sown in 9 and placed in a cold frame or by division in early spring. Balearic Is. **1295**, p. 162.

'Defender' ❋ Early Summer   P.
Fl. satiny crimson with large central mass of golden anthers, single, 5–6 in. across, borne on sturdy stems. *L.* large, glossy green. 3½ ft. A hybrid raised in Clinton, New York, USA. **1296**, p. 162.

lactiflora, syn. **P. albiflora** ❋ Early Summer   P.
Fl. pure white, fragrant. *L.* dark green, sometimes hairy beneath. Siberia, Mongolia.
A large number of so-called Chinese peonies have been raised from this sp. and good varieties include:
  'Albert Crousse', shell-pink with carmine centre, 3 ft;
  'Bowl of Beauty', single, pale pink, large, with upright creamy petaloids, 3 ft, **1297**, p. 163;
  'Festiva Maxima', pure white with deep red blotch, double, 3 ft;
  'Sarah Bernhardt', apple blossom pink, very large, double, 2½ ft;
  'Wiesbaden', coral pink edged white, double, 2½ ft.

lutea ❋ Late Spring–Early Summer   Sh.
Shrub with bare stems up to 5 ft, widespreading. *Fl.* deep golden-yellow with central boss of stamens, cup-shaped up to 4 in. across. *L.* large deeply divided. Full sun or semi-shade, does well also on chalk. A valuable tree peony where there is ample space; specimens up to 15 ft across have been grown. S.E. Tibet.
  var. *ludlowii* is a great improvement on *P. lutea* both in the size of *fl.* and in the distance by which they stand away from the foliage, **1718**, p. 215.

mlokosewitschii ❋ Mid Spring   P.
Fl. citron-yellow, cup-shaped. *L.* dark bluish-green above, pale glaucous beneath. 2 ft. Plant 10–11. Caucasus. **1298**, p. 163.

officinalis ❋ Late Spring–Early Summer   P.
Fl. red, solitary, up to 5 in. across. *L.* green, deeply cut, sometimes slightly hairy beneath. 1½–2 ft. France to Albania. **1299**, p. 163.
Good forms include:
  'Alba Plena', double white, 2 ft;
  'Rosea Plena', double pink, 2 ft;
  'Rubra Plena', double crimson, 2 ft.

suffruticosa Moutan ❋ Late Spring–Early Summer
                                                           Sh.
This tree peony sp. contains some of the most magnificent flowering shrubs possible to grow, either full sun or semi-shade but best where they are sheltered from early morning sun after spring frosts. In type, shrub (often known as Rock's tree peony after the American traveller of that name) grows up to 8 ft and 10 ft across but usually seen as less. *Fl.* large, white or blush pink with dark maroon spots at the base of each petal surrounding boss of golden stamens, up to 8 in. across and one of the finest of all shrubs. Named forms are usually shorter in height and tend to die back part of their branches after flowering. Grows well on chalk.
Among finest forms are:
  'Black Pirate', *fl.* deep maroon-crimson with large boss of golden stamens in centre, very large up to 8 in. across. **1719**, p. 215;
  'Hakuo-Jishi', *fl.* semi-double, white with golden stamens, *l.* large, deeply divided, **1720**, p. 215.

PAINTER'S PALETTE see **Anthurium**, **408**, p. 51.

PALM see **Chamaerops**, **1510**, p. 189; **Phoenix**, **626**, p. 79; **Trachycarpus**, **1930**, p. 242.

PAMIANTHE (AMARYLLIDACEAE)

peruviana ❋ Late Winter–Mid Spring   GBb
Fl. large, tubular with campanulate corona and flattish perianth. Tube up to 4½ in. long, green, perianth segments to 4½ in. long, white with green stripe, corona 2 in. wide, 3 in. long, white. In heads of three or four. *L.* strap-shaped, evergreen, to 12 in. Rich well-drained compost needed and a warm, moist atmosphere. The plant will rest between 10 and 12 when it must be kept on the dry side. Minimum winter temp. 55°F. but higher readings preferred. Propagate by offsets or by seed sown as soon as ripe. Peru. **585**, p. 74.

Abbreviations and Symbols used in the text.
The following abbreviations may sometimes be used in conjunction as HA. indicating Hardy annual or GBb indicating Greenhouse bulb.

A. = Annual	P. = Perennial
Aq. = Aquatic	R. = Rock or
B. = Biennial	Alpine plant
Bb = Bulb	Sh. = Shrub
C. = Corm	Sp., sp. = Species
Cl. = Climber	Syn. = Synonym
Co. = Conifer	T. = Tree
Fl., fl. = Flower(s)	Tu. = Tuber
G. = Greenhouse or	var. = variety
house plant	× = Hybrid or
H. = Hardy	hybrid parents
HH. = Half-hardy	❋ = Flowering time
L., l. = Leaf, leaves	❧ = Foliage plant
Mt(s) = Mount,	
mountain(s)	

The following have been used also in the descriptions of Alpines, Bulbs, Trees and Shrubs.

  * = slightly tender
  † = lime hater
  ☼ = highly recommended

The illustration numbers are in **bold type** and the page numbers in light type preceded by p.

PAMPAS GRASS see **Cortaderia, 1057,** p. 133.

PANCRATIUM (AMARYLLIDACEAE)

illyricum ✳ Early Summer *Bb
Fl. white, star-shaped in clusters, with a central cup and pointed outer segments on end of a long tube. Fragrant. Stem 1½ ft, L. wide, strap-shaped. Bulb very large. Plant in sunny warm position if possible under a S. wall or in colder regions in a frame. A striking fl. common in S. Italy and Central Mediterranean regions. **872,** p. 109.

maritimum Sea Lily ✳ Late Spring–Early Summer
Bb
Similar to P. illyricum, with white fl. and glaucous l. usually lying flat along ground and growing literally in the sand of the sea shore by the Mediterranean. Slightly more tender than P. illyricum and only successful in open in very warm gardens.

PANSY see **Viola tricolor, 221,** p. 28; **395-396,** p. 50.

PAPAVER (PAPAVERACEAE)

alpinum Alpine Poppy ✳ Summer A. or B.
4–8 in. Fl. in many colours from white, yellow, orange or orange-red, singly on short stems, delicate on thin stems. L. glaucous, much divided. A very beautiful miniature poppy. Best sown either in autumn or early spring in position where it is to fl. Full sun but requires well-drained or scree position on rock garden. Once established often spreads freely and maintains itself by self-seeding. European Alps, Carpathians. **126,** p. 16.
var. rhaeticum, deep yellow, a beautiful form with slightly larger fl. E. Alps, Dolomites.

nudicaule Iceland Poppy ✳ Summer HB.
Fl. large single, orange, salmon, yellow and white. 1½ ft. Sow under glass in 2–3 and plant out in 4–5 to fl. as annuals. Arctic regions.

orientale Oriental Poppy ✳ Late Spring–Early Summer P.
Fl. scarlet, often with a black blotch at the base of each petal. L. grey-green, hairy, up to 1 ft long. 2–3 ft. Any well-drained garden soil of good depth to accommodate the plant's long, fleshy roots, and a sunny postion. Propagate named varieties by root cuttings taken in the autumn or winter and placed in boxes of sandy soil in a cold frame, or seed may be sown in the open ground in 3–4. There are many splendid hybrids in shades of orange-scarlet, salmon pink, fiery red and white. Armenia. **1300,** p. 163.
Good varieties include:
'Indian Chief', deep bronze-red, 2½ ft;
'Marcus Perry', orange-red with black blotches, 2½ ft;
'Mrs Perry', salmon-pink, darker blotches, 3 ft, **1301,** p. 163;
'Sultana', peach pink, 2½ ft, **1302,** p. 163.

rhoeas Corn Poppy ✳ Midsummer–Mid Autumn HA.
Fl. scarlet, of the corn field. L. about 6 in. long, irregular toothed. A wide range of garden varieties with double, semi-double and single fl. is available in shades of scarlet, pink, red with black blotches, what are known as art shades. Begonia-flowered strain has large double fl. in many colours. 1½–2 ft. The sp. is widely distributed in the N. Temperate Zone. **355,** p. 45.

PAPERBARK MAPLE see **Acer griseum, 1431,** p. 179.

PAPHIOPEDILUM see **Cypripedium**

PAPYRUS see **Cyperus papyrus, 492,** p. 62.

PARROTIA (HAMAMELIDACEAE)

persica Iron Tree ✳ Early Spring T.
Wide-spreading tree up to 30 ft. Branches grey tending to grow horizontally thus making fine contrast with upright fastigiate conifers such as Libocedrus. Fl. without petals consisting of boss of red stamens. L. large, ovate or obovate, up to 5 in. long. Conspicuous for brilliant orange-red and scarlet autumn colouring. N. Persia and slopes of Caucasus by Caspian. **1721,** p. 216.

PARROT'S BILL see **Clianthus puniceus, 1974,** p. 247.

PARTHENOCISSUS (VITACEAE) Virginia Creeper

tricuspidata 'Veitchii', syn. **Ampelopsis veitchii, Vitis inconstans** ☙ Cl.
Very vigorous climber self-adhesive to walls. Grown for autumn colouring of l. which is brilliant scarlet or deep crimson. L. large up to 5 in. across, three-lobed. One of the most popular wall creepers owing to the brilliance of autumn colouring, vigorous and hardy. China, Japan. **1985,** p. 249.

PARTRIDGE-BREASTED ALOE see **Aloe variegata, 407,** p. 51.

PASSIFLORA (PASSIFLORACEAE) Passion Flower

caerulea ✳ Summer *Cl.
Vigorous evergreen climber but tender in cold districts. Fl. conspicuous up to 2½ in. wide, sepals star-shaped, numerous, greenish-white, inside is corona composed of filaments which are blue at top, white in the middle and deep purplish-blue towards base. Stamens and styles form conspicuous centre with corona said to resemble the wounds of Christ hence name Passion Flower. L. five to seven-lobed up to 7 in. across. Fruits ovoid, fleshy deep yellow or orange up to 1½ in. long. Hardy as a wall shrub in S. and W. England and in warmer areas. May be pruned hard if too vigorous. Central W. S. America. **1986,** p. 249.
'Constance Elliott', is form with ivory-white fl.

PASSION FLOWER see **Passiflora, 1986,** p. 249.

PAULOWNIA (SCROPHULARIACEAE)

tomentosa, syn. **P. imperialis** *T.
Deciduous tree up to 50 ft but usually less, does not fl. when small. Fl. foxglove-like in panicles, each pale lilac-mauve up to 2 in. long and 1½ in. across, borne on bare branches. Owing to habit of making fl. buds in autumn and overwintering them, fl. are often destroyed by hard frosts in winter; branches also rather brittle. L. very large especially on hard-pruned specimens which may be grown for foliage, up to 1 ft long, ovate and 10 in. across, lobed. A fine tree for milder counties but best planted in a position sheltered from strong winds. China. **1722, 1723,** p. 216.

PEA, GLORY see **Clianthus formosus, 473,** p. 60.

PEA, SWEET see **Lathyrus odoratus, 316-321,** pp. 40, 41.

PEACH see **Prunus persica, 1759,** p. 220.

PEACH-LEAVED BELLFLOWER see **Campanula persicifolia, 1014, 1015,** p. 127.

PEANUT CACTUS see **Chamaecereus silvestrii, 446,** p. 56.

PEAR see **Pyrus, 1771,** p. 222.

PEAR, PRICKLY see **Opuntia, 583,** p. 73.

PEAR, WILLOW-LEAVED see **Pyrus salicifolia** 'Pendula', **1771,** p. 222.

PEARL EVERLASTING see **Anaphalis, 960-962,** pp. 120, 121.

PELARGONIUM (GERANIACEAE)

crispum 'Variegatum' ✳ Summer ☙ GP.
Shrubby plant to 3 ft. Fl. mauve in few-flowered peduncles. L. fan-shaped, fragrant, tipped with white in variegated form, up to 1½ in. long. Normal potting compost. Winter temp. 40–45°F. Propagate by stem cuttings, which can be taken at any time, although hard to root in winter. S. Africa. **586,** p. 74.

× **domesticum** ✳ Late Spring–Early Summer GP.
The Regal or Martha Washington Pelargoniums have a fairly involved hybrid ancestry and a history of at least 150 years. It would appear that the principal parents were P. angulosum, P. cucullatum and P. grandiflorum. Other sp. included were P. acerifolium and P. fulgidum. Both P. acerifolium and the related P. angulosum have dark purple fl. often with darker markings. P. cucullatum has red fl. with deeper veins, while P. grandiflorum has white fl. with purplish veins. It may be assumed roughly that the dark cultivars show the influence mainly of P. angulosum, the white petalled cultivars, that of P. grandiflorum, while the red fl. comes from P. cucullatum. This is, however, only a rough approximation as to how the race emerged as many of the earlier hybrids were of unknown parentage. The plants require a cool, airy, rather dry atmosphere and are generally pruned hard back when flowering is complete. Pelargoniums are propagated easily from cuttings, while seed is used for the creation of fresh cultivars. A fairly rich soil mixture suits the Regals, while the other hybrid races, the Zonals and the Ivy-leaved, will do well in a poorer mixture. All that is necessary in the winter months is to keep the plants frost-free. If early fl. are required, some heat must be given from 2 onwards and the plants must receive plenty of water when making their growth. Unlike the

Zonals, the Regals have only one season of flowering, but this is extremely spectacular. Unfortunately there is a hybridity bar between the section Pelargium, to which the Regals belong and the section Ciconium, from which the Zonals spring and it has not been possible to combine the striking colours of the Regals with the continuous flowering of the Zonals. All the sp. from which all the hybrid races have sprung, come from S. Africa.

'Applause', soft pale pink, very frilled, reasonably compact, **587**, p. 74;

'Aztec', white, blotched crimson, compact habit, **588**, p. 74;

'Braque', bright shrimp pink, good habit, **589**, p. 74;

'Carisbrooke', soft rose pink, the most popular regal variety, branching habit, **590**, p. 74;

'Cezanne', purple upper petals on pale lavender ground, very compact, **591**, p. 74;

'Degas', orange-red shading to crimson, fairly compact, **592**, p. 74;

'Doris Frith', white with vivid markings, branching habit, **593**, p. 75;

'Grand Slam', rosy-red shading to crimson, very compact, **594**, p. 75;

'Renoir', glowing orange-pink, compact, **595**, p. 75;

'Rogue', mahogany-crimson, outstandingly dwarf and compact, **596**, p. 75;

'South American Bronze', burgundy red, white picotee edge, rather loose habit, **597**, p. 75.

× **hortorum** ✸ Summer–Early Spring or 🍂 GP.
The parentage usually given for this race is *P. inquinans* crossed with *P. zonale*, but recently doubts have been cast as to whether the other parent was *P. zonale* as it is recognised today. The plant that is known as *P. zonale* has not, in spite of its name, a very distinct horseshoe mark on its *l.* and this is to be found more accentuated in the sp. *P. scandens* and *P. frutetorum*. ('Gazelle' is a modern hybrid using *P. frutetorum*.) These may well have all been cultivated under the name of *P. zonale* and it is possible that all three sp. have been used in the evolution of the race. Another sp. that may have been employed is the salmon-pink flowered *P. salmoneum* (*P. hybridum* L.), which has unmarked *l.*, and in recent years the strap-petalled *P. acetosum* has contributed to the so-called Cactus-flowered Geraniums. Some of the dwarfer cultivars may have *P. monstrum* in their ancestry. This has zoned *l.* and rather small pale pink *fl.* It has never been found in the wild, but has been in cultivation since 1784 and breeds true from seed. The Zonal Pelargoniums can roughly be divided into three sections; the Bedding Geraniums, which *fl.* well out of doors and of which 'Paul Crampel' is the best known; the Greenhouse Zonals, which do not do well out of doors, although they require little heat and the Tricolors, which have been bred for beauty of foliage rather than *fl.* These date from the late 1850's. In the Tricolors it is the sp. with the zoned *l.* that has been the main influence, but in the cultivars raised for their *fl.* the most important sp. is the handsome *P. inquinans*, which has nearly round, broad-petalled, scarlet *fl.* with unzoned *l.* If left for some time many of the cultivars will make large shrubby plants which are often trained on conservatory walls, but for pot work they are usually propagated yearly, cuttings being taken in early autumn. Normally little winter heat is required, but if winter *fl.* are wanted, a temp. around 50°F. should be maintained and better results are obtained if some artificial light is used to prolong the short hours of daylight. Some cultivars are difficult to *fl.* even with additional lighting. It is possible to obtain *fl.* throughout the year by these means. Too rich a soil mixture should not be used, as this tends to encourage *l.* growth at the expense of *fl.* The plants should at all times be well-lit and in a dry airy atmosphere. Many of the Tricolors are very shy-flowering and 'Madame Salleroi' has never been known to *fl.* at all. A giant tetraploid strain came into existence in France in 1872 and double-flowered plants have been known since 1860. Zonals will not cross with Regals, but it has been possible to cross them with the Ivy-leaved Geraniums derived from *P. peltatum*, although such hybrids are usually sterile. Coming from a series of sp. with predominantly scarlet *fl.* the range that has been evolved is surprising and the Zonal Pelargonium must be regarded as one of the most satisfactory of all cool greenhouse plants.

Tricolor:

'A Happy Thought', magenta, *l.* green with a creamy-yellow 'butterfly' in the middle, **598**, p. 75;

'Flower of the Day', intense scarlet, semi-prostrate habit, **599**, p. 75;

'Mrs Henry Cox', pale pink, best-known tricolor, *l.* outer edge light green, zone red, shading to dark green to black, inner zone lavender-green, slow grower, **600**, p. 75;

'The Czar', red, small *fl.*, *l.* with very heavy bronze zone, **601**, p. 76.

Zonal:

'Elaine', cerise pink, single, tall, **602**, p. 76;

'Elizabeth Angus', bright orange, bold white centre, very vigorous, **603**, p. 76;

'Festiva Maxima', purple, double, the best of its type, fairly strong grower, **604**, p. 76;

'Gazelle', bright orange pink, small *fl.*, tall, free-flowering, **605**, p. 76;

'Gustave Emich', fiery red, double;

'Irene Genie', orange-pink, vigorous, tall, **606**, p. 76;

'Jane Campbell', orange, large single *fl.*, strong grower, **607**, p. 76;

'King of Denmark', bright rose pink, semi-double;

'Lief', soft orange-pink, semi-double, fairly dwarf, **608**, p. 76;

'Muriel Parsons', bright pink, very vigorous, **609**, p. 77;

'Orangesonne', orange, double, dwarf habit, **610**, p. 77;

'Paul Crampel', brilliant red, single;

'Xenia Field', white, with a scarlet eye, **611**, p. 77;

'Zinc', scarlet, double, one of the best dwarf varieties, **612**, p. 77.

peltatum and hybrids Ivy-leaved Pelargonium
✸ Mid Spring–Mid Autumn GP.
The Ivy-leaved pelargoniums derive almost entirely from *P. peltatum*, which forms the only member of the section Dibrachya. At one time it was thought that there was a second sp., *P. lateripes*, but this is now considered to be a hybrid between a zonal Pelargonium and *P. peltatum*. If this is so, it suggests that the Ivy-leaved pelargonium must have had some zonal blood in it from an early stage. The plants form climbing or pendant stems of great length and *fl.* throughout the summer and autumn; indeed in warm climes they are rarely out of *fl.* They thrive in rather stony soil, but for pot work a moderately rich mixture is used. Winter temp. should keep the plants frost-free, but great heat would be detrimental. During the summer dry well-lit conditions are the best. In the wild the colour of the *fl.* of *P. peltatum* varies from deep pink to white with violet veins and the cultivar 'L'Elegante' is identical with the wild type apart from its variegated *l.* The Zonals will cross with *P. peltatum* and with the tetraploid forms the hybrids may well be fertile. Hybrids appear to combine the climbing habit of *P. peltatum* with the shape and colour range of the Zonals. Unless they can be given a wall to cover, the peltatum group are best in hanging baskets or placed out of doors in the summer in urns, from which they can depend. Owing to their straggling habit, they are of more use in warmer climes such as California or the Mediterranean, when they can be left outside permanently to make large masses. Many cultivars which sound very attractive have been lost and this race seems to offer the best prospects for the modern breeder.

'Claret Crousse' (in USA known as 'Mexican Beauty'), claret-red the best of its colour group; rather tall, **613**, p. 77;

'Crocodile', pale pink, *l.* white and green, veined like a crocodile's skin, **614**, p. 77;

'King Edward VII', cherry-rose, large flowered, robust, **615**, p. 77;

'L'Elegante', pale blush pink, *l.* green and white variegated, turning deep mauve when mature, **616**, p. 77;

'Mexican Beauty', see 'Claret Crousse';

'Trotting Hill', deep cerise pink, almost the largest of its type in cultivation, good habit, **617**, p. 78.

PELTIPHYLLUM (SAXIFRAGACEAE) Umbrella Plant

peltatum, syn. **Saxifraga peltata** ✸ Mid Spring P.
Fl. white or pale pink in large clusters, before the elegant foliage appears. 2–3 ft. *L.* large, rounded, lobed. Deep moist soil beside a pool or stream in sun or light shade. Very invasive and unsuitable for small gardens. Propagate by division in the early spring, or by seed. California. **1303**, p. 163.

PENNISETUM (GRAMINEAE)

alopecuroides ✸ Late Summer P.
Fl. heads purplish, up to 6 in. long. *L.* bright green, long and narrow. 2–4 ft. A most decorative grass for a well-drained soil and a sunny position. Transplant 4. Propagate by division or seed. China. **1304**, p. 163.

longistylum see **P. villosum**

orientale see **P. ruppelii**

ruppelii, syn. **P. orientale** Fountain Grass USA ✸ Summer HHA.
Fl. white to purplish, in feathery spikes 10–12 in. long on graceful stems 1–3 ft. *L.* 1–2 ft long, smooth or hairy. Sow under glass in 3 and plant out in 5, in a sunny position and ordinary garden soil. Abyssinia. **356**, p. 45.

villosum, syn. **P. longistylum** ✸ Summer P.
Fl. white to purplish feathery plumes up to 6 in. long. *L.* narrow, arching. 1½–2 ft. For a sheltered sunny position in well-drained ordinary garden

soil, may prove tender in cold areas. Sow in boxes in spring under glass and transplant in the open in 4–5. Abyssinia. **1305**, p. 164.

PENSTEMON (SCROPHULARIACEAE)

barbatus, syn. **Chelone barbata** ✳ Summer   P.
Fl. coral-red, tubular. *L.* lance-shaped, smooth. 2½–3½ ft. Needs sun and a well-drained soil. Propagate by division in the spring or by seed. There are various garden forms in shades of pink, salmon and scarlet. Mexico. **1306**, p. 164.

fruticosus ✳ Summer   RP.
6–10 in. Spreading sub-shrubby plant making enormous mats where suited. *Fl.* variable from pale lilac-pink to rosy-purple up to ½ in. long with pronounced lip, on short stems. *L.* small, lanceolate. Best in well-drained sunny position on rock garden or in scree or cleft between rocks with foliage in sun. Mountains of Pacific Coast States of N. America.
    var. *crassifolius*, close to type but with entire *l.*, **127**, p. 16.

gentianoides see **P. hartwegii**

hartwegii, syn. **P. gentianoides** ✳ Summer   P.
Fl. deep red to scarlet, drooping, tubular. *L.* oval-lance-shaped. 2–2½ ft. Sunny, sheltered bed and well-drained soil. Propagate by cuttings of basal shoots in 9 and overwintered in a cold frame. Plant out in 5 to early 6. Mexico.
    Named hybrids include:
    'Firebird' (Schönholzeri'), brilliant crimson, **1307**, p. 164;
    'Ruby', deep crimson.

newberryi ✳ Summer   RP.
4–6 in. *Fl.* bright purplish-crimson, tubular, usually horizontal, up to 1 in. long, numerous. *L.* small but branchlets often form a large mat. Good drainage is very important. A very beautiful sp. for its intensity of colour. Mountains of N.W. America but requires cooler position than *P. fruticosus*. **128**, p. 16.

scouleri ✳ Summer   RP.
8–10 in. Forms large prostrate clumps or mats of bright green foliage. *Fl.* rosy-purple, long-tubed with prominent lip in small clusters. There is also a fine white form. Close to *P. fruticosus* and requires similar well-drained position. Mts of N.W. America. **129**, p. 17.

'Six Hills Hybrid' ✳ Early Summer   P.
Fl. deep rosy-lilac. *L.* oval, small. 6–9 in. Plant 3–4 in well-drained soil with some lime and a sunny position. Propagate by cuttings taken in 9 in a cold frame. A hybrid between *P. davidsonii* × *erianthera*. **1308**, p. 164.

PEONY see **Paeonia**, **1295-1299**, pp. 162, 163; **1718-1720**, p. 215.

PEPEROMIA (PIPERACEAE)

A genus of small herbaceous plants, found throughout the tropics, although most cultivated sp. come from S. America. They are nearly epiphytic and need very little soil, although a good potting compost is to be preferred. Winter temp. should ideally be around 55°F., but lower readings are possible if the plant is kept dry. All sp. will tolerate periods of drought, as they have fleshy stems and *l.*

argyreia, syn. **P. sandersii** Rugby Football Plant ❧   GP.
Plant about 6 in. high. *L.* elliptic, banded in silver and dark green, up to 4 in. long and 3 in. across. If used as a house plant, avoid draughts and keep on dry side. Propagation by *l.* cuttings. Brazil. **618**, p. 78.

caperata ✳ Autumn ❧   GP.
The *fl.* are borne in forked, white inflorescences. About 4 in. high. *L.* heart-shaped, ridged, dark

---

green with purplish and grey sheen. Sometimes infected by a virus causing leaf-distortion. All affected plants should be destroyed. Propagate by leaf-stem cuttings. **619**, p. 78.

hederaefolia ❧   GP.
Similar to *P. caperata*, but larger, up to 6 in. high. *L.* not corrugated, up to 2½ in. long and 2 in. across. Inflorescence unbranched. Propagation by leaf-stem cuttings. **620**, p. 78.

magnoliifolia see **P. obtusifolia** '*Variegata*'

obtusifolia 'Variegata' ❧   GP.
Much branched plant up to 9 in. *L.* evergreen, oval 2 in. long, 1½ in. across, with a cream edge. As the *l.* ages, the cream portion tends to disappear. Propagate by stem cuttings. The plant is usually offered in the UK under the name *P. magnoliifolia*. Tropical America. **621**, p. 78.

sandersii see **P. argyreia**

PEPPER BUSH, SWEET see **Clethra alnifolia** under **C. barbinervis**

PEPPER, RED see **Capsicum annuum**, **256**, p. 32.

PERILLA (LABIATAE)

frutescens ✳ Summer   HHA.
Fl. white, small, in whorls. Ornamental foliage plants. Effective for summer bedding. 1½–2 ft. Sow in a warm greenhouse in 2–3 and plant out in late 5–6. India, China.
    'Nankinensis', a selected form with elegant purple-red *l.* with a bronze centre, **357**, p. 45.

PERIWINKLE see **Vinca**, **1420**, p. 178; **1951**, p. 244.

PERNETTYA (ERICACEAE)

mucronata ✳ Early Summer   Sh.
Dwarf evergreen shrub spreading freely by suckers up to 3 ft but often less. *Fl.* small white flask-shaped followed by *l.*, small, leathery, evergreen, shining. Berries large up to ½ in. wide, white, glistening or pink or purple or deep crimson. One of the finest autumn berrying shrubs for semi-shade and preferably grown on lime free areas and thrives in peaty soil. Chile. **1724**, p. 216.
    Various named strains of selected forms have been raised; among the best are 'Bell's hybrids' and 'Davis's hybrids'.

PEROVSKIA (LABIATAE)

atriplicifolia ✳ Late Summer   P.
Fl. soft blue borne on crest spikes. *L.* grey-green, aromatic, coarsely toothed, up to 2½ in. long. Of shrubby habit. 3–5 ft. Plant 1 1–3 in a dryish soil and a sunny open position. Propagate by cuttings taken with a heel in the spring. Afghanistan to Tibet. **1309**, p. 164.

PERUVIAN LILY see **Alstroemeria**, **957**, **958**, p. 120.

PETROCOSMEA (GESNERIACEAE)

kerrii ✴ Late Summer ❧   *RP.
Fl. white with yellow centre each about ¾ in. across, in clusters on stems about 2½ in. long, opening flat. *L.* thick, velvety, slightly purplish, and silvery below, cordate, decorative as a foliage plant. Best grown as alpine house plant and requires careful watering. Thailand. **130**, p. 17.

PETUNIA (SOLANACEAE)

hybrida ✴ Summer   HHA.
Fl. in shades of crimson, scarlet, pink, deep and

---

light blue, violet, cream, yellow, also pure white. *L.* entire, rather small. 9–18 in. Sow in 2–3 in a warm greenhouse and plant out in a sunny position and well-drained soil in late 5–6. Admirable for pots, bedding or window boxes. S. America.
    There are numerous named hybrids including:
    'Blue Bedder', **358**, p. 45;
    'Lavender Queen';
    'Pink Satin', **359**, p. 45;
    'Salmon Supreme', bright salmon;
    'Snowball', pure white.
    Vigorous F2 hybrids include:
    'Blue Lagoon';
    'Gypsy Red', bright salmon-scarlet;
    'Moonglow', yellow;
    'Pink Beauty';
    'Red Cap', crimson-scarlet;
    'Starfire', scarlet and white;
    'Sugar Plum', deep lavender veined rich purple;
    'White Magic', pure white.
There are also various mixtures and types developed from year to year and good seedsmen should be relied upon to provide the latest developments for specialists.

PFITZER JUNIPER see **Juniperus** × **media** 'Pfitzeriana'

PHACELIA (HYDROPHYLLACEAE)

campanularia ✳ Summer   HA.
Fl. brilliant gentian-blue, bell-shaped. *L.* greyish, egg-shaped, irregularly notched. Of compact habit. 9 in. Sow in 3–4 in a sunny border with a light well-drained soil. Fast growing, may start to *fl.* in six weeks of sowing. In mild areas can be sown in the open in 9. S. California.
    'Blue Bonnet', an intense blue variety, **360**, p. 45.

PHALARIS (GRAMINEAE)

arundinacea ✳ Summer   P.
Fl. green or purplish spikelets *L.* narrow, green. 2–4 ft. Any ordinary garden soil in sun or light shade. Propagate by division of the creeping rootstock in spring. Temperate N. hemisphere.
    'Picta', a form, known as Gardener's Garters, or Ribbon Grass, with longitudinal white stripes on the narrow green leaves, **1310**, p. 164.

Abbreviations and Symbols used in the text.
The following abbreviations may sometimes be used in conjunction as HA. indicating Hardy annual or GBb indicating Greenhouse bulb.

A. = Annual	P. = Perennial
Aq. = Aquatic	R. = Rock or Alpine plant
B. = Biennial	
Bb = Bulb	Sh. = Shrub
C. = Corm	Sp., sp. = Species
Cl. = Climber	Syn. = Synonym
Co. = Conifer	T. = Tree
Fl., fl. = Flower(s)	Tu. = Tuber
G. = Greenhouse or house plant	var. = variety
	× = Hybrid or hybrid parents
H. = Hardy	
HH. = Half-hardy	✳ = Flowering time
L., l. = Leaf, leaves	❧ = Foliage plant
Mt(s) = Mount, mountain(s)	

The following have been used also in the descriptions of Alpines, Bulbs, Trees and Shrubs.

    * = slightly tender
    † = lime hater
    ✿ = highly recommended

The illustration numbers are in **bold type** and the page numbers in light type preceded by p.

PHARBITIS TRICOLOR see **Ipomoea tricolor**

PHEASANT EYE NARCISSUS see **Narcissus** Div. 9.

PHILADELPHUS (SAXIFRAGACEAE) Mock Orange

Sometimes placed in Hydrangeaceae and often erroneously called Syringa thus confusing it with lilacs which belong to the genus *Syringa*. Tall deciduous shrubs up to 10 ft. *Fl.* white, single or semi-double, mostly very fragrant. Will grow well on light soils. Prune by cutting out shoots which have flowered in late 7 or 8 or in winter and occasionally taking out older wood right to base.
Among the finest are:

'Avalanche' ✳ Summer Sh.
Small fragrant *fl.* weighing down arching branches.

✿**'Beauclerk'** ✳ Summer Sh.
Fl. large up to 2½ in. across, milky-white with small amount of cerise colour around stamens, very strongly scented. Less tall growing than many forms usually not more than 6 ft, one of the finest hybrids. **1725**, p. 216.

'Belle Etoile' ✳ Summer Sh.
Fl. single 2 in. across flushed maroon in centre, strongly scented, tall arching growth. **1726**, p. 216.

'Bouquet Blanc' ✳ Summer Sh.
Fl. double snow-white with orange scent. **1727**, p. 216.

coronarius ✳ Summer Sh.
One of the original sp. *Fl.* single smaller than in many hybrids but freely borne with conspicuous yellow stamened centre, very strongly scented. Tall shrub up to 15 ft, very vigorous. Looks well in *fl.* arrangements when stripped of rather large oval *l.* S. Europe, Asia Minor. **1728**, p. 216.

'Manteau d'Hermine' ✳ Summer Sh.
Rather more dwarf up to 5 ft. *Fl.* creamy white, double, fragrant. **1729**, p. 217.

microphyllus ✳ Summer Sh.
Small leafed sp. forming a twiggy bush not often above 3 ft. *Fl.* small white but very strongly scented.

'Virginal' ✳ Summer Sh.
Fl. double white, scented very popular variety.

PHILESIA (LILIACEAE) *†

magellanica, syn. **P. buxifolia** ✳ Summer †Sh.
Dwarf evergreen shrub spreading freely by underground suckers and making large patch in milder areas. Up to 2 ft. *Fl.* deep crimson, long bell-shaped like those of a Lapageria, pendulous, up to 2 in. long with slight bloom over crimson colouring. One of the most beautiful dwarf evergreen shrubs. *L.* narrow, stiff, deep green but glaucous beneath, slightly enrolled. Only suitable for peaty and rather moist soils. Excellent in S.W. countries but hardy in other places as well in sheltered positions. S. Chile. **1730**, p. 217.

PHILODENDRON (ARACEAE)

Most sp. including all those illustrated, are climbers. They produce aerial roots at every joint and do best when allowed to climb up a cylinder of wire stuffed with moss, or trained on the bark, so that additional nourishment can be obtained from the aerial roots. An open fairly rich soil compost is required and a moist atmosphere is necessary. Many sp. are grown for room decoration and will survive in very shady conditions. The growing tip should be taken off in early spring and any etiolated winter growth removed. Propagation is by taking sections of the stem, which are already carrying roots, and potting them up in heat.

andreanum see **P. melanochrysum**

bipinnatifidum 🍂 GP.
Herbaceous plant with *l.* up to 2 ft long and 18 in. across. Often grown as a house plant and will appreciate the same conditions as *P. scandens*.

cordatum see **P. scandens**

erubescens 🍂 GP.
L. sagittate, dark green with purple underside. Petioles and stipules wine-red. Vigorous grower to 10 ft or more. Winter temp. about 50°F., although 55°F. is preferable. Useful as a room plant, when it should be frequently sponged to keep *l.* clean. Colombia.
The clone known as 'Burgundy', is the best-coloured and has *l.* up to 12 in. long.

hastatum 🍂 GP.
L. bright green, shaped like a spear-head, heart-shaped at base, up to 6 in. long. Fairly slow-growing, but ultimate height usually about 8 ft. Winter temp. about 50°F. Brazil. **622**, p. 78.

laciniatum 🍂 GP.
L. five-lobed, the lower four lobes deeply-lobed themselves. Up to 9 in. long and 6 in. across. Vigorous climber needing ample room. Minimum winter temp. 55–60°F. Guiana, Brazil. **623**, p. 78.

melanochrysum 🍂 GP.
L. heart-shaped, up to 6 in. long. Dark green with golden sheen on upper side, pale purple-pink on underside. The plant is not a true sp. but the juvenile form of *P. andreanum*. The adult *l.* are an elongated heart-shape, up to 3 ft long and are produced after the plant has climbed about 5 ft. Winter temp. 65°F. Colombia. **624**, p. 78.

scandens 🍂 GP.
L. green, heart-shaped, up to 4 in. long and 2½ in. across. Fairly vigorous climber to 10 ft or more with long internodes. Will tolerate drier conditions and lower temp. than most other sp. Minimum winter temp. 45°F. This is the most popular foliage house plant in the USA where it goes under the wrong name of 'Philodendron cordatum' among florists. Panama, W. Indies. **625**, p. 79.

PHLOMIS (LABIATAE)

fruticosa Jerusalem Sage ✳ Early Summer *Sh.
Evergreen shrub up to 4 ft, vigorous grower and spreading widely. Branches rather soft and covered with grey hairs. *Fl.* deep yellow in whorls at ends of branches. Tubular 1¼ in. long two-lipped. *L.* grey-green, hairy rather wrinkled like those of a sage. Should be planted in warm sunny position and does well in light sandy soils. In very hard winters may be cut back to ground level. Valuable for its grey foliage and strong yellow *fl.* in 6. Mediterranean regions and S. Europe where it is abundant. **1731**, p. 217.

PHLOX (POLEMONIACEAE)

adsurgens ✳ Early Summer †RP.
6–8 in. Prostrate spreading stems with short erect *fl.* stems. *Fl.* pale shell-pink with deeper eye, 1 in. across in clusters. *L.* small, ovate. A very beautiful plant for cool, rather moist position with plenty of leaf-mould, but dislikes lime. N.W. America. **131**, p. 17.

amoena ✳ Early Summer RP.
6–10 in. *Fl.* deep pink or reddish-purple or white, variable in colour, saucer-shaped with deepest eye, up to 1 in. across in clusters. *L.* linear, hairy. Needs well-drained position on rock garden and more sun than preceding sp. S.E. USA. **132**, p. 17.

bifida ✳ Spring RP.
6–8 in. *Fl.* white or pale violet-purple, petals narrow, more star-like than other sp., with deeply cleft lobes, in small clusters on short stems forming a small dome of *fl.* *L.* linear, hairy. Requires good drainage in sunny position. E. USA. **133**, p. 17.

divaricata ✳ Early Summer P.
Fl. lavender-blue. *L.* green, oblong about 2 in. long.

9–15 in. For the front of a border or on the rock garden in well-drained, moist soil and partial shade. Propagate by cuttings taken after flowering and inserted in sandy soil in a cold frame, or by division in spring. E. N. America. **1311**, p. 164.

douglasii ✳ Late Spring–Summer RP.
2–6 in. Forming large mats, inclined to be straggling in shade. *Fl.* very variable in colour and many forms have been named. Very free-flowering. Rock garden either in sun or semi-shade. Easily propagated from summer cuttings. W. N. America.
Good forms are:
'Beauty of Ronsdorf', deep pink with deeper eye, **134**, p. 17;
'Boothman's variety', pale mauve;
'Snow Queen', white;
'Supreme', lavender-blue, large.

drummondii ✳ Summer HHA.
Fl. in shades of crimson, scarlet, pink, mauve, some with various white markings, fragrant. *L.* up to 3 in. long, lobes three-dentate. 6–12 in. Sow in 3–4 under glass and plant out in late 5–6 in a moist sunny border, or in partial shade. Texas.
'Cecily mixed', dwarf habit, white eyed strain, various colours, 9 in.;
'Cuspidata Twinkle' mixed contains many different coloured, star-like *fl.*, 6 in., **361**, p. 46;
'Dwarf Beauty', large flowered, compact strain with bright colours, 6 in.

maculata ✳ Summer P.
Fl. violet-purple. *L.* opposite, slender-pointed, 2–4 in. long. 2½–3 ft. Sunny border and a well-drained soil. Propagate by division or cuttings. E. N. America.
Good varieties include:
'Alpha', pink in tapering spikes, 2½ ft, **1312**, p. 164;
'Miss Lingard', pure white, 3 ft;
'Purpurea', purple, 3 ft.

mesoleuca see **P. nana** var. *ensifolia*

nana var. *ensifolia*, syn. **P. mesoleuca** ✳ Late Spring–Early Summer RP.
4–8 in. Probably the most beautiful and probably the choicest of all the dwarf phlox in the eyes of the keen alpine gardener. Stem loose and straggling. *Fl.* large, bright shell-pink with white deepset eye, rather star-like up to 1½ in. across, in small clusters. *L.* narrow, linear, 2 in. long. Usually grown in scree

mixture in alpine house and rarely very vigorous in cultivation. Usually propagated by root cuttings. S. USA, Texas and New Mexico. **135**, p. 17.

paniculata ✸ Summer   P.
Fl. violet-purple in dense terminal clusters. *L.* oblong, slender-pointed 3–4 in. long. 2–4 ft. Requires a well-cultivated soil that does not dry out during the growing season and a position in sun or light shade. Propagate by root cuttings taken in the autumn and inserted in boxes of sandy soil in a cold frame. Cuttings are not recommended because of possible eelworm infestation. E. USA.
There are many named hybrids in shades of crimson, mauve, pink, and white, including:
  'Brigadier', salmon-scarlet, 4 ft, **1313**, p. 165;
  'Chintz', pink with a red eye, 3 ft;
  'Mother of Pearl', white, 3 ft, **1314**, p. 165;
  'Norah Leigh', notable for its creamy-buff and green foliage, the mauve *fl.* are of little account, 3 ft, **1315**, p. 165;
  'Prince of Orange', orange-scarlet, 3 ft, **1316**, p. 165;
  'Starfire', striking red, 2½ ft, **1317**, p. 165.

subulata Moss Phlox ✸ Spring   RP.
2–4 in. Forms large tufted spreading mats. *Fl.* very variable in colour with many named forms up to ¾ in. across and usually very floriferous. Full sun on rock garden and usually easy of cultivation, but needs trimming after flowering to keep compact. Among finest forms are:
  'Brilliant', deep rose;
  'Camla', salmon-pink, large *fl.* and very beautiful but not so vigorous as some;
  'G. F. Wilson', pale lavender-blue, an old favourite;
  'Temiscaming', shocking bright magenta-crimson, the most striking form, **136**, p. 17;
  'Vivid', pale crimson, rather dwarf.

PHOENIX (PALMACEAE)

roebelinii Palm   GT.
Up to 2 ft in height. *L.* feathery up to 12 in. long with individual leaflets up to 7 in. long. Winter temp. 50°F. and a well-lit position in the house. Rarely fruiting in cultivation, propagation is by off-shoots ascending from the roots, which should be removed in any case. They are best taken for propagation in late spring. The Date Palm, *P. dactylifera* belongs to the same genus. Assam, Viet-Nam. **626**, p. 79.

PHORMIUM (LILIACEAE)

tenax New Zealand Flax ✸ Summer   Sh.
Sub-shrubby with large glaucous sword-like *l.* growing from base, chiefly grown for striking architectural foliage effect. *Fl.* in large spike up to 10 ft, dull red, long lasting. Spike is headed with branching horizontal panicles. *L.* large glaucous up to 6 ft in length, sharp at points, very tough and from them valuable fibre is extracted. Plant in moist position. Hardy in most areas but unsuitable for very cold regions. New Zealand. **1732**, p. 217.
Several forms have been named including:
  purpureum, *l.* bronzy-purple;
  'Veitchii', *l.* bright green with broad creamy-white stripe up middle of *l.*

PHOTINIA (ROSACEAE)

beauverdiana ✸ Late Spring   T.
Deciduous large shrub or small rather slender tree up to 30 ft usually less. *Fl.* white hawthorn-like in clusters 2 in. across followed by deep red small hip-like fruits. *L.* narrowly obovate rather slender, finely toothed up to 5 in. long, colouring scarlet in autumn and chiefly grown for this reason. Hardy. W. China. **1733**, p. 217.

serrulata ✸ Spring   Sh.
Slightly tender evergreen shrub. *Fl.* white in clusters up to 6 in. across followed by globose small red fruits. *L.* oblong up to 8 in. long and 3 in. across.

Young foliage is lustrous red with bronzy tinge and conspicuous feature in late spring and lasting through earlier part of the year. Only suitable for milder areas where it will make large shrub. China. **1734**, p. 217.

PHYGELIUS (SCROPHULARIACEAE)

aequalis ✸ Late Summer   Sh.
Evergreen sub-shrub with woody base up to 3 ft spreading widely but tender and liable to be cut to ground in bad winter. *Fl.* tubular with small spreading lobes, 1¼ in. long and ½ in. wide, five-lobed, salmon-scarlet with yellow colouring in throat, in large racemes set more closely than those of *P. capensis* which is slightly hardier and grows up to 4 ft but may be more against a wall. Valuable plant for milder areas for its late flowering, does best in full sun, easily increased by cuttings in late summer. S. Africa. **1735**, p. 217.

capensis Cape Figwort ✸ Late Summer   Sh.
  'Coccineus', has slightly brighter scarlet *fl.* than type and is best form to select, **1736**.

PHYSALIS (SOLANACEAE)

franchetii Cape Gooseberry, Chinese Lantern ✸
Early Summer   P.
Fl. small, whitish, insignificant, followed by decorative orange-red inflated calyx. Useful when cut and dried. *L.* large, long-stalked. 1½ ft. Plant 11–3 in well-drained loamy soil, sun or partial shade. Propagate by division of the long, fleshy roots in spring. Japan. **1318**, p. 165.

PHYSOSTEGIA (LABIATAE) Obedient Plant

virginiana ✸ Summer   P.
Fl. deep pink, tubular. *L.* lanceolate, deeply toothed. 1½–2 ft. Plant 3–4, in sun or partial shade. Propagate by division in the spring. N. America.
  'Vivid', a brighter rose and more compact, **1319**, p. 165.

PHYTEUMA (CAMPANULACEAE)

comosum ✸ Summer   RP.
3–4 in. *Fl.* in clusters shaped like small flasks with narrow ends pointing outwards, pale lilac-blue, deeper in colour at tips, up to 1 in. long, one of the most peculiar *fl.* in this section. *L.* sharply toothed, glossy, ovate. A plant of the limestone rock crevice, best grown in a scree or crack in rock or in a hole in tufa block. Not difficult in alpine house. With it in front of picture is *Jankaea heldreichii*. Austrian, N. Italian Alps. **137**, p. 18.

PICEA (PINACEAE) Spruce

Evergreen trees usually rather conical in habit, easily distinguished from *Abies* by the pendulous cones and the small peg-like projections left where needles have fallen off branchlets. Most Spruces do not do well on hot dry land.

abies, syn. **P. excelsa** Norway or Common Spruce   Co.
Tree usually grown as Christmas Tree but also widely grown for forestry purposes.

alba see **P. glauca**

breweriana Brewer's Weeping Spruce   Co.
Tall evergreen tree up to 120 ft in native habitat but much less in cultivation. One of the most beautiful of all conifers. Distinguished by rather horizontal branches from which descend long pendulous branchlets up to several ft long, *L.* dark green above glaucous below about 1 to 1¼ in. long. Cones oblong up to 5 in. long by 1 in. broad, purple before ripening and then becoming brown. Scales reflexed when ripe. Very slow growing especially when young but where old established trees are seen they always attract considerable attention, looking especially fine after rain when pendulous branchlets

---

glisten with water as with dew drops. Does not assume pendulous habit until several years old. Two very fine specimens are to be seen in the arboretum at Westonbirt in Glos. W. USA, Mts of N.W. California, S.W. Oregon. **2026**, p. 254.

canadensis see **P. glauca**

excelsa see **P. abies**

glauca, syn. **P. alba**, **P. canadensis** White Spruce   Co.
Tall tree up to 100 ft. Form usually seen in gardens is:
  var. *albertiana* 'Conica', Alberta Spruce, dwarf slow-growing evergreen conifer from Canadian Rockies, best in a moist sheltered position slowly reaching 6 ft by 4 ft across at base with absolutely conical outline, *l.* light glaucous green. Valuable for large rock garden and for making formal effect. **2027**, p. 254.

likiangensis   Co.
Tree up to 100 ft in native habitat but much less in cultivation. Bark deeply furrowed, rather thick. Distinguished in cultivation for bright pink cones, narrow when immature, pendulous but becoming ovate oblong in later stages. Leaflets thick, stiff, dark green above and glaucous below in two overlapping ranks along sides of young shoots. A rather variable sp. slightly tender when young becoming hardier as it matures. W. China where it is a mountain tree. **2028**, p. 254.

omorika Serbian Spruce   Co.
Tall very slender evergreen with spire-like effect, growing up to 100 ft in native habitat but usually less in cultivation. Branches usually feathered well right to ground giving narrow conical effect. Needles horizontally arranged overlapping, deep green above, glaucous below. Cones ovoid about 2 in. long, pendulous, bluish-black when young becoming dark brown as ripe. **2029**, p. 254.
  'Pendula', very beautiful form with drooping branchlets. One of the most valuable sp. for garden purposes owing to its narrow upright habit and nearly always making a beautiful and distinctive tree.

pungens Blue or Colorado Spruce   Co.
Rather slow growing tree up to 100 ft in native habitat but rarely over 15 or 20 ft in cultivation. *L.* prickly, stout and stiff spreading round shoot up to 1¼ in. long, variable in colour from dull green to

---

bright glaucous blue. Cones cylindrical, narrower at ends up to 4 in. long with reddish tinge when young then pale brown. Grown mostly for its blue leaved forms of which best known are 'Glauca' and 'Kosteriana', these are very similar and may be synonymous, foliage conspicuously glaucous especially in young trees, branching tends to be horizontal. Usually best specimens are seen in young trees and tends to become misshapen as trees age but valuable garden tree for its very glaucous blue effect.
'Glauca', **2030**, p. 254.

PICKEREL WEED see **Pontederia cordata**, **1327**, p. 166.

PIERIS (ERICACEAE) †

✿**formosa**. var. *forrestii*, syn. **P. forrestii** ✳ Mid Spring *Sh.
Evergreen shrub up to 8 ft. *Fl.* creamy-white in drooping panicles urn-shaped about ⅓ in. across but numerous rather like small Lily of the Valley *fl.* Young foliage bright scarlet as it opens in spring sometimes with the *fl.* in 4, becoming paler as it ages through shrimp-pink to green. *L.* oval lanceolate finely and regularly toothed up to 4 in. by 1½ in. wide, glabrous and slightly glossy. Best planted in semi-shade and prefers peaty soil with leaf mould and unsuitable for very dry or very cold positions. Where growing well one of the most spectacular spring shrubs for its combination of *fl.* and foliage. W. China, N.E. Burma. **1737**, p. 218.

forrestii see **P. formosa** var. *forrestii*.

japonica ✳ Spring Sh.
Evergreen shrub up to 15 ft. *Fl.* creamy-white pendulous in long branching panicles, very numerous. *L.* lanceolate or narrowly oval up to 3½ in. long, slightly toothed and dark glossy green above. Hardier and more vigorous in growth than *P. formosa* var. *forrestii*. Japan. **1738**, p. 218.

taiwanensis ✳ Mid Spring Sh.
Evergreen shrub up to 10 ft. *Fl.* horizontal or erect in short racemes up to 3 in. long on which *fl.* are nodding or pendulous, corolla pure white urn-shaped nearly ½ in. long. *L.* leathery, dark, glossy green, up to 5 in. long. Hardy and very desirable shrub for lime-free areas. Young foliage red but not so brilliant as in *P. formosa* var. *forrestii*. **1739**, p. 218.

PIG SQUEAK see **Bergenia**, **1002**, **1003**, p. 126.

PILEA (URTICACEAE) Aluminium Plant

cadierei 'Nana' ❧ GP.
Plant 6–9 in. *L.* oblong-oval, pointed, bluntly toothed, up to 3 in. long, 1½ in. across, dark green with silvery patches between veins. Tolerant of indoor conditions. Propagate by cuttings in heat; stop frequently to maintain bushy shape. Feed frequently for good *l.* colour. **627**, p. 79.

PINCUSHION FLOWER see **Scabiosa atropurpurea**, **373**, p. 47.

PINCUSHION PLANT see **Cotula barbata**, **277**, p. 35.

PINE see **Pinus**, **2031-2036**, pp. 254-255.

PINE, AUSTRIAN see **Pinus nigra**, **2033**, p. 255.

PINE, BHUTAN see **Pinus wallichiana**, **2036**, p. 255.

PINE, BLACK see **Pinus nigra**, **2033**, p. 255.

PINE, CHILEAN see **Araucaria araucana**

PINE, JAPANESE UMBRELLA see **Sciadopitys verticillata**, **2037**, p. 255.

PINE, MEXICAN WHITE see **Pinus ayacahuite**, **2031**, p. 254.

PINE, MONTEREY see **Pinus radiata**, **2034**, p. 255.

PINE, ROUGH-BARKED MEXICAN see **Pinus montezumae**, **2032**. p. 254.

PINE, SCOTS see **Pinus sylvestris**, **2035**, p. 255.

PINEAPPLE SCENTED SAGE see **Salvia rutilans** under **Salvia grahamii**

PINK HORSE CHESTNUT see **Aesculus × carnea**, **1441**, p. 181.

PINKS see **Dianthus**, **49-52**, p. 7; **283-286**, p. 36; **499-510**, pp. 63, 64; **1092-1107**, pp. 137-139.

PINUS (PINACEAE) Pine
Evergreen trees usually rather conical when young but when older with top branches spreading horizontally. Pines do best when planted in open sites and are unsuitable for establishing in shady positions. Most require light, well-drained soil. Bark usually thick furrowed and in some sp. distinguished for its reddish colouring. Needles in groups of two, three or five and sp. may be distinguished in this way. All pines are resinous. Cones upright or horizontal, variable in size.

austriaca see **P. nigra**

ayacahuite Mexican White Pine Co.
Fast growing tree up to 100 ft often widespreading with graceful habit and long needles in clusters of five, up to 8 in. long, slightly glaucous below. Cones large, usually solitary but sometimes clustered up to 1½ ft long but usually less and 6 in. wide at the base. One of the most beautiful conifers and hardy in all except very cold situations. **2031**, p. 254.

excelsa see **P. wallichiana**

griffithii see **P. wallichiana**

insignis see **P. radiata**

montezumae Rough-barked Mexican Pine
Probably the most beautiful Pine for cultivation in Britain but unsuitable for cold areas. Tree up to 100 ft in native country but usually much less in cultivation. Bark reddish-brown, rough and fissured. Leaflets in groups of five but occasionally eight in cluster usually arranged at ends of short branches in large groups, bluish-green, spreading up to 10 in. long. Cones solitary or occasionally clustered, cylindrical up to 10 in. long, dark brown. Mexico on mountains. **2032**, p. 254.
var. *hartwegii*, is probably the hardiest form, but with *l.* less glaucous.

nigra Black Pine Co.
Form usually grown is *P. nigra* var. *nigra* the Austrian Pine syn. *P. nigra* var. *austriaca* or *P. austriaca*. Large tree up to 150 ft tending to have flattish head with horizontal branching as it ages. Bark rough, very dark brown appearing black in shadow. *L.* in pairs occasionally singly, greenish-blue when young with brown tips to scales, becoming light brown with darker scale tips on maturity. Widely grown as forest shelter belt but timber is not coarse and not very valuable, however, good wind resister and very hardy, but somewhat sombre in appearance for garden use. **2033**, p. 255.

radiata, syn. **P. insignis** Monterey Pine Co.
Very fast growing tree, evergreen and up to 100 ft with wide horizontal branching. *L.* in clusters of

three densely crowded on young branchlets, bright yellowish-green up to 6 in. long. Cones shortly stalked, ovoid, usually solitary sometimes in clusters of three to five round branch, up to 6 in. long by 3½ in. wide and remaining persistent on branches for several years. Very valuable tree for making a quick effect and rapidly assumes character of an old tree. It is very wind resistant particularly by seaside and so much used for shelter belts. It transplants badly and should be planted in permanent position when young, not more than 1½ ft, or planted preferably out of pots. **2034**, p. 255.

sylvestris Scots Pine Co.
One of our finest native trees up to 100 ft often with straight trunk and crown of branches horizontally arranged at top. Bark deeply fissured, thick and reddish-brown especially where scales have been shed. *L.* in pairs, grey-green, stiff up to 4 in. long. Cones two or three or solitary, ovoid up to 3 in. long, greyish when young then dull brown. Useful for planting as forestry tree on poor sandy sites and valuable also as wind break. Forms from N.W. of Scotland are notoriously wind and salt spray resistant. **2035**, p. 255.

wallichiana, syn. **P. excelsa**, **P. griffithii** Bhutan Pine Co.
Sometimes also known as Blue Pine or Himalayan Pine. Large tree up to 150 ft in native habitat. Bark greyish-brown with shallow fissures on old trees. *L.* in 5 lasting up to four years, long greyish-green usually spreading or drooping up to 8 in. long. Cones solitary or in clusters up to 3, pendulous when mature up to 12 in. long by 2 in. across, light brown with lighter tips to scales. Unsuitable for lime soils. Distinguished by large horizontal lower branches and glaucous young shoots and smooth cones. One of the finest pines for its long needles and distinct habit of growth. **2036**, p. 255.

PITTOSPORUM (PITTOSPORACEAE)

crassifolium Karo ✳ Spring *Sh.
Evergreen shrub up to 20 ft, too tender except for gardens in warmer areas and Isles of Scilly. May be used for hedging in warm climates. *L.* rather leathery with pale brown or greyish indumentum below, obovate, up to 4 in. long. *Fl.* dark purple in small terminal clusters, unisexual. Photograph shows plant with young seed heads which are pale grey. New Zealand. **1740**, p. 218.

PLAGIORHEGMA DUBIA see **Jeffersonia dubia**

PLANE see **Platanus**, **1741**, p. 218.

PLANTAIN LILY see **Hosta**, **1175–1179**, pp. 147, 148.

PLATANUS (PLATANACEAE) Plane

orientalis Oriental Plane   T.
Very large tree up to 80 ft and widespreading with short trunk in open situations, one of the finest and most long lived trees which can be grown in England. *L.* deeply lobed with five to seven lobes, large up to 9 in. wide, dark glossy green. *Fl.* small inconspicuous followed by globular slightly bristly fruits on pendant stalks each being 1 in. wide. **1741**, p. 218. More often seen is *P. × acerifolia*, the London Plane, a hybrid between *P. orientalis* and *P. occidentalis*, tree up to 100 ft with tall clean trunk and bark peeling to give mottled effect. *L.* usually five-lobed up to 10 in. wide, coarsely toothed. Fruit bristly in globular heads, pendulous. One of the most popular trees especially in public parks and making magnificent effect. Autumn foliage deep yellow.

PLATYCODON (CAMPANULACEAE)

grandiflorum Balloon Flower, Chinese Bell Flower ✻ Summer   RP.
8–12 in. *Fl.* like a small balloon or spineless sea urchin in bud, open to shallow saucer-shape, deep blue-mauve, 2–2½ in across, several to a stem. *L.* grey-green, broadly ovate. Suitable for sunny situation in rock garden but should be planted in final position when young as it moves badly. W. China, Japan. Two good named forms are:
‘Apoyama’, dwarf, 4–5 in. but with large deep mauve *fl.*;
‘Mariesii’, with large deep purplish-blue *fl.*, **138**, p. 18.

PLATYSTEMON (PAPAVERACEAE)

californicus Cream Cups ✻ Summer   HA.
Fl. cream or pale yellow, saucer-shaped. *L.* narrowly oblong, roughly hairy. 6–12 in. Sow in 3–4 in light soil and a sunny position where they are to *fl.*, or in 9. California. **362**, p. 46.

PLEIONE (ORCHIDACEAE)

bulbocodioides see under **P. limprichtii**

formosana ✻ Spring   *RP.
Beautiful dwarf orchids for the alpine house that may be occasionally wintered outside successfully if covered with pane of glass. *Fl.* light magenta-rose with large creamy fringed lip marked buff yellow inside, up to 3 in. across, on short stem from a dark green, fleshy pseudobulb. *L.* developing after *fl.*, broad, pleated, light green. 3–4 in. Should be planted in a mixture of peat, humus, grit and chopped sphagnum with plenty of drainage at base of pan. Keep fairly dry in winter, but water plentifully in late spring and summer when in growth. Pans should be covered with *fl.* Very variable. Formosa. **139**, p. 18.
Numerous forms have been named, such as:
‘Alba’, with white *fl.* and yellow lip, **140**, p. 18;
‘Pricei’, with deeper coloured *fl.* and darker pseudobulbs;
Some have been given vernacular names such as ‘Polar Sun’ and ‘Oriental Splendour’.

limprichtii ✻ Spring   *RP.
Has brighter *fl.* deep cerise-pink with orange-crimson markings inside lip. In warm areas may be hardy outside if covered in winter with pane of glass. **141**, p. 18.

The latest botanical treatment considers the above two sp. and forms as variants of one very polymorphic sp. *P. bulbocodioides.*

PLEOMELE (LILIACEAE)

reflexa ‘Song of India’ ➤   GSh.
Shrub to, apparently, about 3 ft, branching at base. Related to *Cordyline* and *Dracaena*. *Fl.* not seen in cultivation. *L.* sword-shaped, to 10 in. long, 1½ in. across, golden yellow with green streak in centre. Winter temp. 55°F. Propagation by stem cuttings in heat. Keep dry in winter and well-lit; moist and slightly shaded in summer. Introduced from Botanic Garden in Ceylon. **628**, p. 79.

PLUM, CHERRY see **Prunus cerasifera**, **1754**, p. 220.

PLUMBAGO see **Ceratostigma**, **1505**, **1506**, p. 189.

PLUME POPPY see **Macleaya**, **1260**, **1261**, p. 158.

POCKET HANDKERCHIEF TREE see **Davidia involucrata**, **1558**, p. 195.

PODOCARPUS (TAXACEAE)

gracilior ➤   GT.
A graceful evergreen, eventually making a very large tree, but attractive in juvenile state. *L.* 4 in. long, ¼ in. wide on young trees; shorter and broader on older specimens. Winter temp. around 55°F. Propagate by cuttings in late summer or, preferably, by seed. Tropical Africa. **629**, p. 79.

PODOPHYLLUM (BERBERIDACEAE) Himalayan Mayflower
(Sometimes included in new family Podophyllaceae)

emodii ✻ Spring   P.
Fl. large, whitish or pale pink. *L.* bronze-red in spring, large wedge-shaped. Brilliant red fruits in autumn. 6–12 in. Plant 11–2 in shade and a soil rich in peat or leaf mould. Propagate by division or by seed sown in pans in a cold frame. India. **1320**, p. 165.

POISON IVY see **Rhus toxicodendron** after **R. typhina**

POISON OAK see **Rhus radicans** after **R. typhina**

POLEMONIUM (POLEMONIACEAE)

foliosissimum ✻ Late Spring–Early Autumn   P.
Fl. blue, narrowly bell-shaped, in bold clusters, long lasting. *L.* oval, or lance-shaped. 1½–2½ ft. Plant 11–3, in ordinary soil. Propagate by seed or division in the autumn. Rocky Mountains. **1321**, p. 166.
‘Sapphire’, bright blue in 5–6, 1½ ft, **1322**, p. 166.

POLIANTHES (AMARYLLIDACEAE)

tuberosa Tuberose ✻ Summer   GBb.
Fl. white, fragrant, trumpet-shaped in type, but shapeless in the double form ‘The Pearl’. *L.* long grass-like. Bulbs planted at intervals from 2 to 5 will give a succession of *fl.* They need rich soil and a temp. ranging from 60 to 70°F. Bulbs are usually discarded after one year, but offshoots can be grown on. A winter temp. of 50°F. is adequate if bulbs are kept dry. Mexico. **630**, p. 79.

POLYANTHUS see **Primula Polyanthus**, **364**, p. 46.

POLYGALA (POLYGALACEAE)

calcarea Milkwort ✻ Summer   RP.
3–6 in. A beautiful native, especially of the Chalk Downs. Very variable in colour from magenta-pink to brightest blue. *Fl.* stems often tend to lie prostrate. *Fl.* in short spikes with two petaloid wing-like coloured sepals. Plant in as sunny a position as

possible. It probably only develops really good blue colour on chalk. **142**, p. 18.

chamaebuxus Bastard Box ✻ Spring   RP.
4–6 in. Dwarf shrublet with many compact branchlets. *Fl.* conspicuously bicolored, wings pinkish-purple, centre of *fl.* white and keel bright yellow. *L.* small, oblong-lanceolate, rather dark green. Sub-alpine woodlands but suitable for either sunny position or semi-shade in the rock garden.
‘Rhodoptera’, is finest coloured form with deep cerise-carmine wings and bright yellow keel. **143**, p. 18.

POLYGONATUM (LILIACEAE) Solomon's Seal

multiflorum ✻ Early Summer   P.
Fl. small white, pendulous, borne on arching branches. *L.* 3–5 in. long, oval oblong. 2–3 ft. Ordinary soil and a shady position. Propagate by division in the autumn. Europe, including Britain. **1323**, p. 166.

POLYGONUM (POLYGONACEAE) Knotweed

affine ✻ Summer   RP.
4–6 in. *Fl.* rosy-red in dense erect spikes. *L.* basal and forming a dense mat. Spreading freely in sunny position on rock garden. Himalayas.
Best form is:
‘Donald Lowndes’, after famous plant collector and traveller in Nepal, **144**, p. 18.

amplexicaule Late Summer–Mid Autumn   P.
Fl. bright crimson, forming slender pokers on erect stems. *L.* heart-shaped, pointed. 3–4 ft. Ordinary soil in sun or partial shade. Propagate by division in spring. Himalayas. **1324**, p. 166.
Good varieties include:
‘Album’, white, tinged pink, 3 ft;
‘Firetail’, carmine-scarlet, 4 ft;
‘Speciosum’, deep claret, 3 ft.

bistorta Snakeweed ✻ Summer   P.
Fl. soft pink spikes. *L.* oblong-oval. 1½ ft. Plant 10–3. Propagate by division in spring. Europe.
‘Superbum’, light pink, up to 3 ft, **1325**, p. 166.

campanulatum Himalayan Knotweed ✻ Midsummer–Mid Autumn   P.
Fl. pale pink, fragrant, in drooping panicles. *L.* narrowly oval, 3–6 in. long. 2½–3½ ft. Ordinary soil

in sun or partial shade. Propagate by division in spring. Himalayas. **1326**, p. 166.

vacciniifolium ✴ Late Summer–Mid Autumn RP. 4–6 in. A voracious mat-forming spreader over rocks but valuable for its late-flowering. *Fl.* deep shell-pink in narrow spikes on wiry crimson stems. *L.* small, ovate. This usually does best rooting in semi-shade behind boulder and then spreading over it. **145**, p. 19.

POMEGRANATE see **Punica granatum, 174**, p. 22; **1768**, p. 221.

PONCIRUS (RUTACEAE)

trifoliata, syn. **Aegle sepiaria, Limonia trifoliata, Citrus trifoliata** Japanese Bitter Orange, Golden Apple ✴ Spring   T.
Deciduous spiny shrub or small tree up to 15 ft with wide-spreading head. Branches are flattened and have very stout spines up to 2½ in. long and extremely sharp. *Fl.* white up to 2 in. across with five petals. Fruit globose like small oranges, deep yellow when ripe, up to 2 in. across and downy, smelling citrus-like. *L.* trifoliate. Valuable as produces hardy small oranges although these are not very suitable for eating. Hybrids have been raised between this and *Citrus sinensis* and are called Citranges, other hybrids are Kumquats. Useful as hedging plants where complete barrier is required. N. China, Japan. **1742, 1743**, p. 218.

PONTEDERIA (PONTEDERIACEAE) Pickerel Weed

cordata ✴ Summer   HAq.
Fl. blue, in closely packed spikes. *L.* bright green, thick, on long stalks, 1½–2 ft. Plant beside a pool where the water is 6–9 in. deep. Propagate by division in the spring, although this is possible at almost any time. N. America. **1327**, p. 166.

PONDWEED, CAPE see **Aponogeton distachyus,, 972**, p. 122.

POPLAR see **Populus, 1744**, p. 218.

POPPY, ALPINE see **Papaver alpinum, 126**, p. 16.

POPPY BUSH, CALIFORNIAN see **Dendromecon rigidum, 1560**, p. 195.

POPPY, CALIFORNIAN see **Eschscholzia californica, 294**, p. 37.

POPPY, CELANDINE see **Stylophorum diphyllum, 1392**, p. 174.

POPPY, CORN see **Papaver rhoeas, 355**, p. 45.

POPPY, HAREBELL see **Meconopsis quintuplinervia, 1267**, p. 159.

POPPY, HIMALAYAN BLUE see **Meconopsis betonicifolia, 1263**, p. 158.

POPPY, HORNED see **Glaucium flavum, 299**, p. 38.

POPPY, ICELAND see **Papaver nudicaule**

POPPY, ORIENTAL see **Papaver orientale, 1300-1302**, p. 163.

POPPY, PLUME see **Macleaya, 1260, 1261**, p. 158.

POPPY, PRICKLY see **Argemone, 240**, p. 30.

POPPY, TREE see **Romneya, 1837**, p. 230.

POPPY, WELSH see **Meconopsis cambrica, 1264**, p. 158.

POPULUS (SALICACEAE) Poplars
Large deciduous trees several native to British Isles or North America.
Among those frequently seen are:

alba White Poplar   T.
Conspicuous tree owing to the glistening whiteness of undersurfaces of *l.*

candicans Ontario Poplar, Balm of Gilead   T.
L. broader than in true Balsam Poplar which is *P. tacamahaca* but which is rarely grown. Wide-headed tree *l.* having strong small of balsam in spring, widely suckering.

canescens Grey Poplar   T.
Handsome vigorous tree with greyish *l.* and good on chalky soils.

lasiocarpa   T.
Small tree but with very large *l.* up to 1 ft long and 9 in. wide, with conspicuous red veins and *l.* stalks. Catkins 9 in. long and woolly. China.

nigra Black Poplar ✴ Mid Spring   T.
Large deciduous tree up to 100 ft. Distinguished by dark rough bark, often with deep fissures. *L.* ovate or diamond-shaped, up to 4½ in. long. Male catkins red, up to 2 in. long.
    var. *betulifolia*, with dense bushy top and downy young twigs is form most often seen, widely distributed in Europe and W. Asia, too large for most gardens.
    var. *italica*, syn. *P. pyramidalis*, Lombardy Poplar, one of the most useful trees for columnar effect but roots tending to spread widely and very greedy.

× **serotina** Black Italian Poplar   T.
Vigorous hybrid between *P. deltoides* and *P. nigra* with conspicuous male catkins and young *l.* coppery.

tremula The Aspen   T.
Large tree native to N. Europe and E. to Asia Minor to the Caucasus. *L.* up to 4 in. across broadly ovate on very slender petioles thus making them move constantly in the wind hence the name Aspen. Male catkins up to 4 in. long brownish-pink 2, the most conspicuous part of the tree before the *l.* appear. **1744**, p. 218.

tremuloides American Aspen   T.
Close to *P. tremula* but with *l.* rather smaller and more regularly toothed.

trichocarpa Western Balsam Poplar   T.
Large tree said to be up to 200 ft in native habitat. *L.* up to 10 in. long ovate. Male catkins up to 3 in. long. N. America.

PORTUGAL LAUREL see **Prunus lusitanica**

PORTUGUESE HEATH see **Erica lusitanica, 1585**, p. 199.

PORTULACA (PORTULACACEAE) Purslane

grandiflora Sun Plant, Rose Moss ✴ Summer–Mid Autumn   HHA.
Fl. double and single, in shades of scarlet, rose-pink, rosy-purple, yellow, also white. 6–8 in. of spreading habit. Sow in a warm greenhouse in 3, or in the open in 5–6 in a sunny position where they are to *fl.* This is preferable as seedlings do not transplant easily. Brazil.
    'Flore Pleno', the double form, comes in many colours, **363**, p. 46.

POT MARIGOLD see **Calendula officinalis, 248**, pp. 31, 32.

POTATO TREE, CHILEAN see **Solanum crispum, 1993**, p. 250.

POTENTILLA (ROSACEAE) Cinquefoil

✿**arbuscula** ✴ Mid Spring–Early Autumn   Sh.
Close to *P. fruticosa* but distinct from the hairy shaggy branches and large brown stipules. *Fl.* deep yellow up to 1½ in. across. Foliage greyish. One of the most valuable summer flowering shrubs with very long season of *fl.* Plant in full sun. Himalayas, N. China.

atrosanguinea ✴ Summer   P.
Fl. reddish-purple, single, on branching stems. *L.* strawberry-like. 1–1½ ft. For a dry, poorish soil and a sunny position. Propagate by division in spring or basal cuttings in autumn. Himalayas.
There are numerous hybrids with this and other sp.:
    'Etna', deep crimson, silver-tinted leaves, 1½ ft;
    'Gibson's Scarlet', blood-red, 1–1½ ft, **1328**, p. 166;
    'Mons. Rouillard', copper-red, double, 1½ ft, **1329**, p. 167.

fruticosa ✴ Mid Spring–Early Autumn   Sh.
Dense deciduous bushes up to 4 ft. *Fl.* variable in colour deep golden-yellow to white and in one case, orange. Valuable for long flowering season. A rare native in Britain and otherwise widely spread through N. hemisphere of both Europe, Asia and N. America.
Among numerous named varieties are:
    'Elizabeth', *fl.* deep canary yellow, large. One of the most valuable forms, **1745**, p. 219;
    'Katherine Dykes', *fl.* primrose yellow, slightly smaller, **1746**, p. 219;
    'Mandshurica', *fl.* creamy-white with small yellow centres, **1747**, p. 219;
    'Moonlight', *fl.* creamy-white slightly larger than in 'Mandshurica', **1748**, p. 219;
    'Tangerine', *fl.* variable but becoming rusty-orange especially when developed in shade, up to 1¼ in. across, **1749**, p. 219;
    'Vilmoriniana', *fl.* very pale primrose-yellow, foliage silky hairy with silvery-grey effect. One of the most valuable forms, **1750**, p. 219.

nepalensis ✴ Summer   P.
Fl. cherry-red. *L.* coarsely toothed, leaflets up to 3 in. long. 2 ft. Similar in appearance to and requiring the same conditions as for *P. atrosanguinea*. W. Himalayas.

Good varieties include:
'Miss Willmott', carmine, 1 ft;
'Roxana', orange-scarlet, 1 ft.

nitida ❋ Early Summer   RP.
2–3 in. *Fl.* deep shell-pink, like small dog rose, 1 in. across, arising from mats of bright silvery leaflets, deeply divided into three lobes. Sunny position in scree or tufa or in alpine house. *Fl.* freely in its native mountains but tends to be much more sparse in *fl.* in cultivation, however, it is a beauty. E. Alps, Dolomites on limestone rocks.
'Rubra', deeper pink, freer flowering than type, **146**, p. 19.

recta ❋ Summer   P.
Fl. lemon-yellow about 1 in. across in terminal sprays. 1½–2 ft. *L.* finger-like, finely cut. Thrives in dryish soil and in sun or dappled shade. Propagate by division in spring or autumn or by seed sown in well-drained soil in the open in 4. Europe.
'Warrenii', also known as 'Macrantha', *fl.* golden, large, single, 1½ ft, **1330**, p. 167.

POTERIUM CANADENSE see **Sanguisorba canadensis**

PRICKLY PEAR see **Opuntia**, **583**, p. 73.

PRICKLY POPPY see **Argemone**, **240**, p. 30.

PRIMROSE see **Primula vulgaris**, **163**, p. 21.

PRIMROSE, EVENING see **Oenothera**, **1287-1291**, pp. 161, 162.

PRIMULA (PRIMULACEAE)
A large genus of the most beautiful and valuable plants with bell-shaped erect or pendulous *fl.* They vary tremendously in conditions required for cultivation; some like *P. allionii* being saxatile plants of the rock crevices while others are plants of moist boggy places or damp woodlands. The Petiolarid primulas of the Himalayas and W. China contain some of the most beautiful members but are some of the most difficult in cultivation usually growing better, however, in the cooler climate of the North of England and Scotland than in the South where it is warmer and drier in summer. Most are quite hardy as regards winter cold but while resting many require protection from winter wet.

allionii ❋ Spring   *RP.
Dense domed tussocks in a well-grown specimen covered with erect, wide open *fl.* 1 in. across, white, shell-pink to deep pink or purplish magenta-pink, usually white in centre. *L.* broad, spathulate, slightly sticky. 1–2 in. Best grown in pans in alpine house or frame in gritty, almost scree mixture with base of rosette wedged between two small pieces of rock. A treasure for the keen alpine plant grower. Marvellous old specimens up to 1 ft across are frequently seen at Shows. Good forms can be propagated from cuttings in summer. Limestone rock crevices of Italian and French Maritime Alps. **147**, p. 19.

auricula Alpine Auricula, Bears Breeches ❋ Spring   RP.
Fl. deep yellow, narrowly bell-shaped and pendulous, up to 1 in. across in clusters on white mealy stem, centre eye white with yellow centre. *L.* large, slightly fleshy, obovate, often covered with white mealy farina especially along edges. 4–8 in. Best grown in semi-shady position. European and E. Alps, usually saxatile in rocky crevices. **148**, p. 19. Numerous hybrids have been raised between this and other allied sp. and much intercrossing has produced two separate races, the garden auriculas and the alpine auriculas, both with very variable range of colour. They are mostly easier garden plants than the wild sp.
Among best forms of alpine auricula are:

'Blairside Yellow', a beautiful dwarf;
'Mrs J. H. Wilson', with deep lilac-mauve *fl.* and yellow centre is a popular form of easy cultivation;
'Queen Alexandra', pale yellow and cream, with larger *fl.* heads and less farina on *l.* than the wild sp., **149**, p. 19.
These are sometimes placed in *pubescens* hybrid group.

beesiana ❋ Early Summer   P.
Fl. purple-lilac in whorls. 1½–2 ft. *L.* about 8 in. long, toothed. Plant 10–3 in deep moist soil, sun or partial shade. Propagate by seed sown as soon as ripe and overwinter in a cold frame. W. China. **1331**, p. 167.

bhutanica see **P. whytei**

denticulata ❋ Spring   RP.
6–12 in. *Fl.* pale mauve, deep mauve, rosy-mauve or white with yellow eye in large clusters in rather round globose heads on stout stems up to 1 ft before *l.* are much developed, later spathulate up to 1 ft long, toothed. One of the easiest of the primulas for sun or semi-shade but unsuitable for very dry position. Himalayas. **150**, p. 19.

edgeworthii, syn. **P. winteri** ❋ Spring RP.
2–4 in. One of the most lovely and also one of the easiest to grow of the rather difficult Petiolarid section. *Fl.* pale lavender-blue with white eye, up to 1 in. across, singly on short stems. *L.* broadly obovate, toothed, covered with white farina when young. Best grown in semi-shade in cool vertical rock crevice or as an alpine house plant. All this section are sensitive to winter wet in resting crown or to water around collar of rosette. W. Himalayas. **151**, p. 19.

farinosa Bird's Eye Primula ❋ Spring   RP.
Fl. pale pink or lilac-pink with yellow and white eye, ½ in. across, in loose clusters at ends of slightly mealy stems up to 8 in. but often much less. Very variable. *L.* oblanceolate in a basal rosette, up to 4 in. long. 3–6 in. Often abundant in higher alpine meadows, usually in rather moist places. Needs good drainage in cultivation and rarely *fl.* so freely as in the Alps. Usually not very long lived in cultivation. A very widely distributed plant, including Britain. **152**, p. 19.

florindae Himalayan Cowslip ❋ Summer   P.
Fl. sulphur-yellow, in large drooping fragrant heads. 2–3 ft. *L.* broadly lance-shaped, shiny. Moisture-loving, in sun or partial shade. Propagate by seed. S.E. Tibet. **1332**, p. 167.

forrestii ❋ Early Summer   RP.
8–12 in. Makes a sub-shrubby base. *Fl.* deep orange-yellow with orange eye, up to 1 in. across, in a cluster of eight or more. *L.* rugulose, crinkled, long stalked, ovate-elliptic. Seems to grow best in a vertical cleft between rocks and intolerant of winter wet on its rosette. Stock may be raised from seed. China, Yunnan. **153**, p. 20.

'Garryarde Guinevere' ❋ Late Spring   RP.
4–6 in. Like a pale blush-pink primrose, *fl.* with deep yellow eye in clusters at the end of very short stems, pedicel long, reddish, calyx pale crimson. A very free-flowering hybrid which quickly establishes itself. It is best, however, to divide the clumps every other year. Sun or semi-shade. **154**, p. 20.

gracilipes ❋ Spring   RP.
3–4 in. *Fl.* lilac-pink with a green eye, primrose-like but larger up to 1½ in. across, petals slightly fringed. *L.* spathulate, coarsely toothed and without mealiness. One of the Petiolarid section. Best grown vertically between crevices of a peat wall garden; most of this section do better in cooler climate of Scotland rather than in the warmer south. One of easiest, however, of its section. Himalayas. **155**, p. 20.

helodoxa ❋ Summer   P.
Fl. bright yellow in whorls. 2–3 ft. *L.* tapering, up to 1 ft or more long, toothed. Plant 11–3. Moisture loving. Yunnan. **1333**, p. 167.

japonica ❋ Late Spring–Early Summer   P.
Fl. purplish-red in whorled tiers. 1½ ft. *L.* up to 1 ft long, irregularly toothed. Waterside, bog garden or moist woodland plants requiring ample moisture in sun or partial shade. Propagate by seed sown in moist soil and a shady place as soon as ripe, or by self-sown seedlings. Japan. **1334**, p. 167.
Good varieties include:
'Miller's Crimson', crimson, 1½ ft;
'Postford White', white with pink eye, 1½ ft, **1335**, p. 167.

× **kewensis** ❋ Spring   GP.
A chance hybrid with yellow *fl.* which was raised at Kew Gardens.

littoniana see **P. vialii**

malacoides ❋ Spring   GP.
Fl. of wild type, lavender, but now available in shades of carmine, purple and white, up to 1 in. across. *L.* oblong oval, bright green. Plant up to 1 ft high. Seed is sown in late 6 to early 7, pricked out as soon as possible and the plants potted on, usually ending in 5 in. pots. During the summer they are kept in frames, housed in 9 and kept at a temp. around 45°F. in airy conditions. A tetraploid strain has been bred and double *fl.* are sometimes seen. Introduced by Forrest in 1908. China. **631**, p. 79.

nutans ❋ Summer   RP. or B.
Fl. pale mauvish-blue in spikes, bell-like, drooping on stems covered with white farina. *L.* velvety, elliptic and hairy up to 6 in. long. 6–12 in. Soldanelloid Section. One of the most beautiful of all primulas, but seldom long-lived. Usually can be raised easily from seed. Semi-shade in peaty situation with leaf-mould where it is rather moist but not boggy. W. China. **156**, p. 20.

obconica ❋ Spring   GP.
Fl. mauve, reddish or bluish, up to 1½ in. across in an umbel. *L.* broad-ovate, with glandular hairs on underside, which often cause dermatitis. Seed is sown in late 5 or 6 and the plants are progressively pricked out and then potted. Any good potting compost serves for this and *P. malacoides*. A winter temp. of 50–55°F. is desirable, but lower readings possible. Plant is about 9 in. high when in *fl.* China. **632**, p. 79.

Polyanthus ❋ Spring   HP.
Fl. crimson, pink, yellow, blue and white. *L.* similar

to *P. vulgaris*. 9–12 in. Sow in a cool greenhouse in 2–3, and plant out in cool, shady place in 5, or sow in the open in 6 in moist soil. Polyanthuses may also be increased by division but they do not usually *fl.* so well as those raised from seed. In either case plant out in 10 where they are to *fl.* A garden race derived mainly from *P.* × *vulgaris* × *P. veris*. **364**, p. 46.

There are several good strains available, including:
'Pacific hybrids', very early, large *fl.* in brilliant colours, specially suited to cold glass culture.

× **pubescens** ❋ Spring RP.
3–6 in. A large group of hybrids, very variable in colour. Parentage includes *P. rubra* and *P. auricula* but may include also *P. viscosa* and *P. villosa*. Auricula-like in clusters on short stems. *Fl.* usually with distinct eye. Semi-shady position or in cleft of rock. All are best lifted and divided and replanted in fresh soil or position every other year.
Among finest are:
'Christine', old rose;
'Faldonside', bright crimson;
'Marlene', violet purple;
'Rufus', with deep terracotta-red *fl.*, **157**, p. 20.

pulverulenta ❋ Summer P.
Fl. claret-red with darker eye in whorled tiers. 2–3 ft. *L.* narrow, up to 1 ft long. Easily grown in rich loamy soil and half shade. Propagate by removing side offsets in the spring or by seed sown as soon as ripe. W. China. **1336**, p. 167.
'Bartley Strain', is a pleasing soft pink, **1337**, p. 168.

reidii ❋ Late Spring RP. or B.
3–4 in. One of the most beautiful of the Soldanelloid section. *Fl.* large, bell-like, ¾ in. across in group of two or three on short farinose stems, white or pale bluish-lilac in var. *williamsii*. *L.* oblong, shallowly lobed, up to 6 in. long. Alpine house or in cool position in peaty soil with leaf-mould. May be raised from seed but usually rather difficult to keep long. N.W. Himalayas. **158**, p. 20.

rosea ❋ Spring RP.
3–6 in. *Fl.* very bright rose-pink or strong magenta-pink with yellow eye, ¾ in. across, in clusters on short stems, early in year when *l.* are only slightly developed. *L.* later oblanceolate with slight toothing up to 8 in. Needs a damp position as at edge of stream or in slightly boggy ground. One of the most striking plants of early spring and not difficult to grow providing it has ample moisture. N.W. Himalayas.
Best form is:
'Delight', also known as 'Visser de Greer', **159**, p. 20.

sieboldii ❋ Spring RP.
6–9 in. *Fl.* pink, purplish-pink or white up to 1½ in. across, very variable in loose clusters up to six on rather slender stems, deep divisions between petals. *L.* ovate or oblong-ovate up to 3 in., puckered. Belongs to rare Cortusoides section but not difficult in leaf-mould in positions which are not too dry. In Japan many named forms have been developed. Japan. **160**, p. 20.

sinensis, syn. **P. stellata** ❋ Spring GP.
Another primula requiring similar treatment to *P. obconica*, with *fl.* of red, pink, scarlet and white. The dark green lobed *l.* are attractive in themselves and some 'fern-leaved' forms have been bred. The plant is only known from Chinese gardens and has never been found in the wild.

spectabilis ❋ Late Spring RP.
4–6 in. *Fl.* deep rose-red or purplish-red with white eye, slightly cup-shaped, up to 1 in. across in small clusters. *L.* fleshy, ovate-lanceolate. Usually growing in N. facing shady crevices of rock. Requires good drainage in cultivation and unsuitable for hot dry situations. Belongs to Auricula section. E. Alps. **161**, p. 21.

vialii, syn. **P. littoniana** ❋ Summer RP. or B.
1–1½ ft. One of the most beautiful of all primulas

and probably easiest of its section, the Muscarioides. *Fl.* bluish-violet, pendulous, rather tubular in dense spike of which top consists of scaly-crimson buds, making an unusual colour contrast. *L.* primrose-like, but larger up to 8 in. long. Valuable also for its late-flowering. Requires a cool position with plenty of leaf-mould or peat. Not often long-lived but usually can be easily raised from seed. N.W. China. **162**, p. 21.

vinciflora see **Omphalogramma vinciflorum**

vulgaris Primrose ❋ Spring RP.
4–5 in. Common primrose but still one of the finest garden plants in the genus. *Fl.* creamy-yellow with dark yellow eye. *L.* puckered. Grows best on soils of heavy or medium loam in sun or semi-shade. **163**, p. 21.

whytei, syn. **P. bhutanica** ❋ Spring RP. or B.
4–5 in. One of the finest of the Petiolarid group and also one of the easiest to grow. *Fl.* pale lilac-blue with yellowish-green eye surrounded by creamy-white ring, corolla lobed, 1 in. across. *L.* green but young *l.* with some mealy farina, deeply toothed, elliptic enlarging up to 8 in. after flowering. Best grown in shelter of rock in semi-shade in peaty leaf-mould mixture or in alpine house. Must not be allowed to become dry in summer. Himalayas, Bhutan. **164**, p. 21.

winteri see **P. edgeworthii**

PRIVET see **Ligustrum**

PROBOSCIDEA JUSSIEUI see **Martynia louisiana**

PROPHET FLOWER see **Arnebia echioides**, **975**, p. 122.

PROSTANTHERA (LABIATAE) Mint Bush

ovalifolia ❋ Spring *Sh.
Evergreen shrub only hardy in very warm areas excellent on Riviera and under Californian conditions. Up to 6 ft but usually less. *Fl.* very freely borne, lilac-purple, bell-shaped and pouched at base up to ½ in. across on short racemes. *L.* small oval, scented when bruised. Shrub should be pruned hard after flowering in order to keep bushy habit. Australia. **1751**, p. 219.

rotundifolia
Close to *P. ovalifolia* but with rounded *l.* Tasmania.

PRUNELLA (LABIATAE)

webbiana ❋ Summer P.
Fl. rose-purple, in short spikes. 1 ft. *L.* dark green bluntly oval, often toothed. Ordinary garden soil that does not bake dry in summer. Propagate by division in the spring. This is sometimes regarded as a horticultural form probably of *P. grandiflora*. The type plant is very easily raised from seed and may become troublesome. Europe.
Other varieties include:
'Alba', white, 1 ft;
'Loveliness', pale violet, 9 in., **1338**, p. 168;
'Rosea', pink, 1 ft.

PRUNUS (ROSACEAE) Flowering Cherry

Deciduous trees grown for their quantities of white or pale pink *fl.* in 3, 4, 5. Some of the most valuable trees of our gardens especially where they can be protected from birds taking the buds in winter. Many of them also valuable for brilliant autumn colouring of foliage, thus making them dual purpose trees.
Among the finest for gardens are:

'Accolade' ❋ Spring T.
A hybrid of *P. sargentii* × *P. subhirtella*. Rather erect tree up to 20 ft. *Fl.* semi-double, pink in bud,

opening white about 1¼ in. across in clusters. **1752**, p. 219.

× **amygdalo-persica** 'Pollardii' Almond ❋ Early Spring T.
This tree is said to have been derived from a hybrid of the Almond and Peach and is preferable to Common Almond with larger *fl.*, deep pink, single. All Almonds suffer badly from bird damage but are valuable where they can be grown, making small tress up to 20 ft. It is useful to include Almonds when spraying for Peach leaf-curl.

avium Gean, Mazzard ❋ Spring T.
One of the most beautiful native British trees. Tall deciduous tree up to 50 ft. Wild form with single white *fl.* in clusters up to 2 in. across.
❀'Plena', best for gardens, semi-double white *fl.* in large clusters borne freely. One of our most beautiful flowering garden trees in late 4–5, **1753**, p. 220.

cerasifera Cherry Plum, Myrobalan ❋ Early Spring T.
Valuable early flowering tree, *fl.* borne before *l.*, small white star-shaped but very numerous. **1754**, p. 220.
A form with deeper pink *fl.* is:
'Atropurpurea', often known as 'Pissardii' which also has dark plum-red coloured foliage throughout summer and is best when in *fl.* Small tree up to 20 ft.

conradinae ❋ Early Spring T.
Small rather open tree up to 30 ft. *Fl.* before *l.* pink in bud, opening white, very early. **1755**, p. 220.
Best form is:
'Semi-plena', with semi-double *fl.* which last longer than type. *L.* slightly bronzy when young appearing usually after but sometimes with *fl.* One of the most valuable early flowering Cherries.

incisa Cut-leaved Cherry, Fuji Cherry ❋ Spring T.
Shrub or small tree early flowering and usually covered in *fl.* *Fl.* pink in bud, opening white. Many forms also have fine autumn colouring as is shown by picture, other forms have weeping habit such as 'Moerheimii', also valuable as parent to many other flowering Cherries. Japan. **1756**, p. 220.

laurocerasus Common Laurel ❋ Early Summer Sh.
Evergreen shrub or small tree. Valuable for hedges but should be pruned with secateurs rather than

clipped. *Fl.* white in short racemes, scented rather strongly.

lusitanica Portugal Laurel T.
Evergreen tree beautiful in foliage. *Fl.* white in short spikes, hawthorn scented.

mume Japanese Apricot ❋ Early Spring T.
Fl. pink, pale pink semi-double, or white in some forms, before *l.* One of the most valuable early flowering trees especially for a sheltered warm position. **1757**, p. 220.

padus Bird Cherry ❋ Early Summer T.
Deciduous tree up to 30 ft rather open habit. *Fl.* in short racemes up to 6 in. slightly drooping or spreading, white strongly scented. Valuable tree not seen as often as it should be. N. Europe, including Britain. **1758**, p. 220.

persica Peach ❋ Early Spring T.
Deciduous tree, early flowering. All peaches, flowering and fruiting, need to be sprayed for peach leaf-curl in 2–3 before *l.* open.
Among best varieties for flowering but not for fruiting are:
'Clara Meyer', double, pink;
'Helen Borchers', double, bright sugar-pink;
'Iceberg', semi-double, white large. One of the best and most vigorous, **1759**, p. 220;
'Russell's Red', double, crimson, not very vigorous but the best in colour.

prostrata ❋ Spring RSh.
6 in.–1½ ft. Small but dense twiggy semi-prostrate shrub. *Fl.* deep rose-pink up to ¾ in. across, crimson in bud. Usually solitary or in pairs. *L.* small at flowering time, later up to 1½ in. long, ovate, toothed. Plant in as sunny and warm a position as possible to cover rocks or in alpine house. A lovely plant but it rarely *fl.* as well in cultivation as it does in wild. E. Mediterranean. **165**, p. 21.

✡**sargentii,** syn. **P. serrulata sachalinensis** ❋ Early Spring T.
One of the finest of flowering Cherries. Medium sized and rather round-headed tree up to 20 ft but said to be larger in Japan. *Fl.* single pink up to 2 in. across. Foliage bronzy when it first opens and turning brilliant red early in autumn 9–10, one of the earliest autumn colouring trees and most valuable as dual purpose tree, thought by some authorities to be of hybrid origin. **1760**, p. 220.

serrula ❋ Mid Spring T.
Most valuable tree for its fine polished mahogany-coloured bark which peels in late summer. *Fl.* small white. Should be planted where sun can be reflected off the bark and low branches pruned off at early age. W. China. **1761**, p. 221.

serrulata Japanese Flowering Cherry, Satozakura ❋ Spring T.
Horticultural varieties, mostly hybrids derived mainly from *P. serrulata* and also from *P. speciosa*, flowering freely.
Among the finest are with white *fl.*:
'Kojima', see 'Shirotae';
'Longipes', see 'Shimidsu Sakura';
'Mount Fuji', see 'Shirotae';
'Nobilis', see 'Yedo-Zakura';
'Oku-miyako', see 'Shimidsu Sakura':
✡'Shimidsu Sakura', also known as 'Oku-miyako' and 'Longipes', *fl.* pink in bud opening white, semi-double large borne in pendulous clusters with long pedicels. Late flowering mid-5 and young foliage appearing with *fl.* Small tree up to 15 ft with widespreading branches and usually a rather flattish crown. One of the finest and seldom attacked by birds, **1762**, p. 221.
'Shirotae', *fl.* large, snow-white, single or semi-double pendulous, early 4. Young foliage bronze-green. Also known as 'Mount Fuji' or 'Kojima'.
✡'Tai-Haku', *fl.* very large up to 2½ in. across, single, white. Mid-season 4 to early 5. When flowering late *fl.* appear with coppery young foliage. One of the most vigorous and free flowering of these cherries and in most gardens not attacked badly by birds, **1763**, p. 221.
'Yedo-Zakura', *fl.* semi-double red in bud, opening pale pink or white. Mid-season 4 to early 5. Usually small tree with rather upright branches sometimes known as 'Nobilis', **1764**, p. 221.
Among the best of the pink flowering cherries is:
'Kanzan', 'Sekiyama' T.
Often mistakenly described as 'Hisakura'. Probably the most popular of all the Japanese cherries. Strong growing tree with rather erect branches. *Fl.* large, double, deep sugary pink in great masses, pendulous on rather long stems. One of the few varieties which do not seem to be attacked by birds. Much planted as street tree but should not be underrated because of its commonness. Against blue sky when first coming out it is very beautiful. Foliage bronzy when first appearing.

subhirtella Spring Cherry ❋ Spring T.
Bush or small tree usually not more than 15 ft. *Fl.* white or pale pink, rather small but very numerous. Best forms are 'Ascendens', 'Fukubana' and 'Pendula Rubra'. Japan.
var. *autumnalis* ❋ Late Winter–Early Spring
Medium sized tree with spreading branches, deciduous. *Fl.* small pink in bud opening white. Best form is 'Rosea' with *fl.* tinged pale pink hanging on long pedicels but shorter in early part of season. Valuable for its winter flowering habit on bare branches from 11–4 at favourable spells of mild weather during winter. **1765**, p. 221.

tenella Dwarf Russian Almond ❋ Spring Sh.
Low shrub up to 4 ft often less, suckering freely. *Fl.* bright pink on bare branches, early flowering.
Best form is:
'Fire Hill', also known as 'Gessleriana', *fl.* rosy-crimson very numerous, does well on chalk, **1766**, p. 221.

tomentosa Manchu or Nanking Cherry ❋ Mid Spring Sh.
Shrub, 5–10 ft high, with long wand-like branches growing from the base. Ornamental in *fl.* and fruit. *Fl.* white or pinkish. The attractive red fruit is ½–¾ in. in diameter and edible. Extremely hardy. Often used as a flowering hedge with its show of profuse white *fl.* on bare branches in spring. China, Japan.

triloba ❋ Spring Sh.
Small shrub up to 6 ft sometimes grown as a wall shrub. *Fl.* large, bright pink rosette-like, deeper pink in bud. Early flowering without foliage. Often used for forcing. Form usually grown is 'Multiplex' or 'Flore Pleno'. **1767**, p. 221.

PULMONARIA (BORAGINACEAE)

angustifolia, syn. **P. azurea** ❋ Spring RP.
6 in.–1 ft. *Fl.* very bright Royal blue, funnel-shaped in small clusters. *L.* narrowly elliptic, becoming large and a bit coarse after *fl.* unspotted. Plant either in sun or semi-shade, usually spreading freely and too large for choicest space in small rock garden but valuable for its very strong colour early in the year. Central Europe. **166**, p. 21.

PULSATILLA (RANUNCULACEAE)

alpina, syn. **Anemone alpina** Alpine Anemone ❋ Spring RP.
1–1½ ft. One of the glories of the Alps forming large clumps. *Fl.* large, white with large mass of yellow stamens in centre up to 3 in. across, petals wide, overlapping, sometimes tinged blue on outside, *fl.* cup-shaped at first, then opening almost flat. Buds woolly-hairy. *L.* much divided, fern-like, mostly basal but with an involucre on stem, up to 1 ft. Seed heads with long feathery styles like a 'Struwelpeter' very decorative. Rootstock woody and thick and growing deep. Best grown from seed and planted in final position as early as possible and then never moved. **167**, p. 21.

✡**halleri,** syn. **P. vulgaris** 'Budapest', **P. vulgaris** var. **slavica** ❋ Spring RP.
6 in.–1 ft. Perhaps the most beautiful form of Pasque Flower. Usually sold under the name 'Budapest', which may be a particularly fine clone. *Fl.* pale violet-mauve, with wide overlapping petals and large central boss of stamens, cup-shaped, up to 3 in. across, very woolly in bud with long tawny golden hairs, opening on short stalks, then elongating up to 1 ft. Distinguished from *P. vulgaris* by the more coarsely divided *l.* and requiring similar conditions. Makes a very fine alpine house plant in deep pot. E. Alps, Carpathians. **168**, p. 21.

sulphurea ❋ Spring RP.
Deep sulphur-yellow, very beautiful. Generally the white form grows on limestone and the yellow on granitic rocks but this is not invariable. Both require considerable moisture in early spring and usually seen at edge of melting snows in Alps. Usually regarded as a subsp. of *alpina*, syn. *P. alpina* subsp. *apiifolia*. **169**, p. 22.

vernalis, syn. **Anemone vernalis** Spring Anemone ❋ Spring RP.
4–8 in. *Fl.* white with broad petals, cup-shaped with large boss of yellow stamens giving appearance of a poached egg up to 2½ in. across. Buds tawny gold, very hairy, on short stems which elongate as *fl.* matures. *L.* developed after *fl.* buds open, basal, deeply divided. The earliest of this group to open in the Alps. Requires very well-drained conditions in rock gardens or pan in alpine house. **170**, p. 22.

vulgaris, syn. **Anemone pulsatilla** Pasque Flower ❋ Spring RP.
4–8 in. *Fl.* violet-purple with narrow starry petals in native form of limestone but many finer forms have been introduced and tend to reproduce their colours from seed. *Fl.* cup-shaped, opening flat, slightly nodding, up to 2½ in. across. *L.* finely divided, fern-like, mostly developing after flowering. Requires sunny well-drained position and generally does best on chalky soils. Good colour forms include 'Alba', white, 'Rubra', brick-red to maroon, while some forms are deep shell-pink. Petals downy on outside. **171**, **172**, **173**, p. 22.

vulgaris 'Budapest' see **P. halleri**

vulgaris var. **slavica** see **P. halleri**

Abbreviations and Symbols used in the text.
The following abbreviations may sometimes be used in conjunction as HA. indicating Hardy annual or GBb indicating Greenhouse bulb.

A.	= Annual	P.	= Perennial
Aq.	= Aquatic	R.	= Rock or Alpine plant
B.	= Biennial	Sh.	= Shrub
Bb	= Bulb	Sp., sp.	= Species
C.	= Corm	Syn.	= Synonym
Cl.	= Climber	T.	= Tree
Co.	= Conifer	Tu.	= Tuber
Fl., *fl.*	= Flower(s)	var.	= variety
G.	= Greenhouse or house plant	×	= Hybrid or hybrid parents
H.	= Hardy	❋	= Flowering time
HH.	= Half-hardy	❧	= Foliage plant
L., *l.*	= Leaf, leaves		
Mt(s)	= Mount, mountain(s)		

The following have been used also in the descriptions of Alpines, Bulbs, Trees and Shrubs.

* = slightly tender
† = lime hater
✡ = highly recommended

The illustration numbers are in **bold type** and the page numbers in light type preceded by p.

PUNICA (LYRTHRACEAE)
(Sometimes placed in separate family Punicaceae)

granatum Pomegranate ✸ Summer *Sh.
Deciduous shrub or small tree up to 15 ft slightly spiny. *Fl.* bright orange-scarlet, cup-shaped with slightly crumpled petals up to 1½ in. across. Fruits, rarely produced and ripened in Great Britain, deep yellow, round up to 3 in. across with juicy pulp and numerous seeds. In most parts of the country should be grown as wall shrub in sunny position. Widely grown for its fruits in S. Europe and Middle E., probably native in Persia, Afghanistan. **1768**, p. 221.
　'Nana', smaller shrub with linear *l.*, free flowering not often above 2 ft. Suitable for alpine house or rock garden in milder areas. *Fl.* through summer up to 10. Unsuitable for cold areas except in alpine house, **174**, p. 22.

PURPLE-LEAF ICE PLANT see **Sedum maximum** 'Atropurpureum', **1371**, p. 172.

PURPLE LOOSESTRIFE see **Lythrum salicaria**, **1258**, p. 158.

PURPLE TOADFLAX see **Linaria purpurea**, **1241**, p. 156.

PURSLANE see **Portulaca**, **363**, p. 46.

PURSLANE, ROCK see **Calandrinia umbellata**, **246**, p. 31.

PUSCHKINIA (LILIACEAE)

libanotica see **P. scilloides**

scilloides, syn. **P. libanotica** ✸ Spring Bb
Close to a *Scilla*, *fl.* very pale blue or whitish with a deeper blue streak down centre of petal, in clusters on stems 3–6 in. Plant in full sun but unsuitable for very dry places. There is also a fine white form. Asia Minor, Lebanon. **873**, p. 110.

PUYA (BROMELIACEAE)

alpestris ✸ Summer P.
Fl. greenish-blue with orange anthers, borne in large panicles. 2–3 ft. *L.* long, tufted, slightly spiny. A loamy, peaty soil and a very sheltered position. Not reliably hardy. Propagate by seed, or by suckers when produced. Chile. **1339**, p. 168.

PYRACANTHA (ROSACEAE) Firethorn

coccinea ✸ Early Summer Sh.
Evergreen shrub or small tree up to 15 ft, densely branched and spineless. *Fl.* white ⅓ in. across in large clusters, followed by red or orange-red berries in large bunches. *L.* narrowly obovate and tapered at end up to 2½ in. long. Often grown as wall shrub making dense covering especially when hard-pruned but equally good as free standing bush or small tree. S. Europe. **1769**, p. 222.
　'Lalandii', berries orange-red the most commonly grown form.

crenulata see **P. rogersiana**

rogersiana ✸ Early Summer Sh.
Spiny evergreen shrub up to 10 ft dense upright habit, also frequently grown as a wall shrub. *Fl.* white ¼ in. wide in small racemose clusters. Berries golden-yellow or reddish-orange.
　'Flava', most commonly seen form with yellow fruit, syn. *P. crenulata* 'Flava'. Slightly less hardy than *P. coccinea* and distinguished by rounded *l.* to the shoots. China, **1770**, p. 222.

PYRETHRUM (COMPOSITAE) Feverfew

parthenium, syn. **Chrysanthemum parthenium**
✸ Summer P.
Fl. white, with yellow disc. *L.* oval, sometimes slightly hairy. 2 ft. Ordinary well-drained soil, full sun. Pyrethrums are best planted in the spring or just after flowering. Propagate by division in the spring. Caucasus.
　'White Bonnet', double white sprays of button-like *fl.*, 2½ ft, **1340**, p. 168.

roseum, syn. **Chrysanthemum coccineum**
✸ Early Summer P.
Fl. double and single in shades of crimson, scarlet, pink, salmon-pink, white. *L.* fern-like. 2½–3 ft, plant 3–4 or immediately after flowering in a sunny position and well-drained soil, preferably on the light side. Propagate by division in spring or in 7. Botanically sometimes included under *Chrysanthemum coccineum* but the garden hybrids have long been known as Pyrethrums. Persia, Caucasus.
　Among many good hybrids are:
　'Brenda', bright cerise, **1341**, p. 168;
　'E. M. Robinson', salmon-pink, **1342**, p. 168;
　'Vanessa', rosy-carmine flushed yellow at the centre, double, **1343**, p. 168.

PYRUS (ROSACEAE) Pear

salicifolia 'Pendula' Willow-leaved Pear ✸ Spring T.
Small tree up to 20 ft, branches pendulous. *Fl.* white, in small clusters, up to 1 in. across. *L.* narrow, willow-like covered with silvery-grey down. One of the finest silvery-leaved small trees. Best pruned to elegant shape when young, branches close to the trunk should be pruned off and others thinned. Vigorous grower, valuable as a specimen lawn tree, quite hardy. Probably most ornamental of true pears. The fruiting pear is *P. communis*. S.E. Europe, Asia Minor. **1771**, p. 222.

Q

QUAKING GRASS see **Briza**, **245**, p. 31.

QUEEN OF THE PRAIRIE see **Filipendula rubra**

QUEEN'S TEARS see **Billbergia nutans**, **432**, p. 54.

QUERCUS (FAGACEAE) Oak

borealis maxima, syn. **Q. rubra** Red Oak T.
Deciduous tree up to 100 ft in native country usually less in Britain. *L.* large with three to five lobes up to 9 in. long and 6 in. broad. Acorns up to 1¼ in. long, flat-bottomed in shallow saucer-shaped cup, scaly. Autumn foliage dark crimson-scarlet. E. N. America.

cerris Turkey Oak T.
Large wide-spreading deciduous tree. One of the finest Oaks which may be grown in this country. Fast growing. *L.* very coarsely toothed or lobed up to 5 in. long by 3 in. wide, rather variable. Valuable as an ornamental tree but timber is inferior. S. Europe, Asia Minor.

coccifera Kermes Oak *T.
Evergreen shrub or small tree. *L.* small, prickly, holly-like. Acorns small in densely hairy scaly cup. Host of Kermes insect from which scarlet dye is obtained. Only possible in very mild areas outside but sometimes grown as a small alpine house shrub. Mediterranean.

coccinea Scarlet Oak T.
Deciduous tree up to 50 ft, usually less. *L.* large, 6 in. long, up to 4 in. wide, seven to nine-lobed. Acorns up to 1 in. long in deep cup. Foliage brilliant scarlet in autumn and probably the best red colouring oak. N. America.
　'Splendens', the best selected form for colour, which needs to be propagated vegetatively. The typical *l.* has more lobes than shown in the illustration, **1772**, p. 222.

ilex Evergreen or Holm Oak T.
Large evergreen tree particularly valuable in coastal areas but slightly tender, unsuitable for very cold districts. Wide-spreading up to 60 ft but may be clipped. *L.* up to 3 in. long by 1 in. broad, narrowly oval or ovate lanceolate. Acorns small up to ¾ in. long but usually produced in clusters of one to three on short stalk. Mediterranean.

pedunculata see **Q. robur**

petraea Durmast Oak T.
With sessile fruits. Britain.

robur, syn. **Q. pedunculata** Common Oak T.
Has acorn cups on short pedicels. Britain.

rubra see **Q. borealis maxima**

suber Cork Oak *T.
Trunk covered with deeply furrowed cork. *L.* dark green but lustrous above and grey beneath. Only suitable for milder areas. Evergreen spreading tree up to 60 ft in native areas but usually much less in Britain. Very long lived. S. Europe, N. Africa.

QUINCE, ORNAMENTAL see **Chaenomeles**, **1508**, **1509**, p. 189.

R

RAGWORT, GIANT see **Ligularia japonica**, **1240**, p. 155.

RAGWORT, SEA see **Cineraria maritima**, **267**, p. 34.

RAMONDA (GESNERIACEAE)

myconii, syn. **R. pyrenaica** ✸ Spring RP.
4–6 in. *Fl.* pale mauve, two to three on short stems, opening flat with overlapping petals and central protruding anther cone, 1 in. across, ovate, toothed, rugulose on upper surface and decorative without *fl.* Best planted in a vertical crevice between rock or in an open wall in cool situation. Often does best facing N. Pyrenees. **175**, p. 22.

pyrenaica see **R. myconii**

Abbreviations and Symbols used in the text.
The following abbreviations may sometimes be used in conjunction as HA. indicating Hardy annual or GBb indicating Greenhouse bulb.

A. = Annual	P. = Perennial
Aq. = Aquatic	R. = Rock or
B. = Biennial	Alpine plant
Bb = Bulb	Sh. = Shrub
C. = Corm	Sp., sp. = Species
Cl. = Climber	Syn. = Synonym
Co. = Conifer	T. = Tree
Fl., fl. = Flower(s)	Tu. = Tuber
G. = Greenhouse or	var. = variety
house plant	× = Hybrid or
H. = Hardy	hybrid parents
HH. = Half-hardy	✸ = Flowering time
L., l. = Leaf, leaves	❧ = Foliage plant
Mt(s) = Mount,	
mountain(s)	

The following have been used also in the descriptions of Alpines, Bulbs, Trees and Shrubs.

　* = slightly tender
　† = lime hater
　✿ = highly recommended

The illustration numbers are in **bold type** and the page numbers in light type preceded by p.

RANUNCULUS (RANUNCULACEAE)

acris Bachelor's Buttons ❊ Late Spring–Early Summer
P.
Fl. bright yellow. *L.* deeply cut and lobed. 2 ft. Plant 11–3 in ordinary moist soil. Propagate by division in spring or by seed. Europe, including Britain.
  'Flore Pleno', is a double yellow form, **1344**, p. 168.

amplexicaulis ❊ Late Spring–Early Summer RP.
Fl. white with yellow centre, usually two to four to a stem but on long pedicels, 1 in. across. *L.* ovate-lanceolate, clasping stem at base, thus distinguishing it from *R. pyrenaeus* which is also smaller. 6–8 in. Easily cultivated on large rock garden in sunny position. Pyrenees. **176**, p. 22.

asiaticus The Turban Ranunculus ❊ Late Winter–Early Summer
Usually grown as a strain of mixed colours with semi-double or double *fl.* up to 3 in. across. Grown much as a cut *fl.* for market and long lasting when cut. Wild forms are single, brilliant scarlet in Asia Minor, Lebanon, Palestine and Rhodes, white in Crete and yellow in Cyprus. Plant in a warm sunny position and give some protection in winter such as a pile of ashes, also suitable for cool greenhouse. In some areas may be stored in winter and planted in late 2 to *fl.* in 5–6. Tubers are irregular in shape with claw-like ends and should be planted with claws pointing downwards. **874**, p. 110.

ficaria Lesser Celandine ❊ Late Winter–Mid Spring RP.
Fl. golden-yellow, with shining petals. *L.* heart-shaped. 2–4 in. A lovely plant for wild garden but tends to spread very freely both by seed and by division of knobbly tubers. Europe including Britain.
Best form is:
  'Major', with larger *fl.* and *l.* and not spreading so freely, **177**, p. 23.
Other good forms have white, primrose or orange-tangerine *fl.* and do not spread so freely. There are also double forms.

glacialis Glacier Crowfoot ❊ Late Spring–Early Summer RP.
High alpine sp. and one of the glories of the Alps. *Fl.* white with large yellow centre and pink or deep crimson on outside, 1 in. across, in clusters. *L.* fleshy, finely divided. 3–6 in. Grows in damp screes and difficult to grow and *fl.* satisfactorily in cultivation. Needs underground watering and very good drainage. European Alps, Pyrenees, Iceland. **178**, p. 23.

gramineus ❊ Summer RP.
Fl. bright yellow, buttercup-like, one to three to a stem, 1 in. across. *L.* narrow, linear, glaucous, thus readily distinguished from common buttercup. 4–8 in. Sunny position on rock garden where it will make large clumps. S.W. Europe. **179**, p. 23.

lingua Great Spearwort ❊ Summer HAq.
Fl. glossy yellow, up to 2 in. in diameter. 2–3 ft. *L.* long, narrow, undivided. In sun or light shade in boggy ground beside water. Propagate by division in spring. Europe, including Britain. **1345**, p. 169.

RAOULIA (COMPOSITAE)

lutescens ❊ Summer *RP.
Forms large grey silvery mats of compact minute rosettes. *Fl.* minute also, bright yellow, liberally covering much of mat. ½–1 in. Usually grown as an alpine house plant in a scree mixture and requiring careful watering from the base. New Zealand. **180**, p. 23.

REBUTIA (CACTACEAE)

A genus of globular cacti with red or orange *fl.* and rather small spines. They seldom exceed 6 in. in height. A very gritty compost is best and practically

no water is required from 10 until the end of 3. Between 3 and 9 water should be applied sparingly. Propagation by seed which germinates rapidly and soon forms flowering-size plants. Offshoots produced sparingly, but can be detached, when produced.

minuscula ❊ Summer GP.
Fl. red, trumpet-shaped at base of plant. Plant globose. Minimum winter temp. 40–45°F. Self-sown seedlings will appear around base if seed is allowed to ripen and spill. Argentina. **633**, p. 80.

xanthocarpa ❊ Summer GP.
Fl. orange-red. Plant globose. Fruits yellow. Treatment as for *R. minuscula*. Bolivia. **634**, p. 80.

RED-BARKED DOGWOOD see **Cornus alba**, **1524**, **1525**, p. 191.

RED BUCKEYE see **Aesculus pavia**

RED BUD see **Cercis canadensis** and **C. occidentalis**

RED CEDAR see **Libocedrus decurrens**, **2024**, p. 253.

RED CEDAR, WESTERN see **Thuja plicata**, **2046**, **2047**, p. 256

RED ELDER see **Sambucus racemosa**, **1898**, p. 238.

RED FIR see **Abies procera**

RED MAPLE see **Acer rubrum**, **1440**, p. 180.

RED OAK see **Quercus borealis maxima**

RED PEPPER see **Capsicum annuum**, **256**, p. 32.

RED SILVER FIR see **Abies amabilis**

REDHOT CATSTAIL see **Acalypha hispida**, **401**, p. 51.

REDWOOD see **Sequoia sempervirens**, **2038**, p. 255.

REDWOOD, DAWN see **Metasequoia**, **2025**, p. 254.

REGAL PELARGONIUM see **Pelargonium** × **domesticum**, **587–597**, pp. 74, 75.

RESEDA (RESEDACEAE)

odorata Mignonette ❊ Summer–Mid Autumn HA.
Fl. yellowish-white, delightfully fragrant. *L.* bluntly lance-shaped. 1–1½ ft. Sow in the open in 4–5 in a sunny position where they are to *fl.* Add lime to the soil if deficient and make the ground firm before sowing. Mignonette does not transplant readily. N. Africa, Egypt.
  'Goliath', has reddish spikes of *fl.*, 1½ ft, **365**, p. 46;
  'Red Monarch', deep red, 1 ft.

RHAZYA (APOCYNACEAE)

orientalis ❊ Summer P.
Fl. deep blue, small, in terminal clusters. *L.* dark green, thickly placed. 1–1½ ft. Plant 11–3 in ordinary soil, sun or half shade. Propagate by division. Orient. **1346**, p. 169.

RHEUM (POLYGONACEAE) Rhubarb

alexandrae ❊ Summer P.
Fl. straw-coloured bracts borne on erect stems, 3–4 ft. *L.* large, pale green, with prominent veins. For sun or partial shade in deep, moist soil. Requires ample space. Propagate by division in spring, or by seed. Tibet, S. Russia. **1347**, p. 169.

palmatum Sorrel Rhubarb ❊ Summer P.
Fl. creamy-yellow, borne on imposing spikes, 5–6 ft. *L.* large, spreading, five-lobed, deeply cut. Tibet, China. **1348**, p. 169.

RHIPSALIDOPSIS (CACTACEAE)

rosea Easter Cactus ❊ Spring GP.
Fl. rosy-pink. Stems flat, leaf-like, spineless. Plant about 9 in. high much branched. A rather rich compost is desirable. Winter temp. 50°F. During summer put outside in sunny position to harden off current growth. Protect from continuous rain during this period. During rest of year keep compost moist. Propagate by cuttings. Brazil. **635**, p. 80.

RHODANTHE MANGLESII see **Helipterum manglesii**

RHODODENDRON (ERICACEAE) (Including Azalea) †

One of the largest genera grown in gardens showing great variability from evergreen or deciduous plants and ranging from large trees like *arboreum* and big-leaved sp. such as *sino-grande* or *falconeri* to small alpine shrublets with *l.* only a fraction of an in. long. All are intolerant of lime in the soil and larger leaved sp. do best in semi-shade in moist atmosphere of W. England or Scotland. Alpine small-leaved sp. and most azaleas will grow well in full sun provided there is a certain amount of moisture during summer. Collections can be kept in good health by overhead spray in summer and under those conditions can be grown in fuller sun than otherwise when they *fl.* more freely. It is good practice to dead head rhododendrons after flowering in order to save strength for following year. This is done by snapping off the spent *fl.* heads before seeding at the base of the truss. Rhododendrons are divided into series and sub-series being almost unique in this arrangement although in Germany and Continental Europe they are usually treated in sections and sub-sections as with other genera. Each sp. is variable and sometimes collected many times over a large area. Widest area of rhododendron density is in the Himalayas and W. China but they stretch from W. Europe right round the N. Hemisphere to N. America. A number of sp. are found in New Guinea and there are over 500 sp. in cultivation excluding those found in New Guinea and there is one sp. in N. Australia. The majority of those in cultivation are hardy but the system of hardiness ratings and also *fl.* and *l.* valuation has been worked out and published in the Rhododendron Handbook issued by the Royal Horticultural Society, Part 1 being devoted to sp. and Part 2 to hybrids. This is an essential tool for all who grow rhododendrons in large quantities or breed from them. The range of hybrids is gigantic, probably unparalleled in any other shrubby genus. The value of *l.* character in rhododendrons also is very high and many sp. are valued most for their *l.* throughout the year and may be planted for contrast of this effect.

Species

Series **Azalea**, sub-series **Canadense**

albrechtii ❁ Spring   Sh.
Deciduous, rather bushy shrub, usually about 5 ft. *Fl.* opening before the *l.*, deep rose-pink or sometimes with a touch of deep magenta-pink but deep rose forms are best, up to 2 in. across, rather flat. Japan. **1773**, p. 222.
Very beautiful deciduous Azaleas closely allied to this, in same sub-series, and all valuable garden plants are *R. vaseyi*, *R. pentaphyllum*, *R. quinquefolium* (q.v.) and *R. schlippenbachii* (q.v.) all flowering in 4.

Series **Arboreum**, sub-series **Arboreum**

arboreum ❁ Spring   T.
Tallest member of the genus. Tree up to 40 ft and specimens this height may be seen in Cornish and W. of Scotland gardens. Evergreens with *l.* up to 8 in. long, oblong or lanceolate, 2½ in. wide, dark glossy-green above and silvery-white or cinnamon-red or rusty-brown below. *Fl.* in round very compact trusses of 15–20 *fl.*, individual florets are tubular and about 2 in. long. Best forms are those with deep blood-red *fl.* but these are most tender and suitable only for milder areas. The deep pink form *roseum* is one of the finest while the white form with small purple spots at base is often grown. *R. arboreum* blooms early and *fl.* may be destroyed by early frosts. Does not *fl.* on young plants but is well worth waiting for. Semi-shade or in W. areas may be grown in full exposure. Parent of many hybrids which tend to be hardier than *R. arboreum* itself. Himalayas and W. China. One form *zeylanicum* is found in Ceylon.
  var. *roseum*, **1774**, p. 222.
Closely allied is *R. cinnamomeum* with rusty-brown underneath *l.*

Series **Triflorum**, sub-series **Augustinii**

❁**augustinii** ❁ Spring   Sh.
Evergreen shrub up to 15 ft in an old plant. *Fl.* pale lavender-blue, variable to deep violet-blue which are considered finest, some with green throat and almost red stamens, others with reddish-purple throat; widely funnel-shaped in loose clusters up to 5 *fl.* each and each *fl.* up to 2 in. long. The majority of forms are sufficiently hardy for general planting except in very cold areas and members of this series have been claimed to have a little lime tolerance but this should not be relied on. Some of the most beautiful blue rhododendrons are included in this sp. and numerous excellent hybrids have been raised from it. *Fl.* as quite young plant. Named after Augustine Henry who collected a number of fine plants in China while in Customs service. W. China. **1775**, p. 222.

Series **Barbatum**, sub-series **Barbatum**

barbatum ❁ Early Spring   T.
Large shrub or small tree up to 20 ft, occasionally

more in old specimens. Distinguished by beautiful smooth purplish-red bark. Rhododendrons with this smooth reddish bark should never be cut back into old wood. *Fl.* in round very compact high-domed trusses, bright scarlet or crimson-red, trusses up to 4 in. across. *L.* up to 8 in. long lanceolate. This sp. is distinguished usually by bristles at base of the *l.* stalks and *fl.* stems. It is very valuable for its early flowering and very bright scarlet colour with no trace of blue in the red. Hardy in most areas but in colder areas should be given some shelter. **1776**, p. 222.

bullatum see **R. edgeworthii**

Series **Fortunei**, sub-series **Calophytum**

calophytum ❁ Spring   T.
A very distinctive small tree or large shrub up to 15 ft occasionally more and usually as widespreading as it is tall. *Fl.* in large trusses, white or pale-pink with crimson-red blotch at base and slight speckling in large loose truss of 20 or more *fl.* each up to 1½ in. broad, open campanulate. *L.* long up to 15 in. and narrow making distinctive form. Parent of many valuable hybrids but few have inherited its distinctive foliage. Hardy in most gardens and may be grown in semi-shade. W. China. **1777**, p. 223.

campanulatum see **R. wallichii**

Series **Maddenii**, sub-series **Ciliicalyx**

ciliatum ❁ Spring   Sh.
Rather spreading shrub usually not over 5 ft. Bark peeling, reddish-brown. *Fl.* in small clusters up to 4, campanulate with narrow tubing, white or white tinged with pink or pale blush-pink, up to 2 in. long and 2 in. wide, nodding in loose trusses. *L.* up to 3½ in. long, elliptic or oblong, fringed with hairs hence name. *Fl.* sensitive to early frost damage but plant is otherwise hardy in most areas unlike other members of the *Maddenii* series. A parent of many valuable early flowering hybrids. Himalayas, S.E. Tibet. **1778**, p. 223.

cinnamomeum see under **R. arboreum**

Series **Maddenii**, sub-series **Megacalyx**

dalhousiae ❁ Spring   †Sh.
Rather loose growing shrub usually under 6 ft. *Fl.* very large, tubular, bell-shaped up to 4 in. long and up to 5 to the truss, fragrant, pale yellow or chartreuse yellowish-green or white with some pink flush and usually yellow at the base inside. *L.* oblanceolate up to 6 in. long, scaly below. Tender and only suitable as a cool greenhouse plant except in the mildest areas. Himalayas. **1779**, p. 223.
This sub-series contains some of the most beautiful of all tender rhododendrons and rather similar are *R. lindleyi* with waxy tubular white large *fl.* and *R. taggianum* but the largest of all rhododendrons in general cultivation at present is *R. nuttallii* with *fl.* up to 6 in. long and up to 5 to a truss, this however is the most tender of the sp. As cool greenhouse plants they require little attention and are magnificent in *fl.*

Series **Edgeworthii**

edgeworthii ❁ Spring   *Sh.
This sp. from W. China is now regarded as including also *R. bullatum* from N.E. Burma. One of the most beautiful rhododendrons. Rather loose growing shrub up to 6 ft with soft woolly younger branches. *Fl.* 2–5 in a truss, opening widely, funnel-shaped, up to 4 in. across by 2½ in long, strongly scented, calyx large and red. *L.* up to 5 in. long, ovate, elliptic, dark green and above puckered or bullate, fawn coloured with brown woolly indumentum below. Tender but hardier than *R. dalhousiae* but in colder areas should be grown as a cool greenhouse plant. **1780**, p. 223.

Series **Ferrugineum**

ferrugineum Alpenrose ❁ Spring– Summer in Alps depending on altitude   Sh.
Spreading rather straggly shrub usually under 4 ft. *Fl.* in small trusses, tubular, rosy-crimson and

scaly on outside. *L.* small, up to 1½ in. long, densely reddish-brown, scaly below. Pyrenees, Alps. White form occasionally seen. **1781**, p. 223.
Rather similar to *R. hirsutum* another dwarf rhododendron of the Alps but is distinguished by the bristly hairs on the *l.* and by the short hairs on the lobes of the *fl.* and is tolerant of some lime in the soil which *R. ferrugineum* is not.

Series **Griersonianum**

❁**griersonianum** ❁ Summer   Sh.
Evergreen rather loose growing or straggly shrub up to 6 ft but withstands pruning quite well and will sprout from older wood. *Fl.* in larger rather loose trusses, funnel open bell-shaped, 5-lobed, bright geranium-scarlet and in this character unique among the sp. of rhododendron. *L.* up to 8 in. long and 2 in. broad, lanceolate with some buff coloured woolly indumentum below. Hardy in most areas but in cold areas better grown with some protection but *fl.* better in open situation. Easily distinguished by long tapered *fl.* buds. This sp. has been most valuable in hybridisation and is parent of probably more good hybrids than any other sp. All inherit strong red colouring. Yunnan, N. Burma. **1782**, p. 223.

hirsutum see under **R. ferrugineum**

Series **Azalea**, sub-series **Obtusum**

❁**kaempferi** ❁ Late Spring–Midsummer   Sh.
Semi-evergreen azalea, tending to be deciduous in colder areas. Loosely branched shrub up to 6 ft but may be kept to more compact habit by pruning. *Fl.* in small clusters, funnel-shaped but very numerous often covering bush, very variable in colour from salmon-red to bright orange-red to pink or to rosy-scarlet. *L.* up to 3 in. long, slightly hairy. Very variable in time of flowering as well as in colour of *fl.* This late flowering habit of some forms has given rise to valuable later flowering hybrids. Central and N. Japan. **1783**, p. 223.

lindleyi see under **R. dalhousiae**

Series and sub-series **Triflorum**

lutescens ❁ Late Winter–Mid Spring   Sh.
Evergreen rather loose growing shrub up to 10 ft. Attractive with bronzy-red young growths. *Fl.* in rather loose trusses up to 6, widely funnel-shaped but irregular in form, pale primrose-yellow with some light green spotting. Valuable for its early

flowering habit and for the colour of new growths. Quite hardy. Best forms are those with deeper yellow *fl.* but the deepest of these may be slightly tender in cold areas. W. China. **1784**, p. 223.

Series **Grande**

✿**macabeanum** ✳ Spring   T.
Spreading small tree or large bush, quick growing. Probably the finest for garden purposes of the large-leaved rhododendrons and among the hardiest of this series. Distinguished for its magnificent foliage and trusses of *fl.* *Fl.* yellow, varying from pale cream to deep yellow with purplish blotch at base. In very large fairly compact trusses up to 10 in. across, each *fl.* being broadly bell-shaped somewhat fleshy up to 3 in. long. *L.* large up to 12 in. long by 6 in. across, oblong, elliptic, dark green above but silvery-white or greyish-white below. Another distinguishing feature is the silveriness of the young shoots and bright crimson bud scales which give a second season of colour after *fl.* have shed. Hardy in gardens other than in cold areas but away from W. and S. areas should be planted in semi-shelter. All large-leaved rhododendrons of this series require moisture in order to make full growth. They are particularly valuable as foliage plants throughout the year. India, Manipur State. **1785**, p. 224.

Series **Moupinense**

moupinense ✳ Early Spring   Sh.
Spreading dwarf shrub up to 4 ft but usually less with rather bristly branchlets. *Fl.* in clusters up to 3, funnel-shaped with spreading lobes, up to 1½ in. long by 2 in. across, variable in colour from pure white to pale pink or a few forms deep rose and sometimes spotted near base. *L.* up to 1½ in. long, ovate, elliptic, dark green above and scaly below. Hardy but *fl.* are liable to be frosted, excellent as cool greenhouse plant and parent of a number of valuable early flowering hybrids. This sp. will withstand dry conditions better than the majority of rhododendrons. W. China, Szechwan. **1786**, p. 224.

Series **Dauricum**

mucronulatum ✳ Winter   Sh.
Rather straggly shrub up to 6 ft. Valuable for its very early flowering habit. Deciduous. *Fl.* singly or in small clusters at the ends of the shoots produced before the *l.*, up to 1½ in. long, widely funnel-shaped, variable in colour from bright rosy-purple to deep purple to pale rosy-purple. Quite hardy and valuable for early flowering in conjunction with *Hamamelis* to which it presents a fine contrast but young *fl.* or young growth may be damaged by frost. N.E. Asia.
    var. *acuminatum*, palish forms, usually flowering slightly later than other forms, **1787**, p. 224.

nuttallii see under **R. dalhousiae**

Series **Azalea**, sub-series **Obtusum**

obtusum ✳ Spring   Sh.
Dwarf evergreen or semi-evergreen shrub usually not more than 3 ft. Very free flowering and a parent of many evergreen Azalea hybrids. *Fl.* in clusters up to 3 about 1 in. across, funnel-shaped, variable in colour through bright red, scarlet and crimson, does well either in open situations or semi-shade. N.W. Japan. **1788**, p. 224.
    var. *amoenum*, form frequently grown with rich magenta-purple *fl.*, should be kept on its own and then makes very distinctive shrub in garden;
    var. *amoenum* 'Coccineum', branch sport with more red in the magenta of *fl.*, flowering 5.

Series **Uniflorum**

pemakoense ✳ Spring   Sh.
Dwarf spreading shrublet 6 in. to 1 ft. One form is unusual in rhododendrons in being markedly stoloniferous and spreading to large mat. *Fl.* solitary or in pairs, broadly funnel-shaped, pale rosy-purple or whitish flushed pink. *Fl.* buds are tender to spring frosts but plant is quite hardy.

Some forms have pale rosy-mauve flushing in *fl.* Valuable as rock garden plant and usually very free flowering. S.E. Tibet. **1789**, p. 224.

pentaphyllum see under **R. albrechtii**

praevernum see under **R. sutchuenense**

Series **Azalea**, sub-series **Schlippenbachii**

quinquefolium ✳ Spring   Sh.
Deciduous shrub usually under 6 ft but will grow larger. *Fl.* white in small loose trusses up to 3, campanulate but opening widely, pendulous up to 2 in. across, white with some green spotting at base. *Fl.* appearing with young *l.* *L.* at the ends of branchlets, elliptic up to 2 in. long, valuable for fine scarlet autumn colouring. This is one of the most beautiful of the deciduous azalea sp. when in *fl.* but tends to be rather shy flowering as young plant. Japan. **1790**, p. 224.

Series **Scabrifolium**

racemosum ✳ Spring   Sh.
Small evergreen shrub although in some forms growing up to 5–6 ft but usually less, very variable. *Fl.* in axils of *l.* or forming a raceme along branchlets, about 1 in. long, funnel-shaped, pink-white or white tinged pink, a few forms pale or deep rose. Finest form is a dwarf known under collectors' number as ✿'Forrest 19404' or 'Forrest's Dwarf' which has bright pink *fl.* and reddish branchlets and is excellent for rock garden planting. *L.* small, oblong, elliptic, glaucous below up to 2 in. long but usually less. Very hardy and forming spring-like effect amongst the smaller-leaved sp. China, Yunnan. **1791**, p. 224.

Series **Falconeri**

rex ✳ Spring   T.
Small tree up to 20 ft with large *l.* up to 12 in. long and 4 in. across oblanceolate, dark green with pale buff indumentum below. *Fl.* in large truss up to 10 in. across, each *fl.* tubular, campanulate up to 2½ in. long, widely open at the mouth and slightly frilled, variable in colour usually white or pale lilac-rose with crimson blotch and some spotting but some forms are good pale pink. This is one of the hardiest of the large-leaved rhododendrons and grows satisfactorily in most areas especially given some shelter. It is closely allied to *R. fictolacteum*. W. China. **1792**, p. 224.

Series **Anthopogon**

sargentianum ✳ Spring   Sh.
Dwarf compact evergreen bush not often more than 1 ft, with short twiggy branchlets. *Fl.* in small trusses, each about ½ in. across, tubular at base and opening out to broad funnel-shaped, densely scaly at base, white, pale creamy-yellow or lemon-yellow. *L.* small only up to ¾ in. long, broadly elliptic, very scaly below. One of the most desirable rhododendrons for rock garden use and nearly always remaining compact dwarf plant. China, Szechwan. **1793**, p. 225.

Series **Azalea**, sub-series **Schlippenbachii**

schlippenbachii ✳ Spring   Sh.
Deciduous azalea usually forming wide-spreading shrub to about 4 ft, but occasionally growing up to 8 ft. *Fl.* before *l.* or with first young *l.*, in trusses up to 6, flat or saucer-shaped pale or deep rose-pink with some reddish spotting on upper lobes, large up to 3½ in. wide butterfly-like. *L.* in whorls at the end of branches, obovate up to 3½ in. long. One of the most beautiful sp. among the deciduous azaleas and probably the largest in *fl.*, quite hardy and good growing in open situations. Central Japan, Korea, Manchuria.
    'Prince Charming', one of the finest forms with very large *fl.*, **1794**, p. 225.

Series **Grande**

sino-grande ✳ Mid Spring   *T.
Tree wide-spreading usually and when full grown

up to 30 ft. Remarkable for its very large *l.* which when mature are up to 3 ft long by 12 in. broad, oblong, lanceolate, deep green and shining, rather puckered upper surface and silvery-grey below. *Fl.* up to 20 in large rather loose truss, white or creamy-white with crimson blotch, up to 3 in. long. This rhododendron grows best in milder areas with high rainfall and in E. areas rarely attains sufficient size to *fl.* well, it is however valuable as foliage plant more than as flowering plant and its *l.* are like great elephant ears, probably the largest of any ever-green *l.* grown in Britain. W. China, Upper Burma, S.E. Tibet. **1795**, p. 225.
    There is a N. form known as:
    var. *boreale*, with *fl.* of a soft creamy-yellow with crimson blotch which is said to be slightly hardier than type but there is very little difference between.

Series **Barbatum**, sub-series **Maculiferum**

strigillosum ✳ Spring   Sh.
Evergreen shrub up to 20 ft but usually less. Closely allied to *R. barbatum* but coming from China rather than the Himalayas. *Fl.* very brilliant scarlet in rather loose trusses, large waxy up to 2½ in. long, tubular, campanulate. *L.* up to 7 in. long, oblong, lanceolate bristly at base. One of the most valuable early flowering rhododendrons for brilliant colouring, hardy in most situations but best with some protection in cold areas. W. China. **1796**, p. 225.

Series **Fortunei**, sub-series **Davidii**

sutchuenense ✳ Spring   Sh.
Large shrub or small tree up to 15 ft. *Fl.* very early, in large trusses, tubular, campanulate up to 3 in. long, white or rosy-lilac or rosy-pink with some purple spots at base and in var. *giraldii* with large purple blotch. *L.* long, narrow up to 12 in. by 3 in. broad, oblong, oblanceolate, usually drooping, rather matt-green above. *R. praevernum* is very close and it is suggested it is one of the parents of var. *giraldii* when crossed with *R. sutchuenense* but there is little distinction between the three except for the blotch. One of the most valuable early flowering rhododendrons and quite hardy as bush. W. China. **1797**, p. 225.

taggianum see under **R. dalhousiae**

Series **Anthopogon**

trichostomum ✳ Early Summer   Sh.
Small evergreen shrub usually not over 3 ft with

rather stiff, twiggy branchlets. *Fl.* in globose trusses, small tubular each ¾ in. long, white or rose with pink buds. In type is hairy inside the throat and in var. *ledoides* it is without hairs, otherwise only slight differences. *L.* linear, lanceolate up to 1 in. long, scaly below. One of the most useful dwarf rhododendrons especially for the aromatic character of the shrub. Valuable for large rock garden but slightly tender in cold areas. China, Yunnan, Szechwan.

var. *ledoides*, **1798**, p. 225.

vaseyi see under **R. albrechtii**

Series **Campanulatum**

wallichii ✲ Mid Spring   Sh.
Evergreen shrub up to 10 ft. *Fl.* in trusses up to 10, lilac-blue spotted with rose, open campanulate and slightly frilled at mouth. *L.* up to 5 in. long, elliptic or obovate, distinguished by the reddish-brown tufts of hairs on under surface. Very closely allied to *R. campanulatum* and sometimes difficult to distinguish but in its best forms probably has slightly better colouring, although *R. campanulatum* 'Knap Hill' is practically as blue as good forms of *wallichii*. Quite hardy and deserves to be grown more widely provided good forms are obtained but these should be seen in *fl.* first since they are variable. Himalayas. **1799**, p. 225.

Series **Thomsonii**, sub-series **Williamsianum**

✿**williamsianum** ✲ Mid Spring   Sh.
Small spreading evergreen shrub rarely over 4 ft and often as much across. Distinguished by the bronzy young shoots and the rounded *l*. *Fl.* usually in a loose truss, drooping bell-shaped, clear shell-pink in best forms, up to 2 in. long. Very attractive sp. excellent for large rock garden or to emphasise junction. May be grown in full exposure although young foliage may be damaged by early frosts. China, Szechwan. **1800**, p. 225.

Series **Cinnabarinum**

xanthocodon ✲ Spring   Sh.
Spreading shrub usually not more than 8 ft but in old specimens may become tree-like up to 15 ft. Distinguished by young foliage which is very glaucous blue and remains so coloured for earlier part of summer. *Fl.* in loose trusses, drooping, narrowly bell-shaped up to 1½ in. long, slightly fleshy, rich creamy-yellow or buff-yellow. Hardy and valuable in best forms both for *fl.* and for foliage. Foliage is distinctly aromatic. Himalayas, S.E. Tibet. **1801**, p. 226.

Series **Ponticum**, sub-series **Caucasicum**

✿**yakusimanum** ✲ Late Spring   Sh.
Dwarf compact evergreen shrub up to about 3 ft and as much across. *Fl.* from compact rounded trusses up to 8 in. across, bell-shaped, deep rose in bud opening white inside when fully expanded. *L.* like those of *R. ponticum* about 3½ in. long, brown tomentose when young, later dark green and glossy above. One of the most valuable recent introductions for its compact and free flowering habit and complete hardiness. It has been used much for hybridisation but none of the hybrids so far have excelled the parent. On native island there are several varying forms. Japan, Island of Yakusima. **1802**, p. 226.

Hybrids
Excluding evergreen and deciduous azaleas which will be treated separately later. Only small selection of large range can be given here, fuller selection will be found in the Rhododendron Handbook Part 2 or in the International Rhododendron Register both published by the Royal Horticultural Society. In the Rhododendron Handbook will be found ratings for *fl.* and also hardiness ratings.

'Azor' ✲ Summer   T.
Fl. deep strawberry-pink in large loose trusses. Valuable for its very late flowering. Makes a small tree, wide-spreading. *R. discolor* × *R. griersonianum*. **1803**, p. 226.

'Britannia' ✲ Early Summer   Sh.
Fl. bright crimson-red in very compact trusses. Very free flowering. One of the best and most regular flowerer of the older hardy hybrids. Rather wide-spreading bush but reaching 8 ft in height and as much across in time. **1804**, p. 226.

'Choremia' ✲ Early Spring   Sh.
Fl. bright scarlet-red in dense compact truss with black glands at base of corolla. *L.* rusty below. One of the most valuable early flowering hybrids being derived from *R. arboreum* × *R. haematodes*. **1805**, p. 226.

✿**'Cilpinense'** ✲ Early Spring   Sh.
Very early, pinkish-white or pale pink *fl.* in loose trusses, open bell-shaped. Dwarf, usually not more than 3–4 ft, rather lax growing. One of the most valuable early flowering hybrids, quite hardy but *fl.* are liable to be damaged by frost. *R. ciliatum* × *R. moupinense*. **1806**, p. 226.

'Crest' ✲ Spring, occasionally Early Summer   Sh.
Finest yellow seedling from the group known as Hawk derived from 'Lady Bessborough' × *R. wardii*. One of the finest yellow flowered rhododendrons, not however so free flowering and vigorous as some other members of the Hawk group but worth every effort for its deep yellow colour and its large open bell-shaped *fl.* in fairly compact truss. **1807**, p. 226.

✿**'Elizabeth'** ✲ Spring   Sh.
R. forrestii var. *repens* × *R. griersonianum*. Dwarf bush but growing up to 5 ft in time. *Fl.* very bright scarlet-crimson. One of the finest hybrids in this group. Very free flowering. Combines well as in photograph with white tree heather *Erica veitchii* where shown backed with hedge of × *Cupressocyparis leylandii*. **1808**, p. 226.

'Elspeth' ✲ Early Summer   Sh.
Hardy hybrid flowering late 5 to 6. Deep rosy-scarlet in bud, fading as *fl.* opens to pink or cream. Vigorous hybrid forming large bush up to 15 ft. Good specimen may be seen at Wisley at edge of hardy hybrid Rhododendron Trial ground. **1809**, p. 227.

'Fragrantissimum' ✲ Spring   *Sh.
Tender hybrid. *Fl.* large white and slightly frilled at the edge, sweetly scented. May be grown outside in milder districts but in other areas best treated as a greenhouse plant. Growing up to 5 ft but often less and flowering freely, excellent as a pot plant. Derived from *R. edgeworthii* × *R. formosum*. **1810**, p. 227.

'Lady Rosebery' ✲ Early Summer   Sh.
R. cinnabarinum var. *roylei* × 'Royal Flush' pink form. Loose growing shrub. *Fl.* deep pink flushed salmon, drooping in loose trusses, rather tubular with spreading lobes. One of the most beautiful of hybrid rhododendrons of this group which includes 'Lady Chamberlain' and 'Lady Berry'. May be grown with some shelter and hardy in most places but doing best in milder areas. **1811**, p. 227.

✿**Loderi 'King George'** ✲ Spring   Sh.
One of the finest forms of the valuable Loderi cross which has yielded a number of excellent plants. *Fl.* truss large rather loose, pale pink fading to flush white as it matures. Vigorous and wide-spreading shrub up to 15 ft. Very free and regular flowering. **1812**, p. 227.
Other good clones of this cross are:
   'Pink Diamond', 'Sir Joseph Hooker', 'Sir Edmund' and 'Venus'.

'Mrs G. W. Leak' ✲ Early Summer   Sh.
One of the most valuable among hardy hybrids. *Fl.* pale blush-pink with deep purplish-crimson blotch at base making conspicuous contrast, in compact trusses, very regular flowering. **1813**, p. 227.

✿**'Penjerrick Cream'** ✲ Spring   Sh.
Regarded by many authorities as the most beautiful rhododendron hybrid yet raised. *Fl.* open bell-shaped, very regular in loose trusses. Also pink form

but many prefer creamy-yellow form. Forming large bush or small tree. Hardy but best where it can be protected from wind since rather loose growing. Parentage *R. campylocarpum* var. *elatum* × *R. griffithianum*. **1814**, p. 227.

✿**'Polar Bear'** ✲ Summer   T.
Very late flowering hybrid. *Fl.* white in large trusses up to 6 in. across. Forming small tree up to 15 ft. Chiefly distinctive as the latest rhododendron hybrid to *fl.* in most gardens. Slightly scented. *R. auriculatum* × *R. diaprepes*. **1815**, p. 227.

'Praecox' ✲ Early Spring   Sh.
Valuable as one of the earliest hybrids to *fl*. *Fl.* lilac-purple varying in colour, owing to cross having been made with varying parents of *dauricum*, some of which were evergreen, others semi-evergreen or deciduous. Makes small shrub usually not more than 5 ft and as much across. Hardy but *fl.* are liable to be damaged by frost. One of the few rhododendrons which will tolerate a moderate amount of lime in soil. There is a famous hedge of this rhododendron in the Royal Botanic Garden, Edinburgh. *R. ciliatum* × *R. dauricum*. **1816**, p. 227.

✿**'Seta'** ✲ Early Spring   Sh.
Fl. white or blush-pink tipped with deeper pink. Hardy but liable to frost damage on *fl.* One of the finest early flowering, smaller growing hybrids. Derived from *R. moupinense* × *R. spinuliferum*. **1817**, p. 228.

'Susan' ✲ Spring   Sh.
Fl. lavender-blue in large compact trusses. One of the finest of the bluish hybrid rhododendrons of this type. Derived from *R. campanulatum*. **1818**, p. 228.

'Tally-Ho' ✲ Summer   T.
Fl. bright scarlet-crimson in rather loose trusses, late. Makes small tree. One of the strongest in colour of the later flowering hybrids. *R. eriogynum* × *R. griersonianum*. **1819**, p. 228.

'Temple Belle' ✲ Spring   Sh.
Dwarf bush but sometimes reaching up to 5 ft and as much across, usually forming rounded mound. *Fl.* pale pink, bell-shaped, drooping, slightly larger than those of *williamsianum*. Early flowering. Valuable for the decorative effect of its rounded *l.* and close habit of growth. *R. orbiculare* × *R. williamsianum*. **1820**, p. 228.

Abbreviations and Symbols used in the text.
The following abbreviations may sometimes be used in conjunction as HA. indicating Hardy annual or GBb indicating Greenhouse bulb.

A. = Annual	P. = Perennial
Aq. = Aquatic	R. = Rock or
B. = Biennial	Alpine plant
Bb = Bulb	Sh. = Shrub
C. = Corm	Sp., sp. = Species
Cl. = Climber	Syn. = Synonym
Co. = Conifer	T. = Tree
Fl., fl. = Flower(s)	Tu. = Tuber
G. = Greenhouse or	var. = variety
house plant	× = Hybrid or
H. = Hardy	hybrid parents
HH. = Half-hardy	✲ = Flowering time
L., l. = Leaf, leaves	➊ = Foliage plant
Mt(s) = Mount,	
mountain(s)	

The following have been used also in the descriptions of Alpines, Bulbs, Trees and Shrubs.

   * = slightly tender
   † = lime hater
   ✿ = highly recommended

The illustration numbers are in **bold type** and the page numbers in light type preceded by p.

Japanese and Evergreen Azaleas ❋ Spring Sh.
These include those known as Kurumes and the colour variants of *R. kiusianum*. Others are variants with *R. obtusum*, while under *R. indicum* come the later flowering hybrid race known as 'Macrantha'. These include those derived from *R. malvatica* × *R. kaempferi* and for those described as Vuykiana; parentage of Kurume × Mollis, a deciduous Azalea, is claimed although they are evergreen and rather dwarf. Among the finest forms out of a very large range are:

'Addy Wery'
Late flowering. *R. malvatica* × *R. kaempferi* hybrid, bright scarlet-red. **1821**, p. 228.

'Apple Blossom' see **'Hoo'**

'Azuma-kagami'
Deep pink. One of the most attractive in this colour range.

'Betty'
Deep pink with a little orange in it.

'Eddy'
Late flowering. *R.* Kurume × *R. indica*. Bright orange scarlet.

✿**'Fedora'**
Dark pink. One of the best and very free flowering. *R. malvatica* × *R.* Kurume. **1822**, p. 228.

'Hi No Degiri'
Bright magenta-crimson, one of the most spectacular.

✿**'Hi No Mayo'**
Soft pink, very free flowering, one of the most attractive. **1823**, p. 228.

'Hoo'
Often known as 'Apple Blossom'. White with a pinkish tinge.

'John Cairns'
Late flowering, bright indian-red. *R. malvatica* × *R. kaempferi*.

'Kirin'
Deep rose but shaded silvery-rose.

'Kure No Yuki'
White, very free flowering.

'Mucronatum'
White, free flowering, Kurume type.

'Orange Beauty'
Strong tangerine-orange, very free flowering. Thought to be *R.* Kurume × *R. kaempferi*.

✿**'Palestrina'**
White with a green eye, rather large *fl.*, one of the finest forms.

'Vuyk's Scarlet'
Late flowering, very large *fl.* deep scarlet-red, usually rather dwarf. Vuykiana.

Deciduous Hybrid Azaleas ❋ Spring Sh.
These are mostly derived from crosses between *R. molle* and *R. japonicum* but some also include Occidentale which are forms or hybrids from the American sp. *R. occidentale*. The Ghent Azaleas are separate and are later flowering than the *molle* × *japonicum* (Mollis) hybrids and are usually smaller in *fl.* The Knap Hill Azaleas have been derived from crosses between *R. molle* and the Ghent Azaleas and *R. calendulaceum* as well as other sp. They were begun in the nursery at Knap Hill and have been carried on since by several breeders, notably in the Exbury strain. There are very numerous named hybrids a list of which is to be found in the Rhododendron Handbook Part 2, under Knap Hill though in some catalogues they are listed separately.
Among the best of the deciduous hybrids are:

'Adrian Koster'
Mollis, deep yellow.

'Avocet'
Knap Hill, white and pink.

'Brazil'
Knap Hill, bright tangerine-orange, a very hot colour.

'Daybreak'
Ghent, marigold-orange but suffused with red, paler in bright sun after some days. **1824**, p. 228.

'Delicatissima'
Occidentale hybrid, cream with a yellow blotch and pink tinged, late flowering and older hybrid.

'Devon'
Knap Hill, bright red.

'Dr M. Oosthoek'
Mollis, bright orange-red, one of the strongest colours.

'Exquisita'
An Occidentale hybrid, cream flushed pink with an orange blotch, late flowering.

'Gog'
Knap Hill, orange-red.

'Golden Oriole'
Knap Hill, deep chinese-yellow with an orange blotch, early flowering.

'Harvest Moon'
Knap Hill, pale yellow with lemon tinge.

✿**'Hotspur Orange'**
Knap Hill, orange-scarlet with a yellow blotch, one of the strongest colours. **1825**, p. 229.

'Hugh Wormald'
Knap Hill, deep orange-yellow. **1826**, p. 229.

'J. C. Van Tol'
Mollis, deep orange-red, strong colour.

✿**'Koster's Brilliant Red'**
Mollis, glowing orange-red, very strong colour, an old favourite.

'Lapwing'
Knap Hill, pale yellow, tinged pink with an orange blotch.

'Narcissiflora'
Ghent, pale yellow, double *fl.*; one of the older forms. All Ghents are sweetly scented.

'Persil'
Knap Hill, strong white with a yellow blotch.

'Ribera'
Mollis, soft pale pink with a white throat, rather long narrow *fl.* **1827**, p. 229.

'Satan'
Knap Hill, bright scarlet-red, very deep strong colour. **1828**, p. 229.

'Scarlet O'Hara'
Knap Hill, deep scarlet-red. **1829**, p. 229.

'Silver Slipper'
Knap Hill, white flushed orange-pink. **1830**, p. 229.

✿**'Spek's Brilliant'**
Mollis, orange-red with a conspicuous yellow base one of the finest forms.

'Spek's Orange'
Mollis, bright orange with deep blotch, very strong colour.

'Strawberry Ice'
Knap Hill, pale pink with slightly deeper blotch.

✿**'Sun Chariot'**
Knap Hill, deep buttercup-yellow and a deeper orange eye. **1831**, p. 229.

RHODOHYPOXIS (HYPOXIDACEAE)

baurei ❋ Spring–Early Summer RP.
Fl. deep pink but variable from white to crimson, opening flat and star-like in two ranks of three petals each, up to ¾ in. across, singly on short stem. 2–3 in. *L.* strap-shaped, hairy, up to 4 in. Makes a short rhizome with fleshy roots. Alpine house or well-drained warm position. It requires to be fairly dry in winter but while growing in summer, requires good moisture. S. Africa, Basutoland. **181**, p. 23.
Various forms have been selected with slightly larger *fl.*, among which 'Margaret Rose', with flesh-pink *fl.*, is one of the best, **182**, p. 23.

RHOICISSUS (VITACEAE)

rhomboidea ☙ GP.
L. trifoliate, each leaflet stalked, dark green. Useful as house plant, as it tolerates shady conditions and oil and gas fumes. Winter temp. should be 50°F. but plant survives at 45°F. Any good potting compost satisfactory. Nip out growing points in spring to encourage side growths. Propagate by cuttings of hard, but not woody, shoots. Water freely in spring and summer, sparingly at other times. It has been suggested that the plant cultivated under this name is really the W. Indian *Cissus rhombifolia*. Until plants *fl.* in cultivation, this will be difficult to determine. Natal. **636**, p. 80.

RHUBARB see **Rheum**, **1347**, **1348**, p. 169.

RHUS (ANACARDIACEAE) Sumach
Small trees or large shrubs distinguished from *Cotinus* by having pinnate *l.*

cotinus see **Cotinus coggygria**

cotinoides see **Cotinus americanus**

glabra see after **R. typhina**

radicans see after **R. typhina**

toxicodendron see after **R. typhina**

typhina Stag's Horn Sumach ❋ Mid Spring T.
Small wide-headed deciduous tree or large shrub. *L.* large pinnate up to 2 ft long with 13 or more leflets which are up to 4½ in. long, oblong lanceolate, toothed. Autumn colouring is brilliant yellow and scarlet and tree is mainly grown for this feature. *Fl.* small, greenish-white. Fruits on female trees only in large panicle covered with crimson hairs and decorative. E. N. America. **1832**, p. 229.
var. *laciniata*, leaflets deeply divided.

Close is *R. glabra* with smooth *l.* and branches also from E. N. America. It is more shrubby than *R. typhina*. *R. toxicodendron*, Poison Ivy, and *R.*

radicans, Poison Oak, natives of E. N. America with brilliant autumn colouring but should be avoided as garden plants owing to the highly irritating and poisonous *l.* which sting badly when they are touched. The main poison element is in the sap. *R. toxicodendron* sometimes seen as a loose climber or deciduous shrub.

RHYNCOLAELIA see Brassocattleya

RIBBON GRASS see Phalaris arundinacea
'Picta', **1310**, p. 164.

RIBES (SAXIFRAGACEAE) Flowering Currant
(Sometimes placed in separate family Grossulariaceae)

fuchsioides see **R. speciosum**

sanguineum ✳ Spring   Sh.
The most widely grown sp. Deciduous shrub wide-spreading up to 8 ft with short downy shoots. *Fl.* deep pink with white centres ½ in. across star-like in upright racemes up to 4 in. long. *L.* three or five-lobed roundish with cordate base. One of the most regular flowering of spring shrubs. Plant either full sun or semi-shade. W. N. America.
Various forms have been described among the best being:
   'Albescens', with *fl.* white tinged with pink. Syn. 'Albidum';
   'Albidum', see 'Albescens';
   'King Edward VII', *fl.* deeper crimson than type and rather dwarfer growing;
   'Pulborough Scarlet', *fl.* bright crimson-red in large clusters, one of the best, **1833**, p. 230;
   'Splendens', *fl.* rosy-crimson with extra long racemes. N. America.

speciosum, syn. **R. fuchsioides** ✳ Spring   *Sh.
Deciduous or semi-evergreen in mild areas, shrub or wall shrub. *Fl.* bright scarlet-red, fuchsia-like and pendulous. Calyx tubular with four sepals and four petals as long as sepals, stamens protruding from end of *fl.* like those of fuchsia. *Fl.* hang in rows or clusters below branches. Should be planted in warm sunny position. California. **1834**, p. 230.

RICHARDIA AETHIOPICA see Zantedeschia aethiopica

RICHEA (EPACRIDACEAE)

scoparia ✳ Early Summer   *Sh.
Evergreen shrub up to 6 ft but usually less, branching from base making thick cluster. *Fl.* orange, flask-shaped in upright racemes up to 6 in. long. *L.* stiff narrow with pointed ends up to 3 in. Probably best planted in lime-free soil in open sheltered position. There is also form with whitish *fl.* edged with pink. Hardy in gardens of the S. of England and S.W., probably also in W. states of N. America. Tasmania. **1835**, p. 230.

RICINUS (EUPHORBIACEAE)

communis Castor Oil Plant ✳ Midsummer HHA.
Fl. green in clusters. *L.* variable in size and colour, palmately-lobed, smooth, with long stalk. The large, pleasingly coloured, bean-like seeds are the source of castor oil. 3–8 ft or more in warm climates; up to 40 ft tree in the tropics. Sow the seed singly in pots in a warm greenhouse in 2–3. Plant out in 6. Trop. Africa.
   'Gibsonii', reddish *l.* and stems, 4–5 ft, **366**, p. 46;
   'Zanzibarensis', bright green *l.* to 2 ft across, 6–8 ft, **367**, p. 46.

ROBEL BEECH see Nothofagus obliqua

ROBINIA (LEGUMINOSAE)

hispida Rose Acacia ✳ Early Summer   Sh.
Deciduous shrub or small tree without spines. *Fl.*

---

deep pink up to 1¼ in. long with rounded standard petals borne in pendulous or arching racemes up to 3 in. long. Probably the largest and most showy of the Robinias. *L.* pinnate up to 10 in. long with up to 13 leaflets. Usually top grafted on standard of *R. pseudoacacia* since otherwise it is very free suckering shrub. E. USA. **1836**, p. 230.

kelseyi ✳ Early Summer   Sh.
Fl. pink. E. USA.

pseudoacacia Locust, False Acacia ✳ Early Summer   T.
Deciduous tree up to 40 ft often less with large pinnate *l.* up to 1 ft. *Fl.* white in pendulous racemes. N. America but naturalised in many parts of Europe.
Numerous varieties have been separated among the best are:
   'Aurea', with *l.* golden-yellow in early summer turning green later;
   'Tortuosa', a curious var. with branches twisted but small racemes of *fl.*

ROCK PURSLANE see Calandrinia umbellata, 246, p. 31.

ROCK ROSE see Cistus, 1513-1516, p. 190; Helianthemum, 84, 85, p. 11.

RODGERSIA (SAXIFRAGACEAE)

pinnata Feathered Bronze Leaf ✳ Midsummer   P.
Fl. clear pink in much-branched panicles. 3–4 ft. *L.* large, long-stalked, green becoming bronze tinged. Plant 11–3 in moist leafy soil and a position sheltered from strong winds. Propagate by division in the spring. China.
   'Superba', is a magnificent form, **1349**, p. 169.

podophylla ✳ Summer   P.
Fl. cream, in bold panicles. *L.* large, handsomely netted. Plant 11–3. Japan. **1350**, p. 169.

tabularis ✳ Summer   P.
Fl. creamy-white, astilbe-like. 3–4 ft. *L.* large, round, scalloped. China. **1351**, p. 169.

ROMNEYA (PAPAVERACEAE) Tree Poppy

All Romneyas are very sensitive to root disturbance and should be planted out of pots when young. Propagate by root cuttings in cool or warm greenhouse.

coulteri ✳ Midsummer–Early Autumn   *Sh.
Sub-shrubby, plant with tall herbaceous stems up to 8 ft, wide-spreading by suckers. *Fl.* large up to 5 in. across with broad overlapping white satin-like petals with centre boss of golden stamens. *L.* glaucous deeply divided. One of the most valuable, late flowering, shrubby plants for warm situation such as base of a wall but sufficiently hardy to stand in the open in most S. areas of England. Plant in as sunny a position as possible. Usually best to cut down stems nearly to the base in spring. California. **1837**, p. 230.

trichocalyx ✳ Summer   Sh.
Close to *R. coulteri*, with rather more erect less branched stems and bristly buds. Probably many of the plants grown are hybrids between the two sp. California.

ROMULEA (IRIDACEAE)

bulbocodium ✳ Late Winter–Mid Spring   C.
Like a small crocus, *fl.* cup-shaped, appearing almost sessile on ground, pale rosy-purple with yellow centre, opening only in the sun or in warmth. Corms small, crocus-like with reticulated (netlike) covering. *L.* narrow, grasslike. Plant in as warm and sunny a position as possible, also good for pans in alpine house. S. Europe. **875**, p. 110.
Other closely related sp. are:

---

columnea with smaller whitish or pale mauve *fl.*
requienii with deep violet-purple *fl.* heavily veined.

ROSA Rose

Roses form a very large group and are most valuable garden shrubs. Here they are placed in five sections. First, the sp. and direct hybrids; second, the old and new shrub roses; third, the Floribundas, one of the most valuable rose races of recent times with several *fl.* to a stem, sometimes the *fl.* are nearly as large as those of the Hybrid Teas and the distinction between the two is tending to be indistinct and much less than formerly; fourth, the Hybrid Teas so popular for garden decoration and cutting; finally we have a small section of climbing and rambling roses.

1. **Species and direct hybrids**
Variable in size from large bushes 15 ft high and as much wide to 2–3 ft in height.

✿ × **cantabrigiensis** ✳ Early Summer   Sh.
A hybrid of *R. hugonis* × *R. sericea* and better as garden plant in *fl.* than either parent. Loose growing tall shrub up to 8 ft of which the long shoots are covered in late spring 5–6 with creamy-yellow single blooms up to 2 in. across. Foliage ferny, orange-red rather small round hips in late summer. One of the most vigorous Modern Hybrid Roses and probably the best of the early flowering ones. **1838**, p. 230.

damascena 'Hebes Lip' ✳ Summer   Sh.
Probably a hybrid from *R. damascena*. *Fl.* semi-double but showing large boss of yellow stamens in centre, creamy-white with some crimson colouring round tips of petals. Non-recurrent 6. A rose of moderate size usually not more than 4–5 ft. Hips in autumn. **1839**, p. 230.

× **highdownensis** ✳ Summer   Sh.
A selected seedling from *R. moyesii*. Very vigorous with long sprays up to 10 ft and as much across in an old bush. *Fl.* very numerous, single cerise-crimson with yellow stamens in centre, very strong colour. Foliage light, ferny with many small leaflets. Hips large bottle-shaped orange-red making very distinctive feature 9–10 and giving it dual purpose quality. One of the most vigorous and beautiful of *moyesii* types. **1840**, p. 230.

---

hugonis see **R. × cantabrigiensis**

✿**moyesii** ✳ Summer — Sh.
Very vigorous shrub up to 10 ft and in old specimens forming clumps as much across with long sprays covered with deep crimson-red single *fl.* up to 2 in. across, stamens creamy. Foliage light, ferny, hips large orange-scarlet to scarlet-crimson, very strong in colour making it a very valuable dual purpose plant flowering 6, hips 9–10. For pruning old woody sprays should be cut right out to base after flowering to encourage new growth and young shoots grown on. Several forms have been named among which is 'Geranium' which has more compact habit not often over 8 ft with lighter green foliage and large orange-red hips. **1841**, p. 231.

pimpinellifolia see **R. spinosissima**

rubrifolia ✳ Summer — Sh.
Vigorous shrub rose up to 5 or 6 ft and as much across. Distinguished for purplish sheen on foliage thus making it valuable plant for all seasons of summer. *Fl.* deep pink white towards centre, single up to 2 in. across. Prune after flowering or in winter to encourage compact growth. **1842**, p. 231.

sericea see **R. × cantabrigiensis**

spinosissima var. **altaica** ✳ Early Summer — Sh.
Burnett Rose or Scots Briar, sometimes included under *R. pimpinellifolia*. Large shrub sometimes up to 6 ft usually less. *Fl.* single, pale creamy-yellow with large boss of golden stamens, petals broad overlapping. Late 5 to early 6. Leaflets small, foliage fern-like. Hips small black. All Burnett roses grow well on sandy soil and will frequently sucker to make large prickly thickets and colonise large areas. W. Europe, W. Asia including native of Britain. **1843**, p. 231.

webbiana ✳ Early Summer — Sh.
Tall shrub up to 6 ft usually rather thin growth. Distinguished by young branches having glaucous purple bloom. *Fl.* single, pale pink up to 2 in. across on long arching sprays, each *fl.* borne singly on a short lateral twig. Hips pitcher-shaped, bright red up to 1 in. long. Distinguished also by its pale yellowish prickles and fine foliage. Valuable both for its flowering and fruiting as dual purpose plant. Closely allied to *R. willmottiae* which has slightly larger *fl.* but not such good hips. Himalayas. **1844**, p. 231.

willmottiae see **R. webbiana**

woodsii ✳ Summer — Sh.
Large shrub up to 6 ft. *Fl.* pink, single, up to 1½ in. across, solitary or in small clusters. *L.* compound with five to seven obovate leaflets. Fruit ovoid, ½ in. across, light orange-scarlet. W. N. America.
var. *fendleri* distinguished by leaflets, stalks and stipules being glandular. *Fl.* lilac-pink. Good hips. W. N. America, **1845**, p. 231.

2. Old and New Shrub Roses

The Old roses, favourites from the 18 and 19 centuries in most cases are noted for their very fine scent but with only one season of flowering. Many of the Modern Hybrid Shrub roses are very fine plants for the garden, more vigorous than some of the Old roses and floriferous while several have a prolonged season of flowering.

'Blanc Double de Coubert' ✳ Summer — Sh.
Vigorous *rugosa* shrub up to 6 ft and as much across in old bushes, sometimes suckering freely. *Fl.* large, white semi-double with small centre, very fine when opening. *L.* typical *rugosa* bright green and slightly puckered turning yellow in autumn. **1846**, p. 231.

'Constance Spry' ✳ Late Spring–Early Summer — Sh.
Loose growing Shrub rose, branches tending to arch over and spreading widely. *Fl.* deep rose pink, large, fully double in form of centifolia rose, very fragrant. *L.* coppery when young. One of the finest Hybrid Shrub roses in the tradition of the Old roses introduced in recent years. **1847**, p. 231.

'Frau Dagmar Hastrup' ✳ Summer — Sh.
Rugosa shrub, often known as 'Frau Dagmar Hartop' but correctly 'Fru Dagmar Hastrup' from the Danish. *Fl.* deep cerise-pink, single, large up to 4 in. across, free flowering. Leaflets rather large, crinkled or rugose on upper surface. Hips very large, brilliant scarlet, glossy, flattened slightly at tip and base. One of the best dual purpose roses for *fl.* and hips. May be trimmed into hedge by hard pruning in winter if required. **1848**, p. 231.

✿**'Fritz Nobis'** ✳ Summer — Sh.
Modern hybrid of vigorous growth reaching 6 ft by 6 ft across. *Fl.* soft salmon-pink slightly darker towards base, beautifully formed like *fl.* of an Old Shrub rose, very floriferous up to 3–4 in. across, 6 to early 7. One of the most valuable of Modern Hybrid Shrub roses. Small reddish hips in autumn. **1849**, p. 232.

✿**'Frühlingsgold'** ✳ Late Spring–Early Summer Sh.
Very vigorous hybrid of *R. spinosissima* reaching 8 ft or more and forming large shrub. Very free flowering. *Fl.* semi-double or single with large boss of golden stamens in centre, creamy-yellow, late 5 and 6. Growth arching with long shoots. These should be pruned by cutting out some of the old wood after flowering. One of the finest of the *spinosissima* hybrids. **1850**, p. 232.

gallica 'Complicata' ✳ Summer — Sh.
Gallica hybrid of great vigour up to 8 ft with long shoots which can be trained to form a pillar. *Fl.* single, very large, bright pink with large boss of yellow stamens and white at base of petals like a very much larger Dog rose. *Fl.* up to 5 in. across, very freely borne. Forms one of the most spectacular shrubs during 6 but not recurrent. Hips red, quite large. Needs careful pruning and training to show off to best effect and plenty of space. **1851**, p. 232.

gallica 'Versicolor' ✳ Summer — Sh.
Also known as Rosa mundi. One of the oldest of the Shrub roses, up to 3–4 ft. Very free flowering. *Fl.* white splashed and striped liberally with crimson or, as some say, crimson splashed with white. Makes a compact bush and may be trimmed in spring to form rose hedge, making a very distinctive feature in gardens. Non-recurrent flowering and somewhat subject to mildew unless sprayed. **1852**, p. 232.

'Gipsy Boy' see **'Zigeuner Knabe'**

'Marguerite Hilling' ✳ Summer — Sh.
Large shrub up to 5–6 ft. *Fl.* semi-double light rosy-purple. A sport from 'Nevada'. **1853**, p. 232.

✿**'Nevada'** ✳ Late Spring–Early Summer, Late Summer — Sh.
Large and very vigorous bush up to 8 ft and as much across. Said to be a hybrid from Tetraploid form of *R. moyesii* named *R. moyesii fargesii* with a Hybrid Tea. *Fl.* semi-double or single, creamy-white up to 4 in. across and large boss of yellow stamens in centre, slightly untidy in *fl.* but valuable for its great mass of blooms in late 5 and 6, often covering whole shrub with long arching sprays. It is somewhat recurrent with few blooms in 8–9. Buds slightly flushed pink and the *fl.* have occasional purplish-crimson splash. Provided there is space available, one of the most valuable shrub roses. Prune by cutting out oldest sprays after flowering right down to base. **1854**, p. 232.

✿**'Penelope'** ✳ Early Summer, Late Summer — Sh.
A Hybrid Musk Shrub rose. Vigorous, 6 ft by the same across. *Fl.* creamy blush-pink semi-double showing boss of yellow stamens in centre fading to pale cream. Foliage grey. Main flowering 6 but somewhat recurrent with second flowering in 8–9, finely scented. **1855**, p. 232.

'Rosa mundi' see **R. gallica** 'Versicolor'

'Zephirine Drouhin' ✳ Late Spring–Early Autumn — Sh.
Old Bourbon rose. Distinguished by being thornless. May be grown either as large bush rose or as a climber up to 10 ft. *Fl.* semi-double or loosely double,

strong cerise-pink, an unusual colour. Foliage coppery-purple when young becoming light green. **1856**, p. 232.

✿**'Zigeuner Knabe'** ✳ Summer — Sh.
Old Bourbon Hybrid, also known as 'Gipsy Boy'. Very vigorous with long arching branches, up to 10 ft, very prickly. *Fl.* very freely borne, deep purplish-crimson, fully double or occasionally semi-double, showing small patch of yellow in the centre. Petals reflexed and *fl.* flat. Very effective especially growing into old tree and cascading down but *fl.* are unfortunately scentless. Flowering 6, non-recurrent. **1857**, p. 233.

3. Floribunda Roses ✳ Summer–Mid Autumn — Sh.
With these are included those sometimes listed as Grandifloras but there is no hard dividing line between them. All these have a number of *fl.* on single stem but some tend to have large *fl.* approaching those of Hybrid Teas.

'Alison Wheatcroft'
Fl. apricot-pink flushed deeper pink towards edges of petals and with some creaminess on inside of petals. Blended colouring which is very effective in garden. Vigorous free blooming grower with very large *fl.* in large clusters. **1858**, p. 233.

'Anna Wheatcroft'
Single, light salmon-vermilion showing large boss of golden stamens in centre in large clusters, very free blooming. Each *fl.* up to 4 in. across. **1859**, p. 233.

✿**'Elizabeth of Glamis'**
Deep terracotta-salmon, paler on outside of blooms. Very large clusters of *fl.* and very vigorous, fragrant. One of the finest Floribunda roses yet raised and makes magnificent bedding rose. **1860**, p. 233.

'Evelyn Fison'
Bright scarlet-crimson in very large clusters, very vigorous grower and free blooming. One of the best of the scarlet-red Floribundas. **1861**, p. 233.

'Golden Slippers'
Bicolor with pointed buds and large *fl.* up to 3 in. across, vermilion-yellow with golden-yellow centre. Vigorous compact grower better known in USA than in England. **1862**, p. 233.

✿**'Iceberg'**
Known in Germany as 'Schneewittchen'. Probably

---

the finest white Floribunda yet raised. *Fl.* large after long pointed buds, pure white, fragrant. Free blooming and remaining in *fl.* late in the season often up to Christmas. Very vigorous upright grower with good glossy light-green foliage. One of the great roses to be raised in recent years. **1863**, p. 233.

'Jan Spek'
Yellow becoming paler at edge of petals in very large clusters. One of the best yellow Floribundas. **1864**, p. 233.

'John S. Armstrong'
Sometimes described as a Grandiflora. *Fl.* large up to 4 in. across, deep crimson-red slightly fragrant in large clusters. More popular in USA than in England. Described as tall bushy with abundant bloom. **1865**, p. 234.

'Masquerade'
Very distinctive rose for its variation in colour. *Fl.* opening bright yellow and turning salmon-pink and then darkening to light red with several colours visible at the same time in the cluster. Vigorous grower and very popular. **1866**, p. 234.

'Orangeade'
Very bright orange-terracotta, semi-double in large clusters. One of the finest Floribundas with this very striking dazzling colour. **1867**, p. 234.

'Pink Parfait'
Large *fl.* sometimes described as Grandiflora. Deep pink with lighter pink colouring on inside petals, up to 4 in. across with high centre. Vigorous and upright grower and free blooming. Probably one of the finest pink roses of this type yet raised and very valuable for bedding owing to compact growth. **1868**, p. 234.

✿**'Queen Elizabeth'**
Grandiflora. *Fl.* large up to 4 in. across like those of the Hybrid Teas. Bud long pointed. *Fl.* deep salmon-pink, fragrant, borne in small clusters with long stems. Very vigorous and tall grower. One of the finest roses raised of this type and unique for its very vigorous growth. **1869**, p. 234.

'Sarabande'
Semi-double, bright orange-red with cluster of yellow stamens in centre, borne in large clusters. Glossy foliage, rather compact habit and free blooming. Very valuable bedding rose. **1870**, p. 234.

4. Hybrid Teas ✳ Summer–Mid Autumn   Sh.

'Blue Moon'
Horticultural synonym but used both in Britain and America of 'Mainzer Fastnacht', the name under which it will be found in German list. Probably the best of the blue-lilac roses, there is as yet no true blue rose. Bud long pointed, *fl.* large. Vigorous and free blooming rose. **1871**, p. 234.

'Charlotte Armstrong'
Long pointed blood-red buds with large *fl.* Very popular in America where it has won many medals, less well known in Great Britain but sometimes seen in exhibitions. **1872**, p. 234.

'Christian Dior'
Large *fl.*, slightly fragrant, deep crimson flushed scarlet. Bud pointed, ovoid. A good strong grower which has received awards in several countries. **1873**, p. 235.

'Eden Rose'
Very large *fl.*, deep cerise-pink lighter on inside of petals, fragrant. Valuable exhibition rose. **1874**, p. 235.

'Ena Harkness'
Deep crimson, strongly scented. One of the old favourites although tends to hang *fl.* owing to weak stem but still worth planting for its strong scent. **1875**, p. 235.

✿**'Fragrant Cloud'**
One of the great roses of modern times. Notable for its very strong scent. Geranium-red opening coral-red, large well-formed *fl.*, very free blooming. Known in Germany as 'Duft Wolke' of which the 'Fragrant Cloud' name used in England and N. America is horticultural synonym. **1876**, p. 235.

'Gail Borden'
Very large good rose, pink flushed cream on outside of petals giving appearance almost bicolor, fragrant. One of the best roses also for exhibition. **1877**, p. 235.

'Grand'mère Jenny'
Large, apricot-yellow suffused pink especially at edges, fragrant and very free blooming like a slightly smaller *fl.* of 'Peace' but slightly deeper in colour. **1878**, p. 235.

'Monique'
Large bell-shaped *fl.* salmon-pink lighter on inside of petals, very free flowering and vigorous upright grower, fragrant. **1879**, p. 235.

✡**'Peace'**
One of the most famous and vigorous of the roses. *Fl.* very large up to 6 in. across, fully double, pale yellow with pink edging or flushed pink, rather variable in colour, slightly fragrant, very vigorous tall bushy grower. **1880**, p. 235.

'Perfecta'
The correct name is 'Kordes Perfecta' but this rose is usually known as 'Perfecta'. Large *fl.* deep pink with pale creamy outer sides to petals thus giving effect of bicolor, petals rolled back near tips, fragrant. Very fine exhibition *fl.* although not always very vigorous grower. **1881**, p. 236.

'Prima Ballerina'
Deep pink lighter inside of petals, fragrant, *fl.* of medium size but free blooming. **1882**, p. 236.

'Rose Gaujard'
Large *fl.* cherry-red but on outside of petals paler pink flushed silvery-white, fragrant, strong grower and free blooming rose. Very distinctive rose of striking colour. **1883**, p. 236.

'Royal Highness'
Large, light pink, fragrant. Beautifully formed *fl.* but a rose more popular in the USA than in England. **1884**, p. 236.

✿**'Super Star'**
Known in USA as 'Tropicana', a commercial synonym. One of the great roses of the century. Deep coral-orange, large *fl.* well formed, fragrant. Vigorous grower and free blooming. A most striking colour which combines well with an underplanting of silver foliage, but not good mixer in all rose beds and usually best seen on its own or planted with a white rose. **1885**, p. 236.

'Tropicana' see **'Super Star'**

'Tzigane'
Conspicuous bicolor, *fl.* medium size, strong orange-red with creamy-yellow on outside petals. Strong upright grower and free blooming. **1886**, p. 236.

'Virgo'
One of the best whites. *Fl.* with tall centre and long bud, snowy-white with slight creaminess on outside of petals. Not such a vigorous grower as some, *fl.* tending to damage in bad weather, this is a characteristic of all the larger flowered white Hybrid Tea roses. **1887**, p. 236.

'Wendy Cussons'
Deep cerise-red, large *fl.* with long pointed bud. Distinguished for its very fragrant scent, free blooming. **1888**, p. 236.

5. Climbing Roses ✳ Summer

'Albertine' Wichuraiana Rambler ✳ Early Summer
Very vigorous making enormous long arching branches, very thorny. Free flowering, pale blush-pink with deeper salmon-pink in centre and with deeper salmon-pink buds. Does best against a wall where it will be covered in *fl.* Should be pruned in winter by cutting out old flowering shoots or may be pruned after flowering. Slightly fragrant. **1987**, p. 249.

'Danse du Feu' ✳ Early Summer
Climber or Pillar Rose usually not over 10 ft. *Fl.* in clusters, bright scarlet-red, double or semi-double, recurrent flowering, main *fl.* 6. One of the strongest colours among Climbing roses. A comparatively modern raised hybrid. **1988**, p. 249.

'Easlea's Golden Rambler' ✳ Early Summer
Vigorous climber. *Fl.* rich buff-yellow paler towards tips of petals sometimes marked crimson, in clusters on long stems, up to 4 in. across, double, fragrant. Foliage rich olive-green and abundant. Flowering 6, not recurrent. **1989**, p. 249.

filipes 'Kiftsgate' see under **R. 'Wedding Day'**

longicuspis see under **R. 'Wedding Day'**

'Mermaid' ✳ Summer
A hybrid *R. bracteata* rose. Vigorous climber, semi-evergreen. *Fl.* large single up to 5 in. across, pale sulphur-yellow with large boss of amber-gold stamens. Foliage dark green, glossy and distinctive. Flowering 6–7 but slightly recurrent with usually good autumn bloom. Best planted against a wall but may be tender in cold areas losing occasional branches. Very beautiful and unusual rose but requires large space. **1990**, p. 249.

'New Dawn' ✳ Early Summer
Vigorous climber. *Fl.* silvery-pink, lighter towards edges, double, in large clusters. Foliage dark glossy green. Main flowering 6 but recurrent. One of the best and most vigorous climbers, growing over large pergola or up into old tree. **1991**, p. 249.

'Wedding Day' ✳ Early Summer
A hybrid from *R. sino-wilsonii*. Very vigorous Rambler, will cover old shed or tree very rapidly with long shoots up to 15 ft in a year. *Fl.* opening creamy-yellow becoming white, single with golden stamen boss in centre, up to 1½ in. across borne in large clusters becoming slightly pinkish when fading, fragrant. Foliage good glossy green. **1992**, p. 249. Others of this type and preferred by some gardeners are *filipes* 'Kiftsgate' and *longicuspis*.

ROSCOEA (ZINGIBERACEAE)

cautleoides ✳ Summer   RP.
Up to 1 ft. *Fl.* creamy or pale lemon-yellow, slightly deeper at centre, irregularly formed with large basal two-lobed lip up to 3 in. high and 2 in. across. Several *fl.* to a stem which is sheathed like

fl. of an iris. *L.* lanceolate, bright green up to 5 in. long. Forms a large clump in sunny well-drained position but unsuitable for very cold areas. China. **183**, p. 23.

humeana ❋ Late Spring–Early Summer RP.
Fl. violet-purple with deeply cleft bilobed lip, two to four on stem. *L.* ovate-lanceolate, enlarging after *fl.* 8 in.–1 ft. Well-drained sunny position. Valuable for its unusual colouring. W. China. **184**, p. 23.

ROSE see **Rosa**, **1838-1888**, pp. 230–236; **1987-1992**, p. 249.

ROSE ACACIA see **Robinia hispida**, **1836**, p. 230.

ROSE BAY see **Nerium oleander**, **1710**, p. 214.

ROSE CAMPION see **Lychnis coronaria**, **1250**, p. 157.

ROSE, CHRISTMAS see **Helleborus niger**, **1164**, **1165**, p. 146.

ROSE ELDER see **Viburnum opulus**, **1945**, **1946**, p. 244.

ROSE, GUELDER see **Viburnum opulus**, **1945**, **1946**, p. 244.

ROSE OF SHARON see **Hypericum calycinum**, **1655**, p. 207.

ROSE, LENTEN see **Helleborus orientalis**, **1166**, p. 146.

ROSE MOSS see **Portulaca grandiflora**, **363**, p. 46.

ROSE, ROCK see **Cistus**, **1513-1516**, p. 190.

ROUGH-BARKED MEXICAN PINE see **Pinus montezumae**, **2032**, p. 254.

ROWAN see **Sorbus aucuparia**, **1905**, p. 239.

RUBUS (ROSACEAE) Bramble

deliciosus ❋ Late Spring–Early Summer Sh.
Deciduous shrub up to 10 ft but usually less with long arching branches without thorns. *Fl.* white up to 2½ in. across with boss of golden stamens in centre, rather like a white Dog rose, borne on short branches previous years growth. Fruit small up to ½ in. across without flavour. *L.* like those of a Blackcurrant, three- to five-lobed. Valuable shrub for open position. N. America, Rocky Mts.

'Tridel' ❋ Late Spring–Early Summer Sh.
More often grown than *R. deliciosus*. A hybrid of *R. deliciosus* and *R. trilobus*. *Fl.* rather larger up to 3 in. across and freely borne, white with golden stamened centre. Raised by Captain Collingwood Ingram of Kent. **1889**, p. 237.

RUDBECKIA (COMPOSITAE) Cone Flower

fulgida, syn. **R. deamii** ❋ Midsummer–Early Autumn P.
Fl. deep yellow with dark centre. *L.* narrow, coarsely toothed. 2½–3 ft. Similar to the better known *R. speciosa* but more erect and makes a bushy plant. Any ordinary garden soil, preferably heavy. Propagate by division in autumn or spring, or cuttings taken in the spring. S.E. USA. **1352**, p. 169.

hirta Black-eyed Susan ❋ Late Summer HA./HB.
Fl. golden-yellow with dark brown centre. *L.*

oblong or lance-shaped, up to 5 in. long. 2–3 ft. Dwarf strains from 1–1½ ft are also available in various shades of yellow and brown. Biennial, often grown as an annual. Sow in 2–3 under glass and plant out in 5, or sow in the open during 6–7 to *fl.* the following year. Ordinary garden soil and a sunny position. N. America.
'Gloriosa', the tetraploid form has large single *fl.* in shades of bright yellow, mahogany and striking bi-colours, 2½ ft, **368**, p. 46.
'Gloriosa Double', has bright golden-yellow, double *fl.*, with dark centres, 2½ ft.

laciniata ❋ Late Summer P.
Fl. golden-yellow, greenish disc. *L.* dark green, deeply cut. 2½–7 ft. Ordinary soil, preferably moist. Propagate by division in autumn or spring. Canada. Good varieties include:
'Golden Glow', double, yellow, 6 ft;
'Goldquelle', double, chrome-yellow, 2½ ft, **1353**, p. 170.

purpurea, syn. **Echinacea purpurea** ❋ Late Summer P.
Fl. purplish-crimson up to 4 in. across. *L.* lance-shaped, roughish, slightly toothed, 2–2½ ft. Plant 11–3 in a sunny position and well-drained, fertile soil. Propagate by division in autumn or spring. E. and N. America. These are now frequently included under Echinacea.
'Robert Bloom', carmine-purple, 3 ft, **1354**, p. 170;
'The King', glowing rosy-red, 3½–4 ft, **1355**, p. 170.

sullivantii ❋ Summer–Autumn P.
Fl. large deep yellow with black centre. *L.* glossy dark green, narrow. 2½ ft. Propagate by division. N. America. Sometimes included under *R. fulgida*.
'Goldsturm', deep yellow, large *fl.* and more vigorous growth than the type, 3 ft, **1356**, p. 170.

RUE see **Ruta graveolens**, **1891**, p. 237.

RUE, GOATS see **Galega**, **1140**, **1141**, p. 143.

RUE, MEADOW see **Thalictrum**, **1395-1397**, p. 175.

RUGBY FOOTBALL PLANT see **Peperomia argyreia**, **618**, p. 78.

RUSCUS (LILIACEAE)

aculeatus Butcher's Broom ❋ Spring Sh.
Sub-shrubby plants up to 3 ft, evergreen. 'Foliage' consists of cladodes which are leaf-like dark green glossy, leathery but made from modified branches while actual *l.* are small and scale-like. *Fl.* usually unisexual borne on separate bushes, inconspicuous. There is a rarer bi-sexual form. Fruits on female bushes only which need male bush for pollination, bright scarlet berries, long lasting. Valuable for planting in shady places, best divided in spring. Some people eat the young shoots. They arise from the base in spring, like asparagus, to which it is closely related. **1890**, p. 237.

RUSH, FLOWERING see **Butomus umbellatus**, **1007**, p. 126.

RUSH, ZEBRA see **Scirpus tabernaemontanus** 'Zebrinus', **1367**, p. 171.

RUSSIAN ALMOND, DWARF see **Prunus tenella**, **1766**, p. 221.

RUSSIAN COMFREY see **Symphytum peregrinum**

RUTA (RUTACEAE)

graveolens Rue, or Herb of Grace ❋ Summer Sh.
Evergreen sub-shrub aromatic and acrid up to 3 ft. *Fl.* rather dull yellow in small terminal clusters up to 2 in. long. *L.* pinnately divided very glaucous plant is usually grown for its foliage and is best in sunny positions.
Best form is:
'Jackman's Blue', where foliage is very glaucous blue. Best pruned back in early spring to ensure bushiness. Makes good dwarf hedge between parts of the garden, **1891**, p. 237.

S

SAGE see **Salvia**, **370**, **371**, p. 47; **1358-1363**, pp. 170, 171; **1896**, **1897**, pp. 237, 238.

SAGE, BOG see **Salvia uliginosa**, **1363**, p. 171.

SAGE, COMMON see **Salvia officinalis**, **1897**, p. 238.

SAGE, JERUSALEM see **Phlomis fruticosa**, **1731**, p. 217.

SAGE, PINEAPPLE SCENTED see **Salvia rutilans** under **Salvia grahamii**

SAGE, SCARLET see **Salvia splendens**, **371**, p. 47.

SAGITTARIA (ALISMATACEAE) Arrow-head

japonica see **S. sagittifolia**

sagittifolia, syn. **S. japonica** ❋ Summer Aq.
Fl. white, with reddish-purple basal markings, 1–1½ ft. *L.* arrow-shaped, 2–8 in. long on erect stems above the water. Plant in spring in pools or ditches in water about 6 in. deep. Propagate by division of the tubers in spring. Europe, including Britain.
'Flore Pleno', an excellent double-flowered form, should be planted no deeper than 4 in., **1357**, p. 170.

Abbreviations and Symbols used in the text.
The following abbreviations may sometimes be used in conjunction as HA. indicating Hardy annual or GBb indicating Greenhouse bulb.

A. = Annual	P. = Perennial
Aq. = Aquatic	R. = Rock or
B. = Biennial	Alpine plant
Bb = Bulb	Sh. = Shrub
C. = Corm	Sp., sp. = Species
Cl. = Climber	Syn. = Synonym
Co. = Conifer	T. = Tree
Fl., *fl.* = Flower(s)	Tu. = Tuber
G. = Greenhouse or	var. = variety
house plant	× = Hybrid or
H. = Hardy	hybrid parents
HH. = Half-hardy	❋ = Flowering time
L., *l.* = Leaf, leaves	➥ = Foliage plant
Mt(s) = Mount,	
mountain(s)	

The following have been used also in the descriptions of Alpines, Bulbs, Trees and Shrubs.

* = slightly tender
† = lime hater
✿ = highly recommended

The illustration numbers are in **bold type** and the page numbers in light type preceded by p.

ST BERNARD'S LILY see **Anthericum liliago, 971**, p. 122.

ST JOHN'S WORT see **Hypericum, 1655-1658**, pp. 207, 208.

ST PATRICK'S CABBAGE see **Saxifraga umbrosa, 200**, p. 25.

SAINTPAULIA (GESNERIACEAE) African Violet

ionantha All the year round — GP.
Plant to 4 in. *Fl.* violet, white or pink, with yellow eye, single or double. *L.* round, stalked, usually dark green, but light green in some cultivars. Warm, shady, moist conditions needed and a light soil mixture, such as three parts peat: one part loam: one part sharp sand. Plants do best in plastic pots. Minimum temp. 60°F. Water always at same temp. about 60°F. recommended. Propagate by seed or by leaf-stem, cuttings. Avoid getting water on *l.* In the home avoid sudden temp. changes. E. Africa. **637-640**, p. 80.

SALIX (SALICACEAE) Willow

All willows are subject to scab or canker which can be controlled by spraying with copper fungicides in early spring.

alba White Willow — T.
Large tree up to 80 ft with branches pendulous at ends, young shoots with silky down appearing grey. *L.* narrow up to 3½ in. long by ½ in. wide, silky-white beneath, unisexual with catkins borne on separate trees up to 2 in. long, late 4-5. Wide-spread throughout Europe, N. Asia, one of the most beautiful of native trees.
Among forms most widely grown are:
'Aurea', with golden branches upright habit and pale yellow *l.*;
'Chermesina', syn. 'Britzensis', young shoots brilliant orange-scarlet;
'Tristis', syn. *S. chrysocoma*, 'Vitellina Pendula' or *S. babylonica* 'Ramulis Aureis', Weeping Willow, large weeping tree usually seen by waterside but growing well in drier situations, up to 60 ft, wide-spreading, lovely in early spring 2-3 with yellow twiglets and yellowish-green *l.* of fresh growth. This has largely replaced the Weeping Willow, *S. babylonica*, for gardens, which has slender pendulous branches, **1892**, p. 237.
'Vitellina', Golden Willow, young shoots deep yellow but less rapid growth.
'Vitellina Pendula' see 'Tristis'.

babylonica 'Ramulis Aureis' see **S. alba** 'Tristis'.

chrysocoma see **S. alba** 'Tristis'.

caprea Goat Willow, Sallow — Sh.
Shrub or small tree usually bushy. *L.* up to 4 in. long, oval or oblong, soft grey below. Male catkins up to 1½ in. long, female up to 2 in., more conspicuous and widely cut in the spring at Easter for 'Palm'. One of Britain's most beautiful native trees. All willows may be pruned hard in order to encourage young growth. Usually best in moist situations. N. Europe including Britain, N.E. Asia. **1893**, p. 237.

daphnoides ❋ Early Spring — T.
Tall deciduous shrub or small tree, young branches covered with distinctive grey-violet bloom. Male catkins furry, silvery-grey maturing to yellow, up to 2 in. long by ¾ in. wide, female smaller and more slender. *L.* narrow, lanceolate, glaucous below. One of the finest of willows for effect of young branches and catkins. Also used for cutting osiers which are known as 'Violets' in the trade. N. Europe, sometimes regarded as naturalised in Gt Britain. **1894**, p. 237.

matsudana ❋ Early Spring — T.
Tall deciduous small tree, resembling *S. alba*

'Tristis', the weeping willow, young shoots yellowish as they mature. China, Korea.
'Tortuosa', branchlets and branches twisted like a corkscrew. Grown for its grotesque effect. Any straight branches should be cut out so as to retain twisted effect, **1895**, p. 237.

reticulata ❋ Early Summer — RSh.
1-3 in. Makes a dense shrubby mat distinctive for its small rounded *l.* with conspicuous net-like puckering, shiny and dark green. Catkins small up to 1 in. long, erect, reddish on first opening. Best grown over small rocks planted in cleft between, it also makes a good plant for alpine house. European Alps, but also found on Scottish mts. **185**, p. 24.

SALLOW see **Salix caprea, 1893**, p. 237.

SALPIGLOSSIS (SOLANACEAE)

sinuata ❋ Summer — HHA.
Fl. crimson, scarlet, yellow, golden, mauve, violet, with beautiful markings. *L.* elliptic-oblong, stalked. 1-3 ft. Sow in a warm greenhouse in 2-3 and plant out in late 5-6. Seed may also be sown in the open in light soil during 4-5. Chile.
'Bolero', a large flowered F^2 mixture, 2 ft;
'Splash', a new dwarfer F^1 mixture of bright colours, 1½ ft;
'Superbissima', a large-flowered, golden-veined strain, 2 ft, **369**, p. 47.

SALVIA (LABIATAE) Sage

grahamii ❋ Late Summer–Mid Autumn — *Sh.
Tender shrub up to 4 ft, often cut to ground in winter. *Fl.* scarlet-crimson in racemes up to 8 in. long, very brilliant and valuable for its late flowering characteristics. *L.* rather aromatic, oval, irregularly toothed. Mexico. **1896**, p. 237.
Close are *S. greggii* with carmine-scarlet *fl.* and *S. neurepia* with scarlet or carmine *fl.* slightly larger but both of these are slightly more tender. Also in the same group is *S. rutilans*, the Pineapple-scented Sage which is sub-shrubby and valuable for its strongly scented foliage, *fl.* bright scarlet but usually developing too late in summer to be of value but easily propagated from cuttings and overwintered. These scarlet shrubby, or sub-shrubby Salvias should be planted in as warm and sunny a position as possible preferably at the foot of a south-facing wall. They are easily propagated by cuttings taken in late summer and overwintered in a cool greenhouse and will *fl.* the next year.

greggii see under **S. grahamii**

haematodes ❋ Summer — P.
Fl. bluish-violet borne on slender branching spikes. *L.* large, about 9 in. long, heart-shaped, hairy. 3 ft. Ordinary, well-drained soil. Not a long-lived perennial, often treated as a biennial. Easily raised from seed in the open in 9. Greece. **1358**, p. 170.

horminum ❋ Summer — HA.
Fl. mauve to purple in large coloured bracts. *L.* oval, hairy, stalked. 1½ ft. Sow in the open in 4 or 9 where the plants are to *fl.* in a sunny position. There are various coloured forms with blue, purple, white or pink bracts. S. Europe.
'Bouquet mixed', contains many shades;
'Oxford Blue', has broad blue bracts;
'Pink Sundae', is a bright rosy-carmine, **370**, p. 47.

neurepia see under **S. grahamii**

officinalis Common Sage ❋ Early Summer — Sh.
Small shrub up to 2 ft wide-spreading, *l.* oblong up to 1½ in. long, wrinkled, grey, rather woolly on both sides, *fl.* purple or white, not very conspicuous. S. Europe where it is grown as herb.
More decorative than type is:
'Tricolor', *l.* grey-green veined at edge yellowish-white and pink, pinkish-purple in young foliage, also to be planted in sunny position, **1897**, p. 238.

rutilans see under **S. grahamii**

sclarea Clary ❋ Summer — HB.
Fl. bluish-white in erect spreading panicles. *L.* large, heart-shaped, sometimes woolly. 3-4 ft. Plant 11-3 in ordinary well-drained soil and sunny position. Biennial, easily raised from seed. Europe. var. *turkestanica*, white *fl.*, tinged pink, **1359**, p. 170.

splendens Scarlet Sage ❋ Summer — HHA.
Fl. brilliant scarlet. *L.* long-pointed, smooth, stalked. 1-3 ft. Sow in a warm greenhouse in 2-3, and plant out in a sunny bed in late 5-6. Brazil.
'Blaze of Fire', very early, brilliant scarlet, 1 ft;
'Harbinger', scarlet, 1½ ft, **371**, p. 47;
'Purple Blaze', reddish-purple, 1 ft;
'Salmon Pygmy', dwarf, deep salmon, 9 in.;
'Scarlet Pygmy', dwarf, early scarlet, 9 in.

× **superba**, syn. **S. virgata** 'Nemorosa' ❋ Summer — P.
Fl. violet-purple spikes. *L.* sage-green, about 3 in. long with small hairs beneath. 3 ft. Any ordinary garden soil in sun or light shade. Propagate by division in autumn or spring. Origin uncertain. **1360**, p. 170.
Good varieties include:
'Lubeca', similar *fl.*, but compact, 1½ ft, **1361**, p. 171;
'May Night' ('Mai Nacht'), of German origin, deep violet, 15-18 in., **1362**, p. 171.

uliginosa Bog Sage ❋ Late Summer–Mid Autumn P.
Fl. azure-blue, borne on 4-5 in. spikes. *L.* deeply toothed, oblong. 3-5 ft. Ordinary garden soil and a sheltered bed. In cold districts the creeping rootstock should be protected with a layer of peat, bracken or similar covering. Propagate by division in late spring. Brazil, Uruguay, **1363**, p. 171.

virgata 'Nemorosa' see × **superba**

SAMBUCUS (CAPRIFOLIACEAE) Elder

racemosa Red Elder ❋ Summer — Sh.
Deciduous shrub or small tree up to 10 ft often less, widespreading. *Fl.* white in large panicles. Berries bright scarlet, does not fruit as freely as Common Elder *S. nigra* in this country. Native of Europe, much of Asia Minor and stretches across to N. China in distribution, has been long in cultivation. Best form is probably:

Abbreviations and Symbols used in the text.
The following abbreviations may sometimes be used in conjunction as HA. indicating Hardy annual or GBb indicating Greenhouse bulb.

A. = Annual	P. = Perennial
Aq. = Aquatic	R. = Rock or
B. = Biennial	Alpine plant
Bb = Bulb	Sh. = Shrub
C. = Corm	Sp., sp. = Species
Cl. = Climber	Syn. = Synonym
Co. = Conifer	T. = Tree
Fl., *fl.* = Flower(s)	Tu. = Tuber
G. = Greenhouse or house plant	var. = variety
	× = Hybrid or
H. = Hardy	hybrid parents
HH. = Half-hardy	❋ = Flowering time
L., *l.* = Leaf, leaves	❧ = Foliage plant
Mt(s) = Mount, mountain(s)	

The following have been used also in the descriptions of Alpines, Bulbs, Trees and Shrubs.

* = slightly tender
† = lime hater
✿ = highly recommended

The illustration numbers are in **bold type** and the page numbers in light type preceded by p.

355

'Plumosa Aurea', slower growing shrub with very finely divided golden-yellow foliage through much of the year. This is one of the finest of the golden-foliaged shrubs available and should be given choice position, **1898**, p. 238.

SANGUINARIA (PAPAVERACEAE)

canadensis ❋ Mid Spring   RP.
Fl. white, single, cup-shaped, up 1½ in. across on very short stem. *L.* heart-shaped with scolloped edge, rather glaucous, below *fl.* like a fan. 2–3 in. Spreading freely in semi-shade from a thick rhizome. N. America. More often grown and much treasured by alpine gardeners is 'Plena', which has double *fl.* globular and with numerous white petals. Although quite hardy it also makes a good alpine house plant. N. America. **186**, p. 24.

SANGUISORBA (ROSACEAE)

canadensis, syn. **Poterium canadense** Burnet ❋ Summer   P.
Fl. whitish, cylindrical, up to 6 in. long. *L.* grey-green, deeply cut. 4–5 ft. Any ordinary soil which does not dry out too rapidly in summer. Propagate by division of the tough roots in spring or by seed. N. America. **1364**, p. 171.

SANSEVIERIA (LILIACEAE)

Rhizomatous plants with erect, leathery *l.*, tolerant of prolonged drought and two sp. are popular as house plants. Here they need a well-lit position and winter temp. around 50°F., but if kept very dry, will tolerate 45°F. Propagation is by *l.* cuttings of unvariegated plants, but variegated ones only by division of the rhizome. The new *l.* appears about six months before roots appear at its base. Ordinary potting compost.

grandis 🍂   GP.
L. very large, to 3 ft, suberect, flat and broad, fleshy, dark green. Not suitable as house plant. Winter temp. around 60°F. Needs moist atmosphere in summer. Africa. **641**, p. 81.

hahnii 🍂   GP.
Low growing plant to 9 in. *L.* in rosette, similar in coloration to *S. trifasciata* but shorter and triangular in shape. The 'golden' form needs a winter temp. of at least 50°F. W. Africa. **642**, p. 81.

trifasciata Mother-in-law's Tongue 🍂   GP.
L. erect, up to 12 in. (occasionally to 4 ft) banded light and dark green. Tropical W. Africa.
var. *laurentii*, the most frequently seen, with gold margins, **643**, p. 81.

SANTOLINA (COMPOSITAE) Lavender Cotton

chamaecyparissus ❋ Midsummer   Sh.
Bushy dwarf ever-grey shrub up to 2½ ft, branches covered with white felt. *Fl.* in deep yellow heads, globular up to ¾ in. across. Foliage divided, very silvery-grey. Plant in as sunny a position as possible, may be trimmed after flowering to keep compact, some growers prefer to take off *fl.* heads to keep grey effect solid. Easily propagated from cuttings in mid or late summer. S. Europe. **1899**, p. 238.
'Nana', is a valuable dwarf form.

SANVITALIA (COMPOSITAE) Creeping Zinnia

procumbens ❋ Summer   HA.
Fl. small, single, yellow with comparatively large purple-black centre. *L.* oval, dark green. 6 in. Sow in 4–5, in the open ground in light sandy soil and a sunny position. Mexico. **372**, p. 47.
'Flore Pleno', is a double form.

SAPONARIA (CARYOPHYLLACEAE)

ocymoides Rock Soapwort ❋ Summer   RP.
Forms wide-spreading rather loose mats covered

with star-like deep pink or purplish-pink *fl.* on shingle banks in the Alps, but not a very high-altitude plant. 3–6 in. Requires a sunny well-drained position and does well in sandy soil.
Finest form is:
'Rubra Compacta', with deeper pink *fl.* and more compact growth, **187**, p. 24.

SATOZAKURA see **Prunus serrulata**, **1762-1764**, p. 221.

SATIN FLOWER see **Sisyrinchium striatum**, **1379**, p. 173.

SATUREIA (LABIATAE)

montana Winter Savory ❋ Summer   P.
Fl. pale lilac, in whorls. *L.* narrow, oblong, 1 in., partially evergreen, strongly aromatic. 1–1½ ft. Useful kitchen herb easily grown in ordinary soil. Propagate by division in spring. S. Europe.
'Coerulea', a deeper shade of lilac, **1365**, p. 171.

SAVIN, KNAP HILL see **Juniperus** × **media** 'Pfitzeriana', **2019**, p. 253.

SAVORY, WINTER see **Satureia montana**, **1365**, p. 171.

SAW-WORT see **Serratula**, **1378**, p. 173.

SAXIFRAGA (SAXIFRAGACEAE) Saxifrage

A very large and variable group very important for the rock garden. Mostly dwarf with silvery rosettes or green tussocks. They include a very large range of colours and a number of hybrids as well as of sp. Mostly sun lovers and require good drainage. Propagate from division or by cuttings in late summer. Apart from the sp. they are best grouped in four separate groups: A. The Silver Saxifrages, sometimes called Encrusted Saxifrages, which have silvery-white thick rosettes and *fl.* in small or large plumes such as *S. aizoon*; B. The Cushion Saxifrages or Kabschias, silvery rosettes with *fl.* on short stems, usually single but sometimes in small clusters, useful for crevices in rock garden or in a pavement but require some shelter from hot sun in summer and good moisture throughout season. Also grown as scree or alpine house plants, flowering very freely; C. The Englerias or Bell Saxifrages such as *S. grisebachii* with silvery rosettes and *fl.* in small clusters on short stems distinguished by the strong coloured purple calyx; D. The Mossy Saxifrages, these are probably the easiest to grow and spread abundantly in the rock garden.

aizoides ❋ Summer   RP.
Common native of sub-alpine regions and also of Britain in mountain regions. *Fl.* bright yellow, star-like covering a large mat of slightly succulent green *l.* Grows usually in damp places or at the edge of small streams, unsuitable for dry areas but one of the most conspicuous plants in the Alps. 2–3 in.

aizoon ❋ Early Summer   RP.
One of the silver or encrusted saxifrages. Large clumps of silvery rosettes. *Fl.* in short plumes up to 1 ft, starry, creamy-white with crimson stamens. Some dwarf forms such as *baldensis* grow only 3–4 in., also pink and pale yellow forms. **188**, p. 24.

× **apiculata** ❋ Spring   RP.
One of the Cushion or Kabschia saxifrages. *Fl.* primrose-yellow in small clusters 2–4 in. *L.* in green cushion. One of the easier hybrids of this section. **189**, p. 24.

baldensis see **S. aizoon**

burseriana ❋ Late Winter–Mid Spring   RP.
Kabschia saxifrage. This is a large group with silvery cushion rosettes and *fl.* singly on short stems

2–3 in. Excellent in alpine house covering large pans with *fl.*
Among finest forms are:
'Gloria', *fl.* white, large on reddish stems, **190**, p. 24;
'Sulphurea', *fl.* lemon-yellow, abundant on pinkish stems 2–3 in., **191**, p. 24;
'Valerie Finnis', is very fine modern hybrid with large clear yellow *fl.*

ferdinandi-coburgii ❋ Spring   RP.
Kabschia. *Fl.* bright yellow with red buds, dwarf 2–3 in., silvery-grey rosettes. **192**, p. 24.

fortunei ❋ Autumn   RP.
Very distinctive sp. for late autumn flowering. Forms large deciduous clumps. *Fl.* on 1–1½ ft stems, branching, numerous, white, star-like, sometimes drooping, rather untidy, stems crimson. *L.* large, glossy, roundish with slight toothing, brownish-red beneath. Suitable for cool place preferably in semi-shade or peat wall garden. Unsuitable for hot, dry or very cold areas. China, Japan. **193**, p. 25.
'Wada's Variety', finest form which has large *l.* deep crimson below.

grisebachii ❋ Spring   RP.
Englerias or Bell section. Rosettes silvery-grey up to 3 in. across. *L.* encrusted with white. *Fl.* stems arching up to 9 in. covered with deep red glandular hairs. *Fl.* small pinkish. Distinctive feature large purplish-crimson calyx often tipped with lighter colour. Usually grown as alpine house plant but possible outside under scree condition or in cleft of rock. Very distinctive plant. Greece, Macedonia, Albania in mts. **194**, p. 25.
'Wisley Variety', finest form.

× **jenkinsae** ❋ Spring   RP.
A hybrid Kabschia with silvery rosettes. *Fl.* blush pink, pale with slightly deeper centre sometimes almost white, 1–3 in., abundant covering whole tussock. Best grown in alpine house but may be grown outside. Close also is *S.* × *irvingii* with slightly smaller *fl.* but probably of the same parentage. **195**, p. 25.

longifolia ❋ Early Summer   RP.
Largest of the encrusted saxifrages of section *aizoon*. Rosettes large, flat up to 6 in. across, numerous strap-shaped, greyish-silvery *l.* growing over one or two years. *Fl.* in large, very handsome plumes up to 18 in. long with great abundance of starry-white *fl.* Monocarpic, dying after flowering, but sometimes

making small offsets. May also be grown from seed. Pyrenees. **196**, p. 25.

    'Tumbling Waters', one of the finest forms.

oppositifolia ❋ Early Summer   RP.
Creeping or mat-forming with small rosettes of rather scale-like *l*. *Fl*. variable from white to deep purplish-crimson, cup-shaped, ¼ in. across, but very numerous, 1–2 in. Usually grows in damp N. facing cleft of rocks or scree. Alpine house in scree mixture or cool cleft between rocks of rock garden or moist scree. Needs to be dry in winter but with plenty of moisture in growing period. European Alps, found in Britain on a few mts.

    'Splendens', has bright purplish-crimson *fl*. slightly larger than type, **197**, p. 25.

'Peter Pan' ❋ Spring   RP.
Hybrid mossy saxifrage forming large mats of green foliage, *fl*. deep pink with white centre, erect, ¼ in. across but very numerous, 2–4 in. This group does well in semi-shade and in cool moist position but is too invasive for small rock garden. **198**, p. 25.
Other good forms include:
    'Elf', pink, dwarf;
    'Pixie', deep red;
    'Red Admiral', bright red;
    'Sanguinea Superba', scarlet;
    'Sprite', crimson.

peltata see **Peltiphyllum peltatum**

'Riverslea' ❋ Spring   RP.
Kabschia with silvery-grey rosettes. *Fl*. purplish-rose with deeper crimson centre, 1–2 in. Alpine house or scree. **199**, p. 25.

umbrosa London Pride, St Patrick's Cabbage ❋ Early Summer   RP.
Fl. blush pink with deeper red spotting, small, star-like, in sprays, 6–12 in. *L*. green, spathulate, slightly leathery in rosettes forming spreading mats. Semi-shade or sun, very adaptable but too invasive for choice places in the rock garden.
    'Primuloides', dwarf form up to 8 in., *fl*. pinker than type, **200**, p. 25.

SCABIOSA (DIPSACEAE) Scabious

atropurpurea Sweet Scabious, Pincushion Flower ❋ Summer   HA.
Fl. dark purple, blue, deep crimson, pink or white, fragrant. *L*. lance-shaped, coarsely toothed. 2½–3 ft, Tom Thumb varieties 9–12 in. Any ordinary soil and a sunny position. Sow under glass in 3 or in the open in 4 for late summer flowering. There is a wide choice of colour shades in both tall and dwarf varieties. S.W. Europe. **373**, p. 47.
    'Blue Moon', large heads of frilled, pale blue petals, 3 ft;
    'Rose Cockade', large, double, rose pink, 3 ft.

caucasica ❋ Summer–Mid Autumn   P.
Fl. light lavender-blue. *L*. lanceolate, glaucous. 1½–2 ft. Plant 3–4 in well-drained limy soil and a sunny position. Propagate by division in spring or by cuttings taken with a heel. Caucasus.
Good named hybrids include:
    'Bressingham White', a good white;
    'Clive Greaves', large mauve, **1366**, p. 171;
    'Loddon Anna', misty blue.

SCABIOUS see **Scabiosa**, **373**, p. 47; **1366**, p. 171.

SCARBOROUGH LILY see **Vallota speciosa**, **941**, p. 118.

SCARLET CANADIAN MAPLE see **Acer rubrum**, **1440**, p. 180.

SCARLET OAK see **Quercus coccinea**, **1772**, p. 222.

SCARLET PLUME see **Euphorbia fulgens**, **526**, p. 66.

SCARLET SAGE see **Salvia splendens**, **371**, p. 47.

SCARLET TRUMPET HONEYSUCKLE see **Lonicera × brownii**, **1981**, p. 248.

SCHIZOCODON (DIAPENSIACEAE)

soldanelloides ❋ Spring   †RP.
Fl. pale pink or rose-pink, bell-shaped, with deeply fringed edge, in small clusters, 6–8 in. *L*. evergreen, shiny, ovate, toothed at margin. Grows best in cool moist position in semi-shade, peaty soil, probably a lime hater. Some authorities refer this plant to *Shortia*.
    'Magnus', is slightly larger form with rose-pink *fl*., previously known as 'Macrophyllus', **201**, p. 26.

SCHIZOSTYLIS (IRIDACEAE)

coccinea Kaffir Lily ❋ Autumn   Tu.
Fl. star-like up to 2 in. across, scarlet, crimson or pink, numerous on stem up to 2½ ft. *L*. like a narrow iris leaf. Plant in a sunny warm position but they are unsuitable for very dry positions and seem to *fl*. best after a damp summer. Readily increased by division of clumps. They are most valuable for their late-flowering and as cut flowers. S. Africa. **876**, p. 110.
Best forms are:
    ✿'Major', large, scarlet-red;
    ✿'Mrs Hegarty', rose pink, **877**, p. 110;
    'Viscountess Byng', pale shell-pink, named after a great rock gardener, usually latest to *fl*. and so unsuitable for cold gardens.

SCHLUMBERGERA (CACTACEAE)

gaertneri Whitsun or Easter Cactus ❋ Early Summer   GP.
Fl. deep pink. Stems flat, leaf-like, spineless, branched. Fairly rich compost required. Winter temp. 45–50°F. When buds appear in 3, move to a warmer position if possible. Water sparingly 9–3, just enough to keep plant turgid; more freely 3–9. Slight shading beneficial in summer. Propagate by cuttings or by grafting on *Pereskia aculeata*. Now included by some authorities under *Rhipsalidopsis*. Brazil. **644**, p. 81.

SCIADOPITYS (TAXODIACEAE) (Formerly included in PINACEAE)

verticillata Japanese Umbrella Pine   Co.
Evergreen tree up to 120 ft in native habitat but usually much less in cultivation, growing rather slowly. Bark greyish-brown. *L*. long linear up to 5 in. in whorls of up to 30 at the ends of short branches thus giving its name of Umbrella Pine, also small triangular scale-like *l*. at base of shoots. Cones up to 4 in. long by 2 in. wide, brown when ripe, terminal at ends of short branchlets, oblong. Valuable and distinct tree for garden purposes but of little value for timber, quite distinct in the arrangement of its *l*. Seems to do best in moist situations. Japan, E. Central Honshu. **2037**, p. 255.

SCILLA (LILIACEAE)

✿bifolia ❋ Early Spring   Bb
Fl. starlike, very bright royal blue, white, pink or purplish on reddish-crimson stem 3–6 in. Useful for their early-flowering. *L*. strap-shaped, only just emerging at time of flowering. Best in sunny position in warm border but will also *fl*. in semi-shade. S. Europe, mountainous regions flowering as snow melts. **878**, p. 110.

campanulata see **Endymion hispanicus**

hispanica see **Endymion hispanicus**

non-scripta see **Endymion non-scripta**

nutans see **Endymion non-scripta**

peruviana ❋ Early Summer   Bb
Sometimes erroniously called 'Cuban Lily' but really native of Spain and Central Mediterranean. A handsome plant with large conical heads of star-shaped lilac-blue *fl*. like the upper half of a small football nestling in broad green strap-shaped *l*. Bulb large. A white form is also known. Sunny warm position. **879**, p. 110.

pratensis ❋ Early Summer   Bb
Fl. bluish-mauve, star-like in large head on stems up to 1 ft, scented. Plant in full sun. Forming large clump when established. Yugoslavia. **880**, p. 110.

✿sibirica Squill ❋ Late Winter–Mid Spring   Bb
Most valuable member of the genus and a favourite bulb for its very brilliant gentian-blue, almost prussian-blue *fl*. in early spring. Stem up to 8 in. with 3–4 drooping *fl*. several stems to a bulb. S. Russia, Caucasus. **881**, p. 111.
    Best form is 'Atrocoerulea' often listed as 'Spring Beauty' with larger *fl*. and more vigorous growth than type.

tubergeniana ❋ Early Spring   Bb
Fl. very pale blue, almost white. Very early-flowering, petals have narrow deeper greenish-blue streak down centre. Stem short when first *fl*. open but then lengthening up to 6 in., several to a bulb. Quite hardy and will *fl*. either in full sun or semi-shade, also suited for pans in alpine house, often increasing freely. N.W. Iran. **882**, p. 111.
    'Zwanenburg', has very slightly more blue in *fl*.

SCINDAPSUS (ARACEAE) Ivy Arum

aureus ☙   GP.
Climber to 15 ft. *Fl*. not seen in cultivation. Juvenile *l*. entire, oblong-oval, pointed, green, mottled with yellow. Adult *l*. large, to 18 in. long, kidney-shaped, incised. Requires similar treatment to climbing Philodendrons. Winter temp. 50°F. Propagate by stem cuttings. Solomon Islands.
    'Silver Queen', *l*. mottled white, **645**, p. 81.

SCIRPUS (CYPERACEAE)

lacustris 'Zebrina' see **S. tabernaemontanus** 'Zebrinus'

tabernaemontanus 'Zebrinus' Zebra Rush ☙   Aq.
Slender, erect stems with green and white bands. 3–5 ft. Strikingly effective when planted in clumps

in shallow water beside a pool. Propagate by division in the spring. Some botanists consider this plant should now be called *S. lacustris* 'Zebrina'. Japan. **1367**. p. 171.

SCOTCH HEATH see **Erica cinerea, 1581-1583**, p. 198.

SCOTS PINE see **Pinus sylvestris, 2035**, p. 255.

SCOTTISH FLAME FLOWER see **Tropaeolum speciosum, 1994**, p. 250.

SCROPHULARIA (SCROPHULARIACEAE)

nodosa Knotted Figwort ✳ Summer   P.
    Fl. small, brownish-red, inconspicuous. *L.* opposite, oval, toothed. 1–3 ft. Plant 11–3 in a shady moist place. Propagate by seed or cuttings. Europe, including Britain.
        'Variegata', light green foliage with yellowish markings, 2–3 ft, **1368**, p. 171.

SEA BUCKTHORN see **Hippophae rhamnoides, 1647**, p. 206.

SEASIDE GRAPE see **Coccoloba uvifera, 475**, p. 60.

SEA LAVENDER see **Limonium, 326, 327**, p. 41.

SEA RAGWORT see **Cineraria maritima, 267**, p. 34.

SEA WORMWOOD see **Artemisia maritima, 978**, p. 123.

SEAKALE see **Crambe, 1058**, p. 133.

SEDUM (CRASSULACEAE)

acre Stonecrop, Wall-pepper ✳ Summer   RP.
    Forms large mat with slightly succulent green *l. Fl.* bright yellow, star-like, up to ½ in. across, several in a cluster, numerous and often covering *l.*, 1–3 in. Easily grown in sunny position or in crevices of wall, but spreading too freely for choice position on rock garden. Europe including Britain, Asia Minor. **202**, p. 26.

aizoon ✳ Midsummer   P.
    Fl. yellow in loose heads about 3 in. across. 1 ft. *L.* oblong, shiny, coarsely toothed. Propagate by division in late summer or autumn. Japan, Siberia. **1369**, p. 172.

caeruleum ✳ Summer   HHA./HA.
    Fl. pale blue, star-like, with a white eye. *L.* glossy green, gradually turning red, alternate, fleshy. 3–4 in. Sow under glass in 3, or thinly in the open in light sandy soil and a sunny position in 4–5 where it is to *fl.* Mediterranean region. **374**, p. 47.

cauticola ✳ Early Autumn   P.
    Fl. rose-purple in lax, flat heads. 3 in., trailing. *L.* glaucous, opposite. Good plant for a dry wall or sunny crevice. Japan. **1370**, p. 172.

maximum Ice Plant ✳ Late Summer
    Fl. greenish-white. *L.* green or red. 2 ft. Propagate by division in spring. Europe.
        'Atropurpureum', purple-leaf Ice Plant, *fl.* deep pink, *l.* and stem deep red, 1–1½ ft, **1371**, p. 172.

sieboldii ✳ Late Summer ☙   GP.
    Fl. small, pink, in terminal cymes. *L.* round, blue-green in type, but golden in centre in the generally grown var. *medio-variegatum*. Often used as house plant. Stems die down in 10, after flowering is complete, and plant should then be left unwatered until 2. Rather gritty compost. Keep just frost-free in winter; high temp. should be disadvantageous.

Stem cuttings root rapidly and are usually taken in spring and 6–7 put in a 3 in. pot. Japan. **646**, p. 81.

spathulifolium ✳ Summer   RP.
    Forms a large mat of tight silvery rosettes. *Fl.* bright yellow, star-like in clusters on end of short erect reddish stems, 2–4 in. Sunny position and useful for covering rocks. W. N. America.
        'Capa Blanca', *l.* very silvery-grey with white farina, sometimes grown as alpine house plant to protect brightness of foliage but quite hardy. **203**, p. 26.

spectabile ✳ Late Summer–Mid Autumn   P.
    Fl. rosy-purple in large flat heads much loved by butterflies and bees. *L.* oval, glaucous green. 1–1½ ft. Plant 11–3. Propagate by division in spring or stem cuttings in 7. China.
    Good varieties include:
        'Atropurpureum', rich pink, 1½ ft;
        'Autumn Joy', rosy-salmon, tinged bronze, 1½–2 ft, **1372**, p. 172;
        'Meteor', carmine-red, 1½ ft, **1373**. p. 172;
        'Ruby Glow', a hybrid with *S. cauticola*, deep ruby red, 1 ft, **1374**, p. 172.

spurium ✳ Late Summer   RP.
    Fl. white or pale pink or crimson, star-like with darker centres and in large clusters on short erect stems, 3–6 in. *L.* green, rounded, slightly succulent, in loose rosettes or on short erect stems, forming mats. Sunny position but too invasive for choice spots but valuable for its late flowering. N. Persia, USSR, Caucasus.
        'Schorbusser Blut', *fl.* deep carmine-crimson, *l.* bronzy in autumn. **204**, p. 26.

SELAGINELLA (SELAGINELLACEAE)

caulescens 'Argentea', S. argentea ☙   GP.
    Plant to 12 in. high, but usually less. Stems covered by appressed, moss-like *l.* with silvery sheen. Peaty compost recommended, possibly topped with sphagnum. A shady, moist warm atmosphere essential. Plant in pans rather than pots. Winter temp. 50–55°F. Keep free from draughts. If stems are pegged down they root at every joint, so propagation is easy. China, Japan, Mexico. **647**, p. 81.

SEMPERVIVUM (CRASSULACEAE)

arachnoideum Cobweb Houseleek ✳ Summer RP.
    Makes a mat of small rosettes entwined with long silvery hairs like a cobweb. Rosettes usually ½ in. across but sometimes up to 1½ in. *Fl.* deep pink or bright crimson, star-like, ½ in. across in small clusters on short stems, 2–6 in. Does well in sunny and well-drained, rather dry position and looks well growing over rocks. Alps, Pyrenees, a common mountain plant. **205**, p. 26.

'Commander Hay' ✳ Summer   *RP.
    Forms large rosettes up to 4 in. across, deep bronzy-crimson. *Fl.* pink up to 1 in. across in large clusters on stout stems, 12–15 in. Rather tender and best grown as a pan plant for alpine house but may be planted outside in sunny position in summer. Probably largest of the houseleeks. Parentage unknown. **206**, p. 26.

montanum Mountain Houseleek ✳ Summer   RP.
    Forms dense green slightly succulent rosettes up to 1½ in. across but variable in size. *Fl.* pinkish-purple or purplish-crimson with central green disc, star-like, 8–12 in. Quite hardy and suitable for dry sunny position or as a plant for an open dry stone wall. Pyrenees, Alps where it is common. **207**, p. 26.

SENECIO (COMPOSITAE)

cineraria see **Cineraria maritima**

clivorum see **Ligularia dentata**

cruentus see **Cineraria multiflora**

doronicum ✳ Summer   P.
    Fl. bright yellow, daisy-like. *L.* oblong, variable,

2–5 in. long. 1½ ft. Ordinary soil. Propagate by division in spring. Central Europe.
        'Sunburst', deep orange-yellow, free-flowering, 15 in., **1375**, p. 172.

greyi ✳ Summer   Sh.
    Evergreen shrub up to 5 ft with thick grey *l.* margined silvery-grey, underneath white felted, young branches also white felted. *Fl.* daisy-like deep yellow with long ray-florets up to 1½ in. across, borne in racemose clusters in mid to late summer. May be pruned hard to keep compact shape otherwise tends to become straggly. Plant in sunny position. Easily propagated from cuttings. New Zealand, N. Ireland.

haworthii see **Kleinia tomentosa**

japonicum see **Ligularia japonica**

laxifolius ✳ Summer   Sh.
    Close to *S. greyi* but with *l.* slightly more undulating and less blunt at the ends. Probably the shrub in general cultivation is a hybrid between *S greyi* and *S. laxifolius*. Cultivate as for *S. greyi* but slightly tender in cold areas. **1900**, p. 238.

przewalskii, syn. **Ligularia przewalskii** ✳ Summer   P.
    Fl. orange, on tall, slender stems. *L.* large, much divided. 4–5 ft. A moist well-drained soil in sun or partial shade. Propagate by division in the spring. N. China.
        'The Rocket', fuller spikes of orange on erect, almost black stems, **1376**, p. 172.

'White Diamond' ✳ Summer ☙   P.
    Fl. bright yellow. *L.* silvery-white, much divided. 2–3 ft. Sheltered sunny bed in dryish soil. Propagate by cuttings taken in spring. Of garden origin. Mainly grown as foliage plant. **1377**, p. 173.

SEQUOIA (TAXODIACEAE)

gigantea see **Sequoiadendron giganteum**

sempervirens Redwood   Co.
    Magnificent evergreen tree up to 300 ft in native habitat of coastal forest of Oregon and N. California where it grows in rather moist positions with moist atmosphere from sea mists and fogs. Trunk reddish-brown, fibrous and spongy in bark. Branches drooping. Distinct from *Sequoiadendron* by *l.* being spirally arranged and of two kinds, those on lateral branchlets having a basal twist and being larger,

up to 1 in. long, than those on leaders and fertile shoots which are only ¼ in. long. Cones small, globose or ovoid about 1 in. across and long. As specimen tree it is valuable in gardens for its rather upright narrow habit and fresh green of the younger *l.* and also red bark. Where grown under forestry conditions in rather moist mild areas it makes magnificent grove, the finest in Britain being the Carl Akers memorial group in Wales, but Californian groups which are rigidly preserved are much larger and a visit to them is one of the greatest experiences possible for tree lovers. Some trees said to be 3000 years old. *Sequoia* is unusual among conifers in that after cutting, it will regenerate from basal shoots.

Various dwarf forms which are sports from side branches have been named including:

'Adpressa', syn. 'Albo-spica', in which the tips of shoots are creamy-white, **2038**, p. 255;

'Prostrata', growing horizontally and prostrate at first but later tending to produce erect and more vigorous upright shoots, *l.* glaucous beneath.

These however tend to become too large for smaller rock garden purposes.

wellingtonia see **Sequoiadendron giganteum**

SEQUOIADENDRON (TAXODIACEAE) Big or Mammoth Tree, Wellingtonia

giganteum, syn. **Sequoia gigantea, S. wellingtonia** Co.
Giant tree up to 320 ft in native habitat of W. slopes of Sierra Nevada in California. Probably the largest coniferous tree in the world and claimed by some to be the largest tree. Young trees have narrow conical habit. Bark deeply furrowed, bright brown. Branches drooping from the trunk. *L.* small, scale or needle-like adhering to the branch closely. Cones terminal and solitary, ovoid, up to 3 in. long by 1½ in. wide, reddish-brown. Widely planted as avenue or specimen tree. Grown best in rather moist situations where it is sheltered. **2039, 2040,** p. 255.

SERBIAN SPRUCE see **Picea omorika, 2029,** p. 254.

SERRATULA (COMPOSITAE) Saw-wort

shawii ✳ Autumn P.
Fl. bright purple, cornflower-like. *L.* deep green, finely cut 6–9 in. Ordinary soil and sunny position. Propagate by division in spring. S. Europe, N. Africa. **1378,** p. 173.

SHADBLOW see **Amelanchier canadensis, 1444, 1445,** p. 181.

SHAGGY HAWKWEED see **Hieracium villosum, 1174,** p. 147.

SHASTA DAISY see **Chrysanthemum maximum, 1049,** p. 132.

SHEEP'S FESCUE see **Festuca ovina, 1134,** p. 142.

SHELL FLOWER see **Moluccella laevis, 346,** p. 44.

SHOO FLY PLANT see **Nicandra physaloides, 350,** p. 44.

SHOOTING STAR see **Dodecatheon, 56,** p. 7; **1112,** p. 139.

SHORTIA (DIAPENSIACEAE)

soldanelloides see **Schizocodon soldanelloides**

uniflora ✳ Spring †RP.
Fl. shell-pink or white, bell-like with fringed margin

up to 1½ in. across, semi-pendulous; calyx reddish, 3–6 in. *L.* large, heart-shaped with shallowly toothed margin, green, tinged with deep crimson, which sometimes spreads all over. Likes a cool position with peaty soil which does not dry out in semi-shade. A variable plant in colour. Japan. **208,** p. 26.

SHOW PINKS see **Dianthus** under Border Pinks and Carnations, **1100-1103,** p. 138.

SHRIMP PLANT see **Beloperone guttata, 431,** p. 54.

SIBERIAN CRAB see **Malus × robusta, 1703,** p. 213.

SIBERIAN WALLFLOWER see **Cheiranthus allionii, 261,** p. 33.

SILENE (CARYOPHYLLACEAE)

oculata see **Lychnis coeli-rosa** var. *oculata*

pendula ✳ Mid Spring–Midsummer, Summer HA.
Fl. rose-pink, freely borne. *L.* oblong, densely fringed. 1 ft, the compact varieties not more than 6 in. There are single and double white forms, as well as double salmon-pink and bright carmine. Sow in the open in 3–4 in light sandy soil where they are to *fl.* Autumn sown plants will *fl.* from 4–7. Useful for edging. S. Europe. A double flowered form is illustrated. **375,** p. 47.

'Triumph Double mixed', a good colour range.

SILVER BIRCH see **Betula pendula, 1462, 1463,** p. 183.

SILVER FIR see **Abies, 2001, 2002,** p. 251.

SILYBUM (COMPOSITAE)

marianum Milk or Holy Thistle ✳ Summer HA/HB.
Fl. rosy-purple. *L.* glossy green, spotted and veined white, spiny, up to 2 ft long. 1–2 ft. Sow in the open in 4 where it is to *fl.*, in sun or light shade. S. Europe, N. Africa, Asia. **376,** p. 47.

SINARUNDINARIA (GRAMINEAE) Bamboo

Both the plants below are among the most attractive hardy bamboos and grow well in semi-shade. Propagation by division.

murieliae ❧ Sh.
Tall bamboo up to 12 ft with green stems, leaflets for the first year and erect, second year becoming leafy at top and arching slightly. *L.* bright green becoming yellowish as older, narrow up to 4½ in. long by ½ in. wide. *Fl.* not so far seen in Britain in cultivation. Many Bamboos die after flowering or are severely crippled but flowering is rare. China. **1901,** p. 238.

nitida ❧ Sh.
Close to *S. murieliae,* distinguished by purplish stems, slightly less strong growth up to 10 ft and leaflets being glaucous beneath. China.

SINNINGIA (GESNERIACEAE)

speciosa Gloxinia ✳ Summer GP.
Tuberous plants up to 9 in. high. *Fl.* large, trumpet-shaped; crimson, violet, white, often spotted with other colours. *L.* rounded, dark green velvety. A compost such as JIP suits these plants. Tubers usually started in 2 in small pots at temp. of 65°F. and potted on into 5 in. pots when large enough. Warm moist shady conditions required. After flowering the plants are dried out and the tubers are stored in dry conditions in a temp. of 50°F. Propagation by seed, which may *fl.* in eight months or by *l.* cuttings. The original Brazilian sp. has been

much improved by selection. The original wild plant has pendulous *fl.* and it was the appearance of 'Fyfiana' in 1860, a form which carried its *fl.* erect, that started the breeders, particularly in Belgium, developing the present race of which the illustrated plant is typical. **648,** p. 81.

SIPHONOSMANTHUS DELAVAYI see **Osmanthus delavayi**

SISYRINCHIUM (IRIDACEAE)

angustifolium see **S. bermudiana**

bermudiana ✳ Summer RP.
Fl. deep bluish-violet with satin-like sheen and prominent central yellow eye, about ½ in. across, in clusters, 8–10 in. *L.* narrow linear, rather like those of a small iris, forming large clumps. Hardy in sunny position in most areas, although native of Bermuda. Close also is *S. angustifolium* from N. America but naturalised in Britain and known as 'Blue-eyed Grass'. *Fl.* brighter blue. **209,** p. 27.

striatum Satin Flower ✳ Early Summer P.
Fl. creamy-white borne on a slender spike. 2 ft. *L.* iris-like, about 1 ft long. Well-drained ordinary garden soil and a sunny position. Propagate by division in the spring which should be done every three years or so. China. **1379,** p. 173.

SKIMMIA (RUTACEAE)

fortunei see **S. reevesiana**

japonica ✳ Early Summer Sh.
Evergreen shrub up to 5 ft wide-spreading. *Fl.* star-shaped, white in large clustered heads. Berries scarlet, shining in large heads throughout winter. Forms of *S. japonica* are unisexual and so it is necessary to plant in groups with a least one male plant for pollination. Valuable evergreens with very dark green narrowly obovate *l.* up to 4 in. long and 1½ in. wide and will grow well in semi-shade as well as open positions. **1902, 1903,** p. 238.
Among named forms are:
'Foremanii', female;
'Fragrans', is a free-flowering male form with *fl.* strongly scented;
'Rogersii', female.

Abbreviations and Symbols used in the text.
The following abbreviations may sometimes be used in conjunction as HA. indicating Hardy annual or GBb indicating Greenhouse bulb.

A. = Annual	P. = Perennial
Aq. = Aquatic	R. = Rock or
B. = Biennial	Alpine plant
Bb = Bulb	Sh. = Shrub
C. = Corm	Sp., sp. = Species
Cl. = Climber	Syn. = Synonym
Co. = Conifer	T. = Tree
Fl., fl. = Flower(s)	Tu. = Tuber
G. = Greenhouse or	var. = variety
house plant	× = Hybrid or
H. = Hardy	hybrid parents
HH. = Half-hardy	✳ = Flowering time
L., l. = Leaf, leaves	❧ = Foliage plant
Mt(s) = Mount,	
mountain(s)	

The following have been used also in the descriptions of Alpines, Bulbs, Trees and Shrubs.

* = slightly tender
† = lime hater
✿ = highly recommended

The illustration numbers are in **bold type** and the page numbers in light type preceded by p.

reevesiana, syn. **S. fortunei** ✳ Early Summer Sh.
Close to *S. japonica* and is valuable in that both sexes of *fl.* are borne on the same shrub. It is, however, a lime hater.

rubella ✳ Spring Sh.
Valuable for its red buds and pinkish, scented male *fl.* in large panicles in spring. As male bears no berries. Probably a hybrid between *S. reevesiana* and a form of *S. japonica* but sometimes placed as var. of *S. reevesiana*.

SLIPPERWORT see **Calceolaria, 22,** p. 3; **247,** p. 31; **438, 439,** p. 55; **1472,** p. 184.

SMILACINA (LILIACEAE)

racemosa ✳ Early Summer P.
Fl. creamy-white, fragrant, borne in feathery terminal clusters, 2–3 ft. *L.* slender, pointed up to 9 in. long, downy beneath. Plant 11–3 in a shady border and moist soil. Propagate by division in the spring. N. America. **1380,** p. 173.

SMOKE TREE see **Cotinus, 1534-1536,** p. 192.

SMOOTH ARIZONA CYPRESS see **Cupressus glabra, 2013,** p. 252.

SMOOTH-LEAVED ELM see **Ulmus carpinifolia, 1932,** p. 242.

SNAKE-BARKED MAPLE see **Acer pensylvanicum, 1437,** p. 180.

SNAKE-ROOT, BLACK see **Cimicifuga racemosa, 1051,** p. 132.

SNAKEWEED see **Polygonum bistorta, 1325,** p. 166.

SNAPDRAGON see **Antirrhinum, 236, 237,** p. 30.

SNEEZEWEED see **Helenium, 1155-1158,** p. 145.

SNEEZEWORT see **Achillea ptarmica, 951,** p. 119.

SNOW GUM, AUSTRALIAN see **Eucalyptus niphophila, 1598,** p. 200.

SNOWBALL BUSH, JAPANESE see **Viburnum tomentosum** 'Sterile'.

SNOWBALL TREE see **Viburnum opulus** 'Sterile', **1946,** p. 244.

SNOWBELL see **Styrax, 1918, 1919,** p. 240.

SNOWBELL, ALPINE see **Soldanella alpina, 210,** p. 27.

SNOWBELL, DWARF see **Soldanella pusilla, 212,** p. 27.

SNOWBERRY see **Symphoricarpus albus, 1920,** p. 240.

SNOWDROP see **Galanthus, 742-746,** pp. 93, 94.

SNOWDROP, COMMON see **Galanthus nivalis, 744, 745,** pp. 93, 94.

SNOWDROP, GIANT see **Galanthus elwesii, 742,** p. 93.

SNOWDROP TREE see **Halesia, 1628,** p. 204.

SNOWY MESPILUS see **Amelanchier, 1444, 1445,** p. 181.

SOLANUM (SOLANACEAE)

crispum Chilean Potato Tree ✳ Summer Cl.
Semi-evergreen sub-shrubby, usually grown as a wall shrub or climber up to 15 ft, slightly tender in cold districts but growing very vigorously in milder areas. *Fl.* deep purplish-blue with yellow centres up to 1 in. across in large clusters up to 4 in. across, semi-pendulous. *L.* ovate up to 4 in. long and 2 in. wide, downy on both surfaces. Fruit globose yellow up to ⅓ in. across, like a small berry. A very valuable plant for its late season of flowering especially in the milder districts but, against a south wall, will grow well in most areas only occasionally being cut hard by a bad winter. Should be pruned in spring back to base of last year's shoots. Chile. Best form is:
  autumnale, sometimes known as 'Glasnevin var.' which has larger *fl.* and a slightly extended flowering season, **1993,** p. 250.

SOLDANELLA (PRIMULACEAE)

alpina Alpine Snowbell ✳ Spring RP.
Fl. pale or deep mauve or lavender, pendulous or nodding, small, open, bell-shaped with deeply fringed edge, ½ in. long, 1–3 per stem, 2–3 in. *L.* small, kidney-shaped. Best grown in alpine house or cool position, requires some shelter from winter wet. Alps, Pyrenees, flowering by melting snow. **210,** p. 27.

montana ✳ Spring RP.
Fl. pale or deep mauve or bluish-lavender, variable, open funnel-shaped, 3–6 in., larger than preceding and on stouter stem, deeply fringed at margin, 1–3 to a stem, each ¾ in. across. *L.* rounded, heart-shaped at base on short stems and forming quite large clumps. Cool moist situation in semi-shade, but usually the most vigorous sp. in cultivation. Alps, Pyrenees, abundant. **211,** p. 27.

pusilla Dwarf Snowbell ✳ Late Spring–Early Summer RP.
Fl. narrow bell-shaped with deeply fringed margin, pendulous, singly on short crimson stems, pale violet or white, 2–3 in. A beautiful and very delicate *fl. L.* kidney-shaped or rounded. Requires moist position but very good drainage and usually grown in alpine house. Requires protection from winter wet. Alps by melting snow in shale or scree or very short grass.

villosa ✳ Late Spring–Early Summer RP.
Fl. purplish-mauve, 6–9 in. *L.* round and covered with short hairs. Often *fl.* well in open.

SOLIDAGO (COMPOSITAE) Golden Rod

canadensis ✳ Summer–Early Autumn P.
Fl. yellow in pyramidal panicles. 3–6 ft. *L.* narrow, 3–6 in. long with a rough upper surface. Ordinary soil and a sunny position. Propagate by division or by cuttings in the spring. E. N. America.
Hybrids, sometimes listed as *S.* × *hybrida*:
  'Crown of Rays', mustard-yellow, in flattish heads, 2 ft, **1381,** p. 173.
  'Goldenmosa', golden-yellow in fluffy mimosalike heads, 2½–3 ft, **1382,** p. 173;
  'Golden Thumb', yellow, fluffy heads, 1 ft, **1383,** p. 173;
  'Golden Wings', *fl.* bright gold in 9–10, 5–6 ft;
  'Lemore', soft primrose in branching heads, 2½ ft, **1384,** p. 173.

× **hybrida** see under **S. canadensis**

× SOLIDASTER (COMPOSITAE)

luteus ✳ Autumn P.
Fl. bright yellow, small but numerous. 2½ ft. *L.* narrow, aster-like. A hybrid plant resulting from a cross between a dwarf aster and a solidago. Ordinary soil in sun or light shade. Propagate by division in the spring. **1385,** p. 174.

SOLOMON'S SEAL see **Polygonatum, 1323,** p. 166.

SONERILA (MELASTOMATACEAE)

margaritacea ✳ Autumn ❧ GP.
8–12 in. *L.* pointed oval, 3–4 in. long, 2–2½ in. wide, dark shining green, but densely covered with pearly-white spots between veins. *Fl.* rose-pink, transient. Warm, moist atmosphere; minimum temp. 60°F. or *l.* will drop. Shade needed; water freely. Propagate by cuttings in spring, in bottom heat. **649,** p. 82.

SOPHORA (LEGUMINOSAE)

tetraptera Kowhai Tree ✳ Early Summer *T.
Small tree up to 40 ft in wild state but much less usually in cultivation. Densely branched. Usually deciduous or semi-deciduous in cultivation but evergreen where grown in greenhouse. Only suitable for milder areas or as a wall shrub but not worth attempting in colder positions. *Fl.* deep yellow in pendulous clusters, tubular up to 2 in. long with reflexed lobes. *L.* frond-like much divided with small leaflets up to 4 in. long. Valuable tree for its bright yellow *fl.* and fern-like foliage where it can be grown. **1904,** p. 238.
  var. *microphylla,* syn. *Edwardsia microphylla,* leaflets smaller and *fl.* up to 1½ in. long, probably slightly hardier, New Zealand, also recorded from Chile.

SORBUS (ROSACEAE)

Genus divided into two groups, the Aria or Whitebeams with large undivided oval or obovate *l.* and white downy foliage in spring often maintained throughout summer and Aucuparia, Mountain Ashes or Rowan, with pinnate divided *l.* and leaflets in opposite rows. With the exception of *S. aria* all those mentioned below belong to this latter group.

aria Whitebeam ✳ Late Spring T.
Deciduous tree up to 40 ft. *Fl.* white in clusters to 4 in. across. *L.* large oval or obovate up to 4½ in. long, white with down beneath, conspicuous and

---

Abbreviations and Symbols used in the text.
The following abbreviations may sometimes be used in conjunction as HA. indicating Hardy annual or GBb indicating Greenhouse bulb.

A. = Annual	P. = Perennial
Aq. = Aquatic	R. = Rock or
B. = Biennial	Alpine plant
Bb = Bulb	Sh. = Shrub
C. = Corm	Sp., sp. = Species
Cl. = Climber	Syn. = Synonym
Co. = Conifer	T. = Tree
Fl., fl. = Flower(s)	Tu. = Tuber
G. = Greenhouse or	var. = variety
house plant	× = Hybrid or
H. = Hardy	hybrid parents
HH. = Half-hardy	✳ = Flowering time
L., l. = Leaf, leaves	❧ = Foliage plant
Mt(s) = Mount,	
mountain(s)	

The following have been used also in the descriptions of Alpines, Bulbs, Trees and Shrubs.

  * = slightly tender
  † = lime hater
  ✿ = highly recommended

The illustration numbers are in **bold type** and the page numbers in light type preceded by p.

valuable for this character. Fruit scarlet-red in autumn. N. Europe including Britain. Valuable native but usually a large tree for gardens. Finest garden variety is:

'Majestica', with *l.* up to 7 in. long and fruits larger than type.

aucuparia Mountain Ash or Rowan ❀ Late Spring T.
Tree up to 50 ft but usually less, a well known native. Deciduous. *Fl.* white in clusters up to 5 in. across. Fruit globular $\frac{1}{3}$ in. across, bright red, pendulous or horizontal in large clusters, shining. *L.* pinnate with rather large leaflets up to 15 lanceolate oblong and sharply toothed up to 2$\frac{1}{2}$ in. long. Valuable tree for wild garden. Usually has good autumn colouring of yellow or scarlet especially in Scotland. **1905**, p. 239.

cashmeriana ❀ Late Spring T.
Small tree usually not more than 15 ft. Leaflets small, fern-like *l.* Fruit large white and persisting often after *l.* have fallen, round like marbles and glistening. One of the most beautiful sp. but rather rarely seen in cultivation. The largest of the white-fruited sp. Himalayas. **1906**, p. 239.

hupehensis ❀ Late Spring T.
Medium sized tree up to 20 ft often wide-spreading. Leaflets rather oblong but up to 3 in. long on *l.* up to 10 in. with up to 17 leaflets. Fruit globose $\frac{1}{4}$ in. wide, white tinged with pink, pink and even red-berried forms sometimes seen. One of the most valuable sp. China. **1907**, p. 239.

'Joseph Rock' ❀ Late Spring T.
Small tree of unknown origin but probably collected by Dr Rock in China. Leaflets small to medium in size on rather long *l.* Fruit deep creamy-yellow in large clusters with red stalks, unique in its colouring. Often persistent until late winter after *l.* have been shed. **1908**, p. 239.

prattii ❀ Late Spring T.
Small tree not often more than 20 ft. Distinguished by very red-brown down on the winter buds and young shoots dark grey-purplish. *L.* up to 5$\frac{1}{2}$ in. long with up to 25 small leaflets. Fruit white, often pearly, globose and shiny. One of the best white-fruited Mountain Ashes but with fruit smaller than in *S. cashmeriana*. China. **1909**, p. 239.

reducta Miniature Mountain Ash ❀ Late Spring Sh.
Not more than 1$\frac{1}{2}$ ft high and often less. Spreading into small thicket by suckers. *L.* up to 4 in. with small leaflets. Fruit deep pink-crimson. Autumn colouring of foliage scarlet. Valuable for large rock garden or front of border. **1910**, p. 239.

sargentiana ❀ Late Spring T.
Majestic and very distinct Mountain Ash up to 30 ft with rather upright branching. *L.* up to 1 ft with large leaflets up to 5 in. long, oblong, lanceolate. Fruit scarlet in large clusters up to 6 in. across slightly pendulous. Autumn foliage is brilliant scarlet, among the best in the genus. Distinguished also for large sticky winter buds like those of a Horse Chestnut. To be planted in full sun to get best colour. China. **1911**, p. 239.

scalaris ❀ Late Spring T.
Vigorous tree up to 30 ft. *L.* up to 8 in. long with numerous small fern-like leaflets. Fruit orange-scarlet, shining, small but in very large clusters up to 8 in. across. One of the most brilliant sp. for fruit. Autumn colouring also good, bright orange-scarlet. China. **1912**, p. 239.

vilmorinii ❀ Late Spring T.
Small tree up to 15 ft, usually less vigorous than most other members of the genus. *L.* up to 5 in. long with numerous small leaflets, fern-like and delicate. Fruit cherry-red or deep pink, later fading to white, in large clusters. China. **1913**, p. 240.

SORREL RHUBARB see **Rheum palmatum**, **1348**, p. 169.

SOUTHERN BEECH see **Nothofagus**, **1711**, p. 214.

SPANISH BLUEBELL see **Endymion hispanicus**

SPANISH BROOM see **Spartium junceum**, **1914**, p. 240.

SPANISH GORSE see **Genista hispanica**, **1622**, p. 203.

SPANISH HEATH see **Erica australis**, **1578**, p. 198.

SPARTIUM (LEGUMINOSAE)

junceum Spanish Broom ❀ Summer Sh.
Shrub often of rather gaunt habit where unpruned, up to 10 ft. Young branches cylindrical rush-like, green and fulfilling function of *l.* which are almost entirely absent or rudimentary. *Fl.* pea-like, large up to 1$\frac{1}{2}$ in. deep with broad standard up to 1 in. across, deep glowing yellow, very fragrant, showy. Seed pod up to 3 in. long. Valuable for covering dry situations and does best in full sun. One of the best late flowering shrubs. Best when hard pruned after flowering or in spring but pruning should not be taken back beyond current year's wood. Spartiums do not transplant easily and should be raised from seeds, which it produces abundantly, and planted out of small pots when young. S. Europe but long introduced to Britain and almost naturalised in some areas. **1914**, p. 240.

SPATHIPHYLLUM (ARACEAE)

wallisii White Sails ❀ Spring and Autumn GP.
To 9 in. high. *Fl.* white, about 3 in. long. *L.* oblong-lanceolate, evergreen, shining. A greedy plant needing a very rich compost. Winter temp. 50–55°F. Often used as a house plant. Likes warm, moist, shady conditions, but is kept drier in winter. Propagate by division. Colombia. **650**, p. 82.

SPEARWORT, GREAT see **Ranunculus lingua**, **1345**, p. 169.

SPECULARIA (CAMPANULACEAE)

speculum Venus's Looking Glass ❀ Summer HA.
Fl. violet-blue, bell-shaped, free-flowering, about 1 in. across. *L.* egg-shaped, entire, upper *l.* lance-shaped, almost entire. There is a white form and several garden varieties. 9 in. Sow in the open in 3–4 in light soil where they are to *fl.* Self-sown seedlings will often appear year after year. Mediterranean region. **377**, p. 48.

SPEEDWELL see **Veronica**, **219**, p. 28; **1414-1419**, pp. 177, 178.

SPIDER FLOWER see **Cleome spinosa**, **270**, p. 34.

SPIDER PLANT see **Chlorophytum comosum**, **447**, p. 56.

SPIDERWORT see **Tradescantia**, **1400**, **1401**, pp. 175, 176.

SPIKENARD, FALSE see **Smilacina racemosa**, **1380**, p. 173.

SPINDLE TREE see **Euonymus**, **1603-1606**, p. 201.

SPIRAEA (ROSACEAE)

aruncus see **Aruncus sylvester**

× **bumalda** ❀ Summer Sh.
Small shrub usually not more than 3 ft, deciduous, valuable for its long season of *fl.* Type *fl.* heads deep pink. Old *fl.* heads should be cut off to induce continuous flowering. Probably a hybrid of *S. japonica* × *S. albiflora*.

'Anthony Waterer', probably best form with bright crimson *fl.*, *l.* lanceolate or narrowly oval up to 4 in. long, coarsely toothed. Some tend to be variegated creamy-white with pink edges. Valuable shrub for sunny position near front of border for its long flowering season in late summer, **1915**, p. 240.

filipendula see **Filipendula hexapetala**

lobata see **Filipendula rubra**

palmata see **Filipendula purpurea**

SPLEENWORT see **Asplenium bulbiferum**

SPOTTED DEAD NETTLE see **Lamium maculatum**, **1231**, p. 154.

SPREADING EUONYMUS see **Euonymus kiautschovica**

SPREKELIA (AMARYLLIDACEAE) Jacobean Lily

formosissima Late Spring–Early Summer *Bb
Fl. single, deep scarlet, crimson, large up to 5 in. across and as much deep, irregular in shape and very striking, with lower petal two-lipped, curving round into a tube, green at base. Somewhat like a large insect on 1 ft stem. Bulb roundish with a long neck. Tender and should be planted in late summer in a warm sunny place or in cold areas treated as a cool greenhouse plant. Mexico, Guatemala. **883**, p. 111.

SPRUCE see **Picea**, **2026-2030**, p. 254.

SPRUCE, ALBERTA see **Picea glauca** var. **albertiana** 'Conica', **2027**, p. 254.

SPRUCE, BLUE see **Picea pungens**, **2030**, p. 254.

Abbreviations and Symbols used in the text.
The following abbreviations may sometimes be used in conjunction as HA. indicating Hardy annual or GBb indicating Greenhouse bulb.

A. = Annual	P. = Perennial
Aq. = Aquatic	R. = Rock or
B. = Biennial	Alpine plant
Bb = Bulb	Sh. = Shrub
C. = Corm	Sp., sp. = Species
Cl. = Climber	Syn. = Synonym
Co. = Conifer	T. = Tree
Fl., *fl.* = Flower(s)	Tu. = Tuber
G. = Greenhouse or	var. = variety
house plant	× = Hybrid or
H. = Hardy	hybrid parents
HH. = Half-hardy	❀ = Flowering time
L., *l.* = Leaf, leaves	❧ = Foliage plant
Mt(s) = Mount,	
mountain(s)	

The following have been used also in the descriptions of Alpines, Bulbs, Trees and Shrubs.

* = slightly tender
† = lime hater
✿ = highly recommended

The illustration numbers are in **bold type** and the page numbers in light type preceded by p.

SPRUCE, BREWER'S WEEPING see **Picea breweriana, 2026**, p. 254.

SPRUCE, COLORADO see **Picea pungens, 2030**, p. 254.

SPRUCE, COMMON see **Picea abies**

SPRUCE, HEMLOCK see **Tsuga, 2048**, p. 256.

SPRUCE, NORWAY see **Picea abies**

SPRUCE, SERBIAN see **Picea omorika, 2029**, p. 254.

SPRUCE, WHITE see **Picea glauca, 2027**, p. 254.

SPURGE see **Euphorbia, 69**, p. 9; **526**, p. 66; **1129-1133**, p. 142.

SQUILL see **Scilla sibirica, 881**, p. 111.

SQUIRREL-TAIL GRASS see **Hordeum jubatum, 308**, p. 39.

STACHYS (LABIATAE)

lanata Lamb's Tongue ✳ Summer ☙　　P.
Fl. purplish-pink borne on an erect spike. 1–1½ ft. L. grey-white, of soft felt-like texture. Its low spreading habit makes it a valuable plant for the front of a border in any ordinary well-drained soil in sun or light shade. Propagate by division in the spring or by seed. Caucasus. **1386**, p. 174.
　'Silver Carpet', form which rarely fl. and is useful ground cover plant.

macrantha, syn. **Betonica grandiflora** Betony ✳ Late Spring–Early Summer　　P.
Fl. purple-violet, large, borne in whorls on an erect stem. 1–2 ft. L. broadly oval, hairy and wrinkled. Any ordinary garden soil. Caucasus. **1387**, p. 174.
　'Rosea', rosy-pink, 1½–2 ft.

spicata ✳ Summer ,　　P.
Fl. light mauve-pink borne on sturdy erect spikes. 1–1½ ft. L. long, pointed, bluish-green, wrinkled. Ordinary garden soil in sun or light shade. Caucasus.
　'Robusta', purplish-pink, 1½ ft, **1388**, p. 174;
　'Rosea', deep pink, 1 ft.

STACHYURUS (STACHYURACEAE)

chinensis ✳ Early Spring　　Sh.
Deciduous shrub up to 6 ft occasionally more and often as much wide. Young shoots greenish or greenish-brown. Fl. in pendulous racemes up to 4 in. long, small, bell-shaped, pale greenish-yellow. L. ovate to oblong ovate up to 5 in. with slight toothing. China. **1916**, p. 240.

praecox ✳ Early Spring　　Sh.
Close to S. chinensis, flowering slightly earlier and distinguished by reddish branchlets. Usually best grown in peaty soil but will tolerate some lime and valuable for their early blooming before l. appear. Japan.

STAR, BLAZING see **Mentzelia lindleyi, 342**, p. 43.

STAG'S HORN SUMACH see **Rhus typhina, 1832**, p. 229.

STATICE see **Limonium, 326, 327**, p. 41.

STEPHANOTIS (ASCLEPIADACEAE)

floribunda Madagascar Jasmine ✳ Mid Spring–Mid Autumn　　GCl.
Vigorous evergreen climber to 10 ft or more. Fl. white, starry, waxy, very fragrant, produced in large bunches. L. oval, to 3 in. long, leathery. Rich compost needed. Winter temp. 55°F. Moist buoyant atmosphere needed in growing season, drier in winter. Propagate by cuttings of year-old wood in spring. Madagascar. **651**, p. 82.

STERNBERGIA (AMARYLLIDACEAE)

lutea ✳ Autumn　　*Bb
Fl. deep yellow like a large crocus fl. but easily distinguished from a crocus by having six stamens instead of three and broader strap-shaped l. than any crocus. Bulb large with a dark brown tunic. One of Britain's finest autumn-flowering bulbs but needs to be planted in a very warm sunny border where it gets good summer ripening, seems to fl. best in Britain in chalky areas. In cold areas best grown in a bulb frame where it can be well baked in summer. E. Mediterranean and Palestine where some have given Sternbergia the title of 'Lilies of the Field', although there are various other floral candidates. **884**, p. 111.
　var. angustifolia, usually more free-flowering in open.

STIPA (GRAMINEAE)

calamagrostis ✳ Summer　　P.
Ornamental grass. L. grey-green, finely bristly with smooth sheath. Violet awns. Forms dense tufts with slender, erect stems. 3 ft. Decorative in the garden and most useful for floral arrangements. Sow in the open in well-drained soil in spring or increase by division. S. Europe. **1389**, p. 174.

pennata Feather grass ✳ Summer　　P.
Ornamental grass. L. narrow, green. Stems 2½ ft, arching and slender. Conspicuous bearded awns. Admirable in the garden and for decorative arrangements. Sow in the open in spring in a sunny position and well-drained soil, or divide tufted clumps. Europe, Siberia. **1390**, p. 174.

STOCK, VIRGINIAN see **Malcolmia maritima, 336**, p. 42.

STOKES' ASTER see **Stokesia laevis, 1391**, p. 174.

STOKESIA (COMPOSITAE) Stokes' Aster

cyanus see **S. laevis**

laevis, syn. **S. cyanus** ✳ Late Summer–Mid Autumn　　P.
Fl. lavender-blue. L. alternate, smooth, dark green. 1–1½ ft. Ordinary soil in sun or light shade. Propagate by seed or division. N. America. **1391**, p. 174. Good varieties include:
　'Alba', white, 1 ft;
　'Blue Star', large, blue, 1 ft;
　'Superba', large lavender-blue, 9 in.

STONECROP see **Sedum, 202-204**, p. 26; **374**, p. 47; **646**, p. 81; **1369-1374**, p. 172.

STRANVAESIA (ROSACEAE)

davidiana ✳ Summer　　Sh.
Vigorous shrub or small tree up to 20 ft, evergreen. Fl. white with red anthers, small but in clusters up to 3 in. across. Fruit dark crimson-red berries, shiny, each fruit ⅓ in. wide. L. lanceolate, pointed at end, up to 4½ in., dark green but in autumn some of the l. turn brilliant scarlet. Valuable as an evergreen for its bright berries in autumn. Sun or semi-shade. China. **1917**, p. 240.

STRAWBERRY TREE see **Arbutus, 1447-1451**, pp. 181, 182.

STRAWFLOWER EVERLASTING see **Helichrysum bracteatum, 305**, p. 39.

STREPTOCARPUS (GESNERIACEAE) Cape Primrose

hybridus ✳ Summer　　GP.
Fl. tubular, to 2 in. long, several on a stem to 9 in. high. Red, purple, blue and white. L. stemless, large, oblong-oval, to 10 in. long, 3 in. across. Good potting compost. Winter temp. 50°F. Although perennial, often treated as annuals with seed sown in autumn and spring to get a succession of flowering. The principal sp. used in the hybrid are the variable S. rexii, with white, blue or lavender fl. and the red-flowered S. dunnii, but many other sp. have been bred in. Especially good plants can be propagated by l. cuttings, otherwise seed. The parent sp. all come from various parts of S. Africa.
　'Constant Nymph', a fine variety, deep lavender-mauve, **652**, p. 82.

STREPTOSOLEN (SOLANACEAE)

jamesonii ✳ Summer　　GP.
Climber to 8 ft. Fl. orange, tubular bell-shaped, about 1 in. across in terminal panicles. L. evergreen, ovate to 2 in. long. Rather gritty compost best. Winter temp. 45–50°F. Propagate by cuttings of year-old wood. Colombia. **653**, p. 82.

STYLOPHORUM (PAPAVERACEAE) Celandine Poppy

diphyllum ✳ Spring　　P.
Fl. golden-yellow, large, poppy-like. 1 ft. L. bright green, deeply cut. Plant 11–3 in ordinary soil and partial shade. Propagate by division, or by seed sown in the open in 4. N. America. **1392**, p. 174.

STYRAX (STYRACACEAE)

Deciduous shrubs or small trees sometimes known in America as Snowbells.

hemsleyana ✳ Early Summer　　†T.
Small deciduous tree up to 20 ft. Fl. white, with yellow centre consisting of boss of stamens, in

racemes often pendulous up to 6 in., 1 in. across. *L.* obovate up to 5 in. long, toothed and pubescent beneath. Valuable for its flowering during 6 period and the pure whiteness of its *fl.* China. **1918**, p. 240.

japonica ❋ Early Summer *T.
Shrub or small tree up to 15 ft. *Fl.* in small clusters, white, 1¼ in. wide with narrow oblong lobes. *L.* and *fl.* stalks pubescent. *L.* broadly oval to ovate up to 2½ in. long. Only suitable for growth in milder areas or S. Europe. Source of storax, a fragrant resin from which an incense is obtained. S.E. Europe, Asia Minor where it is common. **1919**, p. 240.

SUMACH see **Rhus**, **1832**, p. 229.

SUMACH, STAG'S HORN see **Rhus typhina**, **1832**, p. 229.

SUMACH, VENETIAN see **Cotinus coggygria**, **1535**, **1536**, p. 192.

SUMMER CYPRESS see **Kochia**

SUN PLANT see **Portulaca grandiflora**, **363**, p. 46.

SUNFLOWER see **Helianthus annuus**, **304**, p. 38.

SUNFLOWER, MEXICAN see **Tithonia rotundifolia**, **385**, p. 49.

SWAMP BLUEBERRY see **Vaccinium corymbosum**, **1933**, p. 242.

SWAMP CYPRESS see **Taxodium distichum**, **2041**, p. 256.

SWEDISH BIRCH see **Betula pendula** var. **dalecarlica**

SWEET ALYSSUM see **Alyssum maritimum**, **230-231**, p. 29.

SWEET BAY see **Magnolia virginiana**

SWEET GUM see **Liquidambar styraciflua**, **1677**, p. 210.

SWEET PEA see **Lathyrus odoratus**, **316-321**, pp. 40, 41.

SWEET PEPPER BUSH see **Clethra alnifolia** under **C. barbinervis**

SWEET SCABIOUS see **Scabiosa atropurpurea**, **373**, p. 47.

SWEET SULTAN see **Centaurea moschata**, **260**, p. 33.

SWEET WILLIAM see **Dianthus barbatus**, **283**, p. 36.

SYCAMORE see **Acer pseudoplatanus**, **1439**, p. 180.

SYCAMORE MAPLE see **Acer pseudoplatanus**, **1439**, p. 180.

SYMPHORICARPUS (CAPRIFOLIACEAE)

albus Snowberry ❋ Summer Sh.
Small twiggy shrub up to 4 ft suckering freely from

base with young shoots. *Fl.* pink in small clusters. Fruit large berry on very delicate stem.
Best form is:
var. *laevigatus*, with large white marble-like berries throughout winter usually long lasting after foliage has fallen, **1920**, p. 240.
Various new hybrid forms have recently been raised, among the best are:
'Magic Berry', with pink fruits freely produced;
'White Hedger', with strong upright compact growth and smaller white berries, useful as a hedging plant where only a low hedge is required.

SYMPHYTUM (BORAGINACEAE) Comfrey

officinale ❋ Summer P.
Fl. white, pink, dingy purple or yellow, drooping in terminal clusters. *L.* lanceolate, 6–10 in. long, roughly hairy. 2–4 ft. Plant 11–3 in a moist, sunny place in the wild garden. Propagate by division or seed. Europe, including Britain.
'Argenteum', has striking variegated foliage and blue *fl.*, **1393**, p. 175.

peregrinum Russian Comfrey ❋ Summer P.
Fl. pink in the bud stage, changing to pale blue, pendent. *L.* lower up to 10 in. long, upper about 3 in. long. 3–4 ft. In almost any moist soil in sun or partial shade. Propagate by seed. E. Caucasus, naturalised in Britain.

SYRINGA (OLEACEAE) Lilac

All lilacs should be given generous manuring well on lime soils. Propagate from layers or cuttings.

× **josiflexa** ❋ Early Summer Sh.
Deciduous shrubs up to 10 ft with large terminal panicles of scented *fl.* A hybrid between *S. reflexa* × *S. josikaea*. A fine race of hybrid lilacs raised in Canada. **1921**, p. 241.
Best form is:
'Bellicent', with large panicles of clear rose-pink *fl.*, 6. Vigorous shrub which should be pruned by taking out weak growth and *fl.* heads after they are dead.

vulgaris Common Lilac ❋ Early Summer T.
Deciduous shrub or small tree up to 20 ft. Best kept to a single trunk at base and suckers should be pruned out. *Fl.* in large panicles, in various colours from white, cream, pink, shades of lilac to deep violet and mauve, single or double. It is important to take out old *fl.* heads as soon as they die. *L.* heart-shaped or ovate up to 6 in. long.
Among finest garden varieties are:
Single
'Charles X', pale lilac-mauve, **1922**, p. 241;
'Clarke's Giant', lilac-blue, very large *fl.*;
'Esther Staley', carmine-red in bud opening to bright pink, early flowering;
'Massena', deep reddish-purple large *fl.* trusses, **1925**, p. 241;
'Maud Notcutt', white large *fl.* mid-season;
'Primrose', pale primrose-yellow, smaller *fl.* heads than some varieties, mid-season, **1926**, p. 241;
'Souvenir de Louis Spath', deep purplish or wine-red heavily scented large trusses, mid-season. An old variety but still one of the best.
Double
'General Pershing', purple-violet late flowering;
'Firmament', pale lilac-mauve, an older variety but very free flowering, **1923**, p. 241;
'Katharine Havemeyer', deep purplish-lavender but fading to lilac-pink, compact truss;
'Madame Lemoine', white large trusses, **1924**, p. 241;
'Mrs Edward Harding', purplish-red.

SYRINGA see **Philadelphus**, **1725-1729**, pp. 216, 217.

TAGETES (COMPOSITAE)

erecta African Marigold ❋ Summer HHA.
Fl. of sp. are single, yellow or orange, up to 4 in. across, much larger than *T. patula*. Branching plants 1–3 ft high. *L.* feathered, lance-shaped and toothed. There are also tall and dwarf double varieties. Sow under glass in 2–3, planting out seedlings in late 5–6. Sowings can also be made in a sunny bed in the open in 5. Mexico.
'Crackerjack', carnation flowered double, various colours, 2½–3 ft;
'Golden Age', large, to 3 in. across, carnation flowered double, golden-yellow, 1 ft, **378**, p. 48;
'Jubilee series', F¹ hybrids, large double *fl.*, 3½ in. across, various colours, 2 ft;
'Spanish Brocade', large, double gold and crimson, 2 ft, **379**, p. 48.

patula French Marigold ❋ Summer HHA.
Fl. golden-yellow. *L.* feathery, toothed. 6–12 in. Cultivation as for *T. erecta*. Mexico. There are several cultivated strains and varieties in many colours. Good varieties include:
'Dainty Marietta', compact, single, golden-yellow striped and marked maroon, 6 in., **380**, p. 48;
'Harmony', mahogany with orange centre, 9 in., **381**, p. 48;
'Naughty Marietta', large single, golden-yellow striped maroon, 1 ft;
'Sparky', large double, red and gold shades, mixed, 10 in.

signata see **T. tenuifolia**

tenuifolia, syn. **T. signata** ❋ Midsummer–Mid Autumn HHA.
Fl. rich yellow or orange. 6 in. Compact. *L.* deeply toothed, lance-shaped. See *T. erecta* for cultivation. Mexico. Several good varieties have been developed and include:
'Gnome', deep orange-yellow;
'Golden Gem', gold with small copper markings, **382**, p. 48;
'Lulu', canary yellow;
'Pumila', yellow, a good edging plant.

TAMARISK see **Tamarix**, **1927**, p. 241.

Abbreviations and Symbols used in the text.
The following abbreviations may sometimes be used in conjunction as HA. indicating Hardy annual or GBb indicating Greenhouse bulb.

A. = Annual	P. = Perennial
Aq. = Aquatic	R. = Rock or
B. = Biennial	Alpine plant
Bb = Bulb	Sh. = Shrub
C. = Corm	Sp., sp. = Species
Cl. = Climber	Syn. = Synonym
Co. = Conifer	T. = Tree
Fl., *fl.* = Flower(s)	Tu. = Tuber
G. = Greenhouse or	var. = variety
house plant	× = Hybrid or
H. = Hardy	hybrid parents
HH. = Half-hardy	❋ = Flowering time
L., *l.* = Leaf, leaves	✿ = Foliage plant
Mt(s) = Mount,	
mountain(s)	

The following have been used also in the descriptions of Alpines, Bulbs, Trees and Shrubs.

* = slightly tender
† = lime hater
✿ = highly recommended

The illustration numbers are in **bold type** and the page numbers in light type preceded by p.

TAMARIX (TAMARICACEAE) Tamarisk

pentandra ✳ Late Summer   Sh.
Shrub or small tree up to 15 ft with loose rather drooping slender branches. Leaflets small but giving plumose effect. *Fl.* pink in short racemes. Valuable for its late flowering and usually grows especially well in seaside areas. In order to keep compact, tree should be pruned hard in winter. S.E. Europe. **1927**, p. 241.

tetrandra ✳ Late Spring   Sh.
Close to *T. pentandra* with bright pink *fl.* packed in shorter spikes but differs by flowering in 5. S.E. Europe, Asia Minor.

TANACETUM DENSUM AMANI see Chrysanthemum haradjanii

TASSEL FLOWER see Amaranthus caudatus, 232, p. 29.

TASSEL HYACINTH see Muscari comosum var. monstrosum, 826, p. 104.

TAXODIUM (TAXODIACEAE)

distichum Deciduous, Bald or Swamp Cypress   Co.
Tall deciduous tree up to 150 ft, usually rather conical until it gets old. Bark reddish-brown, peeling. Small lateral branches fall with *l.* in autumn. *L.* spirally arranged on branchlets in two ranks up to ¾ in. long, bright apple-green in spring, yellowish-green in summer, becoming rich rusty-brown before falling in autumn. Cones small, globose, up to 1¼ in. across, slightly purplish. Unique among conifers in that it will grow actually standing in water and grows well at the edge of ponds with its roots in very moist or water-logged soils. In such situations base tends to become swollen and tall cylindrical protruberances called 'Knees' arise from the roots up to several ft high. S.E. USA, Mexico but hardy in most parts of the British Isles. Wood contains fragrant oil which is repellent to white ants. **2041**, p. 256.

TAXUS (TAXACEAE) Yew

baccata Common Yew   Co.
Evergreen wide-spreading tree often reaching considerable age and up to 60 ft high, usually less. *L.* linear, narrow up to 1¼ in. long, spirally arranged on erect shoots but on side shoots appearing in two ranks, dark glossy-green above but paler beneath. Female cones are fleshy, cup-shaped and scarlet and eaten by birds which helps distribution of seed. All yews grow well on chalky soils and stand clipping and are very useful for hedges, making very thick dense compact evergreen hedge often surviving to a great age. **2042**, p. 256.
Erect yews are:
    'Fastigiata', the Irish or Florence Court yew from its place of origin, narrow erect tree with deep green foliage;
    'Fastigiata Aurea', foliage yellowish-green, golden in young growth, valuable evergreen for its colour but slower growing than green Irish yew, **2043**, p. 256.

TEA, OSWEGO see Monarda didyma, 1276, p. 160.

TEA TREE see Leptospermum scoparium, 1674, p. 210.

TECOMA see Campsis

TECOPHILAEA (AMARYLLIDACEAE)

cyanocrocus Chilean crocus ✳ Spring   *Bb
Fl. single of deepest gentian blue, the colour of a *Gentiana verna* and with a white throat, about 2 in. across, on stem 3–4 in. tall. *L.* strap-shaped. Plant in sunny position in well sheltered position. Excellent and most striking as an alpine house plant; never very common or abundant, but still worth every effort for its magnificent colour, a stronger blue than in any other spring *fl.* S. America, Chile. **885**, p. 111.
    var. *leichtlinii*, with more white in *fl.*

TEUCRIUM (LABIATAE)

pyrenaicum ✳ Summer   P.
Fl. mauvish and white, hooded, in terminal clusters. *L.* light green, roundish, hairy, 4–6 in., trailing. Plant 11–3 in ordinary soil. Propagate by division in autumn or spring. S. Europe. **1394**, p. 175.

THALICTRUM (RANUNCULACEAE) Meadow Rue

angustifolium see **T. lucidum**

aquilegiifolium ✳ Late Spring—Midsummer   P.
Fl. soft purplish-pink, variable, in spreading panicles. *L.* shiny grey-blue, pinnately divided. 2–3 ft. Any ordinary garden soil that does not dry out too readily, in sun or partial shade. Propagate by seed sown in pans of sandy soil in spring under glass or by division in the spring. Europe, N. America. **1395**, p. 175.
Good varieties include:
    'Album', white, 2½ ft;
    'Purple Cloud', rosy-purple, 2½ ft.

dipterocarpum ✳ Summer   P.
Fl. deep lavender with prominent yellow anthers borne in graceful panicles. *L.* fern-like, graceful. 4–5 ft. A sunny position in well-drained but moist soil. Propagate by seed sown in pans in spring. W. China.
    'Hewitt's Double', fully double, deep lavender *fl.*, propagate by taking off small side shoots in spring, **1396**, p. 175.

lucidum, syn. **T. angustifolium** ✳ Summer   P.
Fl. yellowish-green, in panicles. *L.* dark green, shiny, pinnately divided. 3–5 ft. Europe. **1397**, p. 175.

rocquebrunianum ✳ Summer   P.
Fl. rosy-lavender, in large branching panicles. *L.* dainty, fern-like. 4 ft. Plant in ordinary moist soil in sun or partial shade. Propagate by seed, or division in spring as growth starts. Origin uncertain.

THLASPI (CRUCIFERAE)

rotundifolium ✳ Late Spring–Early Summer RP, RB.
Fl. pale slatey-purple, small, cress-like, star-shaped in clusters, fragrant, 2–4 in. *L.* glaucous-green, slightly succulent, forming tussocky clumps. Best grown in damp scree or alpine house. European Alps in scree. **213**, p. 27.

THUNBERGIA (ACANTHACEAE)

alata Black-eyed Susan ✳ Midsummer–Mid Autumn HHA/GA
Fl. variable, yellow, buff, cream with purple throat. *L.* heart-shaped. 3–6 ft, twining. Sow in a warm greenhouse in 3–4, or in a sunny bed in sheltered gardens in 4–5. In cold districts it makes an admirable plant for a cool greenhouse. S. Africa. **383**, p. 48.

gibsonii differs from *T. gregorii* botanically but is otherwise similar.

gregorii ✳ Midsummer–Mid Autumn   HHA/GA.
Fl. waxy orange. *L.* triangular, 2–3 in. long. 3–5 ft, twining. Similar treatment as for *T. alata*. E. and S. Africa. **384**, p. 48.

THUYA (CUPRESSACEAE) Arbor-vitae

Evergreen trees with small scaly *l.* and flattened branches giving conical shape especially when young.

occidentalis American Arbor-vitae or White Cedar   Co.
Tree up to 60 ft but usually much less in cultivation. Bark reddish-brown, fissured. *L.* dark green above, pale green beneath, when bruised scented like Tansy, sharp pointed. Cones small, ½ in. long, yellowish and erect brown and pendant when mature. Many cultivars have been named but are in the majority of cases insufficiently distinct. E. N. America.

orientalis Chinese Arbor-vitae   Co.
Small tree up to 40 ft, with erect branches and columnar habit, sometimes branching near base. *L.* small, green. Cones ovoid and fleshy, the scales with a strong hook. Less widely grown than other two sp. N. and W. China. A number of forms have been described.
    'Rosedalis Compacta', dwarf form with bright yellow foliage in spring becoming glaucous-green, juvenile foliage, turning brown or glaucous plum-purple in winter, slow-growing, usually compact, **2044**, p. 256;
    'Semperaurea', yellow foliage, makes a round topped bush. Syn. 'Semperaurescens', **2045**, p. 256.

plicata Western Red Cedar or Western Arbor-vitae   Co.
Large tree up to 200 ft in native habitat but usually much less in cultivation. Bark light reddish-brown with shallow fissures. Branches growing horizontally, sometimes pendant at ends. *L.* larger than those of *T. occidentalis* but still small, arranged laterally along shoots. Valuable as forest tree but also much used in gardens for hedging since it stands cutting much better than the *Cupressus macrocarpa* and always shows fresh green. Cones small about ½ in. long, brown. This tree will establish better in shady conditions than the majority of other conifers and can also be moved up to 5–6 ft but preferably plant at 3 ft if possible. It is widely distributed in Pacific coast of N. America and W. Canada.
Various forms have been named and among the best are:
    'Fastigiata', syn. *pyramidalis*, habit erect and narrow with branches arranged in vertical plane, dark green, **2046**, p. 256.
    'Zebrina', rather erect in habit, *l.* tawny-yellow making good contrast to green forms, **2047**, p. 256.

Abbreviations and Symbols used in the text.
The following abbreviations may sometimes be used in conjunction as HA. indicating Hardy annual or GBb indicating Greenhouse bulb.

A. = Annual	P. = Perennial
Aq. = Aquatic	R. = Rock or
B. = Biennial	Alpine plant
Bb = Bulb	Sh. = Shrub
C. = Corm	Sp., sp. = Species
Cl. = Climber	Syn. = Synonym
Co. = Conifer	T. = Tree
Fl., *fl.* = Flower(s)	Tu. = Tuber
G. = Greenhouse or	var. = variety
house plant	× = Hybrid or
H. = Hardy	hybrid parents
HH. = Half-hardy	✳ = Flowering time
L., *l.* = Leaf, leaves	⚘ = Foliage plant
Mt(s) = Mount,	
mountain(s)	

The following have been used also in the descriptions of Alpines, Bulbs, Trees and Shrubs.

    * = slightly tender
    † = lime hater
    ✿ = highly recommended

The illustration numbers are in **bold type** and the page numbers in light type preceded by p.

THYMUS (LABIATAE) Thyme

serpyllum ✳ Late Spring–Midsummer   RP.
Mat-forming and often spreading widely. *Fl.* deep purple, pale purplish-pink or purplish-crimson, very variable, small but in clusters on short erect stems and covering plant, 1–2 in. *L.* small, aromatic. Sunny position and grows well over rocks. Europe including Britain.
Two of the best forms are:
‘Coccineus’, with bright purplish-crimson, darker in bud, **214**, p. 27;
‘Pink Chintz’, with deep rose-red *fl.*

TIARELLA (SAXIFRAGACEAE) Foam Flower

polyphylla ✳ Summer   P.
Fl. white, tinged pink. 1–2 ft. *L.* three-lobed, toothed. Plant 11–3 in partial shade and moist leafy soil. Propagate by seed, or division in early spring. China, Japan. **1398**, p. 175.

wherryi ✳ Late Spring–Midsummer   P.
Fl. creamy, pink-tinged, feathery spikes. 1 ft. *L.* green-bronze, becoming reddish in autumn, slightly hairy, almost heart-shaped. A moist soil and partial shade. Propagate by seed or by division in early spring. S.E. USA. **1399**, p. 175.

TIBOUCHINA (MELASTOMACEAE)

semidecandra, syn. **Lasiandra macrantha**
✳ Early Autumn–Mid Winter   *GT,GSh.
Shrub up to 20 ft usually less, only possible for growth outside in very warm areas such as a wall in Isles of Scilly or warmer parts of Cornwall, but good in S. Europe and S.W. States of USA. Very valuable as greenhouse shrub. *Fl.* rich purple with satin sheen up to 4 in. across, under glass. Very long-flowering shrub. *L.* oblong-ovate to ovate, downy above. Should be pruned after flowering to basal shoots of young wood in order to keep compact. One of the finest cool greenhouse shrubs. Unfortunately, it appears that the true Brazilian sp. under this name is probably not in cultivation and that the plants usually grown belong to *T. urvilleana.* S. Brazil. **1928**, p. 241.

TICKWEED see **Coreopsis**, **274**, p. 35; **1055**, **1056**, p. 132.

TIGRIDIA (IRIDACEAE)

✿ **pavonia** ✳ Summer   *C.
Fl. orange-red, scarlet, yellow or white with three larger spreading petals and spotted cup-shaped centre. Most spectacular *fl.* like great butterflies and often 5–6 in. across. Ephemeral but several *fl.* to a stem 1–1½ ft tall. L. sword-shaped like those of a gladiolus. Plant in spring in sunny position and in colder areas lift for winter like a gladiolus corm. In warmer areas of S. and W. they will often last the winter in the ground. They appreciate, however, a good deal of moisture in summer as do others of the S. American plants. Mexico in the mts and part of Peru. **886**, p. 111.

TILIA (TILIACEAE) Lime, Linden

× **europaea** ✳ Late Summer   T.
Deciduous tree up to 100 ft. *Fl.* yellowish-white, fragrant, in small clusters. *L.* broadly ovate up to 4 in. long. *Fl.* are a source of nectar for bees. One of the most valuable street trees and also much used for pleaching particularly in warmer parts of S. Europe. Probably a hybrid between *P. platyphyllos* and *T. cordata* the only British native sp. **1929**, p. 242.

platyphyllos ✳ Summer   T.
Close to *T.* × *europaea* but tends to be planted more now owing to greater freedom from disease. *L.* roundish ovate up to 5 in. long and wide. Distinguished by its downy shoots. S. Europe.

TITHONIA (COMPOSITAE)

rotundifolia, syn. **T. speciosa** Mexican Sunflower
✳ Summer   HHA.
Fl. orange-scarlet, resembling a zinnia, 2–3 in. across. *L.* heart-shaped, three-lobed or entire. 4–7 ft. Sow under glass in 3 and plant out 2–3 ft apart in late 5, in a sunny position and preferably light soil. Mexico. **385**, p. 49.
‘Torch’, is a brilliant orange-red with golden centre, 4 ft;

speciosa see **T. rotundifolia**

TOADFLAX see **Linaria**, **328**, p. 41; **1241**, p. 156.

TOAD LILY see **Tricyrtis**, **1402**, p. 176.

TOBACCO PLANT see **Nicotiana**, **351**, p. 44.

TORENIA (SCROPHULARIACEAE)

fournieri Wishbone Flower ✳ Midsummer–Mid Autumn   GA.
Fl. antirrhinum-like, pale blue, yellow blotch at base. *L.* narrowly egg-shaped. 9–12 in. Sow in 3–4 in a warm greenhouse and grow as a decorative cool greenhouse plant. Indo-China.
‘Grandiflora’, larger *fl.* with yellow throat, 1 ft, **386**, p. 49.

TOUCH-ME-NOT see **Impatiens**, **311**, p. 39.

TRACHYCARPUS (PALMACEAE)

fortunei, syn. **T. excelsa, Chamaerops excelsa**
Chusan Palm   *T.
The hardiest palm for growth in Britain and sufficiently hardy to be grown in S. and W. without damage. *L.* large fan-shaped up to 2½ ft long and 4 ft across. Rather slow growing but old trees have been known up to 20 ft. Very decorative for sub-tropical gardening. *Fl.* yellow and small but very numerous in large panicles up to 2 ft and long lasting. *Fl.* among young *l.* at top of stem. Trunk, always un-branched, usually clothed with coarse brown fibres and *l.* only borne at top. China. **1930**, p. 242.

TRACHYMENE CAERULEA see **Didiscus caeruleus**

TRADESCANTIA (COMMELINACEAE)

virginiana Spiderwort ✳ Summer   P.
Fl. violet-blue, three-petalled, about 1 in. across. *L.* dull green, strap-like, smooth, about 1 ft long. 1½–2 ft. Ordinary garden soil in sun or light shade. Propagate by seed sown in the open in spring or by division. N. America. **1400**, p. 175.
Good varieties include:
‘Iris Prichard’, white, shaded pale violet;
‘Isis’, deep blue, 2 in. across, **1401**, p. 176;
‘Osprey’, white, with feathery blue stamens.

TREE HEATH see **Erica arborea** and **E.** × **veitchii**, **1577**, p. 198; **1590**, p. 199.

TREE MALLOW see **Lavatera arborea**, **1672**, p. 209.

TREE PEONIES see **Paeonia lutea**, **1718**, p. 215; and **P. suffruticosa**, **1719**, **1720**, p. 215.

TREE POPPY see **Romneya**, **1837**, p. 230.

TREFOIL, BIRD'S-FOOT see **Lotus corniculatus**, **1244**, p. 156.

TRICHINIUM (AMARANTHACEAE)

manglesii ✳ Summer   *RP.
6–10 in. *Fl.* white with purplish-pink tips up to 1 in. long in dense spikes up to 2 in. across and covered with long silvery-white hairs. *L.* narrow linear. Tender and only suited to alpine house, but should be protected against freezing in winter. Australia. **215**, p. 27.

TRICHOCEREUS (CACTACEAE)

candicans ✳ Summer   GP.
Fl. white, large, nocturnal, fragrant. Plant columnar, ribbed, up to 2 ft high or more. Requires a slightly less loamy than that for the epiphytic cacti. Winter temp. 45–50°F., the higher reading being preferable. Keep moist throughout most of the year and in full light. Propagate by seed. Chile.
‘Robustior’, a particularly vigorous form, **654**, p. 82.

TRICOLOR PELARGONIUM see **Pelargonium** × **hortorum**, **598-612**, pp. 75–77.

TRICUSPIDARIA see **Crinodendron**

TRICYRTIS (LILIACEAE) Toad Lily

stolonifera ✳ Late Summer   P.
Fl. mauve with deeper spots. *L.* slender-pointed, 4–5 in. long. 1½–2 ft. Plant 11–3 in partial shade and moist sandy peat. Propagate by seed, or division in spring. Formosa. **1402**, p. 176.

TRILLIUM (LILIACEAE)

Distinguished by the three large petals arranged in a triangle and the three green sepals below. The *l.* are also in threes on the stem. All members of the genus do best in moist peaty situations and will grow in semi-shade.

chloropetalum ✳ Spring   Tu.
Three petals white or greenish-white, erect or spreading, 3 in. across on stems 1–1½ ft. *L.* heavily marbled with purplish-maroon, large, ovate. N.W. America. **887**, p. 111.

Abbreviations and Symbols used in the text.
The following abbreviations may sometimes be used in conjunction as HA. indicating Hardy annual or GBb indicating Greenhouse bulb.

A. = Annual	P. = Perennial
Aq. = Aquatic	R. = Rock or
B. = Biennial	Alpine plant
Bb = Bulb	Sh. = Shrub
C. = Corm	Sp., sp. = Species
Cl. = Climber	Syn. = Synonym
Co. = Conifer	T. = Tree
Fl., fl. = Flower(s)	Tu. = Tuber
G. = Greenhouse or	var. = variety
house plant	× = Hybrid or
H. = Hardy	hybrid parents
HH. = Half-hardy	✳ = Flowering time
L., l. = Leaf, leaves	❧ = Foliage plant
Mt(s) = Mount,	
mountain(s)	

The following have been used also in the descriptions of Alpines, Bulbs, Trees and Shrubs.

* = slightly tender
† = lime hater
✿ = highly recommended

The illustration numbers are in **bold type** and the page numbers in light type preceded by p.

☆grandiflorum Wake Robin ✳ Spring　　　Tu.
Three petals white, spreading, 3–4 in. across on stem 1–1½ ft. *L.* less broad than in previous sp. and unmarbled. Probably the finest garden plant in the genus and sometimes forming large clumps. E. N. America. **888**, p. 111.

sessile ✳ Spring　　　Tu.
Petals of deep crimson-purple or maroon, erect and rather narrow, up to 1¼ in. long, the *fl.* appearing sessile on stem without any pedicel (stalk). Stem 1½ ft with broad oval *l.* heavily marbled. There are also forms with white or greenish-yellow petals. N. America. **889**, p. 112.

TROLLIUS (RANUNCULACEAE) Globe Flower

europaeus ✳ Late Spring–Early Summer　　　P.
Fl. pale lemon, 1½–2 in. across on erect stems, 2 ft. *L.* fresh green, deeply cut. Any ordinary garden soil but moisture is essential, in sun or partial shade. Most effective beside a pool. Propagate by division in early autumn. Plants raised from seed are very variable in shades of yellow and in *l.* formation. Europe, N. Britain.
Good varieties include:
　'Earliest of All', lemon-yellow, 4–6, 1 ft;
　'Golden Monarch', large, rich yellow, 2 ft, **1403**, p. 176;
　'Orange Princess', bright orange, 2 ft, **1404**, p. 176;
　'Superbus', soft yellow, 2 ft, **1405**, p. 176.

ledebourii ✳ Summer　　　P.
Fl. deep orange, cup-shaped. 2 ft. *L.* deeply lobed and toothed. Cultivation and propagation similar to *T. europaeus*. E. Siberia, China.
　'Golden Queen', 2 ft, bright orange with prominent stamens, **1406**, p. 176.

TROPAEOLUM (TROPAEOLACEAE) Nasturtium

majus ✳ Midsummer–Mid Autumn　　　HA.
Fl. orange in the wild state: garden forms in shades of scarlet, mahogany-red, golden-yellow, primrose, creamy-white. *L.* circular. Climbing or trailing. Sow in 4–5 in poorish soil and in full sun where they are to *fl.* Rich soil will only encourage a mass of foliage which may hide the *fl.* Peru. There are single, **387**, p. 49, and double, **388**, p. 49, varieties.
Named low growing strains include:
　'Gleam hybrids', *fl.* semi-double, sweetly scented, various colours, 1–1½ ft;
　'Tom Thumb mixed', single *fl.*, compact plants, 9 in.–1 ft.

polyphyllum ✳ Summer　　　RP.
Forms trailing stems up to 2 ft long with glaucous, lobed *l.* *Fl.* deep yellow with long spur, 1 in. across, numerous along stems, 2–4 in. Dies back in winter to an underground tuberous rhizome. Plant in warm sunny position with good drainage, but too large for choicest places. Unsuitable for very cold areas. S. America, Chile, Argentina. **216**, p. 27.

speciosum Scottish Flame Flower ✳ Summer　Cl.
Perennial climber with rhizomatous base making annual growth up to 12 ft. Very vigorous where growing well. *Fl.* bright scarlet nasturtium-like up to ¾ in. across with long spur up to 1¼ in., borne very freely. *L.* with 5 or 6 lobes, shortly stalked. This plant does best in moist peaty situation, but will tolerate some lime in soil. It can be seen doing well particularly in Scotland against a N. or E. wall. It does not need to be planted in full sun. Also useful for scrambling over evergreen bushes in summer. One of the most brilliant flowered climbers where it succeeds. Moves badly and young rhizomes should be planted directly out of pots with as little disturbance as possible in spring. Chile. **1994**, p. 250.

tricolorum ✳ Summer　　　*Tu.
Climber with numerous orange-scarlet *fl.* tipped with black and orange-yellow centre and a short spur. A very dainty and striking climber for a very sheltered position or for a cool greenhouse, dying

down to the tuber after flowering. S. America, Chile. **890**, p. 112.

tuberosum ✳ Late Summer　　　Tu.
Vigorous perennial climber or scrambler with orange-red *fl.*, yellow in the centre and with long spurs. Plant the large tubers deeply in a warm sheltered position or at base of a hedge. In colder areas lift tubers after flowering in autumn and store in a box of sand or ashes. S. America, Peru. **891**, p. 112.

TRUE COLUMBINE see **Aquilegia vulgaris**

TRUMPET, ANGEL'S see **Datura suaveolens**, **495**, p. 62.

TRUMPET CREEPER see **Campsis**, **1958**, p. 245.

TRUMPET FLOWER, CHINESE see **Incarvillea**, **1183**, **1184**, p. 148.

TRUMPET HONEYSUCKLE, SCARLET see **Lonicera** × **brownii**, **1981**, p. 248.

TSUGA (PINACEAE) Hemlock or Hemlock Spruce

Large evergreen trees with rather horizontal branches and branchlets often pendulous at tips. *L.* short, linear in two ranked arrangement along small branchlets. Cones small at ends of shoot, pendulous.

albertiana see **T. heterophylla**

canadensis Eastern Hemlock, Canadian Hemlock　　　Co.
Tree up to 100 ft in native habitat but usually less in cultivation. Distinguished by trunk which often forks near base. Bark brownish and furrowed in old trees. *L.* arranged in two ranks up to ⅔ in. long, deep green. Cones ovoid up to 1 in. long with few scales. Valuable as ornamental conifer but not very useful for forestry purposes since the wood is very soft. E. N. America, Canada S. to Alabama. **2048**, p. 256.

heterophylla, syn. **T. mertensiana, T. albertiana**
Western Hemlock　　　†Co.
Tall tree up to 250 ft in W. America. Differing from from *T. canadensis* by its straight trunk and leader, otherwise rather similar.

mertensiana see **T. heterophylla**

TUBEROSE see **Polianthes tuberosa**, **630**, p. 79.

TULIP TREE see **Liriodendron tulipifera**, **1678**, p. 210.

TULIPA (LILIACEAE)

A large genus rivalling the daffodils in popularity and ranging from small early-flowering sp. only a few in. tall and flowering in 2 to the large hybrids which make such a magnificent display in 4–5, especially when underplanted with such plants as forget-me-nots.
The majority of tulips are sun lovers, the exception being *T. sprengeri* the latest to *fl.* They need not be planted before mid 10 or even 11 so that their *l.* do not appear too early in the winter. Plant 3–5 in. deep. Most of the sp. and many of the hybrids are more likely to persist if the bulbs are lifted each year in 6 after they have died down and stored dry for the summer. In well-drained and warm areas some, however, will persist if left in the ground and *fl.* well from year to year.
The wild sp. come mainly from Asia Minor and the Mediterranean regions but extend W. into Spain and E. to China. Many of the finest sp. and the ancestors of many of the most recent hybrids come from Russian Turkestan such as *kaufmanniana*, *fosteriana*, *eichleri* and *greigii*. They are nearly all

plants from areas which have a long and cold winter without mild interruption, a short but warm spring with plenty of moisture flowing down from melting snow and a long and very hot dry summer during which the bulbs are dormant. This is why it so often pays to lift the bulbs in the summer. Many of the sp. also grow well in a raised frame which is covered in summer. Tulips seem to be tolerant of a wide range of soils and grow well on chalk.
There are perhaps 100 different sp. and several thousand named hybrids so only a few typical of the main groups can be described here.

batalinii see **T. linifolia**

chrysantha see **T. stellata** var. **chrysantha**

☆clusiana The Lady Tulip ✳ Mid Spring　　　Bb
One of the most delicate and graceful of the tulip sp. *Fl.* medium in size and slender, white with broad pinkish-crimson streaks on outside of petals which are pointed, on tall rather narrow stem. *L.* narrow, almost grass-like. Known in cultivation since the Middle Ages and naturalised in several Mediterranean countries. Bulbs are small and should be planted in very warm, sunny position. 1–1¼ ft. Forms similar have been found in Afghanistan, Iran and Kashmir where it is probably native. Close to *T. stellata* of which it is sometimes considered as a variety or sub-sp. **892**, p. 112.

dasystemon see **T. tarda**

☆eichleri ✳ Spring　　　Bb
Fl. large up to 4 in. across with pointed petals, brilliant scarlet, the three outer petals having a prominent black blotch edged with yellow at the base on the inside. One of the glowing satin-like scarlet tulips from Turkestan and N. Iran. 1–1½ ft. One of the best garden plants among the sp. tulips often spreading and persisting in sunny areas. **893**, p. 112.

☆fosteriana ✳ Spring　　　Bb
Very large *fl.* of brilliant orange-scarlet with yellow base up to 10 in. across when open. One of the most striking of all tulips and with *fl.* as large or larger than most of the hybrids. Stem stout but often not strong enough to hold upright the immense *fl.* *L.* broad. 1–2 ft. Russian Turkestan.
It is apparently variable in colour and various forms and hybrids have been developed which make wonderful garden plants.
These include:

'Golden Eagle', deep yellow with red markings on outside, large *fl.* on tall stem;

'Mme Lefeber', often known as 'Red Emperor', orange-scarlet, one of the finest forms a few bulbs making a very strong mass of colour of almost pillar-box red, **894**, p. 112;

'Purissima', tall up to 2 ft, large creamy-white *fl.*, **895**, p. 112;

'Red Emperor', see 'Mme Lefeber' above.

✿**greigii** ✳ Spring   Bb
Fl. large, scarlet generally with black or yellow base. Distinct by its broad blue-grey *l.* which are heavily marked with deep purplish-maroon. This character has been inherited by many of its hybrid seedlings. 1–2 ft. Russian Turkestan. Forms are variable from yellow to scarlet, several yellow heavily marked with scarlet or crimson on outside. **896**, p. 112.
Among the best are:
'Margaret Herbst', see 'Royal Splendour' below;
'Oriental Splendour', large deep yellow *fl.* with broad splash of scarlet along centre of petal;
'Royal Splendour', sometimes listed as 'Margaret Herbst', large *fl.* of most vivid scarlet.

hageri see **T. whittallii**

humilis see **T. violacea**

✿**kaufmanniana** The Water Lily tulip ✳ Spring Bb
Usually one of earliest to *fl.* and parent of a most valuable race of many coloured hybrids ranging through scarlet-pink, yellow and white often with decorative eye at base. *Fl.* medium-large, usually with pointed petals and opening flat in sunlight. Basic form is probably creamy-white with large yellow centre and corresponding to form listed as 'The First'. Central Asia. **897**, p. 113.
Other good forms, many named after composers and musicians include:
'Alfred Cortot', bright scarlet, opening star-like to show black base, *l.* heavily streaked with purple brown;
'Cesar Franck', deep yellow with a band of orange-red on outer petals;
'Fritz Kreisler', pale pinkish-apricot, inside ivory-white flushed pink near tip of petals;
'Gluck', carmine-red with yellow edge;
'Johann Strauss', ivory-white with red streak on centre of outer petals, orange-yellow at base inside;
'Shakespeare', blended salmon apricot and pink, a very lovely *fl.*, **898**, p. 113;
'The First', see in notes for *T. kaufmanniana* above.

kolpakowskiana ✳ Spring   Bb
Fl. small-medium in size, yellow with dull pinkish-red streak on outside, deep yellow inside, long pointed petals on slender stem. A graceful plant. *L.* crinkled at edge and lying flat along ground. 1 ft. E. Turkestan. **899**, p. 113.

✿**linifolia** ✳ Spring   Bb
Fl. glowing scarlet with black base. One of the strongest colours among tulips. *Fl.* of medium size with long pointed petals of unequal length, starlike when open. 6 in.–1 ft. Russian Turkestan. The yellow counterpart of this is *T. batalinii* with creamy-yellow *fl.* *L.* slightly grey, rather narrow and edged with red. A lovely plant for the rock garden or alpine house. **900**, p. 113.

orphanidea see **T. whittallii**

praestans ✳ Mid Spring   Bb
Fl. medium to large in size, bright pillar-box scarlet with broad petals. Often two or more *fl.* to stem. Like a smaller flowered *T. fosteriana*. *L.* broad like a hybrid tulip. 1 ft. A good plant for the larger rock garden. **901**, p. 113.

princeps ✳ Mid Spring   Bb
Fl. large, rather broad, bright scarlet with creamy-buff flush to outside of three outer petals. *L.* broad, glaucous. Possibly a former hybrid from *T. fosteriana* but without quite such large *fl.* A good plant for bedding since the stem is strong. 1 ft. **902**, p. 113.

pulchella see **T. violacea**

stellata ✳ Spring   Bb
Fl. deep yellow or white flushed red on outside with dark eye. Variable both in colour and height of stem. 6 in.–1 ft. A graceful sp. for the rock garden with star-like *fl.* Afghanistan, Kashmir.
var. *chrysantha*, *fl.* deep golden yellow, broader than in type, flushed deep pink on outside. Syn. *T. chrysantha* of gardens, **903**, p. 113.

tarda, syn. **T. dasystemon** ✳ Mid Spring   Bb
A good dwarf sp. with bunches of creamy star-like *fl.* 1–2 in. across, inside heavily marked with deep orange in centre spreading outwards along petal. 6–8 in. A good plant for the rock garden and often forming large clumps. Russian Turkestan. **904**, p. 113.

turkestanica ✳ Early Spring   Bb
Small but very early flowering. Several *fl.* to a stem. *Fl.* creamy-white flushed on outside green, base inside yellow, petals rather narrow giving star-like appearance to open *fl.* Rock garden or alpine house. Russian Turkestan. **905**, p. 114.

violacea ✳ Early Spring   Bb
Very early flowering. *Fl.* rather globular, deep cerise-violet with dark base, a striking colour, often nestling on *l.* when opening but stem lengthens as *fl.* ages. Long lasting in *fl.* and valuable for rock garden or alpine house. 4–8 in. Often considered as a variety of *T. humilis* a very variable sp. from N.W. Iran, Kurdistan and N.E. Turkey. **906**, p. 114.
T. pulchella is very close and possibly just another variety of *T. humilis*. In colour these sp. all grade into one another. *T. violacea* has rather more blue in *fl.*, *T. pulchella* is deep pinkish-crimson and *T. humilis* infinitely variable.

whittallii ✳ Spring   Bb
Fl. tawny-orange, deeper inside, marked with green near base outside, a striking *fl.* 8–12 in. Sometimes considered a variety of *T. orphanidea* of Greece but slightly larger and more vigorous than this sp. and the closely allied *T. hageri*, also from Greece. It is said to be a tetraploid. Around Smyrna, W. Turkey. **907**, p. 114.

Hybrid Tulips   Bb
The order of the illustrations differs from the numerical order of the divisions for comparative purposes. Thus the Single Early tulips of Division 3 are followed by the Double Early tulips of Division 15. Like the daffodils the tulips have been divided into a convenient classification with classes for the different types and they are arranged here in this order which is now used in many catalogues. The Darwin, the Darwin Hybrids and the Lily-flowered tulips are still the main ones used for bedding and display in 4–5, the other divisions contain some good plants which will help to extend the season and give variety.

Div. 2. **Single Early Tulips** ✳ Mid Spring
These are much used for forcing and growing in bowls. Outside they usually *fl.* early to mid-4 and are not so tall or large in *fl.* as the later varieties.
Among the best are:
'Bellona', deep yellow with a globular *fl.*, good for forcing or growing in bowls;
'Brilliant Star Maximus', bright scarlet and very good for forcing, **908**, p. 114;
'Couleur Cardinal', deep velvety purplish crimson with a dusky bloom on outside, an old favourite;
'General de Wet', a large *fl.* of deep tawny-orange, slightly marked with orange-scarlet on outside;
'Keizerskroon', a very striking yellow and scarlet, looking well with dark wallflowers, **909**, p. 114;
'Prince of Austria', bright orange-scarlet with tawny orange bloom.

Div. 3. **Early Double Tulips** ✳ Mid Spring
These are popular for bowls and also for early displays since they are not very tall, about 1 ft usually and the stems are sufficiently strong to

support the large *fl.* They look well as a mixture, intermingled with low growing plants such as the very early-flowering pansies. **910**, p. 114.
Good named types are:
'Golden Ducat', deep yellow, excellent for forcing;
'Maréchal Niel', tawny orange-yellow also excellent for forcing;
'Murillo', pale pink;
'Peach Blossom', pink.

Div. 5. **Triumph Tulips** ✳ Late Spring
These usually *fl.* a little before the Darwin tulips and are not quite so large or tall. They are useful for beds which need to be cleared early for a summer display.
This is a large group and amongst the best are:
'Korneforos', bright cerise-red;
'Makassar', deep canary-yellow, a strong grower;
'Mary Housley', a yellow tulip heavily flushed with orange-scarlet, large *fl.*, **913**, p. 115;
'Pink Glow', deep pink;
'Ringo', pillar-box scarlet edged with deep yellow and yellow inside, large, rather square *fl.*, **914**, p. 115.

Div. 6. **Darwin Tulips** ✳ Late Spring
Still probably the most popular for display bedding and the largest group. Sometimes described as the 'King of Tulips' although the newer Darwin hybrids have even larger *fl.* Up to 2½ ft with large *fl.* on stout stems.
Some of the best in the various colour groups include:
White, cream and pale yellow:
'Anjou', pale lemon-yellow, early-flowering in its group;
'Glacier', a very fine white, opening pale cream, **924**, p. 116.
'Niphetos', pale creamy-yellow, lemon-yellow inside, **925**, p. 116;
'Sweet Harmony', pale yellow, edged with cream, very delicate colouring, a distinctive *fl.*, **926**, p. 116.
Deep yellow, orange:
'Golden Harvest', deep yellow, an old favourite;
'Golden Hind', deep golden yellow;
'Mamasa', deep golden yellow, a very fine variety, **927**, p. 116.
Pale to deep pink:
'Clara Butt', bright rosy pink, an old favourite, smaller *fl.* than some of the more modern varieties;
'Prunus', deep rose-pink;

'Queen of Bartigons', rich and clear salmon-pink, a great favourite for bedding, **928**, p. 116.

Scarlet and crimson:

'Eclipse', deep crimson-red with violet base, medium height;

'Nobel', geranium or crimson lake, a very bright colour, **929**, p. 117;

'Scarlet O'Hara', deep scarlet-red, one of the strongest tulips for colour, **930**, p. 117.

Mauve, lilac, purple and maroon:

'Ace of Spades', purplish-black, large *fl.*;

'Bishop', deep lavender-purple;

'La Tulipe Noire', deep maroon, appearing almost black, medium sized *fl.*, **931**, p. 117.

Div. 7. **Darwin hybrids** ✳ Spring

These are probably the most magnificent and largest in *fl.* of all tulips yet raised. They are derived from crosses between *T. fosteriana* and *T. greigii* and the Darwin tulips and seem to have inherited the best characteristics of both including the satin sheen of *T. fosteriana*. The *fl.* are 4–5 in. tall and as much across and stand on stout stems up to 2½ ft. Flowering late 4–early 5, slightly before the Darwins but often overlapping with them.

The following are good varieties:

✿'Apeldoorn', bright orange-scarlet with a slight mauvish bloom on outside on first opening, yellow and black at base, a very good tulip for a really striking display, **932**, p. 117;

'General Eisenhower', pillar-box scarlet with yellow base;

'Gudoshnik', cream and very pale apricot-pink splashed and flecked with pale orange-scarlet, a very large *fl.*, **933**, p. 117;

'Holland's Glory', bright orange-red with long pointed petals, early-flowering;

'Jewel of Spring', pale yellow outside with narrow red edge, deeper yellow inside, very large, **934**, p. 117;

'Oxford', bright orange fiery-red, a rather rounded *fl.*, yellow base, one of the brightest in colour, **935**, p. 117;

'Red Matador', intense scarlet, resembling *T. fosteriana* but with black base, large *fl.* with a stout stem.

Div. 9. **Lily-flowered Tulips** ✳ Late Spring

These are my favourites for the long graceful pointed petals opening wide into large *fl.* They are tending to be almost as widely planted as the Darwins and look well either planted solid and unmixed or more-widely spaced in a mass of forget-me-nots.

There is now a large selection from which to choose, among which the following are all good:

'Aladdin', deep crimson-red with a narrow rim of pale yellow;

'Capt. Fryatt', crimson-purple, a very rich colour;

'Dyanito', deep crimson-red with a yellow base inside, **915**, p. 115;

✿'Mariette', deep China pink, very large *fl.* and very long lasting, deservedly one of the most popular tulips for bedding, a vigorous grower, **916**, p. 115;

✿'Queen of Sheba', orange-red with yellow-orange edge and tawny orange inside, one of the largest *fl.* in this section, very striking, **917**, p. 115;

'White Triumphator', a very good and pure white, tall.

Div. 10. **Cottage Tulip** ✳ Late Spring

Late-flowering single with rather long egg-shaped *fl.* Close to the Darwins with which they can be mixed satisfactorily.

Among them are some of the most popular varieties for bedding including:

'Belle Jaune', deep yellow;

'Blushing Bride', pale creamy-yellow with petals edged with red and slightly flecked with red, inside pale yellow, **918**, p. 115;

'Dillenburg', deep salmon-orange, heavily flushed with orange-scarlet, one of the old favourites, **919**, p. 115;

'Grenadier', bright orange-scarlet;

'Marshal Haig', scarlet-red, very reliable and a

strong colour for tulip bedding, **920**, p. 115;

'Mirella', deep rose with raspberry red shading and a dark base, an unusual combination of colour;

'Mrs John Scheepers', deep yellow, a large *fl.* and an old favourite, **921**, p. 116;

'Palaestrina', deep salmon and rose blending, a large and striking *fl.*;

✿'Rosy Wings', clear pink with a white base, a very beautiful *fl.*

Viridiflora Tulips ✳ Late Spring

These are close to the Cottage tulips but the petals are flushed with bright emerald green. They *fl.* in mid-5 at the same time but are not generally such vigorous growers. Their unusual colouring makes them favourites of the *fl.* arrangers.

'Artist', deep rose-pink with green stripe down centre of petal and slightly undulating edge to the *fl.*, cream centre and green flush outside, **922**, p. 116;

'Greenland', pale pink and green, flushed with cream, a most delicate combination of colours, **923**, p. 116;

'Viridiflora praecox', yellow and green, petals slightly frilled and wavy at edges, early-flowering.

Divs. 11, 12 *and* 13. **Bijbloemen, Bizarre and Rembrandt Tulips** ✳ Late Spring

These are the old tulips of the Dutch flower painters, many streaked with strong colours. They are usually not so vigorous as the Darwins or Darwin hybrids but are worth growing for their striking combinations of colour. They are often described as broken tulips, a phrase often associated with virus disease in tulips, but if they have it, they have lived with it for several hundred years. It is advisable, however, to keep them away from the larger hybrids both for this reason and also on grounds of style.

'Cordell Hull', rose-red on white, Rembrandt, Division 11, **936**, p. 117;

'Absalon', deep yellow heavily marked with dull crimson, Bizarre, Division 12, **937**, p. 118;

'May Blossom', creamy-white with deep purplish maroon markings, Bijbloemen, Division 13, **938**, p. 118.

Div. 14. **Parrot Tulips** ✳ Late Spring

Very large *fl.* distinguished by the fringed and crested petals and twisted shapes. In some a little weak stemmed for the size of *fl.* but most effective in *fl.* arrangements and quite distinct.

'Black Parrot', deep maroon, almost black with heavily fringed petals;

'Blue Parrot', deep lavender mauve with heavily fringed edge;

'Fantasy', deep salmon-pink with white or green crests to the petals, heavily fringed and with wavy edges, **939**, p. 118;

'Orange Parrot', mahogany and gold, very large *fl.*, scented, **940**, p. 118.

Div. 15. **Late Double, Paeony-flowered Tulips** ✳ Spring

These are the later types, usually larger and heavier flowered than the double early to which they make a useful succession. Owing to the weight of the *fl.* and longer stems they are more susceptible to wind damage breaking the stem but look very fine in a sheltered position. Among the best are:

'Brilliant Fire', cherry-red flushed with orange, inside bright scarlet;

'Eros', deep pink, an effective *fl.* though with a little blue in the pink, **911**, p. 114;

'Mt Tacoma', a beautiful double white, like a small double paeony, **912**, p. 114.

TUPELO see **Nyssa sylvatica**, **1712**, p. 214.

TURBAN RANUNCULUS see **Ranunculus asiaticus**, **874**, p. 110.

TURKEY OAK see **Quercus cerris**

TURTLEHEAD see **Chelone**, **1024**, p. 128.

TWINSPUR see **Diascia barberae**, **287**, p. 36.

U

ULEX (LEGUMINOSAE) Gorse

europaeus Common Gorse, Furze or Whin ✳ mainly spring   Sh.

Evergreen spiny shrub up to 6 ft with small *l.* *Fl.* yellow. W. Europe.

The only form worth growing in gardens is:

'Plenus', *fl.* double, deep yellow and more compact than type, this sets no seed and must be propagated by cuttings which strike freely in late summer. Plant in dry sandy position, excellent for covering hot banks in full sun, unsuitable for shady positions or places in very rich soil where it does not *fl.* freely, **1931**, p. 242.

ULMUS (ULMACEAE) Elm

campestris see **U. procera**

carpinifolia, syn. **U. nitens** Smooth-leaved Elm T. Tall tree distinguished by small glossy *l.* usually rather pyramidal in habit.

Best form is:

var. *sarniensis*, syn. *U. wheatleyi*, The Wheatley elm, sometimes also called Jersey elm or Guernsey elm, narrow pyramidal tree and one of the finest for roadside planting, *l.* up to 4 in. long, ovate, downy and toothed, colouring bright yellow in autumn. Often found in lists under *U. stricta*.

'Aurea', Dickson's Golden Elm, form of *U. carpinifolia* var. *sarniensis*, slow growing but *l.* with strong yellow-gold, **1932**, p. 242.

glabra Wych Elm   T.

Also valuable and handsome for its winged yellow seed heads in spring.

'Pendula', Weeping Wych elm which forms small flat-topped tree with long pendulous branches and is suitable for wall specimen.

nitens see **U. carpinifolia**

procera, syn. **U. campestris** English Elm   T. Tall tree up to 100 ft with lovely clear yellow autumn foliage. Unfortunately this is very sensitive to

---

Abbreviations and Symbols used in the text. The following abbreviations may sometimes be used in conjunction as HA. indicating Hardy annual or GBb indicating Greenhouse bulb.

A. = Annual	P. = Perennial
Aq. = Aquatic	R. = Rock or
B. = Biennial	Alpine plant
Bb = Bulb	Sh. = Shrub
C. = Corm	Sp., sp. = Species
Cl. = Climber	Syn. = Synonym
Co. = Conifer	T. = Tree
Fl., fl. = Flower(s)	Tu. = Tuber
G. = Greenhouse or	var. = variety
house plant	× = Hybrid or
H. = Hardy	hybrid parents
HH. = Half-hardy	✳ = Flowering time
L., l. = Leaf, leaves	❧ = Foliage plant
Mt(s) = Mount,	
mountain(s)	

The following have been used also in the descriptions of Alpines, Bulbs, Trees and Shrubs.

    * = slightly tender

    † = lime hater

    ✿ = highly recommended

The illustration numbers are in **bold type** and the page numbers in light type preceded by p.

Dutch Elm disease and so planting is now largely being replaced with *U. carpinifolia sarniensis* which is more resistant.

stricta see **U. carpinifolia** var. **sarniensis**

UMBRELLA PINE see **Sciadopitys verticillata**, **2037**, p. 255.

UMBRELLA PLANT see **Peltiphyllum peltatum**, **1303**, p. 163.

UNICORN PLANT see **Martynia louisiana**, **338**, p. 43.

URN PLANT see **Aechmaea fasciata**

URSINIA (COMPOSITAE)

anethoides ✳ Summer   HHA.
Fl. bright orange-yellow, daisy-like, with central zone of deep purple, 2 to 3 in. across. L. feathery, about 1–1½ in. long. 1–2 ft. Sow under glass in 3 and plant out in 5, or sow in a sunny, well-drained border in the open in 5. S. Africa. **389**, p. 49.
'New hybrids', various shades of orange, 1 ft.

pulchra see **U. versicolor**

versicolor, syn. **U. pulchra** ✳ Summer   HHA.
Fl. orange with dark centre. L. slender, much divided. 9 in. Similar treatment as for *U. anethoides*. S. Africa.
'Golden Bedder', light orange with deeper orange centre, **390**, p. 49.

V

VACCINIUM (ERICACEAE)   †

arctostaphylos Caucasian Whortleberry ✳ Early Summer   Sh.
Deciduous shrub up to 9 ft but usually much less in cultivation. Fl. white, waxy, bell-shaped like Lily of the Valley with small second flowering in 9. Fruit egg-shaped berry, black in 9. L. narrow, elliptic, good autumn colour.

corymbosum Swamp or High-Bush Blueberry ✳ Early Summer   Sh.
Deciduous shrub up to 6 ft. Fl. white, tinted pink or pinkish, flask-shaped up to ½ in. long, borne in short racemes. Fruit edible, blue-black with blue bloom, up to 3 in. across. L. ovate or oval or elliptic with pointed tips up to 3 in. long, turning brilliant scarlet in autumn. A number of varieties have been developed with large fruit and make excellent dessert. E. USA. **1933**, p. 242.

cylindraceum   Sh.
Deciduous shrub up to 6 ft. Fl. tubular or bell-shaped up to ½ in. long, red in bud, opening pale yellow-green tinted red. L. elliptic and turning brilliant scarlet in autumn. Fruit blue-black berries, cylindrical. Still rather uncommon in cultivation but valuable for brilliant autumn colouring. Azores. **1934**, p. 242.

glauco-album ✳ Late Spring–Early Summer *Sh.
Evergreen shrub up to 4 ft but usually less, slightly tender. Fl. in short racemes, white tinted pink, up to ¼ in. Fruit dark blue or black with glaucous bloom and globose berry. One of the finest sp. for its berries, in acid damp soil but not suitable for cold areas. Sikkim, Himalayas. **1935**, p. 242.

myrsinites Evergreen Blueberry ✳ Spring   Sh.
Small evergreen shrub with oval l. tapered at base and tip. Fl. in terminal axillary clusters, white or pinkish. Fruit blue-black, small. S.E. USA. **1936**, p. 242.

myrtillus Billberry, Whortleberry ✳ Late Spring   Sh.
Common deciduous shrub semi-prostrate up to 1½ ft with winged stems. Fl. solitary, pale pink with

cup-shaped corolla. Fruit blue-black with grey bloom, round berry which makes excellent tarts. Common British native but makes good ground cover in acid shady or open positions.

nummularia ✳ Spring   Sh.
Evergreen dwarf shrub up to 1½ ft, young shoots clothed with brown bristles. L. ovate or oval leathery, rugose and shiny up to 1 in. long and ½ in. wide. Fl. in small axillary racemes pink, Fruit black, edible. Very attractive dwarf plant for its shiny l. hardy in most areas but unsuitable for very cold ones. Himalayas.

vitis-idaea Cowberry, Mountain Cranberry ✳ Summer   Sh.
Low creeping evergreen shrub usually not more than 6 in. in height. Fl. white or pale pink. Fruit small red berry, edible, making good tarts. Forms good ground cover in acid situations in open or semi-shade. British native and widely distributed in N. Europe, N. Asia, N.E. America. **1937**, p. 243.

VALERIAN see **Kentranthus**, **313**, p. 40; **1222**, p. 153.

VALLOTA (AMARYLLIDACEAE)

speciosa The Scarborough Lily ✳ Autumn   *Bb
Fl. glowing scarlet-red, opening wide and up to 3 in. across, in groups on stem up to 2 ft. L. strap-shaped. Bulb large. Usually grown as a pot plant in a cool greenhouse and should be left undisturbed. It does not require the absolute resting period without water of many other S. African bulbs. **941**, p. 118.

VENETIAN SUMACH see **Cotinus coggygria**, **1535**, **1536**, p. 192.

VENIDIUM (COMPOSITAE)

fastuosum Monarch of the Veldt, Namaqualand Daisy ✳ Summer   HHA.
Fl. large, rich orange with purple-black zone and prominent black centre. L. deeply cut, up to 6 in. long, grey-white hairs on both sides. 2–3 ft. Sow in a cool greenhouse in 4 and plant out in late 5–6, or sow in the open in 5 in dryish soil and a sunny position. S. Africa. **391**, p. 49.

VENUS'S LOOKING GLASS see **Specularia speculum**, **377**, p. 48.

VERBASCUM (SCROPHULARIACEAE) Mullein

chaixii, syn. **V. vernale** ✳ Summer   P.
Fl. yellow, in large branching panicles. L. wedge-shaped, with white or green hairs. 3 ft. Plant 11–3 in a sunny position and well-drained soil, chalky for preference. Not long-lived. Propagate by seed, or by root cuttings taken in the spring. S. and Central Europe. **1407**, p. 176.

dumulosum ✳ Summer   RP.
Dwarf bush, 6–10 in., semi-prostrate and spreading. Fl. bright yellow, mullein-like with reddish "bee" in centre, up to 1 in. across, on short spikes. L. silvery-grey, rather woolly on young l. and stems. Slightly tender, plant in as warm and sunny a position as possible and protect with a cloche against winter wet. Excellent as alpine house plant. Propagate from short cuttings in summer or root cuttings. Asia Minor. Close is *V. pestalozzae*, also from Asia Minor. **217**, p. 28.

hybridum ✳ Summer   P.
Cultivate as for *V. chaixii*. Of garden origin.
'Cotswold Queen', apricot-buff, 3–4 ft, **1408**, p. 176;
'Gainsborough', canary yellow, 3½–4 ft, **1409**, p. 177;
'Pink Domino', rose-pink, with dark centre, 4 ft, **1410**, p. 177.

spinosum ✳ Summer   *RP.
A dense, twiggy and rather spinous dwarf bush, 6–8 in. Fl. pale lemon-yellow, ½ in. across, smaller than preceding sp. L. few, grey-green, lobed but mostly replaced by grey-green branchlets, Usually treated as an alpine house plant, but may be grown outside in warm sunny position and protected by cloche in winter. Crete. **218**, p. 28.
'Letitia', is a fine hybrid of this, raised at Wisley.

vernale see **V. chaixii**

VERBENA (VERBENACEAE)

chamaedrifolia see **V. peruviana**

hybrida ✳ Midsummer–Autumn   HHA.
Fl. scarlet, crimson, royal blue, white. L. lance-shaped, of thick texture, conspicuously veined. Tender perennial usually grown as a half-hardy annual. 6–12 in. Sow in a warm greenhouse in 2–3 and plant out in a sunny position and in well-drained soil in late 5–6. Of garden origin.
'Blaze', dwarf, brilliant scarlet, 9 in.;
'Mammoth Royal Bouquet', is a colourful mixed strain with white auricula-eye, 1 ft, **392**, p. 49;
'Rainbow mixed', compact and very early flowering, 9 in.;
'Sparkle mixed', dwarf spreading habit, bright colours, 6 in.

Italian see **V. tenera**

peruviana, syn. **V. chamaedrifolia** ✳ Summer–Mid Autumn   HHP.
Fl. bright scarlet in dense clusters. 4–6 in., semi-prostrate. L. oblong, greyish-green. For well-drained soil and a sheltered sunny corner. Not reliably hardy and best raised from cuttings each year taken in 8–9 of the current year's growth and inserted in sandy soil. Over-winter in a frost-free greenhouse and plant out in 5–6. S. America. **1411**, p. 177.

rigida, syn. **V. venosa** ✳ Summer   P.
Fl. violet-purple borne on erect, rigid stems. 1½–2 ft. L. oblong, rigid and toothed. Roots tuberous. Effective when planted in bold groups in a sunny border in well-drained garden soil. In exposed gardens the tubers should be lifted and stored in the same manner as dahlias. Propagate in spring by removing young shoots with s small piece of tuber attached. This is best done from tubers in boxes in a warm house. Argentine. **1412**, p. 177.

Abbreviations and Symbols used in the text.
The following abbreviations may sometimes be used in conjunction as HA. indicating Hardy annual or GBb indicating Greenhouse bulb.

A. = Annual	P. = Perennial
Aq. = Aquatic	R. = Rock or
B. = Biennial	Alpine plant
Bb = Bulb	Sh. = Shrub
C. = Corm	Sp., sp. = Species
Cl. = Climber	Syn. = Synonym
Co. = Conifer	T. = Tree
Fl., fl. = Flower(s)	Tu. = Tuber
G. = Greenhouse or	var. = variety
house plant	× = Hybrid or
H. = Hardy	hybrid parents
HH. = Half-hardy	✳ = Flowering time
L., l. = Leaf, leaves	❧ = Foliage plant
Mt(s) = Mount,	
mountain(s)	

The following have been used also in the descriptions of Alpines, Bulbs, Trees and Shrubs.

* = slightly tender
† = lime hater
✿ = highly recommended

The illustration numbers are in **bold type** and the page numbers in light type preceded by p.

tenera Italian Verbena ✳ Summer   P.
Fl. blue or violet. *L.* much dissected, trailing. Plant 3–4 in a sunny position and well-drained soil. Propagate by cuttings taken in the spring. Brazil, Argentine.
    'Mahonettii', deep lilac with white stripes 4–6 in., **1413**, p. 177.

venosa see **V. rigida**

VERONICA (scrophulariaceae) Speedwell

exaltata ✳ Late Summer   P.
Fl. lavender-mauve in slender spikes. 4–5 ft. *L.* narrowly lance-shaped, toothed. Plant 11–3 in ordinary soil, not too dry, in sun or light shade. Propagate by division. Origin uncertain. **1414**, p. 177.

gentianoides ✳ Early Summer   P.
Fl. light blue in slender racemes. 1–1½ ft. *L.* glossy green, lower forming a rosette. Good garden soil in sun or partial shade. Propagate by division in early autumn or spring. Caucasus. **1415**, p. 177.

incana ✳ Summer   P.
Fl. dark blue. 1 ft. *L.* lance-shaped, silvery-grey. Plant 11–3 in a sunny position. Russia. **1416**, p. 177.
'Rosea' is a pink form.

longifolia ✳ Summer   P.
Fl. lilac-blue in dense spikes. 2–3 ft. *L.* opposite, or in whorls of three, slender pointed. Plant 11–3 in sun, but not too dry soil. Central Europe, N. Asia.
    'Blue Giant', lavender-blue, **1417**, p. 178.

prostrata, syn. **V. rupestris** ✳ Early Summer RP.
Forms a large mat, widespreading with small *l.* and erect *fl.* stems. *Fl.* very bright blue in dense racemes, frequently covering whole plant and forming conspicuous blue mass, 6–8 in. Sunny position but too invasive for a very choice place or small rock garden. Good in front of border. Widespread. Europe, N. Asia. **219**, p. 28.
    'Spode Blue', form with paler China blue *fl.*

rupestris see **V. prostrata**

spicata ✳ Summer   P.
Fl. bright blue in dense spikes. 1–2 ft. *L.* opposite, toothed, narrow, up to 1½ in. long. Ordinary garden soil and a sunny position. Europe, including Britain.
Good varieties include:
    'Pavane', deep pink, 1½ ft;
    'Saraband', deep lavender blue, 1½–2 ft.

teucrium ✳ Summer   P.
Fl. lavender-blue in slender spikes. 1–2 ft. *L.* narrow, dark green on slender stems. Plant 11–3 in sun or light shade. Central Europe.
Good varieties include:
    'Blue Fountain', rich blue, 2 ft, **1418**, p. 178;
    'Crater Lake Blue', vivid ultramarine, 12–15 in., **1419**, p. 178;
    'Trehane', light blue with golden-green *l.*, 9 in.

VERONICA, SHRUBBY see Hebe

VIBURNUM (caprifoliaceae)

Deciduous or evergreen shrubs, often large. *Fl.* usually white and in some cases very strongly scented, in flat heads or rounded corymbs. Berries often decorative. All grow well on chalky soils.

✿**betulifolium** ✳ Early Summer   Sh.
Large deciduous shrub up to 12 ft. *Fl.* small white in large clusters. *L.* up to 4 in. long, ovate, coarsely toothed. Fruit small red berries, very shiny, borne in enormous clusters often weighing down the branches. Needs to be planted in groups of at least three, preferably derived from different clones. China. **1938**, p. 243.

× **bodnantense** ✳ Winter–Early Spring   Sh.
Deciduous winter flowering shrub up to 8 ft. *Fl.* in clusters, tubular with spreading lobes white tinged pink in bud, very fragrant, flowering over long season in mild spells of winter. *L.* lanceolate up to 4 in. long. One of the most valuable winter-flowering shrubs which we have. A hybrid between *V. fragrans* and *V. grandiflorum*.
    ✿'Dawn', is the best form of this hybrid, and was the original seedling, **1939**, p. 243;
    'Deben', has pure white clusters of *fl.* with no pink in bud.

× **burkwoodii** see under **V. × juddii**

× **carlcephalum** ✳ Mid Spring   Sh.
More vigorous but with less grace and larger dense *fl.* head with little red colouring than *V. carlesii*. A hybrid between *V. carlesii* × *V. macrocephalum*.

carlesii ✳ Spring   Sh.
Deciduous bushy shrub up to 6 ft but usually less with downy young shoots. *Fl.* in thick clusters up to 3 in. across white but deep pink in bud, very fragrant. *L.* broadly ovate irregularly toothed and pointed, dull green downy beneath. Not usually a very vigorous grower but valuable for its fine heads of very strongly scented *fl.* Korea. **1940**, p. 243.

✿**davidii** ✳ Early Summer   Sh.
Evergreen shrub up to 5 ft usually less but spreading widely. *Fl.* white in flat corymbs. *L.* oval to obovate up to 5 in. long, conspicuously veined and slightly rugulose. Fruit small, dark blue, shining berries. Unisexual, so both male and female plants are needed if berries are desired. Grown mainly as decorative evergreen shrub and one of the finest sp. for foliage effect. China. **1941**, p. 243.

farreri see **V. fragrans**

fragrans ✳ Winter–Mid Spring   Sh.
Thick deciduous shrub up to 10 ft, growing freely from the base and self layering. One of our most valuable winter flowering plants. *Fl.* on small clusters up to 2 in. wide, white tinged pink in bud. Fruit small scarlet. *L.* up to 2½ in. wide and 4 in. long, toothed. Owing to nomenclatural difficulty, in some books this shrub has been re-named *V. farreri* but is usually known in horticultural literature and in gardens as *V. fragrans*. N. China. **1942**, p. 243.

grandiflorum ✳ Mid Winter–Early Spring   *Sh.
Close to *V. fragrans*. Deciduous shrub. *Fl.* deep pink or white flushed rose in clusters up to 3 in. across, tubular and larger than those of *V. fragrans*. Slightly tender in cold areas. Himalayas.

hupehense × Early Summer   Sh.
Deciduous large shrub up to 8 ft. *Fl.* white in clusters 2 in. across. *L.* rounded, ovate up to 3 in. coarsely toothed and downy. Fruit small berries but borne in large masses, scarlet, shiny, clusters are pendulous. Several specimens should if possible be planted together to ensure good fruiting. China. **1943**, p. 243.

× **juddii** ✳ Spring   Sh.
Deciduous spreading shrub up to 6 ft, close to *V. carlesii* but rather more vigorous in growth. *Fl.* in clusters up to 3½ in., white tinged pink in bud. *L.* broad, ovate, downy beneath. Valuable hybrid where *V. carlesii* does not do well. A hybrid between *V. bitchiuense* × *V. carlesii*. **1944**, p. 243.
    Close also but even more vigorous is *V. × burkwoodii* a hybrid between *V. carlesii* and *V. utile*. Large shrub up to 8 ft wide-spreading, semi-evergreen. *Fl.* ½ in. wide, white with pink buds in large clusters, 3–5, fragrant. Vigorous grower and one of the best early spring flowering shrubs.

opulus Guelder Rose, Rose or Water Elder ✳ Early Summer   Sh.
Large deciduous shrub up to 15 ft. *Fl.* in flat or slightly globose heads up to 3 in. across. *L.* deeply toothed and lobed up to 4 in. long and as much wide. Fruit, berry bright red, translucent and shiny globose, in pendulous clusters. Autumn colouring *l.* scarlet to pinkish-red. One of the most valuable shrubs for *fl.*, fruit and autumn colour. N. Europe, widespread including Britain, N. Africa. **1945**, p. 244.
    ✿'Sterile', Snowball Tree, *fl.* in large rounded clusters up to 3 in. across. All *fl.* of the 'Sterile' with white petals, **1946**, p. 244;
    'Xanthocarpum', fruit yellow translucent, best form is 'Notcutt's' var.

rhytidophyllum ✳ Late Spring   Sh.
Large evergreen shrub up to 10 ft sometimes more, forming wide-spreading bush. *Fl.* whitish in large flat clusters up to 8 in. across. *L.* large up to 8 in. long, elliptic, rugulose and deeply veined above, dark green, grey felted beneath. Fruit small oval red berries later ripening black. Grows well in semi-shade or in open and valuable for decorative wrinkled pattern of foliage. China. **1947**, p. 244.

tinus Laurustinus ✳ Winter–Mid Spring   Sh.
Widely grown evergreen shrub up to 10 ft. *Fl.* white with pink tinge on bud in clusters up to 4 in. across. *L.* narrowly ovate up to 4 in. long, shining green above. Fruit deep blue small berries becoming black as they age.
    'St Ewe', a selected form, **1948**, p. 244.

tomentosum ✳ Early Summer   Sh.
Deciduous shrub up to 10 ft high usually less. Branches tend to be horizontal. *Fl.* white in flat clusters up to 4 in. across, at edge of clusters is ring of outer sterile *fl.* up to 1½ in. across with large white petals, centre *fl.* composed of fertile brownish-green *fl. L.* ovate or oval up to 4 in. long sharply toothed. One of the most valuable flowering shrubs, in 6, particularly for its horizontal branching. All specimens of *V. tomentosum* have crimson foliage in autumn. Should be planted in open position and give valuable architectural form to garden. China, Japan.
Among best forms are:
    'Lanarth', stronger in growth than type with large *l.*;
    ✿'Mariesii', very fine, horizontal-growing plant with branches in tiers and abundance of *fl.*, **1949**, p. 244;
    'Rowallane', close to 'Mariesii', one of the finest forms, **1950**, p. 244;
    'Plicatum', see 'Sterile';
    'Sterile', Japanese Snowball Bush, *fl.* heads rounded, all florets sterile with petals, more decorative in *fl.* also known as 'Plicatum'.

VINCA (apocynaceae) Periwinkle

difformis ✳ Winter   P.
Slightly more tender than *V. minor*, dying back in winter except in milder areas. *Fl.* 1½ in. across, pale

lilac-blue. Distinguished by absence of hairs on stem and valuable for its winter flowering habit. S.W. Europe.

major Larger Periwinkle ✳ Late Spring–Early Autumn   Sh.
Evergreen trailing sub-shrubby plant. Flowerless stems spread freely amd make excellent ground cover, rooting at tips from which plant is easily propagated. Erect shoots bear the *fl.*, 1–2 ft high. *Fl.* blue-purple solitary in leaf axils up to 2 in. long, corolla funnel-shaped with broad spreading lobes, white in centre. *L.* opposite, ovate, up to 3 in. long. *Fl.* over long season. Makes one of the best ground cover plants for semi-shady or open positions. Central and S. Europe and occasionally found wild in parts of England. **1951**, p. 244.

minor Lesser Periwinkle ✳ Mid Spring–Early Autumn   P.
Close to *V. major*, more dwarf and with smaller *fl.* over a long period.
   'Variegata', a form with white and green *l.*, blue *fl.*, **1420**, p. 178.

VINE see **Vitis**, **1995-1997**, p. 250.

VINE, GRAPE see **Vitis vinifera**, **1997**, p. 250.

VINE, KANGAROO see **Cissus antarctica**, **469**, p. 59.

VIOLA (VIOLACEAE)

cornuta ✳ Late Spring–Summer   P.
Fl. violet, about 1½ in. long. *L.* broadly oval, somewhat hairy beneath. 4 in. Decorative rock garden plant for a well-drained soil and sunny position. Propagate by cuttings taken in 8 of non-flowering young shoots, and insert in sandy soil in a cold frame. Cut back after flowering. Division is possible in 4. Pyrenees. **1421**, p. 178.
There are many beautiful hybrids and true sp. may be rare in cultivation:
   'Ardross Gem', dusky gold and blue, 4–6 in., **1422**, p. 178;
   'Northfield Gem', purple-violet, free-flowering, 4–6 in., **1423**, p. 178.

gracilis ✳ Summer   RP.
Fl. deep violet or purple with short spur, about 1–1½ in. across, centres yellow, 4–6 in. Variable in cultivation, many forms grown being of hybrid origin. *L.* variable between basal and stem *l.*, shallowly toothed, basal *l.* ovate, ½ in. wide. Forms large clump or a spreading mat. Sunny position. Asia Minor, Balkans.
   'Major', deep violet-purple, large *fl.* with yellow eye, **220**, p. 28.

hybrida Viola ✳ Late Spring–Early Autumn B. or P.
Fl. blue, purple, yellow and white. *L.* oval. Perennial but usually treated as biennial. 6 in. Sow the seed in a cold frame in 6–7, plant out in rows when large enough to handle. Plant where they are to *fl.* in early autumn or early spring. Of garden origin. Mixed strains include:
   'Bambini mixed', miniature *fl.*, bright colours, variously marked;
   'Clear Crystals', is an early-flowering strain of mixed colours without blotches on the petals, **393**, p. 50;
   'Large Flowered mixed', selfs, picotees and fancy shades without blotches.
Good varieties include:
   'Arkwright Ruby', ruby crimson, deeper in centre of *fl.*;
   'Avalanche', pure white;
   'Campanula Blue', large *fl.*, violet blue, well-rounded petals;
   'Chantreyland', apricot, **394**, p. 50;
   'Yellow Bedder', golden-yellow.

saxatilis ✳ Summer   P.
Fl. usually yellow. *L.* nearly oval, hairy. 4–8 in.

leafy stems sometimes prostrate before rising. Cultivate as for *V. hybrida*. Asia Minor, E. Europe. 'Aetolica', with yellow *fl.* is also suitable for the rock garden, **1424**, p. 178.

tricolor (1) Heartsease, Wild Pansy ✳ Summer   RB. or RP.
Fl. 4–6 in., extremely variable in colour, often bicolor as in form shown and with central radiating lines, up to 1 in. across, spur short. *L.* also variable, usually lobed. Stems spreading, prostrate to form large mat. Wide-spread. Usually rather short-lived in gardens but easily propagated from cuttings or seed. Best in sunny position. Europe including Britain, N. Asia. **221**, p. 28.

tricolor (2) Pansy ✳ Late Spring–Summer HB/P.
Fl. red, apricot, deep yellow, blue, velvety-black, white. *L.* bluntly oval. 6 in. Treat as for *V. hybrida*. Europe including Britain.
Numerous large-flowered strains include:
   'Engelmann's Giant', large flowered mixture with small blotches and markings;
   'King Size', dwarf habit, very large heavily blotched *fl.* in rich colours;
   'Majestic Giants mixed', F¹ hybrids, huge blooms to 4 in. across, various colours and markings;
Roggli, a fine strain of Swiss origin, **395**, p. 50;
   'Swiss Giants', large *fl.* with dark velvety blotches in good colour range;
   'Winter Flowering', early flowering, medium sized *fl.* in various colours.
Named varieties include:
   'Alpine Glow', crimson with a black blotch;
   'Coronation Gold', very fine, golden-orange;
   'King of the Blacks', coal black;
   'Ullswater', deep blue, black centre, **396**, p. 50.

VIOLET, AFRICAN see **Saintpaulia**, **637-640**, p. 80.

VIPER'S BUGLOSS see **Echium**, **292, 293**, p. 37.

VIRGINIA CREEPER see **Parthenocissus**, **1985**, p. 249.

VIRGINIAN STOCK see **Malcolmia maritima**, **336**, p. 42.

VISCARIA see **Lychnis**

VITIS (VITACEAE) Vine

coignetiae ☙   Cl.
Very vigorous climber suitable for growing over old trees or hedges, making shoots up to 60 ft. Grown for its autumn colouring of large *l. L.* up to 10 in. long by 8 in. wide, roundish ovate shallowly lobed, downy beneath, brilliant in autumn for its crimson and scarlet colours. Fruit small black berries with purple bloom up to ½ in. across. Probably the finest vine for autumn colouring of foliage but only suitable for places where it can be allowed to ramp. Japan. **1995, 1996**, p. 250.

inconstans see **Parthenocissus tricuspidata**

vinifera Grape Vine ☙   Cl.
Climber up to 50 ft but usually less when hard pruned. Most ornamental form for garden is:
   'Brandt', *l.* deep crimson with purplish sheen over long period, becoming more scarlet in autumn, deeply lobed up to 5 in. across. Fruit purplish black and quite edible, **1997**, p. 250.

W

WAHLENBERGIA see **Edraianthus**

WAKE ROBIN see **Trillium grandiflorum**, **888**, p. 111.

WALDSTEINIA (ROSACEAE)

ternata ✳ Spring   RP.
Fl. yellow, ½ in. across, opening flat with overlapping petals, in short racemes, 3–4 in. *L.* deeply lobed, trifoliate, on rather long stalks. A neat and distinctive little plant for cool position in rock garden, although rather rarely seen. E. Europe to Japan. **222**, p. 28.

WALLFLOWER see **Cheiranthus**, **34**, p. 5; **261, 262**, p. 33; **1021-1023**, p. 128.

WATER ELDER see **Viburnum opulus**, **1945, 1946**, p. 244.

WATER FIR see **Metasequoia**, **2025**, p. 254.

WATER LILY see **Nymphaea**, **1279-1286**, pp. 160, 161.

WATER LILY TULIP see **Tulipa kaufmanniana**, **897, 898**, p. 113.

WATSONIA (AMARYLLIDACEAE)

beatricis ✳ Late Summer   *C.
Variable in colour with deep apricot, orange-red or deep pink *fl.* funnel-shaped opening flat at end of long tube, usually growing in ranks on two sides of stem only. *L.* like those of a gladiolus. Valuable for its summer flowering and requiring good supplies of water while growing. Tender except in warm and sheltered areas but lovely in gardens in W. and S.W. of England. S. Africa. **942**, p. 118.

WATTAKAKA (ASCLEPIADACEAE)

sinensis, syn. **Dregea sinensis** ✳ Summer   Cl.
Deciduous climber up to 10 ft. *Fl.* creamy-white in large clusters up to 3 in. across and ½ in. wide with five lobes, white with red dots round base. *L.* broadly ovate up to 4 in. long, velvety and rather downy beneath, slightly leathery and distinctive. Valuable climber with waxy *fl.* rather like those of a Hoya and only suitable for mild districts, otherwise needs cold greenhouse treatment. China **1998**, p. 250.

Abbreviations and Symbols used in the text.
The following abbreviations may sometimes be used in conjunction as HA. indicating Hardy annual or GBb indicating Greenhouse bulb.

A. = Annual	P. = Perennial
Aq. = Aquatic	R. = Rock or
B. = Biennial	Alpine plant
Bb = Bulb	Sh. = Shrub
C. = Corm	Sp., sp. = Species
Cl. = Climber	Syn. = Synonym
Co. = Conifer	T. = Tree
Fl., fl. = Flower(s)	Tu. = Tuber
G. = Greenhouse or	var. = variety
house plant	× = Hybrid or
H. = Hardy	hybrid parents
HH. = Half-hardy	✳ = Flowering time
L., l. = Leaf, leaves	☙ = Foliage plant
Mt(s) = Mount,	
mountain(s)	

The following have been used also in the descriptions of Alpines, Bulbs, Trees and Shrubs.

   * = slightly tender
   † = lime hater
   ✿ = highly recommended

The illustration numbers are in **bold type** and the page numbers in light type preceded by p.

WAXEN WOAD see **Genista tinctoria**, **1624**, p. 203.

WEEPING ASH see **Fraxinus excelsior** 'Pendula', **1615**, p. 202.

WEEPING BEECH see **Fagus sylvatica** 'Pendula'.

WEEPING BIRCH see **Betula pendula** 'Youngii', **1463**, p. 183.

WEEPING SPRUCE, BREWER'S see **Picea breweriana**, **2026**, p. 254.

WEEPING WILLOW see **Salix alba** 'Tristis', **1892**, p. 237.

WEEPING WYCH ELM see **Ulmus glabra** 'Pendula'.

WEIGELA (CAPRIFOLIACEAE)

floribunda and **florida hybrids** ❋ Early Summer
Sh.
Varieties often found under *Diervilla* in older catalogues. Raised from *W. florida* and *W. floribunda*, from Japan, with deep crimson *fl.* in 6, is fine race of hybrids which form some of the most valuable of midsummer flowering shrubs coming at a time when there is often little colour in the shrub garden.
Among the best of these are:
  'Abel Carrière', soft rose, large flowered;
  'Bristol Ruby', deep ruby-red, free flowering;
  'Eva Rathke', bright crimson to deep crimson, slow-growing and late flowering, **1952**, p. 244;
  'Newport Red', deep red, **1953**, p. 245.

florida, syn. **Diervilla florida, D. amabilis, W. rosea** ❋ Late Spring–Midsummer
Sh.
Deciduous shrub up to 6 ft, branching freely and suckering from base. *Fl.* tubular, rose-pink outside, paler within, in small clusters. Best planted in full sun. Prune by taking out older shoots after they have flowered to allow development of young growth. N. China, Korea. **1954**, p. 245.

WELDENIA (COMMELINACEAE)

candida ❋ Spring
*RP.
Fl. 4–6 in., white with bright yellow stamens and stigma, cup-shaped, erect, singly, on short stems, 1 in. across. *L.* broadly strap-shaped, slightly fleshy, up to 6 in. long. Tender and best grown as alpine house plant but it requires deep pot. S. America, Mts of Mexico. **223**, p. 28.

WELLINGTONIA see **Sequoiadendron giganteum**, **2039, 2040**, p. 255.

WESTERN ARBOR-VITAE see **Thuja plicata**, **2046, 2047**, p. 256.

WESTERN BALSAM POPLAR see **Populus trichocarpa**

WESTERN HEMLOCK see **Tsuga heterophylla**

WESTERN RED BUD see **Cercis occidentalis**

WESTERN RED CEDAR see **Thuja plicata**, **2046, 2047**, p. 256.

WHEATLEY ELM see **Ulmus carpinifolia** var. **sarniensis**

WHIN see **Ulex europaeus**, **1931**, p. 242.

WHITE ARUM LILY see **Zantedeschia aethiopica**, **943**, p. 118.

WHITE CEDAR see **Thuja occidentalis**

WHITE PINE, MEXICAN see **Pinus ayacahuite**, **2031**, p. 254.

WHITE POPLAR see **Populus alba**

WHITE SAILS see **Spathiphyllum wallisii**, **650**, p. 82.

WHITE SPRUCE see **Picea glauca**, **2027**, p. 254.

WHITE WILLOW see **Salix alba**, **1892**, p. 237.

WHITEBEAM see **Sorbus aria**

WHITSUN CACTUS see **Schlumbergera gaertneri**, **644**, p. 81.

WHORTLEBERRY, CAUCASIAN see **Vaccinium arctostaphylos**

WILLOW see **Salix**, **1892-1895**, p. 237.

WILLOW-LEAVED PEAR see **Pyrus salicifolia** 'Pendula', **1771**, p. 222.

× **WILSONARA** (ORCHIDACEAE)

hybrids ❋ Summer
GP.
Orchid hybrid names that end in "ara" indicate that three genera have contributed to the plant. × *Wilsonara* is bred from *Odontoglossum* which gives a large, shapely *fl.*, *Cochlioda*, which contributes a vivid red colouring and *Oncidium*, which gives a many-flowered scape. The resulting plants are all red-flowered, with a very large number of *fl.* on a long scape, but differ in the intensity of the red and in the shape of the *fl.* Winter temp. 50–55°F. and a summer temp. not higher than 70°F. seems the most satisfactory treatment. During the summer quite heavy shading is beneficial and a moist atmosphere should always be maintained. Propagation by means of back bulbs.
'Lyoth', is a typical hybrid, **655**, p. 82.

WINGED EVERLASTING see **Ammobium alatum**, **234**, p. 30.

WINGED SPINDLE TREE see **Euonymus alatus**, **1603**, p. 201.

WINTER HEATH see **Erica cinerea**, **1581-1583**, p. 198.

WINTER JASMINE see **Jasminum nudiflorum**, **1664**, p. 208.

WINTERBERRY see **Ilex verticillata**

WINTERGREEN, CREEPING see **Gaultheria procumbens**, **1620**, p. 203.

WINTERSWEET see **Chimonanthus praecox**, **1511**, p. 189.

WISHBONE FLOWER see **Torenia fournieri**, **386**, p. 49.

WISTERIA (LEGUMINOSAE) Wisteria, Chinese Kidney Bean (sometimes spelt Wistaria after Mr Wistar).

All Wisterias make valuable wall climbers when kept pruned although they do not *fl.* first year or two after planting, they also look well growing up into dark evergreens where they may be allowed to grow without pruning.

floribunda Early Summer
Cl.
Close to but later flowering than *W. sinensis*. Best form is *W. f.* 'Macrobotrys' with very long racemes sometimes up to 3 ft, also known as *W. multijuga*. *Fl.* blue-purple or lilac, more widely spaced on racemes than those of *W. sinensis*. **2000**, p. 250.

multijuga see **W. floribunda**

sinensis ❋ Late Spring
Cl.
Very vigorous deciduous woody climber up to 100 ft when allowed to ramp and often making large trunk, gnarled at base. *Fl.* lilac-mauve, pea-like up to 1 in. long in pendulous racemes up to 1 ft opening together, very fragrant in warm weather. One of the most valuable hardy climbers, very free flowering. Leaflets usually 11 to a stem, oval to ovate-oblong up to 3 in. long, ciliate, downy. After flowering Wisterias usually make many long shoots up to 6 ft length twining round support but these free-flowering should be cut back to two or three buds either in autumn or winter or soon after they have begun to make growth. China. **1999**, p. 250.

venusta ❋ Early Summer
Cl.
Vigorous climber with white slightly fragrant *fl.* slightly larger than those of *W. sinensis*. More easily distinguished by its more downy character.

WITCH HAZEL see **Hamamelis**, **1630-1634**, pp. 204, 205.

WOAD, WAXEN see **Genista tinctoria**, **1624**, p. 203.

WOLF'S BANE see **Aconitum lycoctonum**

WOODBINE see **Lonicera periclymenum**, **1982**, p. 248.

WYCH ELM see **Ulmus glabra**

Abbreviations and Symbols used in the text.
The following abbreviations may sometimes be used in conjunction as HA. indicating Hardy annual or GBb indicating Greenhouse bulb.

A. = Annual	P. = Perennial
Aq. = Aquatic	R. = Rock or
B. = Biennial	Alpine plant
Bb = Bulb	Sh. = Shrub
C. = Corm	Sp., sp. = Species
Cl. = Climber	Syn. = Synonym
Co. = Conifer	T. = Tree
Fl., fl. = Flower(s)	Tu. = Tuber
G. = Greenhouse or	var. = variety
house plant	× = Hybrid or
H. = Hardy	hybrid parents
HH. = Half-hardy	❋ = Flowering time
L., l. = Leaf, leaves	❧ = Foliage plant
Mt(s) = Mount,	
mountain(s)	

The following have been used also in the descriptions of Alpines, Bulbs, Trees and Shrubs.

  * = slightly tender
  † = lime hater
  ✿ = highly recommended

The illustration numbers are in **bold type** and the page numbers in light type preceded by p.

Y

YELLOW BROOM see **Cytisus scoparius, 1548**, p. 194.

YEW see **Taxus, 2042-2043**, p. 256.

YOUTH AND OLD AGE see **Zinnia elegans, 397, 398**, p. 50.

YUCCA (LILIACEAE)

Yuccas should be planted in full sun in warm positions where possible and are valuable for making architectural or semi-tropical effect.

ellacombei see **Y. gloriosa** 'Nobilis'

filamentosa see under **Y. gloriosa**

flaccida see under **Y. gloriosa**

gloriosa Adam's Needle ❀ Midsummer–Mid Autumn Sh.
Sub-shrub with rosette of glaucous *l.* on top of short thick almost woody trunk. *Fl.* white in very large panicles up to 4 ft long by 1 or more across. Spikes up to 15 ft have been recorded. *Fl.* widely bell-shaped, creamy-white, sometimes tinged with red outside, scented. *L.* up to 2 ft long by 3 in. wide, stiff growing erectly and spine tipped glaucous. S.E. USA.
> 'Nobilis', syn. *Y. ellacombei*, is one of the finest forms with more curved and glaucous *l.* and very large panicles, *fl.* with some red at base on outside of petals, **1956**, p. 245.
Close to *Y. gloriosa* are:

filamentosa ❀ Summer Sh.
L. with numerous white thread-like long curly hairs on threads. S.E. USA. **1955**, p. 245.

flaccida ❀ Summer Sh.
Slightly more hardy and with yellowish-white *fl.* but not in such large panicles. S.E. USA.

recurvifolia ❀ Summer Sh.
Stems up to 6 ft sometimes branching. *L.* up to 3 ft long and recurved, spinous at the tip. *Fl.* up to 3 in. wide, creamy-white in large panicles, looser in its growth and more branched than *Y. gloriosa*. S.E. USA.

whipplei ❀ Early Summer *Sh.
Finest sp. of the genus but too tender except for sunny positions in warmest areas. Rosette of stiff very glaucous narrow *l.* spine tipped up to 4 ft across. Spike very large up to 10 ft, greenish-white margined with purple, closely set, long lasting. Extremely decorative in sub-arid conditions in native country. California.

YULAN see **Magnolia denudata, 1683**, p. 211.

Z

ZANTEDESCHIA (ARACEAE)

aethiopica, syn. **Calla aethiopica, Richardia aethiopica** The White Arum Lily, Lily of the Nile ❀ Spring *Tu.
Spathe very large up to 10 in. and recurved in upper part, snow-white, central spadix white at base then creamy-yellow. Stem up to 3 ft but generally less. *L.* broad unmottled. This is grown widely for forcing as a florists' *fl.* but is also hardy in warmer areas and does best growing at the edge of water. It needs generous feeding. S. Africa.
> 'Crowborough', is more hardy form which grows outside satisfactorily in areas around London and does not require so much moisture, should be planted rather deep, **943**, p. 118.

ZAUSCHNERIA (ONAGRACEAE)

californica Californian Fuchsia ❀ Late Summer *RP.
Forms large grey mats spreading by stolons, slightly woody at base, 4–8 in. *Fl.* very bright scarlet, tubular with spreading lobes. Tender but valuable for its very strong colour and late flowering. A stock of cuttings should be over-wintered in cool greenhouse. W. N. America, California where it grows vertically in clefts or rock.

cana ❀ Late Summer *RP.
Distinguished by grey and narrower foliage. **224**, p. 28.

ZEPHYRANTHES (AMARYLLIDACEAE)

candida Flowers of the Western Wind ❀ Autumn *Bb
Fl. white, like a large crocus, 1½–2 in. long, green at base, opening to a broad star. *L.* narrow, rush-like. Valuable as a late-flowering bulbous plant and in a suitable place multiplying freely into large clumps. Should be planted in a warm sheltered border such as that at the base of a greenhouse wall. It is used in such a place at Kew as an edging. S. America. **944**, p. 118.

grandiflora ❀ Autumn *GBb
Fl. rosy-pink, 3 in. long on stems up to 1 ft and larger than *fl.* of *Z. candida* but more tender and in most gardens only grown as a cool greenhouse plant. Pots may be rested dry in summer like a nerine, but watered freely as soon as buds appear. Central America.

ZINNIA (COMPOSITAE)

angustifolia see **Z. haageana**

elegans Youth and Old Age ❀ Summer– Autumn HHA.
Fl. single, lilac, scarlet, crimson, rose, pale buff and white. *L.* stem-clasping, heart-shaped. Parent of a great variety of modern double varieties, tall, medium and dwarf. 1–3 ft. Sow in 3–4 in a warm greenhouse and when large enough to handle, pot singly as they do not transplant readily from boxes. If pricked out the boxes should be about 6 in. deep. Plant out in a sunny bed in early 6 where the soil is well-drained. May also be sown in the open in 5–6 where they are to *fl.* to avoid check. Mexico.
Good strains include:
> Chrysanthemum-flowered, with large double quilled blooms in many brilliant separate colours, 2–2½ ft, **397**, p. 50;
> Dahlia-flowered, with large double blooms up to 5 in. across, 2–2½ ft, **398**, p. 50.

haageana, syn. **Z. angustifolia** ❀ Midsummer– Mid Autumn HHA.
Fl. single, golden-yellow or orange. 1–1½ in. across. Cultivate as for *Z. elegans*. Parent of many dwarf, double varieties including:
> 'Flore Pleno Persian Carpet' strain, a colourful mixture of yellow, orange, crimson and bicolors, 1½ ft, **399**, p. 50;
> 'Thumbelina', a new strain with double and semi-double *fl.* 1–1½ in. across in many bright colours, 6 in., **400**, p. 50.

ZINNIA, CREEPING see **Sanvitalia, 372**, p. 47.

ZONAL PELARGONIUM see **Pelargonium × hortorum, 598-612**, pp. 75-77.

ZYGOCACTUS (CACTACEAE)

truncatus Christmas Cactus ❀ Winter GP.
Fl. red. Stems, flat, leaf-like, spineless. Fairly rich compost. Plant pendant, sometimes grafted on *Pereskia aculeatus*. Winter temp. 50°F., keep in moist atmosphere and water sparingly in winter; more copiously in 6–7 when a little fertiliser is appreciated. Best in cool, airy position from 8 until buds are visible, then resume watering. Propagate by cuttings. Now included by some authorities under *Schlumbergera*. Brazil. **656**, p. 82.